LAW OF REMEDIES

Principles and Proofs

SPECIAL LECTURES
OF THE
LAW SOCIETY OF UPPER CANADA

1995

LAW OF REMEDIES

Principles and Proofs

CARSWELL
Thomson Professional Publishing

Canadian Cataloguing in Publication Data

Main entry under title:

Law of remedies

(Special lectures of the Law Society of Upper Canada ; 1995)
Includes bibliographical references and index.
ISBN 0-459-55356-9

1. Remedies (Law) – Canada.   I. Law Society of Upper Canada.   II. Series.

KE8532.Z85L38 1995   347.71′077   C95-932551-4
KF9010.A75L38 1995

CARSWELL
Thomson Professional Publishing

One Corporate Plaza, 2075 Kennedy Road, Scarborough, Ontario M1T 3V4
Customer Service:
Toronto 1-416-609-3800
Elsewhere in Canada/U.S. 1-800-387-5164
Fax 1-416-298-5094

TABLE OF CONTENTS

THE LAW SOCIETY OF UPPER CANADA
LEGAL EDUCATION COMMITTEE

P.M. EPSTEIN, Q.C., *Chair*
D.H.L. LAMONT, Q.C., *Vice-Chair*
C.D. McKINNON, Q.C., *Vice-Chair*
E.S. ELLIOTT, *Vice-Chair*

W.J. LLOYD BRENNAN, Q.C.   J. LAX
M.C. CULLITY, Q.C.   L.L. LEGGE, Q.C.
S.T. GOUDGE, Q.C.

1995 PLANNING COMMITTEE

Chair

PAUL M. PERELL
Weir & Foulds

Members

THE HONOURABLE MR. JUSTICE GEORGE W. ADAMS
Ontario Court of Justice (General Division)
SHEILA R. BLOCK
Tory, Tory, DesLauriers & Binnington
JOHN A. CAMPION
Fasken Campbell Godfrey
THOMAS A. CROMWELL
Executive Legal Officer, Supreme Court of Canada
JOAN L. LAX
Assistant Dean, Faculty of Law, University of Toronto

DEPARTMENT OF EDUCATION

BRENDA A. DUNCAN
Director of Continuing Legal Education

PAUL S. TRUSTER
LAUREL A. EVANS
Program Lawyers

KATHLEEN WILL
Program Co-ordinator

UBI JUS IBI REMEDIUM

Professor Emeritus G.H.L. Fridman, Q.C., F.R.C.S. *

"That we may ordeyne a remedy for this grete meschyef"
William Caxton, 1483

"Well, what remedy?"
William Shakespeare, 1598

Those who follow me today and tomorrow will be discussing in depth and detail the niceties of the law relating to damages, specific performance, injunctions, rescission and other kinds of relief. Their task is clear: to bring you up to date on what has been happening in respect of these matters. What, however, is my role? The original schedule of events that was sent to me proposed the tentative title of "The Grand Themes in the Law of Remedies and Why They Matter to You". It suggested that I was to discover and expound some profound and perceptive insights into remedies that would otherwise elude the other participants. The organizers of these lectures clearly had in mind that at the present time in the development of our law there were emerging some new notions that could be argued were, or were capable in the future, of making changes to the way in which the courts regarded remedies. The revelation of these ideas was the task entrusted to me.

Flattered by the confidence expressed in my abilities, I gave the matter much thought and endeavoured to dredge the accumulated legal mud of many years of teaching and writing in the hope of locating some nuggets of gold. I can only hope that I have succeeded. Moreover, I hope that you will understand and appreciate why I abandoned the original title for this talk in favour of what I chose.

The maxim *ubi jus ibi remedium*, which Dr. Herbert Broom discussed at length in his book of legal maxims first published in 1845, manifests a distinction between rights and remedies. Broom's explanation or exposition of this maxim maintains and elaborates upon that distinction.[1] A

---

* Faculty of Law, University of Western Ontario.
[1] *Broom's Legal Maxims*, 10th ed. (1939), at 118 *et seq.*

similar approach is inherent in the definition of "remedy" found in *Bouvier's Law Dictionary*, an American work first published in 1839. A remedy is "the means employed to enforce a right or redress an injury."[2] More recently, Professor David Walker of Scotland, in his *Oxford Companion to Law* of 1980, calls a remedy "that which redresses, rectifies, or corrects that which has been done wrongly, or has caused injury, harm, loss or damage".[3] A remedy is a right, a right of a particular kind, namely, to redress or relief which will, so far as possible, rectify the consequences of a breach of duty by another party to a legal relationship.[4] A remedial right is as much a legal right as is a primary right. Hence, as Professor Walker continues,[5] remedies are rarely regarded as a distinct branch of law, the different remedies being usually considered in relation to the kinds of primary rights and the ways in which they may be infringed. What I think is the point made by these various authors is that the inherent contrast between rights and remedies contained in the maxim *ubi jus ibid remedium* is a false contrast. It makes as much sense to say that where there is a remedy there is a right as the other way around.

We know that the history of the common law is really a history of remedies rather than of right. To recognize and protect rights it was necessary to create or invent remedies. An early example from the reign of Henry II is to be found in the Assize of Clarendon which introduced the assize of novel disseisin for protecting possession of land without the need to establish ownership by trial by battle, which was the method employed under the earlier writs of right. An even more vital creation was the invention of the action on the case, from which so much has evolved. From the time of the Norman conquest onwards remedies have emerged to provide a means of dealing with wrongs of various kinds. Now, as Sir William Holdsworth once observed, legal history ended yesterday. There is no moment of time of which it can be said development ceased, nothing new has emerged. The process is ongoing. The evolution of the law is continuous. This is no less true of remedies than of any other aspect of the law. Courts in Canada, if not elsewhere in the common law world, have been busy adapting older remedies to newer kinds of wrongdoing, seeking to provide protection to deserving claimants by enabling them to obtain redress of one sort or another from someone who has behaved in a manner which, in modern times, if not earlier, is treated as wrongful. By so doing the courts, in effect, are recognizing rights which did not exist previously. Is the right producing the remedy or is the remedy giving birth to the right?

---

[2] *Bouvier's Law Dictionary*, 3rd ed. (1914), at 2870.
[3] Walker, *Oxford Companion to Law* (1980), at 1056.
[4] *Ibid.*
[5] *Ibid.*, at 1057.

That, indeed, is the point. Not very profound, perhaps, not very insightful. Nevertheless, it is a point that ought to be made. By providing a remedy where there was none before, or by providing a different remedy from one that was previously available, courts are changing the law. They are creating rights that did not exist; they are imposing duties and obligations upon people when no such duties or obligations bound them earlier. If you prefer to express this in the language originally employed by the organizers of these lectures, one, if not the most important "grand theme" of the law of remedies at the present time, is the power of courts to affect rights and duties by the creation or invocation of a remedy where previously such remedy did not exist or was inapplicable.

In this respect the common law is not beyond the age of childbearing. Nor is equity, as a hasty reference to Mareva or Anton Piller injunctions will prove.[6] Even without the stimulation of the *Canadian Charter of Rights and Freedoms* (which seems to have provided judges with a new burst of inventive energy — sometimes misplaced and dangerously impish), judges have managed to find new ways of helping the deserving — or those they believe are deserving. However, it is only fair to state that some judges are less willing to be innovative than others. That has always been the case with common law judges. Were it not for judges who were willing to make startling "discoveries" (which, in effect, were inventions rather than discoveries) the common law might still be what it was in the reign of Henry IV. It is worth recalling the remark of Mr. Justice Holmes to the effect that he did not think that the fact that a rule had been laid down in the reign of Henry IV was sufficient justification for its acceptance.

By way of illustration or exemplification of what I have been saying, I shall discuss three developments. They are: (1) damages in cases of unjust enrichment or restitution; (2) damages for breach of fiduciary duty; (3) the use of the constructive trust. These involve a sometimes subtle, sometimes crude melange of common law and equity, and what has happened, in my respectful view, reveals the extent to which some judges, in their efforts to achieve "justice", have been ready and willing to ignore history and logic, and have been prepared to commit the deliberate confusion of well-established categories of liability with their attendant and appropriate remedies. Such judges have perpetrated what the Roman lawyers referred to in another, very different context as *specificatio, confusio* and *commixtio*.[7]

The evolution of the law of unjust enrichment or restitution in Canada

---

[6] Sharpe, *Injunctions and Specific Performance*, 2nd ed. (1992), paras. 1.1150, 1.750, 2.1100.

[7] *Institutions of Justinian*, Bk. II. 1.25-28: Moyle, *Institutes of Justinian* (1931), at 201-204; Maddaugh and McCamus, *Law of Restitution* (1990), at 116-18.

reveals lucidly and dramatically how courts, anxious to achieve what they consider to be a "just" result, can mould and refashion not only substantive law but also the law relating to remedies. The history of this evolution illustrates the point made by Walker about the connection between rights and remedies. What Canadian courts have done is to take the classical common law of *quasi*-contract, designed to cope with some anomalous and ill-assorted situations where the law of contract and the law of tort gave no recourse, and turn it into a more flexible doctrine that is capable of being applied in a multitude of circumstances. At the same time the courts have broadened the range of remedies available to a plaintiff in such situations.

Originally *quasi*-contractual claims, for the most part brought by the action for money had and received by the defendant to the use of the plaintiff, entailed claims for the return of money transferred by the plaintiff to the defendant or by some third party to the defendant. Cases of mistake or compulsion are examples of the former; cases of usurpation of an office and its fees exemplify the latter. Equitable ideas entered the field with the development of the constructive trust and the notion of accountability for profits made by the abuse of some position (of which more will be said later in another context). The start of the modern transmogrification of unjust enrichment or restitution is *Deglman v. Guaranty Trust Co. of Canada*.[8] By a process that the late J.H.C. Morris of Magdalen College, Oxford, called "pulling oneself up by one's bootstraps", the Supreme Court of Canada justified an award of monetary compensation for services rendered to a plaintiff who could not establish a valid, enforceable contract by reason of the provisions of the *Statute of Frauds*. From that small beginning a whole new area of legal activity began. This is not the place to go into detail which has been explored elsewhere.[9] Suffice it to say that subsequent decisions, especially by the Supreme Court of Canada, have widened the scope of such recovery, first by creating proprietary rights, whether legal or equitable, in property acquired by a defendant through the assistance of services rendered by a plaintiff where the parties were united in a matrimonial or *quasi*-matrimonial relationship, and then by applying the same principles to more commercial relationships where the remedy was not the recognition of a proprietary interest but an award of money, now referred to as "damages". It has become axiomatic now that if and when a claim of unjust enrichment or restitution is successful the court can grant any remedy that is appropriate, including damages. It would appear that unjust enrichment is a *tertium quid*, as it were. A plaintiff may sue for breach of contract, tort, or unjust enrich-

---

[8] [1954] S.C.R. 725, [1954] 3 D.L.R. 785.

[9] Maddaugh and McCamus, *supra*, note 7, Chapter 2; Fridman, *Restitution*, 2nd ed. (1992), at 12-19.

ment depending on the particular facts of a case. Indeed, as is well-known, a plaintiff may forgo a claim for breach of contract and sue for unjust enrichment or may "waive" a tort and sue in restitution. Whatever his or her cause of action, the plaintiff may be able to recover "damages".

What are those damages? Are they measured or calculated in the same way and by the same principles as damages for tort or breach of contract? At the present time I do not believe that this is at all clear. The courts refer blithely to "damages" without making clear what exactly they mean, in contrast with tort and contract cases where the term "damages" is understood, as are the scope of the term and the conditions under which damages are recoverable and the kinds of damages that may be sought. These are matters which, presumably, the courts will have to resolve and clarify, now that they have established the idea of unjust enrichment and recognized the rights that stem therefrom.

The old law had the merit of being more precise in its scope and effects. There were markers that delineated the path of the law. The modern development has removed those markers. There are no plainly delineated paths. As Morden J. said in *James More & Sons Ltd. v. University of Ottawa*: "The caegories of restitution are never closed."[10] Nor, it would seem, are the categories of remedies in cases of restitution.

The *Deglman* case[11] may have been *fons et origo mali*, but it was the judgments of Chief Justice Laskin and Chief Justice Dickson, in a succession of cases from *Murdoch v. Murdoch*[12] to *Sorochan v. Sorochan*,[13] that really gave impetus to the idea that an award of damages was legitimate and appropriate in actions founded on unjust enrichment or restitution. The various decisions of the Supreme Court, in cases concerned with claims by wives or cohabitees to a share in the property or profits acquired by a spouse or cohabitee during the course of the matrimonial or *quasi*-matrimonial relationship, helped to provide, if not singlehandedly provided, the means whereby the classical concept of *quasi*-contract as developed by the common law was changed into the modern law of unjust enrichment. That change affected not only substantive principles of liability but also the remedies available in such instances. Indeed, it would be difficult if not impossible to conceive of the one development without the other. In the event what has occurred is a significant transformation of the law. A traditional remedy, relevant in certain situations, namely, torts and breaches of contract, has been invoked in an area of the law where historically and even logically it was inapplicable. It is noteworthy

---

[10] (1974), 49 D.L.R. (3d) 666 at 676, 5 O.R. (2d) 162 (H.C.).
[11] *Supra*, note 8.
[12] [1975] 1 S.C.R. 423, [1974] 1 W.W.R. 361, 13 R.F.L. 185, 41 D.L.R. (3d) 367.
[13] [1986] 2 S.C.R. 38, 46 Alta. L.R. (2d) 97, [1986] 5 W.W.R. 289, 2 R.F.L. (3d) 225, 29 D.L.R. (4th) 1, 23 E.T.R. 143, 69 N.R. 81.

that, to the best of my knowledge, no similar development has occurred in England, even though, in recent years, there has been a greater acceptance and recognition of the idea of unjust enrichment or restitution as a ground of recovery.

English courts maintain the distinction between damages and restitution. The Canadian attitude was well-expressed by Lambert J.A. in *Atlas Cabinets & Furniture Ltd. v. National Trust Co.*[14] In that case the relationship between the parties was not matrimonial or *quasi*-matrimonial but commercial, like that in *Hunter Engineering Co. v. Syncrude Canada Ltd.*,[15] where unjust enrichment was also a basis for recovery. Those two cases illustrate the distance travelled by Canadian courts in respect of restitutionary recovery since *Deglman*.[16] There *quantum meruit* was allowed for services rendered otherwise than under contract (still a rarity in English courts). Canadian courts have gone far beyond that, although in the *Atlas* case Southin J.A. was not prepared to accept the wide range of application endorsed by the other members of the British Columbia Court of Appeal, drawing their inspiration from the language and philosophy of Dickson C.J. in the earlier decisions. Southin J.A. was content to let the relationship in question be governed by contract, or, as was the situation, the absence of contract.[17] The judgment of the majority recognizes a need for courts to intervene where parties have not settled the issue for themselves by express or implied agreement. Where that occurs, in Lambert J.A.'s words: "The available remedies include an order to pay money, as damages . . .".[18] Such language is not found in England. The conclusion to be drawn from this, to which I shall return later, is that Canadian courts have embraced a very different approach to rights, duties and remedies from their English counterparts. Trying to explain this to English academics at conferences or meetings is not easy; they do not appear to appreciate that most of their problems do not arise in Canada because of this difference in approach.

I move on to consideration of the second topic: awards of damages for breach of fiduciary duty. This has been the subject of recent decisions by the Supreme Court of Canada. The importance of these, in my opinion, lies in the way in which some, if not all of the judges of that court have, once again in my view, taken what might be termed a traditional remedy (this time one that is equitable in nature, as contrasted with the common law remedy of money had and received that was utilized origi-

---

[14] (1990), 45 B.C.L.R. (2d) 99, 37 E.T.R. 16, 68 D.L.R. (4th) 161 (C.A.).
[15] [1989] 1 S.C.R. 426, 35 B.C.L.R. (2d) 145. [1989] 3 W.W.R. 385, 57 D.L.R. (4th) 321, 92 N.R. 1.
[16] *Supra*, note 8.
[17] *Supra*, note 14, at 191-96 D.L.R.
[18] *Ibid.*, at 174 D.L.R.

nally in cases of *quasi*-contract or restitution) and have changed its nature and effect. Once again, the rationale for this is suggested to be the desire to achieve what the judges in question conceive of as a just result, whether or not it conforms to precedent and principle.

One of the difficulties arising in cases involving this issue is that the fact situations sometimes involve fraud or deceit, negligent misrepresentation or contract, as well as the law relating to fiduciaries and their duties. The significance of this is that fraud, etc., were and still are matters for the common law, entailing the common law remedy of damages, whereas fiduciaries, their obligations and their liability for breach of those obligations were originally within the exclusive jurisdiction of courts of equity. Those courts probably could not award damages until the passage of Lord Cairns' Act in 1858.[19] But a court of equity could award monetary compensation for infraction of a purely equitable right in the nature of restitution — which probably could not be classified as a power to award damages.[20] In the words of three Australian authors:

> Damages is the term used to describe the monetary compensation awarded for invasion of the plaintiff's common law rights or failure to perform obligations owed him at common law. . .; damages was never an equitable remedy for breach of purely equitable obligations.[21]

They go on to say:

> . . . it is not correct to speak of "damages" as a single concept which readily in a "reforming" spirit may now be transposed from law into equity. . .[22]

Yet that is precisely what appears to have been perpetrated by the Supreme Court of Canada.

The two decisions that require consideration in this regard, especially the judgments of LaForest J. therein, are *Canson Enterprises Ltd. v. Broughton & Co.*[23] and *Hodgkinson v. Simms.*[24] What has now happened in Canada is the transformation of "compensation" as originally understood in equity into "damages".

In the *Canson* case LaForest J. considered the relationship between

---

[19] *Chancery Amendment Act*, 21 & 22 Vict. c. 27.

[20] On compensation, see Davidson, "The Equitable Remedy of Compensation", (1981/1982), 13 Melbourne U.L.R. 349.

[21] Meagher, Gummow and Lehane, *Equity: Doctrine and Remedies*, 3rd ed. (1992), at 634.

[22] *Ibid*.

[23] [1991] 3 S.C.R. 534, 61 B.C.L.R. (2d) 1, [1992] 1 W.W.R. 245, 9 C.C.L.T. (2d) 1, 39 C.P.R. (3d) 449, 85 D.L.R. (4th) 129, 131 N.R. 321.

[24] [1994] 3 S.C.R. 377, 97 B.C.L.R. (2d) 1, 22 C.C.L.T. (2d) 1, 57 C.P.R. (3d) 1, 117 D.L.R. (4th) 161, 95 D.T.C. 5135, 171 N.R. 245.

equitable and common law remedies, in particular compensation for breach
of fiduciary obligation. As he subsequently noted again in *M. (K.) v.
M. (H.)*,[25] in equity there was no capacity to award damages, but the
remedy of compensation evolved. The distinction between damages and
compensation was often slight, and the courts tended to merge the principles of law and equity when necessary to achieve a just remedy. The tenor
of the learned judge's judgment in the *Canson* case[26] is that there is little,
if any need to differentiate the common law remedy of damages from the
equitable remedy of compensation, since common law and equity have
fused, mingled, merged or interacted (these various terms are employed
by LaForest J. in the judgment). The result of this is to provide "a general,
but flexible, approach that allows for direct application of the experience
and best features of both law and equity, whether the mode of redress
(the cause of action or remedy) originates in one system or the other".[27]
So, depending on the type of fiduciary obligation that was breached,[28]
the court could adopt equitable principles of compensation, *i.e.*, disgorg-
ing of profits — in other words restitution — or common law principles
of putting the plaintiff back into the position he or she was in before the
breach (much as in a case of deceit or negligent misrepresentation).[29] In
such a situation the court could invoke common law doctrines of causation and contributory negligence when determining the extent of the defendant's liability. Hence in the *Canson* case[30] the solicitor's liability could
be limited.

McLachlin J. arrived at the same conclusion, but seemingly without the
necessity to merge, fuse, mingle or cause to interact common law and
equitable principles or remedies.[31] Moreover, Stevenson J., in a pithy but
interesting judgment, also seems to have accepted and endorsed the difference between common law damages and equitable compensation. He
reached the same conclusion on the facts by stating that a court of equity
would arrive at that conclusion by applying principles of fairness.

---

[25] [1992] 3 S.C.R. 6, 14 C.C.L.T. (2d) 1, 96 D.L.R. (4th) 289 at 336-37, 142 N.R.
321.

[26] *Supra*, note 23, at 143-53 D.L.R.

[27] *Ibid.*, at 152 D.L.R.

[28] For example, (1) where a person had control of property belonging to another,
and (2) where one person was under a fiduciary duty to perform an obligation
to another: *ibid.*, at 146 D.L.R.

[29] Cp. *Jacks v. Davis* (1983), 39 B.C.L.R. 353, [1983] 1 W.W.R. 327, 22 C.C.L.T.
266, 141 D.L.R. (3d) 355; *Rainbow Industrial Caterers Ltd. v. Canadian
National Railway Co.*, [1991] 3 S.C.R. 3, 59 B.C.L.R. (2d) 129, [1991] 6
W.W.R. 385, 8 C.C.L.T. (2d) 225, 84 D.L.R. (4th) 291; *Burns v. Kelly Peters
& Associates Ltd.* (1987), 16 B.C.L.R. (2d) 1, [1987] 6 W.W.R. 1, 41 C.C.L.T.
257, [1987] I.L.R. 1-2246, 41 D.L.R. (4th) 577.

[30] *Supra*, note 23.

[31] *Ibid.*, at 154-64 D.L.R.

Accordingly he rejected what he termed the "so-called fusion of law and equity" as being relevant and categorically rejected the idea that such fusion had introduced contributory negligence and remoteness of damage, as understood and applied by the common law, into equitable principles of compensation.[32]

If you regard the judgment of Stevenson J. as being closer to that of McLachlin J. than to that of LaForest J., the result is that, on the subject of the fusion or merger of common law and equity with regard to remedies, the Supreme Court was divided equally, four one way and four the other. In *Hodgkinson v. Simms*[33] the court was divided four to three; however, the division was rather over the question whether the defendant was liable for breach of fiduciary duty or breach of contract than on the question of the nature of the remedy and the equation of common law and equity in this respect. Nevertheless, once again, LaForest J. enunciated his views about this, while at the same time distinguishing the *Hodgkinson* case from *Canson* when it came to deciding the principles upon which the extent of the plaintiff's recovery should be based.[34] In this he returned to the point made in *Canson* about the differences between various kinds of fiduciary duty and the effect of those differences upon the extent of the plaintiff's recovery and the basis upon which such recovery was to be determined. What kind of breach occurred determined the nature of the wrong committed by the defendant. If the wrong in issue was like a common law wrong, then equity would adopt common law principles relating to the appropriate remedy. If the wrong were not akin to a common law wrong, then equitable principles of restitution should be applied (as was held by the majority with respect to the situation in *Hodgkinson*).

In the *Canson* case[35] the question of damages revolved around the issue whether the defendants, guilty of breach of fiduciary duty, should be liable for all the subsequent consequences, including the loss caused by the negligence of engineers who built a warehouse on the land in question, as well as for the secret profit made by the defendants. As already noted, the Supreme Court all agreed that there was a limit on the liability of the defendants, but they were not in agreement as to the reasons for that limit. I suggest that the court all felt that justice would not be done if the defendants were held liable for something caused by a third party's negligence but were in difficulties when it came to determining the juridical reason for denying that liability. Once the court held that liability was based on equitable, not common law, wrongdoing, it became a matter of some concern to discover principles on which a court could base the

---

[32] *Ibid.*, at 165-66 D.L.R.
[33] *Supra*, note 24.
[34] *Ibid.*, at 52-53 C.C.L.T.
[35] *Supra*, note 23.

calculation of equitable damages. Where the court, or at least LaForest J. and those who concurred with him, went wrong, I suggest, is in making the transition from the equitable notion of compensation, or indemnity as it was termed in the context of innocent misrepresentation, to the common law concept of damages.

In *Hodgkinson v. Simms*[36] the trial judge, holding the defendant liable for breach of fiduciary duty, held that the plaintiff should be put back in the position he was in before he made the investments recommended by the defendant. The British Columbia Court of Appeal allowed the appeal and held that the defendant was liable only for breach of contract, by reason of which he should only pay over the fees received from the investors.[37] The majority of the Supreme Court restored the trial judge's decision both as to liability and remedy. In doing so they stressed the deterrent effect of the kind of award of damages ordered in this case by the trial judge and approved by the majority of the Supreme Court. They also adverted to the need to uphold the social utility of the idea of fiduciary duty. The language of LaForest J. indicates that underlying the invocation and application of the notice of damages in equity is not so much the notice of compensation that is the fundamental rationale of common law damages but the moral idea of preventing a defendant from gaining by his wrongdoing or improper behaviour.[38] If this indeed is what is at the root of the approach favoured by LaForest J. in these two cases, then it would seem that he and those who agree with him are not simply applying settled law, they are reinterpreting, or perhaps inventing the law to achieve certain ends or policies. What is said in these cases, particularly in the *Hodgkinson* case, is consistent with the admitted policy of the Supreme Court, as set out by McLachlin J., extra-judicially, when she said: "In recent years, courts in Canada have moved to introduce a new standard of morality in commercial dealings."[39] The way that LaForest J. has expounded the idea of damages in equity seems to me to partake of the same attitude. By this evolution of an equitable remedy that originally served another purpose, and fulfilled a different policy, LaForest J. and those who concurred with him are seeking to achieve a different purpose and to promote a different policy. They have identified a right which they regard as worthy of protection and have fashioned a remedy to protect and preserve that right.

The last matter I wish to consider is the way the courts in Canada

---

[36] (1989), 43 B.L.R. 122 (B.C.S.C.).

[37] (1992), 65 B.C.L.R. (2d) 264, [1992] 4 W.W.R. 330, 5 B.L.R. (2d) 236, 6 C.P.C. (3d) 141, 45 E.T.R. 270.

[38] *Supra*, note 24, at 58-59 C.C.L.T.

[39] McLachlin, "The Place of Equity and Equitable Doctrines in the Contemporary Common Law World: a Canadian Perspective", in Waters, ed., *Equity, Fiduciaries and Trusts* (1993), at 40.

have made use of the concept of constructive trust in their search for new remedies to deal with new rights. In this respect Canadian judges have taken what was an institution of the substantive law of equity and utilized it as a remedy for the purpose of more effectively protecting rights which the courts recognized, or, perhaps more correctly, invented.

It is unnecessary for present purposes to retell the story of the way in which the modern law of unjust enrichment or restitution evolved. What is pertinent here is the process by which Canadian courts determined that, in appropriate circumstances, the only effective way to safeguard a party's right to prevent an unjust enrichment of the defendant or compel the latter to make restitution was to subject certain property to a constructive trust in favour of the claimant, thereby making the defendant a constructive trustee on behalf of such claimant. By such means the claimant would obtain more than a right to enforce a money judgment, which could be defeated or outflanked in various ways. At least that is what it would seem the courts thought, though the unfortunate fate of Miss Becker[40] may reveal that their intentions may nonetheless be thwarted.

It was in *Pettkus v. Becker*[41] that the movement in this direction finally reached its objective, as Dickson C.J., the chief protagonist in this development himself stated in *Hunter Engineering Co. v. Syncrude Canada Ltd.*[42] As McLachlin J. declared in *Rawluk v. Rawluk*,[43] the constructive trust is now a general remedy for unjust enrichment. It is not the only available remedy. As noted previously, damages may be appropriate in some instances, but it is certainly an available remedy. Once again, Canadian courts have taken a path apparently not open to use by judges in England. Indeed, one distinguished English academic in the field of restitution has stated that he does not like or approve of the constructive trust.[44] According to him it has "no active role". It is "an inert description". That is not the opinion of the Supreme Court of Canada. On the contrary, the constructive trust is embraced by that court and, accordingly, by provincial courts as a most useful and highly effective means to enforce rights arising under the law of unjust enrichment or restitution.

Perhaps the true origins of this approach in Canada are to be found in the judgment of Dickson J., as he then was, in *Rathwell v. Rathwell.*[45]

---

[40] [1980] 2 S.C.R. 834, 8 E.T.R. 143, 19 R.F.L. (2d) 165, 117 D.L.R. (3d) 257, 34 N.R. 384.

[41] *Ibid.*

[42] [1989] 1 S.C.R. 426, 35 B.C.L.R. (2d) 145, [1989] 3 W.W.R. 385, 57 D.L.R. (4th) 321 at 348-49.

[43] [1990] 1 S.C.R. 70, 38 O.A.C. 81, 71 O.R. (2d) 480n, 36 E.T.R. 1, 23 R.F.L. (3d) 337, 65 D.L.R. (4th) 161 at 184, 103 N.R. 321.

[44] Birks, *An Introduction to the Law of Restitution*, at 89-90.

[45] [1978] 2 S.C.R. 436, [1978] 2 W.W.R. 101, 1 E.T.R. 307, 1 R.F.L. (2d) 1, 83 D.L.R. (3d) 289 at 305-07.

Although the majority of the Supreme Court held that Mrs. Rathwell was entitled to a half-interest in all the real and personal property owned by her husband, the majority was not *ad idem* as to the reason for this conclusion. Ritchie and Pigeon JJ. relied on resulting trust. Dickson and Spence JJ. and Laskin C.J. favoured the novel use of the constructive trust. In the course of this part of his judgment Dickson J. relied on a quotation from something written by Professor Austin Scott,[46] the great American authority on trusts, where the constructive trust has long been recognized as remedial, on a quotation from what might be called a maverick opinion by Lord Denning in *Hussey v. Palmer*[47] and a quotation from Lord Diplock's speech in *Gissing v. Gissing*[48] in which he stated "whenever the trustee has so conducted himself that it would be inequitable to allow him to deny to the *cestui que trust* a beneficial interest in the land acquired". From this Dickson J. concluded that the "constructive trust, *as so envisaged*, comprehends the imposition of trust machinery by the Court in order to achieve a result consonant with good conscience".[49]

I venture to suggest that this passage in the judgment of Dickson J. in *Rathwell* reveals the quantum leap taken by him (and those who concurred with him) from the original English concept of the constructive trust and the circumstances in which a person will be treated by the law as a constructive trustee to the view of constructive trust that was alien to English and Canadian law prior to that judgment, although accepted in the United States. The very next sentence after the one quoted above puts it in a nutshell: "As a matter of principle, the Court will not allow any man unjustly to appropriate himself the value earned by the labours of another".[50] But that is not what the English and previous Canadian idea of constructive trust was all about. If you want to see in great detail what that doctrine entails, look in Volume 2 of the 1994 All England Law Reports. There are seven cases, at first instance and in the Court of Appeal, that really examine and explain what constructive trust *a l'Anglais* is all about.[51] You will quickly and readily discover that it is not quite what Dickson J. had in mind. His attitude, however, is succinctly summarized

---

[46] Scott, "Constructive Trusts", (1955) 71 L.Q.R. 39 at 41.

[47] [1972] 1 W.L.R. 1286.

[48] [1970] 2 All E.R. 780 at 789-90.

[49] *Supra*, note 45, at 306 D.L.R.

[50] *Ibid.*

[51] *Baden v. Societe Generale pour Favoriser le Developpement du Commerce et de l'Industrie en France SA*, [1992] 4 All E.R. 161; *Re Montagu's Settlement, ibid.* at 308; *Lipkin Gorman (a firm) v. Karpnale Ltd., ibid.*, at 311; *Agrip (Africa) Ltd. v. Jackson, ibid.*, at 451; *Eagle Trust plc v. SBC Securities Ltd., ibid.*, at 488; *Cowan de Groot Properties Ltd. v. Eagle Trust plc., ibid.*, at 700; *Polly Peck International plc v. Nadir (No. 2), ibid.*, at 769.

in his remarks in the later decision in *Pettkus v. Becker*,[52] where he said: "The great advantage of ancient principles of equity is their flexibility: the judiciary is thus able to shape these malleable principles so as to accommodate the changing needs and mores of society, in order to achieve justice. The constructive trust has proven to be a useful tool in the judicial armoury." Yes, but only because he and others with like attitudes have been willing to refashion substantive law and the law of remedies to fit their views on what should and can be done.

A return to orthodoxy is now impossible. Perhaps it is even undesirable. What concerns me, and is relevant to the present discussion, is that in the various judgments referred to earlier, Dickson J., and later C.J., caused the law in Canada to take a turn towards a more flexible method of relieving a successful plaintiff and compelling a defendant to disgorge gains that the court, for other reasons, conceived as being ill-gotten. As we now know, despite the dissent of Southin J.A.,[53] the remedy employed by the Supreme Court to cope with husbands and significant others who refused to render to their cohabiting partners their proper share in gains and economic advantages may now be utilized in more commercial, less matrimonial or familial situations and relationships. To the extent that this may be possible, it seems to me, the law in Canada has wandered a long way from the original path of equity.

So, whether we are thinking in terms of a common law or an equitable remedy, there can be no doubt that Canadian courts have been more than willing to make use of classical doctrines in new ways and to deal with novel situations and relationships. From a pragmatic point of view there is much to be said in favour of such originality and imaginative lawmaking. To the practising lawyer seeking to advance his client's claims and protect his client's interests and property, the approach of the courts offers great opportunities. He or she now has much more flexibility when it comes to deciding what kind of remedy to seek. To use the language of Dickson C.J., the "armoury" of the law has been extended or supplemented. To the wrongdoer the courts have broadcast the stern message that they cannot hide behind former technical barriers to prevent a wronged party from obtaining suitable and satisfactory redress.

From the technical or doctrinal point of view, however, what has happened may be regrettable. It is all well and good to strive to achieve justice and a just result; to do this at the expense of long-accepted principles means playing fast and loose with the law. In the long run is this in the best interests of the law and of the society for whose benefit the law exists? We are faced with what has become the classical issue: Should the law

---

[52] *Supra*, note 40, at 273 D.L.R.
[53] In *Atlas Cabinets & Furniture Ltd. v. National Trust Co.* (1990), 45 B.C.L.R. (2d) 99, 37 E.T.R. 16, 68 D.L.R. (4th) 161 (C.A.).

be certain or flexible? That question seems to resemble the famous question posed by Richard Strauss in his opera *Capriccio*: "In opera, which is more important, the music or the words?" I shall answer neither question.

THE GENERAL PRINCIPLES OF
THE LAW OF DAMAGES

*Professor S. M. Waddams**

It is often thought that the general principles of the law of damages are extremely simple, and hardly worthy of extended discussion. The object of an award of damages, as is well known, is to put the party complaining, so far as it can be done by money, in the position that that party would have occupied if the wrong had not been done.[1] But, as with other apparently self-evident legal propositions, difficult problems lie underneath. Throughout the law of damages there runs a tension, never fully resolved, between the notion that it is the duty of the court to pursue a potentially limitless inquiry into the precise circumstances that would have attended the plaintiff if the wrong had not been done and, on the other hand, a search for rules that are clear, predictable, workable, fair between one claimant and another in similar circumstances, and reasonably inexpensive of application.

Very often the former notion, that is, of potentially limitless inquiry, has been perceived as a desirable objective, failure to achieve it being attributed to institutional or individual imperfections that ideally should be overcome. Thus, Lord Wright in *Liesbosch, Dredger v. S.S. Edison*[2] said:

> In these cases [ship collisions] the dominant rule of law is the principle of restitutio in integrum, and subsidiary rules can only be justified if they give effect to that rule.[3]

The willingness of the court to inquire into the plaintiff's particular circumstances is supported by appeal to the single general principle; "subsidiary" rules are called rigid,[4] and arbitrary,[5] and are degraded to mere

---

* Faculty of Law, University of Toronto.
[1] *Livingstone v. Rawyards Coal Co.* (1880), 5 App. Cas. 25 at 39 (H.L.).
[2] [1933] A.C. 449.
[3] *Id.*, at 463.
[4] *Admiralty Com'rs v. S. S. Susquehanna*, [1926] A.C. 655 at 662.
[5] *Liesbosch Dredger v. S. S. Edison, supra,* note 2, at 462.

rules of convenience or of practice.[6] Departures from a fully individual-
ized inquiry are often accompanied by apologetic statements, such as that
"rules as to damages can in the nature of things only be approximately
just".[7]

A more forthright assertion of the necessity, and indeed of the virtue, of departure, on occasion, from the single general principle appears
in a judgment of the High Court of Admiralty, in 1849. Dr. Lushington
said:

> As a general proposition, undoubtedly the principle [of *restitutio in integrum*]
> is correctly stated; and not only in this court, but in all other courts, I appre-
> hend the general rule of law is that where an injury is committed by one
> individual to another . . . the party receiving the injury is entitled to an indem-
> nity for the same. But although this is the general principle of law, all courts
> have found it necessary to adopt certain rules for the application of it; and
> it is utterly impossible, in all the various cases that may arise, that the remedy
> which the law may give should always be to the precise amount of the loss
> or injury sustained. In many cases it will, of necessity, exceed, in others fall
> short of the precise amount.[8]

An example close to home may perhaps illustrate the force of Dr.
Lushington's point. My university, like many other organizations, allows
a fixed sum per kilometre for the use of a private automobile on university business. It is, I would suggest, highly unlikely that the sum of, say,
25¢ per kilometre represents precisely the cost incurred by any particular
claimant. It would be possible to imagine a system where the claimant
had to establish the actual cost, with expert evidence and evidence as to
disputable facts on both sides, and where a tribunal would hear argument
and settle disputes. The amount payable would vary according to the evidence of the age and actual value of the car, the method used by the claimant for financing its purchase, with evidence of actual interest rates paid
on money borrowed, evidence of the actual interest or other profit that
the claimant might have made on money not borrowed, the actual cost
of insurance, the actual cost of fuel, the actual cost and frequency of maintenance, the proportion of use of the car devoted to university business,
the reasonableness of the claimant's expenditures on all these items, and
the proper actuarial and accounting theories to reduce these factors to
the allowable sum.

Compared with such a careful inquiry, the flat rate rule is certainly
"rough and ready" and possibly "arbitrary" and "inflexible". But one

---

[6] *Admiralty Com'rs v. S. S. Chekiang*, [1926] A.C. 637 at 643.

[7] *Rodoconachi v. Milburn* (1886), 18 Q.B.D. 67 at 78 *per* Lindley L.J.

[8] *The Columbus* (1849), 3 W. Rob. 158 at 162. The actual decision in the case
was later overruled, however.

only needs to contemplate the alternative for a moment to see the merits of the flat rate. It is far more economical for the university to pay even a somewhat excessive flat rate than to bear the costs of such an inquiry as has just been contemplated. The system benefits claimants, too. Though in rare cases a claimant would benefit from a detailed inquiry, the flat rate system is obviously preferable for claimants generally, especially if, as members of the university, they have themselves to bear the costs of elaborate inquiries. No one would hesitate for a moment to say, paraphrasing Dr. Lushington, that as a general proposition undoubtedly the principle is that the party incurring the expense is entitled to an indemnity for the same; but that, although this is the general principle, all institutions have found it necessary to adopt certain rules for the application of it, and it is utterly impossible, in all the various cases that may arise, that the reimbursement which the institution may give should always be to the precise amount of the expense sustained; in many cases it will of necessity exceed, in others fall short, of the precise amount.

There are several examples of cases where the law gives a remedy that exceeds the amount of the plaintiff's loss. Rules for the valuation of property supply one example, as in a case where the defendant wrongfully cuts down timber on the plaintiff's land that the plaintiff could not, or would not, have used herself. In such cases, the plaintiff is generally entitled to the full market value of the property wrongfully taken, even though, in some cases, this undoubtedly puts the plaintiff in a better position than if the wrong had not been done.[9] Another well-known example is the case where the defendant misappropriates the plaintiff's property, which declines in value before the plaintiff discovers the loss. The measure of damages is the value of the property at the time of the wrong.[10] A seller is entitled, on default by a buyer, to recover the difference between the contract price and the market price at the date of breach, even if the goods or shares are in fact resold at a higher price.[11] In all these cases the award of the court probably has the effect of putting the plaintiff in a better position than he would have occupied if the wrong had not been done. Nevertheless, the results can be justified on the grounds of simplicity, convenience, and the avoidance of expensive inquiries into the precise circumstances of particular parties.

Cases where the award of damages falls short of the plaintiff's loss are even more common, the legal principles of certainty, mitigation and remoteness all tending in the direction of denying full compensation. These

---

[9] See *Bilambil-Terranora Pty Ltd.* v. *Tweed Shire Council*, [1980] 1 N.S.W.L.R. 465 at 479 (C.A.) (example given by Reynolds J.A.).

[10] *Solloway* v. *McLaughlin*, [1938] A.C. 247 (J.C.).

[11] *Jamal* v. *Moolla Dawood Sons & Co.*, [1916] 1 A.C. 175 (J.C.); *Campbell Mostyn* v. *Barnett*, [1954] 1 Lloyd's Rep. 65 (C.A.).

well-recognized limiting principles can be explained by the need to balance against the search for perfect compensation in the individual case the merits of a system that will, in general, yield results perceived to be reasonably predictable, consistent, workable and convenient.

The purpose of Lord Wright, in making the comment quoted at the beginning of this lecture, was to support an award for destruction of a dredger that took into account the value to the owner of the contract in performance of which the dredger was engaged at the time of its destruction. Lord Wright said that the value of the dredger was not just its "intrinsic" value, but the value to its owner in the particular circumstances.

This line of thinking appears attractive, but if all the circumstances of the particular plaintiff are taken into account, the principle of remoteness would be destroyed. It might be said, for example, that the actual value to the millowner of the millshaft in *Hadley v. Baxendale*[12] included the profits that the owner expected to derive from its use, or that the actual value of goods to a buyer included the prospect of reselling them at an exceptionally large profit.[13] It cannot be supposed, however, that Lord Wright intended to abolish the principle of remoteness, because on another point in the same case he denied recovery of a loss on the ground that it was too remote.[14]

One of the most extensively discussed issues in the assessment of damages for personal injuries has been the question of whether, in assessing damages for loss of earning capacity, to take into account the plaintiff's liability for income tax. The House of Lords held, in *British Transport Com'n v. Gourley*,[15] that the award was to be reduced to take account of the income tax that the plaintiff would have had to pay on his earnings if he had not been injured. Gourley paid income tax at a very high rate, and the decision had the effect of reducing his award by more than 80 per cent. The case has been rejected in Canada,[16] and was at first rejected,[17]

---

[12] (1854), 9 Ex. 341.

[13] See *The Arpad*, [1934] P. 189, denying compensation for a lost sub-sale in these circumstances. Contrast *France v. Gaudet* (1871), L.R. 6 Q.B. 199 and the dissenting judgment of Scrutton L.J. in *The Arpad*.

[14] It was held that the plaintiff's impecuniosity could not be taken into account to increase the damages, even where the plaintiff suffered an actual loss on that account, because it was too remote.

[15] [1956] A.C. 185.

[16] *R. v. Jennings*, [1966] S.C.R. 532, 57 D.L.R. (2d) 644; *Guy v. Trizec Equities Ltd.*, [1979] 2 S.C.R. 756 at 766, 32 N.S.R. (2d) 345, 10 C.C.L.T. 197, 99 D.L.R. (3d) 243, 27 N.R. 301.

[17] *Atlas Tiles Ltd v. Briers* (1978), 144 C.L.R. 202.

but later accepted,[18] by the High Court of Australia. It has been rejected in the context of wrongful dismissal in New Zealand.[19]

Support for the result reached in *Gourley* is derived from the idea that the general principle of assessment of compensation requires an inquiry into the plaintiff's precise individual circumstances (in this case to the plaintiff's disadvantage). The opposite result is supported by the idea that leaving income tax considerations out of account will produce a clear and relatively straightforward rule that will be fairer to litigants (both plaintiffs and defendants) over the long run and will save costs to litigants and to the court. These considerations, if soundly based, are not defeated by the contemplation of an individual case in which the application of the more general principle would lead to a different result.

Briefly stated, the arguments for the Canadian position on this point are as follows. Any undue enrichment of the plaintiff is caused, not by the award of the court, but by the decision of Parliament not to tax the award itself as income. If Parliament is dissatisfied with the result, it has only to amend the taxing statute. The wrongdoer causes an actual economic loss (to the plaintiff and the Revenue jointly) and should pay it in full. The plaintiff's earning capacity may properly be treated as a capital asset (for this and certain other purposes) and it is not unjust to award a capital sum for the loss. The plaintiff will presumably invest the proceed of the award in some way and will pay tax on the income derived from the investment. If the plaintiff is to be treated fairly, the award, after reduction on the *Gourley* principle,[20] would then have to be "grossed up" to allow for the income tax payable by the plaintiff on the invested proceeds of the award.[21] This is a complex, expensive and unpredictable process, which would often result in bringing the award back to about the amount of lost gross income (discounted for advance payment) or, in the case of very high tax rates, even more. If the process of "grossing up" is not conscientiously undertaken, the result for a high rate taxpayer, as no doubt in the *Gourley* case itself, will be severe under-compensation. When these considerations are taken into account, the Canadian rule on the point can be seen to be a very desirable one, not because it promotes convenience at the expense of justice, but because convenience is itself an important part of a working system of justice.

The choice of the proper discount rate for advance payment of money awarded in respect of future losses offers another illustration. In the

---

[18] *Cullen v. Trappell* (1980), 146 C.L.R. 1.

[19] *North Island Wholesale Groceries Ltd. v. Hewin*, [1980] 2 N.Z.L.R. 176 (C.A.); confirmed in *Horsburgh v. New Zealand Meat Processors Industrial Union of Workers*, [1988] 1 N.Z.L.R. 698 at 704 (C.A.).

[20] *Supra*, note 15.

[21] See *infra*, notes 36 to 42, and accompanying text.

"trilogy" of personal injury cases in 1978, and in a fatal accident case decided at the same time, the Supreme Court of Canada used a discount rate (7 per cent) that (as all commentators now agree) was much too high.[22] The consequence was severe under-compensation to the plaintiffs. Great uncertainty followed. During a period of some years the law required evidence in each individual case of the anticipated future rate of inflation and of anticipated future rates of interest. It soon became obvious that this process was unreliable, inconsistent from one case to another, and expensive to the court and to the community at large. Consequently, in most Canadian jurisdictions, including Ontario, the discount rate is now fixed by regulation. (In Ontario it is 2.5 per cent, fixed by the Rules of Court[23]). Of course it may be said that there is an element of the "rough and ready" and even of the "arbitrary" in fixing the rate, and denying to the parties the opportunity of calling expert evidence on the point. But such inquiries are very costly, and experience plainly suggested that they did not lead to greater justice. Few persons knowledgeable in the field of personal injury compensation would favour a return to the former practice of assessment of the discount rate in each individual case.

Another related example is the award of interest. Where the defendant wrongfully deprives the plaintiff of wealth, for example by destroying property, the plaintiff is nowadays entitled, in all Canadian jurisdictions, to have included in the award interest at a known or ascertainable rate on the value of the property from the date of its destruction. It is very unlikely that interest at a predetermined rate (statutory or common law) will precisely match the pecuniary benefit that the plaintiff would have derived from the property if the wrong had not been done: in many cases it will (to borrow again Dr. Lushington's words[24]) exceed, in others fall short of, the precise amount. Nevertheless the predetermined rate of interest will usually approximate with reasonable accuracy to what plaintiffs generally can be said to lose by being deprived of wealth between the date of the wrong and the date of the award. There are many advantages to both parties, and to the court, in a rule that entitles the plaintiff to interest at a predictable rate.

A long-standing puzzle in the law of compensation for personal injuries has been the question of how to deal with collateral benefits. A plaintiff's earning capacity is impaired, but he or she receives money benefits from sources other than the defendant. Should these be taken into account

---

[22] *Andrews v. Grand & Toy (Alberta) Ltd.*, [1978] 2 S.C.R. 229; *Thornton v. Prince George School Dist. No. 57*, [1978] 2 S.C.R. 267, [1978] 1 W.W.R. 607, 3 C.C.L.T. 257, 83 D.L.R. (3d) 480, 19 N.R. 552; *Arnold v. Teno*, [1978] 2 S.C.R. 287, 3 C.C.L.T. 272, 83 D.L.R. (3d) 609; *Keizer v. Hanna*, [1978] 2 S.C.R. 342, 3 C.C.L.T. 316, 82 D.L.R. (3d) 449, 19 N.R. 209.

[23] R.R.O. 1990, Reg. 194.

[24] *Supra*, note 8.

to reduce the damages? The benefits may take the form of sick pay, of disability insurance, of pensions of various sorts, or simply of continuing salary. Some payments may be gratuitous; others will have been paid for in one way or another by the plaintiff. The payments may come from the plaintiff's friends, from the plaintiff's employer, from insurers, or from the state. Courts throughout the Commonwealth have had much difficulty with these issues. Until 1990 the Canadian position was fairly clear: collateral benefits were generally excluded from the calculation (*i.e.*, damages were not reduced). This was objected to by some as over-compensatory: the plaintiff appeared to receive payment twice over. Against this it was argued that a wrongdoer should bear the full cost of the wrong; other arguments against reducing damages were simplicity and the consideration that, in appropriate cases, arrangements could be made between the plaintiff and the source of the benefit for ultimate repayment to the source of any excess indemnity. Several legal devices exist for this purpose, the best known of which is subrogation.

The position changed in 1990 with the decision of the Supreme Court of Canada in *Ratych v. Bloomer*.[25] There the court held that an injured plaintiff who received pay by the terms of his employment agreement during the period of disability was bound to bring the pay into account so as to reduce damages. But the court expressly said that insurance benefits where the plaintiff had made "a contribution equivalent to payment of an insurance premium"[26] were not to be deducted, nor were gratuitous payments.[27] Further, the court said that if there were a legal, or even a moral obligation on the employee to repay the employer out of the damages, the former would be entitled to full recovery.[28] Evidence will frequently be forthcoming that the payments were gratuitous, or that they were paid for in some way and so equivalent to insurance, or that the recipient had a legal obligation, or recognized a moral obligation to repay. Competent counsel must now be ready with evidence to establish these points. It will often be possible to adduce evidence to establish at least one of the conditions for full recovery. Another possibility is a separate action by the employer, either for loss of services, or simply for negligently caused economic loss.[29] Consequently, the net effect of the decision in *Ratych v. Bloomer* was unclear; it certainly did not simplify this branch of the

---

[25] [1990] 1 S.C.R. 940, 39 O.A.C. 103, 73 O.R. (2d) 448n, 30 C.C.E.L. 161, 3 C.C.L.T. (2d) 1, 69 D.L.R. (4th) 25, 107 N.R. 335.

[26] *Id.*, at 47 D.L.R.

[27] *Ibid.*

[28] *Id.*, at 54 D.L.R.

[29] See *Canadian Nat'l Railway Co. v. Norsk Pacific Steamship Co.*, [1992] 1 S.C.R. 1021, 11 C.C.L.T. (2d) 1, 91 D.L.R. (4th) 289, 137 N.R. 241; *Winnipeg Condominium Corp. No. 36 v. Bird Construction Co.*, [1995] 1 S.C.R. 85.

law, and whether it did greater justice by reducing the plaintiff's damages must be regarded as very doubtful in view of the subsequent treatment of the decision by the Supreme Court itself.

Last year the Supreme Court of Canada modified the effect of *Ratych v. Bloomer* by holding that employment benefits were not deductible if paid for by the employee directly or indirectly, and that evidence that the benefits formed part of the collective bargaining process was sufficient to establish indirect payment by the employee.[30] As such evidence will usually be forthcoming, it may be said that *Ratych v. Bloomer*, though not technically overruled, is very substantially limited in effect.

This sequence of events surely indicates that we are missing an important perspective. The law on this point was relatively clear until 1990. Then the Supreme Court of Canada completely altered the approach, only to retreat in 1994. The retreat, however, does not restore the relative clarity of the pre-1990 law, because *Ratych v. Bloomer* is not overruled, but must be distinguished in each case. This gives us the worst of both worlds. Lip service is paid to *Ratych v. Bloomer*, but in the great majority of cases it will not be applicable, provided that the plaintiff's counsel takes care to present evidence of what everyone knows to be universally true, that is that employment benefits can be said to have a certain cost to the employer and so, indirectly, to the employee. Even if that argument should fail, there are the various other devices mentioned for distinguishing *Ratych v. Bloomer*. The vast majority of personal injury claims are settled, and the introduction of uncertainty on the measure of damages for loss of earning capacity has a high cost to insurers, and so to the public at large. It would have been far preferable, I would suggest, for the court to have left in place the pre-1990 position, namely, that collateral benefits are generally to be left out of account, or, having recognized that *Ratych v. Bloomer* was unworkable, frankly to have restored the pre-1990 rule. It may be that such a rule does not yield perfect compensation, but the experience of the two Supreme Court cases shows that the pursuit of perfection has a very high cost, and that a simple rule on the point is the most effective way of doing justice in the long run.

In Ontario, and a few other jurisdictions, courts are empowered to award damages in fatal accident cases for intangible losses such as loss of guidance care and companionship. This is an area, like non-pecuniary loss in personal injury cases, where damages are, in a real sense, unquantifiable. The Ontario Court of Appeal, while urging restraint, has said

---

[30] *Cunningham v. Wheeler*, [1994] 1 S.C.R. 359, 88 B.C.L.R. (2d) 273, 113 D.L.R. (4th) 1, 164 N.R. 81.

that there can be no fixed conventional limit on this portion of the award.[31] The Manitoba Court of Appeal, on the other hand, has held that modest sums only are to be awarded under the corresponding Manitoba provision.[32] The New Brunswick Court of Appeal has also stressed the need for objectivity, predictability, and certainty.[33] In Ontario there have been widely varying awards in apparently similar circumstances, and plaintiffs' counsel are required to adduce actual evidence of the degree of affection felt by the survivors for the deceased, and vice versa. In favour of this process may be adduced the general notion of the pursuit of perfect compensation in the individual case, but, as in the case of non-pecuniary loss in personal injury cases, there are strong contrary arguments. The evidence of plaintiffs on these questions is often, of necessity, unreliable and self-serving; it is incapable of rebuttal by the defendant. The inevitable variation in awards will be rightly perceived as unfair between plaintiff and plaintiff. The pressure on a plaintiff to give evidence of emotional attachment and affection to and by the deceased, and the reward in money for doing so convincingly, are, to my mind, highly objectionable. The requirement of such evidence in each case is expensive to the parties and to the court. The uncertainty on this question greatly increases the difficulty of settlement and (since the vast majority of cases are settled) the over-all cost to the system. Uncertainty increases the cost of liability insurance. Such costs are not borne by morally guilty defendants, since liability is often imposed without proof of moral fault, and the costs of the system are imposed upon a wide section of the community. In an important decision in 1991, *Hamilton v. Canadian Nat'l Railway*,[34] the Ontario Court of Appeal reduced a jury award to a mother for the death of her nine-year-old daughter from $150,000 to $50,000 and also reduced smaller awards to the deceased's brothers and sister. This decision clearly recognizes the need both for a rough upper limit for high awards in this field, and for some sort of scale for ensuring consistency and fairness in smaller awards.[35]

---

[31] *Mason v. Peters* (1982), 39 O.R. (2d) 27, 22 C.C.L.T. 21, 139 D.L.R. (3d) 104; *Nielsen v. Kaufman* (1986), 26 D.L.R. (4th) 20; *Reidy v. McLeod* (1986), 15 O.A.C. 200, 54 O.R. (2d) 661, 36 C.C.L.T. 307, 27 D.L.R. (4th) 317, though saying, at 318 D.L.R., that the assessment should be "objective and unemotional".

[32] *Lawrence v. Good*, [1985] 4 W.W.R. 652, 33 Man. R. (2d) 312, 31 C.C.L.T. 236, 18 D.L.R. (4th) 734; *Larney v. Friesen*, [1986] 4 W.W.R. 467, 41 Man. R. (2d) 169, 29 D.L.R. (4th) 444.

[33] *Nightingale v. Mazerell* (1991), 121 N.B.R (2d) 319, 9 C.C.L.T. (2d) 186, 87 D.L.R. (4th) 158 (C.A.).

[34] (1991), 47 O.A.C. 329, 50 C.P.C. (2d) 271, 80 D.L.R. (4th) 470 (Ont. C.A.).

[35] See *id.*, at 473 D.L.R. where the court spoke of a "general range" of damages. See also *Levesque v. Lipskie* (1991), 45 O.A.C. 313, 3 O.R. (3d) 98, 29 M.V.R. (2d) 99, 80 D.L.R. (4th) 243 (C.A.).

Canadian courts have had much difficulty in personal injury cases with calculation of the "gross-up", *i.e.*, the supplement to allow for the income tax that the plaintiff will presumably have to pay in the future on the proceeds of investment of the portion of the award for cost of future care. In *Scarff v. Wilson*,[36] and in *Watkins v. Olafson*,[37] the Supreme Court of Canada held that the plaintiff was entitled to have an income tax supplement included in the award, but the court did not establish the precise method to be used in making the calculation. It might be thought that experts would agree on this question, but this is very far from being the case, because there are five or six crucial assumptions that lie behind the calculations, and slight variations in the assumptions lead to enormous variations in the final figures. In many cases it is clear that judges have seen their task as selecting either the figure offered by the plaintiff's expert, or that offered by the defendant's expert. Many of the judges, naturally, are not at ease with mathematical calculations, and regard the details of the calculations as a mysterious "black box" the internal workings of which they do not pretend to understand.

This points to a more general question that the courts must face in many areas of the law of damages, namely, the degree to which they should defer to the evidence of accountants and other financial experts. In a British Columbia case involving lost business profits, the Court of Appeal said, in drastically reducing the trial judge's award, "It was not for the accountants to estimate the lost profits, but the court."[38] This suggests that the courts cannot allow themselves to be put in the position of failing to understand, and being unable to explain crucial aspects of their awards. I realize that this limits the courts' acceptance of actuarial evidence to what the judges can be expected to understand, but I think that this limitation is the price that must be paid for maintaining reasoned decisions. If it be objected that this is to turn our back on useful expert assistance, I would answer that there is seldom in fact a simple answer on which experts agree. Usually different experts support different conclusions, according to the assumptions they make and the degree of sophistication to which their analysis aspires. The idea that, just beyond the range of amateur understanding, there lies a simple solution endorsed by expert unanimity is usually false. If there is such an expert unanimity on any point, it quickly becomes a part of the generally accepted knowledge of the community, and so of general judicial understanding.

---

[36] [1989] 2 S.C.R. 776, [1989] 6 W.W.R. 500, 39 B.C.L.R. (2d) 293, 61 D.L.R. (4th) 749, 100 N.R. 189.

[37] [1989] 2 S.C.R. 750, 61 D.L.R. (4th) 577.

[38] *Houweling Nurseries Ltd. v. Fisons Western Corp.* (1988), 37 B.C.L.R. (2d) 2, 49 D.L.R. (4th) 205 at 207 (B.C.C.A.) *per* McLachlin J.A.; leave to appeal to S.C.C. refused 37 B.C.L.R. (2d) 2n, 29 C.P.C. (2d) 168.

The Supreme Court of Canada, in establishing the necessity for awards to include a supplement for income tax, expressed the hope that there would develop "a computer model which would yield an estimate of the gross-up on the basis of the factors relevant to the particular case".[39] But there are difficulties. If it is not for accountants to estimate lost profits, can it be for computer programmers to determine compensation for personal injuries? Given our experience of law generally, is it not likely that sets of circumstances will arise that have not been foreseen by the computer programmers, and that would lead to bizarre results in particular cases? Computer programs produce substantially different results according to the assumptions that are used in designing them. The question of the proper assumptions must, unless all considerations of consistency and rationality are to be abandoned, be a question of law. It is certainly not a question of arithmetic. Some of the crucial factors are matters not specific to the plaintiff, such as the estimated future rate of inflation,[40] and the details of future income tax rules;[41] Other assumptions crucial to the calculation vary from one plaintiff to another. These include such matters as the nature of the investments to be made with the capital sum,[42] the rate of withdrawal from the fund,[43] and the amount of the plaintiff's other income.[44] This question illustrates a tension that runs throughout the law of damages: the imposition of rules, or irrebuttable presumptions, on these question ignores the situation of the individual plaintiff; but the failure to impose such rules increases the expense of litigation, complicates the settlement process, and leads to apparent inconsistencies in awards. When it is added that the questions in issue are inherently uncertain, and there is no control over how the plaintiff in fact will use the award, it may be suggested that "perfect" assessment of this aspect of the award is illusory, or at any rate, that pursuit of this perfection has a high price, and that it must be balanced against other considerations equally important to the attainment of justice.

A difficult question faced by the courts in personal injury cases is how to calculate compensation for lost housekeeping capacity. In *Fobel*

---

[39] *Watkins v. Olafson*, *supra*, note 37, at 588-89 D.L.R.

[40] This is now fixed by rule 53.09(2).

[41] See *Tucker (Public Trustee) v. Asleson* (1992), 62 B.C.L.R. (2d) 78, 86 D.L.R. (4th) 73 (S.C.); revd in part [1993] 6 W.W.R. 45, 78 B.C.L.R. (2d) 173, 44 M.V.R. (2d) 178, 102 D.L.R. (4th) 518.

[42] See *Scarff v. Wilson*, *supra*, note 36. It is now provided in Ontario, by rule 53.09(2)(*a*) that it is to be assumed that the entire award will be invested in fixed income securities.

[43] See *Tucker (Public Trustee) v. Asleson*, *supra*, note 41.

[44] *Ibid.*, *Cherry (Guardian) v. Borsman*, [1992] 6 W.W.R. 701, 70 B.C.L.R. (2d) 273, 12 C.C.L.T. (2d) 137, 94 D.L.R. (4th) 487 (C.A.).

v. Dean [45] the plaintiff had a full-time paid job (six days a week) and, in addition, spent 40 hours per week "to manage the home and perform housekeeping duties". Her housekeeping capacity was reduced by the defendant's wrong, and the question was how compensation for this loss should be measured. No replacement services were actually purchased during the pre-trial period. The Saskatchewan Court of Appeal held that the plaintiff was entitled to an award of $15,000 in respect of the pre-trial period, which was described as compensation for "non-pecuniary loss", that compensation for future loss was appropriate, based on a replacement cost theory, whether or not the proceeds of the award were likely to be spent for this purpose, and that (in contrast to the usual practice with awards for loss of earning capacity) the award was to be "grossed up" for income tax. This approach does not fit easily the framework established by the Supreme Court of Canada in the 1978 "trilogy". It blurs the line between pecuniary and non-pecuniary loss, and that between compensation for loss of earning capacity and compensation for the cost of future care. In laying down the principles of compensation in this area I would suggest that it is desirable to bear in mind the cost to parties and to the community at large of unpredictability. No rule will be found that satisfies all interests in this controversial area, but I would suggest that there is much to be said for a rule that is predictable, fair between one plaintiff and another, reasonably inexpensive to apply and that is likely to facilitate settlements.

Another area where the amount of awards is difficult to predict is that of mental distress for breach of contract. Recent English cases have suggested that damages for mental distress on breach of contract are only recoverable when the subject-matter of the contract is to provide peace of mind,[46] but not all of the Canadian cases making such awards fall into this category,[47] and it seems unlikely, therefore, that the English cases will be followed on this point. Again, the issue, it may be suggested, is the tension, running through the whole law of damages, between, on the one hand, perfect compensation in the individual case, and, on the other hand, the need for rules that are predictable, fair between one plaintiff and another, workable and reasonably inexpensive of application.

Recent cases have shown the need for rules for measuring damages

---

[45] [1991] 6 W.W.R. 408, 93 Sask. R. 103, 9 C.C.L.T. (2d) 87, 83 D.L.R. (4th) 385 (C.A.).

[46] *Hayes v. Dodd*, [1990] 2 All E.R. 815 (C.A.); *Watts v. Morrow*, [1991] 1 W.L.R. 1421 (C.A.).

[47] See *Ribeiro v. Canadian Imperial Bank of Commerce* (1989), 24 C.C.E.L. 15, 67 O.R. (2d) 385, 89 C.L.L.C. 14,033 (H.C.); vard. (1992), 44 C.C.E.L. 165, 13 O.R. (3d) 228 (C.A.); leave to appeal to S.C.C. refused (1993), 65 O.A.C. 79n, 157 N.R. 400n where the Ontario Court of Appeal increased an award in a wrongful dismissal case from $10,000 to $20,000.

in defamation cases that will satisfactorily balance the plaintiff's interest in fair compensation against the defendant's interest, and that of the community, in free speech. In *Derrickson v. Tomat*[48] the British Columbia Court of Appeal, in setting aside an award of $350,000 general and $50,000 exemplary damages, remarked that, in case of politically motivated comment, damages should be restricted to a sum sufficient to indicate that the comment was unwarranted. Exemplary damages would rarely, if ever, be appropriate on such a theory. There is an important case currently before the Supreme court of Canada on this question.[49] I would suggest that much of the criticism levelled at the current law of defamation would be muted if awards of damages were moderate, consistent and predictable. It is in the interest of litigants in general, and of the community at large that, here as elsewhere, the rules for assessment of damages should be predictable, fair between one plaintiff and another, workable, and reasonably inexpensive of application.

We must not seek from our system of civil litigation more than can be reasonably expected of it. It might be said that the purpose of all law is to do justice, and that rules of law can be supported only insofar as they tend towards justice. There is truth in that proposition, but it could not be adopted as a working principle of law, partly because it would have the effect of superseding all legal rules, but more importantly because it begs the question of what is meant by justice. The considerations mentioned, that favour predictability, regularity and practicability of legal rules are not to be opposed to justice: they are part of the concept of justice itself, at least in the context of civil litigation. It must be remembered, too, that the ability of courts to find facts is very severely limited, even in relation to actual past facts, and most especially in relation to the hypothetical facts on which damage assessment usually depends. There is no guarantee, therefore, that the pursuit of an elaborate inquiry will lead to a result that is more just, even in an individual case, particularly where there is an inequality of resources between the parties.

We do not need to be reminded that the cost of litigation is a serious concern to everyone, and that it is emphatically not true that the greater the cost the better the result. Dr. Lushington made another comment, in another context, that is worth bearing in mind here:

> We must ever remember that though truth and justice are the aim and end of all courts, still they must not be sought through the aid of too expensive

---

[48] (1992), 88 D.L.R. (4th) 401 (B.C.C.A.).

[49] *Hill v. Church of Scientology of Toronto* (leave to appeal granted 20 O.R. (3d) xv, 180 N.R. 240*n* (S.C.C.)) on appeal from (1994), 18 O.R. (3d) 385, 20 C.C.L.T. (2d) 129, 114 D.L.R. (4th) 1, where the Ontario Court of Appeal upheld an award of $1.6 million. The decision has now been affirmed by the Supreme Court of Canada: (1995), 126 D.L.R. (4th) 129.

machinery. The true principle is, not to adopt that system which, in special cases, may best arrive at the truth, regardless of delay and expense, but to choose that course which, on the whole, will best administer justice with a due regard to the means of those who seek it.[50]

---

[50] *The Resultatet* (1853), 17 Jur. 353 at 354 (on an evidentiary point).

NON-PECUNIARY DAMAGES

C. Scott Ritchie, Q.C.

1. *Introduction*

In 1978 three catastrophic personal injury cases came before the Supreme Court of Canada,[1] and the court took the opportunity to establish new guidelines for both pecuniary and non-pecuniary damages. The concern over the spectre of excessive million dollar verdicts seen in the United States figured prominently in establishing these new guidelines. Whether the concern was real or imagined in the Canadian setting has been the subject of debate.[2] Mr. Justice Dickson in *Andrews* expressed the concern as follows:

> However, if the principle of the paramountcy of care is accepted, then it follows that there is more room for the consideration of other policy factors in the assessment of damages for non-pecuniary losses. In particular this is the area where the social burden of large awards deserves considerable weight. The sheer fact is that there is no objective yardstick for translating non-pecuniary losses, such as pain and suffering and loss of amenities, into monetary terms. This area is open to widely extravagant claims. It is in this area that awards in the United States have soared to dramatically high levels in recent years. Statistically, it is the area where the danger of excessive burden of expense is greatest.[3]

In *Arnold v. Teno* Mr Justice Spence expressed the same concern as follows:

---

[1] *Andrews v. Grand & Toy Alberta Ltd.*, [1978] 2 S.C.R. 229, [1978] 1 W.W.R. 577, 3 C.C.L.T. 225, 83 D.L.R. (3d) 452, 19 N.R. 50; *Thorton v. Prince Edward Board of Education* [1978] 2 S.C.R. 267, [1978] 1 W.W.R. 607, 3 C.C.L.T. 257, 83 D.L.R. (3d) 480, 19 N.R. 552, and *Arnold v. Teno*, [1978] 2 S.C.R. 287, 3 C.C.L.T. 272, 83 D.L.R. (3d) 609, 19 N.R. 1.

[2] Cherniak, "Commentary on Professor Feldthuseen's Paper on Punitive Damages" (1990), 16 Canadian Business Law Journal 281 at 281.

[3] *Andrews, supra*, note 1, at 261.

In the case of many verdicts in the United States, it may well be said that
they have been soaring. . . . . Certainly, such awards, which one might characterize as exorbitant, fail to accord with the requirements of reasonableness,
a proper gauge for all damages.

. . . . .

The very real and serious social burden of these exorbitant awards has been
illustrated graphically in the United States in cases concerning medical malpractice. We have a right to fear a situation where none but the very wealthy
could own or drive automobiles because none but the very wealthy could
afford to pay the enormous insurance premiums which would be required
by insurers to meet such exorbitant awards.[4]

The Canadian response to personal injury reform has been both legislative and judicial. In the United States reform has been almost exclusively legislative with what can only be described as dramatic and
fundamental reform coming in the past few months when the House of
Representatives passed three Bills[5] that limit punitive damages in civil law
suits to three times the monetary award with a cap of $250,000; limit non-
pecuniary damages in medical malpractice cases to $250,000; eliminate
the right of recovery if a plaintiff had alcohol in the system and was more
than 50 per cent responsible for his or her own injuries; limit recovery
in product liability cases for non-economic damages to the proportion of
harm assessed against a particular defendant leaving open joint and several
liability for economic damages; limit liability for retail sellers to damages
caused by their actions; set new standards for personal injury and products
liability cases; and set a limitation period of 15 years in product liability
cases. Whatever fate lies in store for these Bills in the Senate and White
House there is a strong impetus for change in the direction of moderation
in non-pecuniary and punitive damages.

In Canada the traditional approach to punitive damages and non-
pecuniary damages for defamation, libel and slander has been conservative.[6] However, two recent decisions from Ontario call into question
whether this moderate trend will continue. In *Clairborne Industries Ltd.
v. Nat'l Bank of Canada*[7] punitive damages in the amount of $4,800,000
were upheld, and the Court of Appeal upheld an $800,000 award for puni-
tive damages in the case of *Hill v. Church of Scientology of Toronto*.[8]
The Supreme Court of Canada heard the appeal in *Hill* in

---

[4] *Teno, supra*, note 1, at 332-33.
[5] *Attorney Accountability Act; Securities Litigation Reform Act;* and the *Common Sense Product Liability and Legal Reform Act.*
[6] Ontario Law Reform Commission, *Report on Exemplary Damages* (1991), at 47.
[7] (1989), 34 O.A.C. 241, 69 O.R. (2d) 65, 59 D.L.R. (4th) 533 (C.A.).
[8] (1994), 18 O.R. (3d) 385, 20 C.C.L.T. (2d) 129, 114 D.L.R. (4th) 1 (C.A.);
leave to appeal to S.C.C. granted 20 O.R. (3d) xv, 180 N.R. 240n.

February, 1995 and the decision is still under reserve.[9]

The law of exemplary damages is evolving in Canada and the recent and very valuable contribution of the Ontario Law Reform Commission[10] on the topic will provide a useful frame work for the courts as they deal with exemplary damages.

This paper will examine current questions relating to non-pecuniary damages and punitive damages in both the personal injury and non-personal injury setting. In personal injury cases, there has been considerable debate regarding the theoretical model adopted by the Supreme Court

---

[9] Subsequent to the delivery of this paper the Supreme Court of Canada released their decision in *Hill vs The Church of Scientology of Toronto*. The court was unanimous in upholding the jury's verdict wherein the following awards were made:

Compensatory General Damages	$300,000
Compensatory Aggravated Damages	$500,000
Punitive Damages	$800,000

The tests for aggravated damages and punitive damages established by our Court of Appeal in *Walker v. CFTO Ltd.* (1987), 59 O.R. (2d) 104, 37 D.L.R. (4th) 224, 39 C.C.L.T. 121, was affirmed. Cory J. delivering the judgment for the court on this issue made the following observation:
"Damages can and do serve a useful purpose. But for them, it would be all to easy for the large, wealthy and powerful to persist in libelling vulnerable victims. Awards of general and aggravated damages alone might simply be regarded as a license fee for continuing a character assassination. The protection of a person's arising from the publication of false and injurious statements must be effective. The most effective means of protection will be supplied by the knowledge that fines in the form of punitive damages may be awarded in cases where the defendant's conduct is truly outrageous. In rejecting the imposition of a cap on damages for defamation Cory, J. observed that "First, the injuries suffered by a plaintiff as the result of injurious false statements is entirely different from the non-pecuniary damages suffered by a plaintiff in a personal injury case. . .Second, at the time the cap was placed on non-pecuniary damages, their assessment had become a very real problem for the courts and for society as a whole. The damages awarded were varying tremendously not only between the provinces but between districts of a province. Perhaps as a result of motor vehicle accidents, the problem arose in the courts every day of every week. The size and disparity of assessments was affecting insurance rates and, thus, the cost of operating motor vehicles and, indeed, businesses of all kinds throughout the land. In those circumstances for that one aspect of recovery, it was appropriate to set a cap. The court observed that from 1987 to 1991 there were only twenty-seven reported liable judgments in Canada with an average award of $30,000. The court further observed that "a cap would operate in a manner that would change the whole character and function of the law of defamation. It would amount to a radical change in policy and direction for the courts".
[10] *Supra*, note 6.

of Canada in setting the $100,000 cap[11] on non-pecuniary damages.[12] The fact is that the Supreme Court did not adhere to their own theoretical model when assessing damages in the Trilogy cases. The present practice of non-pecuniary damage assessment in personal injury cases appears to be little different from the pre-Trilogy practice, with the difference being that the courts now set such damages in the presence of a cap. An issue to be considered is whether or not there is a need for the Supreme Court to provide further clarification as to how non-pecuniary damages are to be assessed given the reality that the lower courts have not strictly followed the functional approach adopted by the Supreme Court in the Trilogy cases and *Lindal v. Lindal*.[13] This paper will also examine the question of whether the judicial cap on non-pecuniary damages is appropriate under Bill 164,[14] where the principle of full economic recovery does not apply. Recent punitive and non-pecuniary awards for defamation have risen well beyond previous conservative levels for such awards. The Supreme Court recently heard argument in Hill, a non-pecuniary and punitive damage case, and we will know shortly whether a limit will be placed on such damages.

2. *The Trilogy and Personal Injury Non-pecuniary Damages*

In the hands of imaginative lawyers the principle of *restitutio in integrum* has resulted in multi-million dollar awards. An award by Zuber J. of $6,000,000[15] for a seventeen-year-old quadriplegic has recently been upheld by the Ontario Court of Appeal.[16] It is unlikely that the Supreme

---

[11] Adjusted for inflation, the present value of the cap is approximately $250,000.

[12] See for example Cooper-Stephenson and Saunders, *Personal Injury Damages in Canada* (Toronto: Carswell, 1981), Klar, "The Assessment of Damages for Non-Pecuniary Losses" (1979), 5 C.C.L.T. 262, and Charles, *Charles Handbook on the Assessment of Damages in Personal Injury Cases*, 2nd ed. (Toronto: Carswell, 1990).

[13] [1981] 2 S.C.R. 629, [1982] 1 W.W.R. 433, 34 B.C.L.R. 273, 19 C.C.L.T. 1, 129 D.L.R. (3d) 263, 39 N.R. 361.

[14] *An Act to amend the Insurance Act and certain other Acts in respect of Automobile Insurance and other Insurance Matters*, S.O.1993, c. 10, amending the *Insurance Act*, R.S.O. 1990, c. I.8.

[15] *Stein v. Sandwich West (Twp.)*, [1993] O.J. No. 1772 (Q.L.) (Ont. Gen. Div.).

[16] [1995] O.J. No. 423 (Q.L.) (C.A.). Other recent examples of large awards in personal injury cases include $4,600,000 exclusive of prejudgment interest and *Family Law Act* claims in *Mortimer v. Cameron* (1992), 9 M.P.L.R. (2d) 185 (Ont. Gen Div.); affd 17 O.R. (3d) 1, 19 M.P.L.R. (2d) 286, 111 D.L.R. (4th) 428 (C.A.); $3,000,000 in *Bain v. Calgary Board of Education*, [1994] 2 W.W.R.

Court intended or foresaw that the guidelines adopted in the Trilogy cases would result in such large awards. In *Andrews*[17] the Supreme Court reduced the damages for a 21-year-old quadriplegic from just over $1,000,000 to $740,000. The non-pecuniary award was reduced to the "rough upper limit" established by the court of $100,000 from a trial award of $150,000. In *Thorton*[18] the award for a 15-year-old quadriplegic was reduced from over $1,000,000 to $859,000. The non-pecuniary portion of the award was reduced from $200,000 to the cap of $100,000. In *Teno*[19] the award for a severely brain damaged young girl was reduced from $950,000 to $540,000 with the non-pecuniary portion being reduced from $200,000 to $100,000. Some commentators at the time argued that such awards substantially under-compensated severely injured plaintiffs.[20] Recent large damage awards based upon different actuarial assumptions have corrected most concerns about compensating economic shortfalls.

Chief Justice Dickson, in *Andrews*,[21] articulated what was meant by the principle of full compensation for pecuniary loss in the context of a severe personal injury. The court held that

> . . . there is no duty to mitigate, in the sense of being forced to accept less than real loss. There is a duty to be reasonable. There cannot be "complete" or "perfect" compensation.[22]

You will recall that in *Andrews* the debate related to home care versus institutional care. Chief Justice Dickson went on to say:

> I do not think the area of future care is one in which the argument of the social burden of the expense should be controlling, particularly in a case like the present, where the consequences of acceding to it would be to fail in large measure to compensate the victim for his loss.[23]

It was only upon the premise of full compensation for economic loss that the court, as a matter of policy, limited non-pecuniary damages in

---

468, 14 Alta. L.R. (3d) 314, 18 C.C.L.T. (2d) 249 (Q.B.), and $2,500,000 in *Macdonald v. Neufeld* (November 7, 1991), Doc. Vancouver B894421 (B.C.S.C.), quantum increased in *Macdonald v. Neufeld*, [1994] 2 W.W.R. 113, 85 B.C.L.R. (2d) 129, 17 C.C.L.T. (2d) 201 (C.A.).

[17] *Andrews, supra*, note 1.

[18] *Thorton, supra*, note 1.

[19] *Teno, supra*, note 1.

[20] See for example Braniff and Pratt, "Tragedy in the Supreme Court of Canada: New Developments in the Assessment of Damages for Personal Injuries" (1979), 37 U. of T. Fac.L.Rev. 1.

[21] [1978] 2 S.C.R. 229, [1978] 1 W.W.R. 577, 3 C.C.L.T. 225, 83 D.L.R. (3d) 452, 19 N.R. 50.

[22] *Ibid.*, at 242.

[23] *Ibid.*, at 248.

the most severe injury cases to $100,000 measured in 1978 dollars. The court reasoned:

> However, if the principle of the paramountcy of care is accepted, then it follows that there is more room for the consideration of other policy factors in the assessment of damages for non-pecuniary losses.[24]

The court feared the importation to Canada of what they saw as exorbitant non-pecuniary awards in the United States, and it acted preventively by imposing the $100,000 cap on such damages.

3. *The Theoretical Basis for Non-pecuniary Damage Awards*

In discussing the basis upon which the courts should make an award for non-pecuniary damages, Dickson C.J. examined the three different theoretical models for such compensation as outlined in the article by A. I. Ogus entitled "Damages for Lost Amenities: For a Foot, A Feeling or a Function?".[25] The first approach described by Ogus is the conceptual approach, which involves placing an objective value on the "asset" that had been lost by the plaintiff. The second approach is the personal approach, which starts from the premise that measurement can be made in terms of human happiness, and that no price can be placed on different parts of the human body without reference to an individual's feelings. Therefore the award should reflect the loss of human happiness by the particular injured plaintiff. The third approach is the functional approach, which also focuses on the individual, but adopts a measure based upon how an award can be effectively employed by the plaintiff to purchase some measure of solace. Under this approach the court should not attempt to put a value on happiness.

Of the three theoretical approaches the court concluded that it preferred the functional approach, stating:

> To my mind, this last approach [the functional approach] has much to commend it, as it provides a rationale as to why money is considered compensation for non-pecuniary losses such as loss of amenities, pain and suffering, and loss of expectation of life. Money is awarded because it will serve a useful function in making up for what has been lost in the only way possible,

---

[24] *Ibid.*, at 261.
[25] (1972), 35 Mod.L.Rev. 1.

accepting that what has been lost is incapable of being replaced in any direct way.

. . . . .

If damages for non-pecuniary loss are viewed from a functional perspective, it is reasonable that large amounts should not be awarded once a person is properly provided for in terms of future care for his injuries and disabilities. The money for future care is to provide physical arrangements for assistance, equipment and facilities directly related to the injuries. Additional money to make life more endurable should then be seen as providing more general physical arrangements above and beyond those relating directly to the injuries. The result is a coordinated and interlocking basis for compensation, and a more rational justification for non-pecuniary loss compensation.[26]

The court continued however, to state that regardless of the theoretical model adopted, non-pecuniary damage awards were still largely arbitrary and conventional, and there was a need for consistency across the country for similar non-pecuniary damage awards.[27] The court awarded $100,000 for non-pecuniary damages in each of the Trilogy cases, and stated this amount be regarded as a rough upper limit in similar cases, save for exceptional circumstances.[28]

In Lindal[29] the Supreme Court was asked to find that the injuries were exceptional and that "the rough upper limit" of $100,000 should be exceeded. The trial judge assessed the non-pecuniary damages at $135,000 and justified that award by reasoning that the injuries suffered by the plaintiff were more grievous than those suffered by the plaintiffs in the trilogy cases, thus qualifying for the "exceptional circumstances" referred to by Chief Justice Dickson in Andrews. The court used this opportunity to re-affirm both the upper limit of $100,000 and the functional approach to the assessment of non-pecuniary damages in these words:

Pain and suffering and loss of amenities are intangibles. They are not possessions that have an objective, ascertainable value. Professor Kahn-Freund in his brilliant essay "Expectation of Happiness", 5 Mod. L. R. 81 (1941), cites the example of philosopher Poseidonios, who, when tormented by pain, is reported to have exclaimed [at p. 86] "Pain, thou shalt not defeat me. I shall never admit that thou art an evil." How, Professor Kahn-Freund asks, could we award damages for pain and suffering to this philosopher who welcomed his misery as a test of his own power to resist it? Is the Stoic

---

[26] Andrews, supra, note 21, at 262.
[27] Ibid., at 263.
[28] Ibid., at 265.
[29] Lindal, supra, note 13.

entitled to less compensation than the weak-willed person who recoils at the slightest suggestion of pain or unhappiness?[30]

Chief Justice Dickson explains further:

> Thus the amount of an award for non-pecuniary damage should not depend alone upon the seriousness of the injury but upon its ability to ameliorate the condition of the victim considering his or her particular situation. It therefore will not follow that in considering what part of the maximum should be awarded the gravity of the injury alone will be determinative. An appreciation of the individual's loss is the key and the "need for solace will not necessarily correlate with the seriousness of the injury" (Cooper-Stephenson and Sanders, *Personal Injury Damages in Canada* (1981), at 373).
>
> . . . . .
>
> I have already indicated that the social costs of the award cannot be controlling when assessing damages for loss of income and the cost of future care. The plaintiff must be provided with a fund of money which will provide him with adequate , reasonable care for the rest of his life. The social impact of the award must be considered, however, in calculating the damages for non-pecuniary loss. There are a number of reasons for this. First, the claim of a severely injured plaintiff for damages for non-pecuniary loss is virtually limitless. This is particularly so if we adopt the functional approach and award damages according to the use which can be made of the money.There are an infinite number of uses which could be suggested in order to improve the lot of the crippled plaintiff. Moreover, it is difficult to determine the reasonableness of any of these claims. There are no accurate measures available to guide decision in this area.
>
> A second factor that must be considered is that we have already fully compensated the plaintiff for his loss of future earnings. Had he not been injured, a certain portion of these earnings would have been available for amenities. Logically, therefore, even before we award damages under the head of non-pecuniary loss, the plaintiff has certain funds at his disposal which can be used to provide a substitute for lost amenities. This consideration indicates that a moderate award for non-pecuniary damages is justified.
>
> A third factor is that damages for non-pecuniary loss are not really "compensatory". The purpose of making the award is to substitute other amenities for those that have been lost, not to compensate for the loss of something with a money value. Since the primary function of the law of damages is compensation, it is reasonable that awards for non-pecuniary loss, which do not fulfil this function, be moderate.[31]

---

[30] *Ibid.*, at 635-36.
[31] *Ibid.*, at 637-40.

It has been argued[32] that the Supreme Court simply chose the functional approach because it had the best prospect of moderating damages.

4. *The Functional Approach in Practice*

In neither the Trilogy cases or *Lindal* does the Supreme Court provide any guidance as to how the functional model is to be applied.[33] In arriving at the award of $100,000 in *Andrews* the Supreme Court does not point to any evidence with respect to how this sum is expected to purchase solace for the plaintiff. In "Charles Handbook on Assessment of Damages in Personal Injury Cases"[34] the author notes that most lower courts do not even refer to solace and if they do it is a token reference without a detailed analysis of the plaintiff's situation[35]

An issue left unresolved in the Trilogy was how lesser injuries should be compensated.[36] Were judges and juries to simply scale down from the limit of $100,000 for less than catastrophic injuries or was the cap intended as a ceiling that could be reached or approached with less serious injuries? The Supreme Court attempted to clarify this issue in *Lindal*, where Chief Justice Dickson states:

---

[32] See for example, Cooper-Stephenson and Saunders, *Personal Injury Damages in Canada* (Toronto: Carswell, 1981).

[33] Cooper-Stephenson and Saunders, *ibid.*, at 369 state:

"Though the Court undoubtedly espoused the functional theory in principle, actual quantification in *Andrews*, *Arnold* and *Thorton* resembled more closely the conceptual view. Thus in *Andrews* 'It was said: 'It is difficult to conceive of a person losing more than Andrews has lost' — apparently the loss of an asset approach. And in *Arnold* and *Thorton*, calculation was based heavily on a comparison of the plaintiff's injury and its consequences with those in Andrews. In none of the cases was there discussion of the plaintiff's actual need for solace and of his potential substitute activities. In the result, the Supreme Court trio of decisions must be viewed as only a beginning towards a functional theory of non-pecuniary damages in Canada."

[34] Charles, *Charles Handbook on Assessment of Damages in Personal Injury Cases*, (Toronto: Carswell, 1990).

[35] *Ibid.*, at 55.

[36] Waddams, *The Law of Damages*, 2nd ed. (Toronto: Canada Law Book Inc., 1990), at 3-31, states:

"A question not expressly dealt with in the 1978 trilogy is whether compensation for lesser injuries than those suffered by the plaintiffs in those case is to compensated on a sliding scale, so that $50,000 would be the appropriate award for a plaintiff suffering half of the loss suffered by the 1978 plaintiffs, and so on, assuming that proportionate losses could be estimated."

Thus the amount of an award for non-pecuniary damage should not depend alone upon the seriousness of the injury but upon its ability to ameliorate the condition of the victim considering his or her particular situation. It therefore will not follow that in considering what part of the maximum should be awarded the gravity of the individual's loss is the key and the "need for solace will not necessarily correlate with the seriousness of the injury."[37]

In spite of this clarification in *Lindal*, confusion remains and, with limited exceptions,[38] judges have continued to employ the yardstick of the gravity of the injury compared to the rough upper limit of $100,000.[39]

---

[37] *Lindal v. Lindal*, [1981] 2 S.C.R. 629 at 637, [1982] 1 W.W.R. 433, 34 B.C.L.R. 273, 19 C.C.L.T. 1, 129 D.L.R. (3d) 263, 39 N.R. 361.

[38] Charles, *supra*, note 34, at 60 cites the case of *Lapensee v. Ottawa Day Nursery Inc.* (1986) 35 C.C.L.T. 129 (Ont. H.C.J.) as an example where the court took the functional approach seriously and tried to outline the remedial measures that would make life more bearable for the victim.

[39] In recent decisions involving catastrophic injuries resulting in large awards, the courts often grant the maximum non-pecuniary award with very little discussion. The discussion that does occur is directed to comparing the condition of the plaintiff to the plaintiff's in the trilogy cases. For example, in *Bain v. Calgary Board of Education*, [1994] 2 W.W.R. 468, 14 Alta. L.R. (3d) 314, 18 C.C.L.T. (2d) 249, the court, after making a brief reference to the trilogy decisions, stated at 277 C.C.L.T.:

" I accept the evidence of Dr. Bruce that the equivalent value of $100,000 in 1993 dollars is $233,600. Kevin's injuries and permanent disabilities are not the most severe case that one could imagine although they can only be described as massive. In my view they represent 80% of the most severe case, an approach which in accord with the submissions of both parties, and accordingly under this head of damages the plaintiff's non pecuniary damages are assessed at $186,880."

In *Pittman Estate v. Bain* (1994) 19 C.C.L.T. (2d) 1, 112 D.L.R. (4th) 257, the court assessed the non-pecuniary damages of a women who had contracted the HIV virus from her husband due to the negligence of various parties in this manner at 169-70:

This [the HIV status of the plaintiff] must be compared to a person at the height of their youth who is rendered quadriplegic. For many decades that person will be trapped in a useless body, totally alert and totally dependant on others for their day to day care.

and at 170:

. . . Mrs Pittman's injury, in my view, is somewhat less so than that of a young person trapped in an unresponsive body for a lifetime of dependency, or a burn victim who will experience a lifetime of pain. While Mrs. Pittman's disease has eventually appalling consequences and requires constant monitoring and vigilance, she will probably live a relatively normal, self-sufficient life until the final stages, and those final stages will be, mercifully, relatively brief.

I assess Mrs. Pittman's non-pecuniary damages at $180,000. While her disease cannot be recompensed, that amount of money may offer her some solace during her remaining years.

I suspect that whether one treats the cap as a ceiling or an amount from which the courts should scale down is a distinction without much practical difference because of the court's desire for uniformity and the strong role played by precedents.

The real problem with the strict application of the functional approach in less than catastrophic claims is that it would lead to unpredictability and a lack of uniformity.[40] It is because of this lack of predictability and uniformity that courts have rejected the strict functional approach and adopted what one commentator has called the modified conceptual approach,[41] which is essentially the damage assessment method the courts employed prior to the Trilogy. The modified conceptual approach looks to the severity of the injury for the range of damages and then decides where in that range the facts of the case dictate the award should fall. I believe that the authors of *Personal Injury Damages In Canada* were right when they posed the question:

> In general, is measurement really any different from that under the conceptual and personal theories? Is measurement on the functional view, after all the theorising, simply a matter of identifying the acceptable range of compensation for a particular injury, in light of the "rough upper parameter?"[42]

In England, courts have imposed a judicial cap on non-pecuniary damage awards which is roughly equal to the cap established in Canada.[43] The measure of damages is arrived at using a conceptual approach, which starts out by measuring the severity of the injury and then turning to previous awards in similar cases, and modifying the awards as dictated by the particular facts of the case. The Canadian practice, as opposed to the theory, is more closely aligned with the English approach and I predict will remain so for reasons of uniformity and predictability.

5. *The Unaware Plaintiff*

One area where the application of the strict functional approach will produce a markedly different result from the asset or conceptual approach is where the victim is unaware of his or her plight. It follows from the functional approach that unless the non-pecuniary award will bring

---

[40] Osbourne, Annotation of *Lindal v. Lindal* (1981), 19 C.C.L.T. 3 at 7.

[41] *Ibid.*, at 5.

[42] (Toronto: Carswell, 1981), at 368-69.

[43] See Waddams, *supra*, note 36, at 3-37, and Brazier, *The Law of Torts*, 9th ed. (London: Butterworths, 1993), at 532, who states that the cap at that time was about 90,000-95,000 pounds.

solace no award should be made. Although the Supreme Court in the Trilogy cases did not point to evidence of how the non-pecuniary award would purchase solace there must have been an assumption that, at least at the catastrophic level of injury, the conventional award would purchase appropriate solace. Where the plaintiff is unconscious the assumption that money can purchase solace is not appropriate and the court will, on the functional approach, limit the non-pecuniary award.[44]

6. *Bill 164 and the Functional Approach*

Absent the principle of *restitio in integrum* is the imposition of a cap limiting non-pecuniary damages appropriate? In *Lindal* the Supreme Court stated, in justifying the moderate awards for non-pecuniary damages;

> A second factor that must be considered is that we have already fully compensated the plaintiff for his loss of future earnings. Had he not been injured, a certain portion of these earnings would have been available for amenities. Logically, therefore, even before we award damages under the head of non-pecuniary loss, the plaintiff has certain funds at his disposal which can be used to provide a substitute for lost amenities.[45]

Section 267.1(8)[46] of the *Insurance Act*, directs the court to calculate non-pecuniary damages as if the amendments under Bill 164 did not exist.

---

[44] *Lindal*, *supra*, note 37, at 637; *Khan v. Salama*, [1986] O.J. No. 619; affd [1988] O.J. No. 2226 (C.A.), where Holland J. awarded $10,000 in non-pecuniary damages to a 20-year-old plaintiff who suffered irreversible brain damage and had no understanding of her state or the injury suffered.

[45] *Lindal*, *ibid.*, at 639.

[46] Section 267.1(8) of the *Insurance Act*, as amended by Bill 164 (*An Act to amend the Insurance Act and certain other Acts in respect of Automobile Insurance and other Insurance Matters*, S.O.1993, c. 10, amending *Insurance Act*, R.S.O. 1990, c. I.8), reads as follows:

> "(8) Subject to subsections (2) and (5), in a proceeding for loss or damage from bodily injury or death arising directly or indirectly from the use or operation of an automobile, the court shall determine the amount of damages for non-pecuniary loss to be awarded against the owner of an automobile, an occupant of the automobile or a person present at the incident in accordance with the following rules:
>
> 1. The court shall first determine the amount of damages for non-pecuniary loss for which the owner of the automobile, the occupant of the automobile, or the person present at the incident would be liable without regard to this Part.
> 2. The determination under paragraph 1 shall be made in the same manner as a determination of the amount of damages for non-pecuniary

Did the legislature, with these provisions, intend to maintain the cap on non-pecuniary damages and the Trilogy method of calculating damages for awards less than the cap, or did the legislature simply preserve the guidelines established by the Trilogy, leaving open the right to establish evidence of a meaningful economic shortfall?[47] Evidence of economic shortfall, under the Trilogy guidelines, could overcome the public policy rationale for moderation in non-pecuniary damages. If the courts accepted this argument they would still have to grapple with the problem of the degree of shortfall required to overcome the Trilogy's call for moderation. As well as the question of the level to which damages should rise in such cases predictability and uniformity of damages awards would be victims if the courts were to accept increased damages for pain and suffering in cases of less than full economic recovery.

If the courts reject claims for increased non-pecuniary damages in cases where there was less than full economic recovery, it is at least reasonable to predict that judges and juries will reach for the upper end of the appropriate range for damages.

7. *Non-pecuniary Damages in a Non Personal Injury Setting*

The last time the Supreme Court of Canada had an opportunity to deal with the troubling subject matter of punitive, aggravated and non-pecuniary damages in a non-personal injury setting was in the case of *Vorvis v. Ins. Corp. of British Columbia*[48] where the Supreme Court sought to clarify the law relating to aggravated and punitive damages in a breach of contract action. *Vorvis* involved a wrongful dismissal claim where damages for mental distress flowing from the wrongful termination was asserted. The question before the court was whether punitive damages could be awarded in an action for breach of contract, based on

---

loss in a proceeding to which this section does not apply, and, in particular, without regard to,

   i. the statutory accident benefits provided for under subsection 268(1),

   ii. the provisions of this section that protect the owner of the automobile, the occupants of the automobile and the persons present at the incident from liability for damages for pecuniary loss, and,

   iii. the provisions of paragraph 3 (the provisions with regards to the deductible amount for non-pecuniary loss damages).

[47] McLeish, "Strategies for Expanding the Scope of Non-Economic General Damages", *Practical Strategies For Advocates III* (Toronto: The Advocates' Society, 1993), at 18.

[48] [1989] 1 S.C.R. 1085, 36 B.C.L.R. (2d) 273, 42 B.L.R. 111, 25 C.C.E.L. 81, 90 CLLC 14,035, 58 D.L.R. (4th) 193, 94 N.R. 321.

wrongful dismissal of an employee. The area of the law has been subject
to much judicial comment and there were two lines of authorities. One
line of authorities stands with the proposition that in some contracts the
parties may well have contemplated at the time of the contract that a breach
in certain circumstances would cause a plaintiff mental distress.[49] Insofar
as punitive damages were concerned, the Supreme Court held that although
the English Courts tightly circumscribed the ambit of punitive damages
to two areas, namely, abuse of power by government and torts committed for profit, the law in Canada, and the balance of the Commonwealth
countries, was not as restrictive.[50] *Vorvis* confirmed that the basis for an
award of punitive damages was a finding of the commission of an actionable wrong which caused the very injury complained of by the plaintiff.[51]
The conduct complained of must also be of such a nature as to be deserving of punishment because of its harsh, vindictive, reprehensible and malicious nature.[52] Although the Supreme Court held that punitive damages
were available in a civil context, the discretion to award them should be
"most cautiously exercised".[53] The contentious problem with punitive
damages is that civil courts are imposing fines, which is the traditional
jurisdiction of criminal courts.[54] Not only is it an exception for civil courts
to impose fines, but the fines imposed are paid to the individual as opposed
to the state.[55] Carruthers J., in the case of *Ribeiro v. Canadian Imperial*

---

[49] *Addis v. Gramophone Co.*, [1909] A.C. 488; *Peso Silver Mines Ltd. (MPL)
v. Cropper*, [1966] S.C.R. 673; affg 56 D.L.R. (2d) 117 (B.C.C.A.). These cases
stand for the proposition that in contract actions the only damages that may
be awarded are damages for the breach of contract itself and in a wrongful
dismissal case those damages would be measured by the appropriate notice.
  Jarvis v. Swans Tours Ltd., [1973] Q.B 233; *Brown v. Waterloo Regional
Board of Com'rs of Police* (1983), 43 O.R. (2d) 113 stand for the proposition
that where it was foreseeable by the parties in a contract action that mental
anguish could result if the contract was breached. Confusion remains based
on the following comment by Mr. Justice McIntyre in *Vorvis* "I would not
wish to be taken as saying that aggravated damages could never be awarded
in a case of wrongful dismissal, particularly where the acts complained of were
also independently actionable, a factor not present here". The court held that
any damages for mental distress in this case pre-dated the actual dismissal and
on that basis a claim for aggravated damages was rejected.

[50] *Rookes v. Bernard*, [1964] A.C. 1129, as quoted in *Vorvis, supra*, note 48, at
1105.

[51] *Vorvis, ibid.*, at 1106.

[52] *Vorvis, ibid.*, at 1107.

[53] *Ibid.*

[54] Waddams, *supra*, note 36, at 3-27.

[55] The Supreme Court of Canada decision in *Hill v. Church of Scientology* [see
note 8] where Cory J. outlines the importance of punitive damages as follows:
  "Punitive damages may be awarded in situations where the defendant in
  his conduct is so malicious, oppressive, and high-handed that it offends
  the court's sense of decency. Punitive damages bear no relation to what

Bank of Commerce[56] awarded by damages for mental distress and punitive damages. The punitive damage award of $10,000 was increased on appeal to $50,000 and the award of damages for mental distress was increased from $10,000 to $20,000.[57]

In *Vorvis* the facts and conduct of the defendant did not justify punitive damages for wrongful dismissal. However, the court acknowledged that punitive damages could be awarded in such cases on the right facts and thus the long debate as to whether punitive damages were available in contract cases was resolved in favour of such awards. It can be said that *Vorvis* reinforced the exceptional nature of punitive damages while enlarging the types of cases where such awards are available.

8. *Reform Movements in Canada and the United States*

It has been noted that in Canada, the emphasis in awarding punitive damages appear to be on the retribution relative to the plaintiff only, rather than deterrence at large.[58] The focus in the United States on economic deterrence as opposed to retributive punishment accounts in part for the much higher awards in the United States. This is especially so in products liability cases where the wealth of the defendant is often a major factor in setting damages. The larger awards in the United States is in no small

---

the plaintiff should receive by way of compensation. Their aim is not to compensate the plaintiff, but rather to punish the defendant. It is a means by which the jury or judge expresses its outrage at the egregious conduct of the defendant. They are in the nature of a fine which is meant to act as a deterrent to the defendant and to others from acting in this matter. It is important to emphasize that these damages should only be awarded in those circumstances where the combined award of general and aggravated damages would be insufficient to achieve the goal of punishment and deterrence."

[56] *Ribeiro v. Canadian Imperial Bank of Commerce* (1992), 13 O.R. (3d) 278, 44 C.C.E.L. 165 (C.A.); revg 67 O.R. (2d) 385, 24 C.C.E.L. 225, 89 CLLC 14,033; leave to the Supreme Court of Canada was refused ([1993] 2 S.C.R. x).

[57] High Court decision of Carruthers J.; *Ribeiro v. Canadian Imperial Bank of Commerce, ibid.*, at 278 O.R. (C.A.). Carruthers J. provides a rather exhaustive review of the law in the area of aggravated and punitive damages in breach of contract actions.

[58] Ontario Law Reform Commission, *Report on Exemplary Damages* (1991), at 14. But see the July 20th decision of the Supreme Court of Canada in *Hill v. Church of Scientology of Toronto* where Cory J. speaking on the purpose to be served by punitive damages stated: "They are in the nature of a fine which is meant to act as a deterrent to the defendant and to others from acting in this manner".

part due to the predominance of jury trials.[59] Perhaps, however, the single most important difference relates to the limitation in Canadian law that the plaintiff cannot recover punitive damages unless he or she is the victim of the punishable behaviour, and the award must relate to the actual harm of the plaintiff and not to others.[60]

In the United States, multi-million dollar punitive damage awards have invited constitutional challenge, which have recently been the subject of United States Supreme Court decisions. In *Browning-Ferris Industries of Vermont Inc. v. Kelco Disposal Inc.*,[61] a majority of the Supreme Court refused to find that the Excessive Fines Clause of the Eighth Amendment applied to punitive damage awards in civil cases, and the punitive damage award of $6 million was allowed to stand.[62] A strong dissent by Justice O'Connor and Justice Stevens would have found that the Excessive Fines clause did apply to civil punitive damage awards.[63] Of more significance however, is the fact that both the majority and minority opinions indicated that the court would look favourably on a proper constitutional challenge to excessive civil punitive damages based upon the Due Process Clause,[64] having concluded that this issue had not been properly raised in *Browning*.[65]

Commentators have questioned whether the court's invitation to challenge civil punitive damages under the Due Process Amendment would be successful, and even if successful whether the potential limits that could be imposed judicially would significantly impact on excessive awards.[66]

---

[59] *Ibid.*, at 14.

[60] *Vorvis, supra*, note 48, at 106, and *Cassell & Co. Ltd. v. Broome*, [1972] A.C. 1027, [1972] 2 W.L.R. 645 (H.L.).

[61] 109 S. Ct. 2909 (1989).

[62] U.S. Const. amend. VIII ("Excessive bail shall not be required, nor excessive fines imposed, nor cruel and unusual punishment inflicted.").

[63] *Supra*, note 61, at 2931, "In my view, the $6 million award of punitive damages imposed on BFI constitutes a fine subject to the limitations of the Eighth Amendment."

[64] U.S. Const. amend. XIV ("nor shall any State deprive any person of life, liberty or property without due process of law").

[65] Fry, "Recent Developments: The US Supreme Court 1989 Term: Constitutional Limits to Punitive Damage Awards", 13 Harv. J.L. & Pub. Pol'y 369 (1990). Fry also notes, at 379, that the case of *Browning-Ferris* was the second time that a concurring opinion had indicated a willingness to entertain the argument that punitive damage awards attract due process protection, and quotes the concurring decision of Justice O'Connor in *Bankers Life & Casualty Co. v. Crenshaw*, 108 S. Ct. 1645, 1655-56 (1988) where it was stated, "Appellant has touched on a due process issue that I think is worthy of the Court's consideration."

[66] *Ibid.*, at 381-82. Fry states that if the court did conclude that excessive punitive damages did in fact violate the due process clause, it would most likely adopt a broad test of reasonableness and than leave it to legislatures to articulate what factors would make a punitive damage award unreasonable.

The recent legislative enactments of the United States House of Representatives becomes the most likely road to effective reform in this area in the United States.[67]

In Canada traditional damage awards for punitive damages have, until very recently, been modest.[68] The Ontario Law Reform Commission Report, after making reference to the arguably anomalous case of *Clairborne Industries Ltd. v. National Bank of Canada*[69] where there was an award of $4,800,000 on the principle that the defendant bank should not profit from their wrong, states that:

> It is the practical concern with enormous awards that has so influenced the debate in the United States. Such awards have not manifested themselves in Canada. Moreover, there are a number of reasons to believe that awards will be controlled, and therefore will not become a problem here in the future.[70]

The correctness of the Law Reform Commission's statement would appear to be put to the test by the recent case of *Hill v. Church of Scientology of Toronto*.[71] In *Hill* the Ontario Court of Appeal upheld a jury award for defamation where the plaintiff was awarded $300,000 for non-pecuniary compensatory damages for the defamation which did not cause pecuniary loss; $500,000 for compensatory aggravated damages, and $800,000 for punitive damages, for a total of 1.6 million dollars. Hill, who was employed with the Crown Law Office, Criminal Division, was

---

[67] *Attorney Accountability Act; Securities Litigation Reform Act;* and the *Common Sense Product Liability and Legal Reform Act.*

[68] *Supra*, note 58, at 13.

[69] (1989), 34 O.A.C. 241, 69 O.R. (2d) 65, 59 D.L.R. (4th) 533 (C.A.). The Ontario Law Reform Commission Report, *supra*, note 58 at 65, stated:
   "There may well exist a valid case for punitive damages in *Clairborne* to punish advertent wrongdoing committed for the purpose of making a profit. In the circumstances, such an award might be considerably larger than is common in Canada. Given the exceptional facts in this case, and the way in which the court rationalized the use of punitive damages, we are not convinced that the amount of the award itself reflects a new pattern in the awarding of punitive damages."

[70] *Supra*, note 58, at 47.

[71] (1994), 18 O.R. (3d) 385, 20 C.C.L.T. (2d) 129, 114 D.L.R. (4th) 1 (C.A.); leave to appeal to S.C.C. granted 20 O.R. (3d) xv, 180 N.R. 240*n*. Also of note is the decision of *Derrickson v. Tomat* (1992), 88 D.L.R. (4th) 401 (B.C.C.A.). In the latter decision, the trial judge awarded general damages of $350,000 and $50,000 in punitive damages for defamation to one of the plaintiffs. The award was set aside by the British Columbia Court of Appeal and a new trial directed, with a majority of the court concluding that punitive damages should rarely be awarded in cases of politically motivated defamatory statements.

defamed when counsel for the Church of Scientology stood before Osgoode Hall in his gown and read for the press from a proceeding for contempt that was to be launched the next day against Hill. The allegations alleged improprieties against Hill that impugned his character and honesty and, as later found by the Court, the Church knew the allegations to be false. The allegations were widely published and in the conduct of the trial, character attacks on Hill continued, in what the court described, as a most egregious manner. The attacks were found to be knowingly without foundation and were repeated even after the conclusion of the trial and the defendant had to be permanently enjoined from such conduct.[72] One of the Church's documents produced at trial showed Hill to be an "enemy" of the Church and the inference that was probably drawn by the jury was that the Church would stop at nothing to neutralize their "enemy". In affirming the jury award the Court of Appeal took into account new evidence of the defendants' post trial conduct of repeated defamation against Hill.

Given that there were no pecuniary damages proven, and given that Hill's reputation was largely, if not fully, rehabilitated by the decision, can it be said that an award of $300,000 for non-pecuniary compensatory damages was appropriate? Can aggravated compensatory damages that exceed by $200,000 the non-pecuniary compensatory award comply with the edict that all damages must be reasonable? Is there a question raised by the size of all three separate awards that perhaps each contained an element of punitive damages? In many ways questions relating to the non-pecuniary and aggravated awards are more troublesome than the award of $800,000 for punitive damages, where the evidence seems clear that such an award was required to deter the defendant in its conduct towards the plaintiff.

Given the marked departure from the tradition of moderation, the awards in *Hill* creates the same type of atmosphere that existed in 1978 when the Supreme Court of Canada expressed their concern over what they termed excessive awards and imposed a cap of $100,000 on non-pecuniary damages in personal injury cases. Of note on the question of whether the Supreme Court of Canada will apply similar reasoning in the area of non-pecuniary damages, aggravated damages and punitive damages is the dissenting opinion of Justice Lamer, as he than was, and Justice McIntyre, in the case 1988 of *Snyder v. The Montreal Gazette Ltd.*[73]

In *Snyder*, the plaintiff was a nationally known personality who had been called a member of the Jewish Mafia in an article published by the defendant. The jury awarded non-pecuniary damages in the amount of $135,000. The Quebec Court of Appeal held that the verdict was

72 7 O.R. (3d) 489 (Gen. Div.).
73 [1988] 1 S.C.R. 494, 43 C.C.L.T. 216, 49 D.L.R. (4th) 17, 82 N.R. 371.

unreasonable, particularly in light of the fact that the plaintiff sued a number of other parties for the same defamation in actions still outstanding, and substituted and award of $13,500.

A majority of the Supreme Court held that the trial judge in *Snyder* did not err in holding that the jury award was not so unreasonable that it should be set aside.[74] The minority decision written by Lamer J. would have imposed a cap (reference level) of $50,000 measured in 1978 dollars, for non-pecuniary damages in cases of defamation under Quebec civil law.[75] Lamer J. appeared to be borrowing from the language and arguments of the trilogy when he stated:

> The amount awarded is necessarily arbitrary, in view of the difficulty in measuring objectively such loss in pecuniary terms, especially when it concerns someone else's reputation. It is precisely because this exercise is based on empirical considerations rather than on a mathematical and scientific operation that extravagant claims for this type of loss should not be allowed by the courts.[76]

Professor Waddams states that it is very clear the Supreme Court in *Andrews* was concerned with finding a principle that would justify moderation in awards and anxious to establish a sharp distinction between American and Canadian non-pecuniary damages.[77] Given the present composition of the Supreme Court[78] and given the large damages in *Hill*, it would not be surprising to see the court consider the imposition of a cap on non-pecuniary compensatory and aggravated damages as well as punitive damages in a manner similar to the Trilogy. See the Supreme Court of Canada decision in *Hill v. Church of Scientology*, released July 20, 1995 where the court rejected the imposition of a cap on pecuniary compensatory, aggravated and punitive damages.

---

[74] There were only five members of the Supreme Court sitting on this appeal. Dickson C.J. and Beetz and Wilson JJ. formed the majority, with McIntyre and Lamer JJ. dissenting in part.

[75] *Supra*, note 73, at 506.

[76] *Ibid.*, at 505.

[77] Waddams, *The Law of Damages*, 2nd ed. (Toronto: Canada Law Book, 1990), at 3-27.

[78] Justice L'Heureux-Dubé was sitting on the Quebec Court of Appeal when it considered the appeal in *Snyder*. In her opinion, the jury award was considerable and far in excess of amounts awarded for defamation in Canada, but concluded that the award ought not to be varied because it was not so unreasonable that the Court of Appeal should substitute its opinion for that of the jury. *Snyder, supra*, note 73, at 501.

9. *The Ontario Law Reform Commission Report on Exemplary Damages*

The Supreme Court will no doubt be aided by the valuable work of the Ontario Law Reform Commission *Report on Exemplary Damages*, completed in 1991.[79] Following a comprehensive analysis of the law and the problems presented when civil courts "impose what is in effect a fine for conduct it finds to be worthy of punishment, and then to remit the fine, not to the State Treasury, but to an individual plaintiff who will, by definition, be over-compensated",[80] the Ontario Law Reform Commission made a number of recommendations. Some of these recommendations include:

1. Aggravated damages, as they are currently understood, should be abolished and the court empowered to award compensatory damages for injuries to pride and dignity as part of the award for non-pecuniary loss.
2. Exemplary damages should continue to be available in Ontario and should be referred to as punitive damages.
3. Questions of whether to award punitive damages, and the quantum of such damages, should be restrained by retributive principles.
4. Punitive damages should be awarded only where the defendant has advertently committed a wrongful act deserving of punishment and where the defendant's conduct was exceptional.
5. Exceptional conduct should include conduct engaged in for the purpose of making a profit as well as for malicious, high-handed, outrageous or cynical conduct.
6. Punitive damages should apply equally to corporations and to individuals.
7. The trial judge should be empowered to give guidance to the jury concerning quantum of damages.
8. An appellant court should have the power to substitute its own assessment for punitive damages when the trial award is being set aside.

10. *Conclusion*

No doubt the Supreme Court of Canada will take the opportunity in *Hill* to provide some additional guidelines in the troubling area of non-pecuniary compensatory damages, aggravated damages and punitive damages. The circumstances currently prevailing are remarkably similar

---

[79] *Supra*, note 58.
[80] Waddams, *supra*, note 77, at 11-2.

to the circumstances that existed when the Trilogy came before the Supreme Court of Canada in 1978. In 1978 the spectre of $1,000,000 awards caused the Supreme Court to invoke policy considerations based upon the burden to society imposed by excessive awards. Presently before the Supreme Court is a case that is clearly out of sync with the traditional, moderate approach to damages in this area. Until the *Clairborne* and *Hill* cases, punitive damages awards in Ontario had not exceeded $50,000.[81] In *Snyder*, Lamer J. (now Chief Justice) was of the view that non-pecuniary compensatory damages should be limited to one half the cap imposed in non-pecuniary personal injury claims. While Lamers J., in *Snyder*, was of the view that damages in this area should be limited, he noted that such a restriction would not denigrate from the principle of *restitutio in integrum*, as it would be still open to plaintiffs to prove actual pecuniary loss.[82] Absent insurance coverage for punitive damages and being mindful of the fact that the imposition of fines by civil courts is a extraordinary remedy, the case for moderation is persuasive.

If, as suggested by Professor Waddams, the Supreme Court in *Andrews* was primarily concerned with finding a principle that would justify moderation in awards and establish a sharp distinction between American and Canadian non-pecuniary damage awards, would it not be tempting for the court to act similarly in *Hill* respecting other types of non-pecuniary damages?

The area of non-pecuniary damages for personal injury claims continues to be in a state of uncertainty, and will require further clarification by the Supreme Court of Canada as the law evolves.

In spite of the recommitment in *Lindal* to functional non-pecuniary damages, the courts have resisted, for good reason, adhering to the strict functional approach. Until the Supreme Court of Canada or the Court of Appeal further clarifies non-pecuniary personal injury damages we will continue to see damages set with reference to the severity of injuries and the cap of roughly $250,000 in 1995 dollars. Perhaps the most current challenge to be met by the courts is whether, absent the principle of full economic recovery under Bill 164, non-pecuniary damages should increase significantly in appropriate cases.

---

[81] *Supra*, note 58, at 23.
[82] *Snyder, supra* note 73, at 506.

AN OVERVIEW OF PECUNIARY DAMAGES IN PERSONAL INJURY CLAIMS*

Robert B. Munroe[1]

1. *Introduction*

In 1978, in the now well-known "trilogy" the Supreme Court of Canada placed a limit on general damages for pain and suffering awards in personal injury actions.[2] It did not, however, place a monetary limit on provable pecuniary losses. In fact, full compensation for pecuniary losses was part of the rationale used by the Supreme Court for limiting general damages.[3] As a result, plaintiffs' counsel have directed their energy and creativity toward the proof of pecuniary losses upon the foundation of principles set out in the "trilogy". The result has been a substantial increase in personal injury damage awards.[4] Significant refinements have

* The invaluable contribution of Peter Lawson, D. Phil., LL.B., to the research and stylistic editing of this paper is gratefully acknowledged.

[1] B.A., McMaster University (1972); L.L.B., Osgoode Hall Law School (1975); called to the Bar of Ontario (1977); certified by the Law Society of Upper Canada as a specialist in Civil Litigation (1991); partner, Ross & McBride, practice restricted to civil litigation with an emphasis on personal injury litigation for plaintiffs. He has spoken and instructed at a wide variety of education programmes for lawyers, including the Law Society of Upper Canada; the Ontario Centre for Advocacy Training; and Insight. He is a member of numerous professional organizations including the Advocates Society and the Canadian Instutute for the Administration of Justice and a Past Trustee of the Hamilton Law Association (1979-84).

[2] *Andrews v. Grand & Toy Alta.Ltd.*, [1978] 2 S.C.R. 229, [1978] 1 W.W.R. 577, 8 A.R. 182, 3 C.C.L.T. 225, 83 D.L.R. (3d) 452, 19 N.R. 50; *Arnold v. Teno*, [1978] 2 S.C.R. 287, 3 C.C.L.T. 272, 83 D.L.R. (3d) 609, 19 N.R. 1; *Thornton v. Prince George School Dist. No. 57*, [1978] 2 S.C.R. 267, [1978] 1 W.W.R. 607, 3 C.C.L.T. 257, 19 N.R. 552.

[3] *Andrews, ibid.*, at 262; *Teno, ibid.*, at 333; *Lindal v. Lindal*, [1981] 2 S.C.R. 629 at 639, [1982] 1 W.W.R. 433, 34 B.C.L.R. 273, 129 D.L.R. (3d) 263, 39 N.R. 361.

[4] Earl Cherniak and Mary Anne Sanderson predicted these advances in their important review entitled "Tort Compensation — Personal Injury and Death

been made in the principles of law and techniques of proving pecuniary damages, particularly future income loss and future care costs.

Legislators have responded in quite direct ways to the increase in personal injury damage awards. Important aspects of pecuniary damage awards have been modified by amendments to the *Insurance Act*[5], *Courts of Justice Act*[6], and *Rules of Civil Procedure*[7] to the extent of substituting limited no-fault insurance benefits for the right to claim pecuniary damages in tort for injuries caused in motor vehicle accidents. Ironically, the exclusion of the right to claim pecuniary damages in motor vehicle accidents after January 1, 1994, by s. 267.1 of the *Insurance Act* stands in sharp contrast to the increasing pecuniary damage awards in non motor vehicle, personal injury tort claims.

The judicial response has been more subtle. Nonetheless its significance is undeniable. In two decisions of the Supreme Court of Canada since 1990, Madame Justice McLaughlin has raised fundamental questions about double recovery and collateral benefits in pecuniary damage claims in tort actions.[8] Her decisions in *Ratych*[9] and in *Cunningham*[10] may foreshadow the future treatment of aspects of pecuniary damage awards. On the other hand this may encourage further legislation.

This turbulent interplay between escalating awards and the legislative and judicial responses to that escalation forms the background to the following examination of principles and proofs of pecuniary damage awards in tort actions in Ontario. This overview is confined to personal injury claims, and not the separate issue in claims arising from fatalities.

Damages'' in *Special Lectures of the Law Society of Upper Canada, 1981: New Developments in the Law of Remedies* (Toronto: De Boo, 1981) at 197. That study has been helpful in the preparation of the present article. The following studies have also been helpful: Cherniak, ''Proof of Pecuniary Damages'' (1983), 4 Advocates Q. 257; Engelhart ''Proof of Future Events: In Support of the 'Simple Probability' Burden of Proof'' (1987-88), 8 Advocates' Q. 163; Waddams, *The Law of Damages*, 2nd ed. (Aurora: Canada Law Book Inc., 1994).

[5] *Insurance Act*, R.S.O. 1990, c. I.8.
[6] *Courts of Justice Act*, R.S.O. 1990, c. C.43.
[7] R.R.O. 1990, Reg. 194.
[8] *Ratych v. Bloomer*, (1990) 1 S.C.R. 940, 39 O.A.C. 103, 73 O.R. (2d) 448*n*, 30 C.C.E.L. 161, 3 C.C.L.T. (2d) 1, 69 D.L.R. (4th) 25, 107 N.R. 335; *Cunningham v. Wheeler*, [1994] 1 S.C.R. 359, 88 B.C.L.R. (2d) 273, 113 D.L.R. (4th) 1, 164 N.R. 81.
[9] *Ibid.*
[10] *Ibid.*

2. *What Does the Term "Pecuniary Damages" Mean?*

Pecuniary damages are awarded to compensate a plaintiff for past, present and future financial, economic and monetary losses caused by the fault of the defendant. They are awarded to restore the injured person to the position he or she would have been in if the injury had not occurred. The oft-repeated principle guiding the courts in this regard was set out by the Supreme Court of Canada in *Andrews*,[11] quoting from *Livingston v. Rawyards Coal Yard*[12] as follows:

> . . . where any injury is to be compensated by damages, in settling the sum of money to be given for reparation of damages you should as nearly as possible get at that sum of money which will put the party who has been injured, or who has suffered, in the same position as he would have been in if he had not sustained the wrong for which he is now getting his compensation or reparation.

The purpose of the award is thus full restoration to the plaintiff's pre-injury economic condition as best as can be done with money.[13] It follows that the plaintiff should receive no more nor less than his actual pecuniary loss. If there is no provable financial or economic loss then there can be no recovery for this category of damages.[14]

In the *Cunningham v. Wheeler* trilogy, Mr. Justice Cory summarized the principles of compensation as follows:

> At the outset, it may be well to state once again the principle of recovery in an action for tort. Simply, it is to compensate the injured party as completely as possible for the loss suffered as a result of the negligent action or inaction of the defendant. However, the plaintiff is not entitled to a double recovery for any loss arising from the injury.[15]

These principles were earlier characterized by the Supreme Court of Canada in *Ratych v. Bloomer* as amounting to a "functional" approach to compensation:

> The functional rational for the award of damages adopted in the trilogy of *Andrews*, *Thornton* and *Teno* underlines the necessity of using the plaintiff's actual loss as the basis of his or her damages. The award is justified,

---

[11] *Supra*, note 2, at 241.

[12] (1880), 5 App. Cas. 25 at 39.

[13] *Andrews*, *supra*, note 2, at 240-42; *Engel v. Salyn*, [1993] 1 S.C.R. 306 at 313, [1992] 2 W.W.R. 373, 105 Sask. R. 81, 15 C.C.L.T. (2d) 245, 99 D.L.R. (4th) 401, 147 N.R. 321.

[14] *Ratych*, *supra*, note 8, at 962-64; *Cunningham*, *supra*, note 8, at 396-97.

[15] *Ibid.*, at 396.

not because it is appropriate to punish the defendant or enrich the plaintiff, but because it will serve the purpose or *function* of restoring the plaintiff as nearly as possible to his pre-accident state or alternatively, where this cannot be done, providing substitutes for what he has lost.[16]

At common law the plaintiff has the right to receive the damages as a lump-sum award due from the defendant at the moment of judgment.[17] Once received, there is no restriction on how the money is spent or whether it is used for the purposes for which it was awarded. As the Supreme Court of Canada noted in *Andrews*, "The plaintiff is free to do with the sum as he likes." [18]

The common law generally maintains a fiction that the plaintiff and the defendant are redistributing the plaintiff's pecuniary loss between themselves as individuals based upon fault for the loss. The courts recognize "economic reality" in that the award may simply be redistributing the loss from one "loss pool" such as a disability insurer, the social welfare system, or a publicly funded medical system, to another "loss pool", the latter being a liability insurer or some other publicly funded entity.[19] The redistribution results in economic benefit to the plaintiff by providing a higher standard, more secure fund under the plaintiff's direct control.

3. *What are The Limits on the Amount that Can Be Awarded for Pecuniary Damages?*

Theoretically, there is no upper limit to the amount which can be awarded as damages for pecuniary loss. According to the Supreme Court of Canada in *Ratych*, "It is the actual pecuniary loss sustained by the plaintiff which governs the amount of the award".[20] Beyond that basic rule, the case-law suggests a series of considerations which, when taken together, can be seen to set the outer limits of an award. The most important of these considerations is of course the purpose of the award itself.

---

[16] *Ibid.*, at 963.
[17] *Watkins v. Olafson*, [1989] 2 S.C.R. 750 at 761, [1989] 6 W.W.R. 481, 61 Man. R. (2d) 81, 50 C.C.L.T. 101, 61 D.L.R. (4th) 577, 100 N.R. 161.
[18] *Ibid.*, at 247.
[19] *Andrews, ibid.*, at 248; *Ratych, supra*, note 8, at 974.
[20] *Ibid.*, at 963.

(1) Full Indemnification

As has been noted, the purpose of a pecuniary damage award is full indemnification.[21] Through the damage award the court seeks to restore the plaintiff's loss, not just provide for a need.[22] Therefore, the limit on the award is the plaintiff's actual loss.[23] The calculation of a pecuniary damage award is not governed by considerations of "frugality" or stinginess but by the provable losses of the plaintiff.[24] Moreover, the plaintiff has no obligation to mitigate by accepting a lesser standard than payment for his real loss.[25]

Indemnification for the actual loss is made without reference to sympathy, social cost, insurance premium increases, punishment or the financial consequence to the defendant.[26]

(2) Fairness and Reasonableness

The amount of the award may also be tempered by concerns for fairness and reasonableness.[27] Compensation must be "full but fair".[28] Moreover, as the Supreme Court of Canada noted in *Thornton*, "Fairness . . . is achieved by assuring that the plaintiff's claims are legitimate and justifiable" and not by "arbitrary" increase or reduction.[29] In other words fairness is achieved at a particular point of balance; it arises when the result neither over-compensates nor under-compensates the plaintiff for his loss.[30]

Where the court is faced with two "acceptable alternatives" for restoring the plaintiff then it makes sense that fairness and reasonableness require

---

[21] *Andrews, ibid.*, at 240-41.

[22] *Ibid.*, at 246.

[23] *Engel, supra*, note 13, at 313; *Ratych, supra*, note 8, at 963.

[24] *Lewis v. Todd*, [1980] 2 S.C.R. 694 at 708, 14 C.C.L.T. 294, 115 D.L.R. (3d) 257; *Stein (Litigation Guardian of) v. Sandwich West (Twp.)*, unreported, June 30, 1993, O.J. No. 1772 at 54 (Ont. Gen. Div.), trial decision.

[25] *Andrews v. Grand & Toy Alta. Ltd.*, [1978] 2 S.C.R. 229 at 240, 242, [1978] 1 W.W.R. 577, 8 A.R. 182, 3 C.C.L.T. 225, 83 D.L.R. (3d) 452, 19 N.R. 50.

[26] *Ibid.*, at 240-43, 248; *Arnold v. Teno*, [1978] 2 S.C.R. 287 at 333, 3 C.C.L.T. 272, 83 D.L.R. (3d) 609, 19 N.R. 1; *Thornton v. Prince George School Dist. No. 57*, [1978] 2 S.C.R. 267 at 277-78, [1978] 1 W.W.R. 607, 3 C.C.L.T. 257, 19 N.R. 552; *Lindal v. Lindal*, [1981] 2 S.C.R. 629 at 634, [1982] 1 W.W.R. 433, 34 B.C.L.R. 273, 129 D.L.R. (3d) 263, 39 N.R. 361; *Ratych, supra*, note 8, at 963.

[27] *Andrews, ibid.*, at 242.

[28] *Watkins, supra*, note 17, at 757.

[29] *Supra*, note 24, at 278.

[30] *Ratych, supra*, note 8, at 963.

choice of the least expensive alternative.[31] However, fairness cannot be used to justify inadequate compensation.[32] Rather, proper compensation ". . . ensures a measure of fairness to both sides".[33] Moreover, the "fairness and reasonableness" standard retains a discretionary flexibility. Thus in *Lewis v. Todd*, Justice Dickson reserved the freedom of a trial judge to adjust figures which seemed to a trial judge to be "inordinately" high or low.[34]

Finally, the question arises as to precisely what will be treated as falling below the "fairness and reasonableness" standard. Some guidance may be found in *Thornton*. There Justice Dickson indicated that the test for "unreasonableness" is evidence ". . . which would lead any right thinking person to say 'That would be a squandering of money — no person in his right mind would make such an expenditure'".[35]

(3) Evidence and Proof

The amount awarded for pecuniary damages depends entirely upon the evidence presented at trial.[36] "A plaintiff must prove his loss".[37] Expert evidence is often "vital" to proof of these claims.[38] The courts have repeatedly indicated the importance of proof and evidence in considering these awards; however, they have stressed that pecuniary damages will be awarded if proven, notwithstanding the size of the amount.

(4) Legislated Limits

There are many legislated restrictions on the courts' ability to award pecuniary damages in tort. These include ss. 266, 267 and 267.1 of the *Insurance Act*, s.116 of the *Courts of Justice Act,* and rule 53.09(1) and (2) which will be dealt with below. Of course the most restrictive provision is s. 267.1 of the *Insurance Act*, as amended by Bill 164, S.O. 1993,

---

[31] *Thornton, supra,* note 25, at 280-81.

[32] *Andrews, supra,* note 25, at 248.

[33] *Lindal v. Lindal, supra,* note 26, at 634.

[34] *Ibid.,* at 708-09.

[35] *Supra,* note 25, at 280.

[36] *Ibid.,* at 277-78.

[37] *Ratych v. Bloomer,* [1990] 1 S.C.R. 940 at 973, 39 O.A.C. 103, 73 O.R. (2d) 448n, 30 C.C.E.L. 161, 3 C.C.L.T. (2d) 1, 69 D.L.R. (4th) 25, 107 N.R. 335.

[38] *Lewis, supra,* note 24, at 708-09.

c. 10, in force January 1, 1994, which prohibits pecuniary damage awards in tort actions for personal injuries arising from motor vehicle accidents.

(5) Practical Limits

The most obvious practical limits arise where it would not matter if these claims were unlimited in potential because the defendant has insufficient assets or insurance with which to satisfy an award. For this reason the high pecuniary damage assessments generally arise in those cases where there is a defendant with a "deep pocket" such as a large corporation, a government authority, or a physician.[39]

4. Where is the Upper Limit of Pecuniary Damage Awards: Stein v. Sandwich West

A comparison of the recent decision in Stein with the "trilogy" highlights the extent of growth in pecuniary damage awards since 1978.

In 1978, the Supreme Court of Canada awarded $817,344 to 21-year-old James Andrews, a single, apprentice CNR carman of above average intelligence. The award was by way of total disability arising from C5-6 quadriplegia suffered in a car accident. On February 22, 1995, the Ontario Court of Appeal upheld an award of 8,670,277 to 17-year-old John Stein, a single, part-time university student. The award was by way of compensation for his total disability arising from C4-C5 quadriplegia suffered as a result of a fall at an ice rink, the latter being held to have been caused by the negligent maintenance of the ice surface.

Table 1: Comparison of damage awards in Andrews and Stein

	Andrews (1978)	Stein (1995)
Non-Pecuniary		
Plaintiff	$100,000	$ 243,700
Family Law Act	nil	70,000

---

[39] As in Stein, supra, note 23; affd February 22, 1995, O.J. No. 423 (C.A.), unreported (municipal corporation); Mortimer v. Cameron (1994), 17 O.R. (3d) 1, 19 M.P.L.R. (2d) 286, 111 D.L.R. (4th) 428 (C.A.) (muncipal corporation); leave to appeal to S.C.C. refused 19 O.R. (3d) xvi, 23 M.P.L.R. (2d) 314, 178 N.R. 146n; Kenyeres (Litigation Guardian of) v. Cullimore (1992), 13 C.P.C. (3d) 385 (Ont. Gen. Div.) (physician).

	Andrews (1978)	**Stein (1995)**
Pecuniary		
Specials	$ 77,344	$ 10,000
Family	nil	494,582
Cost of Future Care	571,432	6,273,164
	(no gross up)	(includes gross up)
Lost Future Earnings	69,981	1,200,000
CPP Benefit Lost		25,138
Investment Expense		75,000
Interest		278,693
Total award	**$817,344**	**$8,670,277**

Table 1 demonstrates the size of the gulf between *Andrews* and *Stein*. In gross terms the *Stein* award is ten times higher than the award in Arnold. Moreover a comparison of the awards shows that the increase is largely the result of increased compensation for pecuniary losses; and, more to the point, a close inspection of Table 1 makes it clear that the increased awards cannot be accounted for by inflation alone. As the increase in general damages indicates, inflation alone would yield no more than a 143 per cent increase. Thus the increase must be directly related to the principles and proof of damages in the following areas of pecuniary loss:

(a) loss of earning capacity
(b) future care costs
(c) *Family Law Act* claims
(d) the discount rate
(e) gross up for income tax.

These topics are dealt with below following a discussion of the standard of proving future and contingent events.

5. *Valuing Future Events and Contingencies: Simple Probability*

The largest components of pecuniary damage awards, as can be seen in *Stein*, relate to future care and future income. Quantifying these awards requires the court to attempt to predict not only what the future will be for the injured plaintiff but what it would have been if the injury had not happened.[40]

(1) Future Events

In contrast to assessing the value of a loss which has occurred prior to the date of assessment, evaluation of compensation for future events is of necessity an uncertain exercise. Similar uncertainty relates to reconstructing events which would have happened had the injury not occurred. An award for future losses is thus an attempt to forecast many different and variable factors because the plaintiff is entitled to a once-and-for-all damage award.

Past events which are alleged to have occurred prior to trial must be proven on a balance of probabilities as having "probably" happened before they will be accepted by the court. If past events are not proven to this standard then the trier of fact will make no allowance for them. In contrast, future pecuniary losses are not an "all or nothing proposition".[41] They are established by proving that there is a realistic or substantial possibility of the event happening. To obtain compensation a plaintiff in a personal injury action is required to establish only a substantial risk, or a "reasonable" or "realistic" possibility of future pecuniary loss.[42] The Ontario Court of Appeal reaffirmed this principle in *Meyer v. Bright* as follows:

> . . . in cases involving personal injuries where a court must try to determine what will happen in the future, a plaintiff can satisfy the onus of proof resting upon her by showing upon "expert or cogent evidence" that there is a substantial possibility that the event may occur.[43]

In *Graham* the Ontario Court of Appeal adopted the following passage from Cooper-Stephenson and Saunders, *Personal Injury*

---

[40] The issues relating to the burden of proving future and contingent events is thoroughly reviewed by Engelhart in his excellent article "Proof of Future Events: In Support of the 'Simple Probability' Burden of Proof" (1987-88), 8 Advocates Q. 257. The latter has provided valuable insights in the preparation of the present paper.

[41] *Graham v. Rourke* (1990), 40 O.A.C. 301, 75 O.R. (2d) 622 at 634, 74 D.L.R. (4th) 1 (C.A.).

[42] *Ibid.*, at 634-35 O.R.; *Giannone v. Weinberg* (1989), 33 O.A.C. 11, 68 O.R. (2d) 767 at 774 (C.A.); leave to appeal refused.

[43] (1993), 15 O.R. (3d) 129 at 153, 110 D.L.R. (4th) 354, 48 M.V.R. (2d) 1 (C.A.); leave to appeal to S.C.C. refused 17 O.R. (3d) xvi, 172 N.R. 160*n*.

Damages in Canada[44] to describe how future pecuniary losses are dealt with:

> The different standard of proof which governs most of a damage assessment may be termed "simple probability". It involves the valuation of possibilities, chances and risks according to the degree of likelihood that events would have occurred, or will occur. This contrasts with "the balance of probabilities", more familiar in civil actions, which involves an "all-or-nothing" approach.[45]

Once established, the degree of possibility is quantified as a percentage. In determining the percentage the court considers ". . . the degree of risk, the time when it will materialise . . .".[46] The percentage is then used as the factor by which the assessment, if it were a certainty, is reduced.[47]

In neither *Graham* nor *Meyer* did the Ontario Court of Appeal refer to the Supreme Court of Canada decision in *Janiak v. Ippolito*[48]. However, that decision bears in useful ways on the present issue. In his excellent article, "Proof of Future Events: In Support of the 'Simple Probability' Burden of Proof", Engelhart concludes that "The simple probability test would therefore appear to be firmly entrenched . . .".[49] In reaching that conclusion he cites the following from *Janiak*:

> . . . the balance of probabilities test is confined to determining what did in fact happen in the past. In assessing damages the court determines not only what will happen but what would have happened by estimating the chance of the relevant event occurring, which chance is then to be directly reflected in the amount of damages.[50]

Engelhart rightly notes that the above passage from *Janiak* is also authority for applying the simple probability approach to the calculation of the effect of "what would have happened".[51]

If a party is relying on a finding that an event "would have happened *if* . . ." then it seems reasonable to use the simple probability test as the burden of proof of the event and its effect on pecuniary damages even if the event could have taken place in the past.

---

[44] (Toronto: Carswell, 1981), at 84.

[45] *Graham, supra,* note 41, at 634.

[46] *Longeuay v. Thomas* (1982), 35 O.R. (2d) 660 at 662 (C.A.), citing *Moeliker v. A. Reyrolle & Co. Ltd.*, [1977] 1 All E.R. 9 at 17.

[47] *Graham, supra,* note 41, at 634-37, 644.

[48] [1985] 1 S.C.R. 146, 9 O.A.C. 1, 31 C.C.L.T. 113, 16 D.L.R. (4th) 1, 57 N.R. 241.

[49] *Supra,* note 40, at 173.

[50] *Ibid.,* at 170-71.

[51] *Ibid.,* at 181.

Finally, and it follows logically from the foregoing, no account should be taken of risks which are unproven, purely speculative or unquantifiable remote possibilities. It should also be noted that the Ontario Court of Appeal has rejected the application of simple probability to the calculation of general damages.[52]

(2) Contingencies

Contingencies are the reasonably foreseeable but uncertain events which could effect the actual occurrence of a pecuniary loss. In *Graham* the Ontario Court of Appeal defined contingencies as follows:

> Factors affecting the degree of risk of future economic loss and the possibility that all or part of those losses may have occurred apart from the wrong which is the subject of the litigation are referred to as contingencies.[53]

Contingencies are "positive" if they make the occurrence of the event more likely, and "negative" if they make the event less likely. Contingencies may also be "general" or "specific" in nature. These last two terms were interpreted in quite specific ways by the Ontario Court of Appeal in *Graham*.

(a) *General Contingencies*

In *Graham* general contingencies were interpreted as including uncertain future events which are "likely to be the common future of all of us".[54] They include the occurrence of illness, chances of promotion or layoffs. The degree to which a general contingency would effect a given plaintiff is difficult if not impossible to prove and may be considered in the absence of evidence. Hence the trier of fact *may* — not must — take general contingencies into account to adjust a pecuniary award upwards or downwards, "but where the adjustment is premised only on general contingencies it should be modest".[55]

From the above it appears that great care ought to be taken to protect against double counting in the application of general contingencies.

---

[52] *Graham, supra*, note 41, at 643-44.
[53] *Ibid.*, at 635.
[54] *Ibid.*, at 636.
[55] *Ibid.*

For example, if the witnesses have used life expectancy tables, economic statistics or epidemiological evidence in presenting their opinions, and the court accepts the opinions, no further adjustment for these general factors would normally be made.

The adjustment of a pecuniary damage award for a general contingency is consistent with the desire of the judiciary to reserve some modifying influence over the final calculation of the pecuniary award. For example in *Lewis* the Supreme Court of Canada specifically reserved ". . . a large measure of freedom" to the trial judge to modify awards upwards or downwards to prevent an award from being inordinately high or low.[56] However, in *Andrews* Justice Dickson specifically mentioned that there should be ". . . some degree of specificity, supported by the evidence . . ." and not an arbitrary reduction.[57]

Finally, it should also be remembered that an adjustment for contingencies depends very much upon the facts of the case and is not mandatory.[58]

(b) *Specific Contingencies*

In *Graham* specific contingencies were interpreted as including factors ". . . which are peculiar to a particular plaintiff, *e.g.*, a particularly marketable skill or a poor work record". A trier of fact must ". . . be able to point to evidence which supports an allowance for . . ." a specific contingency. Evidence of a specific contingency ". . . must be capable of supporting the conclusion that the occurrence of the contingency is a realistic as opposed to a speculative possibility."[59]

From this it appears that, life expectancy calculations and contingencies may require considerable expert evidence including evidence from medical, economic, actuarial and epidemiological experts to justify a departure from average life expectancy tables.

The courts apply a simple probability factor to calculating the effect of a specific contingency. If the trier of fact determines that there is a reasonable possibility that a contingency will affect the occurrence of a future event then it must be applied to adjust the assessment of damages. The possibility of a contingency's occurrence is quantified as a percent-

---

[56] *Lewis v. Todd*, [1980] 2 S.C.R. 694 at 709, 14 C.C.L.T. 294, 115 D.L.R. (3d) 257.

[57] *Andrews v. Grand & Toy Alta. Ltd.*, [1978] 2 S.C.R. 229 at 253-54, [1978] 1 W.W.R. 577, 8 A.R. 182, 3 C.C.L.T. 225, 83 D.L.R. (3d) 452, 19 N.R. 50.

[58] *Thornton v. Prince George School Dist. No. 57*, [1978] 2 S.C.R. 267 at 283, [1978] 1 W.W.R. 607, 3 C.C.L.T. 257, 19 N.R. 552.

[59] *Supra*, note 41, at 636 O.R.

age by the trier of fact. It is then applied as a factor to increase or reduce the pecuniary award.

6. *Loss of Earning Capacity*

(1) Principles

A plaintiff must be compensated for interference with his ability to work. The purpose of the award is to restore the plaintiff's loss. But what is the loss of ability to work; and how can it be quantified?

In *Andrews*, the inability to work resulting from an injury was described as "not loss of earnings but, rather, loss of earning capacity for which compensation must be made", and the court continued: "A capital asset has been lost: what was its value?"[60] By way of answering its own question the court took note of a series of factors, including earning levels, working life expectancy, contingencies, duplication of the necessaries of life and the discount rate.

More recently, in *Stein* the Ontario Court of Appeal described the task of valuing a future income loss as follows:

> The calculation of future loss of income is extremely difficult and obviously, as in the present case, it has to be based on reasonable assumptions supported by the evidence, and not based on mere speculation.[61]

Certain reasonable assumptions can be made in valuing the asset. These were described in *Conklin v. Smith*[62] as follows:

(a) if the plaintiff proves that he was working at the time of the accident and that his employment would have continued then damages are awarded based upon that job and wage;

(b) if the plaintiff was not working at the time of the accident but intended to be and would have been capable of working at some point then the plaintiff receives compensation for the lost earning opportunity.[63]

---

[60] *Supra*, note 57, at 251.

[61] *Stein (Litigation Guardian of) v. Sandwich West (Twp.)*, unreported, February 22, 1995, O.J. No. 423 (C.A.) at 22.

[62] *Conklin v. Smith*, [1978] 2 S.C.R. 1107, 6 B.C.L.R. 362, 5 C.C.L.T. 113, 88 D.L.R. (3d) 317, 22 N.R. 140.

[63] *Ibid.*, at 1114.

Furthermore, there is virtually a presumption, unless there is cogent evidence to the contrary, that a plaintiff injured at a very young age would have worked, if only for wages equivalent to average industrial earnings.[64]

(2) The Importance of Evidence in Calculating Loss of Earning Capacity

The task of constructing the plaintiff's earning prospects is an evidentiary question which requires the assistance of a wide variety of witnesses to establish what the future prospects of the plaintiff would have been.

For example, in *Mortimer*[65] the plaintiffs' counsel were masterful in their construction of the future income prospects of a quadriplegic 32-year-old male student in his second year of a Certified Management Accountants Course at Fanshaw College. That portion of the award was assessed at $986,717 after a 15 per cent contingency discount. A detailed picture of the plaintiff's lost prospects was created by piecing together evidence derived from a wide variety of sources, including the plaintiff, family members (including evidence as to their aptitudes and achievements), fellow students, past employers, Fanshaw College (including evidence as to the employment prospects of its students), and the Society of Management Accountants. This evidence was then combined with the evidence from economists as to income averages, as well as actuarial evidence, to provide a picture of the plaintiff's unique characteristics, his ability to succeed and the income profile of a Certified Management Accountant.

Similarly, in *Kenyeres* the plaintiffs' counsel[66] succeeded in obtaining an assessment of $1,060,000 for loss of the future earnings of a five-year-old, brain injured child. The task was particularly difficult given the young age of the plaintiff and the lack of school records or pre-accident aptitude testing. A neuropsychologist provided opinion evidence of the infant's pre-accident educational prospects based upon intelligence and aptitude studies on the infant's parents. An economist correlated the educational prospects with average lifetime earning patterns for various levels

---

[64] *Arnold v. Teno*, [1978] 2 S.C.R. 287 at 329, 3 C.C.L.T. 272, 83 D.L.R. (3d) 609, 19 N.R. 1; *Stevens and Stevens (Litigation Guardian of) v. Forney*, unreported, March 31, 1993, O.J. No. 759 at 97 (Ont. Gen. Div.).

[65] At trial the plaintiffs' counsel were J.R. Morse, J.C. Kennedy, and P. Downs: *Mortimer v. Cameron* (1992), 9 M.P.L.R. 185 (Ont. Gen. Div.); revd in part 17 O.R. (3d) 1, 19 M.P.L.R. (2d) 286, 111 D.L.R. (4th) 428, leave to appeal to S.C.C. refused 19 O.R. (3d) xvi, 23 M.P.L.R. (2d) 314, 178 N.R. 146n.

[66] *Kenyeres (Litigation Guardian of) v. Cullimare* (1992), 13 C.P.C. (3d) 385 (Ont. Gen. Div.), addundum to O.J. No. 540 (Ont. Gen. Div.) The plaintiffs' counsel were David Smye and Michael Winward.

of education. The court ultimately arrived at its assessment by averaging these earning patterns.

The scope of evidence which will assist in the reconstruction of future earning prospects is limited only by the energy, ingenuity and resourcefulness of counsel. The evidence will usually include medical evidence of disability, psychological evidence of aptitude and interests, evidence from family members, functional assessments of physical restrictions and abilities, education record and achievements, labour market statistics and profiles, evidence of the actual occupation including income, benefits and retirement statistics, economic and actuarial evidence.

(3) Deductions From Loss of Future Earning Capacity

(a) *Necessaries of Life*

To the extent that basic necessaries of life which will be required by the plaintiff are included in the cost of care award, then they must be deducted from the future income allowance of the plaintiff.[67] Thus in *Stevens*, the future loss of earnings award of $588,965.33 was reduced by 50 per cent to offset the room and board which would be supplied to the plaintiff in the provincial group home setting.[68] In *Kenyeres*, the deduction was limited to 10 per cent because the future care award included very little for the "normal necessaries of life".[69] In both *Stevens* and *Kenyeres* there was no difference between the infant plaintiffs' pre- and post-injury working life expectancy.

(b) *The Lost Years*

In some cases the plaintiff's post-injury life expectancy will be shorter than the pre-injury life expectancy. The difference between these two life terms is often referred to as the "lost years".

Future care awards are calculated on the basis of post-injury life expectancy. However, lost economic opportunity awards are calculated on the basis of pre-accident working life expectancy. If the pre-injury working life expectancy is longer than the post-injury life expectancy then the

---

[67] *Thornton, supra*, note 58, at 282.

[68] *Supra*, note 64, at 97.

[69] *Supra*, note 66, at 103.

lost economic opportunity award may include compensation for a period of time after the expected death of the plaintiff when the plaintiff would obviously not be incurring any living expenses.

In *Toneguzzo-Norvell v. Savien*,[70] the Supreme Court of Canada confirmed that a deduction for necessaries of life should be made from that part of the future economic loss which has been awarded for the "lost years" for the following reason:

> . . . had the plaintiff been in a position to earn the moneys represented by the award for lost earning capacity, she would have had to spend a portion of them for living expenses. Not to recognize this is to introduce an element of duplication and to put the plaintiff in a better position than she would have been in had she actually earned the moneys in question.

In *Toneguzzo* the deduction for the "lost years" was 50 per cent of the award for lost earning capacity. In *Dube v. Penlon*,[71] Justice Zuber applied *Toneguzzo* to reduce lost earning capacity for the "lost years".[72] However, he indicated that, in his view, the percentage deduction of 50 per cent was not mandatory and instead awarded a 30 per cent deduction based upon the evidence before him.

7. Future Care: Best Interests of the Plaintiff

(1) Principles

The large awards for future care costs have been the result of clear statements by the courts concerning the superior level of care to which a plaintiff is entitled combined with the evidence which has been marshalled by the plaintiffs' bar. As the Supreme Court of Canada noted in *Thornton*, "Each case must proceed on its own evidence."[73]

The focus of the assessment of compensation for future care is the provision of reasonable and adequate physical, psychological and emotional care for the plaintiff. At the same time the assessment is not to be

---

[70] [1994] 1 S.C.R. 114, [1994] 2 W.W.R. 609, 87 B.C.L.R. (2d) 1, 18 C.C.L.T. (2d) 209, 110 D.L.R. (4th) 289, 162 N.R. 161 (S.C.C.).

[71] Unreported, July 28, 1994, O.J. No. 1720 (Ont Gen. Div.).

[72] *Ibid.*, at 25.

[73] *Thornton v. Prince George School Dist. No. 57*, [1978] 2 S.C.R. 267 at 278, [1978] 1 W.W.R. 607, 3 C.C.L.T. 257, 19 N.R. 552.

construed as "an exercise in frugality".[74] In *Andrews*, the Supreme Court of Canada said the following about compensation for future care:

> Money is a barren substitute for health and personal happiness, but to the extent within reason that money can be used to sustain or improve the mental or physical health of the injured person it may properly form part of a claim.[75]

The court must assess what type and standard of care is required to put the plaintiff as best as can be done by money into the position she would have been in if the injury had not happened.[76] The sum awarded is "a self extinguishing sum" being sufficient to pay for the future needs of the plaintiff, leaving no surplus capital when these needs have been met.[77] Reasonable compensation includes full provision for the physical, psychological and emotional needs of the plaintiff which are the direct consequence of the injury including but not limited to,the need for equipment, attendant care, transportation and medical care.[78] The courts require a high standard of standard of care. For example, in *Giannone* a more expensive prosthesis was permitted on the basis of evidence that it was "the best prosthesis available".[79] The plaintiff need not accept second best care.

(2) Home or Institutional care

For example, if it can be shown that the plaintiff was or would have been able to purchase and live independently in his own home had the accident not happened then care in a home, and not an institutional setting, is the appropriate standard.[80] Furthermore, care in a home setting is justifiable if it can be shown that it will improve the plaintiff's mental and physical health, prolong his life, or provide a decent quality of life.[81]

If the defendant can show that it would be contrary to the best interests of the plaintiff to attempt to live in a home setting, or that an institutional environment would provide an equally beneficial environment,

---

[74] *Stein*, June 30, 1993, O.J. No. 1772 (Ont. Gen. Div.), at 54.
[75] *Supra*, note 57, at 241-42.
[76] *Ibid.*, at 241.
[77] *Ibid.*, at 260.
[78] *Ibid.*, at 239-42, 262.
[79] *Giannone v. Weinberg* (1989), 33 O.A.C. 11, 68 O.R. (2d) 767 at 770 (C.A.).
[80] *Andrews v. Grand & Toy Alta. Ltd.*, [1978] 2 S.C.R. 229 at 242, [1978] 1 W.W.R. 577, 8 A.R. 182, 3 C.C.L.T. 225, 83 D.L.R. (3d) 452, 19 N.R. 50.
[81] *Ibid.* at 238, 242-46; *Thornton*, *supra*, note 73, at 277, 280; *Kenyeres*, *supra*, note 66, at 96.

then an institutional setting might be the appropriate standard. In *Stevens*, for example, the severe mental incapacity of the infant plaintiff combined with the dissolution of the family unit led to a finding that a provincial group home was in the best interests of the plaintiff once she reached the age of 21. This claim was settled for $1,300,000 without a gross up by the Ministry of Community and Social Services. By contrast, in *Stein*, the plaintiff was awarded care in a home environment on the basis that this was "reasonable and adequate". Moreover the court in *Stein* stressed that the assessment "under this head is not an exercise in frugality".[82] The amount to be awarded for future care in a home environment depends very much on the evidence presented. In *Mortimer*,[83] a 32-year-old, c4-c5 quadriplegic plaintiff was awarded $3,446,364 for future care costs which was reduced to $2,811,172 after a discount for contingencies.

(3) Publicly Funded Care as an Alternative

There is ample authority for the proposition that the plaintiff's future care should not become a public responsibility, nor should the plaintiff be required to mitigate his future care cost by accepting the standard of care provided by publicly funded chronic care facilities. In *Andrews*, the standard of care provided by the legislature was found to be of only "marginal assistance".[84] In *Stein*, the Ontario Court of Appeal rejected resort to publicly funded services. In so doing it upheld the following principles:

- (a) service levels provided by publicly funded programmes do not set the standard for tort compensation;
- (b) the plaintiff should not be forced to accept publicly funded care where this does not meet the plaintiff's reasonable needs;
- (c) where the evidence proves that a "self directed full-time attendant care program" is reasonable then the plaintiff will not be required to resort to publicly funded services;
- (d) government provided services may be an uncertain source of assistance which are "drying up".[85]

Future care and equipment awards have included the estimated cost of paying for future medical improvements to a prosthesis[86], house-

---

[82] *Stein*, *supra*, note 74, at 54.
[83] *Supra*, note 64.
[84] *Supra*, note 80, at 246.
[85] *Supra*, note 74, at 28-30.
[86] *Giannone*, *supra*, note 79, at 773-74.

keeping and gardening services,[87] a home,[88] home renovations, equipment replacement costs, and attendant and nursing care. The trial decision in *Mortimer* contains an excellent example of the detail required in assessing future care requirements in a catastrophic injury case. The schedule of future care costs awarded in *Mortimer* is found at Appendix "A", below.

(4) No Betterment or Duplication of Expense

In calculating care and equipment costs only that portion of the expense which the plaintiff would not have had but for the injury is allowed. For example, in *Mortimer* only home renovation costs related to care were allowed and not the actual purchase of the home which would have been made by the plaintiff in any event. Similarly, the court awarded the retrofitting cost of a van and not the full purchase price of the van. A deduction from the loss of earning capacity award for necessaries of life has been discussed above.

(5) Management Fee

If the fund awarded for future care is not wisely invested there will be insufficient income from the fund to meet the care requirements of the plaintiff. If there is evidence of the plaintiff's inability to manage and invest the fund then an award will be made to pay professional managers the reasonable and proven cost of obtaining this assistance so that the fund will not be prematurely extinguished.[89]

8. *Family Law Act Claims*

Part V of the *Family Law Act* provides a derivative claim for recovery of pecuniary losses by a specified class of relatives of a person who has been injured or killed. The recoverable pecuniary damages are set out in s. 61(2) of the Act as follows:

---

[87] *Ibid.*, at 776.

[88] *Dube, supra,* note 71, at 104.

[89] *Mandzuk v. Vieira,* [1988] 2 S.C.R. 650 at 651, [1989] 5 W.W.R. 131, 36 B.C.L.R. (2d) 371, 47 C.C.L.T. 63, 53 D.L.R. (4th) 606.

(a) actual expenses reasonably incurred for the benefit of the person of the person injured or killed;

(b) actual funeral expenses reasonably incurred;

(c) a reasonable allowance for travel expenses actually incurred in visiting the person during his or her treatment or recovery;

(d) where, as a result of the injury, the claimant provides nursing, housekeeping or other services for the person, a reasonable allowance for loss of income or the value of the services;

In awarding pecuniary losses under this section care must be taken not to compensate for expenses, time or services which would normally have been expended by the claimant for the injured or deceased person.[90] For example in *Kenyeres*, the court accepted evidence of the market value of services rendered by the parents of a brain damaged child; however, it reduced the award to about 66 per cent to account for the fact that ". . . parents have an obligation to care for their child including housekeeping and nursing care . . .".[91]

Of course care must be taken to provide proof of the expenditures and to avoid duplication with the damages awarded to the primary claimant. For example it would be a double recovery for the primary plaintiff to receive damages for attendant care costs and to award compensation to a relative for the same attendant care "services".

9. *The Discount Rate and Rule 53.09(1)*

(1) Background

In a pecuniary damage award, the plaintiff receives money in the present for future losses. This present payment for future losses may confer a benefit on the plaintiff unless an allowance is made for inflation and the rate of return on investment. To do this ". . . the court applies a . . . 'discount factor' . . . the real rate of return which the plaintiff can expect to receive on the damage award".[92]

Factors other than price inflation and projected interest rates may also result in erosion or inflation of the fund compared to the loss it is

---

[90] *Mortimer v. Cameron* (1992), 9 M.P.L.R. 185 (Gen. Div.); revd in part 17 O.R. (3d)1, 19 M.P.L.R. (2d) 286, 111 D.L.R. (4th) 428; leave to appeal to S.C.C. refused 19 O.R. (3d) xvi, 23 M.P.L.R. (2d) 314, 179 N.R. 146n.

[91] *Kenyeres (Litigation Guardian of) v. Cullimore* (1992), 13 C.P.C. (3d) 385, addendum to O.J. No. 540 (Ont. Gen. Div.) at 107.

[92] *Lewis v. Todd*, [1980] 2 S.C.R. 694 at 709-12, 14 C.C.L.T. 294, 115 D.L.R. (3d) 257.

provided to replace. For example, evidence at trial might show that attendant care expenses have increased at a rate which is historically higher than the Consumer Price Index. Alternatively, the plaintiff may have been in an occupation where historically the increases in income have lagged behind inflation.

Prior to enactment of rule 53.09(1) the discount rate to be applied was "a factual issue which will turn on the evidence advanced in individual cases".[93]

(2) Rule 53.09(1) and Its Interpretation

Rule 53.09(1) provides:

> 53.09(1) The discount rate to be used in determining the amount of an award in respect of future pecuniary damages, to the extent that it reflects the difference between estimated investment and price inflation rates, is 2.5 per cent per year.

In *Giannone* the Ontario Court of Appeal held that when the rate of interest on future investments and the price inflation rate are the only factors being taken into account, the use of the discount rate of 2.5 per cent in rule 53.09(1) is mandatory and a different rate cannot be used.[94] This provides consistency between decisions and saves the expense of proving these issues at trial.[95]

Factors other than investment rates and price inflation rates may affect the discount rate. These may include increased productivity in the work force, wage increases over inflation, and health care costs changing at different rates than inflation. The court may depart from the rate of 2.5 per cent if ". . . there is evidence one way or the other on the factors other than future investment rates and price inflation rates."[96] Evidence of this type must be very specific to the facts of the case and the profile of the plaintiff's loss; generalities based upon the average industrial wage will not suffice.[97] As a matter of strategy counsel should have their economic experts review components of the consumer price index to see whether or not there are economic aspects of the plaintiff's case which have not been included in the Consumer Price Index and which historically have

---

[93] *Ibid.*, at 709.
[94] *Supra*, note 79, at 776-77 O.R.
[95] *Ibid.*, at 777.
[96] *Ibid.*, at 778.
[97] *Mortimer*, *supra*, note 90, at 280-82.

changed at a different rate than price inflation to determine whether evidence should be led to prove a more beneficial rate.[98]

10. *The Gross Up and Rule 53.09(2)*

As indicated above, the sum awarded for future care is "a self extinguishing sum" it being sufficient to pay for the future needs of the plaintiff, leaving no surplus capital when these needs have been met.[99] The investment income which the plaintiff will earn on the fund is included in the calculation of the amount of the award. However, the plaintiff may be required to pay tax on the income earned from the investment of the award for his future care. If the effect of taxation on this income is not counteracted then the fund will be extinguished before the needs of the plaintiff are met. Therefore, an allowance or "gross up" must be added to the award for future care to offset the effects of income tax.[100]

The calculation of the effect of income tax on the fund by the courts has been extremely complicated,[101] and for fairly obvious reasons. It involves a prediction of the interrelationship between inflation rates, income to the plaintiff from other sources, the nature of the investments, tax rates, tax policy, the lag between deductions and tax credits compared to rates of inflation, the pattern of expenditure of the lump-sum award and the effect of contingencies. These complexities require the assistance and evidence of economists, actuaries and accountants.[102] The complex nature of this calculation has led to repeated requests by the judiciary for legislative reform of the gross up calculation.

Against this background, rule 53.09(2) came into effect on October 4, 1993.[103] It applies to causes of action after that date, and it attempts to standardise some aspects of the gross up calculation as follows:

---

[98] Discussion with Michael Winward, counsel in *Kenyeres*, *supra*, note 91.

[99] *Andrews*, *supra*, note 80, at 260.

[100] *Watkins v. Olafson*, [1989] 2 S.C.R. 750, at 764-68, [1989] 6 W.W.R. 481, 61 Man. R. (2d) 81, 50 C.C.L.T. 101, 61 D.L.R. (4th) 577, 100 N.R. 161; *McErlean v. Sarel* (1987), 22 O.A.C. 186, 61 O.R. (2d) 396 at 432-33, 42 C.C.L.T. 78, 42 D.L.R. (4th) 577 (C.A.).

[101] *Giannone v. Weinberg* (1989), 33 O.A.C. 11, 68 O.R. (2d) 767 at 779-87.

[102] At trial in *Mortimer*, *supra*, note 90, Justice McDermid raised these issues and considered their effect in calculating the gross up: supra at 299-305. See also the decision of the Ontario Court of Appeal in the same case: *supra* at 18.

[103] Professor Watson gives a thorough review of the background to this rule, as well as rule 53.09(1) and s.116 of the *Courts of Justice Act*, in Watson and Perkin, *Holmstead and Watson: Ontario Civil Procedure*, 5 vols. (Toronto: Carswell, 1995). The latter has been very helpful in the preparation of this paper.

(2) In calculating the amount to be included in the award to offset any liability for income tax on income from investment of the award, the court shall,
(a) assume that the entire award will be invested in fixed income securities; and
(b) determine the rate to be assumed for future inflation in accordance with the following formula;

$$g = \frac{1+i}{(1+d)} - 1$$

where "g" is the rate to be assumed for future inflation; "i" is the average yield on Government of Canada marketable bonds for durations of over ten years, as published in the edition of the Bank of Canada's Weekly Financial Statistics appearing on or not more than six days before the date that the trial commenced, rounded to the nearest half of one per cent; and "d" is the discount rate specified in subrule (1).[am. O. Reg. 465/93, s. 5]

Applying the reasoning in *Giannone* concerning the mandatory nature of rule 53.09(1), it may be concluded that the provisions of rule 53.09(2) are also mandatory[104] and require use of the definitions in the rule concerning the nature of the investment and the assumed rate of inflation.

11. *Periodic and Lump Sum Payment of Damages: s. 116 Courts of Justice Act*

(1) Background

As outlined above at common law the plaintiff has the right to receive pecuniary damages as a lump-sum award due from the defendant at the moment of judgment. Once received, there is no restriction on how the money is spent or on whether it is used for the purposes for which it was awarded.[105] As the Supreme Court of Canada noted in *Andrews*, "The plaintiff is free to do with the sum as he likes."[106]

The advantages of this approach for the plaintiff are obvious. For one thing it provides flexibility of expenditure and personal control of resources. The plaintiff will have ". . . the flexibility to plan his life and to plan for contingencies".[107] In addition, the fund is securely in the plain-

---

[104] See *Wilson v. Martinello*, unreported, May 18, 1995, Action No. C17594 (Ont. C.A.), reasons for judgment of Finlayson J.A., at 18.

[105] *Ibid.*; *Lewis, supra*, note 92, at 710.

[106] [1978] 2 S.C.R. 229 at 247, [1978] 1 W.W.R. 577, 8 A.R. 182, 3 C.C.L.T. 225, 83 D.L.R. (3d) 452, 19 N.R. 50.

[107] *Ibid.*

tiff's possession and is therefore not threatened by any possible future insolvency of the defendant. Finally, a lump-sum payment brings an end to the process and prevents indefinite periodic assessments of the plaintiff by the defendant.

There are, however, many serious disadvantages to the "once and for all" lump-sum pecuniary damage award as a means of compensating for future losses.[108] The lump-sum award for future care costs requires a "gross up" to offset the effect of taxation on future investment income from the award; by contrast, periodic payments for personal injury damages are not taxed in the hands of the plaintiff. In addition, one must calculate the risks entailed in future events: will future inflation rates, fluctuations of investment income, changes in tax rules, unforseen material changes in nature of the injury, or unpredicted contingencies result in the plaintiff receiving a "shortfall" or "windfall"?[109] In *Andrews* Mr. Justice Dickson stated the following:

> When it is determined that compensation is to be made, it is highly irrational to be tied to a lump sum system and a once-and-for-all-award . . .It should be possible to devise some system whereby payments would be subject to periodic review and variation in light of the continuing needs of the injured person and the cost of meeting those needs.[110]

In response to these concerns the *Courts of Justice Act* was amended in 1984 to permit, by s. 129, a court, with the consent of the parties in an action claiming damages for personal injury or death, to order payment of the award by way of periodic payments.[111] In addition, the amendment permitted the court with the consent of the parties to order that the award be subject to review and revision. While s. 129 thus provided a method of solving some difficulties associated with lump-sum payments, it must be stressed that it could not be used without the consent of all the parties.

---

[108] *Ibid.*, at 236; *Thornton v. Prince George Schoool Dist. No. 57*, [1978] 2 S.C.R. 267 at 283, [1978] 1 W.W.R. 607, 3 C.C.L.T. 257, 19 N.R. 552. Waddams provides a thorough analysis of these issues in his *Law of Damages*, 2nd ed. (Aurora: Canada Law Book, 1994), at 3-1 to 3-10.

[109] *Andrews, supra*, note 106, at 236; *Thornton, ibid.*, at 283-84.

[110] *Ibid.*, at 236.

[111] See Watson, *Holmstead and Watson, supra*, note 103, for a discussion of the legislative history of ss. 129 and 116.

(2) Section 116 of the Courts of Justice Act

It is against this background that s. 116 of the *Courts of Justice Act* was passed, significantly amending s.129 by providing for court imposed periodic payment awards if the plaintiff requests an award to compensate for income tax payable on the award. The provisions of this section should be carefully considered by counsel engaged in a personal injury action for the reasons set out below. For example, in *Baynton v. Rayner*,[112] Mr. Justice Philp applied the provisions of s. 116 thereby avoiding the need to award a gross-up which evidence at trial indicated could have been as high as $12,218,483.

Section 116 applies to all causes of action which have arisen since October 23, 1989.[113] It provides as follows:

116(1) In a proceeding where damages are claimed for personal injuries or under Part V of the Family Law Act for loss resulting from the injury to or death of a person, the court,

   (*a*) if all affected parties consent, may order the defendant to pay all or part of the award for damages periodically on such terms as the court considers just; and

   (*b*) if the plaintiff requests that an amount be included in the award to compensate for income tax payable on the award, shall order the defendant to pay all or part of the award periodically on such terms as the court considers just.

No order

(2) An order under clause (1)(b) shall not be made if the parties otherwise consent or if the court is of the opinion that the order would not be in the best interest of the plaintiff, having regard to all of the circumstances of the case.

Best interests

(3) In considering the best interests of the plaintiff, the court shall take into account,

   (*a*) whether the defendant has sufficient means to fund an adequate scheme of periodic payments;

   (*b*) whether the plaintiff has a plan or a method of payment that is better able to meet the interests of the plaintiff than periodic payments by the defendant; and

   (*c*) whether a scheme of periodic payments is practicable having regard to all the circumstances of the case.

Future review

(4) In an order made under this section, the court may, with the consent of all the affected parties, order that the award be subject to future review

---

[112] Reasons for judgment delivered by Mr. Justice Philp, May 17, 1995, Hamilton, No. at 64-65 (Gen. Div.).

[113] On the legislative history see Watson, *Holmstead and Watson, supra*, note 103.

and revision in such circumstances and on such terms as the court considers just.

Amount to offset liability for income tax

(5) If the court does not make an order for periodic payment under subsection (1), it shall make an award for damages that shall include an amount to offset liability for income tax on income from investment of the award.

The following elements of s. 116 should be particularly noted:

(a) Section 116 applies to personal injury and death actions only.
(b) The plaintiff can control the court's application of the section either by:
  (i) withholding the consent required in section 116(1)(*a*); or,
  (ii) not advancing a claim for income tax payable on the award under s. 116(1)(*b*).
(c) The defendant can refuse to enter into a voluntary periodic payment under s. 116(1)(*a*) but cannot avoid the application of s. 116(1)(*b*) if the plaintiff advances the income tax claim.
(d) An order for future review of the order cannot be made without the consent of both parties.
(e) Once application of the section is triggered then the court has responsibility for ensuring that the payment scheme is "just". The court would require some evidence and argument to assist its decision.
(f) Once the application of s. 116(1)*(b)* is triggered, the court must insure not only that the order is just but "in the best interests of the plaintiff" including the items set out in s. 116(3). The court would require evidence and argument to assist in this decision.
(g) If the court decides not to make the order then it shall make an order including an amount to offset tax liability.

The difficulty with s. 116, however, is that its language is in many respects "badly drafted" and unclear.[114] It is therefore open to a wide variety of interpretations. In this connection the following questions — answered in part by the Court of Appeal recently in *Wilson v. Martinello*[115] — may be noted:

(a) When, how and in what form must the plaintiff's request under s. 116(1)(*b*) be made to trigger the section? If a request is made in a pleading does this trigger the section? Can a request be implied if the plaintiff leads evidence of the effect of income tax on the potential award? Must the request be made at the outset of trial or can the plaintiff reserve his decision on the request until the conclusion of the evidence?

---

[114] *Wilson v. Martinello*, *supra*, note 104, at 10.
[115] *Ibid.*

These difficulties were clarified by Mr. Justice Finlayson in *Wilson v. Martinello* as follows:

> To my mind it is clear that s.116 is not engaged until the end of the trial when the court has decided all issues of liability and has assessed damages in the conventional manner. It is only then that the issue of whether to structure some or all of the damages arises if there is no consent under s.116(1)(*a*). At that stage the plaintiff is in a position to determine "request" a gross-up. Once the findings of fact have been made as to those heads of compensation which would attract gross-up, hopefully the parties can agree to the results that flow from the calculation of gross-up as prescribed by rule 53.09(2) of the Rules, *supra*. If they cannot, evidence would have to be led on the issue having in mind the formula set out in rule 53.09(2). Once the calculation has been made, the defendant would either have to agree to the lump-sum award with gross-up as found by the court or put forward a scheme of periodic payments (a structure) for the consideration of the court under s.116(1)(*b*) of the Act.[116]

(b) Do the words "income tax payable *on the award*" in s. 116(1)(*b*) include income tax payable on *investment income* earned on the award after it is made?

This distinction was noted by Mr. Justice Philp who delivered the trial judgment in in *Wilson v. Martinello*.[117] His comments at para. 52 of the judgment suggest that the request for a "gross up" might be a request for compensation for tax on income earned from the award and not "on the award". However, Mr. Justice Finlayson held, in the appeal decision in *Wilson v. Martinello*, that s.116(1)(*b*) contains a "patent drafting error" and should be interpreted as if the section read ". . . a request for tax *on income earned* from the award . . ."[118] (emphasis added).

(c) Is periodic payment of the "award" confined to that part of the award upon which the plaintiff claims tax compensation or on the entire award thus resulting in the possibility of periodic payment of general damages and income loss?

This question is not dealt with in *Wilson v. Martinello*. The wording of s.116(1)(*b*) is certainly broad enough to suggest that the entire award for damages may be paid periodically in that the subsection uses the words ". . . *all or part* of the award . . ." (emphasis added).

(d) Who bears the onus of proving the best interests of the plaintiff? In *Wilson v. Martinello* Justice Finlayson concluded as follows:

> The hearing under s.116(3) of the Act raises interesting considerations as to which party bears the onus of establishing whether periodic payments are

[116] *Ibid.*, at 11-12.
[117] Unreported, December 20, 1990, O.J. No. 3361 (Gen. Div.).
[118] *Supra*, note 104, at 9-10.

in the best interests of the plaintiff. For instance, the defendant is in the best position to demonstrate that it has "sufficient means to fund an adequate scheme of periodic payments" as required by ss.3(a). However, as a practical matter this will likely become a non-issue because invariably the structure proposed will involve the purchase by the defendant's casualty insurer of an annuity from a life insurer: see Osborne Report, supra at p. 417. Certainly, under ss.3(b), the onus would be upon the plaintiff to establish affirmatively in evidence that he has a plan or a method of payment that is better able to meet the interests of the plaintiff than periodic payments. The issue under ss.3(c) as to whether structuring is practicable would also appear to be the responsibility of the plaintiff. Broadly speaking, it appears to me that the focus of the section is that where gross up is requested by the plaintiff, a structure is mandatory unless the plaintiff can satisfy the court that the one proposed by the defendant is not in the plaintiff's best interests.[119]

Justice Finlayson further decided that in a jury trial the jury decides "the quantum of damages in the usual manner including those awards that attract gross up. The trial judge could then deal with the calculation of gross up and the issues under s. 116 as to the availability of structuring."[120]

It should be noted that it would be open for the plaintiff to propose a plan for periodic payments as an alternative to the defence proposal, or in the absence of any specific proposal from the defendant.

(e) If a request is not made by the plaintiff under s. 116(1)(b) should the judge award an amount for the "gross up" pursuant to s. 116(5) in any event? In *Wilson* at trial, Justice Philp concluded that:

> If no request is made or implied or it is not in his best interests, the plaintiff is entitled to a gross-up in accordance with subsection 5. . .I find that no request by the plaintiff as set out in subsection (1)(b) has been made and I must therefore order a gross -up pursuant to s. 116(5).[121]

On appeal Mr. Justice Finlayson held that: ". . . if it is the decision of the court that the plaintiff is to have a lump-sum award, everything that follows thereafter is determined by the Act or the Rules. Section 116(5) provides that the gross up is mandatory and rule 53.09(2) instructs the parties how to calculate the gross up."[122]

(f) In making an award for periodic payments counsel and the court should be alert to the effects of inflation on periodic payments and the consequent need for an indexing of the payments. In *Kenyeres*, Justice Philp ordered periodic payment of an award with the consent of both

---

[119] *Ibid.*, at 12.
[120] *Ibid.*, at 16.
[121] *Supra*, note 117, paras. 54-55.
[122] *Supra*, note 104, at 18.

parties. In so doing he specifically noted that the discussion of this ". . .should include the question of indexing the annual costs to provide for inflation. . .".[123] Although the parties consented to the order for periodic payments they could not agree on the indexing or guarantee period. After hearing evidence Justice Philp ordered periodic payments for a guaranteed period of 15 years or the plaintiff's life, whichever was longer and ordered a 5 per cent per annum indexing of payments.

(g) How will the court interpret "the best interests of the plaintiff? The court's role is ". . . to determine on the facts of each case whether the plaintiff has demonstrated that a structured award in his case would not be in his best interests."[124]

In *Socha v. Miller*,[125] Justice Kovacs applied s. 116 and ordered periodic payment of a future care award without the consent of the plaintiff. He considered the periodic payments to be in the plaintiff's best interests because the defendant had sufficient means to secure payment, the plaintiff had no plan better able to meet the interests of the plaintiff, and the plaintiff's condition was subject to unpredictable change.

Taken together these questions make it clear that the effects of s. 116 must be carefully considered by counsel before advancing a claim for compensation for income tax liability. Specifically counsel must decide whether the possibility of periodic payments and future review are in the best interest of their clients and be prepared with supporting evidence and arguments at trial. A practical solution is for counsel to agree prior to trial on the way in which the award will be dealt with, and to agree on a structure of the award in advance.

It may be concluded that s. 116 opens up significant possibilities for correcting some of the difficulties accompanying lump sum awards.

12. *Collateral Benefits and Double Recovery in the Supreme Court of Canada: Ratych v. Bloomer and Cunningham v. Wheeler*

Two recent Supreme Court of Canada decisions, *Ratych v. Bloomer*[126] and *Cunningham v. Wheeler*,[127] have considered the extent to which

---

[123] (1992), 13 C.P.C. (3d) 385 at 388-90, addendum to O.J. No. 540 at 103.
[124] *Wilson v. Martinello, per* Mr. Justice Finlayson, *supra*, note 104, at 20.
[125] *Socha (Public Trustee of) v. Millar*, unreported, February 1, 1995, O.J. No. 371 (Ont. Gen. Div.).
[126] [1990] 1 S.C.R. 940, 39 O.A.C. 103, 73 O.R. (2d) 448n, 30 C.C.E.L. 161, 3 C.C.L.T. (2d) 1, 69 D.L.R. (4th) 25, 107 N.R. 335.
[127] [1994] 1 S.C.R. 359, 88 B.C.L.R. (2d) 273, 113 D.L.R. (4th) 1, 164 N.R. 81.

pecuniary damages will be reduced by payments which a plaintiff receives from sources other than the defendant. An analysis of these decisions reveals a difference of approaches between Madam Justice McLaughlin and Mr. Justice Cory regarding not only this issue but also several other issues arising from the general topic of compensation for pecuniary loss. This difference is significant because both decisions were "bare majority" decisions of the court.[128] This in itself suggests that the issue may be a source of continuing debate. Indeed one might speculate that as the composition of the court changes the issue may not only be revisited, but may be extended to other areas of collateral benefits.

(1) The Background in Ontario: Boarelli v. Flannigan

Prior to the decision in *Ratych*, the leading authority in Ontario regarding the deduction of collateral benefits was the Ontario Court of Appeal decision in *Boarelli v. Flannigan*[129]. In *Boarelli*, in considering whether or not welfare benefits paid to the plaintiff following the injury should be deducted from damages, the Court of Appeal arrived at the following conclusions:

(a) A wide range of "collateral benefits" such as social welfare benefits, private insurance benefits, and employment related benefits are available to the plaintiff quite apart from rights against a tortfeasor for loss.[130]

(b) Benefits received by the plaintiff as a result of public benevolence, such as welfare benefits, unemployment insurance and as a result of private benevolence are not to be taken into account in assessing damages for lost earning capacity because they are provided "independent of any cause of action" and are not for the benefit of the wrongdoer.[131]

(c) Benefits received from employment are part of the wage package and should not be treated differently than benefits received from a private policy of insurance which are not deductible.

(d) Proof of consideration for wage benefits is not required in each case but can be assumed. The defendant should not obtain the advantage of these benefits "earned" by the plaintiff.[132]

---

[128] *Ratych* was decided by a 5-4 majority; *Cunningham* was decided by a 4-3 majority.

[129] *Boarelli v. Flannigan*, [1973] 3 O.R. 69, 36 D.L.R. (3d) 4 (C.A.).

[130] *Ibid.*, at 70.

[131] *Ibid.*, at 73-75.

[132] *Ibid.*, at 79.

(e) Ex gratia payments from an employer are no different than the non-deductible ex gratia payments from a friend or relative.[133]

(f) Collateral benefits including, welfare payments, unemployment insurance benefits, disability income from an insurance or employment contracts, ex gratia payments from third parties will not be taken into account in calculating the plaintiff's award for loss of earnings.[134]

(2) Ratych v. Bloomer

In *Ratych*, the Supreme Court of Canada was called upon to determine whether or not salary paid to a police officer while he was unable to work as a result of an injury caused by the defendant's negligence should be deducted from his award for income loss. There was no evidence that the police officer had given any consideration for the continuation of his salary benefit. The lower court decisions applied *Boarelli* and refused to deduct the salary benefits. The Supreme Court of Canada adopted a different approach. In her decision for the majority Madam Justice McLachlin held that the wage benefit of the plaintiff should be deducted from the pecuniary damage award because ". . . neither a loss nor a contribution equivalent to payment of an insurance policy is established . . .".[135] In reaching that conclusion she adopted a position which runs contrary to the position adopted by the Ontario Court of Appeal in *Boarelli* with respect to employment benefits:

> As a general rule, wage benefits paid while a plaintiff is unable to work must be brought into account and deducted from the claim for lost earnings. An exception to this rule may lie where the court is satisfied that the employer or fund which paid the wage benefits is entitled to be reimbursed for them on the principle of subrogation.

As to *Boarelli* itself, Justice McLaughlin stressed that while the issue there was the deductibility of welfare benefits the Court of Appeal had gone beyond that issue, and indeed went "much further" than the precedent relied upon to "pronounce on a wide variety of other benefits".[136]

Finally, Madam Justice McLachlin's obiter comments underline her continuing concern over the issue of double recovery of compensation for pecuniary damages. In particular, the following comments may be noted:

---

[133] *Ibid.*, at 79-80.
[134] *Ibid.*, at 75, 82.
[135] *Ratych, supra*, note 126, at 972.
[136] *Ibid.*, at 969-70.

(a) There is often a tenuous link between the moral culpability of the tortfeasor and the obligation to pay damages. Risks of certain activities may be a social and not individual burden.[137]

(b) Courts should not assume that because a benefit has been conferred by a third person the plaintiff has suffered an equivalent loss.[138]

(c) "[The] deduction of collateral benefits can be justified on a loss-distribution analysis".[139]

(d) "Considerations relating to allocation of loss do not negate and indeed tend to support the deductibility of wage benefits, where that deductibility is otherwise properly founded in legal principle."[140]

(3) Cunningham v. Wheeler

Cunningham v. Wheeler,[141] *Cooper v. Miller*, and *Shanks v. McNee* constitute a trilogy of cases wherein the Supreme Court of Canada revisited the question of the deductibility of wage benefits paid to plaintiffs while off work as a result of the injuries caused by a defendant's negligence. In all three cases there was some evidence of consideration for the benefits in the collective bargaining process.

(a) *The Majority Decision*

In the *Cunningham* trilogy, the Supreme Court of Canada reaffirmed that ". . . the plaintiff is not entitled to double recovery for any loss arising from the injury".[142] However, the majority decision found in all three cases that the wage benefits were not deductible because there was sufficient evidence of consideration from the plaintiffs to place the benefits within the insurance exemption to the general rule against double recovery.

In his decision for the majority Mr. Justice Cory held:

(a) that payments received by a plaintiff which are in the nature of insurance benefits paid for by the plaintiff ought not to be deducted from the lost income award;[143]

---

[137] *Ibid.*, at 963.
[138] *Ibid.*, at 973.
[139] *Ibid.*, at 977.
[140] *Ibid.*
[141] *Supra*, note 127.
[142] *Ibid.*, at 396.
[143] *Ibid.*, at 406, 410, 415.

(b) where there is proof of "some type of consideration given up"[144] by the plaintiff in return for benefits, the benefits will be treated as being in the nature of insurance benefits and will not to be deducted in calculating lost income;

(c) no deduction shall be made for benefits which are not "insurance" if there is a subrogated right by the payer of the benefits to recover the benefits, even if the subrogation right has not been exercised;[145]

(d) the court reserved consideration of situations where the payer of benefits which are not insurance has released its subrogation right.[146]

In the result, income replacement disability benefits received pursuant to collective agreements were not deducted from an award for lost income. In reaching this result Mr. Justice Cory stressed that the insurance exemption should be maintained because,

> It has a long history. It is understood and accepted. . . . More importantly it is based on fairness. All who insure themselves for disability benefits are displaying wisdom and forethought in making provision for the continuation of some income in case of disabling injury or illness.[147]

He continued,

> I can see no reason why a tortfeasor should benefit from the sacrifices made by a plaintiff in obtaining an insurance policy to provide for lost wages. . . . It makes little sense for a wrongdoer to benefit from the private act of forethought and sacrifice of the plaintiff.[148]

He concluded that "if any action is to be taken, it should be by legislatures."

As for the court's decision in *Ratych*, Cory J. confined its significance to the realm of evidentiary matters.[149]

Finally, it should be noted that Mr. Justice Cory did not distinguish *Boarelli*,[150] but rather made passing mention of it as one of the cases in Canada which affirmed the insurance exception.

---

[144] *Ibid.*, at 407.
[145] *Ibid.*, at 415-16.
[146] *Ibid.*, at 416.
[147] *Ibid.*, at 400.
[148] *Ibid.*, at 401.
[149] *Ibid.*, at 406.
[150] *Supra*, note 128.

(b) *The Minority Decision*

The minority decision rendered by Madam Justice McLaughlin held that the wage benefits paid pursuant to a collective agreement should be deducted for the following reasons:

> I conclude that principle, precedent and policy all favour the conclusion that wage benefits paid pursuant to employment plans should be deducted from damages for loss of earnings claimed against the tortfeasor, except where it is established that a right of subrogation will be exercised, thereby avoiding double recovery. The only exceptions that should be endorsed are charity and cases of non-indemnity insurance or pensions. Any benefits which indemnify the plaintiff against wage loss must be brought into account in a damage claim for that loss against a tortfeasor because, to the extent the plaintiff has been indemnified, no loss arises. On the other hand, benefits which are not in the nature of indemnification for the loss claimed against the tortfeasor need not be brought into account.[151]

Madam Justice McLaughlin interpreted her majority decision in *Ratych* as more than ". . . a case about evidence . . .". Specifically she held as follows:

> Ratych v. Bloomer is not merely a ruling on evidentiary sufficiency. Rather, following on the lead in other common law jurisdictions, it pronounces on the general requirement for deduction of employment wage benefits from claims for loss of wages against a tortfeasor.[152]

More importantly, while giving limited acceptance to the non-deductibility of gratuitous payments and non-indemnity insurance proceeds, MacLachlin J. offered a clear reminder[153] that in the majority decision in *Ratych* the court had specifically *left open* questions relating to the non-deductibility of both gratuitous or charitable contributions to the plaintiff, and the private insurance exception.

In the end Madam Justice McLaughlin concluded that a plaintiff's loss of benefit from contribution to a benefit plan does not avoid the problem of double recovery.

---

[151] *Supra*, note 127, at 392-93.
[152] *Ibid.*, at 378-79.
[153] *Ibid.*, at 378-80.

(4) The Future Course of the Collateral Benefit Issue

Boarelli v. Flannigan[154] provided broad statements supporting the non-deductibility of a wide range of collateral benefits. *Ratych*,[155] obliquely revised *Boarelli*; but it did not overrule *Boarelli*. Of course *Ratych* also contains a good many obiter statements favouring deduction of collateral benefits. For its part, *Cunningham*[156] restores the insurance exemption with respect to wage benefits; however, the *Cunningham* decision, like *Ratych*, deals only with employment benefits. Boarelli has not been over-ruled by the Supreme Court of Canada. Although *Boarelli* survives, it dealt with a slightly different question, that being the treatment of social welfare benefits arising from public benevolence.

Clearly many questions relating to the issue of double recovery are still left to be resolved. How will the Supreme Court of Canada deal with questions relating to the deductibility of social welfare benefits? How will the question relating to release of subrogation rights be answered? To what extent will lower courts interpret Cunningham and extend its reasoning beyond the employment benefit context?[157]

It is likely, that the deductibility of collateral benefits will be revisited by various appeal courts and the Supreme Court of Canada to determine the limits of these questions. For example, in *Stein*,[158] arguments were made in the Ontario Court of Appeal for the deduction as collateral benefits of future OHIP benefits to which the plaintiff was entitled. While the Court of Appeal rejected this submission, they did so for a number of reasons (issue not raised at trial, no evidentiary basis, agreement at trial that private agency required, no overlap of medical services, subrogation right existing) which make it difficult to predict how the argument might be dealt with in other circumstances. Interestingly, the court did not consider the "waiver" of subrogation by OHIP to be equivalent to a "release" of subrogation rights, which Cunningham has left open.

Counsel in personal injury cases will need to be sensitive to these issues when considering the pleading of cases, preparation and evidence at trial.

---

[154] [1993] 3 O.R. 69, 36 D.L.R. (3d) 4.

[155] [1990] 1 S.C.R. 940, 39 O.A.C. 103, 73 O.R. (2d) 448n, 30 C.C.E.L. 161, 3 C.C.L.T. (2d) 1, 69 D.L.R. (4th) 25, 107 N.R. 335.

[156] [1994] 1 S.C.R. 359, 88 B.C.L.R (2d) 273, 113 D.L.R. (4th) 1, 164 N.R. 81.

[157] See for example *Dalex v. Schwartz* (1994), 19 O.R. (3d) 463 (Gen.Div.). where the principles in *Cunningham*, *ibid.*, are extended beyond the employment context.

[158] Unreported, June 30, 1993, O.J. No. 1772 (Gen. Div.).

13. *Collateral Benefits and s. 267(1) of the Insurance Act*

As a consequence of s. 267(1) of the *Insurance Act,* the deduction of collateral benefits is required in actions arising from motor vehicle accidents occurring after October 23, 1989. The Act provides in part as follows:

> 267(1) The damages awarded to a person in a proceeding for loss or damage arising directly or indirectly from the use or operation of an automobile shall be reduced by,
>
> > (a) all payments that the person has received or that were or are available for no-fault benefits and by the present value of any no-fault benefits to which the person is entitled;
> >
> > (b) all payments that the person has received under any medical, surgical, dental, hospitalization, rehabilitation or long-term care plan or law and by the present value of such payments to which the person is entitled;
> >
> > (c) all payments that the person has received or that were available for loss of income under the laws of any jurisdiction or under an income continuation benefit plan and by the present value of any such payments to which the person is entitled; and
> >
> > (d) all payments that the person has received under a sick leave plan arising by reason of the person's occupation or employment.
>
> . . . . .
>
> (4) A person who has made a payment or who has a liability to pay a benefit described in clause (1)(a), (b) ,(c) or (d) is not subrogated to a right of recovery of the insured against another person in respect of that payment or benefit.
>
> . . . . .
>
> (6) This section applies to damages awarded for loss or damage arising directly or indirectly from the use or operation, after the 23rd day of October, 1989, of an automobile.

In *Cugliardi v. White,*[159] Justice Caswell held that the payments listed in s. 267(1)(c) are deducted from all damages awarded at trial, and not just from the pecuniary damage award. He further indicated that s. 267(1)(c) was enacted to implement the recommendations in the *Osborne Report* that the collateral source rule be eliminated, except with respect to "non-indemnity payments and gifts". In consequence, before ruling on the deductibility of Canada pension plan disability benefits he first determined that the disability payments were ". . . payments made for

---

[159] *Culiardi v. White* (1994), 21 O.R. (3d) 225 (Gen. Div.).

loss of his income in order to indemnify the plaintiff. Therefore these payments are caught by the provisions of s. 267(1)(c) and must be deducted from the award of damages at trial.''[160] While Justice Caswell was considering s. 267(1)(c), his comments are applicable to the treatment of all of the payments listed in s. 267(1).

In this connection it might also be noted that in his decision at trial in *Meyer v. Bright*,[161] Justice Browne held that the "plain reading" of s. 267(1)(a) must be followed and deducted disability and automobile insurance no-fault benefits from the damages assessed.[162]

14. *Collateral Benefits and s. 63 of the Family Law Act*

In contrast to s. 267(1) of the *Insurance Act*, the *Family Law Act* specifically permits non-deduction of insurance benefits from damages awarded under Part V of the Act as follows:

> 63. In assessing damages in an action brought under this Part, the court shall not take into account any sum paid or payable as a result of the death or injury under a contract of insurance.

The plain wording of this section suggests that it applies to *Family Law Act* derivative claims for personal injury or death. In *Dube v. Penlon*,[163] Mr. Justice Zuber indicated that the section "contemplates sums payable on the death or injury of the primary claimant" and not because of disability of the derivative claimant.[164]

In *Dall Estate v. Adams*,[165] the Ontario Court of Appeal indicated that s. 63 of the *Family Law Act* is not altered by s. 267(1)(c) of the *Insurance Act*. In holding that survivorship benefits under the Canada Pension Plan and the *Public Service Superannuation Act*[166] were not deductible from the plaintiff's claim for pecuniary loss under s. 61 of the *Family Law Act* the court said:

---

[160] *Ibid.*, at 235.
[161] (1992), 9 O.R. (3d) 225, 38 M.V.R. (2d) 138, 94 D.L.R. (4th) 648 (Gen. Div.); affd 15 O.R. (3d) 129, 48 M.V.R. (2d) 1, 110 D.L.R. (4th) 354 (C.A.); leave to appeal to S.C.C. refused 17 O.R. (3d) xvi, 172 N.R. 160*n*.
[162] *Ibid.*, at 254-55.
[163] Unreported, July 28, 1994, O.J. No. 1720 (Ont. Gen. Div.).
[164] *Ibid.*, at 83.
[165] (1994), 19 O.R. (3d) 93, 116 D.L.R. (4th) 189 (C.A.).
[166] R.S.C. 1985, c. P-36.

In my view, having regard to the degree to which the non-deductibility of the type of benefits in issue in these proceeding has been established in Ontario, as well as elsewhere in Canada, it would have taken the clearest of language to displace it.[167]

In *Woodside Estate v. Snyde Estate*,[168] Justice Daudlin followed *Dall* and so found Automobile No-Fault Death Benefits paid to the derivative claimants, as well as weekly benefits paid to the deceased prior to her death, to be non-deductible from damages awarded for death.

15. *Legislative Restrictions on the Right to Recover Pecuniary Loss*

Ironically, while plaintiff's counsel have succeeded in obtaining increasing and substantial multi-million dollar judgments for catastrophically injured plaintiffs, the Ontario legislature first restricted then extinguished the right to claim pecuniary damages in motor vehicle accidents by amendments to s. 266 of the *Insurance Act*. The review of the full effect of these amendments is beyond the scope of this paper. However, some comment follows regarding the effects of these two amendments on pecuniary damage claims in motor vehicle actions.

(1) Ontario Motorist Protection Plan: June 21, 1990 — December 31, 1994

In 1990, the *Insurance Act* was amended to provide immunity to certain individuals from civil actions for personal injury damages arising from car accidents. Section 266 provides as follows:

266(1) In respect of loss or damage arising directly or indirectly from the use or operation, after the 21st day of June, 1990, of an automobile and despite any other Act, none of the owner of an automobile, the occupants of an automobile or any person present at the incident are liable in an action in Ontario for loss or damage from bodily injury arising from such use or operation in Canada, the United States of America or any other jurisdiction designated in the No-Fault Benefits Schedule involving the automobile unless, as a result of such use or operation, the injured person has died or has sustained,

(a) permanent serious disfigurement or,

---

[167] *Supra*, note 165, at 96.
[168] Unreported, August 31, 1994, O.J. No. 2114 (Ont. Gen. Div.), under appeal.

(b) permanent serious impairment of an important bodily function caused by continuing injury which is physical in nature.

This section remained in force from June 21, 1990 until January 1, 1994.

Although s. 266 prevents any claim — including a claim for pecuniary loss — unless the plaintiff falls within one of the exceptions to the immunity provided by the section, the question of pecuniary loss is important in determining whether or not a plaintiff can fit into one of the exceptions. However, in order to understand the importance of pecuniary loss as an indicator that the plaintiff fits into a statutory exception it is necessary to review briefly the decisions of the Ontario Court of Appeal in the trilogy of cases which have interpreted s. 266, these being *Meyer v. Bright*, *Dalgleish v. Green*, and *Lento v. Castaldo*.[169]

In its decision in *Meyer* the Court of Appeal held that while s. 266 immunized certain defendants from action it also created three exceptions to that immunity, one of which was that,

> . . . the injured person has sustained permanent, serious impairment of an important bodily function caused by a continuing injury which is physical in nature.[170]

In analyzing this exception the court noted that the words which would cause most difficulty in considering the applicability of this exception were the words "serious" and "important". The court then posed three questions to be answered in sequence so as to determine if the exception was met:

(1) Has the injured person sustained permanent impairment of a bodily function caused by continuing injury which is physical in nature?
(2) If the answer to question number 1 is yes , is the bodily function, which is permanently impaired, an important one?
(3) If the answer to Q. 2 is yes, is the impairment of the important bodily function serious?

The court indicated that the word "important" in Q. 2 means important to the particular injured person. Similarly, the court indicated that the word "serious" in Q. 3 means serious to the particular plaintiff. It is surely significant that in using examples to clarify the interpretation of the words"important" and "serious" the court used examples which relate to vocational aspects of a persons life. Thus injury to a finger is "impor-

---

[169] *Meyer v. Bright* (1993), 15 O.R. (3d) 129 (C.A.).
[170] *Ibid.*, at 136.

tant" to an operator of a word processor but not to a judge because it interferes with the operator's work. Similarly, a finger injury to a highly skilled violinist will not be "serious" if the violinist plays only for his own enjoyment; however it would be serious if it prevented continuation of a professional career.

Thus, the determination of "important" and "serious" will often turn on the occupational consequences resulting from the injury. A permanent serious impairment of an important bodily function may well not be accompanied by any significant pecuniary loss. However, serious impairment of an important bodily function will often be accompanied by pecuniary loss. Furthermore, significant pecuniary loss will no doubt be at least one indication that there has been a serious impairment of an important bodily function.

For example, in the *Lento* decision, the court found that the bodily function was "important" because it was important to Lento's occupation and that the injury was "serious" because it ". . . compromised Mr. Lento's ability to function in his chosen occupation".[171]

The Court did indicate that proof of economic loss is not determinative of seriousness and that an injury may be serious "regardless of financial consequences". But for the reasons set out above the pecuniary impact of the injury is very relevant to the inquiry.

(2) Bill 164

The amendment to s. 266, by what is now s. 267.1, does prevent any court action for pecuniary damages in motor vehicle accidents by providing as follows:

> 267.1(1) Despite any other Act and subject to subsections (2) and (6), the owner of an automobile, the occupants of an automobile and any person present at the incident are not liable in a proceeding in Ontario for loss or damage from bodily injury or death arising directly or indirectly from the use or operation of the automobile in Canada, the United States of America or any other country designated in the Statutory Accident Benefits Schedule.

> (2) Subsection (1) does not relieve a person from liability for damages for non-pecuniary loss, including damages for non-pecuniary loss under clause 61 (2)(e) of the *Family Law Act*, if as a result of the use or operation of the automobile the injured person has died or has sustained,

---

[171] *Ibid.*, at 157.

(*a*) serious disfigurement; or

(*b*) serious impairment of an important physical, mental or psychological function.

16. *Conclusion*

The cap on general damages set by the Supreme Court Canada in the "trilogy" focused the energy and creativity of counsel on the principles and proofs of pecuniary damages with outstanding results for plaintiffs. These results are evident in decisions such as those in *Stein*,[172] *Mortimer*[173] and *Kenyeres*.[174] At the same time the legislature of Ontario has responded to the tort system by extinguishing the rights of victims of motor vehicle accidents to claim pecuniary damages. The next decade will undoubtedly see the continuation of this tension. The issue to be determined is deceptively simple: will pecuniary losses in personal injury claims be remedied in accordance with the traditional principles of tort law, or will the scope of plaintiff's claims be further limited by legislative action? Two equally extreme answers present themselves: either we embrace traditional tort principles, or we embrace some variation on the "end of torts" solution, such as Bill 164. However, one may be forgiven for suggesting a third option — a compromise solution. On the one hand tort law, as the most robust mechanism for protecting plaintiff's right to full compensation for pecuniary losses, ought to be allowed to survive. At the same time, escalating demands on public and private financial resources requires some restraint. As a start one may suggest a greater sensitivity to the sorts of issues highlighted in the recent developments in the law of pecuniary damages, these including avoidance of double recovery, use of periodic payments, and mechanisms for mandatory review of awards.

---

[172] *Supra*, note 158.

[173] (1994), 17 O.R. (3d) 1, 19 M.P.L.R. (2d) 286, 111 D.L.R. (4th) 428 (C.A.); leave to appeal to S.C.C. refused 19 O.R. (3d) xvi, 23 M.P.L.R. (2d) 314, 178 N.R. 146*n*.

[174] (1992), 13 C.P.C. (3d) 385 (Ont. Gen. Div.); addendum O.J. No. 540 (Ont. Gen. Div.).

Appendix "A"

FUTURE CARE COSTS:

	Initial	Annual
(1) ATTENDANT CARE (annual cost)		
(i) Attendant care		$111,938.08
(ii) Housekeeping		2,500.00
(iii) Home maintenance and repair		2,000.00

(2) TRANSPORTATION		
(a) Extraordinary expense of purchasing van	8,000.00	
(b) Van alterations	18,950.00	
(c) Cellular telephone	500.00	
(d) Difference in annual operating cost of van		4,500.00
(e) Portable ramps	498.00	49.80
	27,948.00	4,459.80

(3) ACCOMMODATION		
Conversion cost	55,000.00	

(4) EQUIPMENT, SUPPLIES AND MEDICATION

Items	Unit Cost	Use/Life	Initial Cost	Annual Cost
Electric Wheelchair	$ 2,750.00 (25%)	5 years	2,750.00	$ 550.00
Manual Wheelchair	$ 1,300.00	5 years	$ 1,300.00	260.00
Wheelchair Maintenance				300.00
Battery Replacement	120.00	1 year	120.00	120.00
Tubes, Tires and Bearing Replacement				300.00
Seating Insert	225.00	5 years	225.00	45.00

Items	Unit Cost	Use/Life	Initial Cost	Annual Cost
ROHO Cushion (2)	93.75 25%	3 years	187.50	62.50
Shower Commode Chair	250.00	7 years	35.71	35.71
	4,738.75		4,618.21	1,673.21
Brought Forward	4,738.75		4,618.21	1,673.21
Air Mattress & Pump	380.00	5 years	76.00	76.00
Mediman Lift & Sling	2,250.00	10 years	225.00	225.00
Extra Sling	250.00	5 years	250.00	50.00
Bowel & Bladder Needs				2,000.00
Directal Telephone	588.00	10 years	58.80	58.80
Medications				1,320.00
Washbasin	38.00	10 years	38.00	3.80
K Basin	16.50	10 years	16.50	1.65
Shampoo Set	81.00	10 years	81.00	8.10
Overbed Table	325.00	10 years	325.00	32.50
Bedpan	6.65	5 years	6.65	1.33
Drawsheets: Vinyl (2)	15.00	3 years	30.00	10.00
Drawsheets: Cotton (5)	10.00	3 years	50.00	16.67
Bed Sore Treatment				50.00
Sheepskin: booties	10.64	5 years	10.64	2.13
pads (2)	30.90	5 years	61.80	12.36
Extraordinary Clothing Expense				1,200.00
TOTAL	$8,740.44		$5,847.60	$6,741,55

(5) VOCATIONAL REHABILITATION AND COMMUNICATIONS

Items	Unit Cost	Use/Life	Initial Cost	Annual Cost
DragonDictate System	$12,000.	4 years	$12,000.	3,000.
Computer Hardware	6,000.	4 years	6,000.	1,500.
Service Contract	1,000.	1 year	1,000.	1,000.
Microphone	200.	4 years	200.	50.
Trackball	300.	4 years	300.00	75.
Tape Backup System	900.	4 years	900.	225.
Ergonomic Work Station	3,000.	10 years	3,000.	300.
Replacement of Moving Parts (every 2 years)				2,000.
Reference Carousels	3,000	4 years	3,000	750.
Service				100.
Environmental Control System	5,000	5 years	5,000.	1,000.
Professional Assignment	800.		800.	800.
Training for DragonDictate	1,350			1,350.
	$33,550.		$32,200.	$10,350.

PECUNIARY DAMAGES FOR LOST PROFITS AND OPPORTUNITIES

Ronald G. Slaght, Q.C.
Perry Hancock

Confronting counsel retained to prosecute or defend a lawsuit is the question of remedy. While the importance of establishing the right sought to be protected cannot be minimized, neither can the development of the remedy. In particular, where a claim is made for damages, counsel must consider, among other things, the nature of the right for which protection is sought, and the availability and extent of the damages that may be recovered for infringement of that right. Some of these issues involve profound questions of law (for example, establishing liability for economic loss in tort) while others involve predominately questions of proof, and the application of generally accepted legal principles to the evidence put before the court. The law governing the recovery of pecuniary damages for lost profits and opportunities raises all these issues. This paper will review generally the state of the law governing a claim for damages for lost profits and opportunities in tort, contract and equity and will address notable recent developments in this area. It will also touch on practical problems of proving damages for lost profits and opportunities.

1. *Availability of Damages for Lost Profits in Contract*

It will become apparent throughout this paper that the approach to determining whether particular types of damages are recoverable in an action depends upon their availability in law, and, in general terms, the plaintiff's ability to prove them. That damages are recoverable for lost profits in contract is of course well-accepted but it is helpful to set out the general and familiar rules to assist in demonstrating their application.

(1) General Principle

A right to damages for breach of contract arises as a consequence of the breach of the parties' original bargain; it is not a part of the contract, but an incident which the law attaches to a breach of the contract.[1] The general rule in awarding damages for breach of contract is that the plaintiff should, so far as it can be done by money, be placed in the same position as he or she would have been in if the contract had been performed.[2] This right to damages is broadly circumscribed by the concept of remoteness of damage.[3]

Remoteness of damage asks the question of whether the damage incurred by the innocent party as a result of a breach of contract is properly remediable by or recoverable in an action for breach of contract, that is, whether the types of consequences of losses suffered by the innocent party may be compensated.[4] Quantification of damages, by contrast, involves the determination of how to measure the loss incurred by the innocent party for a particular consequence or loss which has been held not to be too remote.[5]

(2) Remoteness of Damage

The classic statement of the principle is set out in *Hadley v. Baxendale*[6] in which Alderson B. stated:

---

[1] K.P. McGuinness, *The Law of Guarantee* (Toronto: Carswell, 1986) at 305; *Birmingham R. Dist. Land Co. v. London R. North Western Railway Co.* (1886), 34 Ch. D. 261 at 274-75 (Bowen L.J.), 276 (Fry L.J.) (C.A.); G.H.L. Fridman, *The Law of Contract in Canada*, 3rd ed. (Scarborough: Carswell, 1994) at 702-03.

[2] *Sally Wertheim v. Chicoutimi Pulp Co.*, [1911] A.C. 301 at 307 (P.C.); *Asamera Oil Corp. Ltd. v. Sea Oil & General Corp.*, [1979] 1 S.C.R. 633, [1978] 6 W.W.R. 301, 5 B.L.R. 225, 89 D.L.R. (3d) 1 at 8, 23 N.R. 181.

[3] Fridman, *The Law of Contract in Canada, supra,* note 1, at 711; Guest, gen. ed., *Chitty on Contracts*, 27th ed., vol. I (London: Sweet & Maxwell, 1994) at para. 26-021, note 75. Remoteness of damage has been said to include the concepts of remoteness and quantification of damages. While there is some question of the appropriate terminology in English law, for ease of reference, this paper will use the terms remoteness of damage and quantification of damages to represent two issues to be canvassed in determining a plaintiff's right to damages for breach of contract.

[4] Fridman, *The Law of Contract in Canada, ibid.*, at 711; *Chitty on Contracts, ibid.*, at para. 26-021, note 75.

[5] Fridman, *The Law of Contract in Canada, ibid.*, at 711; *Chitty on Contracts, ibid.*, at para. 26-021, note 15.

[6] (1854), 9 Ex. 341, 156 E.R. 145.

Where two parties have made a contract which one of them has broken, the damages which the other party ought to receive in respect of such breach of contract should be such as may fairly and reasonably be considered either arising naturally, i.e., according to the usual course of things, from such breach of contract itself, or such as may reasonably be supposed to have been in the contemplation of both parties, at the time they made the contract, as the probable result of the breach of it. Now, if the special circumstances under which the contract was actually made were communicated by the plaintiffs to the defendants, and thus known to both parties, the damages resulting from the breach of such a contract, which they would reasonably contemplate, would be the amount of injury which would ordinarily follow from a breach of contract under these special circumstances so known and communicated. But, on the other hand, if these special circumstances were wholly unknown to the party breaking the contract, he, at the most, could only be supposed to have had in his contemplation the amount of injury which would arise generally, and in the great multitude of cases not affected by any special circumstances, from such a breach of contract.[7]

As every first year contract law student knows, that case involved an action by the owners of a mill against a carrier for failing to deliver a broken shaft to the manufacturer when promised so that a new one could be prepared. Significantly, for our purposes, the plaintiffs sought damages for profits lost in the period that the replacement of the shaft was delayed because of the defendant's failure to deliver the damaged shaft in a reasonable time. The court held that these damages could not be recovered since the facts known by the defendant were insufficient to show that the mill would lose profits if the delivery of the broken shaft to the manufacturer were delayed. In setting out the remoteness principle, however, the case implied that a claim for lost profits could be successful if it were shown that such losses were within the reasonable contemplation of the parties as a consequence of the breach of contract.

The principles set out in *Hadley v. Baxendale*[8] have been interpreted and restated in *Victoria Laundry (Windsor) Ltd. v. Newman Industries Ltd.*[9] and in *Koufos v. C. Czarnikow Ltd. (The Heron II).*[10] The combined effect of these cases has been summarized as follows: A type or kind of loss is not too remote a consequence of a breach of contract if, at the time of contracting (and on the assumption that the parties actually foresaw the breach in question), it was within their reasonable contemplation

---

[7] *Ibid.*, at 354-355 Ex.

[8] *Ibid.*

[9] [1949] 1 All E.R. 997 (C.A.).

[10] [1967] 3 All E.R. 686 (H.L.); this sentence is taken from *Chitty on Contracts, supra,* note 3 at para. 26-023, pp. 1217-1218.

as a not unlikely result of that breach.[11] These principles have now long been accepted in Canada.[12]

Upon review of these principles, it is clear that the task of counsel for the plaintiff in an action for damages for breach of contract includes developing a case that establishes the liability of the defendant for the type of damage incurred. In a straightforward case, it will be relatively easy to convince the court that the particular loss suffered by the plaintiff was within the defendant's reasonable contemplation. The words of Cory J.A. (as he then was) in *Canlin Ltd. v. Thiokol Fibres Canada Ltd.*[13] are apposite in most cases:

> It is the position of the appellant Thiokol that the loss of future business profits was not a foreseeable consequence of the breach of warranty. Alternatively, it is said that such a loss is not a consequence directly and naturally resulting from the breach of warranty.
>
> . . . . .
>
> The appellant's proposition appears to me to be one that flies in the face of reason and common sense. Most commercial contracts pertaining to the sale and delivery of materials or goods must, of necessity, be entered into with a view to making a profit in the future. To say otherwise amounts to a denial of the profit motive in the free enterprise system.

In other cases, it will be necessary to prove that the defendant had special knowledge of the plaintiff's intended use of the subject matter of the contract to satisfy the court that the loss of a profitable contract as a consequence of the defendant's breach is not too remote to give rise to an obligation to compensate the plaintiff.

(3) Quantification of Damages

This aspect of damages generally receives the most attention from counsel. It involves the proof of the consequences of the defendant's breach of contract for the purpose of establishing the amount of money that the defendant must pay the plaintiff to put it in the position it would have been in if the contract had been performed. Unlike a simple claim, for

---

[11] *Chitty on Contracts, ibid.*, at para. 26-023, p. 1218.

[12] See, for example, *Brown & Root Ltd. v. Chimo Shipping Ltd.*, [1967] S.C.R. 642, 63 D.L.R. (2d) 1 at 6; *Asamera Oil Corp. Ltd. v. Sea Oil & General Corp., supra,* note 2, at 8-9; *Houweling Nurseries Ltd. v. Fisons Western Corp.* (1988), 37 B.C.L.R. (2d) 2, 49 D.L.R. (4th) 205 at 211 (B.C.C.A.); leave to appeal to S.C.C. refused (1988), 37 B.C.L.R. (2d) 2*n*, 29 C.P.C. (2d) 168, 89 N.R. 398*n*.

[13] (1983), 40 O.R. (2d) 687 at 690, 22 B.L.R. 193, 142 D.L.R. (3d) 450 (C.A.).

example, by a vendor for the unpaid purchase price of goods, a claim for lost profits necessarily involves speculation on what might have happened if the contract had been performed. The courts, however, repeatedly emphasize that the speculative nature of a claim for lost profits does not deprive the plaintiff of a right of recovery. In *Chaplin v. Hicks,*[14] Vaughan Williams L.J. stated:

> [T]he fact that damages cannot be assessed with certainty does not relieve the wrong-doer of the necessity of paying damages for his breach of contract.[15]

Similarly, Cory J.A. in *Canlin Ltd. v. Thiokol Fibres*[16] stated:

> Why should not damages be awarded for the loss of the contemplated future profit? The court, I believe, would be shirking its duty if it were to say that no damages should flow because of the difficulty of calculating and assessing such damages and that they are therefore too remote. An assessment of future loss of profits must, of necessity, be an estimate. Whether such damages are awarded will depend entirely upon the court's assessment of the evidence put forward. The clearest case might base the loss of future profits upon past history of sales to the same or similar customers for same or similar items. It may be developed from evidence given by customers of a plaintiff as to what orders they would have given had the product not been defective over a period of time in the future which is deemed by the court to be reasonable and proper. The task will always be difficult but not insurmountable.

The law on the approach a court should take to assessing damages for lost profits was helpfully summarized by McLachlin J.A. (as she then was) in *Houweling Nurseries Ltd. v. Fisons Western Corp.*[17]:

> In order to recover damages for breach of contract, a plaintiff must establish two things. First, he must prove on a balance of probabilities that the defendant's breach of contract resulted in the damages claimed. Second, he must establish that the damages are not too remote — that is, that they represent a type of loss which was reasonably foreseeable to the defendant when the contract was made . . .
>
> What constitutes proof of loss of profits on a balance of probabilities? The defendant says the elements of the loss must be established with reasonable certainty, and must not be speculative or conjectural. It goes so far as to contend that damages for loss of future business must be confined to contracts existing at the time of breach and cannot be awarded for future contracts . . .

---

[14] [1911] 2 K.B. 786 (C.A.).
[15] *Ibid.,* at 792.
[16] *Supra,* note 13, at 691.
[17] *Supra,* note 12, at 209, 210.

That proposition is not in accord with the general tenor of English and Canadian authority, which has long recognized the right to recover damages for the loss of future business which have not been established with specific certitude . . .

. . . . .

In my view, the law may be summarized as follows. The basic rule is that damages for lost profits, like all damages for breach of contract, must be proven on a balance of probabilities. Where it is shown with some degree of certainty that a specific contract was lost as a result of the breach, with a consequent loss of profit, that sum should be awarded. However, damages may also be awarded for loss of more conjectural profits, where the evidence demonstrates the possibility that contracts have been lost because of the breach, and also establishes that it is probable that some of these possible contracts would have materialized, had the breach not occurred. In such a case, the court should make a moderate award, recognizing that some of the contracts may not have materialized had there been no breach.

McLachlin J.A.'s judgment in *Houweling Nurseries Ltd. v. Fisons Western Corp.*[18] is also useful for emphasizing that it is the duty of the trial judge, not the expert witness, to assess the plaintiff's damages:

The judge seems to have taken the view that it was up to one or other of the accountants to come up with a package estimate of damages which he could accept. This approach, which no doubt resulted quite naturally from the way in which the case was presented, discloses a basic fallacy. It was not for the accountants to estimate the lost profits, but the court.

. . . . .

The trial judge property rejected both sets of assumptions [submitted by the accountants for the parties]. But it was not right to ignore the evidence put forward on those issues and the framework of assessment offered by the parties. What then had to be done was to review the evidence in detail in order to find the facts which could be used within the framework in place of the rejected assumptions . . .

. . . . .

Assessment of damages for lost profits caused by breach of contract is, in this respect, analogous to assessment of damages for personal injury resulting from a tortious act. In so far as mathematical figures and calculations can aid in arriving at a fair and realistic estimate of damages, they should be used. At the same time, it must be recognized that aspects of the claim may not be capable of precise mathematical calculation; this is particularly true of claims for losses in the future. Even when this is the case, however, mathematical calculations may serve as a useful guide. In this case, the parties having based their cases on precise mathematical calculations, it was essen-

---

[18] *Ibid.*

tial that the trial judge consider the validity of the factual assumptions upon which calculations were based.[19]

Rather than downplaying the importance of expert evidence in an action seeking damages for lost profits, McLachlin J.A.'s judgment emphasizes the need for counsel to provide, through the expert witnesses, a proper framework to assist the court in analysing the evidence in support of the claim for damages. This involves ensuring that expert witnesses base their conclusions on justifiable assumptions. In *Houweling Nurseries Ltd. v. Fisons Western Corp.*,[20] the court rejected the expert witnesses' assumptions in determining (i) amount of sales lost as a result of the breach; (ii) capacity of the plaintiff to supply the lost sales; and (iii) rate of profit on the lost sales. Obviously, the assumptions made in any particular case will depend upon the nature of the claim.[21]

A recent instructive example of the court's approach to the calculation of lost profits in an action for breach of contract is *Nathu v. Imbrook Properties Ltd.*[22] In that case, the court considered the damages to be awarded to a lessee for breach of a restrictive covenant in a lease of commercial premises. The court upheld the trial judge's finding of liability and the real issue in the case was "how to arrive at a defensible estimate of the [tenant's] loss".[23]

The court reviewed the standard principles for determining remoteness of damage in contract, noting:

> Because the loss of projected business profits generally invites consideration of contingencies, these calculations are, to some degree, an exercise in conjecture. However, that has not resulted in the courts declining the task.

---

[19] *Ibid.*, at 207, 208. Wakeling J.A. for a majority of the Saskatchewan Court of Appeal has accepted this approach: *Regina Sticks Ltd. v. Sask. Gov't Ins.*, [1993] 7 W.W.R. 572, 113 Sask. R. 40, [1994] I.L.R. 1-3011, 106 D.L.R. (4th) 484 at 500-501.

[20] *Ibid.*, at 208.

[21] The analysis of the evidence can become very detailed. In *Houweling Nurseries Ltd. v. Fisons Western Corp, ibid.*, McLachlin J.A. reviewed for 10 pages the evidence of lost sales in arriving at the calculation of damages, and appended a chart setting out the calculations over the relevant period. For an interesting analysis setting out a framework for quantifying business losses, see Bigen and Rosen, "A Framework for the Assessment of Business Damages for Breach of Contract" (1980-81), 5 C.B.L.J. 302 in which the authors critique the approach taken by the courts (and by academics in reviewing those decisions) in a number of notable cases assessing damages.

[22] [1992] 4 W.W.R. 373, 9 Alta. L.R. (3d) 48, 41 C.P.R. (3d) 458, 23 R.P.R. (2d) 188, 89 D.L.R. (4th) 751 (Alta. C.A.), additional reasons at [1992] 6 W.W.R. 373, 4 Alta. L.R. (3d) 149, 96 D.L.R. (4th) 223.

[23] *Ibid.*, at 754 D.L.R.

Unsettled circumstances, including the probable and future volition of third parties, can be estimated if not measured.[24]

The court noted that the onus to prove loss of profits is on the plaintiff. The process of assessing lost profits is twofold and involves determining: (1) the loss of past profits (usually to the date of trial), and (2) the loss of future profits (from the date of trial for a future period determined by the court).[25] The court continued:

The assessment of past profits can be formalized:

Anticipated profits if no breach to date of trial	*less* earned profits despite breach to date of trial	*plus* reasonable interest on lost income

The calculation of future profit/loss employs a slightly different formula:

Anticipated profits if no breach during future period	*less* anticipated earned profits despite breach during future period	x contingency factor and discount rate[26]

The court noted that the discount rate, or capitalization rate, recognizes both the loss to the plaintiff due to inflationary pressures on the value of money and the obvious benefit to the plaintiff arising from the accelerated use of that money, and is usually calculated to approximate the difference between current rates of return on investment and the estimated rate of inflation over the future period in question.

The court also stated that the assessment of the contingency factor is more complex and, in a commercial setting, is a deduction to account for "various vicissitudes of the market-place, the major ones being competition and swings in business cycles".[27] This risk factor is expressed as a percentage, and the selection of the rate is a matter of estimation by the court from its consideration of the evidence it is given and its understanding of the realities of commercial life. Such contingencies may be either positive or negative, either increasing or decreasing a plaintiff's loss of prospective earnings.

Finally, the court emphasized that, while evidence from professional accounting experts is of assistance in assessing damages, the "final assessment is not shackled to the evidence of those professionals alone".[28]

---

[24] *Ibid.*, at 756.
[25] *Ibid.*
[26] *Ibid.*, at 756-57.
[27] *Ibid.*, at 757.
[28] *Ibid.*

2. *Availability of Damages for Lost Profits in Tort*

In determining issues of damages for lost profits in tort, it is necessary to consider the fundamental nature and basis for such an award. The usual measure of damages in tort is to put the plaintiff in the position it would have been in before the defendant damaged its interests.[29] The fundamental distinction therefore between contract and tort, one however that is blurring with time, is that a right to damages in contract is to be determined as of the date of the contract while in tort, it is the date of the breach which governs.[30]

While a claim for damages for breach of contract frequently, and perhaps usually, includes compensation for lost profits, a claim for damages for a tortious wrong may be strictly limited in its right to include such damages, even where it is clear that the defendant's actions have precipitated the plaintiff's losses. While this paper will not canvass every tort claim that may give rise to a claim for damages for lost profits, it will discuss some of the more usual claims where these damages are sought, and when they may awarded.

Most of the debate and controversy over the recovery of damages for pure economic losses, including profit, arises in the context of negligence. Accordingly, this paper will consider these issues more specifically. However, it should be remembered that damages for economic losses can be recovered in a number of tort actions, including for an intentional wrong or where the plaintiff incurs economic loss as a result of a negligent injury to the plaintiff's person or property.

(1) Intentional Torts

It is clear that the type of wrong committed by the defendant influences the court's evaluation of the plaintiff's damages. The usual rule of remoteness, for example, may be relaxed where the plaintiff's claim

---

[29] S.M. Waddams, *The Law of Contracts in Canada*, 3rd ed. (Toronto: Canada Law Book, 1993), at para. 691, p. 479. This is in contrast with the rule in contract which is to put the plaintiff in the position it would have been in had the contract been performed as agreed: *BG Checo Int'l Ltd. v. B.C. Hydro & Power Authority*, [1993] 1 S.C.R. 12, [1993] 2 W.W.R. 321, 75 B.C.L.R. (2d) 145, 14 C.C.L.T. (2d) 233, 99 D.L.R. (4th) 577 at 591, 147 N.R. 81. In that case, the court contrasted the measure of damages in an action for breach of contract with the measure of damages in an action for negligent misrepresentation. The statement of the appropriate approach to the measure of damages applies also to torts other than negligence.

[30] See, for example, the discussion by Adams J. in *Murano v. Bank of Montreal*, [1995] O.J. No. 883 at paras. 152-153 (Gen. Div.).

against the defendant is based in fraud or deceit rather than negligence. Thus, in *Doyle v. Olby (Ironmogers) Ltd.*,[31] Lord Denning M.R. held that, in an action for fraud, the defendant is bound to make reparation for all the actual damages flowing from the fraudulent inducement:

> On principle the distinction seems to be this: in contract, the defendant has made a promise and broken it. The object of damages is to put the plaintiff in as good a position, as far as money can do it, as if the promise had been performed. In fraud, the defendant has been guilty of a deliberate wrong by inducing the plaintiff to act to his detriment. The object of damages is to compensate the plaintiff for all the loss he has suffered, so far, again, as money can do it. In contract, the damages are limited to what may reasonably be supposed to have been in the contemplation of the parties. In fraud, they are not so limited.[32]

Professor Waddams notes that Lord Denning's judgment should not be taken as always excluding considerations of remoteness in cases of fraud:

> The position seems to be not that the rules of remoteness and mitigation are entirely excluded, but that the defendant will not be permitted to claim as too remote or to say that the plaintiff should have avoided loss arising from reasonable attempts (even if unsuccessful) to salvage something out of the financial difficulties the defendant has caused.[33]

To the extent that the defendant's fraud has caused a consequential loss of profits, the plaintiff will benefit from the relaxed rule of remoteness in determining damages.

It seems clear that in other cases involving intentional torts short of fraud or deceit, a plaintiff who has suffered a loss of profits as a result of an intentional wrong inflicted by the defendant may recover damages on that basis. For example, a plaintiff whose chattel has been wrongfully converted may claim special compensation for any special damage which the law does not regard as too remote.[34] Conversion of a profit-making machine, like a dredger employed on work in a harbour, entitles its owner to compensation for loss in its business prior to getting a replacement.[35]

In general the test for recovery in this case is, as Professor Waddams states, that "all compensatory rules of damage measurement are restricted

---

[31] [1969] 2 All E.R. 119 (C.A.).

[32] *Ibid.*, at 122.

[33] S.M. Waddams, *The Law of Damages*, 2nd ed. (Toronto: Canada Law Book, 1994), at para. 5.600, p. 5-27.

[34] J.G. Fleming, *The Law of Torts*, 8th ed. (Sydney, Australia: The Law Book Company, 1992), at 70.

[35] *Ibid.*, at 70-71, citing *Liebosch (Dredger) v. The Edison*, [1933] A.C. 449.

by considerations of remoteness''.[36] Thus, what is an appropriate case for the award of damages for lost profit for an intentional wrong will depend upon the application of the rules of remoteness.

Lost profits may also be claimed in a tort action based on a claim falling under the umbrella of interference with economic relations. Professor Fleming has stated:

> [O]ur legal tradition has displayed no . . . coyness in furnishing legal sanctions against conduct aimed at impairing advantageous relations or causing other kinds of financial loss.[37]

For example, it seems clear that an award of damages representing lost profits is available where a defendant intentionally interferes with the plaintiff's contractual relations.[38] Where the conduct of the defendant is directed at the economic interests of the plaintiff, it is reasonable to impose liability on the defendant for the harm done to those interests, as represented by the profits lost by the plaintiff.

(2) Negligence

The right of a plaintiff to successfully claim damages for lost profits in negligence depends upon the nature of the claim asserted. The law accords different treatment to a plaintiff whose person or property is injured by the negligence of another and who claims lost profits than to a plaintiff whose loss is purely financial and unconnected to injury to person or property. These issues will be addressed separately.

(a) *Recovery of Lost Profits in Action for Damages for Personal Injury*

In general, in an action for personal injury, a plaintiff may recover special and general damages. Special damages include elements of damage capable of quantification, including lost earnings up to the date of trial while general damages include losses for future earnings.[39] Where a plaintiff runs a business in lieu of or in addition to receiving a salary,

---

[36] *Supra,* note 33, at para. 1.1280, p. 1-61.
[37] *Supra,* note 34, at 684.
[38] See, for example, *Ed Miller Sales & Rentals Ltd. v. Caterpillar Tractor Co.*, [1994] 5 W.W.R. 473, 17 Alta. L.R. (3d) 251, 54 C.P.R. (3d) 1 (Alta. Q.B.).
[39] *Supra,* note 34, at 229.

loss of business profits may be compensable if they are attributable to the injury caused by the defendant.[40] As in any claim, it is necessary to establish the claim for lost profits on the evidence. In *Alexandroff v. R.*[41] the injured plaintiff, a doctor who was the sole shareholder of a drug company and its principal customer, included in his claim for damages an amount representing the decrease in his income from the company resulting from the reduction in his business with the company caused by his personal injury. The Court of Appeal set aside the trial judge's award for this head of damage on the basis that the plaintiff had failed to adduce satisfactory evidence to establish the net profit of the company for the purpose of calculating the plaintiff's loss of income.

(b) *Recovery of Lost Profits in Action for Damages for Injury to Property*

Where the defendant's negligence causes a profit-making chattel to be withheld from use for a period of time, the plaintiff is entitled to be compensated for lost profits.[42]

Professor Waddams notes that a distinction is drawn between a claim for loss of value, and a claim for loss of use:

> In the former kind of case the full value is allowable even if the plaintiff would not in fact have put it to profitable use. In the latter kind of case the starting point is different, for it is usually said that the plaintiff claiming a loss of profits must prove the loss.[43]

While this distinction seems anomalous, Professor Waddams defends it on the basis that the distinction rests not on what profit the plaintiff makes but on its reason for owning the property. A person who owns the property to make a profit and in fact makes none has lost nothing by being deprived of the use; a person who owns the property for any other reason, however, suffers a practical loss by being deprived of the use.[44]

The principle of remoteness must also be considered in assessing the ability to recover damages for profits lost by damage to property. Damages

---

[40] L.D. Rainaldi, ed., *Remedies in Tort*, vol. 4 (Scarborough: Carswell, 1987), at §66.

[41] (1968), 70 D.L.R. (2d) 162 (Ont. C.A.); revd on other grounds 14 D.L.R. (3d) 66 (S.C.C.).

[42] *Supra,* note 33, at para. 1950, p. 1-93; *Remedies in Tort*, vol. 4, *supra,* note 40, at §141; *Pacific Elevators Ltd. v. Canadian Pacific Railway Co.*, [1974] S.C.R. 803, 41 D.L.R. (3d) 608.

[43] *Supra,* note 33, at para. 1.1960, p. 1-93.

[44] *Ibid.*, at para. 1.1970, p. 1-94.

have been given in respect of profits that the plaintiff might normally have been expected to earn, while excluding as too remote compensation for exceptionally lucrative uses.[45]

(c) *Recovery of Lost Profits in Action for Damages for Negligent Misrepresentation*

A plaintiff seeking damages in an action for negligent misrepresentation is entitled to be put in the position he or she would have been in if the misrepresentation had not been made.[46] What that position would have been is a matter that the plaintiff must establish on a balance of probabilities.[47] The plaintiff's damages are usually best captured by assessing the plaintiff's out-of-pocket losses incurred in reliance on the representation, taking into account the principles of foreseeability, remoteness and mitigation.[48]

Nonetheless, it is possible to claim damages for lost profit in an action for negligent misrepresentation. In *V.K. Mason Construction Ltd. v. Bank of Nova Scotia*,[49] the defendant bank was sued for misrepresenting to the plaintiff construction company that financing would be provided to a developer sufficient to cover the cost of constructing a proposed development. In reliance upon this assurance, the plaintiff entered a construction contract with the developer and completed the work, but was not fully paid. The plaintiff sued the defendant bank which was held liable for negligent misrepresentation. Wilson J. held that the plaintiff was entitled to include in its damages a claim for lost profit, representing what it could have earned on another project if it had not entered into a contract with the developer as a result of the bank's misrepresentation:

> The learned trial judge awarded damages for misrepresentation on the basis that they were equal to contract damages minus [the plaintiff's] anticipated profit. Counsel for [the plaintiff] submits that the trial judge was wrong in subtracting the anticipated profit because damages in contract and tort are the same. . . .While I tend to the view that there is a conceptual difference between damages in contract and in tort, I believe that in many instances the same quantum will be arrived at, albeit by some different routes.

---

[45] *Ibid.*, at para. 1.1990, p. 1-95.

[46] *Rainbow Industrial Caterers Ltd. v. C.N.R. Co.* (1991), 84 D.L.R. (4th) 291 at 296 (S.C.C.).

[47] *Ibid.*, at 297.

[48] B. Feldthusen, *Economic Negligence*, 3rd ed. (Scarborough: Carswell, 1994) at 128-129.

[49] (1985), 16 D.L.R. (4th) 598 (S.C.C.).

I agree with the submission of counsel for [the plaintiff] that the trial judge was wrong in subtracting profit. I believe that in principle one is entitled to assume that [the plaintiff] would have found a profitable means of employing itself had it not been induced to work on [the developer's] project by the Bank's misrepresentation. This, in my view, is a reasonably foreseeable head of damage . . . In equating [the plaintiff's] lost profit with the profit estimated on the [developer's] project we are simply saying that this is a reasonable estimate of what [the plaintiff] would have been likely to have made if it had decided to abandon the [developer's] project and find other work. That is to say, the lost profit on *this* contract represents the lost opportunity for profit on *any* contract. If [the plaintiff] had made an exceptional profit on the [developer's] project it might be disentitled to an award of the entire amount of that profit in tort damages, but this would be so only because it was not reasonably foreseeable that it would have made a similarly exceptional profit on some other contract.[50]

The scope for creativity in the determination of damages for negligent misrepresentation is illustrated by the Supreme Court's decision in *BG Checo Int'l Ltd. v. British Columbia Hydro & Power Authority*:

> In tort, Checo is entitled to be compensated for all reasonably foreseeable loss caused by the tort. The Court of Appeal was of the view that Checo, had it known the true facts (*i.e.*, had the tort not been committed) would have increased its bid by an amount equal to the cost of the extra work made necessary by the improperly cleared worksite plus profit and overhead. Such loss was not too remote, being reasonably foreseeable. But to compensate only for the direct costs of clearing is to suggest that the only tort was the failure to clear. The real fault is that Hydro *misrepresented* the situation and Checo may have relied on that representation in performing its other obligations under the contract. For example, having to devote its resources to that extra work might have prevented Checo from meeting its original schedule, thereby resulting in Checo incurring acceleration costs in order to meet the contract completion date. Such costs would also arguably be reasonably foreseeable. In our view, the matter should be referred back to the trial division for determination of whether any such indirect losses were the foreseeable results of the misrepresentation.[51]

Counsel's role is to bring before the court the evidence necessary to make findings of what position the plaintiff would have been in but for the negligent misrepresentation.

---

[50] *Ibid.*, at 607-08.
[51] [1993] 1 S.C.R. 12, [1993] 2 W.W.R. 321, 75 B.C.L.R. (2d) 145, 14 C.C.L.T. (2d) 233, 99 D.L.R. (4th) 577 at 593-594, 147 N.R. 81 (S.C.C.); reassessment of damages reported at (1994), 109 D.L.R. (4th) 1 (B.C.S.C.).

(d) *Recovery of Lost Profits in Action for Damages for Pure Economic Loss*

Recent decisions by the Supreme Court have begun to temper the traditional prohibitions on claims for pure economic loss, leaving open the possibility of liability for lost profits in an appropriate case.

Professor Feldthusen has defined pure economic loss as follows:

> A *pure* economic loss is a financial loss which is not causally consequent upon physical injury to the plaintiff's *own* person or property.[52]

He distinguishes pure economic loss from consequential economic loss which is causally consequent upon physical damage to the plaintiff or the plaintiff's property.[53] He then refers to a categorization of cases in which plaintiffs have sought damages for pure economic loss, of which, for our purposes, the most relevant is relational economic loss.[54] This type of case has been the subject of a recent Supreme Court of Canada decision which attempted to clarify this area of the law.

In a case of this type, a plaintiff attempts to recover from a tortfeasor whose actions have damaged the property of a third person, which in turn caused pure economic losses to the plaintiff. In *Canadian National Railway Co. v. Norsk Pacific Steamship Co.*,[55] the court considered whether C.N.R. could sue the owner of a barge for economic loss incurred by C.N.R. in rerouting its traffic while a railway bridge with which the barge had collided and which was used by C.N.R., was under repair. While C.N.R. had a contract with the federal Crown, which owned the bridge, it had no such relationship with the barge owner. The Supreme Court, by a 4:3 margin, held that C.N.R. could recover its pure economic loss in this case. Because Stevenson J. concurred with McLachlin J. in the result, but for different reasons, none of the reasons for judgment delivered in the case received the support of a majority of the panel. As a result, the law in this area remains unsettled, although McLachlin J.'s judgment is the likely starting point for an analysis of when pure economic loss is recoverable in negligence.[56]

---

[52] *Supra,* note 48, at 1.

[53] *Ibid.* Consequential economic loss is the type of claim discussed in 2(2)(a), (b) above.

[54] *Ibid.,* at 2.

[55] (1992), 91 D.L.R. (4th) 289 (S.C.C.).

[56] Professor Feldthusen suggests that after the division of opinion in *Canadian National Railway Co. v. Norsk Pacific Steamship Co., ibid.,* "one can only say that there exists no Canadian exclusionary rule for relational loss:" Feldthusen, *Economic Negligence, supra,* note 48 at 4-5. In *Winnipeg Condominium Corp. No. 36 v. Bird Construction Co.,* [1995] 1 S.C.R. 85, [1995] 3 W.W.R.

In brief, McLachlin J. held that pure economic loss is *prima facie* recoverable when, in addition to negligence and foreseeable loss, there was sufficient proximity between the negligent act and the loss. In McLachlin J.'s view:

> Proximity is the controlling concept which avoids the spectre of unlimited liability. Proximity may be established by a variety of factors, depending on the nature of the case . . . [T]he categories are not closed. As more cases are decided, we can expect further definition on what factors give rise to liability for pure economic loss in particular categories of cases. In determining whether liability should be extended to a new situation, courts will have regard to the factors traditionally relevant to proximity such as the relationship between the parties, physical propinquity, assumed or imposed obligations and close causal connection. And they will insist on sufficient special factors to avoid the imposition of indeterminate and unreasonable liability . . .
>
> . . . . .
>
> While proximity is critical to establishing the right to recover pure economic loss in tort, it does not always indicate liability. It is a necessary but not necessarily sufficient condition of liability. Recognizing that proximity is itself concerned with policy, the approach adopted in *Kamloops*[57] (paralleled by the second branch of *Anns*[58]), requires the court to consider the purposes served by permitting recovery as well as whether there are any residual policy considerations which call for a limitation on liability. This permits courts to reject liability for pure economic loss where indicated by policy reasons not taken into account in the proximity analysis.[59]

In *Canadian National Railway Co. v. Norsk Pacific Steamship Co.*,[60] McLachlin J. held that C.N.R.'s operations were so closely connected with

---

85, 100 Man. R. (2d) 241, 23 C.C.L.T. (2d) 1, 43 R.P.R. (2d) 1, 121 D.L.R. (4th) 193, 176 N.R. 321, La Forest J., for a unanimous seven member panel, held that pure economic loss for the cost of repair of a building with dangerous defects could be recovered by a subsequent purchaser from the contractor that built it, accepting the dissenting judgment of Laskin J. in *Rivtow Marine Ltd. v. Washington Iron Works*, [1974] S.C.R. 1189. While *Winnipeg Condominium Corp. No. 36 v. Bird Construction Co., supra,* does not raise issues of availability of damages for lost profits, it represents another statement by the Supreme Court of Canada that the law of recovery of economic loss in Canada is derived from *Anns v. Merton London Borough Council*, [1977] 2 All E.R. 492 (H.L.), as adopted by the Supreme Court in *City of Kamloops v. Nielsen*, [1984] 2 S.C.R. 2, [1984] 5 W.W.R. 1, 66 B.C.L.R. 273, 29 C.C.L.T. 97, 26 M.P.L.R. 81, 10 D.L.R. (4th) 641, 54 N.R. 1 (which approach was followed by McLachlin J. in *Canadian Railway Co. v. Norsk Pacific Steamship Co., supra,* note 55).

[57] *City of Kamloops v. Nielsen, ibid.*

[58] *Anns v. Merton London Borough Council, supra,* note 56.

[59] *Supra,* note 55, at 369-70, 371.

[60] *Supra,* note 55.

the operations of the Crown that they were, in effect, joint venturers, and should be entitled to recover its economic loss.

Focusing on the liability issue, McLachlin J. did not review the nature of the damages that might be claimed by C.N.R. She noted that the rerouting of traffic necessitated by the accident raised the cost of C.N.R.'s operation and may have diminished the amount of freight hauled.[61] The claim, however, was described only as for the additional cost incurred as a result of the bridge closure. It is unclear whether the claim included lost profits, although there is no apparent reason why business losses resulting from the rerouting should not be recoverable, provided they can be proven with reasonable certainty.[62]

The Supreme Court may soon have an opportunity to clarify the proper approach to another category of pure economic loss. It recently granted leave to appeal a decision of the British Columbia Court of Appeal in *D'Amato v. Badger*[63] in which the Court of Appeal considered whether the corporate plaintiff was entitled to recover damages arising out of injuries suffered in a motor vehicle accident by a 50 per cent owner of the corporation who also worked for the corporation. The trial judge held that, on the principles set out in *Canadian National Railway Co. v. Norsk Pacific Steamship Co.*,[64] the corporation was entitled to claim its loss of profits as a result of the shareholder's injury if there were sufficient proximity between the negligent act and the loss. He held that, in view of the nature of the corporation's operation and the manner in which its income was earned, there was sufficient proximity to recover any proven loss. This decision was overturned on appeal.

The Court of Appeal reviewed McLachlin J.'s judgment in *Canadian National Railway Co. v. Norsk Pacific Steamship Co.*[65] as well as another British Columbia Court of Appeal decision[66] and rejected the trial judge's analysis:

> The reasoning of the learned trial judge does not examine whether the loss claimed by [the corporate plaintiff] must have been reasonably foresee-

---

[60] *Supra,* note 55.

[61] *Ibid.*, at 358.

[62] Subsequent proceedings to resolve certain damage claims did not discuss whether C.N.R.'s claim included a claim for profits: *Canadian National Railway v. Jervis Crown (The)*, [1994] 2 F.C. 318, 71 F.T.R. 47 (T.D.). According to the reasons of Reed J., prior to the hearing to assess damages, the parties had agreed on all but $263,610.20 of the $1,681,315.58 claim, exclusive of interest.

[63] (1994), 95 B.C.L.R. (2d) 46, [1994] 10 W.W.R. 141 (C.A.); leave to appeal to S.C.C. granted March 2, 1995, S.C.C. Bulletin, 1995, at 463.

[64] *Supra,* note 55.

[65] *Ibid.*

[66] *Kripps v. Touche Ross & Co.* (1992), 84 D.L.R. (4th) 284 (B.C.C.A.); leave to appeal to S.C.C. refused (1993), 101 D.L.R. (4th) vii.

able to the defendants or must have followed so closely and directly from the defendant driver's negligent conduct that the defendants ought reasonably to have been concerned for any loss that [the corporate plaintiff] might suffer if deprived of [the individual plaintiff's] services. There was no evidence that the defendants were aware of [the individual plaintiff's] employment by [the corporate plaintiff] which might have established that a loss suffered by [the corporate plaintiff] was reasonably foreseeable to the defendants or resulted so closely and directly from the defendant driver's negligent act or omission that the defendants ought to have had [the corporate plaintiff] in mind when contemplating that action or omission.

In my opinion the learned trial judge erred in concluding that there was sufficient proximity between the defendants' negligence and [the corporate plaintiff's] loss of profits to justify the award of $73,299.[67]

This case may afford the Supreme Court the opportunity to decide whether McLachlin J.'s approach is the appropriate way to determine liability in economic loss cases. Until then, the scope of creativity for counsel in advancing a claim for pure economic loss remains wide.

3. *Availability of Damages for Lost Profits in Equity*

The relationship between remedies available at common law and those in equity is neither settled nor easy to state. However, recent decisions of the Supreme Court have attempted to explore this relationship, and to establish the rules to be applied in determining the remedy for breach of an equitable duty. This paper will not explore the complexity of the issues raised by the courts in determining appropriate equitable remedies, but will discuss one cause of action in which an award representing lost profits may be granted in equity.[68]

It appears that a beneficiary of a fiduciary duty may claim compensation for profits lost as a result of the wrongful conduct of the fiduciary. In *Maghun v. Richardson Greenshields of Canada Ltd.*,[69] the plaintiffs

---

[67] *Supra,* note 63, at 53-54.

[68] Even terminology can cause some difficulty in discussing equitable remedies. The expression "damages" is traditionally used to describe the remedy available at common law for invasion of a right, while the remedy of compensation was one of a variety of remedies available in equity to restore a person to whom a duty was owed to the position in which he or she would have been had the duty not been breached: La Forest J. in *Canson Enterprises Ltd. v. Boughton & Co.,* [1991] 3 S.C.R. 534, [1992] 1 W.W.R. 245, 61 B.C.L.R. (2d) 1, 9 C.C.L.T. (2d) 1, 39 C.P.R. (3d) 449, 43 E.T.R. 201, 85 D.L.R. (4th) 129 at 145, 131 N.R. 321.

[69] (1986), 18 O.A.C. 141, 58 O.R. (2d) 1, 34 D.L.R. (4th) 524.

sued their broker for losses incurred because of trading advice given by the broker on the acquisition of short contracts for sugar. The court held that the broker owed fiduciary duties to the plaintiffs, including the duty to exercise care, skill and diligence in the transaction of the plaintiffs' business and was liable for the loss resulting from the breach of this duty.[70] Brooke J.A. for the court stated:

> In assessing the plaintiffs' damages, this case must not be regarded simply as one for breach of contract, rather as found for breach of fiduciary duty and so the plaintiffs are entitled to compensation for their loss and not necessarily to be determined on principles of common law and remoteness of damages . . .
>
> . . . . .
>
> In any event . . . there should be a causal connection between the breach of fiduciary duty and the losses sustained. Profits that might reasonably have been expected to have been made but for the breach can be recovered, however, speculative profits cannot. In this case, as of late February no profits had been lost by the plaintiffs . . . Profit might have come at the conclusion of the contract period, but it is speculation whether, notwithstanding that the plaintiffs would have held their short until that time in the face of rising prices and greater margin requirements.[71]

While the court in *Maghun v. Richardson Greenshields of Canada*[72] suggested that the only factors to be considered by the court in assessing compensation for breach of fiduciary duty are causation and certainty, the Supreme Court has held that such factors as remoteness may also be considered where necessary to reach a just and fair result. In *Hodgkinson*

---

[70] *Ibid.*, at 15 O.R.

[71] *Ibid.*, at 18 O.R. The quoted passage is not entirely clear. Professor Fridman states the effect of the passage as follows:

> "The plaintiffs were to be compensated for their loss. All that had to be established was a causal connection between the breach of fiduciary duty and the losses sustained. This meant that profits that might reasonably have been expected to have been made could be recovered, but not speculative profits. Hence, the plaintiffs were entitled to recover from the brokers the amount they would have had to pay if they had been properly advised by the brokers so as to restore their position, i.e., in relation to their short sugar contracts. They could not claim loss of profits because none had been lost by them at the material time; profits might have come at a later date, but it was speculation whether the plaintiffs would have held their short sugar contracts until then in the face of rising prices and greater margin requirements. Equally speculative was the value of the money the plaintiffs might have invested to protect their short position by meeting margin calls. Hence, such money was also not recoverable: G.H.L. Fridman, *Restitution*, 2nd ed. (Scarborough: Carswell, 1992), at 382."

[72] *Supra*, note 69.

v. Simms[73], La Forest J. for a majority of the seven-member panel summarized the principles applicable to calculating damages for breach of fiduciary duty:

> It is well established that the proper approach to damages for breach of fiduciary duty is restitutionary. On this approach, the appellant is entitled to be put in as good a position as he would have been in had the breach not occurred. On the facts here, this means that the appellant is entitled to be restored to the position he was in before the transaction . . .
>
> The respondent advanced two arguments against the trial judge's assessment of damages for breach of fiduciary duty. Both raise the issue of causation . . .
>
> The respondent first submitted that given the appellant's stated desire to shelter as much of his income as possible from taxation, and his practice of buying a wide variety of tax shelters, the appellant would still have invested in real-estate tax shelters had he known the true facts. The main difficulty with this submission is that it flies in the face of the facts found by the trial judge . . .
>
> What is more, the submission runs up against the long-standing equitable principle that where the plaintiff has made out a case of non-disclosure and the loss occasioned thereby is established, the onus is on the defendant to prove that the innocent victim would have suffered the same loss regardless of the breach . . .
>
> The respondent also argued that even assuming the appellant would not have invested had proper disclosure been made, the non-disclosure was not the proximate cause of the appellant's loss . . . The respondent submits that it is grossly unjust to hold him accountable for losses that, he maintains, have no causal relation to the breach of fiduciary duty he perpetrated on the appellant.
>
> . . . . .
>
> On the finding of facts, these investors would not have been exposed to *any* of the risks associated with these investments had it not been for their respective fiduciary's desire to secure an improper personal gain. In short, in each case it was the particular fiduciary breach that initiated the chain of events leading to the investor's loss. As such it is right that the breaching party account for this loss in full.
>
> Contrary to the respondent's submission, this result is not affected by the *ratio* of this court's decision in *Canson Enterprises* . . .[74] *Canson* held that a court exercising equitable jurisdiction is not precluded from considering the principles of remoteness, causation, and intervening act where necessary to reach a just and fair result. *Canson* does not, however, signal a retreat from the principle of full restitution; rather it recognizes the fact that a breach

---

[73] (1994), 97 B.C.L.R. (2d) 1, 16 B.L.R. (2d) 1, 22 C.C.L.T. (2d) 1, 57 C.P.R. (3d) 1, 95 D.T.C. 5135, 117 D.L.R. (4th) 161, 171 N.R. 245 (S.C.C.).

[74] *Supra,* note 68.

of a fiduciary duty can take a variety of forms, and as such a variety of remedial considerations may be appropriate . . .

Put another way, equity is not so rigid as to be susceptible to being used as a vehicle for punishing defendants with harsh damage awards out of all proportion to their actual behaviour. On the contrary, where the common law has developed a measured and just principle in response to a particular kind of wrong, equity is flexible enough to borrow from the common law. . . . Thus, properly understood *Canson* stands for the proposition that courts should strive to treat similar wrongs similarly, regardless of the particular cause or causes of action that may have been pleaded . . . In other words, the courts should look to the harm suffered from the breach of the given duty, and apply the appropriate remedy.[75]

La Forest J.'s review of the law suggests that courts will be flexible in awarding remedies for breach of an equitable duty, thereby permitting an award for lost profits in a proper case.

4. *Availability of Damages for Lost Opportunities*

To a great extent, the right to claim damages for lost opportunities presents the same issues that are addressed in the discussion on the right to claim damages for future lost profits. Indeed, McLachlin J.A. stated in *Houweling Nurseries Ltd. v. Fisons Western Corp.*:

Even though the plaintiff may not be able to prove with certainty that it would have obtained specific contracts but for the breach, it may be able to establish that the defendant's breach of contract deprived it of the opportunity to obtain such business. The plaintiff is entitled to compensation for the loss of that opportunity. But it would be wrong to assess the damages for that lost opportunity as though it were a certainty.[76]

Professor Waddams describes the problem in this way:

Where the defendant's wrongful conduct deprives the plaintiff of a chance of profit that is fifty per cent or less, it might be thought that the plaintiff has failed on the balance of probabilities to prove any loss at all. As likely as not, it could be said, the plaintiff has suffered no loss at all by the defendant's wrong and so should be entitled only to nominal damages. This line

---

[75] *Supra,* note 73, at 199-200, 201-202 D.L.R.

[76] (1988), 37 B.C.L.R. (2d) 2, 49 D.L.R. (4th) 205 at 210-211 (B.C.C.A); leave to appeal to S.C.C. refused 37 B.C.L.R. (2d) 2n, 29 C.P.C. (2d) 168, 89 N.R. 398n.

of reasoning however fails to give weight to the common sense view that in some contexts at least, chances of fifty per cent or less do have a real value.[77]

The leading case in this area is *Chaplin v. Hicks*.[78] The facts are well-known and involved an action by an aspiring performer for damages for loss of a chance to obtain an acting engagement. The defendant ran a contest in which photographs of selected applicants were published in newspapers, and 50 finalists were selected based upon votes from readers of the newspapers. From this group, the defendant was to interview and select the 12 winners. The plaintiff was one of the 50 finalists, but did not receive an interview because, as the court found, the defendant did not take reasonable steps to give the plaintiff an opportunity to be interviewed. The plaintiff was awarded £100 for loss of the opportunity to win the contest, which award was upheld by the Court of Appeal.

Vaughan Williams L.J. rejected the defendant's argument that the damages for loss of chance were impossible to assess:

> It was said that the plaintiff's chance of winning a prize turned on such a number of contingencies that it was impossible for any one, even after arriving at the conclusion that the plaintiff had lost her opportunity by the breach, to say that there was any assessable value of that loss. It is said that in a case which involves so many contingencies it is impossible to say what was the plaintiff's pecuniary loss. I am unable to agree with that contention.[79]

Similarly, Fletcher Moulton L.J. stated:

> [The defendant's counsel] says that damages are difficult to assess, because it is impossible to say that the plaintiff would have obtained any prize . . . Is expulsion from a limited class of competitors an injury? To my mind there can be only one answer to that question; it is an injury and may be a very substantial one. Therefore the plaintiff starts with an unchallengeable case of injury, and the damages given in respect of it should be equivalent to the loss. But it is said that the damages cannot be arrived at because it is impossible to estimate the quantum of the reasonable probability of the plaintiff's being a prize-winner. I think that, where it is clear that there has been actual loss resulting from the breach of contract, which it is difficult to estimate in money, it is for the jury to do their best to estimate; it is not necessary that there should be an absolute measure of damages in each case.[80]

---

[77] S.M. Waddams, *The Law of Damages*, 2nd ed. (Toronto: Canada Law Book, 1994), at para. 13.270, p. 13-13.

[78] [1911] 2 K.B. 786 (C.A.).

[79] *Ibid.*, at 791.

[80] *Ibid.*, at 795.

Chaplin v. Hicks[81] has been frequently followed and cited with approval in Canada,[82] including recently by the Ontario Court of Appeal in *Eastwalsh Homes Ltd. v. Anatal Developments Ltd.*[83]

In that case, Griffiths J.A. for the court summarized the law relating to recovery of damages for loss of a chance as follows:

> The general rule is that the burden is on the plaintiff to establish on the balance of probabilities that as a reasonable and probable consequence of the breach of contract, the plaintiff suffered the damages claimed. If the plaintiff is not able to establish a loss, or where the loss proven is trivial, the plaintiff may recover only nominal damages.
>
> A second fundamental principle is that where it is clear that the breach of contract *caused* loss to the plaintiff, but it is very difficult to quantify that loss, the difficulty in assessing damages is not a basis for refusal to make an award in the plaintiff's favour. One of the frequent difficulties in assessing damages is that the plaintiff is unable to prove loss of a definite benefit but only the "chance" of receiving a benefit had the contract been performed. In those circumstances, rather than refusing to award damages the courts have attempted to estimate the value of the lost chance and awarded damages on a proportionate basis.
>
> . . . . . .
>
> The burden rests on the plaintiff alleging breach of contract to prove on the balance of probabilities that the breach and not some intervening factor or factors has caused loss to the plaintiff. In this respect the courts have not relaxed the basic standard of proof. Where it is clear that the defendant's breach has caused loss to the plaintiff it is no answer to the claim that the loss is difficult to assess or calculate. The concept of the loss of a chance then begins to operate and the court will estimate the plaintiff's chance of obtaining a benefit had the contract been performed. But even in this situation . . . proof of the loss of a mere chance is not enough; the plaintiff must prove that the chance constitutes "some reasonable probability" of realizing "an advantage of some real substantial monetary value".[84]

In *Eastwalsh Homes Ltd. v. Anatal Developments Ltd.*[85], the Court of Appeal considered an appeal from a trial judgment in which a developer had been held liable for damages for breaching an agreement to sell lots on a proposed plan of subdivision by failing to use best efforts to obtain registration. The trial judge held that there was a 50 per cent chance that

---

[81] *Ibid.*

[82] Waddams, *The Law of Damages, supra*, note 77, at para. 13.280, p. 13-14.

[83] (1993), 12 O.R. (3d) 675, 30 R.P.R. (2d) 276, 100 D.L.R. (4th) 469; leave to appeal to S.C.C. refused (1993), 15 O.R. (3d) xvi, 34 R.P.R. (2d) 90*n*.

[84] *Ibid.*, at 687, 689-90.

[85] *Ibid.*

the subdivisions could have been registered on time if the developer had used its best efforts to obtain registration, and awarded damages to the plaintiff of $2,020,780. The Court of Appeal, while accepting that the trial judge applied the correct approach in separating the question of causation from the question of loss and in concluding that the developer's breach of contract denied the plaintiff the chance of closing the transaction, disagreed with the trial judge's assessment of the evidence that the plaintiff had a 50 per cent chance of closing the sale. After reviewing the evidence, Griffiths J.A. concluded that the plaintiff had failed to discharge its burden of proving that, had the developer discharged its obligation to use its best efforts to secure registration of a plan of subdivision, there was a reasonable probability that the plan could have been registered within the time frame provided in the contract. Accordingly, the plaintiff was entitled only to nominal damages, and award was reduced to $1000.

Eastwalsh Homes Ltd. v. Anatal Developments Ltd.[86] is a useful case in a number of ways. It provides a clear, concise summary of the law on the availability of damages for loss of a chance. It also illustrates the importance of proving that the plaintiff had a substantial chance that was taken away by the defendant's breach of contract to justify more than an award of nominal damages. It also gives hope to the defendant in a breach of contract case that the court will discharge its duty to assess the damages claimed by the plaintiff in a principled way, and will not allow its findings on liability to colour its judgment on damages.

It appears that the Supreme Court of Canada may soon consider the scope and application of the law on loss of an opportunity. It recently granted leave to appeal the decision of the Saskatchewan Court of Appeal in *Cohnstaedt v. University of Regina*.[87] In that case, the court considered the application of the loss of a chance doctrine to the assessment of damages that flowed from the breach of the employment contract of a tenured professor appointed under a statute. After a long period of conflict between the professor and the university, the parties entered into an agreement under which the professor was to be assigned academic duties for a time, at the end of which the professor's performance was to be assessed. If the assessment were positive, the professor was to be treated as a tenured professor; if not, he was to retire in accordance with a prior agreement. Ultimately, the professor's work was held to fall below the standard and he was required to retire. The professor sued, and it was held that the university had breached the settlement agreement by failing to provide appropriate work to the professor to allow for a proper

---

[86] *Ibid.*

[87] (1994), 16 Sask. R. 241, 2 C.C.E.L. (2d) 161, 13 D.L.R. (4th) 178; leave to appeal to S.C.C. granted Oct. 13, 1994, S.C.C. Bulletin, 1994, at 1568.

assessment. The issue before the Court of Appeal was the basis upon which the professor's damages were to be calculated.

The differences in the judgments of the majority and the minority of the court illustrate the importance of the characterization of the nature of the wrong done to the plaintiff in assessing the appropriate damages.

Vancise J.A. for the majority characterized the university's breach as "the failure to assign the [plaintiff] the type and quality of work to permit the university . . . to make a proper assessment of [his] performance".[88] The breach was characterized as "the lost opportunity for a full and fair assessment and, consequently, the loss of the possibility of reinstatement to full tenureship".[89] After reviewing the evidence, Vancise J.A. calculated the damages using the following formula:

1. The probability the [plaintiff] would have been favourably assessed and reinstated as a full professor; multiplied by,

2. The probability the [plaintiff] would have worked to the age of normal retirement at the university if he had been reinstated; multiplied by,

3. The value of the benefits (salary and pension) the appellant would have received by working to the age of normal retirement.[90]

This formula, applied to the evidence, resulted in a sum of $74,340 before mitigation of damages was taken into account.

By contrast, Sherstobitoff J.A. in dissent characterized the university's breach as a termination without cause of an employment contract. Accordingly, the plaintiff's loss "was not merely the loss of the right to have his work assessed, but actual and unjustified loss of his employment".[91] In Sherstobitoff J.A.'s view, whether the plaintiff could have established his competence became irrelevant when his employment was terminated without cause or justification. Moreover, to permit the university to rely on its failure to provide a proper basis for assessment of the plaintiff's ability as grounds for arguing that the plaintiff could not have established his competence even had he been given an opportunity to do so would allow the university to take advantage of its own wrong.[92] Sherstobitoff J.A. calculated the damages on the basis of the amount the plaintiff would have earned between the date of termination of his employment and the date of his normal retirement, arriving at a figure of $313,309 before mitigation.

---

[88] *Ibid.*, at 196 D.L.R.
[89] *Ibid.*, at 196.
[90] *Ibid.*, at 201.
[91] *Ibid.*, at 213.
[92] *Ibid.*, at 213-214.

The characterization of the wrong done was crucial to the analysis in *Cohnstaedt v. University of Regina*:[93] damages for loss of an opportunity to be fairly assessed were only one quarter the damages for wrongful dismissal.

5. *Conclusion*

Cohnstaedt v. University of Regina[94] dramatically illustrates the scope for imaginative advocacy by counsel in a loss of profits case. The rules are still being written, and lawyers who adopt a thinking approach to damage issues from the outset of a case can achieve a result that reflects the evidentiary foundation laid by them, assisted by the flexibility of current legal principles.

---

[93] *Ibid.*
[94] *Ibid.*

THE QUANTIFICATION OF DAMAGES FOR LOST PROFITS

William C. Dovey[1]

The arithmetic calculations supporting an accounting expert's opinion as to the damages for lost future profits suggest a level of precision in the conclusion that may not be appropriate. While "numbers" are precise and reliable, 2 plus 3 always equals 5, the selection of the most appropriate numbers to be used by the expert is not usually capable of such precision. The expert is, after all, providing an "opinion" and with an opinion based on what may have happened necessarily comes uncertainty.

In calculating damages for lost profits the accounting expert typically:

(1) establishes the amount of lost future profits on a yearly basis, and
(2) converts that lost stream of future profits to a capital sum.

That capital sum in a perfect world forms the basis of the "award" made by the court in respect of lost future profits.

Conceptually, the calculation is simple and somewhat mechanical. In practice, however, the opposite is true, particularly when attempting to isolate and identify the impact of "risk" on those simple mechanical calculations. It is in the treatment of "risk", being the probability that estimated future lost profits would not have been realized for reasons other than those before the court, that the professional opinion of experts can differ substantially.

Before proceeding with our explanation of "risk", it may be useful to consider a simple damages model.

Assume a claim is made with respect to lost future business profits for a five-year period on an inflation-free basis as follows:

[1] Price Waterhouse — Chartered Accountants.

	Year					
	1	2	3	4	5	Total
Lost Profits (1)	$47	$52	$68	$46	$55	$268
Present Value at 9%	45	46	55	34	37	217
6%	46	48	59	38	42	233

(1) Assuming profits earned uniformly throughout the year.

While lost profits total $268 over the five-year period, to award such an amount would result in the overcompensation of the plaintiff as it would not recognize the time value of money. In this example, the plaintiff would be financially better off with an immediate award of $268 as compared to receiving the same amount over the five-year period of the loss. Hence the need to establish present value of the lost future profits to recognize that a dollar received today is "worth" more than a dollar received a year or five years from today.

A present value calculation is essentially the reverse of a mortgage style calculation as it works backwards from the future annual cash flow amounts or lost profits (the annual principle and interest amounts) to the principal or capital sum (the amount of the mortgage).

In our overly simple example, the present value ("PV") of the lost future profits is $217 at an assumed discount rate of 9 per cent, and $233 at 6 per cent. Put in the reverse, if $233 were put in the bank at 6 per cent at the beginning of year one, it would yield a cash flow (of combined principle and interest) equal to the lost future profits in the year indicated. At the end of year five the bank balance would be NIL.

In theory, the plaintiff is equally well off, from a financial perspective, with an award of $233 (which could be invested immediately at, say, 6 per cent) or the lost profits received over a five-year period.

In practice, it is not the methodology or its application that gives rise to disputes between experts, but the underlying calculation components, being the lost profits and the discount rate — "garbage in, garbage out".

1. *Lost Future Profits*

Beyond some assurance that it will get dark tonight, there is little certainty in the future. The financial press is littered with examples of business failures where only a few years prior ongoing future profits seemed assured or certain. At a personal level, a job for life with a certain income is scarce and getting scarcer.

Even with the best of intentions, two accounting experts working with exactly the same information are not likely to totally agree on the level of future lost profits. We should expect this where judgment is involved, judgment about the risks associated with the forecast profits or the certainty that the profits would have been realized but for the wrongful act.

Again, by way of example:

	Year					
	1	2	3	4	5	Total
Expert A — Lost Profits	$47	$52	$68	$46	$55	$268
Present Value at 9%	45	46	55	34	37	217
Expert B — Lost Profits	94	104	136	92	110	536
Present Value at 9%	90	91	110	68	75	434
Present Value at 52%	76	55	48	21	17	217

While it may be argued that Expert B has an overly optimistic view of the future, it might be similarly argued that Expert A was overly pessimistic. What is certain, however, is that there is substantially less risk that the lower profits forecast by Expert A will not be achieved or conversely there is a higher risk that Expert B's forecast of much higher profits will not be achieved.

Use of a similar discount rate of, say, 9 per cent is not consistent with a finding that the forecast profits are not of equal certainty. Use of a higher discount rate reflects more assumed risk in the forecast profits. Just as a junk bond demands a higher interest rate to compensate the holder for the additional risk of loss (as compared to say a Government of Canada bond) high risk future cash flow demands a higher discount rate.

In our example, the present value of the future profits projected by Experts A and B would be equalized through the use in Expert B's calculation of a 52 per cent discount rate. Whereas Expert A dealt with some portion of the risk by way of a low level of projected lost profits, Expert B could similarly deal with the same risk by applying a higher discount rate (52 per cent) against higher, but riskier earnings.

2. Selection of a Discount Rate

As should now be evident, the selection of a discount rate cannot be divorced from the cash flow against which it is to be applied.

It might be argued that no judgment is required in selection of a discount rate as the *Rules of Civil Procedure*[2] require the use of 2.5% on

---

[2] R.R.O. 1990, Reg. 194.

an inflation-free basis. Using Expert A's estimated lost profits, a 2.5 per cent discount rate would drive a present value as follows:

	Year					
	1	2	3	4	5	Total
Expert A — Lost Profits	$47	$52	$68	$46	$55	$268
Present Value at 2.5%	46	50	64	42	49	251
Present Value at 9%	45	46	55	34	37	217

However, the use of the 2.5 per cent discount rate assumes that the lost profits against which it is applied are relatively risk-free, that is, they are no riskier than the Government of Canada bonds. Few, if any, businesses or individuals can boast incomes that secure.

Accordingly, there is a need to deal with and quantify this uncertainty in assessing damages. The risk inherent in the future profits or income can be accounted for by way of (1) a lump-sum "contingency" adjustment, or (2) an adjustment to the discount rate.

Lump-sum contingency adjustments are both difficult to establish and difficult to criticize. There is seldom a mechanical or obvious logical basis in support of the adjustment. If, in our example, a lump-sum negative contingency adjustment of $34 was applied to the present value of $251 (being the present value of the lost profits at 2.5 per cent), the resulting loss of $217 would be the equivalent of the use of a 9 per cent discount rate (as used in a prior example).

With respect to accounting for contingencies by way of an upward adjustment of the 2.5 per cent discount rate or adjustment in the risk inclusive discount rate used by the expert in calculating the loss, we understand the courts have been somewhat reluctant. Certainly, it is an area where expert evidence, say by a business valuator, can be put forward as to the appropriate risk adjusted discount rate. Again, however, it is a matter of professional judgment, and differences should be expected in attempting to build up the discount rate components as follows:

Real return	2.5%
Risk – say	6.5
	9.0%*

* on an inflation free basis

While the risk element of the discount rate is clearly judgmental, there are many who would argue that the 2.5 per cent "kick off" point is no longer realistic. Even at the time it was established in 1980, it was recommended that it be reviewed every five years. No review has taken place to reflect economic changes in the past 15 years.

Accounting experts often differ dramatically in their opinions of damages. Seldom, in my view, is the difference the result of methodology or mechanical/arithmetic issues. Rather, it is in the expert's understanding of relevant facts and selection of key assumptions, both of which impact on risk, that those differences arise. Small differences, particularly where the loss period is lengthy, can drive substantial differences in damages.

The accounting expert's opinion is as "good" as the underlying facts and assumptions. It is a truism that is sometimes lost on both counsel and their clients.

GOOD INTENTIONS, REASONABLE ACTIONS: RECOVERY OF PECUNIARY DAMAGES FOR PROPERTY LOSSES

Denis J. Power, Q.C.
Duane E. Schippers

1. *Introduction*

This paper accompanies a panel discussion at the 1995 Law Society of Upper Canada Special Lectures focusing on the issue of remedies. The paper is not meant to be an exhaustive treatise on the law of damages.[1] Rather, the purpose of this paper is to provide the reader with a solid understanding of the general principles followed by the courts in awarding pecuniary damages for property losses and recent developments in the law of restitution. This paper addresses the appropriate measure and methods for quantifying damages as well as the practical issues of proving the case for damages. In this context, the issue of damages will also be addressed from the perspective of remoteness, impecuniosity, mitigation and the appropriate date for the assessment of damages.

Needless to say, the award of pecuniary damages for property losses is not a novel concept. Our inherited British legal tradition and most legal systems in the world, have developed around the concept of protecting property rights. The courts have long dealt with claims for damages to property as a result of fires, floods, accidents and trespass. A body of legal principles has been developed over time which is supposed to compensate the victims for the actions of the culpable. These legal principles provide for methods of quantifying losses so as to adequately compensate the victim with money where the victim has suffered damage to or loss of property.

This paper will demonstrate that the appropriate measure of damages should be, and in fact is, the diminution in the value of the property to

---

[1] For a very thorough analysis of the Law of Damages in Canada the reader should refer to Waddams, *The Law of Damages*, 2nd ed. (Aurora: Canada Law Book Inc., 1994) or to Pitch and Snyder, *Damages for Breach of Contract*, 2nd ed. (Toronto: Carswell, 1989).

a reasonable person in the plaintiff's circumstances. The measure of damages, diminution in value, has been confused with the appropriate method of quantifying the damages suffered by the plaintiff. The result has been the development of a "pigeon hole" approach to the issue of pecuniary damages for loss of property. It will be shown that, despite the restrictive "pigeon hole" approach to quantifying damages, the courts can nevertheless deal with new situations that arise by applying the same principles that have resulted in the development of this "pigeon hole" approach. The advocate must understand what these principles are and what must be done to prove or disprove damages in the more difficult cases. In this context, damages for property losses must be examined in connection with the limits that courts traditionally apply to awards of damages, namely, remoteness, mitigation and the date for assessment of damages.

2. *The Purpose of Damages*

Halsbury's Laws of England defines the purpose of damages as follows:

> The general rule is that of restitutio in integrum: so far as money can do it, the injured person should be put in the same position as he would have been in if he had not sustained the wrong, namely if the tort had not been committed or the contract had been performed.[2]

This definition would seem to suggest that the purposes of damages in tort and contract are generally the same. However, the purposes of an award for damages in contract and in tort are clearly distinct. Lord Blackburn in *Livingstone v. Rawyards Coal Co.*[3] referring to the purposes for damages in *tort* stated that:

> I do not think that there is any difference of opinion as to its being a general rule that, where any injury is to be compensated by damages, in settling the sum of money to be given for payment of damages you should as nearly as possible get that sum of money which will put the plaintiff who has been injured, or who has suffered in the same position as he would have been in if he had not sustained the wrong for which he is now getting his compensation or reparation.[4]

---

[2] Lord Hailsham of St. Marylebone, *Halsbury's Laws of England*, 4th ed. (London: Butterworths, 1975), Vol. 12, at para. 1129.

[3] (1880), 5 App. Case 25 (H.L.).

[4] *Ibid.*, at 39.

In tort then, the purpose of damages is to put the person back in the position they would have been in *but for* the conduct of the defendant as far as money can do. The focus of tort damages is on moving the clock back in time to before the damage had occurred and then comparing the victim's pre-accident state to his or her post-accident state. In other words the focus is on the losses suffered by the plaintiff.[5]

The purpose of the measure or assessment of damages for breach of contract, on the other hand, was described in *Wertheim v. Chicoutimi Pulp Co.*[6] where the Privy Council wrote:

> . . . it is the general intention of the law, that in giving damages for breach of contract, the party complaining should so far as it can be done by money, be placed in the same position as he would have been in if the contract had been performed.[7]

In contract the purpose of damages is to focus on the actual performance of the contract, to look to some time in the future in order to determine what situation the contract would have placed the plaintiff in if it had been performed (as opposed to putting the plaintiff in the position he would have been in had the contract never been created). In other words an award of damages considers future benefits to the plaintiff under the terms of the contract.[8]

On the surface one might argue that there is in reality very little difference between the purpose of damages in contract and in tort. However, when examined from the perspective of the quantum of damages and remoteness of damages, the distinction between the purpose of damages for tort and contract becomes very relevant and must be considered in the preparation of the advocate's case.

3. *The Measure of Damages for Property Losses*

(1) Definition of the Measure of Damages

For the purposes of understanding the development of the law in the area of recovery of pecuniary damages for property losses it is necessary to make the conceptual distinction between the "measure of damages"

---

[5] Pitch and Snyder, *Damages for Breach of Contract, supra,* note 1, at 1-2.
[6] [1911] A.C. 301 (P.C.).
[7] *Ibid.,* at 307.
[8] Pitch and Snyder, *Damages for Breach of Contract, supra,* note 1, at 1-2.

and the "quantification" of damages. In other words there is a difference between *what* the damages should compensate for and *how* that compensation should be calculated.

Halsbury's Laws of England distinguishes between the measure of damages and the quantification of damages:

> The "measure of damage" or "measure of damages" is concerned with legal principles governing recoverability, remoteness being the negative aspect of this measure. The assessment of quantum of damages, not being concerned with the legal principle, is distinct from the measure of damages.

> "Quantum of damage" and "quantum of damages" are both phrases in current use. They are used in more than one sense, the usual characteristic being that no question of legal recoverability is involved, but merely the assessment or calculation in terms of money of non-pecuniary damage. . . Quantum of damage or of damages is thus distinguished from "measure of damage", which involves considerations of the law.[9]

If the case-law is examined with the distinction between measure of damages and quantification of damages in mind, the cases can, for the most part, be viewed from the perspective of awarding the diminution in value of the property to the plaintiff. Where other measures of damages are mentioned by the courts the appropriate measure of damages is still diminution in value, but that diminution in value is quantified by considering diminution in market value, cost of repair, restoration or replacement.

(2) Real Property

(a) *Diminution in Market Value*

In cases involving loss of or damage to interests in real property, the approach adopted by the courts is usually to compensate the owner by awarding damages equal to the diminution in value of the property to the owner.[10] The quantification of the diminution in value from the plaintiff's perspective, where the damage is physical in nature, will usually be the cost of restoration of the property to its original state. The assump-

---

[9] *Halsbury's Laws of England* , *supra*, note 2, paras. 1104, 1106.
[10] *Ibid.*, para. 1168.

tion is that the cost of restoration reflects the actual diminution in the value of the real property.[11]

The measure of the actual value of the property usually refers to the market value[12] which is the price that a willing purchaser would pay for the property to a willing vendor.[13] An award of damages based on the diminution in market value is the difference between the pre-injury market value of the property and the post-injury market value of the property.[14]

Where the cost of restoration is less than the diminution in the actual value of the property there is no difficulty in determining the appropriate measure of damages: the plaintiff should receive the cost of restoration.[15] The problem in determining the appropriate measure of damages arises when the cost of the restoration exceeds the diminution in the market value of the property.

The leading Canadian case is *Canadian Nat'l Fire Ins. Co. v. Colonsay Hotel Co.*[16] where the Supreme Court of Canada dealt with a loss suffered as a result of the tortious conduct of the defendant. In discussing the appropriate measure of damages Anglin J. wrote that

> . . ."the actual value of the property to the insured at the time of the loss," having regard to all the conditions and circumstances then existing — not

---

[11] Waddams, *The Law of Damages, supra,* note 1, at 1-111, para. 1.2330; see also *Regnier v. Nelson* (1956), 19 W.W.R. (N.S.) 36 at 39, 64 Man. R. 56 per Freedman J.:

> "I take it to be law that where injury is done to real property the true measure of damage is the diminished value of the property. The cost of repairs may or may not coincide with such diminished value. At best the cost of repairs is an indirect method of ascertaining diminished value. Sometimes, however, it is a convenient and practical method to be employed. Where the repairs have the effect of restoring the property to its condition prior to the damage, the cost thereof may, and very often will, correspond with the diminished value. But even though judgment in such cases may be given in the amount expended for repairs, it is only so given because the court has found it to represent the diminished value of the property, which still remains the true yardstick. Hence, where the cost of repairs is not in line with the actual diminished value of the property ... it cannot be safely relied on as indicating the amount of damages."

[12] "Market Value" is an inaccurate description of the value of the property, but it serves to describe the forces at work in determining the objective value of the property for the purposes of the courts. Professor Waddams more accurately describes it as the "capital value".

[13] Cane, "Negligence, Economic Interests and the Assessment of Damages" (1984), 10 Monash Univ. Law Rev. 17, at 23.

[14] A discussion of the three main methods of calculating the market value of real property is discussed later in this paper.

[15] Waddams, *The Law of Damages, supra,* note 1, at 1-110, para. 1.2320.

[16] [1923] S.C.R. 688, [1923] 2 W.W.R. 1170, [1923] 3 D.L.R. 1001.

necessarily its market value on the one hand and certainly not, on the other, its "replacement value" which, while it may sometimes be less than its actual value to the insured, will more often exceed that value and sometimes, as in the present instance, very grossly exceed it. The right of recovery by the insured is limited to the actual value destroyed by fire.[17]

Canadian Nat'l Fire Ins. Co. was followed by the Ontario Court of Appeal in *Montreal Trust Co. v. Hercules Sales Ltd.*[18] where the plaintiff had purchased land for the purposes of subdividing and developing it. A farm building erected on the land was destroyed as a result of the defendant's negligence. The Court of Appeal, *per* Schroeder J.A., found that the appropriate measure of damages was the diminution in the actual value of the property, not the replacement cost of the building as claimed by the plaintiff. The court held that evidence of the purposes for which the plaintiff owned the property was a relevant factor in determining the measure of damages:

The learned trial Judge excluded all evidence as to the purpose for which Monarch held this property which, it was said, envisaged the eventual demolition of the farm buildings to clear the land for housing construction, and based the damages on the replacement cost of the barn less depreciation. With much deference to the learned trial Judge's views we are of the opinion that he erred in adopting this measure. The action was framed in tort, and the true measure of damage is the difference between the money value of the property *to the plaintiff* before the damage and its value afterwards.[19] [Emphasis added.]

The Court of Appeal in *Montreal Trust Co.* clearly felt that the purpose of the use of the property by the owner, its value to the owner, was a determining factor in awarding damages. Had the plaintiff been awarded the replacement cost of the farm building it would have received a windfall because it was intending to demolish the building in any event. It hardly makes economic sense to award a plaintiff the cost of restoration for property that the plaintiff ultimately intends to destroy. The assumption then, is that the plaintiff in that situation would have been unjustly enriched at the expense of the defendant, the effect of which is to put the plaintiff in a better position than he would have been but for the defendant's actions.

The concern of over-compensation and the true intentions of the plaintiff was expressed in the famous English decision of *Tito v. Waddell*

---

[17] *Ibid.*, at 694 S.C.R., 1007 D.L.R.
[18] [1969] 1 O.R. 661, 3 D.L.R. (3d) 504 (C.A.).
[19] *Ibid.*, at 505 D.L.R.

(No. 2)[20] in which the plaintiffs claimed the cost of restoration where a phosphate mining company had failed to restore the land to its original state after the mining by carrying out improvements and planting trees. The plaintiffs in that case were members of the Banaban tribe on Ocean Island. As a result of the phosphate mining and war time occupation the island was rendered virtually uninhabitable, the Banabans were moved to another island and did not wish to return to Ocean Island. The former Banaban land owners on Ocean island sued for damages for the cost of replanting trees and restoring the land. Megarry V.-C. expressed his concerns about the true intentions of the plaintiffs. He was prepared to allow the cost of restoration of the property if a plaintiff could prove to the court's satisfaction that the plaintiff's true intention was to restore the property:

> The tastes and desires of the owner may be wholly out of step with the ideas of those who constitute the market; yet I cannot see why eccentricity of taste should debar him from obtaining substantial damages unless he sues for specific performance. Per contra, if the plaintiff has suffered little or no monetary loss in the reduction of value of his land, and he has no intention of applying any damages towards carrying out the work contracted for, or its equivalent, I cannot see why he should recover the cost of doing work which will never be done. It is a mere pretence to say that this cost was a loss and should be recoverable as damages.[21]

If the plaintiff could not prove "a sufficient fixity of intention"[22] then the plaintiff should be awarded only the diminution in value. Megarry V.-C. in *Tito v. Waddell (No.2)* found that the plaintiffs had no intention of returning to Ocean Island and, accordingly, awarded damages based on the diminution in the actual value of the property.

In *Peevyhouse v. Garland Coal & Mining Co.*,[23] a decision familiar to all first year contracts students, the majority of the Oklahoma Supreme Court considered a situation where the plaintiff had leased land for strip mining purposes. The defendant had specifically contracted to perform remedial and restoration work on the property as part of the lease agreement. The defendant intentionally[24] breached its contract with the land owner claiming that the cost of restoration was out of all proportion to the actual diminution in value of the property suffered by the plaintiffs. Jackson J. writing for the majority of the court stated that:

---

[20] [1977] 3 All E.R. 129 (Ch.D.).

[21] *Ibid.*, at 316.

[22] *Ibid.*, at 317.

[23] 382 P. 2d 109 (1963) (Okla. Sup. Ct.).

[24] In dissent, Irwin J. wrote that "... in my opinion the [the] defendant's breach of contract was wilful and not in good faith", *Ibid.*, at 115.

. . . where, in a coal mining lease, [the] lessee agrees to perform certain remedial work on the premises concerned at the end of the lease period, and thereafter the contract is fully performed by both parties except that the remedial work is not done, the measure of damages in an action by [the] lessor against [the] lessee for damages for breach of contract is ordinarily the reasonable cost of performance of the work; however, where the contract provision breached was merely incidental to the main purpose in view, and where the economic benefit which would result to lessor by full performance of the work is grossly disproportionate to the cost of performance, the damages which [the] lessor may recover are limited to the diminution in value resulting to the premises because of the non-performance.[25]

The *Peevyhouse* decision has been criticized for its apparent inequities. However, when the evidence is examined it is clear that, although not expressly stated, there was some concern over the "true intentions" of the plaintiffs. Jackson J. noted that although the plaintiffs had introduced expert evidence that it would cost $29,000 to restore the property, the plaintiffs were claiming only $25,000 in damages. It is suggested that this, along with the fact that the diminution in value of the property was only about $300, militated against the plaintiffs proving "a sufficient fixity of intention". The real inequity on the face of the *Peevyhouse* decision is that it appears the corporation has taken advantage of an unsophisticated farmer, and has escaped its obligations by breaching the contract and as a result is unjustly enriched.[26]

The diminution in market value approach is less than ideal as it fails to consider the subjective value of the property to the plaintiff as stated by Professor Muris:

The diminution in value measure is objective; that is, observers external to the contract, such as the judge or jury in a lawsuit, can ascertain its amount with reasonable accuracy at tolerable cost. Yet this objective measure can undercompensate the aggrieved party, thereby contradicting contract law's

---

[25] *Ibid.*, at 114.

[26] This argument was considered in *Tito v. Waddell (No.2)*, *supra*, note 20, at 316 where Megarry V.-C., wrote that:

"... it is fundamental to all questions of damages that they are to compensate the plaintiff for his loss or injury by putting him as nearly as possible in the same position as if he had not suffered the wrong. The question is one of making the defendant disgorge what he has saved by committing the wrong, but one of compensating the plaintiff. ... if the plaintiff has suffered monetary loss, as by a reduction in the value of his property by reason of the wrong, that is plainly a loss that he is entitled to be recouped [*sic*]. On the other hand, if the defendant has saved himself money, as by not doing what he has contracted to do, that does not of itself entitle the plaintiff to recover the saving as damages; for it by no means necessarily follows that what the defendant has saved the plaintiff has lost."

principle that damages should place the injured party in the same position as if the contract were performed.[27]

Professor Muris examined the *Peevyhouse* decision from the perspective of a contract in which the defendant had failed to complete performance.[28] While Professor Muris suggests a slightly different test focusing on the comparative quantum of damages in cases of failed completion of contract, it appears that the purpose remains that of avoiding the over-compensation of the plaintiff. The subjective value to the plaintiff is valid, it is suggested, only in so far as the subjective value claim is reasonable.

From the solicitor's perspective it is essential to examine the motive of the plaintiff to ensure that the plaintiff has a "sufficient fixity of intent". This can be accomplished by proving the plaintiff's past and intended future use of the property. A plaintiff will be far more likely to succeed if he can show that the restoration of the damaged property will indeed occur. Where possible the plaintiff might commence the restoration to prove that fixity of intent.[29] A word of caution, however, the "sufficient fixity of intent" principle is but one factor to consider before committing resources to the restoration of the damaged property and should be limited by considering what a "prudent owner" would do.[30] This notion of reasonableness often arises in the context of claims for specific performance.[31] If it is imprudent or unreasonable for a person

---

[27] Muris, "Cost of Completion or Diminution in Market Value: The Relevance of Subjective Value", (1983) 12 Journal of Legal Studies 379, at 379.

[28] Muris, *ibid.*, at 392-93.

[29] Dore and Veitch, "Guarding Against Over-Compensation when Measuring Damages by the Cost of Repair, Replacement or Performance: The Role of Undertakings" (1994), 23 Can. Bus. L.J. 432. The authors write at 439 :

"The surest way to prove that the victim thinks it worthwhile to incur the cost is for the victim actually to incur it. However, the courts will accept other methods of proving a 'sufficient fixity of intention' to carry out repair, replacement or performance. The intention may be proved by words as well as actions. The victim may have some strong personal interest in the subject matter. Or the victim may be under some duty, public or private, to carry out the work. Or, weakest of all, the victim may simply say that he or she intends to carry it out. The evidence need not establish certainty but it must 'carry conviction'. The victim's actions may also tell against him. For example, the victim may have sold the property on which the work was to be done. Or it might be a case where the victim was in a position to seek specific performance but did not do so."

[30] *Scarborough Golf & Country Club Ltd. v. Scarborough (City)* (1988), 31 O.A.C. 260, 66 O.R. (2d) 257, 41 M.P.L.R. 1, 1 R.P.R. (2d) 225, 54 D.L.R. (4th) 1 at 15 (C.A.). The court reduced damages since a prudent owner would more likely undertake selective work on certain portions of the creek rather than reinforcing the banks of the entire creek on the golf course.

[31] See the discussion on specific performance, *infra*.

in the plaintiff's position to restore the property, there will not be any entitlement to the cost of restoration simply because the plaintiff has acted on intentions that are objectively unreasonable.

(b) Exceptions to the Diminution in Market Value Rule: Cost of Repair, Restoration and Replacement

(i) Statutory Provisions: Environmental Damage

Concern over damage to the environment has received a great deal of public attention over the last several years. Accordingly, both the federal and provincial legislatures have passed legislation dealing with the clean-up and restoration of the physical environment.

At common law in determining the appropriate measure and quantum of damages, the general rule for tort claims based on the *Rylands v. Fletcher*[32] principle of strict liability for recovery of pecuniary damages where there is property damage is the same as for the other forms of damage to property discussed in this paper; the proper measure of damages is the diminution in value which may be quantified by the diminution in market value or the cost of repair or replacement.[33] Legislative action, however, has moved the quantification of damages beyond the common law. The Ontario *Environmental Protection Act*,[34] for example, provides for an order to be made for a clean up where there has been environmental damage to property:

> 17. Where any person causes or permits the discharge of a contaminant into the natural environment, so that land, water, property, animal life, plant life, or human health or safety is injured, damaged or endangered, or is likely to be injured, damaged or endangered, the Director may order the person to,
>
> (a) repair the injury or damage;
> (b) prevent the injury or damage . . .[35]

Under the legislation, therefore, the owner or tenant of property may be ordered to bear the cost of the clean up.[36] The case-law surrounding statu-

---

[32] (1868), L.R. 3 H.L. 330.

[33] See *Jens v. Mannix Co. Ltd.*, [1986] 5 W.W.R. 563, 30 D.L.R. (4th) 260 (B.C.C.A.).

[34] R.S.O. 1990, c. E.19 as amended. See also *Canadian Environmental Protection Act*, R.S.C. 1985, c. 16 (4th Supp.), ss. 131 and 136.

[35] *Environmental Protection Act, ibid.*, s. 17; see also ss.43, 97(2), (3) and 99.

[36] See, for example, *ibid.*, s. 97(1).

tory orders for clean up has centred on the authority of the statute to hold parties, such as owners of the property and banks with security interests in the property, responsible for the clean-up costs where these parties were not the actual polluters.[37]

There is no statutory provision which limits damages to diminution in value; clearly that kind of approach would make environmental damage a question of the cost of doing business.[38] Companies would be able to dump toxins damaging streams, rivers and lands, the destruction of which, if viewed from the basis of diminution in market value of the property, would be more economical for the company committing the wrong and would not represent the true extent of the damage to society as a whole. The harsher penalty of full cost of clean-up or restoration of the property to its pre-accident condition may be a more appropriate method of quantifying damages in order to provide an incentive to individuals and companies to avoid damaging the environment.

Where the land owner has cleaned up a spill or other environmental hazard and then seeks to recover from the polluter, what is the appropriate quantum of damages? Based on the principles discussed above, the land owner would have shown its fixity of intent by having already cleaned up the spill or being under a statutory duty to do so. The reasonableness of the activity cannot be questioned as a public duty is involved and is mandated by the statute. Therefore, the appropriate quantum of damages ought to be the cost of restoration since that is the amount that the land owner is out of pocket. Again the diminution in value *to the owner* is the appropriate measure of damages, but the proper way to quantify it is the cost of restoration.

---

[37] See for example, *King (Twp.) v. Rolex Equipment Co.* (1992), 8 O.R. (3d) 457, 23 R.P.R. (2d) 313, 90 D.L.R. (4th) 442 (Gen. Div.), where the costs of clean-up resulting from the dumping of waste on certain property were found to be in priority to the bank's security interest in the property.

[38] But see s. 136(1), *Canadian Environmental Protection Act, supra*, note 34, which provides that:

"136(1) Any person who has suffered loss or damage as a result of conduct that is contrary to any provision of this Act or the regulations may, in any court of competent jurisdiction, sue for and recover from the person who engaged in the conduct an amount equal to the loss or damage proved to have been suffered by the person and an amount to compensate for the costs of any investigation in connection with the matter and of proceedings under this section."

This would suggest that the common law approach to the measure of damages applies.

(ii) *Fixity of Intention must be Reasonable*

Some courts appear to have had difficulty with the *Tito v. Waddell*[39] principle of awarding damages for cost of restoration only where there was a "sufficient fixity of intent". One such example is *Ziehlke v. Amisk Drilling Co. Ltd.*[40] In Ziehlke, the defendants negligently caused a fire at the plaintiff's gold mine destroying and damaging buildings and equipment. The trial judge awarded damages on the replacement costs of the buildings. The Manitoba Court of Appeal reduced the damages by one-third given that there was a good chance that the mine would never reopen. The buildings that were destroyed had not been used since the early 1970s and the mine had produced only 851 ounces of gold during its 70-year history. The court cited *Mallet v. McMonagle*[41] in which Lord Diplock wrote that:

> The role of the court in making an assessment of damages which depends upon its view as to what will be and what would have been is to be contrasted with its ordinary function in civil actions of determining what was. In determining what did happen in the past a court decides on the balance of probabilities. Anything that is more probable than not it treats as certain. But in assessing damages which depend upon its view as to what will happen in the future or would have happened in the future if something had not happened in the past, the court must make an estimate as to what are the chances that a particular thing will or would have happened and reflect those chances, whether they are more or less than even, in the amount of damages which it awards.[42]

In Ziehlke it appears that the destruction of the buildings either did not alter the value of the land or the cost of restoring the buildings was less than the diminution in the value of the land, although it did alter the economical "intended" operation of the mine. It is apparent that the court was convinced that some damage had resulted, but there was a question as to whether the plaintiff had the "reasonable" intent of using the buildings in the operation of the mine. The court therefore pro-rated the damages based on the plaintiff's "reasonable" intent reflecting the chances of the buildings ever being used in the operation of the mine. Again, the court had to consider the measure of damages as being the diminution in value to the owner.

The different approaches by the courts depending on the intended

---

[39] [1977] 3 All E.R. 129 (Ch.D.).
[40] [1994] 2 W.W.R. 107, 92 Man. R. (2d) 83, 110 D.L.R. (4th) 172 (C.A.).
[41] [1970] A.C. 166 (H.L.).
[42] *Ibid.*, at 176.

use and nature of the damaged property can best be illustrated by the following cases dealing with the unlawful removal of trees from the plaintiff's property.

(iii) *The Wrongful Harvest or Mining of Property: Advantage to the Wrongdoer*

The British Columbia Court of Appeal in *Shewish v. MacMillan Bloedel Ltd.*[43] considered an action for damages caused by a trespass. The defendant, MacMillan Bloedel, had negligently, by failing to obtain the proper survey and field notes, clear cut logged approximately one hectare of the Tse-oo-wa Indian Reserve No. 4 on Vancouver Island. There was no consideration of whether diminution in the value of the property was the appropriate measure of damages.[44] The court found that two measures of damages were available: the market value of the timber logged without any deductions[45]; or the net market value of the timber after deducting the costs of severance of the logs.[46] The court cited *McGregor on Damages* where it is stated that:

> The trend of these decisions and of the dicta in them indeed suggests that the strict rule in *Martin v. Porter* will now apply only where the trespass is wilful or fraudulent, and that the qualification as stated by Parke B. in *Wood v. Morewood* is now to be enlarged so as to include cases of negligence. This trend stems from the approach laid down by Lord Halsbury L.C. in *Jegon v. Vivian*. "Now it strikes me," he said, "as a strong measure to give a man,

---

[43] [1991] 1 W.W.R. 27, 48 B.C.L.R. (2d) 290, 3 C.C.L.T. (2d) 291, 74 D.L.R. (4th) 345 (C.A.).

[44] It is fairly evident that the market value of the property had not declined. However, MacMillan Bloedel had trespassed and gained a pecuniary advantage by the act of the trespass.

[45] *Livingstone v. Rawyards Coal Co.* (1880), 5 App. Cas. 25; *Wood v. Morewood* (1841), 3 Q.B. 440.

[46] *Martin v. Porter* (1839), 151 E.R. 149, *per* Parke B., at 150:
"The plaintiff is entitled to be placed in the same situation as if these coals had been chattels belonging to himself, which had been carried away by the defendant, and must be paid their value at the time they were begun to be taken away. He had a right to them, without being subject to the expense of getting them, which was a wrongful act by the defendant, and for which the defendant cannot claim to be reimbursed."
see also *Union Bank of Canada v. Rideau Lumber Co.* (1902), 4 O.L.R. 721 (C.A.); *Last Chance Mining Co. v. American Boy Mining Co. Ltd.* (1904), 2 M.M.C. 150 (B.C.S.C.); *Kirkpatrick v. Mcnamee* (1905), 36 S.C.R. 152; *Chew Lumber Co. v. Howe Sound Lumber Co.* (1913), 4 W.W.R. 1308, 18 B.C.R. 312, 13 D.L.R. 735 (B.C.C.A.).

instead of the value of his coal, the great advantage of having it worked without any expense for getting and hewing. . . It seems a rough and ready mode of doing justice, though the remark that a wilful trespasser ought to be punished is worthy of observation . . . and it seems to me that the judges have founded their decisions upon the ground of wilful trespass.'' And later he said: ''I think that the milder rule of law is certainly that which ought to guide this court, subject to any case made of a special character which would induce the court to swerve from it. Otherwise, on the one hand, a trespass might be committed with impunity if the rule *in poenam* were not insisted upon; so, on the other hand, persons might stand by and see their coal worked, being spared the expense of winning and getting it.'' This has been interpreted by the courts as putting the burden on the plaintiff of showing that the stricter rule applies. Re United Merthyr Collieries is a strong case, for it was one not of bona fide belief in titled or expected title but of inadvertently crossing the boundary of the plaintiff's adjoining mine: yet the milder rule was applied in the absence of any evidence of fraud. So too in *Livingstone v. Rawyards Coal Co.* all of their lordships spoke of the stricter rule as applying in cases of trespass which as wilful or fraudulent.[47]

The British Columbia Court of Appeal in *Shewish*[48] treated the negligent trespass of the defendant as equivalent to a wilful act and awarded the plaintiff the market value of the timber without a deduction for the cost of severance. However, other market expenses were permitted to be deducted from the market value of the timber.[49] Rather than treating this type of situation as one of a loss of real property (or damage to real property), the courts, it would seem, are treating cases such as *Shewish* as the loss of a chattel.[50] To treat the quantification of damages as the diminution in the market value of the property would effectively deny relief to the plaintiff for the trespass and encourage trespass by the defendant. For this reason, the court appeared to assume that the plaintiff's purpose would have been to harvest the lumber or minerals in the land himself thereby imputing a purpose to the use of the property and a diminution in the value of the property to the plaintiff.

(iv) *The Nature and Purposes of Use of the Damaged Property*

In *Scarborough v. R.E.F. Homes Ltd.*[51] the defendant cut down several maple trees on the plaintiff city's road allowance. The court awarded damages for the trespass noting that:

---

[47] McGregor, *McGregor on Damages*, 15th ed. (London: Sweet & Maxwell Limited, 1988), at 826.

[48] *Supra*, note 43.

[49] *Ibid.*, at 353.

[50] *Martin v. Porter, supra*, note 46, at 150.

[51] (1979), 9 M.P.L.R. 255 (Ont. C.A.).

The normal measure of damages for a trespass causing physical harm to the land, such as felling grown trees, has traditionally been the diminution in value of the land which is often calculated as the cost of replacing it to its previous state . . .

. . . . .

The diminution in value of a road allowance, which normally is not marketable land, must necessarily differ from that of privately owned, landscaped property, even if the trees on both properties are intrinsically similar.[52]

The court criticized the fact that expert evidence was not called to attempt to quantify the monetary loss and diminution in value of the road allowance.

The British Columbia Court of Appeal in *Dykhuizen v. Saanich (District)*[53] considered the *R.E.F. Homes Ltd.* decision when faced with a similar situation and stated that:

In the case of trees used for the purpose of public or private enjoyment, damage for their deliberate destruction is not limited to the resulting diminution in value of the land, or the value of the wood as lumber or firewood, or the value which might be awarded in respect of them as compensation for expropriation. The damages in such cases may extend to the cost of restoration or restitution, within reasonable bounds, together with compensation for loss of amenity to the extent that complete restoration cannot reasonably be affected.[54]

In *Dykhuizen* expert evidence was introduced dealing with the cost of replacing and maturing a tree over a number of years. Thus the court was better able to quantify the value of the damage to the plaintiff.

The intrinsic value of the property to the plaintiff must also be considered where the loss is one of enjoyment, such as in *Peters v. Diamond et al.*,[55] a situation where a few fruit trees on the plaintiff's property were destroyed by the defendant. The court said:

I do, however, find that the defendants must place the plaintiff as nearly as possible in the same position as he was before he sustained the damage by the defendant's tort. This can only be done by assessing the probable cost of planting similar trees of as near a size as possible and practicable, and such as will afford to the plaintiff a similar amount of screening, privacy, beauty and of attraction to his children.[56]

---

[52] *Ibid.*, at 256-57.
[53] (1989), 63 D.L.R. (4th) 211 (B.C.C.A.).
[54] *Ibid.*, at 215 *per* Taylor J.
[55] [1964] 1 O.R. 139, 41 D.L.R. (2d) 311 (Co.Ct.).
[56] *Ibid.*, at 143.

In the cases discussed above, it can be seen that the courts are concerned with ensuring fair and adequate compensation to the victim who has suffered a loss of property. In deciding upon the appropriate measure of damages the courts seem to be willing to make assumptions about the intent and purposes of the plaintiff in claiming the damages. In effect the subjective value based on the use of the property is being considered by the courts where it is reasonable to do so. The equitable quantification of the damages in some cases is to award the cost of replacement or restoration as representing the diminution in the value of the property to the plaintiff as opposed to the diminution in the market value of the property. *McGregor on Damages* in considering this issue focuses on the reasonableness of the plaintiff's actions stating:

> The difficulty in deciding between diminution in value and cost of reinstatement arises from the fact that the plaintiff may want his property in the same state as before the commission of the tort but the amount required to effect this may be substantially greater than the amount by which the value of the property has been diminished. The test which appears to be the appropriate one is the reasonableness of the plaintiff's desire to reinstate the property; this will be judged in part by the advantages to him of reinstatement in relation to the extra cost to the defendant in having to pay damages for reinstatement rather than damages calculated by the diminution in value of the land.[57]

In *Nan v. Black Pine Mfg. Ltd.*[58] it was suggested that the particular nature of the property, for example residential versus commercial, would have an impact on the method of quantification of damages. The diminution in market value may not be appropriate in cases where, for example, the plaintiff's home is destroyed. It is conceivable that simply awarding the diminution in the market value of the property would not truly compensate the plaintiff for his loss, as the diminution in market value approach could effectively leave the defendant with an inferior home.[59] This was the case in *Hollebone v. Midhurst Fernhurst Builders Ltd.*[60] where the court found that given the unique character of the property and lack of comparable properties in the area, the cost of restoration was the appropriate quantification of damages.

Therefore, where the nature and the use of the property is such that the diminution in market value of the property does not adequately reflect

---

[57] *McGregor on Damages, supra*, note 47, at 1396.
[58] [1991] 5 W.W.R. 172, 55 B.C.L.R. (2d) 241, 80 D.L.R. (4th) 153 at 157-58 (C.A.).
[59] See *Jens v. Mannix Co. Ltd.*, [1986] 5 W.W.R. 563, 30 D.L.R. (4th) 260 (B.C.C.A.); *Nan v. Black Pine Mfg. Ltd., ibid.*
[60] [1968] 1 Lloyd's Rep. 38.

the special nature of the property and the reasonably intentioned use of the property by the plaintiff, the appropriate method of quantifying damages is the cost of repair or replacement as a measure of the diminution in the value of the property to the owner. The courts seem to have adopted a quasi-subjective approach making the measure of damages the "reasonable diminution in value to the plaintiff". The method of quantifying the damages, as discussed above, varies depending on what reasonable value the property had to the owner.

(3) Chattels: The Measure of Damages

(a) *The General Approach: Diminution in Value Quantified by Cost to the Plaintiff*

The measure of pecuniary damage for loss or damage to chattels and other goods is the diminution in value to the property owner (as opposed to the cost of restoration). The cost of restoration or cost of the property to the owner is more often utilized as the appropriate method of quantification of the loss in value to the owner. In *Halsbury's Laws of England*, the rule for determining the quantum of damage to goods and chattels is stated as:

> The basic rule is that the measure of damages in the case of damage to a chattel is the cost of repair, but if it is unreasonable from a business point of view to repair the article, or if the article is damaged beyond repair, then the basic measure is the cost of replacement in an available market. If there is no available market and it is reasonable to take steps to have a substitute made, the cost of the substitute may provide the measure of damages; if there is no market and the making of a substitute is unreasonable, it would seem that the measure of damages is the value to the plaintiff at the time of the loss.

> If an article is repaired, but its value is still less than its pre-accident value, the difference may be recovered.[61]

The *Sale of Goods Act*[62] provides that:

> 49(3) Where there is an available market for the goods in question, the measure of damages is, in the absence of evidence to the contrary, to be ascertained by the difference between the contract price and the market or

---

[61] *Halsbury's Laws of England*, 4th ed. (London: Butterworths, 1975), Vol. 12, para. 1163.
[62] R.S.O. 1990, c. S.1, s. 49(3).

current price of the goods at the time or times when they ought to have been delivered, or, if no time was fixed, then at the time of the refusal to deliver.

As in measuring damages for pecuniary losses resulting from damage or loss to real property, regardless of the fact that the measure of damages if often couched in terms of cost of repair or restoration, the true measure is in effect the diminution in value. Cost or available market price is only a convenient method of determining the value of the property. Professor Waddams writes about this remarking that:

> Where the cost of restoration is equal to or less than the diminution of capital value the cost is always recoverable, even if the plaintiff does not actually incur the cost. This has been often described as a way of measuring the capital diminution, and indeed it is arguable that wherever the cost of restoration appears to be less than the diminution of capital value, the two are, on analysis, properly considered to be equal, for a rational purchaser, knowing that perfect restoration can be achieved for a certain sum, will deduct just that sum and no more from the price she would have been willing to pay for the undamaged property.[63]

While the ordinary method of quantifying damages for property losses involving chattels is the cost of replacement or repair, whether the purposes and intentions of the plaintiff are reasonable must be considered, in determining how the diminution in value to the plaintiff will be calculated.

(b) Variations to the Basic Rule of Quantifying by Cost to the Plaintiff

(i) Reseller of Goods: Market value or Cost to the Reseller

Where cost is the appropriate method of quantifying the value of the loss, the question arises as to whether the cost is the retail market value or the wholesale price paid for the item by the plaintiff. If the plaintiff is operating as a retailer of goods, the diminution in value will be reflected by the diminution in the retail sales value of the product.[64] It can be argued

---

[63] Waddams, *The Law of Damages*, 2nd ed. (Aurora: Canada Law Book Inc., 1994), at 1-110, para. 1.2320.

[64] See, for example, *Dor-Al's Specialty Shoppe Ltd. v. Kapuskasing* (1976), 72 D.L.R. (3d) 212 (Ont. C.A.) in which a fire destroyed the plaintiff's in stock inventory. Howland J.A., for the court stated at 218 that:

that items for resale should be valued on the basis of cost to the retailer as opposed to the retail market value of the goods. However, as noted by the Ontario Court of Appeal in *Dor-Al's Specialty Shoppe v. Kapuskasing* the cost to the retailer approach may under-compensate the retailer since costs are incurred by the retailer in making the original purchases and in waiting for replacements for the damaged goods:

> At the time of the fire, there was a stock-in-trade available for the January clearance sale. It was readily saleable and had a profit-earning capacity. Such merchandise was not slow-moving but had a turnover of five to seven times a year. It could not be immediately replaced. Considerable time and travel was required in its selection, and in making it ready for retail sale. The rationale lying behind the American cases which have not adopted market value as the test for valuing stock-in-trade would accordingly not appear to be applicable. Dor-Al as a retailer had given the stock-in-trade the final increment in value. To exclude the profit factor from the value of the stock-in-trade would be to deprive Dor-Al of an element of value to which it is entitled. Dor-Al was entitled to be put in the same position as if it had not suffered the damage.[65]

The maritime shipping cases, which have contributed significantly to the development of the law of damages, have adopted the market value to the owner approach. The quantum of damages for shipped goods which arrive damaged is the difference between the arrival sound market value less the arrival damaged market value of the goods.[66] In these cases, a substantial portion of the costs to the reseller of the product can be attributed to the costs of transportation and the significant delay in time before replacement goods could be received.

In *Ronald Elwyn Lister Ltd. v. Dayton Tire Canada*,[67] the Ontario Court of Appeal valued the damage to a business, where the defendant wrongfully seized the plaintiff's inventory, as the diminution in the value of the business as a going concern. However, the court also remarked that the appropriate measure for damages for the loss of its inventory was its valuation at acquisition cost as opposed to retail sales value.[68] There was

---

"In assessing the money value of the stock-in-trade to Dor-Al as a retailer, the use of market value was in my opinion correct in the circumstances. There was no suggestion that the tagged price was higher than the retail price of similar merchandise in the vicinity."

[65] *Ibid.*, at 218.

[66] *Redpath Industries Ltd. v. The Ship "Cisco"*, [1994] 2 F.C. 279, 70 F.T.R. 136n, 110 D.L.R. (4th) 583 at 585, 163 N.R. 161 (C.A.); leave to appeal to S.C.C. refused 179 N.R. 319n.

[67] (1985), 9 O.A.C. 39, 52 O.R. (2d) 88 (C.A.).

[68] *Ibid.*, at 112 O.R.

evidence that the plaintiff would have encountered serious difficulty in selling its inventory in any event. Morden J.A. wrote that:

> The basic principle is that the plaintiff is to be compensated for its loss result-
> ing from the conversion. A result that furnishes the plaintiff with the total
> cost to it of the inventory seized, in the particular circumstances of this case,
> comes close to accomplishing this result. I think that it is open to the plain-
> tiff to say that regardless of the difficulties it may have had selling the inven-
> tory it is at least entitled to the cost of replacing what was taken. I am not
> persuaded what the normal selling price of this inventory would have been
> or, if it had been obtained, that Lister Limited, having regard to all of the
> attendant costs to be deducted from it, would have been better off than it
> would be by receiving the cost of the goods.[69] [Emphasis added.]

Whether retail market value or wholesale cost is used to quantify the damages suffered by the plaintiff will depend upon whether or not the plaintiff has, in fact, suffered a loss or incurred costs above the whole-sale cost to himself. The court will require proof that the plaintiff would have been able to realize the retail market value of the goods. In addi-tion, the plaintiff should attempt to quantify the costs involved in mak-ing the wholesale purchases and the losses likely to be suffered if the plaintiff is unable to sell the property at the retail price in the normal course of business.

From the defendant's perspective, wherever possible evidence should be produced showing that the product can be replaced at wholesale cost to the plaintiff very quickly with no real additional expense or that the plaintiff would not realize the claimed retail market value of the products. Such evidence will assist the court in determining the actual diminution in value to the plaintiff and effectively reduces the damages that the plain-tiff can claim for, as the courts seek to avoid over-compensating the plaintiff.

(ii) Collectibles

In the case of "collectibles" such as antique cars and works of art that have "special" values, the appropriate quantum of damages is the cost of replacement. In *Scobie v. Wing* a case in which the plaintiff's antique Jaguar car was destroyed in an accident, the British Columbia Court of Appeal held that:

---

[69] *Ibid.*

The rule must, I think, be that the owner of such a chattel is entitled in some circumstances, to replace it and recover all cost and loss reasonably involved in so doing, even though the amount arrived at may exceed the value of the lost chattel at the date of loss, but that to qualify for this basis of assessment of damages it is necessary that the plaintiff in fact replace the lost chattel, or satisfy the court that he or she has elected to do so and has acted reasonably in taking necessary or appropriate steps to that end with reasonable dispatch.[70] [Emphasis added.]

In Scobie, the plaintiff did not meet the higher standard of proof because he delayed for over four years and had not purchased a replacement.

In another "collectibles" case,[71] a mural was destroyed while on loan to a museum. In determining the value, the court considered expert opinions on the sale price of other works by the same artist, but the insured value of the mural as determined by the owner prior to the loss was the determining factor, given that it was reasonable in light of the expert opinions as to value.[72]

In dealing with a "collectibles" case, evidence of the value of the property will need to be adduced by some form of expert evidence. The insured value of the property will be somewhat representative of the value of the property to the owner, but only if the property is restored or replaced as soon as a reasonable person could have done so. The courts will be wary of parties that have not acted with the "sufficient fixity of intent" by showing real attempts to purchase like property. Evidence of the availability and cost of a similar "collectible" on the market should be introduced as indicative of the value of the "collectible" and of the reasonableness of efforts made to replace it.

(iii) *Depreciation in Value of Repaired Chattels*

Depreciation in the value of a chattel or certain forms of real property may result even after the property is repaired. For example, a car that has been in an accident and repaired will usually be of less value than

---

[70] [1992] 2 W.W.R. 514 at 518-19, 63 B.C.L.R. (2d) 76 (C.A.) *per* Taylor J.A.

[71] *Arras Gallery Ltd. v. Ontario* (1985), 29 B.L.R. 253 (Ont. H.C.J.).

[72] The court in *Arras Gallery, ibid.*, was also impressed by the fact that the museum had accepted the insured valuation when it signed the loan agreement. But see *Crayden's Pharmacy Ltd. v. Standard Paving Co.* (1973), 37 D.L.R. (3d) 167 (Ont. C.A.), where the court refused to consider the pay out of the insurer to the insured as evidence of the damage caused by the tortfeasor. The insured value of property may be relevant therefore only if it is a reasonable measure of the value.

a similar car which was never damaged. An allowance for depreciation in cases where even after repair the property is of lessor value simply by the fact of the damage and the repair may be appropriate. Professor Waddams cites Salter J. in *Moss v. Christchurch Rural District Council* on this point considering that even after repair there may be a decline in the value of the property from its pre-damaged state, for example, where part of the value of the property was based upon its historical construction:

> There may conceivably be cases where the true measure of damage is less than the cost of replacement, and it is easy to imagine cases where the damage may be far greater. Suppose irreparable damage has been done to some historic building. No one would suggest that the mere cost of putting new bricks in place of the old would be the full measure of damage or would fairly represent the actual loss.[73]

The courts will make allowance for accelerated depreciation and other circumstances where repair is insufficient to restore the property's value, when awarding the cost of repairs as the quantum of damages on certain items. The plaintiff must still prove that such depreciation will likely result.[74] However, evidence of the amount of depreciation will by its very nature be difficult to obtain.

(4) Solicitor's Negligence Cases

Situations involving recovery of pecuniary damages for property loss frequently arise in the context of solicitor's negligence in real estate transactions. There are three important decisions of the Ontario Court of Appeal dealing with the appropriate measure of damages in these cases.[75]

In *Messineo et al. v. Beale*,[76] the Court of Appeal established the basic principles with respect to quantifying damages for loss of an interest in property as a result of a solicitor's negligence. In *Messineo*, the plaintiffs purchased a large tract of land from the vendor. The purchasers thought that included in the land they were purchasing was land known as "Murch's Point". In fact this piece of land was not conveyed as the

---

[73] [1925] 2 K.B. 750 at 752.

[74] *Sea-Lease Inc. v. Pfeifer* (1991), 8 B.C.A.C. 209 (C.A.).

[75] See *Messineo v. Beale* (1978), 5 C.C.L.T. 235, 20 O.R. (2d) 49, 86 D.L.R. (3d) 713 (C.A.); *Kienzle v. Stringer* (1981), 35 O.R. (2d) 85, 21 R.P.R. 44, 130 D.L.R. (3d) 272 (C.A.) leave to appeal to S.C.C. refused; *Toronto Industrial Leaseholds Ltd. v. Posesorski* (1994), 21 O.R. (3d) 1, 42 R.P.R. (2d) 1, 119 D.L.R. (4th) 193 (C.A.).

[76] *Ibid.*

vendor did not have title to it. The purchasers' solicitor was found to be negligent in failing to review the survey of the property being conveyed and failing to advise the purchasers. The purchasers, however, were able to purchase the remaining lands at less than market value. The purchasers argued that the appropriate measure of damages was the value of Murch's Point. The Ontario Court of Appeal disagreed, Arnup J.A. wrote that:

> In my view it is obvious that *the defendant's breach of duty was not the cause of the plaintiff's getting no title to Murch's point. The vendor had no title to Murch's point, and could give none. Nothing the defendant could have done would have changed that situation.*
>
> It is to be observed that if the defendant had discovered, before closing, that Miss Finley had no title to Murch's Point, it would have been his duty to communicate the fact at once to his clients. Their options then would have been to refuse to close, to close and take title to what Miss Finely could convey, or to try to negotiate, once more, for a lower price.[77] [Emphasis added.]

The attention of the Court of Appeal in *Messineo* was on causation. At most, the solicitor caused the plaintiffs to complete a contract for purchase and sale which they would not have completed but for the solicitor's breach of duty. Damages then ought to put the plaintiffs into the position they would have been in but for the solicitor's error, meaning not having completed the contract for purchase and sale. The plaintiffs are entitled to claim only for any loss they suffered as a result of completing the agreement of purchase and sale. Arnup J.A. considered the measure of damages stating that:

> The measure of damages is the difference in money between the amount paid by the client to the vendor, and the market value of the land to which the client received good title.[78]

In *Messineo* the plaintiffs had suffered *no financial loss* as a result of entering into the transaction because they had acquired the property at below market value, therefore no damages were awarded for the failure to receive title to Murch's Point. Given the discussion in the case, it is apparent that the time for considering the diminution in the value of the property was at the time the transaction was entered into. Costs of the appeal by the solicitor were not allowed as an expression of disapproval of his conduct.

It is interesting to note in *Messineo* that Arnup J.A. based his analysis of liability and assessment of damages on the basis of breach of contract. In the same decision, Zuber J.A. found that the solicitor was liable

---

[77] *Ibid.*, at 51-52 O.R.
[78] *Ibid.*, at 52 O.R.

in both tort and contract, however it did not, in his view, change the measure of damages:

> With great respect, however, I do not agree that the liability of a solicitor is based only on breach of contract. A solicitor, being one of those who profess skills in a calling, is liable for failure to exercise those skills in both tort and contract.
>
> . . . . .
>
> However, in this case, the liability of the defendant in tort as well as contract does not advance the plaintiff's position. The negligence of the defendant did not cause the plaintiffs to lose Murch's Point. Since Finley, the vendor in the subject transaction never had title to Murch's Point it was never within the grasp of the plaintiffs, and hence could not have been lost. The defendant's negligence simply caused the plaintiff's to complete a transaction that they otherwise would have avoided. Therefore, it is the responsibility of the defendant to compensate the plaintiffs for the loss suffered as a result of entering this transaction; but as the reasons of Arnup, J.A., demonstrate, there was in fact no loss.[79]

Of course, the extension of liability of solicitors beyond a contractual basis and into tort was finally settled in *Central Trust v. Rafuse*.[80]

Messineo seemed to be a hard pill to swallow. From our experience acting as counsel for the errors and omissions insurer we can say, without doubt, that plaintiffs' counsel in similar situations have been, and are, reluctant to accept Arnup J.A.'s reasoning.

The second case in the trilogy, *Kienzle v. Stringer,*[81] created some confusion in regard to the appropriate method of quantifying damages. The facts in *Kienzle* were particularly relevant for the purpose of determining the extent of the solicitor's liability for damages. The plaintiff in *Kienzle* was one of three siblings. The plaintiff's sister was the administrix of their parent's estate. The plaintiff offered to purchase the family farm (the "Oxford farm"). The defendant solicitor prepared the documentation for the transfer. The deed prepared by the solicitor was from the plaintiff's sister as administrix of the estate to the plaintiff. Neither the plaintiff nor his two sisters joined in the conveyance in their personal capacity. Unfortunately, at the time of conveyance, title to the Oxford farm had already vested in the plaintiff and his two sisters. Therefore the plaintiff's sister as administrix had no legal authority to convey the farm. This was not noticed by the solicitor. One year later the plaintiff agreed to purchase another farm, the purchase of which was conditional on his selling the Oxford farm. In anticipation of the sale the plaintiff did not renew

---

[79] *Ibid.*, at 54 O.R.
[80] [1988] 1 S.C.R. 1206.
[81] *Supra*, note 75.

the lease of the land adjoining the Oxford farm which was necessary in order to make the plaintiff's farming operation economical. The sale of the Oxford farm could not be completed since one of the plaintiff's sisters refused to convey her interest to the plaintiff.

Mr. Justice Zuber attempted to define the law as set down in *Messineo*. The first issue was the issue of the time of assessment of damages. Mr. Justice Zuber dealt with the time for assessment of damages by stating that:

> I take it to be clear as well that the market value spoken of is the market value at the time of the transaction, otherwise rising values would wipe out the plaintiff's damages but leave him with his problems unresolved.[82]

Mr. Justice Zuber, therefore, held that the difference in value must be quantified at the time the transaction was entered into. This, quite properly, allows the plaintiff to obtain an allowance in the form of interest for the decrease in the purchasing power of the money which he over paid to the vendor, and still retain the benefit of any increase in the market value of the property that was conveyed to him. This may prove unsatisfactory, however, where the market prices of other properties in which the plaintiff might have invested the money have risen faster than the court awarded interest rate.

Mr. Justice Zuber emphasized that the decision in *Messineo* did not preclude a plaintiff from claiming damages beyond simply the difference in the value of the land as a result of the error:

> It appears that in many of the cases, as a matter of fact, the damages amount to no more than the difference between the purchase price and the market value of what is received, but I find no case binding on this Court compelling the acceptance of such a measure as a rule of law.
>
> In my view the law should not support a rule which gives exceptional protection to solicitors from the general principles of damages which flow from either contractual or tortious responsibilities.[83]

The plaintiff was awarded the cost of rectifying the plaintiff's title by paying an additional sum of money to the sister who refused to convey to purchase her interest. Mr. Justice Zuber found that the solicitor had caused this loss to the plaintiff.[84]

---

[82] *Ibid.*, at 88.

[83] *Ibid.*

[84] In order for the solicitor to have *caused* the loss to the plaintiff in *Kienzle*, it must be assumed that *but for* the negligence of the solicitor the plaintiff would have acquired title to the Oxford farm. It was found as a fact at trial (14 R.P.R. 29) that the plaintiff's sister would have conveyed her interest in 1977 when the solicitor drew up the original deed.

Where *Kienzle* contributes most to the development of the law of recovery for pecuniary loss is in the allowance for recovery of consequential losses suffered by the plaintiff as a result of the plaintiff's having relied upon the solicitor's certification of good title. The Court of Appeal allowed the plaintiff to recover consequential losses in the form of lost profits for one year from having to operate the Oxford farm at a loss (one year was found to be sufficient time to allow the plaintiff to mitigate his damages). The court did not, however, permit the plaintiff to recover for the difference in price of purchasing the other farm as a result of the time passing since the solicitor's error. Wilson J.A. disagreed on this point and would have allowed the recovery for the extra cost in acquiring the new farm.[85] Zuber J.A. did leave the door open for other forms of recovery for damage suffered by the plaintiff writing that:

> It may be helpful to recognize that in using the terms "reasonably foreseeable" or "within the reasonable contemplation of the parties" courts are not often concerned with what the parties in fact foresaw or contemplated. (*I leave aside those cases where the disclosure of special facts may lead to the conclusion that a party has assumed an extraordinary risk.*) The governing term is reasonable and what is reasonably foreseen or reasonably contemplated is a matter to be determined by a court. These terms necessarily include more policy than fact as courts attempt to find some fair measure of compensation to be paid to those who suffer damages by those who cause them.[86] [emphasis added.]

While *Messineo* dealt only with a claim for damages for loss of property, that the plaintiff would not have purchased but for the solicitor's negligence, *Kienzle* establishes that the plaintiff can claim additional damages where there is foreseeable reliance on the solicitor's certificate resulting in financial injury to the plaintiff. *Kienzle* also establishes that a solicitor is liable to pay for the cost of rectifying title *where the solicitor*

---

[85] Wilson J.A. would have found that the plaintiff's impecuniosity and therefore his inability to mitigate his damages by purchasing the other farm thereby increasing cost of acquiring the farm at a later date was not too remote and was reasonably foreseeable. She argued that damages would have been recoverable and reasonably foreseeable if the plaintiff had lost his deposit or had to pay damages to the vendor of the farm he intended to purchase. On this basis, Wilson J.A. found it reasonable to expect that the ability of a homeowner or farmer to purchase a new home or farm often rests on his ability to sell his current home or farm. In the view of Wilson J.A. the plaintiff should have been able to recover for the loss in appreciation in value on farm the plaintiff intended to purchase less the appreciation in value of the Oxford farm. She would not have allowed the plaintiff's claim for loss profits on the new farm, finding that loss to be too speculative. (*Kienzle, supra*, note 75, at 91-92).

[86] *Kienzle, ibid., per* Zuber J.A., at 90.

is the cause of the error on title, even if that expense exceeds the diminution in value of the property as a result of the negligent error.

The final case in the trilogy is *Toronto Industrial Leaseholds Ltd. v. Posesorski*.[87] In that case the plaintiffs sued the owner of a building for a declaration that an option to lease premises from owners of an industrial property was valid and binding. The owners added, as a third party, the solicitor who acted for them on the purchase of the property. The solicitor was admittedly negligent in failing to inform the owners, at the time of the purchase, of the option to lease the premises on extremely favourable terms following the expiration of the plaintiff's current lease. The Court of Appeal in a 2-1 split decision found that the measure of damages is the *Messineo* formula where the plaintiff is to be compensated for an overpayment on the purchase price of the property as a result of the solicitor's negligence. Doherty J.A. wrote that:

> . . . I do not regard *Kienzle* as a departure from *Messineo*. As indicated above, the two cases demonstrate that the initial measure of damages will depend in part on the nature of the solicitor's error. If the error caused the client to lose an interest in property he or she otherwise would have had, *Kienzle* is the appropriate starting point. If the error did not cause the client to lose an interest in property, but instead caused the client to enter into a contract that he or she otherwise would not have entered into, then *Messineo* is the appropriate starting point in the assessment of the clients damages. Further, as the Court of Appeal in *Kienzle* indicates, even where *Messineo* is the appropriate starting point, that measure of damages does not necessarily exhaust the client's claim. Consequential damages are recoverable if they are reasonably foreseeable.[88]

Therefore, the Ontario Court of Appeal has determined that the *Messineo* principle is the proper starting point for determining the appropriate measure of damages. Some of the English cases[89] provide that other measures of damages may be appropriate where the diminution in value approach does not satisfactorily compensate the plaintiff for his losses. In those cases the nature of the property was such that it was difficult to restore the plaintiff to the pre-purchase diminution in value position. In those circumstances, the cost of reparation or removal of the defect on title was the more appropriate quantification of damages. However, in the absence of such special circumstances, the *Messineo* principle will govern.

---

[87] *Supra*, note 75.

[88] *Ibid.*, at 25.

[89] *County Personnel (Employment Agency) Ltd. v. Alan R. Pulver & Co. (a firm)*, [1987] 1 All E.R. 289 at 298 (C.A.); *Hayes v. James &Charles Dodd (a firm)*, [1990] All E.R. 815 at 819 (C.A.).

(5) Summary of Approaches to "Quantification" of Value

The quantification of damages focuses on the different methods of determining the actual amount of damages that will adequately compensate plaintiffs for the loss in value of their property. Based upon the discussion above and considering the plaintiff's fixity of intention, reasonable actions, and the nature of the property, the methods of quantifying the diminution in value to the plaintiff can be summarized into four basic principles where there is damage to either real property or a chattel.[90]

First, if the cost of repair or replacement is equivalent to the diminution market value of the property then there is no problem because the quantum of damages will be the same under either method of quantification. In these situations, the cost of repair or replacement will provide a fair assessment of the quantum of damage suffered by the plaintiff.

Second, if the cost of repair or replacement is less than the diminished market value of the property, then damages should be quantified by cost. This approach, if an allowance for any proved accelerated depreciation in the value of the property is permitted to the plaintiff, will return the plaintiff not only to the same financial position but also effects the restoration of the plaintiff's damaged property. This approach, where it is possible to adopt it, best puts the plaintiff into his pre-loss position.

Thirdly, where the cost of repair or replacement is more than the diminished market value of the property, but a reasonable person in the plaintiff's circumstances would incur the cost given the nature of the property and if the plaintiff can prove that he or she will or has incurred the cost, damages will be quantified by the cost of repair or replacement of the property. Sufficient proof of fixity of intent may be considered in light of the actions taken by the plaintiff or if the plaintiff is bound by some other duty, such as a statutory duty, to a third party to make the repairs. The plaintiff's delay in replacing or repairing the property, however, may be construed as evidence of his lack of intent to actually carry out the repairs to or the replacement of the property.

Finally, if the cost of repair or restoration is greater than the diminished market value of the property and if a reasonable person in the plaintiff's circumstances would *not* incur the cost, then damages will be quantified by the diminution in market value of the property. The fact that the plaintiff may have actually incurred or intended to incur the cost will not be relevant.

From the discussion of the leading cases involving recovery of pecuniary damages for property losses, one observation is very much apparent:

---

[90] Dore and Veitch, "Guarding Against Over-Compensation When Measuring Damages by the Cost of Repair, Replacement or Performance: The Role of Undertakings" (1994), 23 Can. Bus. L.J. 432, at 438.

all too often the parties have not met the burden or onus of proving their damages. Where a party wishes to be excluded from the usual "diminution in market value" quantification of damages, meeting the burden of proving the sufficient fixity of intention, the particular nature of the property and the reasonableness in claiming a method of quantification other than diminution in market value is critical to the success of the action. The courts are not willing to go beyond the traditional approach of diminution in market value without feeling secure that the plaintiff will indeed be more properly compensated if another method of quantification of damages is utilized. A careful practitioner, therefore, on first being retained by the claimant should concentrate not only on the issue of liability but, as well, and equally as important, on the issue of how damages will be claimed, quantified, and proven, all of which leads to a discussion on proving the damages.

4. *Proving the Damages: The Expert*

The general rule regarding proof of damages was stated by Mr. Justice Gale in *T.T.C. v. Aqua Taxi Ltd.*:

> The general rule is that the plaintiff must prove sufficient facts to enable the Court to calculate the loss with reasonable certainty. To this must be added the qualification that, where damages are, by their intrinsic nature, incapable of assessment with any degree of certainty, the plaintiff must prove the facts and the Court will approximate a sum, even although it may be little better than a guess.[91]

If the court has to venture a guess at the damages suffered by the plaintiff, it is very likely that the court will retreat to the more conservative estimate of damages based on the lesser of restoration and diminution in market value of the property. The result could be that the client is seriously under-compensated. Counsel must, therefore, demonstrate some ingenuity.

Expert evidence from economists, accountants, business valuators, land appraisers, antique experts, art experts and the like is becoming more common. A party, whether pursuing a claim or defending against a claim, must adduce expert evidence otherwise his or her position will be seriously prejudiced. Production of this kind of evidence allows the court to more accurately compensate plaintiffs for their true losses.

However, expert evidence must be approached with caution. First of

---

[91] [1957] O.W.N. 65, 75 C.R.T.C. 42, 6 D.L.R. (2d) 721, at 745 (Ont. H.C.).

all, economic factors must be considered, specifically, the cost of the expert. Secondly, the assumptions made by the experts must be understood and tested to see if they are reasonable assumptions. Thirdly, make sure that you retain a properly qualified expert. A careful lawyer will discuss the expert's conclusions with at least one legal colleague and, if possible, another qualified expert.

There are at least three different approaches that generally may be used to calculate the diminution in value, where the issue is the diminished value of real property: the comparable sales approach, income capitalization approach and cost approach.[92] The choice of approach depends upon the nature of the property that has been damaged.

In cases involving residential property, the comparable sales approach to the assessment of market value will usually be used. This approach is based upon comparing data from recent sales of similarly situated properties and adjusting the value for any differences between the properties (*i.e.*, the number of bedrooms, square footage, fireplaces, etc.) This is by no means an exact science; assumptions based upon the factors that impact upon the market value and the nature of the comparables will have an impact upon the accuracy of this approach. It is no surprise that there are often widely varying opinions between land appraisers as to the value of the same property.

If the property is an income producing property, the value of the property can usually be best ascertained by utilizing the income capitalization approach to valuation. Essentially, the income approach values the present value of net future income streams from the property. This approach is somewhat more scientific given that a mathematical formula is used to determine the value. However, like any formula, it is only as accurate as the data which is plugged into it. Variables such as the discount rate and estimates of future income streams can vary significantly. A small difference in the estimation of the capitalization rate can result in a serious under, or over-valuation of the property.

In some circumstances, it may be entirely inappropriate to value the property loss on either a comparable market or income basis. This type of situation will arise where the property is unique or some other inherent value factor is at work, such as valuing a heritage property. In that type of case the approach used by land evaluators is known as the cost or replacement value approach. This involves determining what it would cost to rebuild the building or repair the land in order to put the property back into the state it would have been but for the damage. Such an approach

---

[92] Brueggeman and Fisher, *Real Estate Investment and Finance*, 9th ed. (Boston: Richard D. Irwin Inc., 1993); see also *Domowicz v. Orsa Investments Ltd.* (1994), 20 O.R. (3d) 722 at 728-29, 43 R.P.R. (2d) 300 (Gen. Div.).

would probably be utilized if, for example, the Parliament buildings were damaged.

Where chattels are damaged it is very often easier to determine their value in terms of cost, replacement or market value because there it is usually a more fluid market for chattels. Unlike real property, chattels have less of a uniqueness to them. In addition, where a party intends to replace a chattel, it is much more feasible to purchase the same or a very similar chattel. But this cannot easily be done in the real property market where the properties are rarely identical and where the cost of replacement is often prohibitive.

While the methods of valuation discussed above are helpful in assessing the appropriate damages to be awarded, the most accurate method of assessment of damages occurs where there is an actual arm's length sale of the property at its diminished value and the pre-accident value is known or the costs of restoration have actually been incurred by the plaintiff so that the court knows with certainty exactly what damage the plaintiff has suffered.

5. *Limits on Recovery for Damages*

While, as aforesaid, the measure of damages is the diminution in value, plaintiffs may still find themselves limited in their recovery of those damages. The advocate must deal with issues of remoteness, mitigation and betterment in order to effectively ensure that the client obtains damages that are representative of the actual loss suffered.

(1) Remoteness of Damages

It is quite obvious that it would be practically impossible and economically undesirable for society to burden the tortfeasor with every consequence regardless of whether such consequences were foreseeable. In addressing the issue of remoteness, Lord Wright in *Liesbosch* said that:

> The law cannot take account of everything that follows a wrongful act; it regards some subsequent matters as outside the scope of its selection, because "it were infinite for the law to judge the cause of causes," or consequences of consequences . . . In the varied web of affairs, the law must abstract some consequences as relevant, not perhaps on grounds of pure logic but simply for practical reasons.[93]

---

[93] *Owners of the Dredger Liesbosch v. Owners of Steamship Edison*, [1933] A.C. 449 (H.L.), at 460.

A body of law has developed which allows recovery for those losses which are not too remote and unforeseeable. To recover the pecuniary damages suffered as a result of a property loss, the plaintiff must show that those losses were not too remote to be recovered. The test for determining whether damages are too remote is generally the same in both contract and tort.[94] However, there are significant differences, particularly in the practical extension of recovery for pecuniary damages consequential on property losses this is mostly related to the nature of the relationship between the parties and what is foreseeable as a result of that relationship.

(a) Remoteness Principles in Tort

The application of the test for determining if losses are too remote to recover under tort principles is far from simple. Mr. Justice Linden notes that confusion exists when concepts such as cause-in-fact and the proximate cause or remoteness issues are considered and that it is difficult to divorce these two concepts. He suggests that these issues should be viewed separately as the latter issue, proximate cause or remoteness, involves a more complicated legal and public policy analysis. He writes that remoteness:

> . . . has become one of the most complex areas of tort law. Many verbal formulae, such as proximate cause, remoteness, natural and probable consequences, risk, duty and foresight, have been advanced at various times to assist the court to distinguish between the consequences which will produce liability and those that will not.[95]

Over the years, directness,[96] reasonably foreseeable consequences,[97] and foreseeability of the possibility of damage[98] have been expressed by the courts as defining which losses were compensable and which losses were not compensable because they were too remote. The current approach

---

[94] *Asamera Oil Corp. v. Sea Oil & General Corp.*, [1979] 1 S.C.R. 633, [1978] 6 W.W.R. 301, 5 B.L.R. 225, 89 D.L.R. (3d) 1 at 30, 23 N.R. 181.

[95] Linden, *Canadian Tort Law*, 5th ed. (Toronto: Butterworths, 1993), at 306.

[96] *Re Polemis and Furness, Withy & Co. Ltd.*, [1921] 3 K.B. 560.

[97] *The Wagon Mound (No. 1)*, [1961] A.C. 388 (P.C.), qualified by *Hughes v. Lord Advocate*, [1963] A.C. 837 in which the House of Lords found that the foreseeability of the exact manner of occurrence of the accident was not required, so long as the general type of consequences that occur was foreseeable.

[98] *The Wagon Mound (No.2)*, [1967] 1 A.C. 617 (P.C.), in which the Privy Council found that liability could be imposed if there was foreseeability of a possibility or a real risk of damage and that the damage did not have to be reasonably foreseeable.

adopted by the courts for defining losses that are too remote, not surprisingly, is a melange of the factors referred to above which focuses more on a, with respect, palm tree justice or Chancellor's foot dispensation of fairness approach as opposed to solid, defined and workable principles. The test is couched in legal language but is perhaps more adeptly described by Mr. Justice Andrews in *Palsgraf v. Long Island Railroad*[99] as the adoption of an expedient and practical approach:

> . . . because of convenience, of public policy, of a rough sense of justice, the law arbitrarily declines to trace a series of events beyond a certain point. This is not logic, it is practical politics.[100]

It is important to realize that the concept of foreseeability is the foreseeability of the reasonable person in the same circumstances at the time of the tortious conduct. In contrast, the relevant time for foreseeability in contract law damages for breach is the foreseeability of the parties at the time the contract was entered into. The advantage of a tort claim then, is the possibility that the defendant has gained additional knowledge of the circumstances of the plaintiff which would extend the foreseeability of the consequences of his acts. Unfortunately all too often the tortfeasor is unknown to the plaintiff, therefore no real advantage is gained.

(b) *Remoteness Principles in Contract*

Strangely enough, the development of the law surrounding remoteness as a basis for limiting recovery in cases of breach of contract has been far less confusing. Perhaps the more defined and principled approach to remoteness in contract law is the result of the fact that the parties usually address their minds to specific issues such as loss, allocate certain risks prior to breach and, by the nature of the contract itself, limit what breaches are foreseeable. Under a contract, there is only so much that can go wrong unlike a tort claim where the unexpected is par for the course.

As all lawyers and judges know, the basic rule governing recoverability and remoteness in contract was established in 1854 by the House of Lords in *Hadley v. Baxendale*[101] and was followed in *Victoria Laundry (Windsor) Ltd. v. Newman Industries*[102] where Lord Asquith wrote:

---

[99] 162 N.E. 99 (1928).
[100] *Ibid.*,at 104.
[101] (1854), 9 Exch. 341 (H.L.).
[102] [1949] 1 All E.R. 997.

In cases of breach of contract the aggrieved party is only entitled to recover such part of the loss actually resulting as was at the time reasonably foreseeable as liable to result from the breach. What was at the time reasonably foreseeable depends on the knowledge then possessed by the parties, or at all events, by the party who later commits the breach. For this purpose, knowledge "possessed" is of two kinds — one imputed, the other actual. Everyone, as a reasonable person, is taken to know the ordinary course of things" and consequently what loss is liable to result from a breach of that ordinary course . . . there may have to be added in a particular case knowledge which he actually possesses of special circumstances outside the "ordinary course of things" of such a kind that a breach in those special circumstances would be liable to cause more loss. Such a case attracts the operation of the "second rule" so as to make additional loss also recoverable. In order to make the contract-breaker liable under either rule it is not necessary that he should actually have asked himself what loss is liable to result from a breach . . . It suffices that, if he had considered the question, he would as a reasonable man have concluded that the loss in question was liable to result . . .[103]

Therefore where the defendant has actual knowledge of some special circumstances of the plaintiff the defendant will be held liable for damages that ordinarily may have been too remote.[104] Imputed knowledge will exist where a reasonable person would have anticipated the loss.[105] Factors to consider in determining the extent of knowledge to be imputed to the parties include the identity of the plaintiff and defendant, their expertise, the subject-matter of the contract, and the quantum of the consideration.[106] These factors will assist the court in determining what was within the reasonable contemplation of the parties at the time the contract was entered into.[107]

Despite the different approaches by the courts to remoteness in contract and tort, it now appears that the actual principles governing the measure of the damages is to be the same whether the action is in contract or in tort. In *Parsons (Livestock) Ltd. v. Uttley Ingham & Co. Ltd.*,[108] Lord Scarman wrote that:

> . . . in a factual situation where all have the same actual or imputed knowledge and the contract contains no term limiting the damages for breach, the amount of damages recoverable does not depend upon whether, as a matter

---

[103] *Ibid.*, at 1002-03.

[104] *Cornwall Gravel Co. v. Purolator Courier Ltd.*, [1980] 2 S.C.R. 118.

[105] *Koufos v. C. Czarnikow Ltd.*, [1969] 1 A.C. (H.L.).

[106] Pitch and Snyder, *Damages for Breach of Contract*, 2nd ed. (Toronto: Carswell, 1989), at 7-13 to 7-21.

[107] *H. Parsons (Livestock) v. Uttley Ingham & Co.*, [1978] Q.B. 791, [1977] 2 Lloyd's Rep. 522 (C.A.).

[108] *Ibid.*

of legal classification, the plaintiffs' cause of action is breach of contract or tort.[109]

The Supreme Court of Canada in *Asamera Oil Corp. v. Sea Oil & General Corp.*,[110] considered the issue of remoteness in contract and in tort where Mr. Justice Estey wrote that:

> . . . the same principles of remoteness will apply to the claims whether they sound in tort or contract subject only to special knowledge, understanding or relationship of the contracting parties or to any terms express or implied of the contractual arrangement relating to damages recoverable on breach.[111]

This position was reiterated by the Ontario Court of Appeal when considering whether the damages suffered by the plaintiff in *Kienzle*[112] were too remote. The Court of Appeal found that there was not any real difference between the tests of foreseeability in contract or in tort.[113] In both *Kienzle* and *Asamera* the plaintiff could have proceeded in its action on the basis of tort or breach of contract. However, Wilson J.A., in *Kienzle* seemed conscious of the special knowledge and added foreseeability that parties to a contract might have of each other's particular circumstances such as impecuniosity, by the very nature of the contractual relationship. In Wilson's view, in contracts of purchase and sale it was foreseeable that the vendor would be entering into another transaction which would depend upon him obtaining the funds from the sale of the currently owned property.

(c) *The Plaintiff's Impecuniosity*

The general rule is that when a plaintiff fails to mitigate the loss suffered, it is no excuse for the plaintiff to blame that failure on his own impecuniosity. The leading case is an English case, *Owners of the Dredger Liesbosch v. Owners of Steamship Edison*[114] in which a dredger was damaged by the negligence of the defendants. The dredger was involved in a contract of service at the time of its loss. The plaintiffs did not have the funds to purchase a new dredger so they had to rent a larger dredger that was more costly to operate. The House of Lords awarded damages

---

[109] *Ibid.*, at 529 Lloyd's.
[110] *Asamera, supra*, note 94.
[111] *Ibid.*, at 30 D.L.R.
[112] (1981), 35 O.R. (2d) 85, 21 R.P.R. 44, 130 D.L.R. (3d) 272 (C.A.).
[113] (1978), 40 D.L.R. (3d) 418, 23 N.R. 221.
[114] [1933] A.C. 449 (H.L.).

calculated as if the plaintiffs had purchased a new dredger within a reasonable amount of time. No damages were awarded for losses and additional expenses suffered as a result of the plaintiffs' financial position. Lord Wright distinguished between the compensable losses suffered as a result of the loss of the dredger and the actual losses that were suffered by the plaintiffs:

> The respondents' tortious act involved the physical loss of the dredger: that loss must somehow be reduced to terms of money. But the appellant's actual loss in so far as it was due to their impecuniosity arose from that impecuniosity as a separate and concurrent cause, extraneous to and distinct in character from the tort; the impecuniosity was not traceable to the respondents' acts, and in my opinion was outside the legal purview of the consequences of these acts.[115]

The Supreme Court of Canada followed the principle set down in *Liesbosch* in *Dawson v. Helicopter Exploration Co. Ltd.*[116] In *Dawson* the plaintiff had been promised a number of shares for guiding the defendants to certain mining claims. The plaintiff did not receive the shares and did not attempt to replace the shares by purchasing shares offered for sale to him, he claimed for the value of the shares as of the date of trial (the shares had risen in value considerably in the interim). It is this decision which, in the authors' view, has made impecuniosity an issue of mitigation as opposed to remoteness (Lord Wright in *Liesbosch* did not go that far).[117] Mr. Justice Rand writing for the Court in *Dawson v.*

---

[115] *Ibid.*, at 460.

[116] (1958), 12 D.L.R. (2d) 1 (S.C.C.).

[117] Lord Wright differentiated between the effect of the plaintiff's impecuniosity and remoteness and the impact of impecuniosity on mitigation citing Lord Collins in *Clippens Oil Co. v. Edinburgh & District Water Trustees*, [1907] A.C. 291. At 461 of the judgment in *Liesbosch* Lord Wright starting with Lord Collins' statement in *Clippens* wrote:

> " 'It was contended that this implied that the defenders were entitled to measure the damages on the footing that it was the duty of the company to do all that was reasonably possible to mitigate the loss, and that if, through lack of funds, they were unable to incur the necessary expense of such remedial measures the defenders ought not to suffer for it. If this were the true construction to put upon the passage cited, I think there would be force in the observation, for in my opinion the wrongdoer must take his victim *talem qualem*, and if the position of the latter is aggravated because he is without the means of mitigating it, so much the worse for the wrongdoer, who has got to be answerable for the consequences flowing from his tortious act.' But, as I think it is clear that Lord Collins is here dealing not with measure of damage, but with the victim's duty to minimize damage, which is quite a different matter, the dictum is not in point."

Helicopter Exploration Co. Ltd. interpreted the *Liesbosch* principle to apply to mitigation:

> Dawson could have purchased the number of shares promised and had he done so his damages would have been made certain. From the point of view of a purchaser, that is really in the nature of mitigation, and it would be no answer that at the time he was not financially able to buy . . .[118]

The Ontario Court of Appeal considered the effect of the plaintiff's impecuniosity on mitigation in *R.G. McLean Ltd. v. Canadian Vickers Ltd.*,[119] where the plaintiff was supplied with a defective printing press. The defendant unconditionally offered to remove the press and refund the plaintiff's money, but the plaintiff refused:

> The plaintiff's answer to this contention was that it had already spent so much money and had sustained such losses that it could not afford to buy another press to replace the one purchased from the defendant. In my opinion, this argument cannot prevail. The plaintiff could not refuse the unconditional offer made, retain the obviously defective press and "run up the damages" to the prejudice of the defendant. The frailties (if any) of the plaintiff's credit, or its inability to purchase a new press from available assets, cannot be set up to destroy the effect of the defendant's offer.[120]

Essentially, the court found that it was completely unreasonable for the plaintiff to have failed to accept the defendant's offer, an offer which did not restrict the right of the plaintiff to claim for additional damages it had sustained.

Shortly after the decision in *Canadian Vickers Ltd.*, the Ontario Court of Appeal revisited the problem of the impecunious plaintiff in *Freedhoff v. Pomalift Industries Ltd.*[121] In that case the plaintiff, the operator of a ski hill, contracted for the purchase and installation of a ski lift. The defendant defaulted on the contract. As a result the plaintiff suffered a serious loss of revenue in the operation of the ski hill and was unable to keep up the mortgage payments on the property. The bank foreclosed on the mortgage and sold the property. The Court of Appeal found that the defendant was not liable for the damages suffered as a result of the plaintiff's impecuniosity holding that the loss was not within the reasonable contemplation of the parties:

> In the instant case, even if the plaintiff be entitled to be compensated for damages in the amount of loss of revenue, the loss of property through the

---

[118] *Supra*, note 116, at 11.
[119] [1971] 1 O.R. 207 (C.A.).
[120] *Ibid.*, at 215-16.
[121] [1971] 2 O.R. 773 (C.A.).

sale by the Industrial Development Bank because of the plaintiff's failure
to keep the mortgage in good standing, does not entitle him to damages measured by the loss he alleges that he suffered in the sale of the property. It
does not meet the test of foreseeability.[122]

We have always been of the opinion that this result was rather harsh and
that the court, with respect, was a little short sighted in concluding what
was foreseeable.

It is suggested that the approach being taken by the courts is really
one of determining whether a failure to mitigate and increased pecuniary
loss caused by a party's impecuniosity is reasonably foreseeable. This
approach received a favourable response in *Dodd Properties v. Canter-
bury City*[123] in which the defendants were liable for damage to the plaintiffs' building, but the plaintiffs delayed in making repairs because of
financial constraints and that in any event it did not make commercial
sense to for them to have repaired the building any earlier. Donaldson
L.J. wrote:

> As I understand Lord Wright's speech, he took the view that in so far as
> the plaintiffs in fact suffered more than the loss assessed on a market basis,
> the excess loss flowed directly from their lack of means and not from the
> tortious act, or alternatively it was too remote in law. In modern terms, I
> think he would have said that it was not foreseeable.[124]

More recently, the Saskatchewan Court of Appeal in *Kozak v.
Gruza*[125] allowed recovery for damages flowing from the plaintiff's
impecuniosity where, as a result of the tortious conduct of the defendant,
the plaintiff did not have sufficient funds to purchase crop insurance and
an uninsured loss resulted. There the court found that the defendant had
actual knowledge of the plaintiff's circumstances and that the plaintiff's
inability to pay was foreseeable. This was the same approach taken by
Duff C.J.C. in *General Securities Ltd. v. Don Ingram Ltd.*[126]

Denying a plaintiff the right to rely on its impecuniosity as a reason
for its failure to mitigate seems too harsh a rule. However, the cases can
be reconciled if approached on the basis of remoteness. The question is
really whether or not it was reasonably foreseeable that the plaintiff was
impecunious and would suffer additional damages as a result of that
impecuniosity. This will entail an examination of any special relationship

---

[122] *Ibid.*, at 778.
[123] [1980] 1 All E.R. 928 (C.A.).
[124] *Ibid.*, at 941.
[125] (1989), 80 Sask. R. 197, 9 P.P.S.A.C. 221, 63 D.L.R. (4th) 129 at 136 (C.A.).
[126] [1940] 3 D.L.R. 641 at 643 (S.C.C.).

or circumstances of the parties. This appears to be the approach suggested by Wilson J.A. in *Kienzle*.[127]

The courts have practically denied recovery for consequential losses which tended to be based on loss of opportunity or loss of profits, losses which appear to be purely economic in nature, and are traditionally dealt with as being too remote. However, where there is tangible physical property loss for which the plaintiff must be compensated the losses are not too remote to be recovered as they are limited to the value of the property lost. From the perspective of mitigation, the question is whether or not a reasonable person *in the plaintiff's* position could have mitigated.[128] If the mitigation approach is adopted the failure to mitigate due to impecuniosity should not diminish the plaintiff's damages on the basis that the tortfeasor takes his victim as he finds him. It is a question of allocation of risks: whether the innocent plaintiff should bear the risk or whether, as a consequence of his wrongful actions, the defendant should bear the risk.

(2) Mitigation

(a) *The Rule*

The party suffering a loss has a duty to act reasonably in mitigating its damages. This rule was set out in *Westinghouse Electric & Mfg. Co., Ltd. v. Underground Electric R. Co. of London, Ltd.* where Viscount Haldane stated the principle that in an award of damages:

> The fundamental basis is thus compensation for pecuniary loss naturally flowing from the breach; but this first principle is qualified by a

---

[127] *Kienzle , supra*, note 112, at 91-92.

[128] See *Marriott v. Carson's Construction Ltd.* (1983), 56 N.S.R. (2d) 665, 146 D.L.R. (3d) 126, at 137-38 (S.C.) where the trial judge wrote:

> It is my view that a man should not be penalized when he has not created the situation simply because he is already carrying a heavy financial burden, as in this case, which prevented him from obtaining additional funds to carry out total repairs. ... The water damage could clearly be anticipated by the defendant and, from the evidence, he sat back and did nothing except give verable assurance that the damages would be repaired...
>
> . . . .
>
> Taking all of the factors into consideration I find that it is unreasonable for the plaintiff to have made full repairs on his own, and that it was reasonable for him to have expected the defendant to either make the repairs or place the plaintiff in funds to do the repairs himself.

second, which imposes on a plaintiff the duty of taking all reasonable steps to mitigate the loss consequent on the breach, and debars him from claiming any part of the damage which is due to his neglect to take such steps. In the words of James L.J. in *Dunkirk Colliery Co. v. Lever* (1898), 9 Ch. D. 20, at p. 25, "The person who has broken the contract is not to be exposed to additional cost by reason of the plaintiffs not doing what they ought to have done as reasonable men, and the plaintiffs not being under any obligation to do anything otherwise than in the ordinary course of business."

As James L.J. indicates, this second principle does not impose on the plaintiff an obligation to take any step which a reasonable and prudent man would not ordinarily take in the course of his business. But when in the course of his business he has taken action arising out of the transaction, which action has diminished his loss, the effect in actual diminution of the loss he has suffered may be taken into account even though there was no duty on him to act.[129]

In Canada this rule was adopted by the Supreme Court of Canada in *Red Deer College v. Michaels*[130] and followed in *Asamera*[131] where Mr. Justice Estey wrote:

Damages which could have been avoided by the taking of reasonable steps in all the circumstances should not and, indeed, in the interests of commercial enterprise, must not be thrown onto the shoulders of a defendant by an arbitrary although nearly universal rule for the recovery of damages on breach of the contract for redelivery of property.[132]

From the perspective of a plaintiff who has suffered a property loss and now claims pecuniary damages for that loss there is a duty to attempt to take all the steps that a reasonable person in the plaintiff's position would take to minimize the pecuniary damages flowing from the loss. In other words, the plaintiff must arrive in court with "clean hands" having done all that was reasonable to mitigate his damages.[133] However, the plaintiff need only act reasonably and there is no obligation to take extraordinary measures to mitigate.

In *Redpath Industries Ltd. v. The "Cisco"*,[134] the Federal Court of Appeal considered a situation where the defendant shipper had damaged

---

[129] [1912] A.C. 673 at 689.

[130] [1976] 2 S.C.R. 324 at 330-31 *per* Laskin C.J.C.

[131] [1979] 1 S.C.R. 633, [1978] 6 W.W.R. 301, 5 B.L.R. 225, 89 D.L.R. (3d) 1, 23 N.R. 181.

[132] *Ibid.*, at 20 D.L.R.

[133] *Redpath Industries Ltd. v. "Cisco" (The)*, [1994] 2 F.C. 279, 70 F.T.R. 136*n*, 110 D.L.R. (4th) 583 at 588, 163 N.R. 161; leave to appeal to S.C.C. refused 179 N.R. 319*n*.

[134] *Ibid.*

raw sugar in transport by allowing it to get wet. The plaintiff claimed the full difference between the arrival sound market value of the sugar to be refined for human consumption and the arrival damaged market value of the sugar, the evidence showing that it was suitable only for animal consumption. The plaintiff, however, took an extraordinary risk in expending $50,000 to modify its refining processes in order to mix the damaged sugar with undamaged sugar in a fashion that enabled the damaged sugar to be marketed as if it had arrived undamaged. Relying on *Westinghouse*,[135] Létourneau J.A. found that the plaintiff, even if it went beyond what a reasonable plaintiff would have done to mitigate, is entitled to be compensated only for its actual losses. Accordingly, the plaintiff was entitled to receive only the $50,000 it had expended in its effort to mitigate.

The plaintiff is *prima facie* assumed to have mitigated his losses; the onus of proving that the plaintiff failed to mitigate his losses rests upon the defendant.[136] Laskin C.J.C. wrote:

> If it is the defendant's position that the plaintiff could reasonably have avoided some part of the loss claimed, it is for the defendant to carry the burden of that issue, subject to the defendant being content to allow the matter to be disposed of on the trial judge's assessment of the plaintiff's evidence on avoidable consequences.[137]

Accordingly, "mitigation" should be pleaded.

(b) *Exception to the Rule: Specific Performance*

The major exception to the general duty to mitigate is if the plaintiff is seeking specific performance. The rationale, of course, is that it is unreasonable to mitigate because there is no substitute for the property as a result of some unique characteristic.[138] These considerations usually arise from breach of contract in the context of conveyance of property. Where the issue is recovery for damage to property or repair of property it is difficult to see how specific performance can be an excuse for a failure to mitigate. In such cases, the loss is purely pecuniary and, as a result of inflation, the costs of repair and effect on the value of the damaged property is likely to increase in magnitude, thus increasing the liability

---

[135] *Supra*, note 129.
[136] *Red Deer College v. Michaels*, [1976] 2 S.C.R. 324 at 331; *100 Main Street Ltd. v. W.B. Sullivan Construction Ltd.* (1978), 88 D.L.R. (3d) 1 at 23 (C.A.) *per* Morden J.A.
[137] *Red Deer College v. Michaels, ibid.*, at 331.
[138] See *Johnson v. Agnew*, [1979] 1 All E.R. 883 (H.L.).

of the defendant. In that type of situation, it is suggested that a claim for specific performance, whether on the basis of completion of a contract or for repairs will not suffice to excuse the plaintiff's failure to mitigate.

Whether or not specific performance will excuse a failure to mitigate will depend on the reasonableness of continuing with a claim for specific performance. In *Asamera*, Mr. Justice Estey discussed the court's concern for the reasonableness of the actions of the plaintiff:

> On principle it is clear that a plaintiff may not merely by instituting proceedings in which a request is made for specific performance and/or damages thereby shield himself and block the Court from taking into account the accumulation of losses which the plaintiff by acting with reasonable promptness in processing his claim, could have avoided. Similarly, the bare institution of judicial process in circumstances where a reasonable response by the injured plaintiff would include mitigative replacement of property, will not entitle the plaintiff to the relief which would be achieved by such replacement purchase and prompt prosecution of the claim. Before a plaintiff can rely on a claim for specific performance so as to insulate himself from the consequences of failing to procure alternate property in mitigation of his losses, some fair, real and substantial justification for his claim to performance must be found. Otherwise its effect will be to cast upon the defendant all the risk of aggravated loss by reason of delay in bringing the issue to trial.[139]

In order to determine whether the plaintiff's claim for specific performance is reasonable the circumstances surrounding the claim will have to be considered. Circumstances such as the uniqueness and nature of the property (if conveyance is an issue);[140] whether there is a substantial risk that discontinuance of a claim for specific performance would aggravate the plaintiff's losses; or whether the parties are in fact in a position to grant specific performance;[141] are all factors which must be considered in assessing the reasonableness of pressing a claim for specific performance.[142]

The recent Ontario case of *Domowicz v. Orsa Investments Ltd.*[143] considered a claim for specific performance arising from the breach of

---

[139] *Asamera, supra,* note 131, at 26 D.L.R.

[140] *Domowicz v. Orsa Investments Ltd.* (1994), 20 O.R. (3d) 722, 43 R.P.R. (2d) 300 (Gen. Div.) *per* Adams J. The issue here was whether an investment property that was not conveyed could be the subject of specific performance. The market varied substantially during the period between the breach and the trial.

[141] See *A.V.G. Management Science Ltd. v. Barwell Developments Ltd.* (1978), 92 D.L.R. (3d) 1 (S.C.C.), *per* Laskin J.; *Ansdell v. Crowther* (1984), 55 B.C.L.R. 216, 11 D.L.R. (4th) 614 (C.A.).

[142] *Asamera, supra,* note 131, at 26 D.L.R.

[143] *Supra,* note 140.

an agreement of purchase and sale of an apartment building which the plaintiff intended to hold as an investment property. Mr. Justice Adams wrote "it is only where a plaintiff reasonably seeks specific performance that it will be permitted to postpone mitigation until trial."[144] Mr. Justice Adams goes on to consider the circumstances in which specific performance will be reasonably sought, thus excusing a failure to mitigate:

> It is clearly reasonable in some circumstances for a plaintiff to await a determination on an action for specific performance before taking steps to mitigate its losses. For example, in the case of a purchase of a home where the property is unique, a plaintiff purchaser would not normally be required to purchase another home while awaiting a determination on the specific performance issue. Thus, no duty to mitigate would arise at the time of breach in such a case.[145]

In determining the appropriateness of mitigation then, the intentions, purposes and nature of the transaction are very relevant to determining whether a plaintiff has acted reasonably in either mitigating or failing to mitigate by claiming specific performance.

(3) Betterment: Over compensation the Plaintiff

As discussed above, the courts are loathe to award damages which have the effect of over-compensating the plaintiff. To address this concern the courts developed the concept of betterment or allowance for depreciation.[146] Betterment is defined by Professor Berryman as:

> . . . a measure of the extent to which a plaintiff has been placed in a position more advantageous than the position enjoyed by the plaintiff, before the breach of contract or commission of the tortious wrong, in respect of an injury to the plaintiff's property.[147]

---

[144] *Ibid.*, at 733; see also *Garbens v. Khayami* (1994) , 17 O.R. (3d) 162, 36 R.P.R. (2d) 244 (Gen. Div.).

[145] *Ibid.*, at 733-34.

[146] In *Kinnard v. C.L. Martin & Co. Ltd.* (1969), 7 D.L.R. (3d) 139 (Ont. C.A.), Laskin J.A. writing for the court, allowed a deduction in damages. The plaintiffs replaced their old barn following a fire with a new more efficient structure. The court awarded a 40 per cent reduction in damages as that was the benefit deemed to have been gained by the plaintiffs.

[147] Berryman, "Betterment Before Canadian Common Law Courts" (1993), 72 Can. Bar Rev. 54 at 54.

The concept of betterment arises when the damages awarded are quantified based on the cost of restoration or replacement. Therefore, betterment may occur only in a situation where the plaintiff receives the value of a new item in place of a used or older item. In effect the defendant pays for a new item with a longer life than the former item which results in a net benefit accruing to the plaintiff since the plaintiff will not have to replace the item as soon as it otherwise would have.

The English decision in *Harbutt's "Plasticine" Ltd. v. Wayne Tank & Pump Co. Ltd.*[148] is the starting point for a discussion on betterment. In that case the defendant's negligence caused the destruction of the plaintiffs' factory. The plaintiffs built a new factory that was different in design from the original factory (the new factory had two floors as opposed to the old factory with five floors) and was more expensive than replacing the original factory. The defendants were held liable for the cost of building the new factory. What complicated the matter was that the plaintiffs could not restore the old factory as a result of new requirements of the planning authorities. In not reducing the damages on account of betterment, Lord Denning wrote:

> The destruction of a building is different from the destruction of a chattel. If a second-hand car is destroyed, the owner only gets its value; because he can go into the market and get another second-hand car to replace it. He cannot charge the other party with the cost of replacing it with a new car. But when this mill was destroyed, the plasticine company had no choice. They were bound to replace it as soon as they could, not only to keep their business going, but also to mitigate the loss of profit (for which they would be able to charge the defendants). They replaced it the only possible way, without adding any extras. I think they should be allowed the cost of replacement. True it is that they get new for old; but I do not think the wrongdoer can diminish the claim on that account. If they had added extra accommodation or made extra improvements, they would have to give credit. But that is not this case.[149]

Lord Denning seems to suggest that so long as there is no unreasonable advantage to the plaintiff as a result of restoring the factory, the plaintiff should not be obliged to suffer the additional expenses incurred as a result of the destruction of the factory and changes by the planning authorities requiring the factory to be rebuilt in a different fashion. This could place the plaintiff at a disadvantage as the plaintiff would not have incurred the added expenses but for the tortious conduct of the defen-

---

[148] [1970] 1 Q.B. 447 (C.A.).
[149] *Ibid.*, at 468, per Lord Denning M.R.

dant.[150] The Federal Court of Appeal followed the decision in *Harbutt's "Plasticine"* in *The Ship "Dumurra" v. Maritime Telegraph & Telephone Co. Ltd.*,[151] where the respondent was awarded the replacement value of two submarine cables that where damaged by the appellant's ship without a deduction for betterment.

The British Columbia Court of Appeal in *Jens v. Mannix Co. Ltd.*[152] considered the loss of a house as a result of a break in the defendant's pipeline on property that was utilized in part for an antique car museum. The property was zoned commercial and there was evidence that the owner was not always in residence. The court found that the plaintiff was entitled to the replacement cost of the house at the time of the loss, but given the nature of the property an allowance for depreciation was permitted.[153]

Today, the leading case is generally thought to be the decision of the Ontario Court of Appeal in *James St. Hardware & Furniture Co. v. Spizziri*,[154] a case in which the plaintiff's building was severely damaged when a welder in the defendant's employ caused a fire. The damaged part of the building was rebuilt in a superior, larger form as exact restoration of the building had been prohibited by the building code.[155] The court wrote that:

> Quite simply, if a plaintiff, who is entitled to be compensated on the basis of the cost of replacement, is obliged to submit to a deduction from that

---

[150] *Harbutt's "Plasticine"* judgment of Lord Cross, *ibid.*, at 476:
"It is not in practice possible to rebuild and re-equip a factory with old and worn materials and plant corresponding to what was there before, and such benefit as the plaintiffs may get by having a new building and new plant in place of an old building and old plant is something in respect of which the defendants are not, as I see it, entitled to any allowance. I can well understand that if the plaintiffs in rebuilding the factory with a different and more convenient lay-out had spent more money than they would have spent had they rebuilt it according to the old plant, the defendants would have been entitled to claim that the excess should be deducted in calculating the damages. But the defendant's did not call any evidence to make out a case of betterment on these lines and we were told that in fact the planning authorities would not have allowed the factory to be rebuilt on the old lines."

[151] (1977), 75 D.L.R. (3d) 766 at 768 (F.C.A.).

[152] [1986] 5 W.W.R. 563, 30 D.L.R. (4th) 260 (B.C.C.A.).

[153] *Ibid.*, at 263, *per* Hinkson J.A.:
"Rather it seems to me that, having regard to the nature of this property and to the type of loss that has occurred, that the usual principle should be applied and that depreciation should be taken into account and ought to have been taken into account by the learned trial judge."

[154] (1987), 24 O.A.C. 42, 62 O.R. (2d) 385, 43 C.C.L.T. 9.

[155] For a good analysis of this case see Bridge, "Damages — Damage to Property — Betterment — Calculation of Damages — Interest on Sums Expended: *James Street Hardware & Furniture Co. Ltd. v. Spizziri*" (1989), 68 Can. Bar Rev. 155.

compensation for incidental and unavoidable enhancement, he or she will not be fully compensated for the loss suffered. The plaintiff will be obliged, if the difference is paid for out of his or her own pocket, whether borrowed or already possessed, to submit to "some loss or burden", to quote from Dr. Lushington. Widgery L.J. in *Harbutt's "Plasticine"* called it "forcing the plaintiffs to invest their money in the modernising of their plant which might be highly inconvenient for them."

These considerations, however, do not necessarily mean that in cases of this kind the plaintiff is entitled to damages which include the element of betterment. As Waddams suggests, the answer lies in compensating the plaintiff for the loss imposed upon him or her in being forced to spend money he or she would not otherwise have spent — at least as early as was required by the damages occasioned to him by the tort. In general terms, this would be the cost (if he has to borrow) or value (if he already has the money) of the money equivalent of the betterment over a particular period of time.[156]

In calculating an allowance for betterment, the defendant is entitled to an allowance for the value of the advantaged gained by the plaintiff by the replacement of new for old, but from that allowance must be deducted the plaintiff's cost of making an unexpected expenditure forcing him to borrow money (in which case the allowance should be the cost of borrowing) or by the opportunity cost to the plaintiff of not being able to invest his money elsewhere. Both the cost of borrowing and the lost opportunity costs should be in the form of a lump-sum deduction calculated on the present value of the future costs; to award the actual cost of borrowing or opportunity cost would fail to recognize the benefit to the plaintiff of being able to invest that award.[157]

The onus of proving the value of an alleged improvement or betterment conferred on the plaintiff rests upon the defendant and, again, we caution that this defence should be pleaded. In *James St. Hardware*,[158] the Court of Appeal reversed the trial judge's allowance for betterment on the basis that the defendant had not produced satisfactory evidence of any betterment, and the defendant's expert was unable to show the effects of the restoration of the damaged part of the building on the value of the building as a whole.[159] However, where the plaintiff claims a loss

---

[156] *James St. Hardware, supra*, note 154, at 404 O.R.

[157] *Upper Lakes Shipping Ltd. v. St. Lawrence Cement Inc.* (1992), 89 D.L.R. (4th) 722 at 724 (Ont. C.A.). In this case the defendant had negligently damaged a three-year-old conveyor belt which had to be replaced with a new one with a life span of 15 years. The plaintiff was awarded the value of a conveyor belt with a 12-year life span, since the additional three years would represent a betterment.

[158] *Supra*, note 154.

[159] *Ibid.*, at 405 O.R.

as a result of being required to make an unexpected expenditure, the plaintiff bears the onus of proving that loss.[160]

The Court of Appeal in *James St. Hardware* left open the question of whether a deduction for betterment was always appropriate:

> . . . each case turns on its own facts and that the process of assessing damages should be a practical one designed to do justice between the parties. The process should not be unnecessarily complicated or rule ridden. The rules applied should be responsive to the particular facts of the case. For example, in some cases, perhaps many, the repair or replacement of property (mere substituting of new for old) may well not involve any increase in the value of the property as a whole.[161]

In *Nan v. Black Pine Mfg. Ltd.*,[162] the British Columbia Court of Appeal considered whether an award for betterment should be granted where the defendants destroyed the plaintiff's home and the cost of restoration was the claimed quantum of damages. The court declined to disturb the trial judge's finding that there was insufficient evidence to make an award for betterment:

> In reaching her conclusion the learned trial judge refused to assume as a matter of course that simply by getting a new house for an old one Mr. Nan had enjoyed some element of "betterment", which had to be deducted from the damages award in order to prevent over-compensation. The learned trial judge did not have before her any direct evidence of "betterment". Even accepting the appraiser's report (the weight of which was clearly suspect) and assuming that the original home and land were worth $47,000 at the time of the fire, there was no evidence to show that the new replacement home had any greater market value.[163]

The decision in *Nan v. Black Pine Mfg. Ltd.* suggests that even where the plaintiff has received new for old, there may not be any real tangible financial advantage to the plaintiff and thus no award for betterment. The issue is somewhat blurred, however, by the fact that the British Columbia Court of Appeal also had to consider whether the appropriate "measure" of damages was the diminution in market value or the cost of restoration. The defendants relied on the fact that simply because the cost of restoration was greater than the diminution in market value there must have been some betterment to the plaintiff. Clearly, then, the defendant must show actual proof of some advantage to the plaintiff; the fact that

---

[160] *Ibid.*
[161] *Ibid.*, at 404 O.R.
[162] [1991] 5 W.W.R. 172, 55 B.C.L.R. (2d) 241, 80 D.L.R. (4th) 153 (C.A.).
[163] *Ibid.*, at 155 D.L.R.

the plaintiff receives new for old alone will not be sufficient for the courts to assume that the plaintiff has gained some advantage.

(4) The Date for Assessing the Plaintiff's Damages

The appropriate date for the assessment of damages is part in parcel of a consideration of the issues of remoteness, impecuniosity and mitigation. The traditional rule was that damages were to be assessed as of the date the damage or loss was suffered by the plaintiff.[164] This was thought to be desirable in order to ensure finality of the claim for damages and to provide for an objective and specific date for the assessment of damages.[165] The exception to this general rule was in a case where a claim for specific performance was abandoned at trial in favour of damages in which instance damages would be assessed as of the date of trial. Both of these rules are extreme in the sense that neither reflects the true loss suffered by the plaintiff.

If damages are awarded as of the date the loss is actually incurred, the plaintiff may be seriously under-compensated particularly in cases involving a loss of property that the plaintiff wishes to replace. Prices may increase before the plaintiff has a reasonable opportunity to obtain a substitute to replace his loss. This problem can be more acute given the nature of the particular property, for example if real estate is involved or if "collectible" items are involved, it depends on the market for such items and how obtainable those items are in the market place.

On the other hand, if damages are assessed as of the date of the trial, the plaintiff's behaviour may not favour the economical mitigation of his loss and instead the plaintiff is encouraged to allow the damages to accumulate at the expense of the defendant.[166]

In *Dodd Properties* Lord Denning's approach to assessment of damages as of the date of breach was said to be no longer good law. Megaw L.J. cited Cantley J.[167]:

". . . the nature and circumstances of the damage may be such that it would be imprudent and possibly wasteful to begin the work before waiting longer to ensure that no further damage is going to develop from the same cause . . . I would put it this way. The appropriate damages are the cost of repairs at the time when it was reasonable to begin repairs."[168]

---

[164] *Phillips v. Ward*, [1980] 1 W.L.R. 433, *per* Denning L.J.
[165] Waddams, "The Date for Assessment of Damages" (1981), 97 L.Q. Rev. 445.
[166] *Ibid.*, at 457.
[167] [1979] 2 All E.R. 118 at 126.
[168] [1980] 1 All E.R. 928 at 932-33.

The proper approach to assessing damages depends upon the reasonable intentions of the parties. If the plaintiff does not have the intention, or if it is unreasonable to replace or restore the lost property, then damages ought to be assessed as of the date the damage was suffered. If however, the plaintiff has the intention, and it is reasonable to replace or restore the damaged property then damages should be assessed at the earliest date the plaintiff could reasonably have replaced or restored the damaged property. In determining what date was the appropriate date for reasonably replacing or restoring the property the court must objectively consider the plaintiff's circumstances and the nature of the property.

This "reasonableness" approach properly co-exists with the principle of mitigation and provides a uniform yet flexible approach to assessing damages. It is the approach that appears to have been adopted by the Supreme Court of Canada in *Asamera*[169] where the court concluded that the damages should be assessed at the date at which the plaintiff could reasonably have been expected to mitigate his losses by purchasing replacement shares which is the date that the plaintiff's damages "crystallized".[170] In reference to the "crystallization" principle Professor Waddams writes:

> The principle of crystallisation does not demand rigid adherence to assessment at the date of the wrong. The crystallisation occurs when the plaintiff could, acting reasonably in all the circumstances, purchase substitute performance. While the plaintiff can reasonably expect actual performance from the defendant, as for example while a justifiable claim for specific performance is awaiting adjudication, or while the defendant is giving assurances of actual performance, the plaintiff cannot reasonably be expected to make a substitute purchase. But when it becomes plain that actual performance will never be forthcoming from the defendant, the plaintiff's damages crystallise.[171]

The date for assessing the plaintiff's damages is no longer fixed to the inflexible time of the date of the wrong or breach. Today, a proper consideration of the date for assessing damages will deal with factors such as when the plaintiff could reasonably have mitigated his damages and the intention of the plaintiff to replace or restore the property. The date at which this occurs is the date that the damages "crystallize" or become fixed for the purposes of compensating the plaintiff.

---

[169] [1979] 1 S.C.R. 633, [1978] 6 W.W.R. 301, 5 B.L.R. 225, 89 D.L.R. (3d) 1, 23 N.R. 181.

[170] *Ibid.*, at 31 D.L.R.; see also *Garbens v. Khayami* (1994), 17 O.R. (3d) 162, 36 R.P.R. (2d) 244 (Gen. Div.); *Domowicz v. Orsa Investments Ltd.* (1994) 20 O.R. (3d) 722, 43 R.P.R. (2d) 300 (Gen. Div.).

[171] Waddams, "Date for Assessment of Damages", *supra*, note 165, at 450.

6. *Conclusion*

Concepts of reasonableness and real intentions of the parties are at the heart of determining the appropriate method for quantifying damages. The "pigeon hole" approach where the method of quantification of damages depends on the nature of the property, while appearing to be somewhat inflexible, developed around the basic principles of reasonableness and an examination of the apparent intentions and circumstances of the parties.

Over time certain methods of quantification of damages based upon the nature of the property have come to be accepted by the courts as the starting point for determining the quantum of damages. It is important that advocates and the courts do not lose sight of the basic concepts upon which the classifications of damages by nature of property is based. As new and more complex situations arise, a strong case can be made for a particular method of quantifying damages where the advocate is able to formulate an argument that addresses these concepts and principles.

The danger of applying a standard "pigeon hole" approach to quantifying damages is that the injured party may be over-compensated or under-compensated. All too often, standard approaches are applied to non-standard situations; this makes for bad law and creates inequities. The courts must not shy from examining each case on its own facts, particularly as they relate to concepts of reasonableness, intention, remoteness and mitigation, the corner stones of any award for damages.

As can be seen in several of the cases discussed in this paper, the courts have had considerable difficulty where the advocates have not addressed their minds to the nature of the proof required to make the case for a particular quantum of damages. This problem also arises in the context of proving betterment and mitigation. The courts are looking for assistance in quantifying damages. It appears that the best way to provide that assistance is for the court to receive expert evidence in relation to the quantum of damages, be it on cost of repair or replacement, or on the diminution in the market value of the property.

It is hoped that this paper will provoke discussion about the issues and concerns raised within it by the authors. It is only by examining where we have been and questioning our past approaches that the law will continue to evolve to be based on truly equitable and manageable principles.

CHOOSING REMEDIES

Sheila Block[1]

1. *Introduction*

The 19th Century cynic, Ambrose Bierce[2] defined the lawsuit as a machine which you go into as a pig and come out as a sausage. Samuel Johnson had warned, more then a century earlier that the law could cure only a small part "of all that human hearts endure".[3]

Realizing that remedies are only available to those hardy few willing to withstand the sausage maker and that, even then, the scope for relief from what ails is limited, I am asked to speak to you about choosing them. Although it is tempting to focus on rights or causes of action, rather than remedies, the task at hand is to look at how lawyers choose remedies for their clients.

It is helpful to have in our minds the categories of remedies. A. S. Burroughs in his 1987 book *Remedies for Tort and Breach of Contract* lists the following categories:

1. Compensation.
2. Restitution: restitutionary damages; accounting of profits; award of money had and received.
3. Punishment: exemplary damages.
4. Compelling performance of positive obligations: specific performance, award of agreed sum; mandatory enforcing injunction; receiver/manager.
5. Preventing wrongful acts: prohibitory injunction; delivery up for destruction or destruction on oath.

---

[1] Tory Tory DesLauriers & Binnington. Thanks to Mark Gannage, Barry Leon and Paul Perell for their helpful ideas and comments.
[2] 1842-1914, author of *The Cynic's Word Book* (1911).
[3] "How small, of all that human hearts endure, That part which laws or kings can cause or cure!" Lines added to Goldsmith, The Traveller (1763-1764), cited in Bartlett's Familiar Quotations, ed. E.M. Beck, (Little Brown and Co. 1980).

6. Compelling the undoing of a wrong: mandatory and restorative injunction; delivery up of goods.
7. Declaring rights: declaration; nominal, contemptuous damages.[4]

Some academics have commented on the unimaginative approach
taken by the practising bar to the topic of remedies. Although every case
must include a claim for a remedy, too often our energies are focused on
questions of liability. The extensive exploration of potential remedies is
an indulgence litigators may not always permit themselves. The focus is
on proving the client has a "jus". The "remedium" will somehow fall
into place if the first hurdle is successfully scaled.

Remedies may also enjoy a lower status in the hands of the practising lawyer because the choice of remedy is often driven by tactical concerns. Many of those choices affect the remedy.

- What is the effect of the remedy sought on settlement?
- What is the effect on third parties?
- What documents will have to be produced if we seek this relief rather
  than that?
- What are the likely effects on future business relations if we seek "anni-
  hilation" as opposed to more limited recovery?
- What retaliation will we trigger if we seek a more draconian remedy?

The tactical tail wags the remedial dog.

Apart from tactical concerns, it may well be a justified complaint
about the practising bar that it does not regularly invest the intellectual
and analytical energy in the subject of remedies that one sees applied to
issues of liability. Little analysis is done about what is the best remedy
for the client.

Law and economics gurus urge us to consider the utility and efficiency
of remedies. They would provide us with endless treatises on the inter-
nalization of costs of various activities, the appropriate shifting of risks,
the prevention of involuntary exchange and other concepts to which we
pay no attention. It is not that the law journals are bereft of articles on
these and other topics on the theory of remedies. Indeed the law of remedies, cutting across as it does so many areas of law, appears to attract
bright and creative young academics. Yet we do not feel the need to understand remedies at the scholarly level as that understanding does not seem,
in any practical way, to inform the choices facing the practising lawyer.

Professor Grant Hammond speculates that "perhaps academic work
is not read, or if it is read, perhaps it does not percolate down to the

---

[4] At 8.

operational level of the law".[5] An English writer on remedies, H.F. Lawson, tentatively lays blame at the door of the bar: "To some extent the fault, if it is one, lies at the door of the bar, which does not explore possibilities that already exist."[6]

Courts, Hammond says, "can only respond to what is put in front of them"[7]. Lawyers seem stuck on the notion that monetary damages are best. Hammond suggests that the monetary bias thrives among the profession because lawyers can better justify their fees against successful monetary claims. This, plus the bar's innate conservatism keeps the bar tied to traditional remedies rooted in common law monetary damages. (Clients, with their enduring preference for money damages, may encourage these attitudes.)

In this paper I want to explore how we (the practising bar) choose remedies. Then I want to consider what else we could persuade the court to do. Can we push the law forward? Can we make it more responsive by taking a more rigorous, creative approach to remedies?

2. How We Choose Remedies

In choosing a remedy the starting point is inevitably to ascertain the client's real goal.

- What does the client want or need?
- Who does the client want or need it from?
- Where should you go in order to get it?
- How does the remedy become available?
- Why should the client get the remedy?
- What else could the client conceivably get?
- How long will it take?
- How feasible is this choice; in other words what effect will the desired remedy have on a myriad of factors that may be important to the client or affect the willingness of the tribunal to grant the remedy?
- Can we persuade the court to grant it?

---

[5] Hammond, "Rethinking Remedies: The Changing Conception of the Relationship Between Legal and Equitable Remedies", at 95 in *Remedies: Issues and Perspectives*, ed. Jeffrey Berryman.

[6] *Remedies of English Law*, 2nd ed. (London: Butterworths, 1982), at 292, cited by Hammond, *ibid.*

[7] *Supra*, note 5, at 95.

What the client wants must always be tested against the hurdle of what counsel can persuade the court is an appropriate remedy, justified by the facts of the case and on the law.

3. *Who Should Provide the Remedy?*

A tricky question for both the client and the lawyer is often who to sue. It is an essential question in the analysis of remedy. In some cases the causes of action may be more extensive against defendant A (leading to wider remedies) than against defendant B. In other cases the consequences of suing a particular defendant may either enhance or detract from the likelihood of obtaining the desired relief. Usually there is little science to the predictions by client or lawyer. Often the discussion is raised in connection with the likelihood of forcing a settlement if individuals working for the corporation or advisors to it are sued in their personal capacities, along with the corporation itself. Clients will say "we should sue the directors" (officers, investment bankers, lawyers, accountants, as the cases may be) "because those individuals will put pressure on the corporate defendant to settle". In fact, it may be just as likely that suit against the individuals or advisors will impede settlement, causing defendants to get their backs up and providing more resources for the defence.

The client and his lawyer must keep their eyes out for potential other parties that might be added as defendants or third parties.[8] In a recent case the plaintiff purchaser of commercial real estate sued the vendor and his agent for misrepresentation. The agent brought the purchaser's lawyer into the suit as a third party, arguing that the lawyer had checked the offer and failed to protect the client, therefore contributing to the loss.[9]

Defendants may be added to the title of proceedings because they provide financial stability. Although a financially sound defendant may have more money to fight with, their presence as someone from whom to collect at the end of the day generally justifies the inconvenience. Yet in some cases such a defendant may be more important for future business relations and, accordingly left out of the suit at the plaintiff's instance. In other cases, it is the added defendant who turns out to be the worst foe — causing the lawyer to regret ever suggesting or acquiescing to the addition.

Retaliation, reputation, and the cost of battling on another front may all affect the choice of who to sue. That choice may affect the available remedies.

---

[8] See e.g. *Canadian Newspapers Co. Ltd. v. Kansa*, unreported, June 27, 1991 (Ont. H.C.J.), Anderson J.

[9] *478649 Ontario Ltd. v. Corcoran* (1978), 20 O.R. (2d) 28 (C.A.).

4. *Where Should You Go to Get the Remedy?*

A fundamental threshold for clients is to determine whether they really want to sue. Are there other routes which can be taken to pursue their cause of action? Can a disciplinary body be invoked in pursuing a claim against a doctor or hospital or other professional? It may be that a prosecution by the professional college (handled and paid for by the professional body itself), will provide useful information for a subsequent civil lawsuit by the complainant. It may well also result in certain remedies, either formal (such as revocation of licence) or informal (such as changes to professional procedures or protocols) which appeal to the client and may not, in fact, be available in a civil suit. The civil suit can then concentrate on the monetary damages arising from the failure to receive competent care or advice. The administrative tribunal's process may also provide information identifying other appropriate defendants from whom to seek relief.

In corporate life, the administrative tribunal choice often arises. Should the client pursue an action in the Commercial Court to have a shareholders' rights plan (a.k.a. poison pill) declared invalid? Should, instead the OSC be asked to cease the trading of the rights promised under the shareholders' rights plan? In the context of an ongoing bid, the effect of either remedy might be the same — *i.e.*, it thwarts the exercise of the poison pill and allows the bid to go forward to shareholders. However the nature of the two remedies is different; the timing and availability of their grant might be quite different; and the appeal routes different again. An appeal from the OSC order would have to be taken to the Divisional Court and may run less risk of success than an appeal from a Commercial Court judge sitting on an application, which appeal would go to the Court of Appeal.

Interventions by other parties are commonly permitted at the Securities Commission and other administrative tribunals (and that may or may not be desired by your client). Interventions are less likely in court. Thus the remedy is chosen because of practical and tactical factors not directly related to the remedy but very much affecting the ability to quickly obtain relief in a particular type of forum.

There are many areas where claims can be pursued either before courts or administrative tribunals (areas such as labour, communications, human rights). When the choices are available, often practical considerations, collateral to the choice of remedy, drive clients to pursue one remedy over another, in one forum rather than another. Those practical considerations can range from cost and timing to precedential value and privacy.

In labour arbitration cases it has been recognized that arbitrators have wider scope for remedial solutions, particularly in the context of discipline and discharge cases. Indeed the courts try not to fetter such remedial power.[10] Arbitrators can reinstate discharged employees as of the date of discharge (something courts would almost never do).[11] They can even require that the employee be treated as if on long-term disability.[12]

5. *How does the Client Get the Remedy?*

It always helps to have a cause of action which supports the remedy sought. Let's assume that is table stakes for this discussion. Next you must consider the advantages or disadvantages of various remedies.

You may have the contract/tort choice. The structuring of the claim in tort may offer greater recovery for your client. For example, rather than suing for damages for breach of contract, a plaintiff might claim breach of fiduciary duty or unjust enrichment and seek compensation measured by the defendant's gain. The innocent party's recovery from a restitutionary order requiring the defendant to disgorge its gain could result in greater recovery than damages for the plaintiff's loss.

It may be that a contractor plaintiff would be better off with a judgment for *quantum meruit* than a judgment for damages for breach of contract if, in fact there would have been no profit from the contract.

Can your client claim special damages as well as general damages for loss of reputation in a libel case? If so, will that require disclosure of corporate financial information that would otherwise be unaccessible?[13]

Should you be leaving something on the table? If you seek rescission of the contract when your real aim is damages, will the more draconian relief cause your opponent to settle faster or fight harder? Your choice of remedy may be dictated by your and your client's assessment of the effect of the claim on the other side. Should you forego the relief from more aggressive causes of action such as fraud, deceit or discrimination because of the effect on the client's future position in a particular community or business sector? Your client's choice of remedy could be affected by concerns about reputation.

---

[10] Brown and Beatty, *Canadian Labour Arbitration*, 2:1400, at 2-7.

[11] In Quebec and under the *Canada Labour Code*, R.S.C. 1985, c. L-2, there is some jurisdiction for court-ordered re-instatement. It is otherwise not done in standard wrongful dismissal actions.

[12] *Heustis v. N.B. Electric Power Com'n*, [1979] 2 S.C.R. 768 at 781-82, 25 N.B.R. (2d) 613, 98 D.L.R. (3d) 622, 27 N.R. 103; *R. v. OPSEU (Fabro) and Crown Employees Grievance Settlement Board*, unreported, March 24, 1994 (Ont. Div. Ct.).

[13] *Reichmann v. Toronto Life Publishing Co.*(1990), 71 O.R. (2d) 719, 41 C.P.C. (2d) 73, 66 D.L.R. (4th) 162, Anderson J. citing *Teskey v. Canadian Newspapers Co.*, unreported, June 19, 1986 (Ont. H.C.J.).

It is often important to consider whether an injunction is available in addition to remedies in damages. Then it becomes important to assess the gravity of the undertaking as to damages — does your client really want to be on the hook for the damages caused by preventing the launch of a new product by the defendant? In the case of departing employees whom the plaintiff alleges breached fiduciary duties and "stole" clients, query whether more pressure is brought to bear by not seeking an injunction. The defendants must carry on their new venture with significant uncertainty hanging over their heads as to whether they will have to account for all their hard work between the time of their departure and judgment in the plaintiff's breach of fiduciary duty case. In some cases the plaintiff will not only save considerable legal fees in foregoing the injunction, but will also get the defendants to the table to settle the matter so the defendants can make a clean break with the past and work in their new venture for their own account, not the plaintiff's.

Perhaps the client could raise an issue as to the constitutional validity of relevant legislation. There may be a number of situations where this is a collateral or additional argument to the main cause of action, but available nonetheless. Counsel will have to advise the client about the additional time, cost and potential inconvenience should the Attorneys General seek to intervene upon receiving notice of a constitutional question.

In some cases the analysis of what else your client could get, results in a determination that you must ask for a certain remedy before you can claim further relief. For example, in a judicial review application complaining about a tribunal decision, it may be that you have to use the provisions in the governing statute which permit a rehearing before you can bring an application for judicial review.[14] In cases like this, it is important to canvass all possible remedies and then consider whether there is a hierarchy which requires some to be exhausted before others are pursued.

Thus the practising lawyer will consider what else might be sought and make decisions as to remedies, again largely driven by tactical considerations.

In some cases the client is not eligible for the remedy unless certain steps have been taken (or, more often than not, pitfalls avoided). Many of the papers in this series of lectures will deal with specific pitfalls in particular areas. A few examples here will illustrate the point that choice of remedy can be taken away from the client by missteps at the outset. Put another way, the lawyer can assist the client in ordering his affairs so as

---

[14] *Ellis-Don Ltd. v. Ont. (Labour Relations Bd.)* (1994), 16 O.R. (3d) 698, at 714, 94 CLLC 14,012, 110 D.L.R. (4th) 731 (Div.Ct.), leave to appeal to C.A. denied; leave to appeal that denial of leave, denied by S.C.C.). See also, *Labour Relations Act*, R.S.O. 1990, c. L.2, s. 108; *Ontario Energy Board Act*, R.S.O. 1990, c. O.13, s. 30.

to keep elections open for as long as possible. Thus, in a specific performance case, it is important not to seek the return of the deposit. In other contract cases the breach may be of sufficient gravity to permit the innocent party to treat the agreement as discharged and sue for damages. The plaintiff can sue in quasi-contract for recovery of benefits or can continue to be bound by the contract and sue only for damages for breach of warranty.

With a non-paying tenant the landlord may distrain, guard the premises and alert the tenant and the tenant's friends that any fraudulent removal of goods will result in liability to pay the landlord double the value of such goods.[15] The landlord may impound the goods on part of the premises but must be careful not to change the locks as he may forfeit the lease and then have no right to distress. If, after the tenant's breach, the landlord accepts rent, this may be seen as a waiver of the breach, leaving the landlord only with a claim for damages.

6. *How Long Will It Take?*

The answer the practising lawyer must give to most clients is "much longer than you can possibly imagine". As noted above, there are choices one makes because of the speed of the procedure. Some administrative tribunals (such as the OSC in certain cases) provide a faster route to remedy. The Commercial Court can be very useful for expeditious determinations in the right circumstance. In the Rogers/Maclean Hunter bid, Mr. Justice Farley was telephoned by counsel on a Wednesday. His Lordship was in Florida at the time and counsel sought to know whether he would be available "next week" to hear an injunction in connection with the takeover bid. Farley J. suggested everyone attend before him that Saturday. He acquiesced to the requests of counsel that it be put over until at least Sunday afternoon (when he promptly heard and disposed of the matter).

Cases suitable for mediation can be disposed of quickly at the Judicial ADR Centre or through private mediation. (When privacy is an important value, mediation is an attractive option.)

However, generally the story is a grim one for plaintiffs. Extensive discoveries and production and then long waits for trial still plague the system. An attitude among counsel that no stone can be left unturned, although theoretically admirable in pursuit of a client's cause, can result in glacially slow determinations.

To some extent, however, cutting out claims against additional

---

[15] *Landlord and Tenant Act*, R.S.O. 1990, c. L.7, s. 50.

parties and narrowing the relief and focus of the case can assist in speeding up the process. Take the dismissal of a second in command from a public corporation. He can simply sue the corporation for wrongful dismissal. Although that will not guarantee quick justice, it is likely to be a lot faster than if he also claims inducing breach of contract against the CEO of the company; claims that the CEO was oppressing him in his capacity as an officer, director and shareholder; and that the CEO conspired with others in the company to oust the plaintiff. Adding those claims to the simple wrongful dismissal damage claim and adding additional parties will result in greater production, longer discoveries and more protracted litigation.

You may want to structure the claim and choose relief with an eye to early disposition through summary judgment. A more modest request for relief may be more conducive to summary judgment, giving the client less than the maximum possible available recovery but providing an accelerated time frame for relief.

To some extent, albeit limited, the choice of remedy may affect the timeliness of recovery.

7. *How Feasible Is the Relief?*

After considering all of the tactical and logistical questions above, counsel must revisit whether the choice of remedy is feasible. Does it achieve what the client wants? Will it backfire in some way, for example by poisoning an existing or future relationship? Do the remedies proposed provide the court with reasonable choices which it may make in your client's favour?

Sometimes this latter factor is difficult to assess. Should you include alternative relief that is less than you want but may be an easy way out for a judge? If you leave it out, you risk losing altogether. If you put it in, you risk not having the relief you truly seek to have granted.

Think too, as well, about whether you will be winning "too big" if you advance an aggressive claim. You may meet judicial resistance in the Court of Appeal, even if you get by the judge or jury.[16]

---

[16] See, *e.g.*, *Walker v. CFTO* (1987), 59 O.R. (2d) 104, 39 C.C.L.T. 121, 37 D.L.R. (4th) 224 (C.A.), where general damages for libel of "a dollar per viewer" failed to hold on appeal.

8. *Can the Court be Persuaded to Grant the Relief?*

The next consideration for counsel and the client is whether the court will grant the relief sought. This is a particularly pertinent consideration when seeking extraordinary or innovative relief since there is almost always an element of discretion in the court that must be activated through an appeal to the justice of your client's cause.

In the majority of cases this issue does not arise, since conventional remedies (mostly damages) are usually claimed. There is, as Hammond pointed out, an innate conservatism in the bar and an abiding bias for money-based remedies over performance-based remedies. The structures of the law conspire to encourage this behaviour. Judges do not "supervise" the implementation of court orders; compelling performance of positive obligations or preventing wrongful acts will only be judicially imposed if damages do not suffice.

These long-standing principles are routinely accepted by the bar as immutable. Yet they have been under long-standing criticism.

Hammond cites Rosco Pound's criticism levelled in 1923 of the tradition of remedial justice through money damages.

> [W]e hesitate to employ restitution or coercion or specific action or prevention until we are convinced that our common law remedial technique will not suffice . . . This attitude colors our whole administration of justice.[17]

For 25 years before, Holmes and Joseph Storey were engaged in the debate, Holmes being of the view that breaching a contract merely meant that you knew you had to pay damages — "and nothing else".[18] Storey on the other hand said:

> It is against conscience that a party should have a right of election whether he should perform his covenant or only pay damages for the breach of it.[19]

By taking the approach that requires damages to be shown to be an inadequate remedy before equitable remedies are invoked, our law has allowed the wrongdoer to make the election, namely, to breach and pay.

Hammond urges the courts to show "greater neutrality between common law and equity remedies".[20] It may be that that, in Canada we are

---

[17] "The Theory of Judicial Decision" (1923), 36 Harv.L.Rev. 641 at 650, cited by Hammond, *supra*, note 5, at 94.
[18] "The Path of Justice" (1897), 10 Harv. L. Rev. 457, at 462, cited by Hammond, *ibid.*
[19] *Equity Jurisprudence*, 14th ed. (Ann Arbor: Univ.of Mich., 1918), s.717a, cited by Hammond, *ibid.*
[20] Hammond, *ibid.*, at 95.

already doing this. Madam Justice McLachlin has said that in Canada we have enthusiastically embraced a new approach to equity "using equity to modify the rigours of contract and tort".[21] This "new approach" could be used to challenge counsel and the courts even more. Perhaps we could unseat the age old principles upon which equitable remedies have often been denied, namely, the notion that if damages suffice there will be no equitable relief, and if supervision is required by the court the relief is not appropriate.

We could argue that there is no reason why the wrongdoer should have the election to breach and merely face monetary damages. It may be much more efficient, more just and perfectly sensible to require the wrongdoer to carry out the bargain or repair the damage if that is what the plaintiff wants. In 1955, the American legal scholar C.A. Wright proposed a hierarchy of remedies that incorporated this thought.

- First, relief should be preventive.
- Secondly, punitive relief should be given if it will deter.
- Thirdly, if a wrong is committed the plaintiff should be able to choose specific relief if the plaintiff so desires (e.g., restitution).
- Fourthly if the plaintiff elects money it should be based on the plaintiff's loss or the defendant's gain, whichever is greater.
- Finally Professor Wright argued that any doubt about whether to use the plaintiff's loss or the defendant's gain as the measure should be resolved against the wrongdoer.[22]

If the approach taken by the court was based on this hierarchy or some home grown version of the hierarchy, the question of whether damages would suffice becomes irrelevant.

Supervision is still an issue but it does not prove as significant an impediment in actual practice as it seems to be in judicial rationalization. The spectre of U.S. judges virtually running prisons, organizing desegregation busing or busting up AT&T is at the extreme end of the continuum. The reality of a system that would mandate the performance of positive obligations would have plaintiffs monitoring the implementation of court orders and bringing any disputes about the inadequacy of the defendant's back before the judge.

This would not be such a bad result. As many good humoured judges point out, they are, in fact, paid to sit there and listen. They can be paid

---

[21] McLachlin, "The Place of Equity and Equitable Doctrines in the Contemporary Common Law World: A Canadian Perspective", *Equity, Fiduciaries and Trusts*, (1993), ed. Donovan Waters.

[22] "The Law of Remedies as a Social Institution" (1955), 18 Univ. of Detroit L.J. at 376.

to hear from the same people again if there are problems with the implementation of their orders. Post-trial "supervision" seems to be no different in fundamental nature than pre-trial "supervision". Our increasing experience with case managed litigation has familiarized the bar with judges who will quickly arrange appointments, telephone conferences or clarification through correspondence. In a recent large and complex commercial case which was case managed to trial in a one-year time frame, our judge met with us frequently, dealt with all of the usual issues concerning production, confidentiality, discovery and timing and it was done in almost a paperless fashion. If my opponent and I were having a difference of view on something we would slide up to Osgoode Hall, talk to the judge and resolve the dispute.

In insolvency and restructurings, judges in the Commercial Court are continually "supervising" ongoing matters including the implementation of various orders of the court. There is little principled reason why courts could not supervise certain mandatory orders requiring performance by the defendant. Discipline can easily be brought to the unseemly spectacle of a party disobeying an order of the court. This is done in exactly the same way as it has been for centuries, through the power of contempt.

Another discipline in the system is a responsible bar. Competent counsel will explain to clients the implications of various remedies being sought and caution and advise clients concerning their obligations to abide by orders granting ongoing remedies. One hopes there is still the ability, among counsel, to convince clients to abide by such orders. Many other tribunals manage to make ongoing orders. There seems little reason why the court, in appropriate cases, cannot do the same — the monitoring being left to the vigilance of the plaintiff for whose benefit the order has been made.

Perhaps there is room for dislodging, at least in the right case, the restrictive notions that put the common law remedy of damages at the top of the hierarchy and discourage remedies which may require more intervention by the court or some ongoing role.

The law has often been moulded to produce justice in particular cases, notwithstanding the fact that it results in unconventional remedies. We can see this in cases where the usual remedy is modified in order to prevent harm to the defendant. In those cases the modifications do not undermine our notions of fairness and justice. Two famous examples from other jurisdictions make the point. In *Patel v. Ali*[23] Goulding J. refused to order specific performance to the purchasers of a house, citing hardship to the defendant as the basis for the refusal. A more deserving case for this remedial modification can scarcely be imagined. The contract for the sale of the house had been subject to a four year delay which was not the fault

---

[23] [1984] 1 Ch. 283.

of either party. During the four years the defendant, a woman who spoke virtually no English found herself in desperate straits. At the time of the contract she had been in good health, living with her husband and one young child. She developed bone cancer necessitating the amputation of her leg; had two further children; her husband went to prison; and she was completely dependent upon friends and relations who lived close by. Goulding J. found a principle for modifying the normal remedy of specific performance in the notion that "in extraordinary and persuasive circumstances . . . hardship [can] supply an excuse for resisting performance of a contract for the sale of immovable property".[24] Mrs. Ali was being asked to do "what she never bargained for, namely to complete the sale after more than four years, after all the unforeseeable changes that such a period entails." He concluded that specific performance would inflict upon her "a hardship amounting to injustice".[25]

The second case comes from the United States, *Boomer v. Atlantic Cement Co.*[26] The defendant operated a large cement plant near Albany. The plaintiffs suffered injury to their property next door from dirt, smoke and vibration emanating from the plant.

Although the plaintiffs were entitled to injunctive relief, the court refused to continue an injunction if the defendant paid permanent damages. The defendant's loss and the loss to its employees and the community at large was extensive. No techniques yet existed to eliminate the nuisance. The economic harm to the plaintiffs' properties was small in comparison to the value of the defendant's operation and the consequences of the injunction to the defendant, its employees and the community. The court looked at the marked disparity in economic consequences and refused the injunctive remedy.

Both these cases, in the negative, demonstrate the flexibility and suppleness of the remedial jurisdiction. We accept it as appropriate in the denial of certain relief and the substitution of another remedy. If we think of these cases as merely examples of the ability of the court to fashion remedies to do justice in the particular circumstances, they can be turned around to support the grant of more innovative (and non-traditional) remedies which would do justice in particular cases.

The examples found on the positive side are less inspiring. Professor Wright includes a catalogue of what can only be described as wacky

---

[24] *Ibid.*, at 288.
[25] *Ibid.*
[26] 40 A.L.R. (3d) 590 (1970) (Court of Appeals, New York).

remedial orders which, as he says, "do little for the dignity and prestige of the courts".[27]

Although as McLachlin J. cautions, "equity is not a panacea for every innocent loss"[28] judges can be persuaded to use more innovative remedies in order to do individual justice.[29] Some of the panelists and presenters in these lectures have suggested stretching existing remedies into other areas. For example, structured settlements are now provided for by s. 116 of the *Courts of Justice Act* in personal injury and wrongful death cases. There may be other substantive areas in which the structured settlement could be used to provide a plaintiff in a commercial case with an income stream.

Constructive trusts and specific performance provide plaintiffs with property rights. In insolvency and restructuring situations, these remedies could be useful to provide a plaintiff with greater security than he or she would have with merely a money judgment and result in a higher priority claim in the insolvency or restructuring.

9. *Role of the Bar*

Should we pursue more adventuresome remedies? Should we think about the application of existing remedies in new types of situations?

---

[27] Wright notes a number of what he describes as "ridiculous" orders which arose from the abandonment by some courts of Lord Eldon's dictate in *Gee v. Pritchard* (1818), 36 E.R. 670 (Ch.) that equity can act only to protect property rights. The sorry results included:

(1) an injunction in favour of a woman against her former lover from seeking to induce her to renew the relationship (Texas, 1924, an early anti-harrassment case);

(2) an injunction against a man from further debauching of the plaintiff's minor daughter (Georgia, 1919);

(3) an injunction against a husband's former mistress, who had been paid off once and had given a release, from molesting the husband and wife (Texas, 1943);

(4) an injunction against a woman from making rude faces at another;

(5) an injunction prohibiting the jilted defendant from committing suicide on his ex-girlfriend's doorstep;

(6) an injunction against a wife, prohibiting her from following her fireman husband to fires.

See Wright, *supra*, note 22, at 385-86.

[28] McLachlin, *supra*, note 21, at 55.

[29] Emily Sherwin in her learned article "An Essay on Private Remedies" Vol. 6, No. 1, Jan. 1993, Canadian Journal of Law and Jurisprudence, at 89, warns, at 109, of the dangers of too much modification at the remedial stage, undermining as it might a system that requires a limit to deviation from announced rights in order to preserve, what she calls, the security of rights. See at 109-88.

McLachlin J. recommends a recipe of "certainty" and "sufficient flexibility" to do justice in the individual case.[30] But certainty is no mean element in the functionality of the law. We cannot promote a system of remedies which results in the court dispensing palm tree justice in individual cases without regard to certainty and the legitimate expectations of private litigants.

This is why the way to promote flexibility in the law of remedies is to use the age old common law system. The practising bar will continue to choose remedies for various practical and tactical reasons, such as those outlined earlier in this paper. If that can be combined with an approach which challenges some of the conservatisim both the bar and bench have displayed on the issue of remedies, the law will be moved forward in the usual, evolutionary way.

Take, for example, the remedy under the corporations statutes of just and equitable winding up. This extreme remedy was the only choice courts used to have if it was determined that an incorporated partnership had to be dissolved. The courts ameliorated this drastic remedy by delaying the implementation of the wind up order for a period of time. The idea behind this was to force the parties to come to their senses and fashion a commercial solution so they did not face a lose/lose result by having the company destroyed.

The jurisdiction developed (and is now enshrined in the corporate statutes[31]) to allow the court to impose a less drastic remedy. Thus the court can require one party to buy out the other, thus keeping the corporation intact but solving the question of "divorce" of the "partners". Now the jurisdiction is even more extensive, allowing the court to impose any of the relief permitted under the oppression remedy.[32]

The oppression remedy itself provides a good example of a jurisdiction in the court to fashion wide-ranging and unusual remedies. The existence of a remedy with such far ranging scope does not seem to have undermined the element of certainty.[33] Even though it is sometimes difficult to predict for a client facing an oppression application the nature of remedial order that may be imposed, corporations still function and business carries on.

There is, I would contend, a fair bit of scope for a less conservative

---

[30] *Supra*, note 21, at 40.

[31] See, e.g., *Business Corporations Act*, R.S.O. 1990, c. B.16, s. 207(2).

[32] *Ibid.*, s. 248.

[33] Sherwin, *supra*, note 29, argues that whenever remedies depart from announced rights, something of the security of rights (which security she asserts is the reason for remedies) is lost. "Frequent discrepancies between right and remedy will produce a cumulative sense of disappointment in law — a sense that it does not live up to its promises.": at 111. It is a mistake, she argues, to try to do perfect justice in every case.

approach than we have been accustomed to in the fashioning of remedies. However a real limiting factor to a departure from money relief will be the client requirements. As long as they must spend significant sums to obtain relief, they will want recovery that makes that expenditure economic. This usually means a large damage award, plus indemnity for at least part of their costs. Remedies that do not make them whole in their pocket book will amount to pyrrhic victories for most clients.[34]

10. *Conclusion*

These are just first thoughts about how the practising bar chooses remedies. As we reflect further on this we should challenge ourselves to see what more we can do to fashion more effective remedies. Arbitrators and even more so, mediators, are continually forging solutions to problems with a great deal more flexibility than courts. Some of that flexibility can be imported into the court system. We should consider whether we can challenge the hierarchy of remedies and obtain more tailormade, case specific, remedies which solve clients' problems more effectively than the blunt instrument of damages.

We should consider carefully the opportunities for use of declaratory relief.

Economic arguments such as the disparity in the *Boomer* case or the hardship in the *Patel v. Ali* case may be useful tools for persuading a court to depart from the standard fare in a particular case.

The moral value of remedies, advanced by Story in the early part of this century and still advanced today by scholars[35] may provide the base for arguments which support more adventuresome remedies in particular cases.

Remedies do not need to continue to be "the step child of the law".[36] In remedies, as in issues of liability, the advocate's task is to persuade the court that the proposed solution achieves justice. It may be time for justice to come in increasingly different packages.

---

[34] See examples in the appendix entitled "Losers, Winners and Pyrrhic Victories", to Block, "The Owners' Perspective: Protecting Information, Opportunity, Clientele and Intellectual Property", Canadian Bar Association programme, June 20, 1985, entitled *Protecting Business Assets: The Tort Remedies.*

[35] See, e.g., Professor Charles Fried, *Contract as Promise* (Harvard Univ. Press, 1981).

[36] Wright, *supra*, note 22, at 376.

SPECIFIC PERFORMANCE

Benjamin Zarnett[1]

1. *Introduction*

In the cast of remedies for breach of contract, specific performance plays a secondary role to damages, and, like many supporting players, sometimes suffers from a lack of attention and appreciation. The 657 page, 8th edition of *Cheshire & Fifoot's Law of Contract*[2] that I trudged around with in law school, devoted a scant seven pages to specific performance (two of which really dealt with injunctions). When the Law Society Special Lectures reviewed "Remedies" for the profession in 1961,[3] specific performance did not even qualify as a topic. Twenty years later, when the Special Lectures canvassed "New Developments in the Law of Remedies", the only mention of specific performance was to applaud an English decision which gave a party who elected specific performance the right to re-elect damages.[4]

Yet when it comes to redressing contractual wrongs, specific performance has a lot going for it. The remedy will often be preferable, from the standpoint of the innocent party, to an award of damages. The advantages of specific performance, and whether they can be secured in any particular case, deserve careful consideration.

In this paper, therefore, I intend to review the positive features of specific performance, and then consider some recent developments related to the availability of the remedy.

---

[1] Of Goodman Phillips & Vineberg, Toronto.
[2] (London: Butterworth's, 1972).
[3] Law Society of Upper Canada Special Lectures, "Remedies" (Toronto: Richard De Boo Limited, 1961).
[4] Law Society of Upper Canada Special Lectures, "New Developments in the Law of Remedies" (Toronto: Richard De Boo Limited, 1981).

2. *Specific Performance Defined*

The best definition of specific performance remains that of Fry:

> The specific performance of a contract is its actual execution according to
> its stipulations and terms; and is contrasted with damages or compensation
> for the non-execution of the contract. Such actual execution is enforced under
> the equitable jurisdiction vested in the Courts of this country by directing
> the party in default to do the very thing which he contracted to do, and,
> in the event of his disobedience, by treating such disobedience as a contempt
> of Court and visiting it with all the consequences of such contempt includ-
> ing imprisonment; and in some cases by doing in one way the thing which
> the defaulter was directed to do in another way, as, eg., by vesting by an
> order of the Court an estate which ought to have been vested by conveyance
> of the party.[5]

3. *The Advantages of Specific Performance*

Why seek specific performance?
A number of positive features attach to, or flow from, the remedy.

(1) Specific Performance Satisfies the Innocent Party's Expectations

Remedies for breach of contract have at least two purposes: to ensure
that an innocent party does not suffer from a breach of contract and to
do so in such a way that persons will continue with confidence to enter
into contracts. These purposes are achieved by granting remedies which
fulfil the innocent party's "expectation interest" in the contract, or, to
put it another way, by putting the innocent party in the position he or
she would have been in if the defaulting party had voluntarily performed
the contract.[6] A remedy which does this ensures that the innocent party
gets what was bargained for, or the equivalent, and the availability of such
a remedy permits parties to confidently contract, secure that their expectations will be fulfilled through voluntary performance or a court imposed
remedy which achieves for them the equivalent.
Specific performance clearly fulfills these two purposes by securing

---

[5] Fry, *Specific Performance of Contracts*, 5th ed. (London: Stevens and Sons,
Limited, 1911).
[6] See Sharpe, *Injunctions and Specific Performance*, 2nd ed. (Toronto: Canada
Law Book Inc., 1992), at para. 7.5.

actual performance of the contract, giving both sides what they bargained for.

(2) Specific Performance is Available with Damages in Addition

The comedian Jackie Mason makes a rather heavy joke at the expense of those who complain about having been cheated out of business opportunities. Offered, as amends, the same opportunities, they protest: "Now . . . now is too late!"

Specific performance also comes late. The court does not intervene until after actual performance was due and undelivered. Therefore, at least in timing, specific performance will differ from voluntary performance. Yet in any case where court ordered performance does not fully equate with voluntary performance, damages or compensation may, in addition to specific performance, be awarded to bridge the gap and to ensure that delayed performance is not less valuable performance.[7]

(3) Specific Performance Avoids Evidentiary Disputes About Damage

Damages (as an alternative to specific performance) are awarded for breach of contract on the principle that, so far as money can do it, the innocent party is to be put in the position he or she would have been if performance had occurred.[8] Some benefits promised by contract and not delivered cannot be measured in money — for these, only specific performance can do justice. But even where attempts can be made to value what was lost, they should be recognized for what they are — attempts. Where performance has not occurred and will not occur, the financial position the innocent party would have been in on performance is a matter of conjecture. Thus, in all but the most simple of cases, opinion evidence of experts — appraisers to establish the value of land at material times, forensic accountants to forecast profits which would have been earned, and so on — must be led. Not surprisingly, different experts, hired by opposing parties, may proffer different opinions. The actual assessment of damages which occurs on the basis of conflicting expert testimony is only

---

[7] *Holmes v. Alexson* (1974), 7 O.R. (2d) 11, 54 D.L.R. (3d) 175 (H.C.); affd 12 O.R. (2d) 431, 69 D.L.R. (3d) 223 (C.A.); *Jones v. Gardinier*, [1902] 1 Ch. D. 191; *Bowes & Cocks Ltd. v. Aspirant Investments Ltd.* (1984), 31 R.P.R. 63 (Ont. H.C.).

[8] Sharpe, *supra*, note 6.

as good as the quality of the experts' presentations, counsels' abilities to test them, and the court's ability to weigh and evaluate them. Whether the result produced in any case actually accords with what the innocent party would have received through actual performance will never be known. What is not open to question is that substantial time and expense are involved in any damage assessment.

(4) Specific Performance Avoids Arguments that Mitigation Has or Should Have Taken Place

Damages are not available to compensate for a loss which the innocent party has either mitigated (by taking steps to reduce or avoid it after it occurred) or would have mitigated if such steps had been taken.[9] In the case of contracts, mitigation generally involves the entering into of a transaction in substitution for the one the defaulting party failed to perform.

In a damages action, the innocent party often faces arguments that a transaction entered into after the breach of the contract is to be taken in mitigation of the loss arising from the breach. Since only transactions which arise out of the consequences of the breach are to be taken into account as mitigation, arguments can ensue as to whether the subsequent transaction was one which the innocent party could have performed in addition to the transaction contemplated by the contract (and therefore is not to be considered as mitigation), or whether it was a true substitution for the aborted transaction (and therefore to be taken into account in mitigation).[10] In such cases the innocent party must try to prove that it could and would have completed both the transactions, while the defaulter points to the similar nature of them and claims that its breach is relieved by the innocent party's subsequent transaction. All of this takes place against the background created by the default, namely, that the innocent party, having been deprived of the opportunity to perform the original transaction, cannot prove it would have performed both transactions by simply pointing to that actually having occurred.

Similarly, in a damages action where no subsequent transaction has been entered into, it is open to the defaulting party to argue that the innocent party should have mitigated. Here again, evidence and opinion can be led and argument made on what are now two hypothetical situations

---

[9] *British Westinghouse Electric & Mfg. Co. v. Underground Electric Railways, Co.*, [1912] A.C. 673 at 689 (H.L.).

[10] *Windmill Place v. Apeco of Canada Ltd.*, [1978] 2 S.C.R. 385, 3 R.P.R. 137, 82 D.L.R. (3d) 1, 19 N.R. 124.

— what position the innocent party would have achieved if the contract had been performed, and what position the innocent party would have been in if the hypothetical mitigation transaction had in fact occurred.

Specific performance avoids the entire issue. No argument of actual mitigation is relevant because the innocent party, by electing to compel actual performance, makes it plain that any transaction performed subsequently to the one which was breached was additional to it, and not a substitute for it. Similarly, arguments that the innocent party should have, but failed to mitigate, are irrelevant if specific performance is decreed.

(5) Specific Performance Is An Electable Remedy for the Innocent Party

A party seeking specific performance may couple that claim with an alternative claim for damages for breach of contract. As long as the innocent party does not foreclose an election of specific performance before or during the course of the proceedings (by, for example, electing to disaffirm the contract sought to be enforced, or electing damages) an election between specific performance and damages may be made at any time until judgment is pronounced.[11]

This right of election provides the innocent party the continuing opportunity, during the lengthy period which can pass between institution of the action and trial, to gauge whether compelling actual performance is still desirable, should changes in the market or in his or her business or personal circumstances, occur.

The making of a claim for specific performance with an alternative claim for damages by the innocent party does not, however, normally permit the defaulting party, who started the ball rolling by the initial refusal to complete, to later "force" specific performance on the innocent party, if performance later appears advantageous to the defaulting party. *Lyew v. 418648 Ontario Ltd.*,[12] was a case which dealt with a motion by a defendant vendor, who had originally refused to close, for summary judgment to "force" specific performance on the plaintiff purchaser who had sued seeking specific performance and damages in the alternative. Presumably, the market had fallen in the interim and the defendant's view of the

---

[11] *Dobson v. Winton & Robbins Ltd.*, [1959] S.C.R. 775, 20 D.L.R. (2d) 164.

[12] (1983), 26 R.P.R. 213*n*, 134 D.L.R. (3d) 384*n* (Ont. C.A.); revg 35 O.R. (2d) 241, 24 R.P.R. 237, 132 D.L.R. (3d) 472; see also Chapman, A Stacked Deck: Specific Performance and the Real Estate Transaction (1994), 16 Adv. Q. 273, at 295-96.

wisdom of closing had changed. The Ontario Court of Appeal held that it was not clear that a defendant could at any time force a plaintiff who had initially claimed specific performance to submit to it. Rather, the matter of the remedy was to be left until trial.

A similar attempt by a defaulting party to force specific performance on the innocent party and avoid the right of election was rejected by the Federal Court of Appeal in the following terms:

> This would not be equity, because it would not be fair, in relation to a contract of which time was of the essence, to abrogate the distinction between the wronged and the wronging party. The election of remedies must remain at the option of the innocent party, and to that extent, the contract will be alive in an unequal way, or, more accurately, it will remain alive but will be enforceable, if at all, only by the originally non-defaulting party on such terms as to compensation as a court of equity may prescribe.[13]

(6) Specific Performance Contemplates Favourable Adjustments in Favour of the Innocent Party

Not only may specific performance be awarded in favour of an innocent party *with* damages to compensate for delayed or defective performance, an innocent party may also obtain very favourable treatment on the adjustment issues of interest and expenses of carrying the property. In a case where the contract is for the purchase of an asset, and the vendor has wrongly refused to complete, the purchaser, until specific performance is later ordered and takes place, retains the purchase price and therefore retains benefit of it including the right to earn interest on it. However, as the law has developed, when completion under the specific performance order actually occurs, the defaulting vendor, having been responsible for the delay, will not receive interest on the purchase price. Nor will the defaulting vendor be able to saddle the purchaser with any losses that the vendor might have incurred in operating the property between the date the transaction should have closed, and the actual closing under the specific performance order. Rather, specific performance will be ordered with adjustments made and calculated as of the actual date of closing pursuant to the specific performance order, "without taking account any monies received or expended and without provision for interest since the date of closing stipulated in the agreement".[14]

---

[13] *Beauchamp v. Coastal Corp.*, [1986] 2 F.C. 298, 26 D.L.R. (4th) 146 at 154, 65 N.R. 336 (C.A.).

[14] *Morgan v. Lucky Dog Ltd.* (1987), 45 R.P.R. 263 at 289 (Ont. H.C.J.).

Where income, attributable to the asset which will be delivered under the specific performance order, has accrued during the litigation but has not been paid to the vendor, the purchaser may be obligated in equity to pay interest on the purchase price if, on receiving the asset under the specific performance award, he or she will also receive the accrued income.[15]

(7) Seeking Specific Performance May Actually Enhance the Damages Which May Be Awarded

The normal date for assessment of damages for breach of contract is the date of the breach. This means, in the case of the non-fulfilment of a purchase agreement, that a purchaser who pursues only damages will normally be entitled to the difference between the value of the asset on the date of the breach, and the contract price. Subsequent increases to the value of the asset, even if realized by the defaulting vendor, are irrelevant to the innocent purchaser's damages.

If, however, the innocent purchaser pursues specific performance with damages in the alternative, and if the claim for specific performance is one for which there is a fair, real and substantial justification,[16] then, if specific performance is refused or elected against at trial (because, for example the contract cannot be performed without the consent of a third party which is not forthcoming) the innocent purchaser may be entitled to elect damages assessed at the date of trial, and therefore obtain the benefit of any increase in the value of the asset between breach and trial.[17]

(8) Specific Performance Provides a Means of Benefitting Third Parties

Our law does not generally recognize a right in a person, not a party to a contract, to enforce it, even when the third party is to be the

---

[15] *Harvelor Investments Ltd. v. Royal Trust Co. of Canada*, [1985] 2 All E.R. 966 (H.C.).

[16] *Asamera Oil Corp. v. Sea Oil & General Corp.*, [1978] 1 S.C.R. 633, [1978] 6 W.W.R. 301, 5 B.L.R. 225, 89 D.L.R (3d) 1, 23 N.R. 181; vard [1979] 1 S.C.R. 677, [1979] 3 W.W.R. 93, 10 C.P.C. 166, 97 D.L.R. (3d) 300, 25 N.R. 451.

[17] *Wroth v. Tyler*, [1974] 1 All E.R. 897; *Metropolitan Trust Co. v. Pressure Concrete Services Ltd.*, [1973] 3 O.R. 629, 37 D.L.R. (3d) 649 (H.C.); affd 9 O.R. (2d) 373, 60 D.L.R. (3d) 431 (C.A.).

recipient of the benefits under the contract. Specific performance provides a means of securing benefits in favour of those third parties in some cases. For example in *Beswick v. Beswick*[18] an agreement between Mr. Beswick and the defendant provided for payments by the defendant to Mr. Beswick for his life, and after his death to Mrs. Beswick. On Mr. Beswick's death, the defendant ceased making any payments. In defence of an action by Mr. Beswick's Estate, the defendant argued (accurately according to the majority of the Law Lords) that the estate suffered no damges as a result of the non-payment to Mrs. Beswick, and although Mrs. Beswick suffered losses, she personally had no rights under the contract. The House of Lords' answer to this was to order specific performance of the defendant's promise to pay Mrs. Beswick. Lord Pearce stated:

> It is argued that since the widow personally had no rights which she personally could enforce the court will not make an order which will have the effect of enforcing those rights. I can find no principle to this effect. The condition as to payment of an annuity to the widow personally was valid. The estate (though not the widow personally) can enforce it. Why should the estate be barred from exercising its full contractual rights merely because in doing so it secures justice for a widow who by a mechanical defect of our law, is unable to assert her own rights? Such a principle would be repugnant to justice and fulfil no other object than that of aiding the wrong doer. I can find no ground on which such a principle should exist.[19]

Specific performance may therefore be ordered of a contract to pay money or transfer property to a third person, notwithstanding (and perhaps because) the damages which could be claimed by the contracting party are nominal or non-existent.[20]

(9) Specific Performance Better Protects the Innocent Party In The Case of The Defaulting Party's Insolvency

An award of damages is only as good as the ability of the defendant to honour it. A judgment for damages for breach of a contract to sell an asset has no particular priority against other creditors of the defendant unless collection under the judgment has occurred. This is so, even if the asset which was the subject of the contract remains in the hands of the defendant. On bankruptcy of the defaulting party, a judgment for damages for breach of contract is no more enforceable than any

---

[18] [1968] A.C. 58 (H.L.).

[19] *Ibid.*, at 89.

[20] See also *Hohler v. Aston*, [1920] 2 Ch. 420.

unsecured debt. Where the contract was one under which the innocent party made prepayments, the innocent party holding a judgment for damages only would have to share, *pro rata* with all the defaulting party's creditors, the advantage of the prepayments under the contract and of the property or rights which were to be delivered under the contract.

However, at least in so far as land is concerned, specific performance may be sought and obtained notwithstanding the bankruptcy of the vendor under the sale agreement. An ordinary executory agreement of purchase and sale of land is an "agreement of purchase and sale" within the meaning of s. 75 of the *Bankruptcy and Insolvency Act*[21] and accordingly, such an agreement, in favour of a *bona fide* purchaser for consideration "is valid and effectual as if no bankruptcy had occurred and the trustee is bound by the contract in the same manner as the bankrupt and has no power to disclaim it."[22] Accordingly, the vendor's bankruptcy does not prevent the purchaser's entitlement to specific performance of the agreement, which may be obtained and enforced against the vendor's Trustee.

Similarly, the fact that a corporate vendor has gone into receivership affords no defence to an action for specific performance of an agreement to sell land. The vendor's trustee or receiver does not obtain the land of the vendor free of the purchaser's equitable right to obtain it on payment of the purchase price.[23]

Accordingly, when an innocent party disclaims, abandons, fails to pursue or is denied specific performance in favour of damages, significant rights and status are also disclaimed, abandoned or denied should subsequent insolvency occur.

(10) Specific Performance is a Remedy Which is Not Stayed By An Appeal

A judgment for damages will be automatically stayed on the filing of a notice of appeal by the defendant, after which no steps may be taken under the judgment or for its enforcement.[24] The delay until an appeal in Ontario is heard can be years. Prejudice can occur to the plaintiff during such a delay, if the defendant's ability to honour the judgment should deteriorate while the appeal is pending.

On the contrary, a judgment for specific performance is not stayed

---

[21] R.S.C. 1985, c. B-3.

[22] *Re Triangle Lumber and Supply Co. Ltd.* (1978), 21 O.R. (2d) 221, 27 C.B.R. (N.S.) 317, 90 D.L.R. (3d) 152 (Ont. S.C.).

[23] *Freevale Ltd. v. Montrose Hldg. Ltd.*, [1984] Ch. 199.

[24] Rules 63.01 and 63.03, *Rules of Civil Procedure*, R.R.O. 1990, Reg. 194.

by the filing of an appeal; rather, the defendant must apply for and obtain such a stay.[25] A stay will be granted only where the balance of convenience favours it, with the most important factor in that balance being that an adjudication has already taken place which is *prima facie* correct.[26] Accordingly, insubstantial appeals may not justify a stay. Even if a stay is granted, terms can be imposed which will protect the innocent party pending the hearing of the appeal. These could include terms as to the preservation and management of the property and to secure the income from it so that no prejudice could accrue to the innocent party pending the hearing of the appeal.[27]

4. *Developments Relating to the Availability of Specific Performance*

Despite its advantages, specific performance is not generally available to remedy a breach of contract. The general principles upon which specific performance is available are carefully canvassed elsewhere.[28] I propose here to review certain recent developments of the law which have impacted on the availability of specific performance.

(1) Interlocutory Considerations

A party claiming specific performance of a contract to convey an asset, must ensure that the asset is available at trial, so that it may be made the subject of a court order for specific performance. The remedy is not available where the property which was the subject of the contract has been conveyed by the defaulting party to a third party whose rights are unaffected by the plaintiff's claims.[29] The court will not make an order which is impossible to perform, nor will it, by an order of specific performance, affect the rights of *bona fide* third parties who have acquired property without notice of the plaintiff's rights. Therefore, to ensure land is not disposed of free of the plaintiff's right, a plaintiff wishing specific performance must obtain and register a certificate of pending litigation against the land, and must be able to successfully oppose a motion to

---

[25] *Ibid.*, rule 63.02.

[26] *Re 820099 Ontario Inc.* (1991), 49 C.P.C. (2d) 239 (Ont. Div. Ct.)

[27] *Supra*, note 24, rule 63.02(1).

[28] Sharpe, *Injunctions and Specific Performance*, 2nd ed. (Toronto: Canada Law Book Inc., 1992).

[29] *Ibid.*, para. 10.650.

discharge it.[30] It is therefore worth considering the relationship between the factors which the court will consider in deciding to discharge a certificate (and effectively foreclose specific performance), and those a court will consider in dealing with the remedy at trial.

Until recently[31] it appeared unquestioned in Ontario that a purchaser suing for specific performance of an agreement to purchase land would, at trial, have it presumed in his or her favour that damages would not be an adequate remedy, and that therefore specific performance would be available as a matter of course. This was so, regardless of the purchaser's purposes for the land.

In *Kloepfer Wholesale Hardware & Automotive Co. Ltd. v. R.G. Roy*,[32] the Supreme Court of Canada stated:

> Finally, as to the suggestion that damages would be sufficient because it is contended that the plaintiff intended to use the property as an investment, it is sufficient to say that generally speaking, specific performance applies to agreements for the sale of lands as a matter of course.

This approach was followed by the Ontario Court of Appeal in *Bashir v. Koper*.[33] There, the trial judge's refusal to grant specific performance on the basis that damages were an adequate remedy for a breach of a contract to sell land was held to be wrong in principle. Further, the trial judge's consideration of factors such as the property being an investment, damages being a complete remedy, the plaintiff having purchased another property, and the lack of any special or unique character to the land for the plaintiff, were deemed by the Court of Appeal to have been a consideration of factors which were immaterial.

One would expect that, if the remedy of specific performance at trial could not be defeated by a consideration of such factors, then the remedy could also not be effectively denied by a consideration of those factors at the certificate of pending litigation stage. Initially, this was the case. According to older cases such as *Galinski v. Jurashek*,[34] the court would consider, in deciding whether to remove a certificate of pending litigation, only whether the action was an abuse of process or whether, on a consideration of the merits of the action, the plaintiff could not possibly succeed on liability and therefore obtain an interest in the land.

Later cases, however, have proceeded on a different basis. It has become established law that a certificate of pending litigation can be

---

[30] *Courts of Justice Act*, R.S.O. 1990, c. C.43, s. 103.
[31] See *Domowicz v. Orsa Investments Ltd.*, *infra*, note 39.
[32] [1952] 2 S.C.R. 465 at 472, [1952] 3 D.L.R. 705.
[33] (1983), 40 O.R. (2d) 758, 27 R.P.R. 297 (C.A.).
[34] (1976), 1 C.P.C. 68 (Ont. H.C.J.).

discharged on the basis of an exercise of the court's discretion in equity considering a number of factors, including:

(1) whether the land is actually, rather than presumptively, unique;
(2) the intent of the parties in acquiring the land (with purposes such as investment or resale counting toward discharge, and purposes such as personal occupation counting against discharge);
(3) whether there is an alternative claim for damages;
(4) the ease or difficulty in calculating damages;
(5) whether damages would be a satisfactory remedy;
(6) the presence or absence of another purchaser;
(7) whether the plaintiff is a shell company; and
(8) the harm to each party if the certificate is maintained or removed.[35]

Clearly many of these factors would, on the authority of *Kloepfer* and *Bashir v. Koper*, be irrelevant, at trial, to the plaintiff's entitlement to specific performance. Conversely, on these factors, the plaintiffs in *Kloepfer* and *Bashir v. Koper* may not have been successful in maintaining certificates of pending litigation if they were challenged, and they, like plaintiffs in other cases, may have lost their certificates on the basis that the lands they were seeking to have conveyed were not unique, or that the lands were being acquired for investment purposes, or that damages were an adequate remedy.[36]

Where the court refuses to grant, or discharge, a certificate of pending litigation, it effectively denies the remedy of specific performance, as a claim for specific performance can thereafter only meaningfully continue if, for some reason, the defendant/vendor does not dispose of the land to a third party prior to trial (and the land therefore remains available, though as a matter of luck, not legal process).

No case has ever addressed why, at the certificate of pending litigation stage, the court should apply a test more restrictive on the issue of the plaintiff's right to land *in specie* than would be used at trial. But these developments in the law relating to certificates of pending litigation have acted and continue to act as a real and meaningful restriction on the availability of the remedy of specific performance, and in a manner not necessarily consistent with the law which governs the grant of the remedy at trial.

---

[35] *572383 Ontario Inc. v. Dhunna* (1987), 24 C.P.C. (2d) 287 (S.C.); *931473 Ontario Ltd. v. Coldwell Banker Canada Inc.* (1992), 5 C.P.C. (3d) 238 (Ont. Gen. Div.).

[36] As did the plaintiffs in *572383 Ontario Inc. v. Dhunna, ibid.*; *Pete & Marty's (Front) Ltd. v. Market Block Toronto Properties Ltd.* (1985), 5 C.P.C. (2d) 97, 37 R.P.R. 157 (Ont. H.C.J.); *Heron Bay Investments Ltd. v. Peel-Elder Developments* (1976), 2 C.P.C. 338 (Ont. H.C.J.).

(2) Developments in the Primacy of Damages Doctrine

At trial, the major impediment to an award of specific performance is the doctrine that specific performance ought only to be ordered where damages are not an adequate remedy.

There can be no doubting the venerability of this doctrine.[37] However, the basis for it will largely determine the extent to which it constricts the availability of specific performance.

(a) *Historical Background*

The original basis for the doctrine was historical. The law of contracts developed within the framework of a divided English Court System. The Courts of Common Law gave and enforced only money awards. Specific performance was granted by Courts of Equity, which would only intervene where the law did not do justice. The subsequent unification of the courts did not alter the presumption that specific performance was available only on a showing of the inadequacy of monetary compensation.[38]

On the historical basis grew historical distinctions. The law developed differently with respect to land than with respect to chattels and other contracts, perhaps because, historically, certain incidents were attached to the ownership of land, such as the right to vote.[39] Consequently, the law came to presume land unique and special, regardless of the particular plaintiff's purposes and intentions for it, and specific performance became available as a matter of course.[40] In cases involving chattels and other contracts, an actual showing of uniqueness and the consequent inadequacy of damages, was required. Still, in other cases, such as contracts for personal service, the law treated those contracts as presumptively not specifically enforceable.

In the cases dealing with assets other than land, the requirement that an actual showing of uniqueness and inadequacy of damages gave rise to a relatively restricted category of cases in which specific performance would be granted. For example:

- In the case of agreements to purchase chattels, if a substitute was available in the market, the purchaser would be restricted to a remedy

---

[37] See *Cuddee v. Rudder* (1720), 1 P. Wms; *Flint v. Brandon* (1803), 8 Ves. 159.

[38] Sharpe, *supra* note 28, paras. 7.10-7.40.

[39] *Domowicz v. Orsa Investments Ltd.* (1993), 15 O.R. (3d) 661 at 683 (Gen. Div.).

[40] *Kloepfer Wholesale Hardward & Automotive Co. Ltd. v. R. G. Roy, supra,* note 32; *Bashir v. Koper, supra,* note 33.

in damages being the difference between the contract price and the price of the substitute on the date of the breach. Specific performance would be restricted to cases of specific and ascertained goods which were rare paintings, antiques, ceremonial ornaments, dresses, decorations and papers, family heirlooms, and the like, where there existed no substitutes, or where the goods had a particular immeasurable value to the plaintiff.[41]

- Contracts to borrow money were not specifically enforceable, because damages (being the loss of interest) were an adequate remedy, but breach of a contract to provide security for a loan was specifically enforceable, since by definition an unsecured obligation to pay money in such a case was not considered adequate.[42]

- A contract to acquire shares where there is a public market for them will not generally be specifically enforceable, but a contract to acquire shares in a private company not otherwise available, or to acquire shares which have a particular incident, such as representing a control block, may be specifically enforceable.[43]

The historical justification for the doctrine of the primacy of damages was obviously subject to the frailty that where the historical reason had ceased to exist, it could no longer justify the doctrine. However, the doctrine has been justified on another basis, and the elucidation of that basis in the case-law has begun to impact on the traditional thinking on specific performance.

(b) The Mitigation Doctrine

The primacy of damages doctrine has been ahistorically justified on the following reasoning.[44] Whereas specific performance as a remedy may satisfy the interests of the innocent party, regard must also be had to the interests of the defaulting party and to society. These interests are appropriately balanced, it is argued, by imposing upon the innocent party a duty, upon being faced with a breach, of taking steps to mitigate or avoid any loss resulting from the breach, and enforcing that duty by limiting the innocent party to claiming only those losses which have not been and could

---

[41] See generally Sharpe, *supra*, note 28, para. 8.230-8.510.

[42] *Bank of B.C. v. Denenfeld* (1973), 38 D.L.R. (3d) 750 (B.C.S.C.).

[43] *Asamera Oil Corp. Ltd. v. Sea Oil & General Corp.*, [1979] 1 S.C.R. 633, [1978] 6 W.W.R. 301, 5 B.L.R. 225, 89 D.L.R. (3d) 1, 23 N.R. 181; vard [1979] 1 S.C.R. 677, [1979] 3 W.W.R. 93, 10 C.P.C. 166, 97 D.L.R. (3d) 300, 25 N.R. 451; *Eansor v. Eansor*, [1946] S.C.R. 54, [1946] 2 D.L.R. 181.

[44] See Sharpe, *supra*, note 28, para. 7.120.

not be avoided or mitigated. In this way, the defaulting party benefits by being subjected only to those claims which the innocent party could not avoid by taking reasonable steps, such as entering into a substitute transaction. Society, as well, benefits, as disputes in general, and resort to the courts in particular, are avoided where losses are completely mitigated, and are limited where losses are partially mitigated. Specific performance neither requires, nor recognizes mitigation, and is thus inconsistent with this theory. Damages recognizes and enshrines the theory; thus it is entitled to primacy.

Stressing the importance of mitigation over specific performance was given judicial sanction by the Supreme Court of Canada in *Asamera Oil Corp. v. Sea & Oil General Corp.*[45] There, in an action for failure to return loaned shares, the plaintiff attempted to justify a failure or a delay to replace such shares by market purchases (which would have mitigated the plaintiff's losses), on the basis that it had made a claim for specific performance of the contract to return the shares. In other words, the plaintiff attempted to justify its failure to make market purchases to replace the shares on the basis that it was seeking specific performance of the contract to return the shares, and had to remain ready, willing and able to perform that contract, and thus should not have its claim limited on the basis that it should have reduced its loss by making market purchases when the market was favourable. The Supreme Court of Canada disagreed, holding that only a real and substantial claim to specific performance could ever justify a plaintiff in failing to mitigate its losses. The principle of mitigation was central to contract law and its administration, and should not lightly be displaced. As the plaintiff did not have a real and substantial claim to specific performance (the shares in question being available on the market) the mere asertion of it could not justify a failure to mitigate.

This approach was expanded upon in *Domowicz v. Orsa Investments Ltd.*[46] In that case, the plaintiffs, who had been investors in several apartment buildings, entered into an agreement to purchase a 123 suite nine-storey apartment building from the defendant. The defendant failed to close in breach of its obligations to do so. The plaintiff sought the remedy of specific performance.

Adams J. denied specific performance. He found that the plaintiffs wished to acquire the apartment buildings to earn income from them, to increase their value, and to re-sell them in the short to mid-term assuming constant market conditions and rent legislation.

On the authority of *Kloepfer* and *Bashir v. Koper*, one would have expected, nonetheless, that specific performance would have been granted. However, Adams J. held that the same principles which apply to specific

---

[45] *Supra*, note 43.
[46] *Supra*, note 39.

performance of other contracts ought to apply to specific performance of contracts for the sale of land. Therefore, the normal remedy to redress breach should be considered damages. Any presumption in favour of the inadequacy of damages in the case of contracts for the purchase of land ought to be considered displaced by examining the principles underlying the choice of remedies as set forth in the Supreme Court of Canada's decision in *Asamera*. The superior efficiencies associated with granting damages (limiting losses to only those which could not have been avoided) required viewing any presumption in favour of specific performance in land cases as rebuttable. Applying a principled approach led to the conclusion that damages would be an adequate remedy for the plaintiffs and to a denial of specific performance.

As for the effect of departing from established precedent and its effect on predictability, Adams J. held that adopting the same principled approach in land and other cases would lead ultimately to more certainty in the law than would following the previously adhered to rigid rule requiring specific performance in land cases.

In subsequent separate reasons dealing with damages[47] Adams J. held that the plaintiffs did not have a fair, real and substantial justification for their claim to specific performance, and were therefore not justified in postponing their mitigation of damages for the seven years which passed between the date of the breach and the date of the court's determination that specific performance was not an appropriate remedy. Adams J. held that the plaintiffs ought to have mitigated within three months of the date of the breach (notwithstanding the state of the law under *Kloepfer* and *Bashir v. Koper*, and notwithstanding that the plaintiffs in fact obtained summary judgment for specific performance which was later overturned, without addressing the remedy issue, by the Court of Appeal). The plaintiffs were limited in their damages to the difference between the contract price and the price of a replacement investment three months after the contract should have been completed.

(c) *Issues For The Future*

It remains to be seen whether the approach to land cases in *Domowicz v. Orsa Investments Ltd.* will be adopted or rejected by a higher court. The decision raises a number of issues as to the scope of specific performance in the future:

- What will be the continuing status of the special treatment of land

---

[47] (1994), 20 O.R. (3d) 722 (Gen. Div.)

previously accorded by the law? The decisions in *Kloepfer* and *Bashir v. Koper* are neither insignificant nor ancient and, as recently as 1992, the Ontario Court of Appeal reaffirmed that "specific performance of a contract involving a sale of land is the general rule."[48]

• What impact will the adoption of the approach in *Domowicz* have on the availability of certificates of pending litigation? The availability of certificates is more restricted than the availability of the remedy of specific performance, at least on the tests for it at the appellate levels. If the *Domowicz* approach is generally accepted, further restricting the basis for the remedy, will the class of cases in which certificates of pending litigation are available also be further restricted?

• If a governing principle is to achieve greater efficiencies, will it be open to argue in particular cases that specific performance is the more efficient remedy, given its enforceability in insolvency; its avoidance of the costs, delay and expense of damage assessments; and its truer satisfaction of expectation interests? Indeed, this appears to be the approach followed recently in *Joseph Chiavatti Construction Ltd. v. Palleshi*.[49] In that case, the plaintiff brought a motion for summary judgment for specific performance of an agreement of purchase and sale of land. The court considered the decision in *Domowicz*. The court went on to state that the remedy of specific performance should be approached in a reasonably broad way, bearing in mind that it is equitable, and in the discretion of the court. After finding that the property at issue was a "money property" which, although possessed of certain advantages could not be considered unique, the court concluded that it was a proper case for an order of specific performance. McNeely J. stated:

> All of that expense (of expert testimony) would be incurred . . . At the end of the day, the Court would be in the position of trying to arrive at an amount of money that was equivalent to performance. We here today are in a position by granting specific performance to see that each of these parties get exactly what they bargained for. In my judgment it is a proper case in every respect to make an order for specific performance and it is for that reason that I have made it.

• Finally, will the principled approach advocated in *Domowicz* lead to the reconsideration of other types of contracts of which specific performance has traditionally been refused? Adams J. thought it would.[50] In England, a decision has been rendered granting specific performance

---

[48] *Mongeon v. Bilapolovich*, unreported, [1992] O.J. No. 1351 (Ont. C.A.).
[49] Unreported, [1994] O.J. No. 1442 (Ont. Gen. Div.), McNeely J.
[50] *Supra*, note 39, at 688.

of a contract for personal service where damages would not have been an adequate remedy, and denying the existence of any inflexible rule that specific performance of such contracts could not be granted.[51] As well, specific performance of a commercial contract for the supply of chattels, though not specific or ascertained, has been granted, where failure to continue to supply could have put the plaintiff out of business.[52] In that case, the court also departed from a well-established rule on the basis of an examination of its underlying principle or purpose, stating:

> Now I come to the most serious hurdle in the way of the plaintiff company which is the well-known doctrine that the court refuses specific performance of a contract to sell and purchase chattels not specific or ascertained. That is a well-established and salutary rule and I am entirely unconvinced by counsel for the plaintiff company when he tells me that an injunction in the form sought by him would not be specific enforcement at all. The matter is one of substance and not of form and it is, in my judgment, quite plain that I am for the time being specifically enforcing the contract if I grant an injunction. However, the ratio behind the rule is, as I believe, that under the ordinary contract for the sale of non-specific goods, damages are a sufficient remedy. That, to my mind, is lacking in the circumstances of the present case. The evidence suggests, and indeed it is common knowlege, that the petroleum market is in an unusual state in which a would-be buyer cannot go out into the market and contract with another seller, possibly at some sacrifice as to price. Here, the defendant company appears for practical purposes to be the plaintiff company's sole means of keeping its business going, and I am prepared so far to depart from the general rule as to try to preserve the position under the contract until a later date. I therefore propose to grant an injunction.

---

[51] *Hill v. C.A. Parsons & Co. Ltd.*, [1972] 1 Ch. 305 (C.A.) at 320.
[52] *Sky Petroleum Ltd. v. VIP Petroleum Ltd.*, [1974] 1 All E.R. 954.

THE INTERLOCUTORY INJUNCTION IN CANADA: READING SMOKE SIGNALS

Nigel Campbell[1]

1. *Introduction*

The "interlocutory injunction"[2] has a lengthy and controversial history. Indeed, this important pre-trial remedy was a catalyst for conflict as early as the 16th century when the English Court of Chancery endeavoured to supplant the strict rules of the common law courts with extraordinary and vigorous tools like the injunction.[3] Even today the subject of the interlocutory injunction draws controversy, particularly in connection with the debate over the appropriate purpose to be served by injunctive relief and the appropriate standard to be applied by a court in deciding whether to grant or refuse the remedy.[4]

The historical and recent[5] controversies are understandable. The issues which the remedy raises are very difficult ones which can range from the

---

[1] Nigel Campbell is a partner with Blake, Cassels & Graydon. The author wishes to acknowledge the valuable research assistance of Paul Adams, Liz Aspinall, Jennifer Horton and Margaret McMullen.

[2] By the term "interlocutory injunction" I will refer to mandatory or prohibitory injunctive relief which is granted after an initial hearing but before the final determination of the merits at trial. In Ontario, s. 101 [am. 1994, c. 12, s. 40] of the *Courts of Justice Act*, R.S.O. 1990, c. C.43, provides that an interlocutory injunction may be granted where it appears to be "just and convenient" to do so. The "just and convenient" language can be traced back to 1881 and s. 17(8) of the *Judicature Act*, 44 Vict., c.5. Rule 40 of the *Rules of Civil Procedure*, R.R.O. 1990, Reg. 194, provides the procedure for obtaining an interlocutory injunction.

[3] Audain, "Of Posner, Newton, and Twenty-First Century Law: An Economic and Statistical Analysis of the Posner Rule for Granting Preliminary Injunctions" (1990), 23 Loy. L.A. L. Rev. 1215 at 1220; Black, "A New Look at Preliminary Injunctions: Can Principles From the Past Offer Any Guidelines to Decisionmakers in the Future?" (1984), 36 Ala. L. Rev. 1 at 3-4.

[4] See, generally, *infra*, footnotes 26, 27 and 28.

[5] By "recent" I mean, in particular, within the last 20 years since the House of Lords decision in *American Cyanamid Co. v. Ethicon Ltd.*, [1975] A.C. 396.

broadly theoretical to the narrowly practical. For example, should the law permit "rights" determinations in advance of full procedural safeguards? What is the proper compromise between the often conflicting goals of judgment accuracy and judgment timeliness?[6] Should the court be concerned with evaluating the "merits" of a case at the interlocutory stage? Is the court competent to evaluate the merits at an early interlocutory stage? If so, how rigorous should the court's evaluation of the merits be? Should the merits evaluation vary where the interlocutory injunction threatens to be dispositive of the dispute?

In Canada, as elsewhere in the Anglo-American law world, the law of interlocutory injunctions continues to develop. Indeed, the law on the subject was recently restated and somewhat clarified in the decision of the Supreme Court of Canada in *RJR-MacDonald Inc. v. Can. (A.G.).*[7] I say "somewhat" clarified because the court approached the task cautiously and in so doing left several troublesome issues open to interpretation. Nevertheless, the *RJR-MacDonald* case is important and it deserves the close attention of the bench and bar. It is possible that the case is a new beginning for future principled decision-making in this country. On the other hand, without due attention, the risk remains that the significance of the case will be overlooked and the courts will continue to resolve whether to grant or refuse interlocutory injunctions based primarily upon a problematic assessment of the likely outcome on the merits and with no real attention to either irreparable harm or the balance of inconvenience.[8]

Accordingly, this article will review and highlight the *RJR-MacDonald* decision. It will then outline the theoretical backdrop against which the decision can be examined. Thereafter, it will offer some observations which will focus on the policy choices made expressly or implicitly by the court. Lastly, this article will make suggestions on how the *RJR-MacDonald* case

---

[6] For a discussion of time as a dimension of justice, see Zuckerman, "Quality and Economy in Civil Procedure: The Case for Commuting Correct Judgments for Timely Judgments" (1994), 14 Oxford J. Legal Stud. 353.

[7] [1994] 1 S.C.R. 311, 60 Q.A.C. 241, 54 C.P.R. (3d) 114, 20 C.R.R. (2d) D-7, 111 D.L.R. (4th) 385, 164 N.R. 1. In brief, Justices Sopinka and Cory, writing for the entire court, concluded that "the *American Cyanamid* standard is now generally accepted by the Canadian courts, subject to the occasional reversion to a stricter standard" (at 335); *American Cyanamid Co.*, *supra*, note 5.

[8] It may be instructive here to recall the way Lord Denning once sought to dismiss the seminal decision of the House of Lords in *American Cyanamid*, *ibid.*: "I think I may say that nowadays all practitioners and judges are so familiar with the *American Cyanamid* case that it is never cited at length. It is taken as read. And the judges grant or refuse interlocutory injunctions in the light of it but they come to just the same result as if the waters had never been troubled". Lord Denning, The Closing Chapter (London: Butterworths, 1983), at 262.

should be applied and built upon, in light of the theoretical choices made by the court.

2. *The RJR-MacDonald Reasons*

In this case the applicants, RJR-MacDonald Inc. and Imperial Tobacco Ltd., attacked the constitutional validity of the *Tobacco Products Control Act*.[9] The complaint was that the legislation was *ultra vires* the Parliament of Canada and invalid as it violated s. 2(*b*) of the *Canadian Charter of Rights and Freedoms*.[10] The applicants had been successful in the Quebec Superior Court. The Court of Appeal, however, allowed the respondents' appeal and found the legislation constitutional. Thereafter, the applicants sought leave to appeal to the Supreme Court of Canada. Before a decision on their leave applications in the main actions had been made, the applicants brought motions for a stay pursuant to s. 65.1 of the *Supreme Court Act*[11] or, in the event that leave was granted, pursuant to r. 27 of the Rules of the Supreme Court of Canada.[12]

The applicants needed the stay from the Supreme Court of Canada to release them from any obligation to comply with impugned new regulations which required expensive redesigning of their packaging to accommodate more prominent health warnings. The stay was to be until the disposition of the constitutional challenge and, also, beyond for twelve months. The applicants argued that the regulations would cause the applicants irreparable harm should the legislation ultimately be found to be unconstitutional. The court characterized the primary issue on the motions as follows:

> . . . whether the applicants should be granted the interlocutory relief they seek. The applicants are only entitled to this relief if they can satisfy the test laid down in *Manitoba (Attorney General) v. Metropolitan Stores (MTS) Ltd.* If not, the applicants will have to comply with the new regulations, at least until such time as the decision is rendered in the main actions.[13]

---

[9] R.S.C. 1985, c. 14 (4th Supp.).

[10] Part I of the *Constitution Act*, 1982, being Sch. B of the *Canada Act*, 1982 (U.K.), c. 11.

[11] R.S.C. 1985, c. S-26. Section 65.1 am. 1990, c. 8, s. 40.

[12] C.R.C. 1978, c. 1512.

[13] *RJR-MacDonald, supra*, note 7, at 333; *Metropolitan Stores (MTS) Ltd.v. Man. (A.G.)*, [1987] 1 S.C.R. 110, 46 Man. R. (2d) 241, 25 Admin. L.R. 20, 87 CLLC 14,015, 18 C.P.C. (2d) 273, 38 D.L.R. (4th) 321, 73 N.R. 341.

In result, the motions for a stay were dismissed. The reasons of the entire court were expressed by Justices Sopinka and Cory.[14] The court specifically concluded that the *American Cyanamid* test (as adopted by Mr. Justice Beetz in *Metropolitan Stores*) should be applied to motions for interlocutory injunctions and, as well, for stays in both private law[15] and Charter cases.

The court expressed the "three-stage test" for granting interlocutory relief as follows:

> First, a preliminary assessment must be made of the merits of the case to ensure that there is a serious question to be tried. Secondly, it must be determined whether the applicant would suffer irreparable harm if the application were refused. Finally, an assessment must be made as to which of the parties would suffer greater harm from the granting or refusal of the remedy pending a decision on the merits.[16]

In connection with the first "stage" of the test the court specifically rejected the need for a moving party to first demonstrate a *prima facie* case on the merits, subject only to two, *possibly* three, generic exceptions. The court adopted instead the threshold of "a serious question to be tried". In so doing the court had this to say:

> What then are the indicators of "a serious question to be tried"? There are no specific requirements which must be met in order to satisfy this test. The threshold is a low one. The judge on the application must make a preliminary assessment of the merits of the case. . . .
>
> Once satisfied that the application is neither vexatious nor frivolous, the motions judge should proceed to consider the second and third tests, even if of the opinion that the plaintiff is unlikely to succeed at trial. A prolonged examination of the merits is generally neither necessary nor desirable.[17]

---

[14] It is interesting to highlight the participation of Justice Cory and also Justice McLachlin. Both learned justices had been responsible for leading interlocutory injunction decisions prior to being elevated to the Supreme Court. Mr. Justice Cory wrote *Yule Inc. v. Atlantic Pizza Delight Franchise (1968) Ltd.* (1977), 17 O.R. (2d) 505, 35 C.P.R. (2d) 273, 80 D.L.R. (3d) 725 (Div. Ct.). Madam Justice McLachlin wrote for the majority in *B.C. (A.G.) v. Wale,* [1987] 2 W.W.R. 331, 9 B.C.L.R. (2d) 333, 120 N.R. 212 (C.A.); affd [1991] 1 S.C.R. 62 [1991] 2 W.W.R. 568, 53 B.C.L.R. (2d) 189, 120 N.R. 208. In this way, particularly, it may be seen that the law of interlocutory injunctions has been restated for the country as a whole.

[15] While the decision in *RJR-MacDonald, supra,* note 7, was in a public law context, I do not believe that this has any limiting effect. It is very clear from the reasons that a broader private law implication was intended.

[16] *Supra,* note 7, at 334.

[17] *Ibid.* at 337-38.

Then, later in the reasons, and in summary, the court stated:

> . . . an applicant for interlocutory relief . . . must demonstrate a serious question to be tried. Whether the test has been satisfied should be determined by a motions judge on the basis of common sense and an extremely limited review of the case on the merits".[18]

As noted just above, and as has recently been acknowledged in the Ontario courts[19] in particular, the Supreme Court of Canada outlined two specific exceptions to the general rule that a moving party need only demonstrate "a serious question to be tried" and that a judge should not engage in a "prolonged" review of the merits. The first exception arises when the result of the interlocutory motion will in effect amount to a final determination of the action. The second exception arises when the question of constitutionality presents itself as a simple question of law alone. Although a third exception was mentioned by the court, it was left in considerable doubt. The third possible exception, "to the extent that this exception exists at all"[20], would be applicable only in the private law context. The third exception may be that the court will engage in a more detailed merits review and require the stronger showing on the merits in circumstances "where the factual record is largely settled"[21] prior to the motion being heard by the court.[22]

At the second stage or the "irreparable harm" stage of the three-stage test, a court must decide whether the potential harm to the plaintiff can be remedied in the future, after the case has been decided on its merits. As the Supreme Court of Canada stated:

> At this stage the only issue to be decided is whether a refusal to grant relief could so adversely affect the applicants' own interests that the harm could not be remedied if the eventual decision on the merits does not accord with the result of the interlocutory application.
>
> "Irreparable" refers to the nature of the harm suffered rather than its magnitude. It is harm which either cannot be quantified in monetary terms or which cannot be cured, usually because one party cannot collect damages from the other.[23]

---

[18] *Ibid.*, at 348.

[19] For example, see *Unitel Communications Inc. v. Bell Canada* (1994), 17 B.L.R. (2d) 63, 29 C.P.C. (3d) 159, 56 C.P.R. (3d) 232 (Ont. Gen. Div.); and *Ont. (A.G.) v. Dieleman* (1995), 20 O.R. (3d) 229, 117 D.L.R. (4th) 449 (Gen. Div.).

[20] *Supra*, note 7, at 340.

[21] *Ibid.*

[22] In connection with this third possible exception, it should be noted that a motion for summary judgment may be a more appropriate procedure in the right case.

[23] *Supra*, note 7, at 341.

In connection with the third stage or the "balance of inconvenience and public interest" stage of the test, the court adopted the description of this stage of the test given by Beetz J. in *Metropolitan Stores*. The court, in that case, determined the third inquiry to involve:

> . . . "a determination of which of the two parties will suffer the greater harm from the granting or refusal of an interlocutory injunction, pending a decision on the merits".[24]

The court expressly adopted Lord Diplock's caution in *American Cyanamid* that the factors to be considered in assessing the balance of inconvenience cannot be and ought not be listed as they are "numerous and will vary in each individual case".[25] Interestingly, and at some peril, the court made no express suggestion how a court might resolve a case where the balance of inconvenience is relatively equal between the parties.

3. *Theoretical Backdrop*

As mentioned in the introduction to this paper, the answers to the question of the rationale for an interlocutory injunction and the question of the best formulation of a standard or test for the granting or withholding of an interlocutory injunction have been the subjects of ongoing controversy. The controversy, embodied in a detailed academic and judicial debate, has perhaps been most animated in the United States.[26] However,

---

[24] *Ibid.*, at 342.

[25] *Ibid.*, at 342.

[26] See generally the following American articles: Audain, *supra*, note 3; Laycock, "The Death of the Irreparable Injury Rule" (1990), 103 Harv. L. Rev. 688; Vaughn, "A Need for Clarity: Toward A New Standard for Preliminary Injunctions" (1989), 68 Or. L. Rev. 838; Santarelli, "Preliminary Injunctions in Delaware: The Need for a Clearer Standard" (1988), 13 Del. J. Corp. L. 107; Heiny, "Formulating a Theory for Preliminary Injunctions: American Hospital Supply Corp. v. Hospital Supply Products Ltd." (1987), 72 Iowa L. Rev. 1157; Black, *supra*, note 3; Wolf, "Preliminary Injunctions: The Varying Standards" (1984), 7 W. New. Eng. L. Rev. 173; Meyer, "Dataphase Systems Inc. v. C.L. Systems, Inc.: Preliminary Injunctions" (1982), 15 Creighton L. Rev. 830; Rendleman, "The Inadequate Remedy at Law Prerequisite for an Injunction" (1981), 33 U. Fla. L. Rev. 346; Shreve, "Federal Injunctions and the Public Interest" (1981), 51 Geo. Wash. L. Rev. 382; Castles III, "Interlocutory Injunctions in Flux: A Plea for Uniformity" (1979), 34 Bus. Law. 1359; Laycock, "Injunctions and the Irreparable Injury Rule" (1979), 57 Tex. L. Rev. 1065; Abrams, "The Fourth Circuit's Liberal Approach to Preliminary Injunctions" (1978), 14 Wake Forest L. Rev. 103, and Leubsdorf, "The Standard for Preliminary Injunctions" (1978), 91 Harv. L. Rev. 525.

Canada[27] and Britain[28] have also had the benefit of a substantial discussion. For the purposes of this paper and as a prelude to further analysis of the *RJR-MacDonald* decision, a summary of these two particular areas of theoretical discussion will be of assistance.

(1) Rationale or Purpose for an Interlocutory Injunction

It seems valid to assert that all the participants in the legal process benefit from laws which are certain and predictable. It is equally logical that the certainty and predictability of the law of interlocutory injunc-

---

[27] See generally the following Canadian articles: Hammond, "Interlocutory Injunctions: Time for a New Model" (1980), 30 U.T.L.J. 240; Carlson, "Granting an Interlocutory Injunction: What is the Test?" (1982), 12 Man. L.J. 109; Stockwood, *American Cyanamid in Ontario Today: A Practical Analysis in Injunctions* (Toronto: The Carswell Company Limited, 1985); Perell, "The Interlocutory Injunction and Irreparable Harm" (1989), 68 Can. Bar Rev. 538; Berryman, "Interlocutory Injunctions and Accessibility Thresholds: Or Once More Round the Mulberry Bush" (1989), 5 I.P.J. 137, and Ahern, "Interlocutory Injunctions in Administrative Law: What is the Test?" (1991-92), 5 C.J.A.L.P. 1.

[28] See generally the following articles from the United Kingdom and Australia: Gray, "Interlocutory Injunctions Since *Cyanamid*" (1981), 40 Cambridge L.J. 307; Zuckerman, "Quality and Economy in Civil Procedure: The Case for Commuting Correct Judgments for Timely Judgments" (1994), 14 Oxford J. Legal Stud. 353; Zuckerman, "Interlocutory Remedies in Quest of Procedural Fairness" (1993), 56 Mod. L. Rev. 325; Spry, "The Myth of the Prima Facie Case" (1981), 55 Austl. L.J. 784; Martin, "Equitable and Inequitable Remedies" (1990), 20 W. Austl. L. Rev. 143; Spry, "Plaintiffs' Undertakings and Equity's Power to Award Damages" (1991), 65 Austl. L.J. 658; Beck, "Interlocutory and Final Orders: A New Kernel in an Old Chestnut?" (1993), 109 L.Q. Rev. 30; Gore, "Interlocutory Injunctions — A Final Judgment?" (1975), 38 Mod. L. Rev. 672; Barav, "Interim Relief and English Law" (1990), New L.J. 899; Lindsay, "Red Hot Issue" (1994), 138 Sol. J. 280.; Zuckerman, "Interlocutory Injunctions on the Merits" (1991), 107 L.Q. Rev. 196; Reville, "Exploring the Limits of Interlocutory Injunctions" (1988), 132 Sol. J. 1575; Forsyth, "Interlocutory Injunctions where there is no legal or equitable right to be protected" (1988), Cambridge L.J. 177; Applegarth, "Interlocutory Injunctions: An Analysis of Recent Developments" (1987), Q.L.S.J. 31; J.G.S., "Principles Governing Grant of an Interlocutory Mandatory Injunction" (1985), 59 Austl. L.J. 630; Sofronoff, "Interlocutory Injunction Having Final Effect" (1987), 61 The Austl. L.J. 341; Chaplin, "Why Give an Undertaking?" (1991), 141 New L.J. 243; Galanisky, "Interlocutory Injunctions and Damages" (1992), 136 Sol. J. 1086; J.G.S., "Can the Crown in Right of the Commonwealth be Required to give an Undertaking as to Damages in Interlocutory Injunction Proceedings?" (1981), 55 Austl. L.J. 102.

tions is advanced by the articulation of a purpose or rationale for the remedy.[29]

Three possible purposes underlying the granting of an interlocutory injunction have emerged.[30] First, maintaining the *status quo*. Second, minimizing the risk of judicial error.[31] Third, preserving the court's ability to render a meaningful final decision.[32]

While maintaining the *status quo* has been expressed often in the past as the goal of an interlocutory injunction, that objective has now been discredited as being unhelpful.[33] For example, Professor Vaughn has this to say about such a purpose:

> Historically, preserving the status quo stands out as the most common justification. Consider the following common statement: "The purpose of the preliminary injunction is to preserve the status quo between the parties pending a final determination of the merits of the action." Maintaining the status quo incorporates several considerations for granting interlocutory relief. Within the context of historical equity, it theoretically afforded the moving party effective relief after a full trial on the merits. The term was often used reflexively and in combination with other equitable principles. Courts did not always fully consider what leaving the parties in the status quo, however defined, might do to their relative positions. For example, blindly invoking the status quo in a situation in which the defendant has already caused some harm to the moving party is not effective relief.
>
> The status quo concept also embraces a timing factor. At some point in the relationship or transactions between the parties the court must identify it. Classically, that time was the last peaceable status between the parties. But when courts attempted to inquire into that peaceable situation, they have tripped over another component of a status quo oriented purpose: the parties' subjective description of that time. One person's last noncontested status was often another's declaration of war.

---

[29] See, for example, Leubsdorf, *supra*, note 26, at 566, where it is noted that a serious defect of preliminary injunction standards has been "the lack of an articulated rationale". The proper purpose for granting preliminary relief has tended to be at the centre of the debate surrounding the appropriate standard for preliminary injunctive relief.

[30] Vaughn, *supra*, note 26, at 849-50.

[31] See Audain, "Of Posner, Newton, and Twenty-First Century Law: An Economic and Statistical Analysis of the Posner Rule for Granting Preliminary Injunctions" (1990), 23 Loy. L.A.L. Rev. 1215; Heiny, *supra*, note 26; and Leubsdorf, *supra*, note 26. See also the decision of Judge Posner in *American Hospital Supply Corp. v. Hospital Products*, 780 F. 2d 589 (7th Cir. 1986).

[32] See Vaughn, *supra*, note 26; and Wolf, *supra*, note 26.

[33] Leubsdorf, *supra*, note 26, at 526, 535-36 and 546 (criticizing this rationale as a "habit without reason"); Wolf, *supra*, note 26, at 173 (suggesting this rationale has caused confusion); and Audain, *supra*, note 31, at 1233.

When these components are added together, it becomes easy to see why the status quo purpose has been so freely abandoned. The doctrine is manipulable and subjective. It rests heavily upon the parties' evaluation of the facts when there is not much time to evaluate them. As a principle, it does not inform the deliberations for a preliminary injunction in any meaningful way.[34]

The Supreme Court of Canada in the *RJR-MacDonald* decision appears to have accepted observations like these by Professor Vaughn and questioned the utility of the concept of maintaining the *status quo* as a helpful principle.[35] Accordingly, little more will be said about it as a viable purpose for an interlocutory injunction.

A second purpose, minimizing the risk of judicial error in granting or refusing an interlocutory injunction, has received some recent support.[36] While, perhaps, this rationale is intuitively appealing it too has been criticized, particularly in connection with its preoccupation with the merits of the case. For example, Professor Vaughn has observed, as follows:

> Professor Leubsdorf has suggested minimizing risk as the justification for the injunctive standard: "The preliminary injunction standard should aim to minimize the probable irreparable loss of rights caused by errors incident to hasty decision". This justification, he argues, fully captures a court's dilemma in making a decision that, because of the truncated hearing, might mistakenly adjust the rights and injuries of the parties. Consequently, Professor Leubsdorf and Judge Posner, who adopts his theory, emphasize success on the merits over the other factors in the injunctive standard. But when courts focus on the merits, they undermine the traditional function of interlocutory relief, that is, relieving the moving party of injuries that cannot be remedied after trial. This forces the preliminary injunction to do procedural work it ought not do — the preliminary injunction hearing becomes a mini-trial on the merits of the case.[37]

A third possible rationale underlying the granting of interlocutory relief is to create an interlocutory order which ensures that effective relief can be rendered when the matter is ultimately heard on its merits.[38] The

---

[34] *Supra*, note 26, at 849-50.

[35] [1994] 1 S.C.R. 311 at 347, 60 Q.A.C. 241, 54 C.P.R. (3d) 114, 20 C.R.R. (2d) D-7, 111 D.L.R. (4th) 385, 164 N.R. 1.

[36] Audain, *supra*, note 31; Leubsdorf, *supra*, note 26; and *American Hospital Supply Corp.*, *supra*, note 31.

[37] *Supra*, note 26, at 850.

[38] Wolf, *supra*, note 26, at 228-29; and Vaughn, *supra*, note 26, at 842 and 853. Although Professor Leubsdorf has been critical of this rationale, his criticism has been directed to the situation in which the granting of an interlocutory injunction would resolve the matter before the merits are heard. See Leubsdorf, *supra*, note 26, at 545-46. In such circumstances, as we have seen, the Supreme Court of Canada seems to have agreed that it is appropriate to

focus of attention under this "effective relief" rationale is away from the merits and towards the minimization of harm pending a final resolution. This rationale is more purposeful than a *status quo* rationale and may often require a material change in the *status quo* between the parties where such change better ensures an effective ultimate decision. This rationale also requires a much more careful analysis of what will constitute irreparable harm and how competing harms will be weighed and measured. Professor Vaughn has succinctly articulated this rationale as follows:

> . . . the preliminary injunction should create a state of affairs that will best give effective relief to the parties when the case has been fully heard on the merits. The court should deliberately engage in a debate as to what will best accommodate the often conflicting interests of the parties, while preserving its ability to render a meaningful final decision. The touchstone here is that the relief be effective.
>
> This approach has several advantages. It ends the resort to outmoded historical formulas such as preserving the status quo or the mandatory/permissive distinction. By forcing the court to focus on the facts and the consequences of relief, it encourages the court to flexibly exercise its discretion. Where the focus is on creating effective interlocutory relief, the court should feel relatively free to experiment with its order.[39]

These three purposes for injunctive relief will be returned to below and considered in the context of further analysis of the Supreme Court's decision in *RJR-MacDonald*.

(2) A Standard for Interlocutory Injunctions

With a worthwhile purpose or rationale for interlocutory injunctions in mind, it becomes necessary and possible to determine the most appropriate way to achieve that purpose. The choice of standard, it would seem, is driven by the purpose to be fostered.[40]

---

analyze the merits of the case in greater detail and to demand that the moving party demonstrate a *prima facie* case.

[39] *Supra*, note 26, at 850-51.

[40] It has been suggested that a good standard should exhibit four qualities. Professor Vaughn has articulated those qualities to be as follows: "First, it should encourage purposeful argument and deliberation by the court and the parties. By focusing their attention on only factually and legally relevant matters, it will allow informed and productive discussions of the case. Second, the standard should attempt to equalize power between the parties, allowing them to present their best case. Third, the standard should promote clarity and candor, both in arguments and decisions. Finally, it should be easy to use" (Vaughn, *supra*, note 26, at 842).

Mr. Justice Cory, who it may be remembered contributed to the reasons in the *RJR-MacDonald* decision, writing for the Ontario Divisional Court in the case of *Yule Inc. v. Atlantic Pizza Delight Franchise (1968) Ltd.*[41] accepted that there were three standards at work in Canada at that time. The first was a "multi-requisite" test. The second was the "multi-factor" test. The third was the *American Cyanamid* approach.

The multi-requisite test required that the moving party clear a number of hurdles; the first hurdle being that the moving party show a *prima facie* case. If no *prima facie* case was demonstrated, then the application was to be dismissed without consideration of any other aspect such as irreparable harm or balance of convenience.

The multi-factor test required the court to weigh the performance of the plaintiff in a number of categories. If the plaintiff failed in one of the six categories, the plaintiff might nevertheless obtain injunctive relief by making a strong showing in other categories. This test also required that the plaintiff establish a *prima facie* case on the merits.

The *American Cyanamid* test was the third standard evident in Canada at the time. As will be further elaborated, the Supreme Court of Canada in the *RJR-MacDonald* decision has now seen fit to require the application of that standard throughout the country but with a difference. We now have the *RJR-MacDonald* test in Canada.

4. Policy Choices

With the foregoing theoretical backdrop in mind it is possible to further consider the decision of the Supreme Court of Canada in *RJR-MacDonald*. In doing so it can be seen that two important policy choices have been made by the court. First, while the court has made no express statement of purpose or rationale for an interlocutory injunction, it appears that the court has adopted an "effective relief" rationale by implication. Second, the court has elected the *American Cyanamid* test and in doing so has been emphatic in discouraging a merits based analysis for interlocutory injunctions. These two policy choices are the key to the proper understanding and future development of the law of interlocutory injunctions in Canada.

In addressing first the question of the purpose for an interlocutory injunction, it may be concluded that the court has drawn very close to the third rationale expressed earlier. That is, the court believes that an interlocutory injunction ought to create a state of affairs that will best ensure effective relief for the parties when the case has been fully heard

---

[41] (1977), 17 O.R. (2d) 505, 35 C.P.R. (2d) 273, 80 D.L.R. (3d) 725 (Div. Ct.).

on the merits. This conclusion may be implied from the *RJR-MacDonald* decision for the following reasons.

The court can be interpreted to have dismissed maintaining the *status quo* as a rationale for an interlocutory injunction by the following expression:

> In the course of discussing the balance of convenience in *American Cyanamid*, Lord Diplock stated at p. 408 that when everything else is equal, "it is a counsel of prudence to . . . preserve the status quo." This approach would seem to be of limited value in private law cases, and, although there may be exceptions, as a general rule it has no merit as such in the face of the alleged violation of fundamental rights. One of the functions of the *Charter* is to provide individuals with a tool to challenge the existing order of things or status quo.[42]

Similarly, the minimization of the risk of judicial error was implicitly rejected as a useful rationale by the court. As previously pointed out, the objective of minimizing risk of judicial error is directly addressed by a detailed evaluation of the merits of the claim. In contrast, the Supreme Court of Canada has gone as far as possible in de-emphasizing the merits, suggesting instead that a merits review generally is "neither necessary nor desirable".[43]

Then, turning to what the court has adopted, it is evident from the reasons that the court has concluded that the parties' relative inconvenience or irreparable harm is a more fruitful and accessible point of inquiry at the interlocutory stage. Such an inconvenience analysis is less consistent with a rationale of minimization of the risk of judicial error than it is with the rationale that a requested injunction should be granted or rejected depending upon which choice most effectively ensures meaningful relief when the case is being heard on the merits. While effective relief will not always result in the avoidance of harm to both parties during the interlocutory period, a court should seek to minimize that harm.

The second important policy choice evident in *RJR-MacDonald* is the choice of the *American Cyanamid* test but with a difference. The difference comes from the court's very clear disenchantment with a merits analysis at the interlocutory stage.

It is to be remembered that in the *American Cyanamid* decision Lord

---

[42] *Supra*, note 35, at 347.

[43] Admittedly, the court leaves some scope for the rationale of minimizing risk of judicial error by the admission of "exceptions" which permit a more detailed merits review. However, these exceptions are to be narrowly construed and resorted to only in rare circumstances. It seems therefore that as exceptions they cannot be taken to evidence the adoption of the rationale of minimizing the risk of judicial error.

Diplock's reasoning reduced the degree of merits analysis at the threshold stage of the test for the granting of an interlocutory injunction by adopting the "serious question to be tried" formula. However, Lord Diplock sent a somewhat contradictory signal when later in the formulation of the test a further merits inquiry was recommended to resolve cases in which the balance of inconvenience inquiry determined the disadvantages between the parties to be equal.[44]

In *RJR-MacDonald* the court has avoided Lord Diplock's circularity. This is clear from the reasons as a whole but particularly from the various strong expressions used by the court to indicate that merits analysis is "neither necessary nor desirable" and also from the court's clear intent to narrowly circumscribe the two acknowledged exceptions and to virtually eradicate the possible third exception.[45] This aversion to merit analysis is likely based upon the court's recognition that most interlocutory injunctions are so fraught with practical limitations as to make merit assessments highly problematic.[46] Without question interlocutory injunction procedure does not ensure factual transparency. The procedure is often high speed. The injunction motion is usually argued without full documentary production, upon affidavit evidence which may have been tested by limited cross-examination outside the court.[47]

Indeed, based upon the court's expressions and the weaknesses inherent in merits analysis at an early interlocutory stage, it would seem that the court would not countenance a return to an evaluation of the merits even in a close case where the inconveniences to be experienced by the plaintiff and the defendant are relatively equal.

5. *The Application of RJR-MacDonald*

The *RJR-MacDonald* reasons were carefully formulated by the Supreme Court of Canada. It would be a mistake to read the decision as a mere duplication of *American Cyanamid*. To the contrary, with an appreciation of the policy choices apparently made by the court, it is demonstrable that the decision represents a new beginning in the development of the law of interlocutory injunctions.

---

[44] [1975] A.C. 396 at 409.

[45] *Supra*, note 35, at 338 and 339.

[46] It should be noted, however, that there is a troubling lack of empirical data to indicate how often interlocutory injunctions granted after a merits assessment turn out to have been incorrectly granted.

[47] The procedure on interlocutory injunctions does vary from province to province. For example, in some provinces cross-examination on affidavits is rare and then only with leave, at the return of the motion.

On one level the decision simply provides a succinct test for the granting of an interlocutory injunction. Unless the case presented to a court engages one of the two exceptions, the reasons require that a court hearing an interlocutory injunction motion ask the following questions in the following order. First, the court must ask whether the plaintiff's case demonstrates a serious question to be tried. The answer to this question is determined by a motions judge "on the basis of common sense and an extremely limited review of the case on the merits"[48]. Second, the court must be satisfied that the plaintiff faces irreparable harm if the injunction is not granted. The quality that makes harm irreparable is that it is unquantifiable or, although quantifiable, possibly unrecoverable.[49] At the third stage of the test the court must evaluate the relative degrees of harm between the parties were an injunction to issue or not.

However, it is at a deeper level that the importance of the *RJR-MacDonald* decision becomes most apparent. The two significant features of the reasons are the determinations by the court that the merits are frequently impenetrable at the interlocutory stage and that the court's decision to grant or refuse an injunction should be guided by the objective of creating a state of affairs which most effectively ensures meaningful relief when the case is heard at trial. These two principles cannot be overlooked and are essential to the proper application of *RJR-MacDonald*, particularly in the more difficult cases. Nevertheless, there is a risk that these principles may not be given the attention which they deserve.

It has been observed, reasonably it would seem, that "when applying *American Cyanamid*, courts readily move towards finding comparable disadvantage to both parties and thus ultimately justifying merit adjudication to tip the balance".[50] This reluctance to stay away from a merits based inquiry may have been due to the fact that, generally speaking, judges and lawyers are more familiar and comfortable with merit evaluations and they are unfamiliar and uncomfortable with inconvenience assessments. However, this reluctance cannot be reconciled with the *RJR-MacDonald* decision. The impact of the reasons does not permit resort to a merits adjudication.

Unfortunately, it is evident that courts dealing with motions for interlocutory injunctions subsequent to the *RJR-MacDonald* decision remain reluctant to move in the direction mandated by the Supreme Court of Canada. For example, *the Federal Court of Appeal, with the benefit of the reasons in RJR-MacDonald*, recently discussed the appropriate test

---

[48] *Supra*, note 35, at 348.

[49] *Ibid.*, at 341.

[50] Berryman, "Interlocutory Injunctions and Accessibility Thresholds: Or Once More Round the Mulberry Bush" (1989), 5 I.P.J. 137 at 148.

for granting or refusing an interlocutory injunction.[51] In that case, the court faced appeals from orders of the Trial Division dismissing a motion for an interlocutory injunction in an action for, *inter alia*, passing off. The appellant had sought an interlocutory injunction to prevent the respondent from carrying out various steps in connection with the sale and distribution in Canada of certain drugs in pill form. The motion judge had refused the injunction following the *American Cyanamid* approach. The motion judge had concluded that a serious issue had been raised and that neither party had demonstrated a greater irreparable harm than the other. In dealing with the issue of the balance of convenience, the motions judge had concluded that he was unable to find any factors "which tip the balance of convenience significantly one way or the other". In consequence, the learned judge felt it appropriate to return to an assessment of the merits of the case. On return to the merits, the motions court judge concluded that the appellant/plaintiff lacked "much substance" to its case.

Mr. Justice Stone gave reasons for the Federal Court of Appeal. Justice Stone concluded that the motions court judge had correctly applied the *American Cyanamid* tests as adopted by the Supreme Court of Canada in *RJR-MacDonald*. Mr. Justice Stone appears to have specifically approved Dean Robert J. Sharpe's synopsis of the *American Cyanamid* test as follows:

> First, as indicated, the court is to ask whether the plaintiff has presented a case which is not frivolous or vexatious but which presents a serious case to be tried. Second, will damages provide the plaintiff with an adequate remedy? If so, no injunction should be granted. If not, third, would the plaintiff's undertaking in damages provide adequate compensation to the defendant should he or she succeed at trial, for loss sustained because of the interlocutory injunction? If so, then there is a strong case for an interlocutory injunction. Fourth, where there is doubt as to the adequacy of the respective remedies and damages, the case turns on the balance of convenience. Fifth, at this point, according to Lord Diplock, weight may be placed on the court's prediction of ultimate success, but only in certain cases.[52]

Mr. Justice Stone also concluded that the motions court judge had underestimated the strength of the appellant's case.[53] The learned justice stated further that "in order for the strength of case factor to tip the

---

[51] *Searle Canada Inc. v. Novopharm Ltd.*, [1994] 3 F.C. 603, 56 C.P.R. (3d) 213, 81 F.T.R. 320*n*, 171 N.R. 48 (C.A.).

[52] See Sharpe, *Injunctions and Specific Performance*, 2nd ed. (Toronto: Canada Law Book, 1993), at 2.190.

[53] This opposite finding reveals the second concern with merits analysis at the interlocutory stage. Not only will the court be concerned whether it has a fair understanding of the facts but there is the additional risk that even the "known" facts may be open to more than one interpretation.

balance in favour of granting an injunction, I would have to be satisfied that the appellant stands a good chance of succeeding at trial"[54]. Mr. Justice Stone went on to indicate that he had difficulty in reliably predicting the outcome of the litigation and, although the question was serious, the outcome at trial remained uncertain. As the appellant had not established a good chance of succeeding, an interlocutory injunction was refused.

It is respectfully submitted that the *Searle* decision is regressive and inconsistent with the proper application of the *RJR-MacDonald* decision, which requires a significantly different approach. First, the Supreme Court of Canada is recommending a much closer and detailed consideration of the harm likely to be experienced by the parties. The practical consequence of this is that the evidence now required upon an interlocutory injunction motion must very carefully demonstrate each party's inconvenience. Weak evidence or mechanical reference to possible harm will be insufficient. The *RJR-MacDonald* decision then requires that the judiciary carefully assess and weigh the evidence of inconvenience and make a determination based upon it. Second, assuming that even after close examination the evidence suggests equality in inconvenience between the parties, the decision in *RJR-MacDonald* requires a court to "break the tie" or "tip the balance", where possible, by means other than a return to merit adjudication. Where other means do not avail, presumably no injunction can be granted.

The decision in *RJR-MacDonald* does not expressly address the alternate means by which close cases may be resolved. However, the means ought to be inferred from the apparent purpose for injunctive relief which the court has adopted. As noted, that purpose can be described as the creation of a state of affairs which most effectively ensures meaningful relief when the case is heard on the merits.

With this purpose in mind it seems that the proper application of *RJR-MacDonald* requires that all cases, though most importantly close cases, should be resolved by careful attention to creative order drafting.[55] In other words, the court should endeavour to devise an order which brings about a satisfactory state of affairs between the parties during the interlocutory

---

[54] *Supra*, note 51, at para. 31.
[55] Vaughn, "A Need for Clarity: Toward A New Standard for Preliminary Injunctions" (1989), 103 Harv. L. Rev. 688 at 854-55 (arguing that the "court should employ the full range of its discretion and be willing to try creative drafting solutions"); and Wolf, "Preliminary Injunctions: The Varying Standards" (1984), 7 W. New Eng. L. Rev. 173 at 230 (suggesting that courts could impose conditions on the moving party in exchange for the injunction). See also Leubsdorf, "The Standard for Preliminary Injunctions" (1978), 91 Harv. L. Rev. 525 at 558 (observing that judicial efforts to make injuries "reparable" or to minimize irreparable injury, if possible, can operate to "simplify" the interlocutory decision).

period so that a meaningful outcome at trial is assured.[56] Accordingly, the imaginative invention of new tools for achieving such a state of affairs is where the next development in the law of interlocutory injunctions should occur.

It can be expected that the most effective tools will usually arise from the particular facts which the court encounters. Some possibilities immediately come to mind. Most apparent would be those tools or variations on those tools which are already found in the court's arsenal. For example, in return for an injunction, the plaintiff could be required to put forward a *substantial* undertaking as to damages involving the posting of security based on a realistic assessment of possible damages.[57] Similarly, the court might require a cross-undertaking from the defendant or, perhaps, a requirement that a monitor be appointed to keep pertinent records which will facilitate subsequent calculations of profits or losses.

Another useful tool might be found in the court's ability to control its processes. As suggested earlier, time is an important dimension of justice. At least in part, the recognition of this dimension underlies recent court initiatives to streamline procedures, manage cases and promote quicker passage to the trial stage. Accordingly, for the proper interlocutory injunction case, the court may wish to resolve uncertainty with an order for an early trial after an expedited discovery and pre-trial process. In other words, the possible harm which might otherwise be experienced because of the interlocutory period can be moderated by shortening that period.[58] Additionally, the court hearing the interlocutory injunction might consider, in the appropriate case, requiring the parties to mediate or, at least, negotiate the terms of an injunction order so as to forge the best compromise over the interlocutory stage. Without any question there is substantial scope for the determination of new and creative interlocutory injunction orders.

---

[56] It should be clarified that a resort to creative order drafting is not simply a mechanical step to be considered and taken only in exceptional circumstances or simply at a late stage in the application of the *RJR-MacDonald* test. Instead, creative order drafting is more "holistic", requiring consideration throughout the decision-making process.

[57] For example, courts in the United States have required the moving party to post a bond pursuant to rule 65(c) of the *Federal Rules of Civil Procedure.* See Leubsdorf, *supra*, note 55, at 558-60; Vaughn, *supra*, note 55, at 853-54; Wolf, *supra*, note 55, at 230; and Meyer, "Dataphase Systems Inc. v. C.L. Systems, Inc.: Preliminary Injunctions" (1982), 15 Creighton L. Rev. 830 at 831.

[58] Leubsdorf, *ibid.*, at 556-58.

6. *Conclusion*

In conclusion, it is possible to summarize the thesis of this paper as follows. It has been suggested that the *RJR-MacDonald* decision is important and worthy of close attention. It would be a mistake to interpret the case as though it did not advance a changed approach to the law of interlocutory injunctions. The court has sounded a very strong warning that merits analysis is neither necessary nor desirable. The court instead has recommended an analysis which requires very careful attention to the matter of relative inconvenience. In all instances but especially in the event that the inconvenience to the parties is reasonably balanced, the court requires detailed attention to the development of an effective and creative order to resolve the motion. It is in this latter area particularly that the *RJR-MacDonald* decision is inviting growth. It will now be for the bench and bar to give life and meaning to this new initiative.

THE OPPRESSION REMEDY: REASONABLE EXPECTATIONS OF SHAREHOLDERS

John A. Campion
Stephanie A. Brown
Alistair M. Crawley[1]

"No rational God guarantees in advance that important areas of practical activity will be governed by elegant theories."[2]

1. *Introduction*

Few would disagree that judicial discretion is necessary and desirable in balancing the interests of corporate stakeholders in the context of applying the oppression remedy. However, in the interests of engendering a degree of predictability in the standards of acceptable corporate conduct, such discretion must be exercised within a developed framework of rules. Too often, the courts, in dealing with the oppression remedy, have operated under the justification guise of vague notions of fairness and have failed to devise a coherent set of principles and standards against which these notions of fairness can be measured. A discernible trend in recent cases, however, has been to look to the reasonable expectations of the corporate stakeholders, particularly shareholders' expectations, to determine whether there has been a breach of those expectations giving rise to a situation which is oppressive.

The proposition that a violation of the reasonable expectations of a shareholder could give rise to relief under the oppression remedy is an interesting one, in that it shifts the analytical emphasis from wrongful or unfair conduct to the determination of whether a situation exists which is unfair to the shareholder concerned. In this respect, it is submitted that the analysis is truer to the scheme of the oppression remedy provisions

---

[1] We would like to acknowledge the generous assistance of Lisa Tracey and Paul Severin, students-at-law, Fasken Campbell Godfrey.
[2] Grey, "Holmes and Legal Pragmatism" (1989), 41 Stan. L. Rev. 787 at 815.

in the business corporation statutes, and more readily achieves the legislative goal of protecting the rights of minority shareholders.

This paper focuses on the concept of shareholders' reasonable expectations. It explores the potential for the analysis of shareholders' reasonable expectations to constitute the conceptual framework of the oppression remedy with respect to its application to shareholders. The theoretical and practical implications of the application of the concept are examined, as are its limitations. The overall thesis of this paper, however, is that an analysis of shareholders' reasonable expectations, while not capable of answering many of the hard questions in oppression cases, provides the most satisfactory theoretical framework upon which to understand, analyze and develop the oppression remedy.

2. *Historical Background*

To understand the modern statutory oppression remedy and the body of law which has developed around it, one must understand its origins. The statutory oppression remedy in Canadian law is derived from s. 210 of the *Company Act (U.K.), 1948.* Section 210 was a far more limited remedy than its modern Canadian counterpart. It was a requirement that the applicant establish the existence of both "oppressive" conduct and circumstances such that it would be "just and equitable" to order a winding-up. The latter requirement placed a significant limitation on the scope of the remedy.[3]

Section 210 was enacted to remedy the injustices which can, in certain limited circumstances, flow from a strict application of the common law principle of majority rule. At common law, a minority shareholder had no remedy against a majority shareholder that abused its control to the prejudice of a minority shareholder. Section 210 provided a remedy which allowed the court to look beyond the "legal rights", rigidly applied at common law, to principles of fairness or "equitable considerations". Lord Wilberforce described these equitable considerations as follows:

> The "just and equitable" provision . . . does . . . as equity always does, enable the court to subject the exercise of legal rights to equitable considera-

---

[3] Relief under the just and equitable winding-up remedy was predicated on the presence of certain requirements, including, (i) a loss of the substratum of the company, (ii) a justifiable loss of confidence in the management of the company, (iii) deadlock in management and (iv) the existence of a partnership in the guise of a corporation. See Huberman, "Winding-up of Business Corporations" in Ziegel, ed., *Studies in Canadian Company Law*, vol. II (Toronto: Butterworths, 1973), at 273.

tions; considerations, that is, of a personal character arising between one individual and another, which may make it unjust, or inequitable, to insist on legal rights, or to exercise them in a particular way.[4]

The first Canadian jurisdiction to enact a statutory oppression remedy was British Columbia in 1960.[5] The provision mimicked s. 210 of the *Company Act (U.K.), 1948*. After considerable agonizing and head scratching both in Ontario[6] and at the federal level,[7] statutory oppression remedies were enacted federally and in several provinces, including Ontario.[8] With the exception of British Columbia, the statutory oppression remedies in the *Canada Business Corporations Act* and the provincial statutes are identical.

Section 210 of the *Company Act (U.K.), 1948* provided no guidance as to the meaning of "oppressive" or "just and equitable". The early English cases tended to define oppression in terms of broad notions of fairness or superficial dictionary definitions. For example, in *Elder v. Elder & Watson*[9], Lord Cooper described oppression in the nebulous terms of "fair dealing" and "fair play":

> . . . the essence of the matter seems to be that the conduct complained of should at the lowest involve a visible departure from the standards of fair dealing, and a violation of the conditions of fair play on which every shareholder who entrusts his money to a company is entitled to rely.[10]

Similarly, and equally unhelpfully, in *Scottish Co-operative Wholesale Society Ltd. v. Meyer*[11], Viscount Simond adopted and purported to apply a dictionary definition of "oppressive":

---

[4] *Ebrahimi v. Westbourne Galleries Ltd.*, [1973] A.C. 360 (H.L.) at 379.
[5] For an overview of the legislative history of the oppression remedy in Canada see: Peterson, *Shareholder Remedies in Canada* (Toronto and Vancouver: Butterworths, 1989), at 18.7.
[6] Ontario *Interim Report of the Select Committee on Company Law* (Toronto: Queen's Printer, 1967) (also known as the "*Lawrence Report*").
[7] Dickerson, *Proposals for a New Business Corporations Law for Canada*, vol. I and vol. II (Ottawa: Information Canada, 1971) (also known as the "*Dickerson Report*").
[8] *Canada Business Corporations Act*, R.S.C. 1985, c. C-44, s. 234 (hereinafter CBCA); Ontario *Business Corporations Act*, R.S.O. 1990, c. B.16, s. 248(2) (hereinafter OBCA); Manitoba *Corporations Act*, R.S.M. 1987, c. C-225, s. 234; Alberta *Business Corporations Act*, S.A. 1981, c. B-15, s. 234; New Brunswick *Business Corporations Act*, S.N.B. 1981, c. B-9.1, s. 166(2); Nova Scotia *Companies Act*, R.S.N.S. 1989, c. 81, s. 5(2). The remaining provinces do not have a statutory oppression remedy.
[9] [1952] Sess. Cas. 49 (Ct. Sess.) (hereinafter *Elder*).
[10] *Ibid.*, at 55.
[11] [1959] A.C. 324 (H.L.) (hereinafter *Scottish Co-op*).

. . . it appears to me incontrovertible that the society have behaved to the minority shareholders of the company in a manner which can justly be described as "oppressive." They had the majority power and they exercised their authority in a manner "burdensome, harsh and wrongful" — I take the dictionary meaning of the word.[12]

Elder and *Scottish Co-op* continue to be cited as if they are enlightening treatises on the meaning of "oppression"; however, clearly their value in this respect is minimal. The early jurisprudence fails to establish a workable standard against which to measure conduct that is alleged to be oppressive. This failing has been carried over into the Canadian jurisprudence, in which judges and counsel have looked to the early English decisions in an attempt to interpret and apply the oppression remedy provisions in Canadian statutes.

3. *The Modern Oppression Remedy*

The modern United Kingdom oppression remedy[13] is a different creature from the original statutory provision. First, there is no requirement that it be just and equitable to wind-up the corporation. Secondly, rather than relief being predicated on the existence of "oppressive" conduct, the question is whether the company's affairs have been conducted in a manner which is unfairly prejudicial to some part of the members of the company. The reference to "unfairly prejudicial" as opposed to "oppressive" suggests an emphasis on the *effect* of the conduct on the shareholder rather than the nature and quality of the conduct itself.

The Canadian oppression remedy contained in the business corporations statutes is even further removed from the original United Kingdom provision. Although a discussion of its various features is beyond the scope of this paper, it is worth noting that the oppression remedy is available to a broad range of corporate stakeholders in addition to shareholders and, furthermore, that the range of remedies available to the court is extremely extensive. Of greater significance to the discussion in this paper, however, is the articulation of the circumstances which may give rise to relief under the section. A court may make an order in the event that an act or omission of the corporation (or an affiliate) effects a *result*, or the business and affairs of the corporation have been *carried on or conducted in a manner*, or the powers of the directors have been *exercised in a*

---

[12] *Ibid.*, at 342.
[13] *Companies Act, (U.K.)*, 1980, c. 22, s. 459.

manner, that is: (i) *oppressive*; or (ii) *unfairly prejudicial* to; or (iii) that *unfairly disregards* the interests of; any stakeholder.

The substantive preconditions of relief encompass three different types of circumstances, which can be characterized as follows:

(1) wrongful conduct;
(2) an unfair result; and
(3) an unfair process.

Accordingly, the scope of the oppression remedy is far broader than the original formulation in the *Companies Act (U.K.)*. For that reason it is questionable whether the pre-business corporations statute jurisprudence defining the circumstances in which relief is available should be applicable in any *restrictive* sense as an aid to interpreting the modern provisions. That is particularly so with cases that predicate relief under the oppression remedy on the presence of egregious conduct. Contemporary analysis must move beyond a focus on the nature and quality of particular conduct and consider also the *effect* of that conduct and the *process* by which the conduct was implemented.

While judicial discretion is inevitable and desirable in adjudicating the various and unique factual contexts which arise in oppression cases, it is unfortunate that no conceptual framework has been devised that can provide a principled approach to the application of the remedy. This failure raises the spectre of indeterminate and arbitrary exercises of judicial power, a point which has not gone unrecognized and has prompted charges of "selective judicial intervention".[14] However, a review of the jurisprudence reveals that there is an underlying theme in oppression remedy cases concerning shareholders' rights that has the potential to rationalize a large part of the judicial activity concerning the oppression remedy. That theme is the protection of shareholders' reasonable expectations.

4. *Shareholders' Reasonable Expectations*

Shareholders' expectations are the expectations that underlie a shareholders' decision to invest in a particular corporation. They include expectations as to the nature of the business invested in, the corporate structure, the ownership structure, the financial structure of the corpora-

---

[14] Welling, *Corporate Law in Canada: The Governing Principles* (Toronto: Butterworths, 1984), at 532.

tion and the source of the control of the business and affairs of the corporation.[15]

In addition to these expectations, which will vary depending on the nature of the corporation invested in, there are various norms of corporate law that shareholders may be presumed to expect:

- that the business and affairs of the corporation will be managed by a board of directors which will act in the best interests of the corporation;[16]
- that shareholders have no right to manage the business and affairs of the corporation except to the extent that they have removed such powers from the board of directors pursuant to a unanimous shareholders' agreement;[17]
- that the extent of any obligations owed by and between shareholders will be pursuant to an agreement between the shareholders;[18] and
- that majority rule is the touchstone of corporate governance.

However, in certain types of corporations, most typically closely-held corporations, shareholders may have various expectations which deviate from the norms referred to above. Specifically, shareholders might expect:

- that their investment in the corporation as a shareholder will entitle them to participate in management;
- that dissolution of the corporation will follow in the event that the shareholder ceases to participate in management;
- that shareholders will receive returns on their investment in the form of salary for the provision of management services rather than through dividends; and
- that majority rule will not prevail over the individual shareholders' wishes.

---

[15] See *Palmer v. Carling O'Keefe Ltd.* (1989), 32 O.A.C. 113, 67 O.R. (2d) 161, 41 B.L.R. 128 at 136, 56 D.L.R. (4th) 128 (S.C.), in which preference shareholders brought an oppression application as a consequence of an amalgamation of Carling O'Keefe and Elders IXL approved by the board of directors. It was significant to a finding of oppression that the shareholders "had invested in a Canadian brewing company, not an Australian conglomerate", and that the debt to equity ratio of Carling O'Keefe had been 1:5, whereas with the amalgamated corporation it became 10:1.

[16] CBCA, *supra*, note 8, s. 102.

[17] *Ibid.*, s. 146.

[18] Majority shareholders do not owe fiduciary duties to minority shareholders. See *Brant Investments Ltd. v. Keeprite Inc.* (1990), 45 O.A.C. 320, 3 O.R. (3d) 289, 1 B.L.R. (2d) 225 at 244, 80 D.L.R. (4th) 161 (C.A.).

This provides a rough, and by no means exhaustive, guide to the kinds of expectations that shareholders may have which are potentially recognizable at law. Corporate action taken in breach of any of those expectations could, if the expectations are "reasonable" expectations, create a situation that is unfair to the shareholder in question and give rise to relief under the oppression remedy on the basis that the interests of the shareholder have been *unfairly prejudiced* or *unfairly disregarded*.

The key question, of course, is which expectations are "reasonable" and worthy of legal protection. The term "shareholders' reasonable expectations" is a term of art which encompasses those expectations that are deserving of legal recognition. Some of the factors which provide a useful guide, at least in the context of a closely-held corporation, are summarized in the American jurisprudence. Four criteria in particular warrant consideration:[19]

(1) *expectations need not be contained in the corporate constating documents* — the courts have recognized that, in the context of a closely-held corporation, it is unlikely that all of the understandings of the participants will be contained in the articles, by-laws or a shareholders' agreement of the corporation;

(2) *expectations must be important to the investor's participation* — an expectation will only be given legal recognition if it was important to the shareholder's decision to invest in the corporation;

(3) *expectations must be known to other parties* — the court will not protect the subjective "hopes and desires" of shareholders. If expectations are not made known to other participants they are not reasonable; and

(4) *expectations exist at the inception of the enterprise and evolve with the concurrence of the shareholders* — the expectations of shareholders are not static and may change over time. Accordingly, what constitutes oppression may change.

Of course the foregoing is not intended to be an exclusive list of the considerations relevant to distinguishing shareholders' reasonable expectations from expectations which are not deserving of legal protection. It is interesting that the analysis promulgated in the United States effectively limits the significance of the reasonable expectations theory to closely-held corporations. In Canada at least, the application of the oppression remedy has been extended to situations involving issuer corporations. In

---

[19] O'Neal and Thompson, *O'Neal's Oppression of Minority Shareholders: Protecting Minority Rights in Squeeze-Outs and Other Intracorporate Conflicts*, vol. II, 2nd ed. (New York: Clark Boardman Callaghan, 1991-93), c. 7, at 90-91.

order to examine the potential for the concept of shareholders' reasonable expectations to explain or justify the oppression remedy with respect to those cases, it is necessary to consider whether, in the case of a corporation that is an issuer, shareholders' reasonable expectations have any role to play in the regulation of corporate conduct and the protection of shareholders' rights. Expectations in the issuer corporation context are likely to be somewhat more abstract and concern the way in which the board of directors or management will manage the business and affairs of the corporation, as opposed to the more direct expectations found in a closely-held corporation, such as an expectation of the right to participate in management. Such expectations are not going to accord with the criteria above to the extent that expectations must be known by and concurred in by all of the shareholders.

These issues and others are developed further in the paper. At this point it is fruitful to study the place of the concept of shareholders' reasonable expectations in the jurisprudence concerning the oppression remedy.

(1) In the beginning: *Ebrahimi*

Legal recognition of the normative importance of shareholders' expectations is largely attributable to the decision of the House of Lords in *Ebrahimi v. Westbourne Galleries Ltd.*[20] The applicant had brought a petition under the oppression section of the *Company Act (U.K.), 1948*[21] for an order directing that the respondent be ordered to purchase the applicant's shares. In the alternative, the applicant sought an order directing a winding-up of the company under s. 222 of the *Company Act (U.K.), 1948* on the ground that it was "just and equitable" to do so. At trial it was held that although oppression had not been made out, a winding-up was nonetheless justified under the "just and equitable" winding-up provision. On appeal to the House of Lords the issue was confined to a consideration of the winding-up order granted under s. 222.

Although a decision based on the "just and equitable" winding-up provision, *Ebrahimi* has become one of the leading authorities cited in oppression remedy cases. In an elegantly crafted judgment, Lord Wilberforce examined the history of the "just and equitable" jurisdiction of the court and delivered a prophetic exposition of the foundation of that jurisdiction and the scope of its application. Lord Wilberforce noted that the words "just and equitable" provide a "bridge" between the winding-up

---

[20] [1973] A.C. 360 (H.L.) (hereinafter *Ebrahimi*).
[21] 11 & 12 Geo. 6, c. 38, s. 210.

cases decided under s. 222 of the *Company Act (U.K.), 1948* and the principles of equity developed in relation to partnerships.[22] The court's jurisdiction to grant a just and equitable winding-up was based on a recognition that circumstances can exist in a corporation such that it is just and equitable to wind-up the corporation, in the same way that circumstances can exist that make it just and equitable to dissolve a partnership. For that reason, and no other, the just and equitable winding-up remedy has developed on the basis of a so-called "partnership analogy".

Lord Wilberforce held that the foundation of the jurisdiction of the court lies in the words "just and equitable". Significantly, His Lordship identified the interests, the protection of which provides the normative justification for the just and equitable jurisdiction of the court, as shareholders' expectations:

> The foundation of it all lies in the "words just and equitable" and, if there is any respect in which some of the cases may be open to criticism, it is that the courts may sometimes have been too timorous in giving them full force. The words are a recognition of the fact that a limited company is more than a mere judicial entity, with a personality in law of its own: that there is room in company law for recognition of the fact that behind it, or amongst it, there are individuals, with rights, expectations and obligations inter se which are not necessarily submerged in the company structure.[23]

Ebrahimi is an extremely significant case because it constitutes an express recognition, at the highest level, that there are various understandings and expectations that are shared by the participants in a corporation that are not necessarily reflected in the articles, by-laws or shareholders' agreements of the corporation, that may, nonetheless, be deserving of legal protection. In so holding, Lord Wilberforce extended the application of the just and equitable winding-up remedy beyond the traditional categories of inquiry into loss of substratum, loss of confidence in management, deadlock and the partnership analogy. Until *Ebrahimi* settled the matter, it was uncertain whether, within the context of those categories, corporate action taken in accordance with the constitution of the corporation could provide a basis for a just and equitable winding-up.

The classic example, which was the case before the House of Lords in *Ebrahimi*, is the lawful expulsion of a shareholder from management. Lord Wilberforce built upon earlier authorities and ruled that, even in the case of action taken in accordance with the constitution of the corporation, the result of such action may justify the invocation of the court's

---

[22] The words "just and equitable" appeared in s. 25 of the *Partnership Act*, 1892 as a ground for dissolution of the partnership.

[23] *Supra*, note 20, at 379.

just and equitable jurisdiction on the grounds that the shareholder's reasonable expectations have been breached.

It is unfortunate that the judgment of Lord Wilberforce has been mis-interpreted as a rationalization of the just and equitable remedy on the basis of the so-called partnership analogy.[24] In fact, Lord Wilberforce quite explicitly pointed out that the reference in many of the cases to "quasi-partnerships" or "in substance partnerships" is at best convenient, at worst confusing, but in reality of no substantive importance.[25] The reason for this being that, "[a] company, however small, however domestic, is a company not a partnership or even a quasi-partnership".[26] The relevance of partnership is limited to the fact that the just and equitable winding-up remedy recognizes obligations and expectations which are common to part-nership.[27]

Lord Wilberforce did not base the foundation of the just and equita-ble winding-up remedy on the "partnership analogy". The factors that Lord Wilberforce considered as giving rise to relief on just and equitable grounds "typically may include one, or probably more, of the following elements":

> (i) an association formed or continued on the basis of a personal relation-ship, involving mutual confidence — this element will often be found where a pre-existing partnership has been converted into a limited company; (ii) an agreement, or understanding, that all, or some (for there may be "sleep-ing" members), of the shareholders shall participate in the conduct of the business; (iii) restriction upon the transfer of the members' interest in the company — so that if confidence is lost, or one member is removed from management, he cannot take out his stake and go elsewhere.[28]

The factors identified above reflect a "shareholders' reasonable expec-tations" analysis. First, two circumstances are identified: (i) an associa-tion based on a relationship of mutual confidence; and (ii) a lack of liquidity of the shareholder's equity. Secondly, it is recognized that those circumstances generate certain expectations. Specifically, each shareholder shall participate in management so long as he or she remains an equity participant. It is the breach of that reasonable expectation and the conse-quential unfairness of that situation that justifies the application of the just and equitable jurisdiction of the court. That was the basis for Lord Wilberforce's decision in *Ebrahimi*.

---

[24] See Huberman, "Winding-up of Business Corporations", in Ziegel, ed., *Studies in Canadian Company Law*, vol. II (Toronto: Butterworths, 1973), at 310-11.

[25] *Supra*, note 20, at 379-80.

[26] *Ibid.*, at 380.

[27] *Ibid.*

[28] *Ibid.*, at 379.

(2) Application of a Shareholders' Reasonable Expectations Analysis

In *Diligenti v. RWMD Operations Kelowna Ltd. (No. 1)*,[29] the first Canadian decision to consider the modern statutory oppression remedy, Fulton J. adopted the reasoning of Lord Wilberforce in considering an application under the then newly-enacted s. 221 of the *Companies Act, 1973* (British Columbia). *Diligenti* is a classic example of the kind of oppressive conduct which may arise in the context of a closely-held corporation. The applicant and the three individual respondents agreed to set up a restaurant business. They incorporated two companies for that purpose in respect of which each was made a director and each acquired one-quarter of the shares in the companies.

The applicant, who had previous experience in setting up restaurant businesses, devoted a great deal of his time to establishing the business, for which he was paid a management fee. Differences arose between the applicant and the three individual respondents relating to the payment of the management fees to the applicant. These differences led to the applicant being ousted from his position as director, excluded from all day-to-day managerial responsibilities and functions and deprived of the management fee previously paid to him for his services. At the same time, the individual respondents, in their capacity as directors, passed resolutions to pay to themselves, among other things, directors' fees and management fees.

The proceeding before Fulton J. was pursuant to a motion brought by the respondents to have the application dismissed. The respondents argued, among other things, that the acts complained of did not oppress the applicant as a *shareholder*. Based on the authorities, it was clear that the removal of the applicant as a director did not "oppress" him in his status as shareholder. It was, therefore, necessary to consider the words "unfairly prejudicial" to determine whether they might afford protection to the applicant in these circumstances. Fulton J. took as his starting point the dictionary definitions of "prejudice", "prejudicial" and "unfair", from which he drew two conclusions: first, that "what is unjust and inequitable is obviously also unfairly prejudicial"; and secondly, the focus, in determining whether there has been unfair prejudice, is on the applicant's *rights* or *interests* as a shareholder and whether such rights or interests have been unfairly prejudiced.

Fulton J. noted that the circumstances before him were "remarkably similar" to those before Lord Wilberforce in *Ebrahimi*.[30] Applying the reasoning in *Ebrahimi*, Fulton J. was prepared to recognize that the applicant could have rights and expectations which were not necessarily

---

[29] (1976), 1 B.C.L.R. 36 (S.C.) (hereinafter *Diligenti*).
[30] *Ibid.*, at 47.

"submerged" in the corporate structure. Specifically, the applicant had an expectation that the shareholders would collectively provide management services to the companies and receive consideration with respect to those services. Accordingly, the removal of the applicant as a director was contrary to his expectations and in breach of his equitable rights as a shareholder. Fulton J. held that, although the breach of the applicant's expectations did not "oppress" him with respect to his proprietary rights as a shareholder, the unjust and inequitable denial of his rights and expectations was "unfairly prejudicial" to him as a shareholder.

The qualification of traditional principles of corporate law in accordance with the reasonable expectations of shareholders was endorsed by McDonald J. in *First Edmonton Place Ltd. v. 315888 Alberta Ltd.*:[31]

> Whereas in the past good faith and the constitutional power of the directors and the majority had been critical, the emphasis shifted to the damaging effect on the interests set out in s. 234. These interests include "equitable rights" based on legitimate expectation . . . [32]

Relying on *Diligenti* and a reasonable expectations analysis set forth by Professor Shapira in an article entitled "Minority Shareholders' Protection", McDonald J. adopted and applied a reasonable expectations standard as the analytical framework within which to consider whether there had been "unfair prejudice".

In *First Edmonton*, the applicant, a creditor, sought leave to bring an action against the respondent corporation and the three individual respondents under s. 234 of the *Alberta Business Corporations Act*. To obtain leave, the applicant was required to establish, among other things, that the conduct complained of was oppressive, unfairly prejudicial to or unfairly disregarded its interests. The individual respondents, three lawyers, were the sole shareholders and directors of the corporate respondent. The corporate respondent leased premises from the applicant's predecessor for a term of ten years. The respondents had been granted various inducements including 18-months free rent, a leasehold improvement allowance of $115,900 and a signing bonus of $140,126. The corporate respondent distributed the signing bonus to the individual respondents. The respondents occupied the premises for 21 months and then reneged on the lease.

McDonald J. set out a number of factors to be considered in determining whether the interests of a stakeholder had been unfairly prejudiced or unfairly disregarded:

---

[31] (1988), 60 Alta. L.R. (2d) 122, 40 B.L.R. 28 (Q.B.) (hereinafter *First Edmonton*).
[32] *Ibid.*, at 144.

- the history and the nature of the corporation;
- the essential nature of the relationship between the corporation and the creditor;
- the type of rights affected; and
- the general commercial practice.[33]

More specifically, McDonald J. held that the foregoing should be examined with a view to considering the following:

- the protection of the underlying expectations of a creditor in its arrangement with the corporation;
- the extent to which the acts complained of were unforeseeable or the creditor could reasonably have protected itself from such acts; and
- the detriment to the interests of the creditor.[34]

These elements focus on the impact of the conduct complained of upon the interests of the stakeholder rather than on the *bona fides* of the conduct.[35] In addition, there are two overriding principles which emerge from the analysis put forward by McDonald J.: first, the underlying expectations of the stakeholder are the interests which the oppression remedy seeks to protect and, secondly, the need to balance the protection of the stakeholder's interests with the right, and duty, of management to act in the best interests of the corporation, even if that entails acting to the prejudice of the stakeholder.[36]

Since the decisions in *Diligenti (No. 1)* and *First Edmonton,* there have been numerous decisions in Canada and elsewhere which have adopted, expressly or impliedly, a standard based on the reasonable expectations of shareholders. A reasonable expectations standard for determining oppression has been adopted by the highest appellate courts in several U.S. jurisdictions: Alaska, Montana, New York, North Carolina, North Dakota and West Virginia.[37] Other states have codified the judicial use of a reasonable expectations standard.[38] Similarly, the English courts have, as noted below, looked increasingly towards a reasonable expectations standard.

An analysis of reasonable expectations was applied in *Re Elgindata Ltd.,* a decision of the English Chancery Division.[39] In adopting an analysis based on reasonable expectations, Warner J. considered, but did not

---

[33] *Ibid.,* at 146.
[34] *Ibid.*
[35] *Ibid.*
[36] *Ibid.,* at 145.
[37] *Supra,* note 18, at 88.
[38] *Ibid.*
[39] [1991] B.C.L.C. 959 (Ch. D.).

follow, authorities in both England and in Canada which formed the basis of the so-called "quasi-partnership doctrine". The doctrine provides that the "equitable considerations" of Lord Wilberforce apply only to those corporations which are found to be "quasi-partnerships" or "in substance" partnerships. Absent such a determination, the shareholders will be held to the strict legal rights applicable to the governance of corporations.

The applicant Mr. Rowland had acquired his stake in the respondent company from the individual respondent, Mr. Purslow, by threatening to terminate a licence agreement controlled by Mr. Rowland which was essential to the company's business. Warner J. described the situation as one in which "Mr. Rowland [had] imposed himself on Mr. Purslow as a shareholder".[40] Thus, a finding of "quasi-partnership" was out of the question. Expressly recognizing that a strict application of the "quasi-partnership" doctrine would deny the applicant a remedy under the oppression remedy, Warner J. rationalized the analysis on the basis of legitimate expectations:

> It was common ground between counsel that, even in the absence of a quasi-partnership, the interests of a member that are relevant for the purposes of s. 459 are not necessarily confined to his legal rights. They extend to any legitimate expectations he may have.[41]

Disputes between the parties led to allegations of unfair prejudice in which Mr. Rowland alleged that Mr. Purslow had: (i) failed to consult him with respect to policy decisions on which he had a right to be consulted; (ii) managed the affairs of the company in a manner that was incompetent; and (iii) misused the assets of the company for his own personal and his family's benefit. The question became one of distinguishing legitimate expectations from illegitimate or unreasonable expectations. Legitimate expectations may arise from the agreements or understandings between the shareholders, whether or not such agreements or understandings have been put in writing. Where understandings are contained in written agreements, however, it becomes a question of construing those agreements to determine whether there are any legitimate expectations which can be superimposed on the legal rights emanating from the written agreements.[42]

Warner J. considered the circumstances which might give rise to legitimate expectations on the part of Mr. Rowland: first, his appointment as a director of the company; secondly, the substantial size of his shareholding

---

[40] *Ibid.*, at 984.
[41] *Ibid.*, at 985.
[42] *Ibid.*

in the company; and thirdly, the nature of his stake in the company which included income from royalties linked to the company's sales.[43] Having regard to all of these circumstances, Warner J. held that Mr. Rowland had certain legitimate expectations which went beyond the legal rights set out in the written agreements. Specifically, Mr. Rowland had a legitimate expectation that he would be consulted and would participate in policy decisions relating to the company.[44]

Although Warner J. found that Mr. Rowland had a legitimate expectation that he would be consulted and would participate in policy decisions, he found little evidence to support the allegations that this expectation had been violated. Similarly, Warner J. agreed that although mismanagement of a company, if serious, could constitute unfairly prejudicial conduct, the evidence of mismanagement was insufficient to conclude that Mr. Rowland had been unfairly prejudiced on this ground. Warner J. concluded, however, that Mr. Rowland's complaint that Mr. Purslow had misused the company's funds for his own personal and his family's benefit was justified.[45] As a consequence, Warner J. held that Mr. Rowland had been unfairly prejudiced and ordered that Mr. Purslow purchase Mr. Rowland's shares.

Significantly, an analysis of shareholders' reasonable expectations was applied in *Westfair Foods Ltd. v. Watt* in the context of an issuer corporation.[46] The applicants were class A preferred shareholders of Westfair Foods Ltd. ("Westfair"). The respondent Kelly Douglas Ltd. ("Kelly Douglas") held 56 per cent of the class A shares and all of the common shares of Westfair. Based on the current capital structure arranged in 1946, the class A shareholders were entitled to a $2 per share preferred dividend per annum, on a non-cumulative basis. In addition, they were entitled to share equally in the distribution of the company's assets on liquidation, dissolution or winding-up.

In 1985 Westfair adopted a "trailing dividend policy" whereby all of the previous year's net earnings were paid out through dividends to Kelly Douglas, the one common shareholder. In conjunction with the dividend policy, Westfair adopted a "borrowing back policy" pursuant to which Kelly Douglas would loan back the dividend amounts paid out to Westfair at a variable bank prime lending rate. The class A shareholders argued that the dividend and the borrowing back policies unfairly prejudiced and unfairly disregarded their interests by breaching their

---

[43] *Ibid.*, at 986.

[44] *Ibid.*

[45] *Ibid.*, at 1004.

[46] [1991] 4 W.W.R. 695, 79 Alta. L.R. (2d) 363, 5 B.L.R. (2d) 160, 79 D.L.R. (4th) 48 (C.A.); affg [1990] 4 W.W.R. 685, 73 Alta. L.R. (2d) 326, 48 B.L.R. 43 (Q.B.) (hereinafter "*Westfair*"). Leave to appeal to the Supreme Court of Canada was refused [1992] 1 W.W.R. lxv (note).

expectation that they would share in the future of Westfair. In addition, the class A shareholders argued that Westfair had unfairly prejudiced or unfairly disregarded their interests by allowing their shares to be delisted by the Toronto Stock Exchange, without opposition and without notice to them, due to lack of sufficient public distribution. Although the class A shares continued to be listed on the Winnipeg Stock Exchange, the delisting on the Toronto Stock Exchange meant that there was no effective market for the shares.

Both the reasons for decision at the trial level and on appeal apply a reasonable expectations analysis and are deserving of consideration. The decisions differ significantly, however, on whether the expectations in question were deserving of protection.

At trial, Moore C.J.Q.B. found that the directors and officers of Westfair had unfairly prejudiced and unfairly disregarded the interests of the class A shareholders on the basis that the latter had acquired their shares with the expectation that they would share in the future of Westfair, subject only to the amount of dividend that they would be paid as provided in the 1946 shareholders' agreement.[47] Moore C.J.Q.B. held that this "expropriation" of the class A shareholders' right to share in the future of the company, contrary to the interests and expectations of the class A shareholders, was unfairly prejudicial to their rights as shareholders.[48] Moreover, the actions of the directors in pursuing these policies constituted an unfair disregard of the interests of the class A shareholders.[49] In so holding, Moore C.J.Q.B. rejected Westfair's argument that it had an expectation that it would be paid all of the retained earnings of the company by way of dividends.[50]

In addition, Moore C.J.Q.B. concluded that the "failure either to act or to inform" the class A shareholders of the delisting from the Toronto Stock Exchange, contrary to the expectations of the class A shareholders, constituted unfair prejudice to or an unfair disregard of the interests of the class A shareholders:

> I have already determined that the creation of the class A shares was accompanied by an undertaking to endeavour to have the shares listed on the Toronto and Montreal Stock Exchanges. Furthermore, the shares were created with the express intention that they should be publicly tradedand that this market activity should provide a valuation for the underlying equity represented by these shares. The holders of the class A shares were fully entitled to the expectation that a market should exist for their shares.
>
> This expectation is important. It provides one significant reason why

---

[47] *Ibid.*, at 76 B.L.R.
[48] *Ibid.*
[49] *Ibid.*
[50] *Ibid.*, at 69.

reason why investors would wish to acquire these shares, which were acquired or disposed of with convenience and ease, and always, of course, dependent upon the fluctuations and demand reflected by the market, which, in turn, can reflect the reasonable expectation of a capital gain based on the corporation's performance. Any reduction of a public market or in the convenience or ease with which these shares may be traded diminishes their attractiveness to investors and, hence, detracts from their value.[51]

Moore C.J.Q.B. ordered that the class A shares be purchased by Westfair at a value to be determined by a court-appointed auditor or accountant.[52]

On appeal, Kerans J.A. agreed with the use of a reasonable expectations analysis to determine whether the directors had unfairly prejudiced or unfairly disregarded the interests of the class A shareholders, but held that any expectation of the class A shareholders that they would share in the success of the company beyond their right to a fixed dividend was an unreasonable expectation.[53] It was a "mere desire"[54] not deserving of protection.

Kerans J.A. held that the question of whether an expectation is reasonable is to be judged on the basis of the words and the deeds of the parties and, in particular, by those words and deeds which would ordinarily raise expectations in the mind of the other party.[55] The words and deeds relevant to an assessment of the reasonable expectations of shareholders are not restricted to those put in writing or, in recognition of the potential for changing expectations, those in existence at the time that the relationship first arose.[56] Kerans J.A. concluded that there was nothing in the evidence before him that could reasonably be said to have encouraged any expectations contrary to those afforded to the class A shareholders under the share structure established in 1946.[57]

Although finding that there had been no oppression with respect to the "substantial" complaint, Kerans J.A. went on to consider whether a finding of oppression could be upheld on procedural grounds. He noted that the directors of Westfair "did not consult or inform the shareholders, did not arrange independent review, did not conduct a careful study and did not even address their minds to the position of the shareholders" with respect to the dividend policy.[58] Moreover, the Westfair directors had

---

[51] *Ibid.*, at 77.
[52] *Ibid.*, at 79.
[53] *Supra*, note 46.
[54] *Ibid.*, at 167 B.L.R.
[55] *Ibid.*
[56] *Ibid.*, at 167-68.
[57] *Ibid.*, at 171.
[58] *Ibid.*, at 175.

allowed the class A shares to be delisted from the Toronto Stock Exchange without notice to the class A shareholders. (As an aside, Kerans J.A. noted in passing that counsel for the shareholders conceded that there was no hope of successfully opposing the delisting.) The interesting question in this respect is what, if anything, flows from such procedural unfairness? Although holding that the "procedural issues" were of insufficient gravity to warrant a winding-up order, Kerans J.A nonetheless ordered that West-fair purchase the class A shares and dismissed the appeal, concluding that "[n]o doubt it would be best for all if the shares were to be sold".[59] Ironically, after expounding at length on the failure of the courts to elucidate defined standards of fairness and advocating, and applying, a standard based on reasonable expectations, it seems that the "best for all" standard carried the day.

Westfair stands for the proposition that a breach of the reasonable expectations of the shareholders of an issuer corporation may justify the invocation of the oppression remedy. The circumstances giving rise to the reasonable expectations reflect none of the elements identified by Lord Wilberforce in *Ebrahimi*: (i) an association based on a relationship of mutual confidence; (ii) an expectation that the shareholder will participate in management; and (iii) a restriction on the transfer of the shareholders' interests in the company. Accordingly, *Westfair* constitutes an extension of the reasonable expectations analysis derived from the principles enunciated by Lord Wilberforce in *Ebrahimi*. While there are obvious limitations to the application of the analysis in the absence of the features of the kind identified by Lord Wilberforce, there is clearly some potential for the application of the reasonable expectations analysis in the context of issuer corporations.

Completing the array of recent cases which have applied an analysis of shareholders' reasonable expectations is *Naneff v. Con-Crete Holdings Ltd.*[60] At trial, Blair J. applied an analysis of the reasonable expectations of the shareholders in order to determine, first, whether there was oppression, and secondly, what remedy to grant. The dispute in *Naneff* involved a family-owned business founded by the applicant's father ("Mr. Naneff") in the 1950s. As part of an estate-freeze, the applicant ("Alex") and his brother ("Boris") each acquired 50 per cent of the common shares of the holding corporation and Mr. Naneff and his wife ("Mrs. Naneff") acquired all of the preference shares of the corporation.

Alex and Boris had worked in the family business since they were young. Blair J. found that up until the events giving rise to the dispute,

---

[59] *Ibid.*, at 176.
[60] (1993), 11 B.L.R.(2d) 218 (Ont.Gen.Div.); revd in part on other grounds (1994), 19 O.R.(3d) 691, 16 B.L.R. (2d) 169 (Div. Ct.); revd 23 O.R. (3d) 481 (C.A.) (hereinafter *Naneff*).

both had contributed significantly to the operation and the management of the business. As a result of a falling out between Alex and his parents and brother, Alex was removed as an employee, manager and officer. Alex continued as a director; however, Blair J. found that he was excluded from the day-to-day management of the business which prevented him from making any meaningful contribution at directors' meetings.

Blair J. considered the reasonable expectations of the parties as they evolved over the years, recognizing that such expectations may change over time. It was found that although the sons had worked in their father's business from a young age, the expectation that they would join in the business did not achieve the status of a "shareholders' reasonable expectation" until some later date when the corporate relationship between the sons and their father had matured. Having regard to the family background and, in particular, the sons' increased role in the family business over time, Blair J. held that Alex's expectation that he would one day take over the family business was "a reasonable one, and one which underlies the entire corporate relationship between the members of the Naneff family".[61] Assessing the respondents' conduct against Alex's reasonable expectation that he would, together with his brother, take over the family business on his father's death, Blair J. made several findings of oppressive conduct; that is, "oppressive" in that it did not conform with Alex's legitimate shareholder expectation, one that he had been led to hold over the years, that control in the business would pass to him and his brother, on their father's death.[62]

Having determined that the respondents had breached Alex's reasonable expectation and hence acted in a manner that was oppressive to him, Blair J. considered the appropriate remedy to be ordered having regard to the circumstances. Alex took the position that he should be reinstated to his former positions within the corporations. The respondents argued that the appropriate remedy was a buy-out of the applicants' shares. Applying a reasonable shareholders' expectations analysis to the question of remedy, Blair J. rejected both submissions:

> It would not, in my view, be "just and equitable" to allow his parents to force Alex out of Rainbow in this fashion. Alex does not want out of Rainbow. It has been the source of his livelihood and the centre of his entire life, and he had a reasonable expectation that it would continue to be those things.[63]

Blair J. considered the possibility that Alex be reinstated and Alex and Boris be permitted to run the corporation, an option which would

---

[61] *Ibid.*, at 248.

[62] *Ibid.*, at 250.

[63] *Ibid.*, at 259.

apparently entail removing Mr. Naneff from his position of voting control. Blair J. rejected this option which, in his view, would defeat Mr. Naneff's reasonable expectation that he would continue to exercise all final decision-making power. After this balancing of reasonable expectations, Blair J. concluded that the appropriate remedy would be for the corporations to be placed on the open market for sale so that "[a]ny family member, singly or in combination, may bid for the companies, as may a third party."[64] Such a remedy provided Alex with "an opportunity to continue in the business"[65] and did not "arbitrarily expropriate" Mr. Naneff's control position.[66] To order otherwise would defeat the reasonable expectations of one or other of the shareholders.

(3) The Scope of the Shareholders' Reasonable Expectations Analysis

The jurisprudence demonstrates that an analysis of shareholders' reasonable expectations is able to provide the theoretical basis for the resolution of cases in which the interests of shareholders have been unfairly prejudiced or unfairly disregarded in the context of a closely-held corporation. The relationship between the principle of shareholders' reasonable expectations and the oppression remedy is notable for its justificatory coherence. In the event that a shareholder's reasonable expectations have been breached, a situation may exist which is unfairly prejudicial to the interests of that shareholder. The unfairness emanates from the breach of the reasonable expectations. The prejudice necessitating relief is the detriment suffered by the shareholder as a result of the breach of their expectations. Often this will arise from the illiquidity of the shareholder's interest.

The difficult question of the reasonableness of the expectation which has allegedly been breached can be determined by analyzing the shared understandings and expectations of the shareholders. Those understandings and expectations which were material to the decision of the shareholder to invest in the corporation, and which are shared or concurred with by the other shareholders, are likely to be considered "reasonable" expectations.[67] The reason why this form of analysis is particularly important to closely-held corporations is because the source of the expectations

---

[64] *Ibid.*

[65] *Ibid.*, at 260.

[66] *Ibid.*

[67] O'Neal and Thompson, *O'Neal's Oppression of Minority Shareholders: Protecting Minority Rights in Squeeze-Outs and Other Intracorporate Conflicts*, vol. II, 2nd ed. (New York: Clark Boardman Callaghan, 1991-93).

— the underlying understandings — is prevalent among associations founded upon personal relationships.

The paradigmatic case is the expulsion of a shareholder from the board of directors or from management, in breach of the shareholders' reasonable expectation that they would be entitled to participate in the management of the business and affairs of the corporation. The corporate action taken to achieve that result may be lawful in itself, but nonetheless contrary to the expectations of the excluded shareholder. A lack of preparedness for such an eventuality in a shareholders' agreement or the like is explained by the fact that the relationship between the participants concealed the possibility that the rules of the corporation could be used in that way. The ultimate injustice of the situation is that the illiquid nature of the investment means that the excluded shareholder has no control over his or her equity. Justice, in this limited sense, is achieved by enabling the shareholder to liberate his or her investment.

It is submitted that the shareholders' reasonable expectations analysis is the most appropriate theory to determine whether the interests of a shareholder have been unfairly prejudiced or unfairly disregarded in the context of a closely-held corporation. The analysis goes to the heart of the unfairness on an intuitive level. It also defines the standard of unfairness in a manner that is conducive to a principled application at law.

Of course other circumstances can attract the remedial scope of the oppression remedy. Corporate action which is contrary to the constitution of the corporation, or which constitutes a breach by the directors of their duties to the corporation, may be considered to be oppressive, or to unfairly prejudice or unfairly disregard the interests of the shareholders. In these situations, an analysis of shareholders' reasonable expectations is arguably of little substantive importance. To say that shareholders have a reasonable expectation that corporate action will be taken lawfully, or that directors will act in accordance with their duties, is a rather banal statement. The conclusion that unlawful conduct should give rise to relief under the oppression remedy could be reached on the basis of an alternative theory.

Having said that, two points should be borne in mind. First, cases involving a breach of an established rule or norm of corporate law do not represent the hard cases in terms of finding unfairness sufficient to justify relief under the oppression remedy. Secondly, it is important to recognize that the reasonable expectations analysis provides the necessary linkage between the theory of directors' duties, for example, and the right of a shareholder to seek relief under the oppression remedy. Directors' duties are owed to the corporation and not to shareholders directly.[68] Some

---

[68] *Brant Investments Ltd. v. Keeprite Inc.* (1990), 45 O.A.C. 320, 3 O.R. (3d) 289, 1 B.L.R. (2d) 255 at 244, 80 D.L.R. (4th) 161 (C.A.).

theory other than "directors' duties", therefore, is required in order to justify the application of the oppression remedy. A conclusion that shareholders reasonably expect that directors will act in accordance with their duties may not be a theoretical breakthrough, but at least it provides a coherent conceptual basis for the application of the remedy.

The next area that requires consideration in order to evaluate the scope of the shareholders' expectations analysis is the application of the oppression remedy in the context of issuer corporations. In this respect it is interesting to note that Lord Wilberforce's seminal exposition of shareholders' expectations did not contemplate the application of the principles outside of a closely-held corporation.[69] However, the decision of the Alberta Court of Appeal in *Westfair*[70] renders any debate about the applicability of an analysis of shareholders' expectations in the context of issuer corporations largely academic. Shareholders' reasonable expectations provided the analytical framework within which that case was decided. The issue was framed as whether the class A preferred shareholders had a reasonable expectation that the dividend policy of the corporation would preserve cash reserves which would be available for distribution to the class A preferred shareholders in the event of the liquidation, dissolution or winding-up of the corporation. The Court of Appeal held that there was no such reasonable expectation. Arguably, the focus on reasonable expectations did not add much substantively to the disposition of the case. The reasonableness of the expectation claimed was more a matter to be determined by reference to the expectations common to shareholders of issuer corporations at large, than an analysis of the expectations which were individual to the shareholders of that corporation. In other words, the reference to reasonable expectations in the context of an issuer corporation will, more often than not, describe a norm of corporate law rather than provide a source of a right recognizable at law. However, it is significant that, in conceptual terms, the analysis allowed for a coherent and principled resolution of the issues.

It is also possible to rationalize the decision in *Palmer v. Carling O'Keefe*,[71] a case concerning an issuer corporation, on the basis of an analysis of shareholders' expectations. It was material to the decision in that case, in holding that the preferred shareholders had been unfairly prejudiced by an amalgamation, that they had expectations with respect to the nature of the corporation they had invested in. Specifically, the

---

[69] See the three elements which Lord Wilberforce identified as typically predicating entitlement to relief, [1973] A.C. 360 at 379.

[70] [1991] 4 W.W.R. 695, 79 Alta. L.R. (2d) 363, 5 B.L.R. (2d) 160, 79 D.L.R. (4th) 48.

[71] (1989), 32 O.A.C. 113, 67 O.R. (2d) 161, 41 B.L.R. 128, 56 D.L.R. (4th) 128 (S.C.).

shareholders had invested in a Canadian brewing company not an Australian conglomerate. They also had expectations about the financial structure of the corporation; specifically, they had invested in a corporation with a debt to equity ratio of 1:5, which was rather more appealing than the amalgamated corporation's ratio of 10:1.[72] Whilst the case could be analyzed as one concerning the duty of the board to act in the best interests of the corporation, a rather banal expectation, it is arguable that the expectations of the shareholders with respect to the nature of the enterprise they had invested in added substantive content to the decision.

It is an interesting feature of the decisions in both *Westfair* and *Palmer v. Carling O'Keefe* that there were issues concerning the liquidity and value of the shares. In *Westfair* the complainants' class A shares had been delisted on the Toronto Stock Exchange, hence there was a liquidity problem. In *Palmer* the market value of the preference shares was well below their redemption value, and arguably the circumstances of the case warranted a redemption of the preference shares. Although not as acute as the liquidity problems faced by shareholders in closely-held corporations, it is conceivable that corporate action affecting the value or liquidity of publicly traded shares may cause injustice to shareholders.

Another interesting feature of the decision in *Westfair,* which introduces a further aspect of the scope of the shareholders' reasonable expectations analysis within the context of the oppression remedy, is the finding of oppression on procedural grounds.[73] Procedural complaints attract the remedial scope of the oppression remedy on the grounds that the interests of the stakeholder have been *unfairly disregarded.* This element of the oppression remedy is also well served by a reasonable expectations analysis. As the decision in *Westfair* exemplifies, minority shareholders have a reasonable expectation that their interests will not be disregarded in a general sense. This point is undramatic. However, more substantively, minority shareholders have reasonable expectations that the majority shareholder and the board of the corporation will not treat the corporation as a wholly-owned subsidiary of the majority shareholder.[74] Minority shareholders can also reasonably expect that the board will not abdicate its duty to act in the best interests of the corporation and act as the majority shareholder's stooge in order to implement its agenda. These situations may not result in unfair prejudice to the interests of the shareholders. However, they may result in a breach of the shareholders' reasonable expectations that their interests will be regarded. Such circumstances could justify some sort of relief.

The final point that requires consideration is the emphasis that the

---

[72] *Ibid.,* at 136 B.L.R.
[73] *Supra,* note 53, at 175-76.
[74] *Ibid.,* at 176.

reasonable expectations analysis places on the *effect* of corporate action rather than the nature and quality of the conduct. Arguably, this feature of the analysis does not accommodate the "oppressive" element of the oppression remedy. By "oppressive" we refer to the "harsh, burdensome and wrongful" overtones of the oppression remedy. This criticism of the reasonable expectations analysis would carry more weight if a focus on egregious conduct was still important. In *Brant Investments Ltd. v. Keeprite*[75] the Ontario Court of Appeal decisively rejected the need to establish any bad faith in an oppression application as a "judicial gloss" that is inappropriate and that distracts attention away from the "difficult question" of whether a stakeholder's rights have been unfairly prejudiced or unfairly disregarded.[76] Accordingly, the focus of the shareholders' reasonable expectations analysis on the effects of corporate action is the correct focus which addresses the real questions.

For the reasons outlined above, it is submitted that an analysis of shareholders' reasonable expectations provides a principled standard of fairness and a coherent framework of analysis for oppression remedy cases, both in the context of closely-held and issuer corporations. Shareholders' reasonable expectations are more likely to give rise to substantive grounds for relief in the context of closely-held corporations than issuer corporations. However, the disparity in that respect is reflective of the greater likelihood of oppression occuring in closely-held corporations. The important point, however, is that the reasonable expectations analysis has a sufficient scope to rationalize the application of the oppression remedy, even in those cases in which it does not add any substantive principles of fairness.

5. *Conclusion*

This paper comprises an examination of the concept of shareholders' reasonable expectations. The thesis of the paper is that an analysis of shareholders' reasonable expectations provides the most satisfactory theoretical framework for the principled application of the oppression remedy as it pertains to shareholders.

Since the celebrated analysis of reasonable expectations in the judgment of Lord Wilberforce in *Ebrahimi*, the importance of the expectations of shareholders in the context of the application of the oppression remedy has grown noticeably. It is the view of the authors of this paper that the recognition given to shareholders' reasonable expectations in the

---

[75] *Supra*, note 68.
[76] *Ibid.*, at 248 B.L.R.

contemporary jurisprudence is an appropriate precursor to a more extensive and rigorous application of the concept.

The concept of shareholders' reasonable expectations provides a principled and coherent framework of analysis on the basis of which the oppression remedy can be understood and applied. First, an analysis of shareholders' reasonable expectations provides an intelligible standard of fairness which can be applied by the courts in oppression cases concerning shareholders. In essence, the analysis equates unfairness with the breach of a shareholder's reasonable expectations. Secondly, the determination of the reasonableness of the disappointed expectations is guided by a relatively determinate standard; specifically, an inquiry into the underlying understandings of the shareholders or established rules and norms of corporate law. Thirdly, the analysis is sensitive to the circumstances warranting relief. In the event that a breach of a shareholder's reasonable expectations gives rise to circumstances that negatively impact on the shareholder, the unfairness will be found to be prejudicial to the interests of that shareholder. Alternatively, the breach of the expectations may be found to unfairly disregard the interests of the shareholder. In either case, relief is available to remedy the results of the unfairness.

Another important feature of the analysis is the focus on the effect of corporate action on shareholders as opposed to the nature and quality of the conduct in question. This focus accentuates the remedial function of the oppression remedy. Finally, the theory has normative force because of the coherence of the analysis and the potential to do justice through its application.

It is an impossible task to remove all uncertainty and subjectivity from the application of the oppression remedy. The recognition of the importance of shareholders' reasonable expectations at least creates some analytical standards which make the uncertainty more bearable.

RESCISSION

Paul M. Perell

1. *Introduction*

Since the word rescission is used variously to refer to a right, a remedy, and a result, its meaning has been the source of confusion.[1] This confusion can be avoided, in part, with the generalization that rescission prescribes when a person may have a contract set aside and be restored to his or her pre-contractual position. Rescission also prescribes when a person may have a gift set aside. Used in this way, rescission is a topic of equity, the common law, restitution, and statute.

Rescission is usually described as an equitable remedy. This description reflects that rescission is a remedy, like specific performance, that was provided originally by courts of equity and is associated with the equitable doctrines of undue influence, unconscionability, misrepresentation, breach of fiduciary duty, and mistake, all of which provide grounds for setting aside contracts or gifts. The description, however, is not exact because rescission has a common law[2] and a statutory side and because, in some circumstances, rescission is better described as the right to set aside a contract or gift rather than the remedy yielding that result. In other words, in some circumstances, a party may simply treat a contract or gift as rescinded and the help of a court is not required.

On the common law side, rescission is available on the grounds of duress, fraud, error *in substantialibus*, and for the common law's treatment of mistake. If these grounds are established, then the common law can set aside a contract, although, before the fusion of law and equity, the common law courts, lacking equity's *in personam* jurisdiction were

---

[1] See Bate, "Rescission" (1955), 19 The Conveyancer and Property Lawyer 116; Weir, "Remedies with Respect to Contracts of Purchase and Sale", [1960] L.S.U.C. Special Lectures 427; Baker and Lanagan, *Snell's Equity*, 26th ed., c. 2; Oosterhoff and Rayner, *Anger and Honsberger Law of Real Property*, 2nd ed., at 1190-1202; Pattillo, "Rectification and Rescission", [1961] L.S.U.C. Special Lectures 211.

[2] See Maddaugh and McCamus, *The Law of Restitution*, at 73.

less able to restore the parties to their pre-contractual position. Also, under the common law, contracts that want for full capacity in a contracting party may be set aside; examples are contracts with infants, mental incompetents, the intoxicated and certain statutory entities. Further, under the common law, contracts may be unenforceable on grounds of illegality, frustration, want of formalities, or for material alteration. While, strictly speaking, these contracts are not set aside, all these grounds raise issues about rescission in the sense that the parties to varying degrees may be restored to their pre-contractual position. Further, on the common law side, rescission may be available as a matter of contract.[3] The paradigm is the "rescission clause" used in standard form agreements of purchase and sale of land. Under this clause, if the vendor is unable to answer a title requisition that the purchaser will not waive, the vendor may end the transaction and the parties are restored to their pre-contractual position.

As a matter of statute law, rescission, again in the sense of restoring a party to his or her pre-contractual position, is sometimes offered as an element of a statutory regime. For example, under the *Condominium Act*, a purchaser has a right to rescind an agreement of purchase and sale within ten days after receiving the disclosure statement required by the Act.[4]

The equitable remedy of rescission and some of the equitable and common law grounds for rescission already mentioned may also be claimed as topics under the law of restitution, which has its roots in both law and equity.[5] Rescission is restitutionary in that it restores the parties to the position that they were in before the contract or gift. Rescission will require the defendant to return the benefit that he or she unjustly received at the expense of the plaintiff, and viewed in this way, rescission is a response to unjust enrichment, the principle now used to rationalize the law of restitution.

The word rescission is sometimes used to describe the legal consequences of a party repudiating a contract or of breaching a contract term classified as a condition. In response to this misconduct, the innocent party

---

[3] Another source of confusion is that termination clauses in contracts are sometimes called rescission clauses; see, for example, *Chitty on Contracts*, 27th ed., paras. 22-022 to 22-028. These clauses, which are not about restoring the parties to their pre-contractual position, provide rights to end a contract usually on notice for default or upon the happening of a defined event, or sometimes simply as a matter of choice.

[4] R.S.O. 1990, c. C.26, s. 52. See *Abdool v. Somerset Place Developments of Georgetown* (1992), 10 O.R. (3d) 120, 27 R.P.R. (2d) 157, 96 D.L.R. (4th) 449 (C.A.).

[5] McCamus, "The Restitutionary Remedy of Constructive Trust", [1981] L.S.U.C. Special Lectures 85 at 90; McCamus, "Restitutionary Remedies", [1975] L.S.U.C. Special Lectures 255 at 255-61.

has the right to treat the contact as at an end. The usage of describing this result as rescission is confusing for at least two reasons. First, in this context, while the innocent party may have the right to treat the contact as at an end, the normal remedies will be damages or specific performance. These remedies are not rescission and are not restitutionary, because the innocent party is not restored to his or her pre-contractual position and there is no return of benefits, but rather the innocent party receives monetary compensation or the completion of the contract.[6] Second, the problem of usage is not solved by simply precluding the use of the word rescission in connection with a repudiation or breach of contract. This solution is not available because, as will be seen below, under the law of restitution, genuine rescission sometimes is an alternative remedy for breach of contract.

One way to minimize confusion about the meaning of the word rescission and the usual approach to explaining the right, remedy, or result of rescission is to describe the grounds or circumstances when it is available and then to describe limits on its availability. This approach is used in this paper, limiting the discussion, however, to contract situations, save for the occasional passing reference to gifts. Thus, the common law and equitable grounds for rescission are discussed in the next section, and the restitutionary grounds are discussed following. The allocation of restitutionary grounds between these two sections is somewhat arbitrary because several topics could be included in either section. The concluding section discusses the limiting principles and the defences to claims for rescission.

2. Equitable and Common Law Grounds for Rescission

(1) Fraudulent Misrepresentation, Innocent Misrepresentation, and Failure to Disclose

An innocent or fraudulent misstatement of fact that induces a party to sign a contract or that misdescribes the nature and effect of the contract being signed may provide grounds for rescission.[7] To ground rescis-

---

[6] *Johnson v. Agnew*, [1980] A.C. 307 (H.L.); *McDonald v. Dennys Lascelles Ltd.* (1933), 48 C.L.R. 457 (H.C. of A); *Milburn v. Dueck*, [1992] 6 W.W.R. 497, 81 Man. R. (2d) 266, 26 R.P.R. (2d) 9, 96 D.L.R. (4th) 107 (C.A.).

[7] *Panzer v. Zeifman* (1978), 20 O.R. (2d) 502, 88 D.L.R. (3d) 131 (C.A.); *Peat Moss Plant Foods Ltd. v. Sutherland* (1983), 43 N.B.R. (2d) 671, 23 B.L.R. 215 (C.A.); *Tejani v. Arbreu* (1994), 38 R.P.R. (2d) 218 (Ont. Gen. Div.); *Toronto Dominion Bank v. Paconiel Investments Inc.* (1992), 6 O.R. (3d) 547 (Gen. Div.).

sion, the misrepresentation must be material and an inducement to the transaction.[8] If there is no reliance on the misrepresentation, which is a question of fact,[9] then there can be no inducement.[10] General salesmanship or puffery will not constitute a misrepresentation.[11]

Fraud is proven when it is clearly and distinctly shown[12] that a false representation has been made knowingly without belief in its truth or recklessly without caring whether the representation be true or false.[13] The dishonest intent is essential and distinguishes fraudulent misrepresentation from innocent misrepresentation.[14] If the person who makes the false

---

[8] *Panzer v. Zeifman, ibid.*; *Proudfoot v. Allen* (1925), 28 O.W.N. 179 (C.A.); *Zigelstein v. Steiner* (1985), 49 O.R. (2d) 308 (H.C.); affd 57 O.R. (2d) 735 (C.A.); *Guest v. Beecroft* (1957), 22 W.W.R. 481, 10 D.L.R. (2d) 657 (B.C.S.C.); *Thorman v. Parnes* (1990), 73 O.R. (2d) 149, 11 R.P.R. (2d) 182 (H.C.); revd 17 O.R. (3d) 622n (C.A.); *Hyndman v. Jenkins* (1981), 29 Nfld. & P.E.I.R. 331, 16 C.C.L.T. 296, 18 C.P.C. 303 (P.E.I.S.C.); *Kingu v. Walmar Ventures Ltd.* (1986), 10 B.C.L.R. (2d) 15, 38 C.C.L.T. 51 (C.A.); *Hinchey v. Gonda*, [1955] O.W.N. 125 (H.C.); *Burns v. Kelly Peters & Associates Ltd.*, [1987] 6 W.W.R. 1, 16 B.C.L.R. (2d) 1, 41 C.C.L.T. 257, [1987] I.L.R. 1-2246, 41 D.L.R. (4th) 577 (C.A.).

[9] *L.K. Oil & Gas Ltd. v. Canalands Energy Corp.*, [1989] 6 W.W.R. 259, 68 Alta. L.R. (2d) 269, 60 D.L.R. (4th) 490 (C.A.); leave to appeal to S.C.C. refused [1990] 1 W.W.R. lxxi.

[10] *Cancarp Construction Ltd. v. P.D.I. Structures Ltd. (1982) Inc.* (1987), 62 O.R. (2d) 161 (H.C.J.); *L.K. Oil & Gas Ltd. v. Canalands Energy Corp.*, ibid.; *Holt, Renfrew & Co. Ltd. v. Henry Singer Ltd.*, [1982] 4 W.W.R. 481, 20 Alta. L.R. (2d) 97, 135 D.L.R. (3d) 391 (C.A.); leave to appeal to S.C.C. refused 39 A.R. 272n.

[11] *Dimmock v. Hallet* (1866), L.R. 2 Ch. App. 21; *Shields v. Broderick* (1984), 46 O.R. (2d) 19, 8 D.L.R. (4th) 96 (H.C.); *Andronyk v. Williams*, [1986] 1 W.W.R. 225, 36 Man. R. (2d) 161, 38 R.P.R. 58, 21 D.L.R. (4th) 557 (C.A.); leave to appeal to S.C.C. refused (1986), 36 C.C.L.T. xxxi (S.C.C.); *Robinson v. McDonald* (1922), 22 O.W.N. 215 (H.C.); affd 22 O.W.N. 471 (C.A.); *Roberts v. Arnott Co.*,[1932] 1 D.L.R. 798 (Alta. C.A.); *Sternberg v. Dunn* (1992), 24 R.P.R. (2d) 54 (B.C.S.C).

[12] *Parna v. G. & S. Properties Ltd.*, [1971] S.C.R. 306, 15 D.L.R. (3d) 336; *Zorzi v. Baker* (1957), 8 D.L.R. (2d) 164 (B.C.C.A.); *Ross v. Hobbis* (1992), 25 R.P.R. (2d) 27 (B.C.S.C.); *Angus v. Clifford* (1891), 2 Ch. 499 at p. 479; *Hjort v. Wilson* (1953), 11 W.W.R. 545, [1953] 2 D.L.R. 705 (B.C.C.A.).

[13] *Derry v. Peek* (1889), 14 App. Cas. 337 (H.L.); *Angus v. Clifford, ibid.*; *Charpentier v. Slauenwhite* (1971), 3 N.S.R. (2d) 42, 22 D.L.R. (3d) 222 (S.C.); *Newton v. Hiscock* (1992), 26 R.P.R. (2d) 99 (Nfld. S.C.); *Sedgemore v. Block Bros.* (1985), 39 R.P.R. 38 (B.C.S.C.).

[14] *BG Checo Int'l Ltd. v. British Columbia Hydro & Power Authority*, [1993] 1 S.C.R. 12, [1993] 2 W.W.R. 321, 75 B.C.L.R. (2d) 145, 14 C.C.L.T. (2d) 233, 99 D.L.R. (4th) 577, 147 N.R. 81; affg [1990] 3 W.W.R. 690, 44 B.C.L.R. (2d) 145, 4 C.C.L.T. (2d) 161 (C.A.); *Rainbow Industrial Caterers Ltd. v. Canadian National Railway Co.*, [1989] 1 W.W.R. 673, 30 B.C.L.R. (2d) 273, 54 D.L.R. (4th) 43 (C.A.); *Le Lievre v. Gould*, [1893] 1 Q.B. 491; *Crozman v. Ruesch*, [1994] 4 W.W.R. 116, 87 B.C.L.R. (2d) 223 (C.A.).

statement proves that he or she had an actual and honest belief in the truth of the statement, then fraud is not established, even if the statement was made negligently or carelessly.[15]

Misrepresentations are not just oral and written false statements. In certain circumstances, conduct and silence may amount to a misrepresentation. Active conduct to conceal and prevent discovery of a defect in the property being sold constitutes a fraudulent misrepresentation.[16] Where there is a duty to disclose, as in the case of material latent defects that make a property dangerous or uninhabitable, it is a fraudulent misrepresentation to fail to disclose defects known to the vendor.[17] If a party makes a representation and subsequently discovers that the representation was false or has become false, then there is an obligation to edify the other party, and, if there is an intent to deceive, the failure to disclose may be conduct equivalent to fraud and provides ground for rescission.[18]

Generally speaking, however, silence by itself does not constitute a

---

[15] *Derry v. Peek, supra*, note 13; *Lowe v. Suburban Developers (Sault Ste. Marie) Ltd.*, [1962] O.R. 1029, 35 D.L.R. (2d) 178 (C.A.); *Roberts v. Montex Dev. Corp.*, [1979] 4 W.W.R. 306, 100 D.L.R. (3d) 660 (B.C.S.C.); *Nesbitt, Thomson & Co. v. Pigott*, [1941] S.C.R. 520, [1941] 4 D.L.R. 353; *Dugas v. Boutilier* (1981), 45 N.S.R. (2d) 98 (T.D.); *P.M Foods Ltd. v. Pizza Hut Inc.* (1985), 6 C.P.R. (3d) 330 (Alta. Q.B.).

[16] *Abel v. Macdonald*, [1964] 2 O.R. 256, 45 D.L.R. (2d) 198 (C.A.); leave to appeal to S.C.C. refused, June 5, 1964; *McCallum v. Dean*, [1956] O.W.N. 873 (C.A.); *Allen v. McCutcheon* (1979), 10 B.C.L.R. 149, 9 R.P.R. 191 (S.C.); *Rawson v. Hammer* (1982), 23 R.P.R. 239 (Alta. Q.B.); *Rowley v. Isley* (1950), 3 W.W.R. (N.S.) 173, [1951] 3 D.L.R. 766 (B.C.S.C.); *Unrau v. Gay* (1983), 61 N.S.R. (2d) 256, 30 R.P.R. 198 (N.S.T.D.); *Gronau v. Schlamp Invts. Ltd.*, [1975] W.W.D. 47, 52 D.L.R. (3d) 631 (Man. Q.B.); *Jakubke v. Sussex Group—SRC Realty Corp.* (1993), 15 C.C.L.T. (2d) 298, 31 R.P.R. (2d) 193 (B.C.S.C.).

[17] *McGrath v. MacLean* (1979), 22 O.R. (2d) 784, 95 D.L.R. (3d) 144 (C.A.); *C.R.F. Holdings Ltd. v. Comor Supplies Ltd.*, [1982] 2 W.W.R. 385, 33 B.C.L.R. 291, 19 C.C.L.T. 263 (C.A.); *Ball v. Gutschenritter*, [1925] S.C.R. 68; *McAleer v. Desjardine*, [1948] O.R. 557, [1948] 4 D.L.R. 40 (C.A.); *Bolton v. McMulroch* (1983), 27 R.P.R. 286 (B.C.S.C.); *Boulderwood Dev. Co. v. Edwards* (1984), 64 N.S.R. (2d) 395, 30 C.C.L.T. 223, 34 R.P.R. 171 (C.A.); *Hartlen v. Falconer* (1977), 28 N.S.R. (2d) 54, 5 R.P.R. 153 (N.S.S.C.); *Sevidal v. Chopra* (1987), 64 O.R. (2d) 169, 41 C.C.L.T. 179, 45 R.P.R. 79 (H.C.J.); *Lix v. Erickson* (1994), 42 R.P.R. (2d) 34 (Ont. Gen. Div.).

[18] *Rainbow Industrial Caterers Ltd. v. Canadian National Railway Co.*, [1989] 1 W.W.R. 673, 30 B.C.L.R. (2d) 273, 54 D.L.R. (4th) 43 (B.C.C.A.); *Hogar Estates Ltd. in Trust v. Shebron Holdings Ltd.* (1979), 25 O.R. (2d) 543, 101 D.L.R (3d) 509 (S.C.); *Defence Construction (1951) Ltd. v. Municipal Enterprises Ltd.* (1985), 71 N.S.R. (2d) 59, 23 D.L.R. (4th) 653 (C.A.); *With v. O'Flanagan*, [1936] Ch. 575; *Davies v. London & Provincial Marine Ins. Co.* (1878), 8 Ch. D. 469; *Holt, Renfrew & Co. Ltd. v. Henry Singer Ltd., supra*, note 10.

misrepresentation,[19] but silence and half truths that mislead or that imply something other than the truth may amount to misrepresentation.[20]

Certain specific types of contracts provide an exception to the general rule that one contracting party is under no duty to make disclosure to the other. The prime examples are insurance contracts and contracts for family settlements; these types of contract are known as contracts *uberrimae fidei*.[21] These contracts require the parties to proceed with good faith, candour, and openness.[22]

There is a special rule for contracts of guarantee. Although contracts of guarantee are not contracts *uberrimae fidei* and the creditor is not obliged to make disclosure to the guarantor of all information material to the risk, a creditor must reveal to the guarantor every fact that under the circumstances the guarantor would ordinarily or naturally expect not to exist.[23] The failure to disclose the unexpected is viewed as a misrepresentation, and the guarantee may be set aside.

Generally speaking, statements of opinion do not qualify for misrepresentations because they are not statements of present or past fact but rather estimates or predictions of future events,[24] but there are

[19] *Fox v. Mackreth* (1788), 2 Cox. Eq. Cas. 320; *Peek v. Gurney* (1873), L.R. 6 H.L. 377; *Brownlie v. Campbell* (1880), 5 App. Cas. 925 (H.L.); *Turner v. Green*, [1895] 2 Ch. 205; *Walters v. Morgan* 3 D.F. & J. 718; *Gabriel v. Hamilton Tiger-Cat Football Club Ltd.* (1975), 8 O.R. (2d) 285, 57 D.L.R. (3d) 669 (H.C.); *Marathon Realty Co. Ltd. v. Ginsberg* (1981), 18 R.P.R. 232 (Ont. S.C.); affd 24 R.P.R. 155 (C.A.), leave to appeal to S.C.C. refused (1982), 42 N.R. 180 (S.C.C.); *Sorenson v. Kaye Holdings Ltd.*, [1979] 6 W.W.R. 193, 14 B.C.L.R. 204 (C.A.).
[20] *Panzer v. Zeifman, supra*, note 7; *C.R.F. Holdings Ltd. v. Comor Supplies Ltd.*, *supra*, note 17; *Graham v. Legault*, [1951] 3 D.L.R. 423 (B.C.S.C.); *449576 Ont. Ltd. v. Bogojevski* (1984), 46 O.R. (2d) 161, 9 D.L.R. (4th) 109 (H.C.J.); *Olsen v. Poirier* (1978), 21 O.R. (2d) 642, 91 D.L.R. (3d) 123 (S.C.); affd 28 O.R. (2d) 744, 111 D.L.R. (3d) 512 (C.A.); *Derry v. Peek*, *supra*, note 13; *Dimmock v. Hallet, supra*, note 11; *Tapp v. Lee* (1803), 3 Bos. & Pul. 367; *Proudfoot v. Allen, supra*, note 8; *Ross v. Hobbis* (1992), 25 R.P.R. (2d) 27 (B.C.S.C.).
[21] *Gabriel v. Hamilton Tiger-Cat Football Club Ltd., supra*, note 19. In *Saul v. Himmel* (1994), 22 C.C.L.T. 292 (Ont. Gen. Div.), a separation agreement was held not to be a contract *uberrimae fidei*.
[22] *Saul v. Himmel, ibid.*
[23] *Hamilton v. Watson* (1895), 12 Cl. & Fin. 109, 8 E.R. 1339 (H.L.); *Canadian Imperial Bank of Commerce v. White*, [1975] 6 W.W.R. 617, 61 D.L.R. (3d) 185 (Alta. C.A.); *Royal Bank of Canada v. Hislop* (1989), 39 B.C.L.R. (2d) 392, 62 D.L.R. (4th) 228 (C.A.).
[24] *Datile Financial Corp. v. Royal Trust Corp. of Canada* (1991), 5 O.R. (3d) 358 (Gen. Div.); affd 11 O.R. (3d) 224n (C.A.); *Foster Advertising Ltd. v. Keenberg*, [1987] 3 W.W.R. 127, 45 Man. R. (2d) 1, 38 C.C.L.T. 309, 35 D.L.R. (4th) 521 (C.A.); leave to appeal to S.C.C. refused [1987] 4 W.W.R. lxvi; *Reid v. Marr's Leisure Holdings Inc.*, unreported, May 6, 1994, Doc. AI 93-30-01570

exceptions to this rule because the existence of the opinion in itself may be a fact, and, to the extent that they presuppose a factual foundation, opinions may constitute statements of fact.[25] Statements of law are treated similarly to opinions. Thus, it will depend on the circumstances whether a statement of law is treated as a statement of fact capable of being treated as a misrepresentation.[26]

If the plaintiff shows a misrepresentation in a matter *prima facie* material to the agreement and likely to operate as an inducement, then the onus falls on the defendant to show that the representation did not so operate.[27] Put somewhat differently, where an untrue representation has been made, the onus of showing that it was not relied upon rests upon the party that made the misrepresentation.[28]

Whether the misrepresentation be innocent or fraudulent, it is no answer for the defendant in defence of the claim based on misrepresentation to say that the falsehood would have been discovered if the plaintiff had exercised due diligence and made his or her own investigation.[29]

(Man. C.A.); *Jacks v. U & R Services Ltd.* (1995), 99 Man. R. (2d) 60, 33 C.P.C. (3d) 201 (Q.B.). The issue of what is an actionable misrepresentation often arises in the context of negligent misrepresentation claims. Opinions are said not to qualify because they are not statements of fact about the present or the past.

[25] *Bisset v. Wilkinson*, [1927] A.C. 177 (P.C.); *Dart v. Rogers* (1911), 19 W.L.R. 326 (Man. K.B.); *Northern & Central Gas Corp. v. Hillcrest Collieries*, [1976] 1 W.W.R. 481, 59 D.L.R. (3d) 533 (Alta. S.C.).

[26] *Rule v. Pals*, [1928] 3 D.L.R. 295 (Sask. C.A.); *Graham v. Legault*, [1951] 3 D.L.R. 423 (B.C.S.C.); *MacKenzie v. Royal Bank of Canada*, [1934] A.C. 468 (P.C.); *Semkuley v. Clay* (1982), 140 D.L.R. (3d) 489 (Alta. Q.B.); *Kavener v. Bowhey*, [1928] 3 W.W.R. 267, 23 Alta. L.R. 530, [1928] 4 D.L.R. 907 (C.A.); *West London Commercial Bank v. Kitson* (1884), 13 Q.B.D. 360 (C.A.).

[27] *Barron v. Kelly* (1918), 56 S.C.R. 455, [1918] 2 W.W.R. 131, 41 D.L.R. 590; *Mailman Bros. v. Nat. Trust Co.*, [1958] O.W.N. 368 (H.C.); *Lowe v. Suburban Developers (Sault Ste. Marie) Ltd.*, [1962] O.R. 1029, 35 D.L.R. (2d) 178 (C.A.); *Siametis v. Trojan Horse (Burlington) Inc.* (1981), 32 O.R. (2d) 782, 123 D.L.R. (3d) 737 (C.A.); affg 25 O.R. (2d) 120, 104 D.L.R. (3d) 556 (S.C.); *Olsen v. Porier, supra*, note 20; *Smith v. Mattacchione*, [1970] 3 O.R. 541, 13 D.L.R. (3d) 437 (Co. Ct.); *Hopkins v. Butts* (1967), 65 D.L.R. (2d) 711 (B.C.S.C.); *Bango v. Holt*, [1971] 5 W.W.R. 522, 21 D.L.R. (3d) 66 (B.C.S.C.); *Chua v. Van Pelt* (1977), 2 B.C.L.R. 117, 74 D.L.R. (3d) 244 (S.C.).

[28] *Redgrave v. Hurd* (1881), 20 Ch. D. 1 (C.A.); *Parallels Restaurant Ltd. v. Yeung's Enterprises Ltd.* (1990), 49 B.L.R. 237, 4 C.C.L.T. (2d) 59 (B.C.C.A.); *Toronto-Dominion Bank v. Paconiel Investments Ltd.* (1992), 6 O.R. (3d) 546 (Gen. Div.).

[29] This principle applies to all forms of misrepresentation including negligent misrepresentations: *Allen v. McCutcheon, supra*, note 16; *Hopkins v. Butts, supra*, note 27; *Smith v. Mattacchione, supra*, note 27; *Labelle v. Bernier* (1911), 18 O.W.R. 444, 20 O.W.N. 634 (H.C.); *Hasham v. Kingston* (1991), 4 O.R. (3d) 514, 19 O.R. (3d) 514 (Div. Ct.); *Nocton v. Lord Ashburton*, [1914] A.C. 932 at p. 962; *Free Ukrainian Society (Toronto) Credit Union Ltd. v. Hnatkiw*, [1964] 2 O.R. 169, 44 D.L.R. (2d) 633 (C.A.); *Redgrave v. Hurd, ibid.*; *Parallels Restaurant Ltd. v. Yeung's Enterprises Ltd.*, *ibid.*

In the context of real property transactions, if the misrepresentation is innocent, then the right to rescission is diminished because, as a general rule, with an exception for what is known as an error *in substantialibus*, discussed later, and subject to other grounds being available, rescission is not available for an innocent misrepresentation discovered after the contract has been executed.[30] By contrast, rescission for fraudulent misrepresentation is available for executed contracts for the sale of real property.

(2) Mistake

In the context of contracts, the law of mistake describes the circumstances where a party is entitled to be relieved of obligations and to be restored to his or her pre-contractual position because there was a misunderstanding at the time of contracting. Both the common law and equity respond to circumstances of contractual mistake with the remedy of rescission, but their theories differ.

A conventional framework for analysis of contractual mistake is to define three types of mistake: unilateral, mutual, and common. Unilateral mistake refers to the situation where one party, but not the other, enters into the contract under a mistake. Mutual mistake refers to the situation where the parties are at cross-purposes and each enters into the contract with a different understanding. Common mistake refers to the situation where both parties enter into the contract under the same mistake.

The common law and equity developed the same rule for unilateral mistake for different reasons. To succeed on a plea of unilateral mistake, a party must establish that a mistake occurred at the time of the signing of the contract and that the other side knew or must be taken to know that the agreement was signed under a fundamental misapprehension.[31]

---

[30] *Redican v. Nesbitt*, [1924] S.C.R. 135, [1924] 1 W.W.R. 305, [1924] 1 D.L.R. 536; *Komarniski v. Marien*, [1979] 4 W.W.R. 267, 8 R.P.R. 229, 100 D.L.R. (3d) 81 (Sask. Q.B.); *Aberg v. Rafuse* (1979), 36 N.S.R. (2d) 56, 64 A.P.R. 56, 8 R.P.R. 216 (T.D.). But see *S-244 Holdings Ltd. v. Seymour Building Systems Ltd.*, [1994] 8 W.W.R. 185, 93 B.C.L.R. (2d) 34 (C.A.).

[31] *Belle River Community Arena Inc. v. W.J.C. Kaufman Co. Ltd.* (1978), 20 O.R. (2d) 447 (C.A.); *Alampi v. Swartz*, [1964] 1 O.R. 488, 43 D.L.R. (2d) 11 (C.A.); *McMaster University v. Wilchar Const. Ltd.*, [1971] 3 O.R. 801, 22 D.L.R. (3d) 9 (H.C.); affd 12 O.R. (2d) 512n (C.A.); *McMillen v. Chapman*, [1953] O.R. 399, [1953] 2 D.L.R. 611 (C.A.); *Farah v. Barki*, [1955] S.C.R. 107, [1955] 2 D.L.R. 657; *Gabriel v. Hamilton Tiger-Cat Football Club Ltd.*, *supra*, note 19; *Stepps Invts. Ltd. v. Security Capital Corp.* (1973), 14 O.R. (2d) 259 (H.C.); *Marathon Realty Co. v. Ginsberg*, *supra*, note 19; *Devald v. Zigeuner*, [1958] O.W.N. 381, 16 D.L.R. (2d) 285 (Ont. H.C.J.); *Beverly Motel*

A party is taken to know what would be obvious to a reasonable person in the circumstances.[32] The actual or constructive awareness of the non-mistaken party is vital and provides the different reasons for the relief for unilateral mistake. At common law, since the creation of a contract involves a process of offer and acceptance producing a meeting of the minds or *consensus ad idem*, the non-mistaken party cannot ignore the fact that the consensus is not real. At common law, a contract signed under unilateral mistake is void, having in theory never actually come into existence. In equity, the non-mistaken party's taking advantage of the contract while aware of the other's mistake was viewed as conduct equivalent to fraud for which equity would provide relief. In equity, a contract signed under unilateral mistake is voidable.

In cases of unilateral mistake, the defendant may be given the option of agreeing to a decree of rectification as an alternative to the judgment for rescission.[33]

The problem presented by mutual mistake is different.[34] At common law, the problem may be solved as an aspect of offer and acceptance theory. This time, however, since neither party is aware of the other's understanding, it is not possible, as it was in the case of unilateral mistake, to use the subjective awareness as precluding *consensus ad idem*. Rather, the common law uses the standard of an objective observer, "the reasonable man,"[35] to test the existence of a *consensus ad idem*. If a reasonable person would find a contract with specific terms, then the contract will stand

---

(1972) Ltd. v. Klyne Properties Ltd. (1981), 30 B.C.L.R. 282, 21 R.P.R. 106, 126 D.L.R. (3d) 757 (S.C.); *449576 Ont. Ltd. v. Bogojevski, supra*, note 20; *Solle v. Butcher*, [1950] 1 K.B. 671 (C.A.); *Defence Construction (1951) Ltd. v. Municipal Enterprises Ltd.* (1985), 71 N.S.R. (2d) 59, 23 D.L.R. (4th) 653 (C.A.); *First City Capital Ltd. v. B.C. Building Corp.* (1989), 43 B.L.R. 29 (B.C.S.C.); *Foderaro v. Future Homes Construction Ltd.* (1991), 17 R.P.R. (2d) 258 (Ont. Gen. Div.); *Santini v. Catenacci* (1992), 21 R.P.R. (2d) 111 (Ont. Gen. Div.); *Wilcox Lake Enterprises Inc. v. Starr* (1993), 30 R.P.R. (2d) 75 (Ont. Gen. Div.).

[32] *First City Capital Ltd. v. B.C. Building Corp., ibid.; Stepps Invts. Ltd. v. Security Capital Corp., ibid.; McMaster University v. Wilchar Const. Ltd., ibid.; Hartog v. Colin and Shields,* [1939] 3 All E.R. 566 (K.B.); *Windjammer Homes Inc. v. Generation Enterprises* (1989), 43 B.L.R. 315 (B.C.S.C.).

[33] *Devald v. Zigeuner, supra,* note 31; *Stepps Inv. Ltd. v. Security Capital Corp., ibid.; Murphy's Ltd. v. Fabricville Co. Inc.* (1980), 117 D.L.R. (3d) 668 (N.S.S.C.); *Windjammer Homes Inc. v. Generation Enterprises, ibid.*

[34] A mutual mistake sometimes may also be characterized as an error *in substantialibus,* which is discussed below.

[35] *Stepps Invts. Ltd. v. Security Capital Corp., supra,* note 31; *Gabriel v. Hamilton Tiger-Cat Football Club Ltd., supra,* note 19.

at common law, otherwise the contract is void.[36] In equity, it is doubtful that the pre-*Judicature Act* courts had a theory for mutual mistake.[37] However, the contemporary approach of equity will allow relief for all kinds of mistake, including mutual mistake, if the mistake is fundamental, the party seeking relief is not at fault, and it would be unfair, unjust, or unconscionable not to grant relief.[38] In equity, the contract is voidable. Thus, the remedy of rescission is more readily available and flexible in equity than at law.[39]

The problem of common mistake, where the parties share the same mistake, is difficult to solve at common law because a response cannot be justified on the basis of offer and acceptance theory. At the time of contracting, both parties intend to contract as they have, there is a *consensus ad idem* and an apparent contract. The common law, however, did respond to some circumstances where the parties contracted under a mistake about a fundamental aspect of their transaction, and it allowed rescission for common mistake if there was a complete difference in substance between what was supposed to be and what was taken, so as to constitute a failure of consideration.[40] As already noted above, equity does not rely on contract formation theory, and equity will allow rescission if the mistake is fundamental, the party seeking relief is not at fault, and it would be unfair, unjust, or unconscionable not to grant relief. Thus, equity's jurisdiction will reach all of the conventional types of mistake.

Whatever the type of mistake, historically, the law drew a distinction between a mistake of fact and a mistake of law and did not provide relief for a mistake of law. This distinction would appear to be no longer

---

[36] *Maida v. Dalewood Invts. Ltd.* (1982), 40 O.R. (2d) 472 (C.A.); affd [1985] 1 S.C.R. 568, 8 O.A.C. 369, 50 O.R. (2d) 223 (S.C.C.); *Brooklin Heights Homes Ltd. v. Major Holdings & Dev. Ltd.* (1977), 17 O.R. (2d) 413, 80 D.L.R. (3d) 563 (H.C.); *Charter-York Ltd. v. Hurst* (1978), 2 R.P.R. 272 (Ont. H.C.); leave to appeal to S.C.C. refused 28 N.R. 616*n*; *Staiman Steel Ltd. v. Commercial & Home Bldrs. Ltd.* (1976), 13 O.R. (2d) 315, 71 D.L.R. (3d) 17 (H.C.).

[37] Slade, "The Myth of Mistake in the English Law of Contract" (1954), 70 L.Q.R. 385 at 390.

[38] *McMaster University v. Wilchar Const. Ltd., supra,* note 31; *Hyrsky v. Smith,* [1969] 2 O.R. 360, 5 D.L.R. (3d) 385 (H.C.); *Stellar Properties Ltd. v. Botham Holdings Ltd.* (1992), 25 R.P.R. (2d) 299 (B.C.S.C.); affd [1994] 8 W.W.R. 639, 94 B.C.L.R. (2d) 42, 37 R.P.R. (2d) 284 (C.A.); *Solle v. Butcher, supra,* note 31; *First City Capital Ltd. v. B.C. Building Corp., supra,* note 31.

[39] An example of mutual mistake occurred in *Maida v. Dalewood Invts. Ltd., supra,* note 36, where the vendor and purchaser of lots on a proposed plan of subdivision had different understandings of what plan of subdivision was to receive approval. The court treated the agreement of sale as unenforceable.

[40] *Bell v. Lever Brothers Ltd.,* [1932] A.C. 161 (C.A.); *R. v. Ontario (Flue-Cured Tobacco Growers' Marketing Board,* [1965] 2 O.R. 411, 51 D.L.R. (2d) 7 (C.A.); *Stellar Properties Ltd. v. Botham Holdings Ltd., supra,* note 38.

sustainable. Taken together, in *Air Canada v. British Columbia*[41] and *Canadian Pacific Airlines Ltd. v. British Columbia*,[42] the Supreme Court of Canada adopted the dissenting judgment of Dickson, J. in *Hydro Electric Com'n of Twp. of Nepean v. Ontario Hydro*,[43] where he rejected the distinction between mistakes of fact and law in an action for moneys had and received. Although these cases involved the law of restitution and the action for moneys had and received, their rationale would apply equally to mistaken contracts.[44]

(3) *Non Est Factum*

The doctrine of *non est factum* focuses attention on a particular kind of mistake by a party signing a contract. The mistake is that the party fundamentally misunderstands the nature of the document being signed. The party believes that a contract of one type has been signed, when in fact a different kind of document has been signed. The mistake vitiates the consent necessary to contract, and the contract is considered void from the outset. A simple example from the case-law is *Taylor v. Armstrong*,[45] where a practically illiterate man signed a deed of land but believed he was signing a will.[46]

There are substantial limits on the availability of a successful plea of *non est factum*. In the House of Lords' decision in *Saunders v. Anglia Building Society*,[47] which was adopted by the Supreme Court of Canada in *Marvco Colour Research Ltd. v. Harris*,[48] the Law Lords held that *non*

---

[41] [1989] 1 S.C.R. 1161, [1989] 4 W.W.R. 97, 36 B.C.L.R. (2d) 145, 41 C.R.R. 308, 59 D.L.R. (4th) 161, 95 N.R. 1. Discussed in Perell, "Restitutionary Claims Against Government" (1995), 17 Adv. Q. 71.

[42] [1989] 1 S.C.R. 1133, [1989] 4 W.W.R. 137, 36 B.C.L.R. (2d) 185, 59 D.L.R. (4th) 218, 96 N.R. 1.

[43] [1982] 1 S.C.R. 347, 16 B.L.R. 215, 132 D.L.R. (3d) 193, 41 N.R. 1.

[44] *Vandekerhove v. Litchfield*, [1994] 1 W.W.R. 596, 84 B.C.L.R. (2d) 252, 103 D.L.R. (4th) 739 (S.C.); revd [1995] 4 W.W.R. 573, 1 B.C.L.R. (3d) 70, 121 D.L.R. (4th) 571 (C.A.); *Stellar Properties Ltd. v. Botham Holdings Ltd.*, *supra*, note 38, at 301 R.P.R. (C.A.).

[45] (1979), 24 O.R. (2d) 614, 99 D.L.R. (3d) 547 (S.C.).

[46] See also *Free Ukrainian Society (Toronto) Credit Union Ltd. v. Hnatkiw*, [1964] 2 O.R. 169, 44 D.L.R. (2d) 633 (C.A.); *Ghadban v. Bank of Nova Scotia* (1982), 132 D.L.R. (3d) 475 (Ont. H.C.J.); *Westerlund v. Ayer*, [1971] S.C.R. 131, 74 W.W.R. 348, 13 D.L.R. (3d) 334. The plea failed in *Royal Bank of Canada v. Gill*, [1988] 3 W.W.R. 441, 23 B.C.L.R. 176, 47 D.L.R. (4th) 466 (C.A.), where the illiterate defendant knew the general nature of the guarantee he had signed.

[47] [1971] A.C. 1004 (H.L.).

[48] [1982] 2 S.C.R. 774, 20 B.L.R. 143, 26 R.P.R. 48, 141 D.L.R. (3d) 577, 45 N.R. 302.

est factum was generally not available where an innocent third party relies on an apparently properly signed contract, and, in all the circumstances the signor was careless or negligent in signing the contract.[49]

In *Saunders v. Anglia Building Society*, the House of Lords held also that to establish *non est factum* it was necessary to show a fundamental or radical difference between the document signed and what was intended to be signed. This test is more liberal and was a departure from earlier authorities that drew a distinction between an error about the nature of the document, for which there was a remedy, and an error about its contents and detail, for which there was not. The Supreme Court did not decide this point in the *Marvco Colour Research Ltd. v. Harris* case, but lower Canadian courts have adopted the test used in *Saunders v. Anglia Building Society*.[50]

(4) Error *in Substantialibus*

As a legal doctrine, error *in substantialibus* is close to the common law's treatment of mistake, but it is an independent doctrine.[51] In a transaction involving the sale of real property, an error *in substantialibus* refers to the situation where there is a difference in substance between the property bargained for and that obtained amounting to or approaching a total failure in consideration.[52]

When the failure in consideration is total, as in *Cole v. Pope*,[53] where the purchaser obtained no title to a mining claim, the court will find that there has been an error *in substantialibus*. In other cases, the results are more problematic. For example, in *Komarniski v. Marien*,[54] the vendor innocently misrepresented his land as being about twice as large as its true

---

[49] *Shoppers Trust Co. v. Dynamic Homes Ltd.* (1992), 10 O.R. (3d) 361, 43 R.F.L. (3d) 97, 26 R.P.R. (2d) 30, 96 D.L.R. (4th) 267 (Gen. Div.).

[50] *Custom Motors Ltd. v. Dwinell* (1975), 2 N.S.R. (2d) 524, 61 D.L.R. (3d) 342 (C.A.); *C.I.B.C. v. Dura Wood Preservers Ltd.* (1979), 14 B.C.L.R. 338, 102 D.L.R. (3d) 78 (S.C.).

[51] See Fridman, "Error in Substantialibus: A Canadian Comedy of Errors" (1978), 56 Can. Bar Rev. 603.

[52] *Freear v. Gilders* (1921), 50 O.L.R. 217 (C.A.); *Hyrsky v. Smith*, *supra*, note 38; *DiCenzo Construction Co. Ltd. v. Glassco* (1978), 21 O.R. (2d) 186, 90 D.L.R. (3d) 127 (C.A.); *Alessio v. Jovica*, [1974] 2 W.W.R. 126, 42 D.L.R. (3d) 242 (Alta. C.A.); *Gronau v. Schlamp Invts. Ltd.*, [1975] W.W.D. 47, 52 D.L.R. (3d) 631 (Man. Q.B.); *Northern & Central Gas Corp. Ltd. v. Hillcrest Collieries*, [1976] 1 W.W.R. 481, 59 D.L.R. (3d) 533 (Alta. S.C.); *Kennedy v. Panama, New Zealand & Australian Royal Mail Co.* (1867), L.R. 2 Q.B. 580.

[53] (1898), 29 S.C.R. 291.

[54] [1979] 4 W.W.R. 267, 8 R.P.R. 229, 100 D.L.R. (3d) 80 (Sask. Q.B.).

size, but the court concluded that the purchaser had not received something totally different than bargained for and it denied the remedy of rescission.[55] A misrepresentation as to the zoning of land has been held not to amount to an error *in substantialibus*.[56] Recently, in *Goldstein v. Davidson*,[57] the court held that a misrepresentation (by silence) about whether a property was subject to the developmental constraints of legislation designed to preserve heritage properties was held not to be an error *in substantialibus*. In other cases, however, similar discrepancies have qualified as errors *in substantialibus*.[58]

(5) Undue Influence

Undue influence is the name of an equitable doctrine that will set aside a contract that is induced by the power or domination of one contracting party over the other.[59] The party alleging undue influence must show that in agreeing to contract, he or she was not a free and voluntary actor because of the domination of the other contracting party,[60] or of the other party's agents,[61] or of a third party if the third party's dominating influence was known or ought to have been known to the other contracting party.[62]

Because of their positions of influence, certain classes of individuals are presumed to have exercised undue influence. So, undue influence is

---

[55] For other similar cases, see *Schonekess v. Bach* (1968), 62 W.W.R. 673, 66 D.L.R. (2d) 415 (B.C.S.C.); *Aberg v. Rafuse* (1979), 36 N.S.R. (2d) 56, 8 R.P.R. 216 (N.S. S.C.).

[56] *Abraham v. Wingate Properties Ltd.*, [1986] 1 W.W.R. 568, 36 Man. R. (2d) 264 (C.A.); varied on reconsideration [1986] 2 W.W.R. 568 (Man. C.A.); *John Bosworth Ltd. v. Professional Syndicated Devs. Ltd.* (1979), 24 O.R. (2d) 97, 9 M.P.L.R. 241, 97 D.L.R. (3d) 112 (S.C.).

[57] (1994), 39 R.P.R. (2d) 61 (Ont. Gen. Div.).

[58] *Hyrsky v. Smith, supra*, note 38; *Freear v. Gilder, supra*, note 52.

[59] *Goodman Estate v. Geffen*, [1991] 2 S.C.R. 353, [1991] 5 W.W.R. 389, 80 Alta. L.R. (2d) 293, 42 E.T.R. 97, 81 D.L.R. (4th) 211; *Taylor v. Armstrong, supra*, note 45.

[60] *Rochdale Credit Union Ltd. v. Barney* (1984), 7 O.A.C. 9, 48 O.R. (2d) 676, 14 D.L.R. (4th) 116 (C.A.); leave to appeal to S.C.C. refused [1985] 1 S.C.R. xii; *Williams v. Downey-Waterbury*, [1995] 2 W.W.R. 609, 97 Man. R. (2d) 307, 11 R.F.L. (4th) 106, 120 D.L.R. (4th) 737 (C.A.).

[61] *Rochdale Credit Union Ltd. v. Barney, ibid.*

[62] *Bank of Montreal v. Stuart*, [1911] A.C. 120; *Hutchinson v. Standard Bank of Canada* (1917), 39 O.L.R. 286, 36 D.L.R. 378 (C.A.); *Chaplin & Co. Ltd. v. Brammall*, [1908] 1 K.B. 233 (C.A.); *Bank of Credit and Commerce International S.A. v. Aboody*, [1992] 4 All E.R. 955 (C.A.).

presumed to have been exercised by solicitors,[63] doctors,[64] trustees,[65] religious advisers,[66] and parents[67] but with an apparent exception for elderly parents.[68] Undue influence is, however, not presumed to have been exercised by spouses[69] or children.[70] But that does not mean that the doctrine cannot be applied to such a relationship or to any *ad hoc* relationship if it is shown that one person was in the position to exercise and did exercise undue influence over the other contracting party.[71]

Recent English authorities, particularly *Bank of Credit and Commerce International SA v. Aboody*,[72] have developed a scheme that differentiates between various classes for the operation of the doctrine of undue influence. Under this scheme, the availability of relief will depend upon whether the undue influence is: (a) actual (class 1); (b) presumed from a recognized relationship of trust and confidence (class 2A); or (c) presumed because the complainant proves the existence of a relationship of trust and confidence (class 2B). For class 2B situations that involve commercial transactions, there is no presumption of undue influence unless the transaction is manifestly disadvantageous to the complainant.[73] Under this English scheme, the requirement of manifest disadvantage does not apply to: (a) class 1 situations, because actual undue influence is a species of fraud and the victim has the right to have the transactions set aside

---

[63] *Rochdale Credit Union Ltd. v. Barney, supra*, note 60; *Malicki v. Yankovich* (1981), 41 O.R. (2d) 160, 125 D.L.R. (3d) 411 (Ont. H.C.), revised reasons at 42 O.R. (2d) 522, 149 D.L.R. (3d) 380 (Ont. H.C.J.); affd 41 O.R. (2d) 160, 145 D.L.R. (3d) 767 (C.A.); *Wright v. Carter*, [1903] 1 Ch. 27 (C.A.).

[64] *Kenny v. Lockwood*, [1932] O.R. 141, [1932] 1 D.L.R. 507 (Ont. C.A.); *Mitchell v. Homfray* (1881), 8 Q.B.D. 587 (C.A.).

[65] *Turnbull & Co. v. Duval*, [1902] A.C. 429 (P.C.); *Ellis v. Barker* (1871), L.R. 7 Ch. 104.

[66] *McKinnon v. McPherson* (1910), 44 N.S.R. 402 (C.A.).

[67] *Cox v. Adams* (1904), 35 S.C.R. 393; *Lancashire Loans Ltd. v. Black*, [1934] 1 K.B. 380 (C.A.).

[68] *Barclays Bank plc. v. O'Brien*, [1992] 4 All E.R. 983 (C.A.); *MacKay v. Bank of Nova Scotia* (1994), 41 R.P.R. (2d) 244, 20 O.R. (3d) 698 (Gen. Div.); *Bertolo v. Bank of Montreal* (1987), 18 O.A.C. 262, 57 O.R. (2d) 577, 33 D.L.R. (4th) 610 (C.A.).

[69] *Bank of Montreal v. Stuart, supra*, note 62; *Hutchinson v. Standard Bank of Canada, supra*, note 62; *Williams v. Downey-Waterbury, supra*, note 60; *McMurchy v. Harper*, [1937] 2 D.L.R. 774 (Man. K.B.).

[70] *Calmusky v. Karaloff*, [1947] S.C.R. 110, [1947] 1 D.L.R. 734; affg [1946] 2 W.W.R. 32, [1946] 2 D.L.R. 513 (Sask. C.A.).

[71] *Vanzant v. Coates* (1917), 40 O.L.R. 556, 39 D.L.R. 485 (C.A.); *Shortell v. Fitzpatrick*, [1949] O.R. 488 (H.C.); *Taylor v. Armstrong* (1979), 24 O.R. (2d) 614, 99 D.L.R. (3d) 547 (H.C.); *Burris v. Rhind* (1899), 29 S.C.R. 498.

[72] [1990] 1 Q.B. 923 (C.A.). See also *Barclays Bank plc v. O'Brien, supra*, note 68.

[73] *Nat'l Westminster Bank Plc v. Morgan*, [1985] A.C. 686 (H.L.); *Bank of Credit and Commerce Int'l SA v. Aboody*, [1990] 1 Q.B. 923 (C.A.).

as of right;[74] (b) class 2A situations because the presumption is made available here as a matter of public policy regulating recognized relationships of trust and confidence;[75] or (c) those class 2B situations about gifts, because this requirement does not sensibly operate in this context.[76] The role of the element of manifest disadvantage, however, is unsettled in Canada.[77]

If there is no presumption of undue influence, the onus of proof will be on the party seeking to set aside the transaction.[78] If, because of the classification of the relationship, there is a presumption of undue influence, then the onus will be on the party seeking to uphold the transaction to establish that the other party was acting with an independent will.[79] The existence or absence of independent legal advice is a factor but not a conclusive factor in assessing the presence of undue influence.[80]

In the recent case of *MacKay v. Bank of Montreal*,[81] where an elderly mother borrowed money to help a daughter and her common-law spouse, both of whom were financially irresponsible, the loan was held to be uncollectible on the grounds of undue influence. The court held that the bank, which had been unwilling to lend directly to the common-law couple because of their credit unworthiness, could not lend money to the plaintiff when it knew that the loan was improvident and that she had not received independent legal advice. It was not sufficient that the bank had recommended independent advice; the bank had to insist upon it or not make the loan. The court held that the unequal bargaining power together with an unfair contract created a presumption of undue influence.

---

[74] *CIBC Mortgages plc v. Pitt*, [1993] 4 All E.R. 432 (H.L.).

[75] *Ibid.*

[76] *Goodman Estate v. Geffen, supra*, note 59.

[77] *Ibid.*, where two judges adopted the requirement, but three judges decided the point did not arise for decision. See also Rafferty, ''Developments in Contract and Tort Law: The 1990-91 Term'' (1992), 3 S.C.L.R. (2d) 73.

[78] *Calmusky v. Karaloff, supra*, note 70; *Shortell v. Fitzpatrick, supra*, note 71; *O'Neill v. O'Neill*, [1952] O.R. 741 (H.C.); affd [1958] O.W.N. 280 (C.A.); *Brooks v. Alker* (1975), 9 O.R. (2d) 409, 22 R.F.L. 260, 60 D.L.R. (3d) 577 (H.C.).

[79] *Treadwell v. Martin* (1976), 13 N.B.R. (2d) 137, 67 D.L.R. (3d) 493 (C.A.); *O'Neill v. O'Neill, ibid.*

[80] *O'Neill v. O'Neill, ibid.*; *Brooks v. Alker, supra*, note 78; *Treadwell v. Martin, ibid.*; *Inche Noriah v. Shaik Allie Bin Omar*, [1929] A.C.127 (P.C.).

[81] *MacKay v. Bank of Nova Scotia, supra*, note 68.

(6) Duress

Duress is a doctrine of the common law concerned about coercion of the consent or free will necessary to establish a binding contract.[82] A contract obtained by duress is voidable.[83] To establish duress, it is not enough to show that one party has taken an unfair advantage of a dominating bargaining position; there must be coercion of the will of the other contracting party.[84] The doctrine of duress originally responded to cases of fear of personal injury or forced confinement of the contracting party, but the doctrine evolved to respond to cases of economic coercion where the conduct goes beyond legitimate commercial pressure so that the contracting is not a voluntary act.[85] Duress will also respond to cases where the will of the contracting party is coerced because of threats made against a third party.[86]

In cases of duress, to determine whether the pressure went beyond tolerable limits, the courts will weigh such factors as whether or not the coerced party protested; whether the coerced party had a realistic alternative to submission; whether the coerced party received independent advice; whether the coerced party affirmed the agreement; and whether the coerced party took any steps after the contract was signed to set it aside.[87]

---

[82] *Underwood v. Cox* (1912), 26 O.L.R. 303, 4 D.L.R. 66 (C.A.); *Brooks v. Alker, supra*, note 78.

[83] *Barton v. Armstrong*, [1975] 2 All E.R. 465 (P.C.); *Brooks v. Alker, ibid.*; *Byle v. Byle* (1990), 46 B.L.R. 292, 65 D.L.R. (4th) 641 (B.C.C.A.).

[84] *Century 21 Campbell Munro Ltd. v. S & G Estates Ltd.* (1992), 89 D.L.R. (4th) 413 (Ont. Div. Ct.) (claim dismissed); *CTN Cash & Carry Ltd. v. Gallaher Ltd.*, [1994] 4 All E.R. 714 (C.A.), where the exercise of commercial muscle to compel payment of a disputed debt subsequently found not to have been payable was held to be legitimate.

[85] *On v. Yiu*, [1979] 3 All E.R. 65 (P.C.); *Ronald Elwyn Lister Ltd. v. Dunlop Can. Ltd.* (1980), 27 O.R. (2d) 168, 9 B.L.R. 290, 32 C.B.R. (N.S.) 4, 50 C.P.R. (2d) 50, 105 D.L.R. (3d) 684 (C.A.); revd on other grounds [1982] 1 S.C.R. 726, 18 B.L.R. 1, 41 C.B.R. (N.S.) 272, 65 C.P.R. (2d) 1, 135 D.L.R. (3d) 1, 42 N.R. 181; *Universal Tankships Inc. of Monrovia v. Int. Tpt. Wkrs. Fed.*, [1982] 2 W.L.R. 803 (H.L.); *Gordon v. Roebuck* (1992), 9 O.R. (3d) 1, 92 D.L.R. (3d) 1 (C.A.) (claim dismissed); *DeWolfe v. Mansour* (1986), 73 N.S.R. (2d) 110, 33 B.L.R. 135 (S.C.) (claim dismissed); *Ben Plastering Ltd. v. Global Dixie Ltd.* (1980), 33 C.B.R. (N.S.) 253,14 R.P.R. 161 (Ont. S.C.) (claim dismissed).

[86] *Byle v. Byle, supra*, note 83.

[87] *On v. Yiu, supra*, note 85; *Universal Tankships Inc. of Monrovia v. Int. Tpt. Wkrs. Fed., supra*, note 85; *Stott v. Merit Investment Corp.* (1988), 25 O.A.C. 174, 63 O.R. (2d) 545, 19 C.C.E.L. 68, 48 D.L.R. (4th) 288 (C.A.); leave to appeal to S.C.C. refused 63 O.R. (2d) x; *Gordon v. Roebuck, supra*, note 85; *Byle v. Byle, ibid.*

The onus is on the person who alleges duress to prove it.[88] The party alleging duress must show that the conduct of the other contracting party or its agent amounted to duress or that the other contracting party was aware that a third party was coercing the execution of the agreement.

(7) Unconscionability

When a contract is unfair because of a disparity in the bargaining strength of the parties, the equitable doctrine of unconscionability may provide the remedy of rescission. The essential elements for relief are a pronounced inequality of bargaining power and a substantially improvident or unfair bargain; both factors must be present.[89] Equity will not intervene merely because a party, acting foolishly, immoderately, or under ordinary bargaining pressure has made a very bad bargain.[90] There must be a stronger party who takes an unfair advantage of the circumstances that hamper the weaker party. Those circumstances may be age, impaired mental health or ability, recklessness, a weak or submissive personality,

---

[88] *Brooks v. Alker, supra*, note 78.

[89] *Waters v. Donnelly* (1884), 9 O.R. 391 (Ch. Div.); *Vanzant v. Coates, supra*, note 71; *Morrison v. Coast Finance Ltd.* (1965), 54 W.W.R. 257, 55 D.L.R. (2d) 710 (B.C.C.A.); *Knupp v. Bell* (1968), 67 D.L.R. (2d) 256 (Sask. C.A.); *Marshall v. Can. Permanent Trust Co.* (1968), 69 D.L.R. (2d) 260 (Alta. S.C.); *Mundinger v. Mundinger*, [1969] 1 O.R. 606, 3 D.L.R. (3d) 338 (C.A.); affd [1970] S.C.R. vi; *Black v. Wilcox* (1976), 12 O.R. (2d) 759, 70 D.L.R. (3d) 192 (C.A.); *Paris v. Machnick* (1972), 32 D.L.R. (3d) 723 (N.S.S.C.); *Laderoute v. Laderoute* (1978), 17 O.R. (2d) 700, 81 D.L.R. (3d) 433 (H.C.); *Harry v. Kreutziger* (1978), 95 D.L.R. (3d) 231 (B.C.C.A.); *Junkin v. Junkin* (1978), 20 O.R. (2d) 118 (H.C.); *Taylor v. Armstrong, supra*, note 71; *Gillett v. Gillett* (1979), 100 D.L.R. (3d) 247 (Alta. S.C.); *Tweedie v. Geib* (1982), 19 Sask. R. 48, 138 D.L.R. (3d) 311 (Q.B.); *370866 Ont. Ltd. v. Chizy* (1987), 57 O.R. (2d) 587, 34 D.L.R. (4th) 404 (H.C.); *Principal Investments Ltd. v. Thiele's Estate* (1987), 12 B.C.L.R. (2d) 258, 37 D.L.R. (4th) 398 (C.A.); *Turner Estate v. Bonli Estate*, [1989] 5 W.W.R. 730, 77 Sask. R. 49 (Q.B.); affd [1990] 5 W.W.R. 685, 86 Sask. R. 235 (C.A.); *Shoppers Trust Co. v. Dynamic Homes Ltd.* (1993), 10 O.R. (3d) 361, 43 R.F.L. (3d) 97, 26 R.P.R. (2d) 30, 96 D.L.R. (4th) 267 (Gen. Div.).

[90] *Brock v. Gronbach*, [1953] 1 S.C.R. 207, [1953] 1 D.L.R. 785; revg 5 W.W.R. (N.S.) 68, [1952] 3 D.L.R. 490 *sub nom. Gronbach v. Petty* (Man. C.A.); revg 4 W.W.R. (N.S.) 49, *sub nom. Gronbach v. Petty* (Man. K.B.); *Calmusky v. Karaloff*, [1947] S.C.R. 110, [1947] 1 D.L.R. 734; affg [1946] 2 W.W.R. 32, [1946] 2 D.L.R. 513 (Sask. C.A.); *Laderoute v. Laderoute, supra*, note 89; *Syed v. McArthur* (1984), 46 O.R. (2d) 593 (H.C.J.); *DeWolfe v. Mansour, supra*, note 85; *Lindsay v. Lindsay* (1989), 59 Man. R. (2d) 186, 21 R.F.L. (3d) 34 (Man. Q.B.); *Williams v. Downey-Waterbury*, [1995] 2 W.W.R. 609, 97 Man. R. (2d) 307, 11 R.F.L. (4th) 106, 120 D.L.R. (4th) 737 (C.A.) (claim dismissed).

intimidation, lack of representation, ignorance, illiteracy, poverty, need, or distress. If the circumstances of inequality exist, the court will set the transaction aside unless the stronger party seeking to uphold the transaction demonstrates that it was a fair and not an improvident transaction.[91]

The principles of unconscionability have been applied in a variety of circumstances. In *Beach v. Eames*,[92] an improvident settlement of an accident claim was set aside; the accident victim was of modest intelligence with little education and did not fully understand the nature and effect of the release he was asked to sign by the claims adjuster. In *Canada Life Assur. Co. v. Stewart*,[93] a lease was set aside because the tenant, an inexperienced businesswoman, was coerced to sign by pressure found to be unconscionable by community standards of commercial morality. A relatively common occurrence in the case-law is the situation where a bank allows a customer or a relative of a customer to assume responsibility for a loan and the customer or relative is not advised about the improvidence of the transaction and the imprudence of assuming liability. In such circumstances, the court in the exercise of its equitable jurisdiction may rescind the transaction.[94]

(8) Breach of Fiduciary Duty

A contract entered into by a fiduciary who is breaching his or her fiduciary duties owed to the other contracting party may be rescinded. The law does not prohibit a fiduciary contracting with a beneficiary, but the contract is subject to being set aside if the fiduciary cannot demonstrate that there has been no breach of duty. For example, in *Hogar Estates Ltd. In Trust v. Shebron Holdings Ltd.*,[95] an agreement to wind up a joint land venture was set aside on the grounds of breach of fiduciary duty when one joint venturer did not disclose that the opposition of planning

---

[91] *Waters v. Donnelly, supra*, note 89; *Vanzant v. Coates, supra*, note 71; *Mundinger v. Mundinger, supra*, note 89; *Black v. Wilcox, supra*, note 89; *Junkin v. Junkin, supra*, note 89; *Harry v. Kreutziger, supra*, note 89; *Moore v. Stygall* (1914), 6 O.W.N. 126 (H.C.); *Trusts & Guarantee Co. v. Fryfogel* (1914), 6 O.W.N. 308, 26 O.W.R. 330 (H.C.).

[92] (1976), 18 O.R. (2d) 486 (Co. Ct.).

[93] (1994), 132 N.S.R. (2d) 324, 40 R.P.R. (2d) 85, 118 D.L.R. (4th) 67 (C.A.).

[94] *Royal Bank of Canada v. Hinds* (1978), 20 O.R. (2d) 613 (H.C.); *McKenzie v. Bank of Montreal* (1975), 7 O.R. (2d) 521, 55 D.L.R. (3d) 641 (H.C.); affd 12 O.R. (2d) 719, 70 D.L.R. (3d) 113 (C.A.); *Lloyds Bank Ltd. v. Bundy*, [1974] 3 All E.R. 757 (C.A.); *Shoppers Trust Co. v. Dynamic Homes Ltd., supra*, note 89; *MacKay v. Bank of Nova Scotia* (1994), 41 R.P.R. (2d) 244, 20 O.R. (3d) 698 (Gen. Div.).

[95] (1979), 25 O.R. (2d) 543, 101 D.L.R. (3d) 509 (S.C.).

authorities had been removed. In *Baskerville v. Thurgood*,[96] a financial
consultant breached his fiduciary duty when he sold shares in his consult-
ing company to his clients without obtaining their fully informed consent
and after providing them with information that was erroneous and misleading. The clients' investment plus the amount of their borrowing costs
was restored to them.

The courts apply a rigorous standard of review. The fiduciary must
show that there has been full disclosure of all material facts within the
fiduciary's knowledge; that the transaction is a just and fair one as far
as the beneficiary is concerned; and that the beneficiary would not have
done better by dealing with an arm's-length party. The presence or absence
of independent advice is a factor, although it is not by itself determinative of whether there has been a breach of fiduciary duty.[97]

Fiduciary duties are incidents of certain relationships; for example,
the relationship between trustee and beneficiary, but fiduciary duties may
arise in other relationships depending on the facts of the particular case.[98]
For example, usually the relationship between a lender and a borrower
is not a fiduciary relationship, but in several cases, banks have been found
to have had a fiduciary relationship with a borrower; in these cases, transactions have been rescinded because of the bank's breach of fiduciary
duty.[99]

(9) Alteration of Document

Where a party to a deed or contract unilaterally alters the instrument
by addition, deletion, interdelineation, or other physical change and the
change is material, then the other contracting parties may treat the deed
or contract as void.[100] The rationale for the law's vitiating the instrument

---

[96] [1992] 5 W.W.R. 193, 100 Sask. R. 214, 46 E.T.R. 28, 93 D.L.R. (4th) 695
(C.A.).

[97] *Ascu Community Credit Union Ltd. v. Dunster* (1990), 75 O.R. (2d) 490 (Gen.
Div.); *Shoppers Trust Co. v. Dynamic Homes Ltd.*, *supra*, note 89.

[98] *Hodgkinson v. Simms*, [1994] 9 W.W.R. 609, 97 B.C.L.R. (2d) 1, 16 B.L.R.
(2d) 1, 22 C.C.L.T. (2d) 1, 57 C.P.R. (3d) 1, 117 D.L.R. (4th) 161, 95 DTC
5135, 171 N.R. 245 (S.C.C.).

[99] *Bank of Montreal v. Hancock* (1982), 39 O.R. (2d) 82, 137 D.L.R. (3d) 648
(H.C.J.); *Hayward v. Bank of Nova Scotia* (1985), 10 O.A.C. 391, 51 O.R.
(2d) 193 , 32 C.C.L.T. 286, 6 C.P.R. (3d) 33, 19 D.L.R. (4th) 758 (C.A.); affg
45 O.R. (2d) 542, 25 B.L.R. 169, 27 C.C.L.T. 298, 7 D.L.R. (4th) 135 (H.C.);
Bank of Montreal v. Jakoujian (1986), 32 B.L.R. 177 (Ont. Dist. Ct.); *Royal
Bank of Canada v. Hinds*, *supra*, note 94.

[100] *Pigot's Case* (1614), 11 Co. Rep. 26b; *Stanbrook v. Ward*, [1965] 2 O.R. 607
(Ont. H.C.); *Spector v. Ageda*, [1973] Ch. 30; *Johnson v. Trobak*, [1977] 6

as opposed to simply ignoring the alteration is that a person should have something to lose by committing what may be a fraud. In any particular case, because the contract has become unenforceable at the option of the innocent party, the result of the application of this principle may approach rescission in the sense of restoring the parties to their pre-contractual situation.

The alteration must be material, which means that it must affect the rights, liabilities, or legal position of the parties.[101] Unilaterally affixing a seal on a document that was not intended to be a deed is a material alteration.[102] Conversely affixing a seal on an instrument intended to be a deed is not a material alteration.[103]

(10) Rescission as a Matter of Contract

The parties to a contract may agree that their contract will come to an end in defined circumstances. If they also agree that they are to be restored to their pre-contractual position, then, in effect, there is rescission as a matter of contract. A similar result is achieved if a contract is lawfully terminated while still executory.[104] As already noted above, the paradigm of rescission as a matter of contract is the rescission clause in the standard form agreement of purchase of sale. This clause allows the vendor to end the transaction if he or she is unable to answer a title requisition that the purchaser will not waive. The cancellation clause was introduced for the relief of vendors who might otherwise be subject to an action for specific performance with an abatement if the title they had promised was impaired by a defect. If available, the cancellation clause allows the vendor to withdraw rather than submit to the abatement.[105]

W.W.R. 289, 79 D.L.R. (3d) 684 (B.C.C.A.); *CIBC v. Skender*, [1986] 1 W.W.R. 284 (B.C.C.A.).

[101] *Roberto v. Bumb*, [1943] O.R. 299, [1943] 2 D.L.R. 613; *Clement v. Renaud*, [1956] O.W.N. 222, 1 D.L.R. (2d) 695; *CIBC v. Skender, ibid.*

[102] *Johnson v. Trobak, supra*, note 100; *Petro Canada Exploration Inc. v. Tormac Transport Ltd.*, [1983] 4 W.W.R. 205, 44 B.C.L.R. 220, 23 B.L.R. 1 (S.C.). But see *Bank of Montreal v. Scott*, [1987] 2 W.W.R. 404, 49 Alta. L.R. (2d) 117, 36 B.L.R. 73 (Q.B.).

[103] *Bank of Nova Scotia v. Spear* (1973), 6 N.B.R. (2d) 377, 37 D.L.R. (3d) 130 (C.A.); *Linton v. Royal Bank*, [1967] 1 O.R. 315, 60 D.L.R. (2d) 398 (H.C.); *Royal Bank v. Bermuda Holdings Ltd.* (1975), 67 D.L.R. (3d) 316 (B.C.S.C.).

[104] See *1061590 Ontario Ltd. v. Ontario Jockey Club* (1995), 21 O.R. (3d) 547, 43 R.P.R. (2d) 161 (C.A.).

[105] *Louch v. Pape Ave. Land Co.*, [1928] S.C.R. 518, [1928] 3 D.L.R. 620; *Lavine v. Independent Builders Ltd.*, [1932] O.R. 669, [1932] 4 D.L.R. 569; *Grant v. Tiercel Digital Ltd.* (1993), 32 R.P.R. (2d) 5 (Ont. Gen. Div.).

The case-law establishes that a vendor must be acting in good faith and must make a *bona fide* and reasonable effort to satisfy the requisition before being able to rely on the rescission clause.[106]

Similar is the law about conditions precedent. Contracts subject to conditions precedent may come to a end and the parties, practically speaking, restored to their pre-contractual position if the condition precedent is not satisfied within the time specified.[107] A party, however, cannot rely on the non-satisfaction of the condition precedent unless he or she is acting in good faith and did not, by default, bring about the non-satisfaction of the condition.[108]

---

[106] *Hurley v. Roy* (1921), 50 O.L.R. 281, 64 D.L.R. 375 (C.A.); *Lavine v. Independent Bldrs. Ltd.*, *ibid.*; *Mason v. Freedman*, [1958] S.C.R. 485; *Paulter Holdings Ltd. v. Karrys Invt. Ltd.*, [1961] O.R. 579, 28 D.L.R. (2d) 642 (H.C.); *Patterson v. Scherloski*, [1971] 3 O.R. 753, 21 D.L.R. (3d) 641 (H.C.); *Mitz v. Wiseman*, [1972] 1 O.R. 189, 22 D.L.R. (3d) 513 (H.C.); *Farantos Development Ltd. v. Canada Permanent Trust Co.* (1975), 7 O.R. (2d) 721, 56 D.L.R. (3d) 481 (H.C.); *J.C. Bakker & Sons Ltd. v. House* (1979), 8 R.P.R. 24 (Ont. S.C.); *Koccoris v. Cordery* (1982), 28 R.P.R. 75 (Ont. H.C.J.); *Re Barnett and Cadillac Fairview Corp.* (1983), 42 O.R. (2d) 461 (C.A.); *Ribic v. Weinstein* (1982), 26 R.P.R. 247, 140 D.L.R. (3d) 258 (Ont. H.C.); affd 4 O.A.C. 234, 47 O.R. (2d) 126, 34 R.P.R. 63, 10 D.L.R. (4th) 717, *sub nom. Weinstein Estate v. A.E. Le Page (Ont.) Ltd.* (C.A.); *Skariah v. Praxl* (1990), 73 O.R. (2d) 1, 11 R.P.R. (2d) 1, 70 D.L.R. (4th) 27 (H.C.); appeal to C.A. dismissed and leave to appeal to the S.C.C. refused, 2 O.R. (3d) xii; *Mink Printing Inc. v. K.J. Choi Ltd.* (1988), 66 O.R. (2d) 737, 2 R.P.R. (2d) 170, 55 D.L.R. (4th) 614 (H.C.); *McCauley v. McVey*, [1980] 1 S.C.R. 165, 9 R.P.R. 35, 98 D.L.R. (3d) 577, 27 N.R. 604. See also Herschorn, "Some Considerations of Fault in Real Estate Transactions" (1989), 11 Adv. Q. 71.

[107] *Rushville Construction Ltd. v. 57231 Ontario Ltd.* (1988), 66 O.R. (2d) 146 (H.C.J.); *Thorman v. Parnes* (1990), 73 O.R. (2d) 149, 11 R.P.R. (2d) 182 (H.C.J.); vard 17 O.R. (3d) 622n (C.A.); *Hicks v. Gelowitz*, [1989] 1 W.W.R. 52, 72 Sask. R. 319 (C.A.); *Cressey Development Corp. v. Breckner* (1991), 20 R.P.R. (2d) 218 (B.C.S.C.); *Blair v. Crawford* (1989), 70 O.R. (2d) 748 (H.C.J.); *Moon v. Metropolitan Toronto Ass'n for Community Living* (1989), 6 R.P.R. (2d) 284 (Ont. H.C.J.); *Lizar v. Chisholm* (1992), 25 R.P.R. (2d) 52 (Ont. Gen. Div.); *Scully v. Lismore* (1994), 37 R.P.R. (2d) 101 (Ont. Gen. Div.).

[108] *Dynamic Tpt. Ltd. v. O.K. Detailing Ltd.*, [1978] S.C.R. 1072; *100 Main St. Ltd. v. W.B. Sullivan Const. Ltd.* (1978), 88 D.L.R. (3d) 1 (Ont. C.A.); leave to appeal to S.C.C. refused (1978), 88 D.L.R. (3d) 1n (S.C.C.); *Aldercrest Devs. Ltd. v. Hunter*, [1970] 2 O.R. 562 (C.A.); *Metro. Trust Co. v. Pressure Concrete Services Ltd.* (1976), 9 O.R. (2d) 375, 60 D.L.R. (3d) 431 (C.A.); affg [1973] 3 O.R. 629, 37 D.L.R. (3d) 649 (H.C.); *Eastwalsh Homes Ltd. v. Anatal Developments Ltd.* (1990), 72 O.R. (2d) 661, 11 R.P.R. (2d) 107, 68 D.L.R. (4th) 46 (H.C.J.); vard 12 O.R. (3d) 675, 30 R.P.R. (2d) 276, 100 D.L.R. (4th) 469 (C.A.); leave to appeal to S.C.C. refused 34 R.P.R. (2d) 90 (S.C.C.); *Melody Enterprises Inc. v. McGregor* (1991), 91 Nfld. & P.E.I.R. 256, 17 R.P.R. (2d) 272 (P.E.I.C.A.).

3. *Rescission and the Law of Restitution*

(1) Introduction

Until relatively recently, the Canadian law of restitution was not governed by any general principle. Rather, the law of restitution referred to certain established categories of claim for which restitutionary remedies were available. The categories included claims for *quantum meruit*, for moneys had and received, and also claims arising from fraud, innocent misrepresentation, mistake, duress, and breach of fiduciary duty. As already discussed above, some of these categories provide grounds for the remedy of rescission.

The modern Canadian law of restitution, without ignoring the established categories, recognizes the principle of unjust enrichment as a rationalizing or governing general principle. The elements of unjust enrichment are:[109] (1) the defendant has been enriched by the receipt of a benefit; (2) the defendant has been enriched at the plaintiff's expense; and (3) there is no juristic reason justifying the enrichment. In the recent case of *Peel (Reg. Mun.) v. Canada*,[110] the Supreme Court of Canada held that the established categories of restitutionary claims remain relevant and that the general principles of unjust enrichment do not govern alone; rather, the general principles inform the established categories and allow the law of restitution to grow and respond to new types of cases.

With this background, the next topics for this paper about rescission may be identified. These topics concern rescission in restitutionary claims arising from breach of contract, from illegal, ineffective, or unenforceable contracts, and from the doctrine of frustration of contract. In considering rescission in the context of the law of restitution, it should be kept in mind that in the particular circumstances restitutionary relief may go beyond rescission. Thus, for example, a defendant who breached his or her fiduciary duty might be obliged to disgorge profits or property that

---

[109] *Pettkus v. Becker*, [1980] 2 S.C.R. 834, 8 E.T.R. 143, 19 R.F.L. (2d) 165, 117 D.L.R. (3d) 257, *sub nom. Becker v. Pettkus*; *Sorochan v. Sorochan*, [1986] 2 S.C.R. 38, [1986] 5 W.W.R. 289, 46 Alta. L.R. (2d) 97, 23 E.T.R. 143, 29 D.L.R. (4th) 1, 69 N.R. 81; *Peter v. Beblow*, [1993] 1 S.C.R. 980, [1993] 3 W.W.R. 337, 77 B.C.L.R. (2d) 1, 48 E.T.R. 1, 101 D.L.R. (4th) 621, 150 N.R. 1.

[110] [1992] 3 S.C.R. 762, 12 M.P.L.R. (2d) 229, 98 D.L.R. (4th) 140, 140 N.R. 1; affg [1989] 2 F.C. 562, 1 O.R. (3d) 97, 41 M.P.L.R. 113, 55 D.L.R. (4th) 618 (C.A.). See also *White v. Central Trust Co.* (1984), 54 N.B.R. (2d) 293, 17 E.T.R. 78, 7 D.L.R. (4th) 236 (C.A.).

never belonged to the beneficiary of the fiduciary duty.[111] Thus, the law of restitution may provide remedies that go far beyond restoring the parties to a pre-contractual position.[112]

(2) Breach of Contract

Recalling the discussion at the outset of this paper, one of the most confusing uses of the word rescission arises in the context of a breach of contract. Here, rescission has been used to refer to the consequences when a party repudiates or breaches a term classified as a condition; these consequences include damages or specific performance but not genuine rescission. However, under the law of restitution, there may be genuine rescission for breach of contract. To avoid the confusion and to understand how there can be genuine rescission for breach of contract, it is necessary first to summarize the situation under the law of contract.

Under the theory of the classification of contract terms, contract promises or terms are classified as warranties, intermediate terms, and conditions.[113] Where the breached term is classified as a warranty, the innocent party may seek the remedies of damages or specific performance, but the innocent party may not lawfully end the contract.[114] Where the

---

[111] Similarly, a tortfeasor may be obliged to disgorge profits if the injured plaintiff "waives the tort": See Maddaugh and McCamus, *The Law of Restitution*, at 432-33; Smith, "Disgorgement of the Profits of Breach of Contract: Property, Contract and Efficient Breach" (1994), 24 Can. Bus. L.J. 121.

[112] An example is *quantum meruit*, which provides compensation rather than the restoration of benefits. See Fridman, *Restitution*, 2nd ed., at 23-26, where, in addition to claims for restoration, Professor Fridman, identifies: (a) restitutionary claims for reimbursement; for example, a surety's claim against the principal debtor; and (b) claims for recompense; for example, a claim for *quantum meruit* for services rendered under an unenforceable contract. Another categorization, suggested by Professor Birks is between restitution for the plaintiff having been deprived (subtraction at the plaintiff's expense) and for the plaintiff having been wronged. This categorization is discussed by Professor McCamus in "Restitution and the Supreme Court: The Continuing Progress of the Unjust Enrichment Principle" (1991), 2 S.C.L.R. (2d) 505.

[113] *Bunge Corp. v. Tradax S.A.*, [1981] 2 All E.R. 513 (H.L.); *Hongkong Fir Shipping Co. v. Kisen Kaisha Ltd.*, [1962] 2 Q.B. 26 (C.A.); *Jorian Properties Ltd. v. Zellenrath* (1984), 4 O.A.C. 107, 46 O.R. (2d) 775, 26 B.L.R. 276, 10 D.L.R. (4th) 458 (C.A.); *First City Trust v. Triple Five Corp.*, [1989] 3 W.W.R. 577, 65 Alta. L.R. (2d) 193, 57 D.L.R. (4th) 554 (C.A.); leave to appeal to S.C.C. refused 62 D.L.R. (4th) vii, 104 N.R. 318n.

[114] *Bentsen v. Taylor, Sons & Co.*, [1893] 2 Q.B. 274 (C.A.); *Field v. Zein*, [1963] S.C.R. 632; *Jorian Properties Ltd. v. Zellenrath, ibid.*; *Penner v. Williamson*, [1993] 6 W.W.R. 340, 78 B.C.L.R. (2d) 237, 101 D.L.R. (4th) 286 (C.A.).

breached term is classified as a condition, the innocent party may treat the breach as if it were a breach of warranty or the innocent party may lawfully end the contract and both sides are discharged from further performance, but the innocent party may claim damages.[115] Where the breached term is classified as an intermediate term, the legal consequences of its breach depend upon the seriousness of the actual consequences of the breach; *i.e.*, for consequences that destroy the heart of the bargain, the intermediate term will be treated as a condition, otherwise, it will be treated as a warranty.[116]

Under the modern Canadian law of restitution, where there is a breach of a term that is classified as a condition of the contract, the innocent party may have the alternative of seeking restitutionary relief instead of a contract law remedy. Thus, subject to an exception, discussed below, where the innocent party has fully performed and claims money, instead of damages or specific performance, the innocent party may claim *quantum meruit, quantum valebat* or moneys had and received.[117] Similarly, although the number of reported cases is few, where there is a breach of a condition, the innocent party may have the alternative of treating the contract as at an end and of being restored to his or her pre-contractual position; *i.e.*, of obtaining genuine rescission.[118] Restitutionary relief may be advantageous because, in the particular circumstances, it may be higher in quantum or easier of proof than a claim for damages.[119]

A simple example will help bring into focus rescission as an alternative remedy for breach of contract. A purchaser contracts to buy a machine

---

[115] *Johnson v. Agnew*, [1979] 1 All E.R. 523 (H.L.).

[116] *Bunge Corp. v. Tradax S.A., supra*, note 113; *Hongkong Fir Shipping Co. v. Kisen Kaisha Ltd., supra*, note 113; *L. Schuler A.G. v. Wickman Machine Tool Sales Ltd.*, [1973] 2 All E.R. 39 (H.L.); Hutchinson and Wakefield, "Contracts—Innominate [Intermediate] Terms: Contractual Encounters of the Third Kind" (1982), 60 Can. Bar Rev. 335.

[117] *Alkok v. Grymek*, [1968] S.C.R. 452, 67 D.L.R. (2d) 718; *Gettle Bros. Const. Co. v. Alwinsol Potash of Canada Ltd.* (1969), 5 D.L.R. (3d) 719 (Sask. C.A.); affd [1971] S.C.R. 320, 15 D.L.R. (3d) 128; *Komorowski v. Van Weel* (1993), 12 O.R. (3d) 444 (Gen. Div.); *Le Sueur v. Morang & Co. Ltd.* (1910), 20 O.L.R. 594 (C.A.); affd 45 S.C.R. 95; *Clermont v. Mid-West Steel Products Ltd.* (1965), 51 D.L.R. (2d) 340 (Sask. Q.B.); Maddaugh and McCamus, *The Law of Restitution*, at 73-74, c. 19; Klippert, *Unjust Enrichment*, at 299-306; Fridman, *Restitution*, 2nd ed., at 212-15; Waddams, *The Law of Contracts*, 3rd ed., paras. 712-19; *Chitty on Contracts*, 27th ed., para. 29-124.

[118] *Fleischhaker v. Fort Gary Agencies Ltd.* (1957), 65 Man. R. 339, 23 W.W.R. 390, 11 D.L.R. (2d) 599 (C.A.); *Bertok (Wilson) v. Patrician School of Personal Arts Ltd.* (1977), 2 B.L.R. 275 (Ont. C.A.); *Gibbons v. Trapp Motors Ltd.* (1970), 9 D.L.R. (3d) 742 (B.C.S.C.); *Lightburn v. Belmont Sales Ltd.* (1969), 69 W.W.R. 734, 6 D.L.R. (3d) 692 (B.C.S.C.); *Jay Trading Corp. v. Ifax Export & Imports Ltd.*, [1954] 2 D.L.R. 110 (N.S.S.C.).

[119] *Chitty on Contracts, supra*, note 117, para. 29-035.

for $1,000. The purchaser pays a deposit of $100. The vendor fails to deliver. Depending on the price of a substitute machine, there may be no damages and indeed the purchaser may have been saved from a bad bargain. The purchaser would be better off with a claim for rescission restoring him or her to the pre-contractual position. In this example, the purchaser's entitlement can be explained by the elements of an action for unjust enrichment. The vendor has been enriched, the enrichment is at the purchaser's expense, and there is no juridical basis for the enrichment.

Palachik v. Kiss [120] provides an example from the case-law. In this case, Mrs. Palachik married Mr. Kiss and purchased a home for them. Title was taken in her name, but she orally agreed that he would receive a half-interest by paying $100 each month until half the purchase price had been paid. He kept his side of the bargain, but she died without performing her side. Mr. Kiss sued for repayment of the moneys he had paid, and his claim was upheld on several different grounds by the Supreme Court of Canada. Approaching the matter as a matter of contract law, Wilson J., who delivered the court's judgment, said that an innocent party who has made payments under a contract can recover them by showing that because the contract was either breached by the other side or frustrated by the circumstances, there has been a total failure of consideration. She explained that a total failure of consideration referred to the performance of the contract and the relevant question was whether the innocent party received the benefit in exchange for which the payments had been made.

The *Palachik* case and old case-law, which precedes the modern development of the principle of unjust enrichment, preclude the restitutionary claim unless there is a total failure of consideration under the contract.[121] The old case-law, however, did not impose this requirement when the innocent party's claim was for the value of property or services supplied, and the total failure of consideration requirement has been both questioned and narrowed by explanation. Arguably, it is no longer a factor for any type of claim under the modern case-law about unjust enrichment.[122]

---

[120] [1983] 1 S.C.R. 623, 15 E.T.R. 129, 33 R.F.L. (2d) 225, 146 D.L.R. (3d) 385, 47 N.R. 148.

[121] *Hunt v. Silk* (1804), 5 East 449, 102 E.R. 1142.

[122] Maddaugh and McCamus, *The Law of Restitution*, supra, note 117, at 73-4, 422-25. *Chitty on Contracts*, supra, note 117, make the point that the concept of total failure of consideration does not mean that the innocent party receives no benefits but rather he or she does not receive the benefits bargained for. Fridman's analysis in *Restitution*, supra, note 117, at 209-215 is that total failure of consideration is still an element of the claim but that failure of consideration here refers to the faulty performance of the promises constituting the consideration; he adds that the contemporary position is for the court to be

The exception to the availability of a restitutionary claim as an alternative remedy for breach of a condition of a contract is the case where the innocent party has completely performed his or her obligations and the breach by the other party is simply the failure to pay.[123]

(3) Frustration

Through the doctrine of frustration, the law recognizes that unexpected events after the creation of the contract may thwart the expectation under which the parties entered into their contract and that in the circumstances it is unfair to hold the parties to their bargain. A recent example is *Can-Truck Transportation Ltd. v. Fenton's Auto Paint Shop*,[124] where a fire destroyed the defendant's auto repair shop along with the plaintiff's truck, which was then in the course of being repaired. The destruction of the specific thing essential to the performance of the contract frustrated the contract for repairs,[125] and the parties were discharged from further performance although subject to the operation of the *Frustrated Contracts Act*, discussed below.

Given that risk and the unexpected are inherent to contracting, not every unexpected event will operate to frustrate the contract. Unexpected hardship, inconvenience, or material loss by themselves do not call for the operation of the doctrine of frustration. In *Davis Contrs. Ltd. v. Fareham Urban Dist. Council*,[126] a construction contract took longer than anticipated because of the unavailability of labour and materials. These circumstances were held insufficient to constitute frustration. The House of Lords held that for frustration, the unexpected event must transmute

---

more realistic and practical about this element. In Waddams, *The Law of Contracts, supra*, note 117, para. 715 a similar view is expressed.

[123] *Morrison-Knudsen Co. Inc. v. British Columbia Hydro & Power Authority* (1978), 85 D.L.R. (3d) 186 (B.C.C.A.). The restitutionary claim, however, is not denied if the innocent party has not completely performed. As Waddams, *The Law of Contracts, ibid.*, para. 717 points out, this may produce anomalies. The innocent party may do better by the guilty party's breach than if the guilty party had performed. There are arguments for and against the justness of these results. See *Chitty on Contracts, supra*, note 117, paras. 29-123 to 29-124; Baer, "Can Contract Damages Based on Wasted Expenses Give the Plaintiff More than the Value of the Promised Performance" (1978-79), 3 Can. Bus. L.J. 198.

[124] (1993), 101 D.L.R. (4th) 562 (Ont. C.A.).

[125] See also *Taylor v. Caldwell* (1863), 3 B. & S. 862; *Laurwen Investment Inc. v. 814693 Northwest Territories Ltd.* (1989), 48 B.L.R. 100 (N.W.T.S.C.); *Turner v. Clark* (1983), 49 N.B.R. (2d) 340, 30 R.P.R. 164 (C.A.).

[126] [1956] A.C. 696 (H.L.).

the undertaking of performance into a radically different kind of obligation.[127]

If the allegedly frustrating event is foreseen and provided for in the agreement, there can be no frustration;[128] for example, there is no frustration where the object of the transaction is destroyed by fire, but the parties have addressed the risk of destruction in their contract.[129] Further, the frustrating event must take place without fault of the parties to the contract.[130]

When augmented by the statutory provisions described below, the remedial response to frustration bears a strong resemblance and approaches the equitable remedy of rescission. As is the case for the remedy of rescission, under the doctrine of frustration, the parties are freed from their contractual obligations, and the issue that remains is whether they may be restored to their pre-contractual position. At common law, when a contract is frustrated, contractual performance is frozen as at the time of the frustrating event. Future performance is discharged, but obligations that have accrued are still required to be fulfilled, and there is no recovery of consideration that has already passed unless there has been total failure of consideration. Further, at common law, there is no adjustment for expenses incurred in anticipation of completion of the contract.[131] However, the rigidity of the common law treatment of frustrated contracts is addressed by the statutory provisions of the *Frustrated Contracts Act*.[132]

---

[127] See also *Gambouras v. Swan* (1993), 37 R.P.R. (2d) 221 (B.C.S.C.); *Lafrenière v. Leduc* (1990), 72 O.R. (2d) 285, 66 D.L.R. (4th) 577 (H.C.J.); *Kesmat Investments Inc. v. Canadian Indemnity Co.* (1985), 70 N.S.R. (2d) 341, 39 R.P.R. 19 (C.A.). In cases about contracts for the purchase of lands, new planning legislation that thwarts a developer's plans sometimes has constituted an event frustrating the contract: *Capital Quality Homes Ltd. v. Colwyn Construction* (1975), 9 O.R. (2d) 617 (C.A.); *British Columbia (Minister of Crown Lands) v. Cressey Dev. Corp.*, [1992] 4 W.W.R. 357, 66 B.C.L.R. (2d) 146, 5 B.L.R. (2d) 1, 23 R.P.R. (2d) 258 (S.C.). There was, however, no frustration in *Victoria Wood Development Corp. v. Ondrey* (1978), 22 O.R. (2d) 1 (C.A.), affg 14 O.R. (2d) 723 (H.C.J.); leave to appeal to the S.C.C. refused (1979), 7 R.P.R. 60n.

[128] *Capital Quality Homes Ltd. v. Colwyn Const. Ltd.* (1975), 9 O.R. (2d) 617, 61 D.L.R. (3d) 385 (C.A.); affg [1973] 3 O.R. 651, 37 D.L.R. (3d) 671 (H.C.); *Dot Devs. Ltd. v. Fowler* (1980), 18 R.P.R. 10, 118 D.L.R. (3d) 371 (B.C.S.C.); *Kesmat Investments Inc. v. Canadian Indemnity Co.*, *ibid.*

[129] *Gambouras v. Swan*, *supra*, note 127.

[130] *Graham v. Wagman* (1976), 14 O.R. (2d) 349, 73 D.L.R. (3d) 667 (H.C.); vard 21 O.R. (2d) 1, 89 D.L.R. (3d) 282 (C.A.); *Paal Wilson & Co. A/S v. Partenreederei Hannah Blumenthal*, [1983] 1 All E.R. 34 (H.L.).

[131] *Krell v. Henry*, [1903] 2 K.B. 740 (C.A.); *Chandler v. Webster*, [1904] 1 K.B. 493 (C.A.); *Goulding v. Rabinovitch*, [1927] 3 D.L.R. 820 (Ont. C.A.); *Fibrosa Spolka Akcyina v. Fairbairn Lawson Combe Barbour Ltd.*, [1943] A.C. 32 (H.L.); *Cahan v. Fraser*, [1952] 4 D.L.R. 112 (B.C.C.A.).

[132] R.S.O. 1990, c. F.34.

Assuming that the contract itself does not provide for the consequences of frustration, the Act discharges future obligations and allows the recovery of sums already paid.[133] The Act gives the court discretionary power to allow sums to be retained or to order sums to be paid as compensation for expenses in connection with the performance of the contract. The court has the discretion to make an allowance for any valuable benefit received other than a payment of money.[134] The court has the discretion to award interest on moneys that one party must return to the other.[135]

(4) Illegality

In certain cases associated with the exceptions to the law's normal treatment of illegal contracts, the consequences of an illegal contract may approach genuine rescission. Subject to several exceptions, if a contract is illegal, then the law will not enforce the contract[136] and the law will not restore either party to their pre-contractual position; there is no rescission or restitution; and the benefits or losses from the contract are not adjusted.[137] If a contract is illegal, a subsequent contract of settlement or compromise is also illegal.[138]

As to what is an illegal contract, the general principle expressed in Latin is *"ex dolo malo non oritur actio"* or *"ex turpi causa non oritur actio"*: no court will lend its aid to a person who founds the cause of action upon an immoral or illegal act. Illegal contracts are of two types: (1) contracts contrary to statute; and (2) contracts contrary to established common law categories of illegality. Example categories are contracts to

---

[133] See Percy, "The Application of the Doctrine of Frustration in Canada," in *Studies in Canadian Business Law*, Fridman, ed. (Toronto: Butterworths, 1971), at 49.

[134] *B.P. Explorations Co. (Libya) Ltd. v. Hunt (No. 2)*, [1979] 1 W.L.R. 783; affd [1981] 1 W.L.R. 232 (C.A.); affd [1983] 2 A.C. 352 (H.L.); *Cassidy v. Canada Publishing Corp.* (1988), 41 B.L.R. 223 (B.C.S.C.).

[135] *British Columbia (Minister of Crown Lands) v. Cressey Development Corp.*, *supra*, note 127.

[136] *Holman v. Johnson* (1755), 1 Cowp. 341; *Perry v. Anderson* (1970), 12 D.L.R. (3d) 414 (B.C.S.C.); *Rogers v. Leonard* (1973), 1 O.R. (2d) 57, 39 D.L.R. (3d) 349 (Div. Ct.); *Stuart v. Kingman* (1978), 21 O.R. (2d) 650 (H.C.J.).

[137] *Re O.S.C. and Br. Can. Commodity Options Ltd.* (1978), 22 O.R. (2d) 278 (H.C.J.); *Rosemay v. Nuberg & Dale Const. Ltd.* (1982), 40 O.R. (2d) 152 (Div. Ct.); *Menard v. Genereux* (1982), 39 O.R. (2d) 55, 138 D.L.R. (3d) 273 (H.C.J.); *Ross v. Jones* (1993), 9 B.L.R. (2d) 299 (B.C.S.C.).

[138] *Vandekerhove v. Litchfield*, [1994] 1 W.W.R. 596, 84 B.C.L.R. (2d) 252, 103 D.L.R. (4th) 739 (S.C.); revd [1995] 4 W.W.R. 573, 1 B.C.L.R. (3d) 70, 121 D.L.R. (4th) 571 (C.A.).

commit criminal or tortious acts including fraud; contracts that interfere with the administration of justice; contracts injurious to the state; contracts that encourage immorality, and contracts in restraint of trade.

Under statutory illegality, unless the statute expressly prohibits the contract, the fact that a contract is contrary to a statutory provision does not automatically make the contract illegal. It is a matter of statutory interpretation whether the doctrine of illegality is to apply. The contemporary approach is to analyse the purpose of the statute and determine whether the legislative purpose would be served or, conversely, frustrated by the application of the doctrine.[139]

While the courts will not enforce a contract wholly tainted by illegality, in some cases, the illegality may relate to a severable part of the contract; in these cases, the court may enforce the agreement in part. In deciding to exercise its discretion to sever and partially enforce, the court will consider the object and policy of the statute, whether that object and policy would be subverted by partial performance, whether one or both of the parties intended to break the law, whether the parties were in an equal bargaining position, whether the parties were professionally advised, and whether one party would be unjustly enriched if the contract were not enforced in part.[140]

There are three exceptions to the rule that illegality will preclude restitution.[141] If there is restitution, then, practically speaking, the parties may be restored to their pre-contractual situation. The three exceptions are associated with the Latin phrases *"ex turpi causa non oritur actio,"* *"in pari delicto, potior est conditio defendentis"* and *"locus poenitentiae"*. As a legal maxim, the first phrase means, as already noted above, that an action cannot be founded on a tainted, that is, an illegal, transaction. The second phrase means that if the fault of the party seeking restitution, that is, the plaintiff, is equal to the fault of the defendant, then the property will remain with the defendant. As a legal maxim, the third

---

[139] *Sidmay Ltd. v. Wehttam Invts. Ltd.*, [1967] 1 O.R. 508 (C.A.); affd on other grounds [1968] S.C.R. 828; *Re O.S.C. and Br. Can. Commodity Options Ltd.*, *supra*, note 137.

[140] *William E. Thomson Associates Inc. v. Carpenter* (1989), 69 O.R. (2d) 545, 44 B.L.R. 125, 61 D.L.R. (4th) 1 (C.A.); *Tartan Development Corp. v. Ottawa (City)* (1993), 14 O.R. (3d) 747 (Gen. Div.); *T.F.P. Investments Inc. Estate v. Beacon Realty Co.* (1994), 17 O.R. (3d) 687 (C.A.).

[141] *Berne Devs. Ltd. v. Havilland* (1983), 40 O.R. (2d) 238, 27 R.P.R. 56 (H.C.J.); *McDonald v. Fellows*, [1979] 6 W.W.R. 544, 9 R.P.R. 168, 105 D.L.R. (3d) 434 (Alta. C.A.); *Menard v. Genereux*, *supra*, note 137; *Ouston v. Zurowski*, [1985] 5 W.W.R. 169, 63 B.C.L.R. 89, 18 D.L.R. (4th) 563 (C.A.); Merkin, "Restitution by Withdrawal from Executory Illegal Contracts" (1981), 97 L.Q.R. 420; Grodecki, "In Pari Delicto Potior est Conditio Defendentis" (1955), 71 L.Q.R. 254.

phrase means that restitution will be granted to a party who repents the illegality while the contract is still executory.

The first exception is associated with the phrase *"ex turpi causa non oritur actio"*, which articulates the basic principle of the doctrine of illegality. Under the first exception, the plaintiff finds a way around the principle; *i.e.*, if the plaintiff can establish an independent claim not tainted by illegality, then the fact that the plaintiff was a party to an illegal transaction will present no obstacle to recovery.[142]

The second exception is a true qualification to the doctrine of illegality. To rely on this exception, a plaintiff will have to show that he or she is not equally at fault or, to use the Latin, not *in pari delicto*, with the defendant. The fact that the plaintiff was ignorant of the illegality of the transaction will not establish that he or she was not *in pari delicto*. However, there are other ways to satisfy this criteria.[143] Circumstances where the plaintiff is under duress or oppression or is the victim of fraud or breach of fiduciary duty will satisfy the criteria.[144] Where the illegality is based on the contravention of a statute, if the plaintiff is among the class for whose protection the statute was designed or if the denial of restitution would be inimical to the statutory policy, then the plaintiff will be allowed restitution.[145]

The third exception will allow recovery if a party repents in time.[146] This exception may be explained as a policy decision to encourage honesty. The exception has been allowed to operate to allow a party out of a disadvantageous transaction.

---

[142] *Elford v. Elford* (1922), 64 S.C.R. 125; *Kirzinger v. Kalthoff* (1964), 46 W.W.R. 547 (Sask. Q.B.); *Tinsley v. Milligan*, [1994] 1 A.C. 340 (H.L.).

[143] *Ouston v. Zurowski, supra*, note 141; *J.M. Allan (Merchandising) Ltd. v. Cloke*, [1963] 2 All E.R. 258 (C.A.); *Lauff v. Cooney*, [1960] O.W.N. 481 (H.C.).

[144] *Ouston v. Zurowski, ibid.*; *Steinberg v. Cohen*, [1930] 2 D.L.R. 916 (Ont. C.A.); *D'Amore v. McDonald*, [1973] 1 O.R. 845, 32 D.L.R. (3d) 543 (H.C.); affd 1 O.R. (2d) 370, 40 D.L.R. (3d) 354 (C.A.).

[145] *Sidmay Ltd. v. Wehttam Invts. Ltd.*, [1967] 1 O.R. 508, 61 D.L.R. (2d) 358 (C.A.); affd [1968] S.C.R. 828, 69 D.L.R. (2d) 336; *Re O.S.C. and Br. Can. Commodity Options Ltd., supra*, note 137; *Hands v. Sutherland* (1976), 66 D.L.R. (3d) 40 (Alta. T.D.); *Re Kasprzycki and Abel* (1986), 55 O.R. (2d) 536 (Dist. Ct.); *Vandekerhove v. Litchfield, supra*, note 138.

[146] *Zimmermann v. Letkeman*, [1978] 1 S.C.R. 1097; *Barrett v. Wright* (1927), 33 O.W.N. 382 (Div. Ct.); *Taylor v. Bowers* (1876), 1 Q.B.D. 291 (C.A.); *McDonald v. Fellows*, [1979] 6 W.W.R. 544, 9 R.P.R. 168, 105 D.L.R. (3d) 434 (Alta. C.A.); *Ouston v. Zurowski, supra*, note 141.

(5) **Want of Contractual Formalities**

Statute law demands that, to be enforceable, certain types of contracts must comply with prescribed formalities. An example is the *Statute of Frauds*,[147] which, among other things, requires that contracts for the sale of land be in writing to be enforceable. When a party is unable to enforce a contract for a want of formalities, he or she may wish to be compensated for any wasted efforts or to be restored to the pre-contractual position; restitutionary relief may be available in these circumstances under the principle of unjust enrichment.[148] Once again, practically speaking, the result may approach that of rescission.

(6) **Want of Contractual Capacity**

In certain circumstances, the common law allows an apparently valid contract to be set aside or treats it as unenforceable because of the want of contractual capacity of one of the parties. Types of incapacity are infancy,[149] mental incompetency,[150] intoxication, and want of statutory authority for certain statutory entities. In some of these cases, the law treats the contract as void, and, other times, the contract is treated as voidable. Since, when a contract is set aside on the grounds of incapacity, the law also may require that benefits received under the contract be restored, the result approaches rescission.

Beginning with contracts with infants, with exceptions for contracts for necessaries and contracts for services that are to the benefit of the infant, a contract with an infant is either void or voidable.[151] Contracts for necessaries include contracts for the necessities of life and also for articles required to maintain the infant in his or her ordinary social

---

[147] R.S.O. 1990, c. S.19.

[148] *Deglman v. Guaranty Trust Co.*, [1954] S.C.R. 725; *Baker v. Guaranty Trust Co. of Canada*, [1956] O.W.N. 120, 1 D.L.R. (2d) 448 (H.C.J.); *Goodwin v. Goodwin* (1958), 13 D.L.R. (2d) 365 (N.S.S.C.).

[149] Percy, "The Present Law of Infants' Contracts" (1975), 53 Can. Bar Rev. 1; Grange, "The Execution of the Agreement of Purchase and Sale-Part 1", [1960] L.S.U.C. Special Lectures 37, at 43-46; *Leonard H. Cook's Construction Ltd. v. Scott* (1988), 92 N.B.R. (2d) 361, 1 R.P.R. (2d) 76 (Q.B.); affd 102 N.B.R. (2d) 395, 9 R.P.R. (2d) 69 (C.A.).

[150] Brown, "Can the Insane Contract?" (1933), 11 Can. Bar Rev. 600; Coutts, "Contracts of Mental Incompetents", [1963] L.S.U.C. Special Lectures (Part 1) 49.

[151] *Toronto Marlboro Major Junior "A" Hockey Club v. Tonelli* (1979), 23 O.R. (2d) 193, 42 C.P.R. (2d) 40, 96 D.L.R. (3d) 135 (C.A.); affg 18 O.R. (2d) 21, 2 B.L.R. 301, 35 C.P.R. (2d) 1, 4 R.F.L. (2d) 246, 81 D.L.R. (3d) 403 (Div. Ct.).

position. There is no absolute standard to judge whether a contract is a contract for necessities. The particular circumstances and needs of the contracting infant at the time of the contract must be considered.[152] If, by its nature, a contract prejudices the interests of an infant contracting party, the contract is treated as void.[153] If an infant is a party to a contract that is neither for necessaries nor by its nature prejudicial to the infant, then the contract is voidable. That the contract is voidable means that the infant may escape the contract at any time during infancy or within a reasonable time after reaching majority. After majority, the contract may be ratified and the right to avoidance is lost.[154]

A major difference between a void contract and a voidable contract is that a void contract cannot be ratified or saved by the doctrine of acquiescence.[155] Another difference is that if the contract is voidable, then, generally speaking, the infant who avoids the contract cannot recover back purchase moneys paid.[156] Purchase money is, however, recoverable by the infant if the contract is void and not just voidable.[157] In either event, for his or her part, the infant must restore any benefits received under the impugned contract.

Turning next to mental incompetency, when there has been a judicial determination that a person is mentally incompetent, so long as the court's order stands unrevoked, the mentally incompetent person does not have the capacity to enter into contracts. This remains true even if the person is no longer actually suffering from any mental disability.[158] Where there is no court order, then with an exception for contracts for necessaries, which are enforceable, and for contracts granting a power of attorney, which are void if there is a lack of mental capacity, a contract with

---

[152] *Peters v. Fleming* (1840), 6 M. & W. 42; *Nash v. Inman*, [1908] 2 K.B. 1 (C.A.).

[153] *Beam v. Beatty* (1902), 4 O.L.R. 554 (C.A.); *Phillips v. Greater Ottawa Dev. Co.* (1916), 38 O.L.R. 315 (C.A.); *McKay v. McKinley*, [1933] O.W.N. 392 (H.C.); *Re Staruch*, [1955] 5 D.L.R. 807 (Ont. H.C.).

[154] *Hilliard v. Dillon*, [1955] O.W.N. 621 (H.C.); *Murray v. Dean* (1926), 30 O.W.N. 271 (H.C.); *Foley v. Can. Permanent Loan & Savings Co.* (1883), 4 O.R. 38 (Div. Ct.); *Lauzon v. Menard* (1923), 25 O.W.N. 387 (H.C.); *Robinson v. Moffatt* (1915), 35 O.L.R. 9 (C.A.).

[155] *McKay v. McKinley*, [1933] O.W.N. 392 (H.C.); *Hill Estate v. Chevron Standard Life*, [1993] 2 W.W.R. 545, 83 Man. R. (2d) 58, 8 B.L.R. (2d) 1, 49 E.T.R. 242 (C.A.); leave to appeal to S.C.C. refused (1993), 10 B.L.R. (2d) 202n, 49 E.T.R. 260n (S.C.C.).

[156] *Short v. Field* (1914), 32 O.L.R. 395 (H.C.); affd 32 O.L.R. 395, at 398 (C.A.); *Robinson v. Moffatt* (1915), 35 O.L.R. 9 (C.A.).

[157] *Phillips v. Greater Ottawa Dev. Co.* (1916), 38 O.L.R. 315 (C.A.).

[158] *Monticello State Bank v. Baillee* (1922), 66 D.L.R. 494 (Alta. C.A.); *Rourke v. Halford* (1916), 31 D.L.R. 371 (Ont. C.A.).

a mental incompetent is voidable.[159] Two elements must be satisfied before the contract is voidable. First, the mental incompetent must at the time of contracting be suffering from a mental condition such that he or she is unable to understand the terms of the contract or incapable of forming a rational judgment of the contract's effect on his or her interests. A mental condition that does not impair the ability to contract will not provide grounds to vitiate the transaction.[160] Second, the other party to the contract must have had actual or constructive knowledge of the disability. The other party will have constructive knowledge where the circumstances are such that he or she should have been put on notice. If there are suspicious circumstances, the party not suffering from any disability may not refrain from inquiring and the court will impute constructive knowledge of the mental disability.[161] It is only the mentally incompetent party who may avoid the contract.[162] The onus of proof is usually on the party seeking to set aside the contract.[163] However, if mental incapacity is established, the onus will be on the party seeking to uphold the contract to show that the contract was executed during a lucid interval.[164]

In *Hill Estate v. Chevron*,[165] the Manitoba Court of Appeal held that a power of attorney is void if executed by a party lacking the mental capacity to contract and any contracts executed pursuant to the impugned power of attorney would also be void even if the other contracting party was unaware of the lack of mental capacity. This result places an onus on persons contracting with a party acting by power of attorney to be satisfied about the validity of the power of attorney.

The law about contracts entered into while one party is intoxicated has some similarity to the law about mental incompetency. The contract is voidable if the sober contracting party has actual or constructive knowledge that the other side's state of intoxication has nullified the ability to understand the terms of the contract and its effect. Once sobriety has

---

[159] *Bank of Nova Scotia v. Kelly* (1973), 41 D.L.R. (3d) 273 (P.E.I.S.C.); *Browne v. Joddrell* (1827), M. & M. 105; *Moulton v. Camroux* (1848), 2 Exch. 487, 154 E.R. 1107; *Imperial Loan Co. v. Stone*, [1892] 1 Q.B. 599 (C.A.); *Conrad v. Halifax Lumber Co.* (1918), 41 D.L.R. 218 (N.S.C.A.); *Re Wilcinsky* (1982), 22 Alta. L.R. 155, 19 B.L.R. 125 (Q.B.).

[160] *Robertson v. Kelly* (1883), 2 O.R. 163 (Q.B.).

[161] *Hunt v. Texaco Exploration Co.*, [1955] 3 D.L.R. 555 (Alta. S.C.); *Bank of Nova Scotia v. Kelly, supra*, note 159.

[162] *Kerr v. Petrolia (Town)* (1921), 51 O.L.R. 74 (H.C.).

[163] *Imperial Loan Co. v. Stone*, [1892] 1 Q.B. 599 (C.A.); *Fyckes v. Chisholm* (1911), 10 O.W.R. 977 (H.C.).

[164] *Hoover v. Nunn* (1912), 3 O.W.N. 1223 (H.C.).

[165] *Supra*, note 155.

returned, the contract can be ratified. If the contract is to be avoided, it must be disaffirmed within a reasonable time.[166]

For certain statutory entities, want of statutory authority to contract is another type of incapacity. Entities created by statute derive their powers from their statute, and some entities, for example municipalities, are not given an unlimited power to contract. If a statutory body contracts outside its mandate, then the contract is *ultra vires* and unenforceable.[167] When this occurs, restitutionary remedies and the doctrine of unjust enrichment may be available to restore benefits transferred under the unenforceable contract.[168]

4. *Limitations on the Remedy of Rescission*

Assuming that the grounds for rescission exist, then several factors limit the availability of the remedy. These factors are noted below.

(1) *Restitutio in Integrum*

Since the goal of rescission is to restore the parties to their pre-contractual position, as a general rule, rescission will be refused when this is not possible. The circumstances must be such that restitution or, in Latin, *restitutio in integrum* is substantially possible.[169] For example, in *Frigidaire,*

---

[166] *Bawlf Grain Co. v. Ross* (1917), 55 S.C.R. 232; *Matthews v. Baxter* (1873), L.R. 8 Exch. 132; *Standard Bank v. Dunham* (1887), 14 O.R. 67 (Q.B.); *Chait v. Harding* (1920), 19 O.W.N. 20 (H.C.).

[167] *Re Hay and City of Burlington* (1980), 31 O.R. (2d) 467, 16 M.P.L.R. 292, 119 D.L.R. (3d) 160 (Div. Ct.); revd 38 O.R. (2d) 476, 22 R.P.R. 108, 131 D.L.R. (3d) 600 (C.A.); *Re Sorokolit and Regional Municipality of Peel* (1977), 16 O.R. 607 (Div. Ct.); *John Mackay Co. v. City of Toronto* (1919), 48 D.L.R. 151 (P.C.).

[168] *First City Development Corp. Ltd. v. Durham (Reg. Mun.)* (1989), 67 O.R. (2d) 665, 41 M.P.L.R. 241 (H.C.J.).

[169] *Redican v. Nesbitt*, [1924] S.C.R. 135, [1924] 1 W.W.R. 305, [1924] 1 D.L.R. 536; *Re Cairns and McNairn* (1922), 60 O.L.R. 194 (C.A.); *Thurston v. Streilen* (1950), 59 Man. R. 55, [1951] 4 D.L.R. 724 (K.B.); *Lowe v. Suburban Developers (Sault Ste. Marie) Ltd.*, [1962] O.R. 1029 (C.A.); *Friesen v. Berta* (1979), 100 D.L.R. (3d) 91 (B.C.S.C.); *Redgrave v. Hurd* (1881), 20 Ch. D. 1 (C.A.); *Kingu v. Walmar Ventures Ltd.* (1986), 10 B.C.L.R. (2d) 15, 38 C.C.L.T. 51 (C.A.); *Baranick v. Counsel Trust Co.* (1994), 12 B.L.R. (2d) 39, 37 R.P.R. (2d) 202 (Ont. Gen. Div.); affd 17 B.L.R. (2d) 39 (Ont. C.A.).

Corp. v. Steedman,[170] where a purchaser of goods sued to set aside the contract on the ground that the vendor had bribed the purchaser's agent, rescission was refused where the purchaser had not offered and was not in a position to offer *restitutio in integrum*.

Because equity maintains a jurisdiction to make allowances and adjustments, restitution need not be perfect and the parties need not be restored exactly to the pre-contractual position.[171] It is quite common for rescission to be granted with compensation for depreciation, deterioration, profits, or use of the property.[172] *Carter v. Golland*[173] provides an example. In this case, the purchaser was misled by a false representation as to the earning power of the business being purchased. The purchaser was entitled to rescission. In order to satisfy the requirement of *restitutio in integrum*, the court ordered that a charge be made for any benefits received from carrying on the business and that there be an allowance for the expense of carrying on the business.

In the recent English case of *Cheese v. Thomas*,[174] the English Court of Appeal set aside a transaction in which the plaintiff and his great-nephew had together acquired a home for the plaintiff to live with title taken solely in the name of the nephew. The transaction was set aside on the grounds of undue influence. The home was sold but, because of a declining real estate market, the resale did not yield sufficient funds to restore the parties to their original position. On the particular facts of this case, the court held that the losses should be proportional to the original contributions of the parties.

The court is not as rigorous in its demand for *restitutio in integrum* where rescission is sought to undo fraud.[175]

---

[170] [1933] 1 D.L.R. 161 (P.C.) (*sub nom. Steedman v. Frigidaire Corp.*); varg [1931] O.R. 285 (C.A.). See also *251798 Ontario Inc. v. R.*, [1980] 1 F.C. 706, 8 B.L.R. 113, 106 D.L.R. (3d) 564, 31 N.R. 10 (C.A.).

[171] *Erlanger v. New Sombrero Phosphate Co.* (1878), 3 App. Cas. 1218 (H.L.); *Lewis v. Howson*, [1928] 4 D.L.R. 207 (C.A.); affd [1929] S.C.R. 174; *Carter v. Golland*, [1937] O.R. 881 (C.A); *Yee v. Durand*, [1939] 2 D.L.R. 167 (N.S.C.A.); *Wiley v. Fortin*, [1946] 2 D.L.R. 712 (B.C.S.C.); *Guest v. Beecroft* (1957), 10 D.L.R. (2d) 657 (B.C.S.C.); *Kupchak v. Dayson Holdings Co.* (1965), 53 W.W.R. 65, 53 D.L.R. (2d) 482 (B.C.C.A.); *Wandinger v. Lake* (1977), 16 O.R. (2d) 362 (H.C.).

[172] *Marwood v. Charter Credit Corp.* (1971), 20 D.L.R. (3d) 563 (N.S.C.A.); *Allen v. McCutcheon* (1979), 10 B.C.L.R. 149, 9 R.P.R. 191 (B.C.S.C.); *Tomoch v. North Br. Can. Invt. Co.*, [1936] 2 D.L.R. 409 (Man. K.B.); *Devald v. Zigeuner* (1958), 16 D.L.R. (2d) 285 (Ont. H.C.).

[173] [1937] O.R. 881 (C.A.).

[174] [1994] 1 All E.R. 35 (C.A.).

[175] *McCarthy v. Kenny*, [1939] 3 D.L.R. 556 (Ont. H.C.); *Kupchak v. Dayson Holdings Co*, *supra*, note 171; *Carter v. Golland*, *supra*, note 171; *Wandinger v. Lake*, *supra*, note 171.

(2) Election and Affirmation

The existence of grounds for rescission does not automatically bring the contract to an end. The innocent party, once aware of the situation giving rise to a claim for rescission, has the choice or election of affirming the contract or of ending the contract by seeking rescission.[176] If the innocent party affirms the contract by word or by conduct, then the right of rescission is lost.[177]

For example, if a party is induced by a fraudulent misrepresentation to enter into a contract, then, rather than seeking rescission, the innocent party may instead decide to affirm the contract and sue for damages for deceit.[178] Or, where a contract is tainted by duress, once the pressure has been removed, the oppressed party may decide by words or conduct to affirm the contract.[179] The doctrine of affirmation also applies to cases where a contract is entered into under a mistake[180] and has been applied in a case where the rule, discussed above, about material alterations to a deed or contract was broken.[181]

In *Barron v. Kelly*,[182] the plaintiff purchaser, who had been fraudulently deceived about the number of other purchasers in a new town project, was allowed to claim damages for deceit but not rescission because he had gone forward with the transaction with knowledge of the deception. Delay in disaffirming may be treated as evidence of affirmation, and

---

[176] In *Bowbriar Investments Inc. v. Wellesley Community Homes Inc.* (1977), 24 R.P.R. 241 (Ont. H.C.J.), the plaintiff claimed rescission or, in the alternative, specific performance. The later claim was protected by a certificate of pending litigation. The court granted an application to compel the plaintiff to make an election so as to not unnecessarily tie up the vendor's land.

[177] *Shortt v. MacLennan*, [1959] S.C.R. 3; affg 6 D.L.R. (2d) 431 (Ont. C.A.); *Timmins v. Kuzyk* (1962), 32 D.L.R. (2d) 207 (B.C.S.C.); *Lowe v. Suburban Developers (Sault Ste. Marie) Ltd.*, [1962] O.R. 1029 (C.A.); *Panzer v. Zeifman* (1978), 20 O.R. (2d) 502, 88 D.L.R. (3d) 131 (C.A.); *Burrows v. Burke* (1984), 49 O.R. (2d) 76 (C.A.); leave to appeal to S.C.C. refused 10 O.A.C. 354n (S.C.C.); *Clough v. London & North Western Ry. Co.* (1871), L.R. 7 Exch. 26; *Kupchak v. Dayson Holdings Co.*, *supra*, note 171; *Thomas v. Crown Trust Co.* (1958), 13 D.L.R. (2d) 425 (Man. C.A.); *Andronyk v. Williams*, [1986] 1 W.W.R. 225, 36 Man. R. (2d) 161, 35 C.C.L.T. 38, 38 R.P.R. 53, 21 D.L.R. (4th) 557 (C.A.); leave to appeal to S.C.C. refused 36 C.C.L.T. xxxi (S.C.C.).

[178] *Barron v. Kelly* (1918), 56 S.C.R. 455; *Gosse-Millard Ltd. v. Devine*, [1928] S.C.R. 101; *Goulet v. Clarkson*, [1949] 1 D.L.R. 847 (B.C.S.C.).

[179] *Stott v. Merit Investment Corp.* (1988), 25 O.A.C. 174, 63 O.R. (2d) 545, 19 C.C.E.L. 68, 48 D.L.R. (4th) 288 (C.A.); leave to appeal to S.C.C. refused 63 O.R. (2d) x.

[180] *Canadian Medical Laboratories Ltd. v. Stabile* (1992), 25 R.P.R. (2d) 106 (Ont. Gen. Div.).

[181] *Johnson v. Trobak*, [1977] 6 W.W.R. 289, 79 D.L.R. (3d) 684 (B.C.C.A.).

[182] *Supra*, note 178.

a long delay may constitute conclusive evidence of an election to affirm. In general, the plaintiff must act promptly to disaffirm a contract once aware of the right to do so.[183]

Affirmation presupposes that the party knows that he or she has both grounds and a right to seek rescission. In other words, the party must be aware that the factual circumstances entail a right to rescind.[184] If the party is not aware of the facts giving rise to the right to rescind, there can be no affirmation. For example, in *Boulter v. Stocks*,[185] the purchaser of farm land was deceived about the size of the property and also about its weed coverage. He could not rescind based on the existence of noxious weeds because he went ahead and leased the lands with knowledge of this deception. However, he was allowed rescission for the other deception. His leasing of the property was made without knowledge of the discrepancy in its size; the leasing being without knowledge of the acreage problem, it was not an affirmation of the contract.

(3) Laches

Laches is an equitable defence that will deny an equitable remedy on the grounds of the plaintiff's delay in asserting or advancing the claim. To establish laches, it is not the length but the consequences of the delay that matter. The court will examine the acts of the parties in the interval of the delay and whether the parties have prejudicially changed their positions. The court will then determine the justice or injustice of allowing the claim to proceed despite the period of delay.[186]

(4) Execution of the Contract

For transactions involving the sale of land, misrepresentation will ground a claim for rescission only if the contract is executory, unless the

---

[183] *Clough v. London & North Western Ry. Co.*, *supra*, note 177; *Consol. Invts. Ltd. v. Acres* (1917), 32 D.L.R. 579 (Alta. C.A.); *Davis v. Whittington* (1918), 15 O.W.N. 160 (Div. Ct.); *Kingu v. Walmar Ventures Ltd.*, *supra*, note 169.

[184] *Byle v. Byle* (1990),46 B.L.R. 292, 65 D.L.R. (4th) 641 (B.C.C.A.); *Peyman v. Lanjani*, [1984] 3 All E.R. 703 (C.A.).

[185] (1913), 47 S.C.R. 440.

[186] *Thomas v. Crown Trust Co.*, *supra*, note 177; *Croft v. Tress* (1967), 61 W.W.R. 201 (B.C.S.C.); *Consol. Invts. Ltd. v. Acres* (1917), 32 D.L.R. 579 (Alta. C.A.); *Alex v. Tiede*, [1986] 5 W.W.R. 599, 43 Man. R. (2d) 1 (Q.B.).

misrepresentation is fraudulent or amounts to an error *in substantialibus*,[187] the nature of which has been discussed above.[188] This rule manifests a concern for the stability and certainty of commercial and property transactions. The execution or closing of a transaction, however, will not bar rescission for duress,[189] undue influence,[190] unconscionability,[191] mistake,[192] or *non est factum*.[193]

(5) Third Party Rights

Where the contract is voidable, rescission is not available if the rights of an innocent third party for value intervene.[194] For example, in *Baranick v. Counsel Trust Co.*,[195] the purchasers of condominium units under a tax shelter scheme sought to set aside the mortgages that financed their purchases. The purchasers relied on the fact that the vendor had failed to provide them with an offering memorandum as required by the Ontario Securities Commission. Among other reasons, the court refused rescis-

---

[187] *Cole v. Pope* (1898), 29 S.C.R. 291; *Redican v. Nesbitt*, [1924] S.C.R. 135, [1924] 1 W.W.R. 305, [1924] 1 D.L.R. 536; *Shortt v. MacLennan, supra*, note 177; *Dalladas v. Tennikat*, [1958] O.W.N. 169 (C.A.); *Schonekess v. Bach* (1968), 66 D.L.R. (2d) 415 (B.C.S.C.); *Fraser-Reid v. Droumtsekas*, [1980] 1 S.C.R. 720, 9 R.P.R. 121, 103 D.L.R. (3d) 385, 29 N.R. 424; *Komarniski v. Marien*, [1989] 4 W.W.R. 267, 8 R.P.R. 229, 100 D.L.R. (3d) 80 (Sask. Q.B.); *Perry v. Thompson* (1957), 7 D.L.R. (2d) 556 (B.C.S.C.); *Shurie v. White* (1906), 12 O.L.R. 54 (H.C.); *Panzer v. Zeifman, supra*, note 177.
[188] But see *S-244 Holdings Ltd. v. Seymour Building Systems Ltd.*, [1994] 8 W.W.R. 185, 93 B.C.L.R. (2d) 32 (C.A.).
[189] *Burris v. Rhind* (1899), 29 S.C.R. 498.
[190] *Taylor v. Armstrong* (1979), 24 O.R. (2d) 614, 99 D.L.R. (3d) 547 (S.C.); *Burris v. Rhind* (1899), 29 S.C.R. 498.
[191] *Waters v. Donnelly* (1884), 9 O.R. 391 (Ch. Div.).
[192] *Solle v. Butcher*, [1950] 1 K.B. 671 (C.A.); *Beverly Motel (1972) Ltd. v. Klyne Properties Ltd.* (1981), 30 B.C.L.R. 282, 21 R.P.R. 106, 126 D.L.R. (3d) 757 (S.C.); *Marwood v. Charter Credit Corp.* (1971), 20 D.L.R. (3d) 563 (N.S.C.A.).
[193] *Prudential Trust Co. v. Cugnet*, [1956] S.C.R. 914, 5 D.L.R. (2d) 1, overturned on other grounds; see *Marvco Color Research Ltd. v. Harris*, [1982] 2 S.C.R. 774, 20 B.L.R. 143, 26 R.P.R. 48, 141 D.L.R. (3d) 577, 45 N.R. 302; *Taylor v. Armstrong, supra*, note 190.
[194] *Morin v. Anger* (1931), 66 O.L.R. 327 (C.A.); *Clough v. London & North Western Ry. Co., supra*, note 177; *Treadwell v. Martin* (1976),13 N.B.R. (2d) 137, 67 D.L.R. (3d) 493 (C.A.); *Consol. Invts. Ltd. v. Acres, supra*, note 186; *Barry v. Stoney Point Canning Co.* (1917), 55 S.C.R. 51; *Kingu v. Walmar Ventures Ltd.* (1986), 10 B.C.L.R. (2d) 15, 38 C.C.L.T. 51 (C.A.).
[195] (1994), 12 B.L.R. (2d) 39, 37 R.P.R. (2d) 202 (Ont. Gen. Div.); affd 17 B.L.R. (2d) 140 (C.A.). See also *Royal Bank of Canada v. Harowitz* (1994), 17 O.R. (3d) 671 (Gen. Div.), an unsuccessful unjust enrichment claim.

sion because the mortgagee was a *bona fide* purchaser without notice or involvement in any wrongdoing.

(6) Clean Hands

One of the maxims of equity is that a petitioner for equitable relief must have "clean hands". This is a reference to the petitioner's conduct in the matter that is the subject of the suit in equity and not a general reference to the petitioner's general character or reputation.[196] Since rescission is associated with equitable principles, a person who calls for rescission must be able to show that his or her conduct with respect to the transaction was honourable.[197]

(7) Change of Position

Claims for unjust enrichment may be denied if the defendant has detrimentally changed its position after the enrichment or for some other reason it would be inequitable that the money or the property alleged to constitute an unjust enrichment be returned.[198] In *Rural Municipality of Storthoaks v. Mobil Oil Canada Ltd.*,[199] the Supreme Court recognized that the equities of the circumstances may be considered and that change of position could constitute a defence to an unjust enrichment claim; however, the defence was not made out on the facts of that case.

---

[196] *Toronto v. Polai*, [1970] 1 O.R. 483 (C.A.); affd [1973] S.C.R. 38; *Moody v. Cox & Hatt*, [1917] 2 Ch. 71 (C.A.). See also *Hongkong Bank of Canada v. Wheeler Holdings Ltd.*, [1993] 1 S.C.R. 167, 6 Alta. L.R. (3d) 337, 29 R.P.R. (2d) 1, 100 D.L.R. (4th) 40, 148 N.R. 1.

[197] *Alex v. Tiede*, [1986] 5 W.W.R. 599, 43 Man. R. (2d) 1 (Q.B.).

[198] *Wilson v. Corp. of District of Surrey*, [1981] 3 W.W.R. 266, 26 B.C.L.R. 28, 14 M.P.L.R. 86 (S.C.); *J.R.S. Holdings Ltd. v. District of Maple Ridge*, [1981] 4 W.W.R. 632, 27 B.C.L.R. 37, 122 D.L.R. (3d) 398 (S.C.); *A.J. Seversen Inc. v. Village of Qualicum Beach*, [1982] 4 W.W.R. 374, 35 B.C.L.R. 192, 135 D.L.R. (3d) 122, 19 M.P.L.R. 39 (S.C.); *Moore (Twp.) v. Guarantee Co. of North America* (1991), 2 O.R. (3d) 370 at pp. 379-80, [1991] I.L.R. 1-2706; supplementary reasons 4 O.R. (3d) 556, [1992] I.L.R. 1654 (Gen. Div.); *Royal Bank of Canada v. Harowitz, supra*, note 195.

[199] [1976] 2 S.C.R. 147, [1975] 4 W.W.R. 591, [1975], 55 D.L.R. (3d) 1, 5 N.R. 23. See also Maddaugh and McCamus, *The Law of Restitution*, at 231-36, 279.

EQUITABLE COMPENSATION AND RESTITUTIONARY REMEDIES: RECENT DEVELOPMENTS

*Professor John D. McCamus**

1. *Introduction*

The object of this paper is to describe and comment on recent developments in the law relating to equitable compensation — principally, equitable compensation in the context of breach of fiduciary obligation — and recent developments in the field now often referred to as the "law of restitution". One of the difficulties that one encounters in attempting to follow recent developments in the field of remedies is the absence of a sufficiently wide consensus on the meaning of such critical terms as "damages", "compensation" and "restitution". As a preliminary matter, then, it may be useful to set out my own understanding of the core meaning or meanings of these terms, if only for the purpose of indicating how these terms are being employed in this paper.

The term "damages" is often used to refer to compensatory relief of a kind made available historically by the courts of common law. There are, of course, different measures of relief for different types of common law damages. For present purposes, it will be useful to keep in mind that contract damages are calculated on the basis of the expectancy principle, which allows the victim of the breach to recover sufficient money to place him or her in the same position he or she would have been in had the contract been performed. They are, in this sense, "forward-looking". Tort damages, on the other hand, do not contain an expectancy element. Damages in tort are designed to repair the injury and to restore the plaintiff to the position he or she was in before the tort occurred. They are, in this sense, "backward-looking".

Perhaps the most common use of the term "restitution", at the present time, is to refer to a relatively new subject of the private law of obli-

---

* Faculty of Law, Osgoode Hall Law School, York University.

gations which was first outlined in the American *Restatement of the Law of Restitution*.[1] This new subject is an amalgamation of the old common law doctrines of *quasi*-contract and a group of equitable doctrines, principal amongst them, doctrines relating to the availability of the constructive trust remedy. The central principle which underlies this new subject or, one might say, this reorganization of these materials, and, which, as well, may serve as the best explanation for the awarding of relief in these cases, is the principle against unjust enrichment: "A person who has been unjustly enriched at the expense of another is required to make restitution to the other".[2] Although the reorganization of doctrine is, in some sense, an academic exercise, it is well-known that the Supreme Court of Canada has given its *imprimatur* to this development in an important series of cases,[3] and has taken the lead in developing and reshaping the Canadian law of restitution or, as is it sometimes called, the law of unjust enrichment.

What is less well-known is that the term "restitution" carries with it some important ambiguities. Restitution scholars have included within the new "law of restitution", one might say, two different kinds of restitution cases. In the typical case, the plaintiff recovers value that has been transferred by the plaintiff to the defendant. The defendant is "in pocket"; the plaintiff is "out of pocket". One scholar refers to this as "unjust enrichment by subtraction".[4] A typical case would be the recovery of money paid by the plaintiff to the defendant by mistake.

As normally conceived, the law of restitution also includes, however, cases where the defendant has acquired benefits wrongfully and in breach of duties owed to the plaintiff but not at the plaintiff's expense in the subtraction sense. A typical example would be a breach of fiduciary duty which enables the fiduciary to earn profits which the person to whom the duty is owed would probably not have been able to earn. The victim of the fiduciary breach would be able to recover those profits either through the imposition of a constructive trust or by the remedy of an accounting of profits. We might refer to this kind of remedy as relief in the "disgorgement measure" in order to distinguish such cases from subtraction cases. Disgorgement cases have been referred to as "unjust enrichment by doing wrong" to the plaintiff.[5] Textbooks on the law of restitution,

---

[1] American Law Institute, *Restatement of the Law of Restitution: Quasi-Contracts and Constructive Trusts* (St. Paul: American Law Institute Publishers, 1937).

[2] *Ibid.*, §1.

[3] For an account of these cases, stretching over the past four decades, see, for example, Maddaugh and McCamus, *The Law of Restitution* (Aurora: Canada Law Book, 1990), c. 2.

[4] Birks, *An Introduction to the Law of Restitution* (Oxford: Clarendon Press, 1985), at 25.

[5] *Ibid.*

then, will typically include accounts of both "subtraction" cases and "disgorgement" cases.[6] The unifying theme, arguably, is that in both types of cases the defendant can be said to be "unjustly enriched".

It is important to note that in the law of trusts, however, the term "restitution" has acquired a third and less precise meaning. In cases where an express trustee has committed a breach of trust with resulting injury to the value of the property held in trust, the trustee is sometimes said to be liable to make "restitution" of the trust property. While this term could refer to relief which is parallel to restitutionary subtraction or disgorgement relief (where, for example, the trustee has misappropriated trust assets or profited from their administration), the term is typically used to refer to remedies that look rather more like tort damages or contract damages. As we shall see, however, it is important to keep in mind that the principles for calculating the quantum of this form of relief are not the same as those developed in common law for calculating damages in tort or contract. The type of compensation that trustees can be required to pay in cases of breach of trust is often referred to as "equitable compensation", by way of distinguishing this type of remedy from "damages" at common law.

A question that has been examined at great length in recent decisions of the Supreme Court of Canada is the extent to which equitable compensation of this kind is to be made available in the context of breaches of fiduciary duty by persons who are not trustees. It is this question that will preoccupy most of this paper. Attention will be devoted as well, however, to the possibility that equitable compensation might be available in the context of other kinds of equitable wrongdoing. Finally, a brief account will be offered of recent developments concerning the kinds of restitutionary remedies that are available in "subtraction" and "disgorgement" cases.

---

[6] See, for example, Maddaugh and McCamus, *supra*, note 3; Fridman, *Restitution,* 2nd ed. (Toronto: Carswell, 1992); Goff and Jones, *The Law of Restitution*, 4th ed. (London: Sweet & Maxwell, 1993); Burrows, *The Law of Restitution* (London: Butterworths, 1993). Cf. Smith, "The Province of the Law of Restitution" (1992), 71 Can. Bar Rev. 672.
One reason for doing so, of course, is that the same type of breach of duty, such as a breach of fiduciary duty, can give rise to enrichment in either one or both of the subtraction and disgorgement modes. Improper profits, which the principal could not have earned, are subject to disgorgement. Other profits, however, which could have been earned, but for the breach, by the person to whom the duty is owed may be considered to constitute a subtraction enrichment. Improper acquisition of the principal's property offers another example of a subtraction enrichment.

2. *Equitable Compensation*

As a general rule, courts of equity did not award damages. The awarding of damages was a device of the common law. Thus, until the enactment of *Lord Cairns' Act* in 1858,[7] a plaintiff who failed in an application for an injunction or for specific performance of a contract in equity would be required to commence a separate action at common law to recover the damages for breach. Under that legislation, of course, courts of equity were enabled in such cases to award "damages" which "may be ascertained in such manner as the Court directs" either in addition to or in lieu of an injunction or specific performance. If, as the House of Lords has indicated, contemporary courts exercising this equitable jurisdiction should calculate damages in the manner indicated by the principles of common law, this equitable jurisdiction is of essentially historical interest.[8]

Although courts of equity did not award damages, then, this is not to say that orders of monetary compensation were unknown to equity.[9] Most obviously, of course, in cases where a breach of trust results in a loss to the trust estate, equitable "compensation" could be awarded to the beneficiaries of the trust.[10] The principles guiding the calculation of equitable compensation for loss resulting from a breach of trust are very generous to the plaintiff beneficiary. It will be useful for present purposes to provide a brief sketch of the trustee's liability to make compensation. Where, for example, a trustee fails to sell trust property in a timely fashion,[11] invests in unauthorized investments which fall in value[12] or fails to make a gain by proper stewardship of the trust property,[13] the trustee is liable to make up the loss sustained by the trust. Although the courts possess a statutory power to relieve from liability a trustee who "has acted honestly and reasonably, and ought fairly to be excused for the breach of trust",[14] the liability of trustees for compensation is otherwise rather strict. More particularly, it appears not to be subject to the kinds of limitations that would restrict the scope of a defendant's liability for damages

---

[7] *Chancery Amendment Act, 1858 (U.K.)*, 21 & 22 Vict., c. 27.

[8] *Johnson v. Agnew*, [1980] A.C. 367 at 400 (H.L.).

[9] See, generally, McDermott, "Jurisdiction of the Court of Chancery to Award Damages" (1992), 108 L.Q.R. 652.

[10] See Waters, *The Law of Trusts in Canada*, 2nd ed. (Toronto: Carswell, 1984), at 987-1005; and Ford and Lee, *Principles of the Law of Trusts*, 2nd ed. (Sydney: The Law Book Company, 1990), at 726-33.

[11] *Fales v. Canada Permanent Trust Co.* (1976), 70 D.L.R. (3d) 257 (S.C.C.).

[12] *Crook v. Smart* (1872), 11 N.S.W.S.C.R. (Eq.) 121.

[13] *Graham v. Gibson* (1882), 8 V.L.R. (Eq.) 43.

[14] For an account of the Canadian experience see Waters, *supra*, note 10, at 1025-31.

for tort or breach of contract at common law. In *Re: Dawson*,[15] Street J. commented as follows:

> The obligation of a defaulting trustee is essentially one of effecting a restitution to the estate. The obligation is of a personal character and its extent is not to be limited by common law principles governing remoteness of damage.
>
> . . . . .
>
> Caffrey v. Darby (1801) 6 Ves. Jun. 488; 31 E.R. 1159 is consistent with the proposition that if a breach has been committed then the trustee is liable to place the trust estate in the same position as it would have been in if no breach had been committed. Considerations of causation, foreseeability and remoteness do not readily enter into the matter.
>
> . . . . .
>
> The principles embodied in this approach do not appear to involve any inquiry as to whether the loss was caused by or flowed from the breach. Rather, the inquiry in each instance would appear to be whether the loss would have happened if there had been no breach.[16]

Consistent with this approach, the beneficiary is entitled to recoup the loss calculated as of the time of trial rather than as of the time of breach.[17] Further, the beneficiary is entitled to the benefit of presumptions — such as the presumption that when a trustee wrongfully withholds securities from the beneficiary, it is presumed that the beneficiary would have sold them at the highest price available during the period of withholding[18] — which ensure that any possible loss to the trust is the subject of compensation. Under these principles, then, the trustee becomes, in effect, a guarantor of the value of the assets held in trust. Against this background, we may turn to the question that has attracted much attention in the recent jurisprudence of the Supreme Court of Canada: the extent to which equitable compensation may be available for breach of fiduciary duties by non-trustees and, if available, the extent to which the comprehensive type of liability imposed on trustees may be extended to such cases.

---

[15] (1966), 84 W.N. (N.S.W.) 399.

[16] *Ibid.*, at 404-05, quoted by Wilson J. in *Guerin v. R.*, [1984] 2 S.C.R. 335, [1984] 6 W.W.R. 481, 59 B.C.L.R. 301, 20 E.T.R. 6, 36 R.P.R. 1, 13 D.L.R. (4th) 321 at 365, 55 N.R. 161.

[17] *Tomkinson v. First Pennsylvania Banking and Trust Co.*, [1961] A.C. 1007.

[18] *McNeil v. Fultz* (1906), 38 S.C.R. 198.

3. *Equitable Compensation for Breach of Fiduciary Duty*

The traditional law of fiduciary obligation imposes certain duties of fiduciary loyalty on individuals who have undertaken either expressly or tacitly to act in the interests of another.[19] No attempt will be made here to grapple with the important question of how one identifies the existence of a fiduciary relationship giving rise to such duties. As is well-known, fiduciary duties arise in the context of a recognized list of categories of relationships such as principal and agent, solicitor and client, executor or administrator and beneficiary, director or officer and the corporation, promoter and investor, partners, joint ventures, doctor and patient, parent and child and so on. Fiduciary duties may also arise, however, in the context of relationships that do not fall within the establish categories, provided that the undertaking or task assumed by the individual has the requisite fiduciary character.

The fiduciary duty of loyalty imposed on such persons is normally expressed in two proscriptions: one who occupies a fiduciary position must not secure a personal profit by virtue of that position (the "profit" rule); and, further, one must not place oneself in a situation where self- interest may come into conflict with the interests of the person to whom the duty is owed (the "conflict" rule). Simply put, one must not engage in undisclosed self-dealing and one must not make a secret profit by virtue of the position held. What is enjoined, then, is a particular kind of exploitation or profiteering. In the event of a breach of duty, the principal remedies available to the victim — constructive trust or an accounting of profits — force the faithless fiduciary to disgorge the profits secured through breach. Both remedies are equitable in nature. Their distinguishing feature is that the accounting of profits leads to a monetary award whereas the constructive trust confers a proprietary remedy by determining that the defendant holds certain assets as a constructive trustee on the plaintiff's behalf. Where the self-dealing involves the transfer of an asset to or from the principal, a decree of rescission may be available.

In this brief sketch of traditional fiduciary doctrine, little space is created for the awarding of compensatory damages. The nature of the duty imposed is not such as to give rise to the kinds of injuries for which compensation would be an appropriate remedy. In cases where fiduciaries have injured their principal through misconduct of some kind — for example, where a solicitor provides careless legal advice to a client — the victim will typically be entitled to compensation in the form of damages

---

[19] See, generally, Maddaugh and McCamus, *supra*, note 3, c. 25, for detailed references to the authorities supporting the brief account of the law of fiduciary obligations set out in this and the next paragraph of the text.

either in contract or in tort. Nonetheless, there does exist a line of authority which holds that equitable compensation is a further remedy potentially available in breach of fiduciary duty cases.[20] The leading authority is *Nocton v. Lord Ashburton*,[21] a decision rendered by the House of Lords in 1914. Nocton was a solicitor who had retained an interest in land that had been sold to a builder. Nocton's client, Lord Ashburton, advanced moneys on a first mortgage given on the property by the builder. In due course, Nocton persuaded his client to release a portion of the security, and in the course of so doing either made misrepresentations or offered careless advice. The release of the client's security had the effect of advancing Nocton's own interest in the land. Upon the builder's default, Lord Ashburton's security proved inadequate and he pursued Nocton for damages. A claim in deceit failed as Nocton's misconduct failed to meet the fraud threshold set out in *Derry v. Peek*[22] for liability for misrepresentation. The client's claim in contract for Nocton's failure to exercise reasonable skill and care was held to be statute-barred. The House of Lords held, however, that the solicitor was liable for breach of fiduciary duty and that the client could recover equitable compensation for the injury sustained.

Before turning to consider more recent developments, a few observations concerning *Nocton v. Lord Ashburton* may be helpful. First, it may be noted that *Nocton v. Lord Ashburton* is a classic instance of fiduciary breach. The solicitor clearly placed his self-interest ahead of his duty to his client. What is unusual about the case, of course, is that compensatory damages, in effect, are awarded. It is of more than passing interest to note that such damages would have been available but for the limitations problem in contract and, under now current law, would be available in tort.[23]

Finally, it is of considerable interest to note that the historical record[24]

---

[20] See generally, Davidson, "The Equitable Remedy of Compensation" (1982), 13 Melb. U.L. Rev. 349; Gummow, "Compensation for Breach of Fiduciary Duty" in Youdan (ed.), *Equity, Fiduciaries and Trusts* (Toronto: Carswell, 1989), at 57.

[21] [1914] A.C. 932 (H.L.).

[22] (1889), 14 A.C. 337 (H.L.).

[23] *Hedley Byrne & Co. Ltd. v. Heller & Partners*, [1964] A.C. 465.

[24] In a letter from Sir Frederick Pollock to Oliver Wendell Holmes in May of 1914, quoted by Gummow, *supra*, note 20, at 57, the following appears:

Haldane asked me last week to a tobacco talk of *Derry v. Peek* and the possibility of minimising its consequences. The Lords are going to hold that it does not apply to the situation created by a positive fiduciary duty such as a solicitor's, in other words, go as near as they dare to saying it was wrong, as all Lincoln's Inn thought at the time.

See, De Wolfe Howe (ed.), *Holmes-Pollock Letters: The correspondence of Mr. Justice Holmes and Sir Frederick Pollock, 1874-1932*, vol. 1 (Cambridge: Harvard University Press, 1941), at 214-15.

strongly suggests that *Nocton v. Lord Ashburton* was the product of a deliberate attempt by the House of Lords to minimize the consequences of the recent and much criticized decision in *Derry v. Peek*. It is not surprising that the House of Lords was unwilling to recant from *Derry v. Peek* only a few decades after its release. But we should observe that, as a reform measure, *Nocton v. Lord Ashburton* may appear cramped and incomplete. It applies only to a very particular kind of careless misstatement — that is, one involved in a breach of the fiduciary duty of loyalty — in the context of a rather particular kind of relationship. More comprehensive and satisfactory reform of *Derry v. Peek* would wait another 50 years until the decision in *Hedley Byrne & Co. Ltd. v. Heller & Partners.*[25] I will return to this point after briefly reviewing the recent Supreme Court jurisprudence.

4. *Equitable Compensation in the Supreme Court of Canada*

Perhaps because a breach of the fiduciary duty of loyalty, by its very nature, would rarely lead to consequential loss, claims for equitable compensation for fiduciary breach appear only infrequently in the law reports. In the series of decisions beginning with *Guerin v. R.*[26] in 1984 and culminating last September in *Hodgkinson v. Simms,*[27] however, the Supreme Court of Canada has devoted considerable attention to the analysis of the jurisdiction to grant equitable compensation for fiduciary breach and has laid the foundation for what could become a much more expansive availability of this form of relief. As will be seen, the current members of the court are not of one mind concerning these developments and the potential future reach of the doctrine cannot be predicted with confidence at the present time. It is possible, however, to identify the main lines of analysis and the areas of potential difficulty. As a prelude to attempting such an exercise, a brief account of the leading cases is required.

(1) *Guerin v. R.*[28]

In *Guerin*, the claim was brought on behalf of the members of an Indian band against the federal Crown with respect to the activities of

---

[25] *Supra*, note 23.
[26] *Supra*, note 16.
[27] [1994] 3 S.C.R. 377, 97 B.C.L.R. (2d) 1, 16 B.L.R. (2d) 1, 22 C.C.L.T. (2d) 1, 57 C.P.R. (3d) 1, 95 DTC 5135, 117 D.L.R. (4th) 161, 171 N.R. 245.
[28] *Supra*, note 16.

officials in the Indian Affairs Branch who had negotiated, on the band's behalf, a lease of a portion of the band's reserve lands to a golf club. The band had agreed with Indian Affairs to surrender the land to the Crown "in trust to lease the same" to the golf club in question on the basis of certain understandings they had reached with the officials with respect to the terms of the proposed lease. In effect, the officials had been instructed to negotiate a lease only on certain agreed terms. In the event, those terms proved to be unattainable and the lands were leased to the golf club on less favourable terms. The band was not consulted with respect to these changes. Indeed, more than a decade passed before the Branch was prepared to make a copy of the lease available to the band. The band claimed successfully at trial that the surrender of the land to the Crown created a trust, the terms of which were to be found in the understandings concerning the proposed lease. The Crown's failure to follow the band's instructions concerning the lease was held to be a breach of trust which entitled the band to compensation.

The Crown argued that the band had suffered no loss since it had made a decision to lease the land and the lease obtained by the Crown was the most favourable that could have been obtained at that time. This submission was rejected by the trial judge[29] who concluded that the band would not have entered into a lease on the less favourable terms agreed to by the Crown, but would, instead, have made a decision to market the property as 99-year leasehold lots for residential development. Such a plan would have generated far more revenue than leasing the land to a golf club. This lost opportunity was assessed by the trial judge to be worth 10 million dollars. The Crown was therefore obliged to restore this lost value to the band.

On the eventual appeal to the Supreme Court of Canada, Dickson J. for a majority of the court, held that the surrender of the land to the Crown did not create a trust. In the majority view, however, the Crown's relationship with the band did attract a fiduciary obligation to deal with the land for the benefit of the band. Although the Indian Affairs Branch officials "did not act dishonestly or for improper motives",[30] their conduct nonetheless constituted a breach of the Crown's fiduciary obligation. The failure of the officials to return to the band "to explain what had occurred and seek the band's counsel on how to proceed"[31] was "unconscionable behaviour in a fiduciary, whose duty is that of utmost loyalty to his principal".[32] With respect to the remedy, the majority indicated that "the quantum of damages [was] to be determined by analogy with

---

[29] [1982] 2 F.C. 385, 127 D.L.R. (3d) 170 (T.D.).
[30] *Supra*, note 16, at 345 D.L.R.
[31] *Ibid.*, at 344.
[32] *Ibid.*

the principles of trust law"[33] and adopted the calculation proposed by the trial judge.

Two further opinions, concurring in result, were offered by members of the court. Wilson J., with whom two colleagues concurred, held that the Crown did indeed become a trustee by virtue of the surrender of the reserve lands and that the Crown breached the terms of that trust when it leased the land on terms which were unacceptable to the band. Wilson J., relying in part on the passages quoted above from Street J.'s judgment in *Re: Dawson*, agreed with the quantum suggested by the trial judge. The band was, in her view, entitled to the benefit of an assumption that it "would have wished to develop its land in the most advantageous way possible during the period covered by the unauthorized lease".[34] In this respect, it was noted, the damages calculation differed from that which would have obtained in a claim for damages for breach of contract. In the latter context, the band would have been obliged to prove that it would have developed land in this way. In trust, the most advantageous use is presumed. In a separate opinion, Estey J., who agreed with his colleagues on the question of quantum, was alone in the view that this result could be achieved on the basis of an agency theory.[35]

In *Guerin*, then, the court held that the principles applicable to claims for equitable compensation against trustees were also applicable in claims against non-trustee fiduciaries whose breach of fiduciary duty caused the principal to suffer a loss of opportunity to profit. We should observe that although Dickson J. characterized the Crown's failure to follow instructions as an "unconscionable" act which constituted a breach of the fiduciary duty of loyalty, the misconduct at issue in *Guerin* does not constitute a classic breach of fiduciary duty. There is no suggestion that the Crown had placed itself in a conflict of interest situation or that it had in any way profited from the transaction. The alleged breach was a failure to follow instructions. If the Crown had simply been acting for the band as an agent on a contractual basis — and it is perhaps important in explaining the approach taken in *Guerin* that this was not so — it seems rather likely that the breach in question would have been characterized as a simple breach of contract sounding in contractual damages. In contract, the quantum of damages would doubtless be substantially less than the amount awarded in *Guerin*. After *Guerin*, then, the cautious view might well have been that the result in this case rests on the somewhat unusual nature of the relationship between the parties.

---

[33] *Ibid.*, at 345.

[34] *Ibid.*, at 366.

[35] *Ibid.*, at 348-49.

(2) *Canson Enterprises Ltd. v. Boughton & Co.*[36]

It was not until 1991 that the Supreme Court was required to confront the question of whether the *Guerin* type of equitable compensation analysis would apply to a more traditional category of fiduciary relationship. In *Canson Enterprises Ltd. v. Boughton & Co.* a claim was brought by a client against a solicitor for an alleged breach of fiduciary obligation and, in the alternative, for deceit in the context of a purchase and sale of land. The plaintiff and another of the defendants had agreed to purchase a property for the purpose of developing it as a joint venture. The defendant solicitor, Wollen, acted for both the vendor and the purchasers on the transaction. A material fact concerning the transaction was unknown to the plaintiff. The promoter of the project had arranged for an intermediate sale or "flip" to a third party. The land was sold by the vendors to the third party for $410,000, whereas the purchasers were to pay $525,000 as the purchase price. The existence of the flip was known to the other defendants, including Wollen. Wollen, who also acted for the third party, to whom the property was flipped, documented the transaction in such fashion as to disguise the existence of the flip from the plaintiff. Wollen's failure to disclose the existence of the flip was held to be a breach of his fiduciary duty of loyalty to the plaintiff.

Following the purchase, the plaintiff proceeded with a warehouse development which was most unsuccessful. The negligent advice of soils engineers and the unsatisfactory work of a pile driving contractor resulted in the warehouse sinking into the soil and suffering substantial damage. A successful claim was brought against the soils engineers and the pile driving contractor leading to an award of damages of $4,920,200.33. The plaintiff was unable to realize completely on that judgement, however, and brought a claim for equitable compensation for breach of fiduciary duty against Wollen to recover the short-fall of approximately $1,000,000. The case was litigated on the basis of an agreed statement of facts which included an agreement that the plaintiffs would not have purchased the property or entered into the joint venture agreement had they known of the flip to the third party.

The trial judge[37] in *Canson* held that Wollen was not liable in deceit but that he was liable for breach of fiduciary duty. In his view, however, compensation for the injury sustained as a result of breach was to be

---

[36] [1991] 3 S.C.R. 534, 61 B.C.L.R. (2d) 1, 9 C.C.L.T. (2d) 1, 39 C.P.R. (3d) 449, 43 E.T.R. 201, 85 D.L.R. (4th) 129, 131 N.R. 321. See, generally, Davies, "Equitable Compensation: 'Causation, Foreseeability and Remoteness'", in Waters (ed.), *Equity, Fiduciaries and Trusts, 199*3 (Toronto: Carswell, 1994), at 297.

[37] [1989] 2 W.W.R. 30, 31 B.C.L.R. (2d) 46, 45 C.C.L.T. 209, 52 D.L.R. (4th) 323.

calculated as it would be in a claim for damages in fraud. The plaintiffs were entitled to the difference between the purchase price and the value of the property, that value being the amount paid by the third party on the flip, as well as unspecified consequential losses relating to the development project prior to the intervention of the wrongful conduct of the soils engineers and the pile driving contractor. This quantum was upheld in the Court of Appeal[38] on the basis that the trial judge had adequately assessed the difference between the purchase price and the actual value of the property on the date of purchase.

On appeal to the Supreme Court of Canada, the plaintiff placed great weight on the *Guerin* decision.[39] It was argued that when one assesses equitable compensation, as opposed to common law damages, concepts such as remoteness, intervening cause and foreseeability simply have no relevance. The defaulting fiduciary — just like the defaulting trustee — must place the plaintiff in as good a position as he or she would have been in had the breach not occurred. The courts below, it was contended — and this was perhaps an unfortunate way of expressing the point — had fallen "into error because of a misplaced concern with concepts of common sense and reasonableness".[40]

The respondent defendants sought to uphold the decision below on essentially two grounds. First, it was argued that the reasoning in *Guerin* should be limited to cases in which a fiduciary exercises control over the principal's property. In short, the application of equitable principles relating to the liability of trustees ought to be extended only to cases where the fiduciary has stewardship of assets and is therefore in a role which is analogous to that of the express trustee. Second, the defendants submitted that the fusion of law and equity had the effect of imposing common law limitations, such as the principles of remoteness and causation, on equitable compensation for breach of fiduciary duty.

In the Supreme Court of Canada the majority of the court accepted both branches of the respondents' argument. La Forest J. observed that there "is a sharp divide between a situation where a person has control of property, which in the view of the court belongs to another, and one where a person is under a fiduciary duty to perform an obligation where equity's concern is simply that the duty be performed honestly and in accordance with the undertaking the fiduciary has taken on".[41] In the latter case, it would be appropriate to look to common law doctrines in determining the scope of liability. La Forest J. noted that there appeared to

[38] [1990] 1 W.W.R. 375, 39 B.C.L.R. (2d) 177, 45 B.L.R. 301, 61 D.L.R. (4th) 732.
[39] [1984] 2 S.C.R. 335, [1984] 6 W.W.R. 481, 59 B.C.L.R. 301, 20 E.T.R. 6, 36 R.P.R. 1, 13 D.L.R. (4th) 321, 55 N.R. 161.
[40] *Supra*, note 36, at 588-89. "I would have thought that these concerns were central to both common law and equity" *per* La Forest J.: *ibid.*
[41] *Ibid.*, at 578.

be no previous cases in which trust principles were applied to the type of fiduciary breach at issue in this case. As he explained:

> The harshness of the result is reason alone, but apart from this, I do not think that the claim for the harm resulting from the actions of third parties can fairly be looked upon as falling within what is encompassed in restoration for the harm suffered from the breach.[42]

The defendant was not to be liable, then, for injuries resulting from the conduct of third parties. In reaching this conclusion, La Forest J. drew support from the fusion or "mingling" of common law and equity which is alleged to be the result of the enactment of the *Judicature Acts*[43] in the late 19th century. La Forest J. quoted at length from Lord Diplock's opinion in *United Scientific Holdings Ltd. v. Burnley Borough Council*[44] in support of the proposition "that the two streams of common law and equity have now mingled and interact".[45] La Forest J. appeared to assume that a strict application of equitable principles might well expose the defendant to liability for the full loss sustained by the plaintiff. Equitable principles were not, however, to be considered to be "frozen in time"[46] and where, as in the present case, there is considerable overlap between common law and equitable principles, it may be appropriate for equitable principles to evolve in the direction of the common law. La Forest J. put this point on the following terms:

> Equitable concepts like trusts, equitable estates, and consequent equitable remedies must continue to exist apart, if not in isolation, from common law rules. But when one moves to fiduciary relationships and the law regarding misstatements, we have a situation where now the courts of common law, now the courts of equity moved forward to provide remedies where a person failed to meet the trust or confidence reposed in that person. There was throughout considerable overlap. In time the common law outstripped equity and the remedy of compensation became somewhat atrophied. Under these circumstances, why should it not borrow from the experience of the common law?[47]

For La Forest J., the underlying policy considerations pertaining to the claim were similar whether the claim were characterized as one at common law or as one in equity, and accordingly, the same result should be

---

[42] *Ibid.*, at 580.
[43] *Supreme Court of Judicature Act, 1873 (U.K.)*, 36 & 37 Vict., c. 66; *1875 (U.K.)*, 38 & 39 Vict., c. 77.
[44] [1978] A.C. 904.
[45] *Supra*, note 36, at 586.
[46] *Ibid.*, at 580.
[47] *Ibid.*, at 587-88.

achieved by adjusting equitable principles in the light of the experience of the common law. "Only when there are different policy objectives should equity engage in its well-known flexibility to achieve a different and fairer result".[48]

In a separate opinion concurring as to result, McLachlin J., with whom Lamer C.J. and L'Heureux-Dubé J. agreed, strongly affirmed the independence of equitable concepts and asserted that damages for breach of fiduciary duty should not be measured by analogy to tort and contract. In her view, the "trust-like nature of the fiduciary obligation manifests itself in characteristics which distinguish it from the tort of negligence and from the breach of contract".[49] The appropriate approach, then, is to "look to the policy behind compensation for breach of fiduciary duty and determine which remedies will best further that policy".[50] McLachlin J. went on to consider a number of aspects of equitable doctrine which might distinguish it from doctrines of contract and tort. Essentially, it would appear that McLachlin J.'s view is that the policy objective of enforcing the fiduciary duty of loyalty is what sets fiduciary law apart from contract and tort. She concluded, however, that, in equity, there was nonetheless the need for "a link between the equitable breach and the loss for which compensation is awarded,"[51] which was lacking on the facts of the *Canson* case. As McLachlin J. explained:

> The construction loss was caused by third parties. There is no link between the breach of fiduciary duty and this loss. The solicitor's duty had come to an end and the plaintiffs had assumed control of the property. This loss was the result, not of the solicitor's breach of duty, but of decisions made by the plaintiffs and those they chose to hire.[52]

While McLachlin J. and LaForest J. thus appear to conclude that both common law and equitable principles lead to the same conclusion on the causation point, there are a number of other points of difference between them to which we shall return in due course. In a separate concurring opinion, Stevenson J. indicated his agreement with the view that the losses were so unrelated to the breach that they should not be recoverable. He added, however, that he did not share the view that "the so-called fusion of law and equity has anything to do with deciding this case".[53]

For present purposes, it is important to emphasize that the breach of duty in issue was not a traditional breach of fiduciary duty. That is

---

[48] *Ibid.*, at 586-87.
[49] *Ibid.*, at 543.
[50] *Ibid.*, at 545.
[51] *Ibid.*, at 551.
[52] *Ibid.*, at 557.
[53] *Ibid.*, at 590.

to say, the defendant solicitor appeared to be neither in breach of the conflict rule nor of the profit rule. Rather, he had engaged in a material non-disclosure of information which, it was claimed, was quite relevant to the client's decision to go through with the transaction. La Forest J. explicitly acknowledged this point in the following terms:

> There was one difference in the nature of the breach by the solicitor in *Nocton* from that complained of in the present case. In *Nocton*, it will be remembered, the breach could give rise to a possible benefit to the solicitor, a situation that does not arise here. However, I have no doubt, and it was not contested, that the situation here also involves a breach of a fiduciary duty sufficient to call upon equity's jurisdiction to compensate the appellants for breach of the duty. It is true that Viscount Haldane specifically referred to the benefit enuring to the solicitor in holding that there was a breach of fiduciary duty.
>
>   . . . . .
>
> This does not mean that a fiduciary duty has not been breached when, as in the present case, the solicitor fails to inform a client of a fact of which he should have informed him, or that he should seek independent advice.[54]

In holding that a material non-disclosure, which is unrelated to a breach of the conflict or profit rules, constitutes a breach of fiduciary duty, La Forest J. gave the court's blessing to a line of previous Canadian decisions which had awarded relief in such circumstances.[55] He acknowledged that "[s]ome academic writings, it is true, argue for limiting fiduciary obligations to situations where the solicitor may benefit from a misstatement".[56] But such views, according to La Forest J. "may to some extent rest on, in my view, a misguided sense of orderliness".[57] This too is a point to which we must return.

---

[54] *Ibid.*, at 571-72.

[55] *Culling v. Sansai Securities Ltd.* (1974), 45 D.L.R. (3d) 456 (B.C.S.C.); *Burke v. Cory* (1959), 19 D.L.R. (2d) 252 (Ont. C.A.); *Howard v. Cunliffe* (1973), 36 D.L.R. (3d) 212 (B.C.C.A.); *Laskin v. Bache & Co.*, [1972] 1 O.R. 465 (C.A.), and *Maghun v. Richardson Securities of Canada Ltd.* (1986), 18 O.A.C. 141, 58 O.R. (2d) 1, 34 D.L.R. (4th) 524 (C.A.).

[56] *Supra*, note 36, at 573, referring to the article by distinguished equity scholar and judge, The Hon. Mr. Justice Gummow, "Compensation for Breach of Fiduciary Duty" in Youdan (ed.), *Equity, Fiduciaries and Trusts* (Toronto: Carswell, 1989).

[57] *Ibid.*

(3) *Norberg v. Wynrib*[58]

Equitable compensation for breach of fiduciary duty next surfaced in the Supreme Court in the context of two cases dealing with sexual assault. The first, *Norberg v. Wynrib*, concerned a claim brought by a former patient of the defendant physician. The patient had developed an addiction to Fiorinal and had approached the defendant with a view to obtaining prescriptions for Fiorinal on the basis of fraudulent misrepresentations concerning symptoms requiring treatment. When the defendant eventually discerned that the plaintiff was addicted to the drug, he confronted her with this information and offered further prescriptions only in exchange for sexual favours. Although this overture was at first rejected, the plaintiff, in desperation, eventually complied with the defendant's demands when her other sources of supply became constricted. The resulting encounters between the physician and patient occurred over the next year or so on as many as a dozen or more occasions. The present claim was brought for damages for assault and battery and, in the alternative, for equitable compensation for the physician's alleged breach of fiduciary duty.

On the battery claim, of course, the principal hurdle confronted by the plaintiff was the issue of consent. La Forest J., for three of a panel of six members of the court, was able to conclude that the general requirement in such a case — that the consent must be genuine — was not met on the present facts. Drawing some support from the law of unconscionable transactions,[59] La Forest J. concluded that, in the circumstances of this case, the plaintiff was not truly in a position to make a free choice and, accordingly, that the defence of consent was unavailable to the defendant physician. Turning to the question of quantum, La Forest J. noted that battery is actionable without proof of damage and that aggravated damages may be awarded if the battery occurred "in humiliating or undignified circumstances".[60] Aggravated damages were appropriate, in his view, on the present facts, and he awarded general damages in the amount of $20,000. It was also his view that the reprehensible nature of the physician's conduct was such that an additional award of $10,000 in punitive damages would be appropriate.

The three other members of the panel disagreed with respect to quantum. Sopinka J. was alone in the view that punitive damages were inappropriate in this case. It was also his view that the proper theory of liability on these facts was in contract rather than tort on the theory that the defendant failed to discharge his contractual obligation to provide medical care

---

[58] [1992] 2 S.C.R. 226, [1992] 4 W.W.R. 577, 68 B.C.L.R. (2d) 29, 12 C.C.L.T. (2d) 1, 92 D.L.R. (4th) 449, 138 N.R. 81.
[59] *Ibid.*, at 457-64 D.L.R. *Cf.* Sopinka J. at 476-80 and McLachlin J. at 494.
[60] *Ibid.*, at 469.

of the requisite standard. McLachlin J., with whom L' Heureux-Dubé J. concurred, was of the view that general damages for suffering and loss during the period of prolonged addiction in the amount of $20,000, and damages for sexual exploitation in the amount of $25,000, together with punitive damages of $25,000, would be more appropriate in circumstances of this case. Moreover, it was her view that "the doctrines of tort or contract [do not] capture the essential nature of the wrong done to the plaintiff".[61] In her view "[o]nly the principles applicable to fiduciary relationships and their breach encompass it in its totality".[62] McLachlin J. reviewed the definition of fiduciary obligation emerging from recent Supreme Court jurisprudence and observed that "[a]ll the classic characteristics of a fiduciary relationship were present".[63] The defendant physician was under a duty to act in the patient's best interest and "not permit any conflict between his duty to act only in her best interests and his own interests — including his interest in sexual gratification — to arise".[64] On this basis, the defendant was said to be in breach of the classic duty of "loyalty, good faith, and avoidance of a conflict of duty and self-interest".[65]

McLachlin J. noted that the type of interest infringed in this case has not been regarded traditionally as a "legal interest" for purposes of fiduciary law.[66] Nonetheless, the interests that both society and individual patients have in access to "professional medical care free of exploitation for the physician's private purposes"[67] are protected by the professional obligations of physicians, breach of which may give rise to professional discipline. McLachlin J. acknowledged that "the interests which the enforcement of these duties protect are, to be sure, different from the legal and economic interests which the law of fiduciary relationships has been used traditionally to safeguard".[68] Drawing support from Wilson J.'s comment in *Frame v. Smith*[69] that "[t]o deny relief because of the nature of the interest involved, to afford protection to material interests but not to human or personal interests would, it seems to me, be arbitrary in the extreme",[70] McLachlin J. concluded that the societal and personal interests

---

[61] *Ibid.*, at 484. Tort and contract, for McLachlin J., do not adequately take into account the "power imbalance inherent in the relationship between fiduciary and beneficiary": *ibid.*, at 499.

[62] *Ibid.*, at 484.

[63] *Ibid.*, at 489.

[64] *Ibid.*

[65] *Ibid.*

[66] *Ibid.*, at 490.

[67] *Ibid.*

[68] *Ibid.*, at 490.

[69] [1987] 2 S.C.R. 99, 23 O.A.C. 84, 42 C.C.L.T. 1, 9 R.F.L. (3d) 225, 42 D.L.R. (4th) 81 at 104, 78 N.R. 40.

[70] *Supra*, note 58, at 491 D.L.R..

at stake in this case constituted a type of practical[71] interest which is to be protected by the law of fiduciary obligation. The defendant breached this fiduciary duty of loyalty "when he prescribed drugs which he knew she should not have, when he failed to advise her to obtain counselling when her addiction became or should have become apparent to him, and most notoriously, when he placed his own interest in obtaining sexual favours from Ms. Norberg in conflict with and above her interest in obtaining treatment and becoming well".[72]

(4) *M.(K.) v. M.(H.)*[73]

The decision in *Norberg* was released in June of 1992. The court had an early opportunity to reconsider the suggestion that sexual assault might constitute a breach of fiduciary duty. The decision in *M.(K.) v. M.(H.)* was released in October of 1992. The plaintiff in this case was an incest victim who brought a claim for assault and battery and, in the alternative, for compensation for breach of fiduciary duty against her father who had perpetrated the abuse. The abuse began when the victim was of tender years and continued for eight years until the victim left home at age 17. Although the victim was very aware of the abuse and its wrongful nature, she did not appreciate the connection between the abuse and her own psychological injuries until she began attending a self-help group for incest victims ten years later. Shortly thereafter, she commenced these proceedings. The defendant sought to rely on the statutory limitations period with respect to the tort claim and to rely on the statutory period by analogy with respect to the claim in equity. At trial, the jury indicated that it would award $50,000 in damages but the trial judge held that the action was statute-barred. At the Supreme Court, the limitations arguments failed. La Forest J., for a majority of the Supreme Court, held that the limitations period with respect to the tort claim would not begin to run until a victim of incest could reasonably discover the connection between childhood abuse and the resulting injuries. This realization did not reasonably occur in the present case until the commencement of counselling. Accordingly, the relief sought by the plaintiff — reinstatement of the jury award — was granted by the court.

---

[71] The notion of a "practical" interest was drawn from *Reading v. Attorney General*, [1951] A.C. 507 (H.L.), where the Crown's interest in not having British soldiers accept bribes for off-duty and unlawful use of uniforms was so described.

[72] *Supra*, note 58, at 495 D.L.R.

[73] [1992] 3 S.C.R. 6, 14 C.C.L.T. (2d) 1, 96 D.L.R. (4th) 289, 142 N.R. 321.

It is of greater interest for present purposes that on this occasion La Forest J., for a majority of the court, offered the view that the father's sexual assault also constituted a breach of fiduciary duty. La Forest J. noted that the fiduciary nature of a parent's responsibility with respect to the economic interests of a child has been well-established in the case law. It was his view that the absence of prior authority did not prevent extending the fiduciary duties of parents to encompass an obligation to protect a child's health and well-being. The defendant's insidious conduct constituted an obvious breach of this fiduciary duty.[74] As one would expect from her *Norberg* opinion, McLachlin J. agreed with her colleague on this issue, as did L'Heureux-Dubé J. in a concurring opinion.

La Forest J. referred to his prior difference of opinion with McLachlin J. on the relationship between sexual assault and breach of fiduciary duty in *Norberg v. Wynrib* in the following fashion:

> In *Norberg*, McLachlin J. and I differed on the path to be followed in upholding recovery. She chose the route of the fiduciary claim whereas I preferred the route afforded by common law tort of battery because in the circumstances of that case there might be difficulties concerning the applicability of fiduciary obligations, an issue I did not find it necessary to decide. I could do this because I did not consider the common law molds to be ill-fitting in that case. Nor, as I will attempt to demonstrate, do I think they are ill-fitting in the present circumstances. Nonetheless, I agree with my colleague that a breach of fiduciary duty cannot be automatically overlooked in favour of concurrent common law claims.[75]

La Forest J. and McLachlin J. did, however, differ on the question of the appropriate remedy. La Forest J. reasserted the proposition he advanced in *Canson* to the effect that if the policy considerations underlying both the common law claim and the equitable claim were the same, the same remedies normally ought to be available. He then reasoned as follows:

> The question in this appeal is whether there are different policy objectives animating a breach of a parent's fiduciary duty as compared with incestuous sexual assault. In my view, the underlying objectives are the same. Both seek to compensate the victim for her injuries and to punish the wrongdoer. The jury award of general damages was made with full knowledge of the injuries suffered by the appellant and her rehabilitative needs. The same concerns would apply in assessing equitable compensation, and as such I would decline to provide any additional compensation for the breach of fiduciary obligation.[76]

---

[74] *Ibid.*, at 61-69.
[75] *Ibid.*, at 61.
[76] *Ibid.*, at 81-82.

It was also La Forest J.'s view that the jury's award of punitive damages would be available in equity. Accordingly, he was not inclined to disturb the jury's award.

McLachlin J., on the other hand, was unable to agree that the measure of damages for battery and assault would necessarily be the same for compensation for breach of fiduciary duty. She went on to explain as follows:

> As I see it, the question is whether the wrong encompassed by the cause of action is the same. The wrong encompassed by the torts of battery and assault may be different from the wrong encompassed by the action for a breach of fiduciary duty. The latter encompasses damage to the trust relationship, for example, which the former does not. The action for breach of fiduciary duty may also be more concerned with imposing a measure which will deter future breaches . . . trustees have always been held to highest account in a manner stricter than that applicable to tortfeasors.[77]

In the present case, however, it was unnecessary to consider this matter further, as the plaintiff appellant merely sought reinstatement of the jury award. In *M.(K.) v. M.(H.)*, then, we have a majority of the court adopting the view that fiduciary law is capable of protecting more than merely economic interests. The court apparently remains seriously divided, however, on the implications of this innovation for remedial issues.

(5) *Hodgkinson v. Simms*[78]

The latest — though surely not the final — chapter in this saga is the decision of the court in *Hodgkinson v. Simms*, released in December of 1994. In *Hodgkinson*, the court returned to consider the potential availability of equitable compensation in an economic context. The plaintiff appellant was a stockbroker who had sought investment advice from the defendant accountant. The defendant had developed a business of providing tax planning and investment advice to small businessmen and professionals. The plaintiff had moved from one employer to another and increased his income from the $50,000 to $70,000 per year he was earning with his former employer to $1.2 million in his second year at his new place of employment in 1981. The plaintiff was an alleged "neophyte" in the field of tax planning who sought advice with respect to such matters from the defendant Simms. The plaintiff shared Simms' view that

---

[77] *Ibid.*, at 86.
[78] [1994] 3 S.C.R. 377, 97 B.C.L.R. (2d) 1, 16 B.L.R. (2d) 1, 22 C.C.L.T. (2d) 1, 57 C.P.R. (3d) 1, 95 DTC 5135, 117 D.L.R. (4th) 161, 171 N.R. 245.

real estate would be a sound investment. Simms recommended four MURB projects to the plaintiff, in which he duly invested.

Simms had not disclosed to the plaintiff, however, that he was in a professional relationship with the developers of these projects. This arrangement entitled the defendant to larger fees from his developer clients if their MURBS were sold to other clients of Simms, a practice described by Mr. Simms as "bonus billing". With the collapse of the real estate market, Hodgkinson suffered losses in the amount of $350,507.62 on the four investments recommended by Simms. Hodgkinson claimed and succeeded in persuading the trial judge that he would not have invested in the MURBs if he had known of Simms' involvement. Hodgkinson was seeking independent advice. On this basis, the plaintiff claimed for damages for breach of contract and, in the alternative, for compensation for breach of fiduciary duty.

The trial judge[79] concluded that there was an implied term in Simms' retainer with the plaintiff imposing a contractual duty of material disclosure. In the trial judge's view, Simms was in breach of this provision and also in breach of his fiduciary duties — the breach here, of course, being a classic breach of non-disclosure of personal interest — and awarded damages for the full amount of the loss sustained. The British Columbia Court of Appeal reversed on the fiduciary duty point and reduced the award to the amount of the fees received by Simms from the developers with respect to the "bonus billing" arrangement. The loss sustained as a result of the collapse of the real estate market, was, in the Court of Appeal's view, unforeseeable and therefore not recoverable.

In the Supreme Court, the panel divided on the question of the existence of a fiduciary relationship. A bare majority, for whom La Forest J. wrote a plurality opinion on this point, held that a fiduciary relationship was established on these facts. In joint dissenting reasons, McLachlin and Sopinka JJ., with whom Major J. concurred, offered the view that the relationship between the parties lacked the element of "total reliance"[80] by the beneficiary on the principal which is necessary to establish the existence of a fiduciary relationship. For the majority, then, it became material to consider the principles applicable to the calculation of equitable compensation, and, further, to determine whether their application yields a different result than the principles for calculating damages for breach of contract.

La Forest J. began his consideration of remedial issues by determining the level of compensation that would be available for the breach of fiduciary duty. The proper approach to calculating such damages, he said, is "restitutionary", by which he meant that the claimant "is entitled to

---

[79] (1989), 43 B.L.R. 122 (B.C.S.C.).
[80] *Supra*, note 78, at 468.

be put in as good as position as he would have been in had the breach not occurred".[81] This approach leads to the conclusion, in La Forest J.'s view, that the plaintiff should be restored to the position he was in before the transaction by recovery equal to the loss of capital as well as all consequential losses. In response to the defendant's submission that the plaintiff would, in any event, have invested in real estate tax shelters, and suffered, therefore, an equivalent loss, La Forest J. noted that this was inconsistent with the factual findings of the trial judge. In any event, this argument was precluded by the equitable principle that the onus would be on the defendant in such a case to prove that the victim would have suffered the same loss even if no breach had occurred.[82]

The defendant further argued that even if it could not be established that the plaintiff would have invested in real estate, in any event, it was inappropriate to now recover the full loss since the defendant's non-disclosure was not the "proximate cause of the plaintiff's loss".[83] The plaintiff's loss was caused by the impact of the general economic recession on the real estate market. La Forest J. was of the view that since the fiduciary breach had "initiated the chain of events leading to the investor's loss [,] . . . the breaching party [should] account for this loss in full".[84] Understandably, the defendant relied on *Canson* for the proposition that the defendant should not be liable for losses that were not caused by the defendant's breach. For La Forest J., however, *Canson* was to be distinguished on the basis that the loss in *Canson* was caused by the acts of third parties which were unrelated to the fiduciary breach, whereas in *Hodgkinson*, the breach of duty was "directly related to the risk that materialized".[85] The defendant Simms had encouraged, indeed had exercised some control over the plaintiff's decision to make these very investments. In *Canson*, on the other hand, the defendant had no control over the risks that eventually materialized.

The application of the "but for" test with respect to the losses that occurred in *Hodgkinson* was strengthened, in La Forest J.'s view, by "the need to put special pressure on those in positions of trust and power over others in situations of vulnerability".[86] By imposing strict obligations on fiduciaries, "the law is able to monitor a given relationship society views as socially useful while avoiding the necessity of formal regulation that

---

[81] *Ibid.*, at 440. This is to use the term "restitution" in the trust law sense referred to in the introductory section of this paper.

[82] *Ibid.*, at 441. A presumption, it would appear, that may not be available in contract at common law.

[83] *Ibid.*, at 442.

[84] *Ibid.*, at 443.

[85] *Ibid.*, at 445.

[86] *Ibid.*, at 452.

may tend to hamper its social utility".[87] In short, La Forest J. appears to have drawn on the well springs of policy supporting the general law of fiduciary obligations in coming to the conclusion that the defendant should be liable to the full extent of the plaintiff's loss in this case.

As La Forest J. noted, it was not strictly necessary to consider how damages for breach of contract should be calculated. Nonetheless, La Forest J. proceeded to the perhaps surprising conclusion that "on the facts of this case, damages in contract follow the principles stated in connection with the equitable breach."[88] For La Forest J., the breach of contract was the failure to provide "independent" investment advice. Thus, the breach of contract was very similar to the breach of fiduciary duty. Moreover, since it was reasonably foreseeable that if the contract was breached, the plaintiff would not have invested and therefore would not have been exposed to the market risks in connection with these four MURBS, the risk which accrued was therefore a reasonably foreseeable consequence of the breach. It was sufficient that the type of loss was foreseeable, even if its extent might not have been. On these particular facts, then, equitable compensation and, damages for breach of contract are to be calculated, according to La Forest J., in the same fashion.

In dissent, McLachlin and Sopinka JJ. rejected the literal application of a strict "but for" compensation principle in the context of both equitable and common law claims. *Canson* was noted as authority for the proposition that "the results of supervening events beyond the control of the defendant are not justly visited upon him/her in assessing damages, even in the context of the breach of an equitable duty".[89] In the context of contractual damages, the "but for" approach was similarly inappropriate. The plaintiff's loss resulted from the economic downturn rather than any inadequacy in the advice provided by the respondent. Further, it was their view that the plaintiff's losses would not reasonably have been contemplated as a consequence of the defendant's failure to make full disclosure and, therefore, that the losses failed to meet the reasonable foreseeability threshold applicable to the calculation of common law damages for breach of contract.

In *Hodgkinson*, then, we are offered two rather different views as to the proper method of calculating damages in this type of fact situation, either in equity or in contract. What the two opinions share, however, is the view that the same principle would apply both at common law and in equity. For the majority, however, the principle that would apply

---

[87] *Ibid,.* at 453. Sopinka and McLachlin JJ. expressed some scepticism with respect to the relative social utility of "advice as to how to add to one's personal wealth while paying the least amount of tax": *ibid.*, at 469.

[88] *Ibid.*, at 454.

[89] *Ibid.*, at 475.

in both cases is the "but for" test, with the result that the defendant is liable for the full restoration of the plaintiff's loss. For the minority, the "but for" approach is inappropriate on these facts in either context.

If one accepts that, as a matter of practicality, it is rather unlikely that either of the parties contemplated the possibility of the collapse of the real estate market, or would, if asked, have assumed that the defendant would bear the risk of such losses in the event that the contract was breached in a way which was unconnected to that collapse, it is tempting to conclude that the view offered by the minority represents a more traditional application of the principle for calculating damages for breach of contract. If one takes this view, La Forest J.'s method of calculating common law damages for breach of contract appears to be much influenced by the equitable considerations that led him to apply the "but for" test in the context of calculating equitable compensation. If, in *Canson*, La Forest J. was overtly indicating that equity should be influenced by common law, it may well be that in *Hodgkinson* equity has covertly influenced his analysis of the common law damages claim.

5. *Equitable Compensation: The Current State of the Art*

This fascinating series of cases offers a rich analytical harvest, the bare surface of which has been scratched in the foregoing exposition. In reading these opinions, the reader is confronted time and again with principled discussions of fundamental issues of civil liability. It is also fair to suggest, however, that this collection of authorities raises more questions than it is able to answer. While the ultimate significance of these decisions must await further developments in the law reports and the law reviews in the years to come, it may be helpful to offer some preliminary and tentative views at the present stage of development.

(1) Equity's Version of the Law of Torts?

Perhaps the most interesting feature of these cases is the extent to which the Supreme Court appears to be reinventing tort law as equitable compensation for breach of fiduciary duty. If it is not misleading to characterize tort law as the body of private law doctrine that defines liability for compensatory damages arising from unprivileged or wrongful conduct, there is a very real sense in which these recent cases are reinventing an equitable body of doctrine with the same objective and policy foundations. Perhaps it is not too late to ask whether this development is a necessary one and, if not, whether it is a truly desirable one. Before raising such questions, however, the reader may need to be persuaded that something of this kind is indeed occurring in this line of jurisprudence.

As a preliminary point, it is important to stress that the traditional role of fiduciary law has been one of lifting the profits secured by breach of the fiduciary duty of loyalty either by placing oneself in the position where duty and self-interest conflict or by profiting from the fiduciary position. True, *Nocton v. Lord Ashburton*[90] demonstrates that equitable compensation can be awarded with respect to injuries sustained as a result of a breach of this type of duty, but such cases appear to be exceptional,[91] perhaps because in meritorious cases damages relief will already be available at common law either in contract or in tort.

Two analytical moves made in the recent Supreme Court jurisprudence have substantially expanded the potential role for equitable compensation as a means for providing compensation for injuries sustained as a result of wrongful conduct. The first move, anticipated, to be sure, by some earlier Canadian decisions,[92] is to recognize that equitable compensation may be available in cases where fiduciaries breach duties other than those comprised in the traditional duty of fiduciary loyalty. In *Guerin*,[93] the breach leading to compensation was a failure to follow the principal's instructions in negotiating a deal. In *Canson*,[94] the breach of duty was a failure to disclose information that would have been material to the principal's decision to enter into a transaction with someone other than the fiduciary and with respect to which the fiduciary had no personal interest. In each case, then, there is no suggestion of conflict of interest or profit from position. Breach of fiduciary duty is thus converted into a claim essentially for failure to take proper care in carrying out the task

---

[90] [1914] A.C. 932 (H.L.).

[91] Canadian illustrations in addition to the Supreme court jurisprudence discussed in this paper include: *Standard Investments Ltd. v. Canadian Imperial Bank of Commerce* (1985), 11 O.A.C. 318, 52 O.R. (2d) 473, 30 B.L.R. 193, 22 D.L.R. (4th) 410 (C.A.); appeal to S.C.C. refused (1986), 53 O.R. (2d) 663n; *Bedard v. James* (1986), 32 B.L.R. 188, 10 C.P.R. (3d) 339 (Ont. Dist. Ct.). See also *Warman Int'l Ltd. v. Dwyer* (1995), 69 Aust. L.J.R. 362 (H.C.) with respect to the question of election between the remedies of compensation and an accounting of profits.

[92] See *supra*, note 55. It should be noted that a broader view of *Nocton v. Lord Ashburton*, consistent with the broader duty of fiduciary care adopted in the Canadian cases, is possible. See, *e.g.*, for example, *White v. Jones,* [1995] 1 All E.R. 691 (H.L.) at 712-14, *per* Lord Browne-Wilkinson, who appears to read *Nocton* thusly.

[93] [1984] 2 S.C.R. 335, [1984] 6 W.W.R. 481, 59 B.C.L.R. 301, 20 E.T.R. 6, 36 R.P.R. 1, 13 D.L.R. (4th) 321, 55 N.R. 161.

[94] [1991] 3 S.C.R. 534, 61 B.C.L.R. (2d) 1, 9 C.C.L.T. (2d) 1, 39 C.P.R. (3d) 449, 43 E.T.R. 201, 85 D.L.R. (4th) 129, 131 N.R. 321.

that has been assigned to the fiduciary. This is a rather important and substantial addition to the traditional list of duties imposed on those who hold a fiduciary office.

The second analytical move which appears to substantially expand the role of equitable compensation as a device for compensating wrongful injury is the decision anticipated in *Norberg* and actually taken by the majority in *M.(K.) v. M.(H.)* to expand the types of interests to be protected by fiduciary law beyond those economic interests protected by the traditional doctrine. Fiduciary duty now appears to embrace the obligation, at least of a parent and perhaps of a physician, to protect the health and well-being of the person to whom the duty is owed by not perpetrating a sexual assault. It is unclear, at this stage, whether the ability of fiduciary law to protect this type of interest will be extended to other kinds of fiduciary relationships and to other kinds of wrongful conduct. In principle, it is not obvious that a lawyer or other fiduciary who committed the torts of non-sexual assault and battery, conspiracy or perhaps defamation with resulting injuries to a client would not similarly be exposed to liability for equitable compensation as an alternative to liability in tort. Similarly, where the fiduciary commits a more traditional type of fiduciary breach — say, non-disclosure of a conflict of interest — it may be interesting to consider whether non-pecuniary loss such as foreseeable psychological injury could be the subject of equitable compensation. Even if the types of interest recognized in *M.(K.) v. M.(H.)* are rather narrowly circumscribed, the shift from economic to other kinds of loss is, again, obviously a move of considerable significance.

As a result of these developments, it is beyond question that the new fiduciary duties have a considerable capacity to overlap with tort duties. It should perhaps be emphasized that the fact that there is some overlap is not new. Some traditional breaches of fiduciary duty would constitute deceit at common law. In such cases, however, the victim who sought compensatory damages would pursue the claim in tort; the victim who sought to lift the profit secured by the wrongdoing would pursue equitable relief for breach of fiduciary duty. Indeed, it is revealing that there appears to be no history evident in the law reports of plaintiffs seeking equitable compensation in cases of common law fraud with a view to persuading the court to ignore common law principles such as those relating to causation, remoteness or foreseeability. What has become possible with the revised model of equitable compensation for fiduciary breach, however, is the possibility of substantial overlap in claims for compensatory relief at common law and in equity.

It is perhaps too early to attempt to assess whether or not the reinvention of tort liability in equitable terms is a useful development. It may be helpful, however, to attempt to identify some of the potential difficulties. In the first place, it may be important to keep in mind that the standards of care designed and imposed by fiduciary law have been developed, in the main, with a rather different form of liability in mind. The principal task of fiduciary law has been to provide a means of lifting profits acquired in an unattractive way. It is one thing, I would suggest, to hold an individual liable to disgorge ill-gotten gains, it is quite another to hold a person liable essentially as an insurer to compensate for injuries sustained by another. It may, of course, be very disappointing to lose one's profits; it may, however, be ruinous to be held to be the insurer of another's losses. Perhaps this is why it is acceptable to impose on fiduciaries a very high standard of duty. The impressive height of the standard was colourfully portrayed by Cardozo C.J. in the following terms:

> Many forms of conduct permissible in a workaday world for those acting at arm's length, are forbidden to those bound by fiduciary ties. A trustee is held to something stricter than the morals of the market place. Not honesty alone, but the punctilio of an honour the most sensitive, is then the standard of behaviour. As to this there has developed a tradition that is unbending and inveterate. Uncompromising rigidity has been the attitude of courts of equity when petitioned to undermine the rule of undivided loyalty by the "disintegrating erosion" of particular exceptions.
>
> . . . . .
>
> Only thus has the level of conduct for fiduciaries been kept at a level higher than that trodden by the crowd.[95]

I appreciate, of course, that express trustees are both subject to such high standards and vulnerable to claims for compensation. Why not extend this approach to non-trustee fiduciaries? It might be argued, however, that the express trustee is likely to have a greater awareness of the nature of the burden being assumed than the average non-trustee fiduciary. More modestly, I would suggest that there is at least the risk that standards designed to deal essentially with the disgorgement of profits will not serve us well as indicators of when it is appropriate to impose the type of liability imposed by the law of torts.

Conversely, if is true that the law of torts is the jurisprudential context within which our legal system has most directly confronted the question of defining the circumstances in which one person should serve as an insurer of another's losses, it may be important for courts grappling with claims for equitable compensation to proceed carefully before addressing these questions in a different manner in their articulation and development of the law of equitable compensation. Such an instinct, of course, is very much consistent with the views expressed by La Forest J. in *Canson* to the effect that equity should, in developing principles of equitable

---

[95] *Meinhard v. Salmon*, 249 N.Y. 458 (C.A. 1928), at 464.

compensation, have regard to the principles developed at common law.

A second and related concern might be referred to as the *Nocton v. Lord Ashburton* problem. As has been mentioned previously,[96] it appears rather likely that the decision in *Nocton v. Lord Ashburton* represents an attempt by the House of Lords to reform the principles of tort liability developed in *Derry v. Peek*.[97] One would not, of course, wish to stand in the path of progress, however it might be achieved. And yet, it may reasonably be asked whether the development of equitable compensation for breach of fiduciary duty is a very satisfactory method of reforming the law of torts. If the standard for liability in *Derry v. Peek* was, indeed, set at too high a threshold, it is a rather cramped and limited reform of the doctrine that creates liability only in the context of certain kinds of non-disclosures made by fiduciaries. Similarly, if the law of torts has developed inadequate doctrine to deal with the limitations problems arising in the context of claims by the victims of sexual assault, it would be a very unsatisfactory reform of that doctrine to suggest that different rules apply only where the perpetrator of the assault was engaged in a fiduciary task on behalf of the victim at the time of the assault. From this perspective, the first branch of the position taken by the majority of the court in *M.(K.) v. M.(H.)* — that of ensuring that a just result could be achieved by adjustment of the principles of tort law — appears to be a more satisfactory response to the type of problem raised by that case than the second branch — characterization of the father's physical abuse of his child as a breach of a fiduciary duty.

Finally, apart from *Guerin* — a case which might be regarded as *sui generis* — it is an interesting fact that in the recent Supreme Court cases dealing with equitable compensation, there is not one decision in which a majority of the court take the view that a different result can be achieved in equity than can be achieved at common law. If, then, we would be wise to keep an open mind on the extent to which equitable principles may have a useful reforming influence to play with respect to the law of torts, the ultimate success of the venture, surely, is to be measured in terms of differences in result, rather than differences in judicial discourse leading to the same result.

(2) Concurrent Liability in Contract and Fiduciary Duty?

Many of the same points can be made with respect to the prospect of increasing overlap between fiduciary duty and contractual liability.

---

[96] See the text, *supra*, at notes 21-25.

[97] (1889), 14 A.C. 337 (H.L.).

Again, the possibility of overlap itself is not new. Many traditional breaches of fiduciary duty — say, those of solicitors who do not disclose a conflict — could be characterized as both a breach of fiduciary duty and a failure to fulfil a contractual obligation to provide a service at a standard of reasonable skill and care. On the traditional approach, of course, the client who sought compensation would sue for damages for breach of contract. Resort would be made to equity only to take advantage of the disgorgement remedies to lift any profits that had been secured by the breach of duty. Under the revised model of equitable compensation, it may be increasingly the case that courts will have to consider, as in *Hodgkinson*,[98] whether the principles for calculating damages for breach of contract are different from the principles for calculating equitable compensation. Again, while it may well be that the principles of the law of contract could be improved by greater reliance on equitable notions, it is nonetheless the case that contract law is the principal forum in which the courts have attempted to develop principles for defining the liability that should be assumed by someone who fails to perform an undertaking. Standards of conduct designed with disgorgement liability in mind may or may not be appropriate for the imposition of contractual expectancy damages.[99] Accordingly, a careful examination of the policy and principles underlying the common law rules would appear to be a desirable prelude to the development of significantly different principles for calculating equitable compensation for failure to perform undertakings. Again, it may be that the better reform device in a particular set of circumstances would be reform of the law of contract itself, rather than the development of an exception to the unsatisfactory rule which is applicable only to fiduciary relationships.[100]

(3) The La Forest/McLachlin Debate

One of the more interesting features of this line of authority is the running debate between La Forest and McLachlin JJ. with respect to the relationship of common law and equity and, more particularly with respect

---

[98] [1994] 3 S.C.R. 377, 97 B.C.L.R. (2d) 1, 16 B.L.R. (2d) 1, 22 C.C.L.T. (2d) 1, 57 C.P.R. (3d) 1, 95 DTC 5135, 117 D.L.R. (4th) 161, 171 N.R. 245.

[99] It may be noted that courts have thus far generally resisted the suggestion that disgorgement relief be available in some sub-set of breach of contract cases. See, Smith, "Disgorgement of the Profits of Breach of Contract: Property, Contract and 'Efficient Breach'" (1994-95) 24 C.B.L.J. 121; and Maddaugh and McCamus, *The Law of Restitution* (Aurora: Canada Law Book, 1990), at 432-38.

[100] *Cf. Johnson v. Agnew*, [1980] A.C. 367 at 400 (H.L.).

to the significance of the so-called fusion of law and equity effected by the *Judicature Acts.*[101] In *Canson,*[102] La Forest J. appeared to suggest that the fusion of law and equity meant that in developing equitable principles to deal with problems which had previously been addressed by the common law, courts ought to accord some deference to the principles developed at common law. McLachlin J., on the other hand, perhaps having adopted the more orthodox view that whatever else it may have accomplished, fusion of law and equity did not effect a merger of the substantive principles of liability of common law and equity, advocated the independence of fiduciary duty and the inappropriateness of tort and contract as a source of analogy in developing principles of equitable compensation.

As Paul Perrell has indicated,[103] it is possible to exaggerate the importance of this apparent difference of opinion with respect to the significance of fusion. Although La Forest J. did indicate that it was appropriate, in some cases, for equity to borrow from the common law, he also stressed that the best approach is one "that allows for direct application of the experience and best features of both law and equity, whether the motive of redress (the cause of action or remedy) originates in one system or the other".[104] For her part, McLachlin J. suggested in the following passage that even though her preference was to work within equity when dealing with equitable issues, borrowing from doctrines of common law might well be appropriate:

> Rather than begin from tort and proceed by changing the tort model to meet the constraints of trust, I prefer to start from trust, using the tort analogy to the extent shared concerns may make it helpful. That said, I readily concede that we may take wisdom where we find it, and accept such insights offered by the law of tort, in particular deceit, as may prove useful.[105]

Thus, it does seem likely that this difference in approach will very often lead to the same result, albeit by somewhat different conceptual routes. On the other hand, this difference of opinion does not appear to be trivial. La Forest J. appears to have consistently opted for solutions that generate the same results at common law and equity, whereas McLachlin J. is evidently attracted to the notion that different solutions might be achieved by relying on the internal logic of equity. It does seem likely that, as this debate unfolds, it will be focused more on fundamental policy

---

[101] *Supreme Court of Judicature Act, 1873(U.K.),* 36 & 37 Vict., c. 66; *1875 (U.K.),* 38 & 39 Vict., c. 77.

[102] *Supra* note 94.

[103] Perell, "The Aftermath of Fusion: Canson Enterprises Ltd. v. Boughton & Co." (1993), 14 Adv. Q. 488.

[104] *Supra,* note 94, at 587.

[105] *Ibid.,* at 545-46.

questions concerning different theories of liability than on a difference of opinion about the precise effect of the fusion or intermingling of law and equity.

(4) Heads of Damage: Pecuniary, Non-Pecuniary and Punitive

It was established in *Nocton v. Lord Ashburton*[106] that equitable compensation for pecuniary losses suffered as a result of a breach of fiduciary duty would be available in an appropriate case. In the recent Supreme Court decisions, it has been established that compensation for non-pecuniary losses may also be available. In *M.(K.) v. M.(H.),*[107] a majority of the court held that equitable compensation for breach of fiduciary duty is available for the psychological injuries resulting from incestuous sexual assault. The potential significance of the difference in approach of La Forest J. and McLachlin J. with respect to the development of equitable compensation is, however, evident in their expressions of opinion on this point in this case. For the majority, La Forest J. expressed the view that as the underlying policy objectives animating the calculation of damages for assault and battery are the same as those that would animate the calculation of equitable compensation, the same amount of general damages should be awarded under either theory. McLachlin J. offered the view that the measure of damages for assault and battery would not necessarily be the same as compensation for breach of fiduciary duty. A similar difference in views is evident in *Norberg.*[108] In that case, La Forest J. calculated damages only on the basis of tort liability. It was his view that the plaintiff was entitled to compensatory damages, including aggravated damages as a result of the particularly offensive nature of the defendant physician's assault. McLachlin J. would have awarded substantially greater damages on an equitable compensation theory. It is possible, however, that these are differences of opinion with respect to the appropriate quantum more than differences in principle. It is not clear that there is much to choose between a theory which suggests that the fact that a perpetrator of sexual abuse has abused a relationship of trust and confidence can be taken into account in calculating aggravated damages in tort, and a theory which takes the view that equitable compensation must reflect the special nature of the fiduciary relationship.

---

[106] *Supra*, note 90.
[107] [1992] 3 S.C.R. 6, 14 C.C.L.T. (2d) 1, 96 D.L.R. (4th) 289, 142 N.R. 321. See also *Mouat v. Clark Boyce*, [1992] 2 N.Z.L.R. 559 at 569 *per* Cooke P., revd on other grounds by the Privy Council at [1993] 4 All E.R. 268.
[108] [1992] 2 S.C.R. 226, [1992] 4 W.W.R. 577, 68 B.C.L.R. (2d) 29, 12 C.C.L.T. (2d) 1, 92 D.L.R. (4th) 449, 138 N.R. 81.

In *M.(K.) v. M.(H.)*,[109] a majority of the court holds that punitive damages may be available in a claim for equitable compensation for breach of fiduciary duty. It is not at all apparent that the controversial nature of such a holding was made clear to the court. Punitive damages are not traditionally available in equity,[110] though it is true that some Canadian courts have made such awards in the past.[111] Nonetheless, I think it is difficult to articulate a principled objection to the extension of the possibility of awarding punitive or exemplary damages in equity cases. Indeed, the Ontario Law Reform Commission has recently recommended that punitive damages be potentially available in such cases, it having been assumed that they were not clearly available under then current Canadian law.[112]

(5) Causation

The enthusiasm demonstrated by plaintiffs in these cases for equitable compensation rather than common law damages is inspired by the thought that principles drawn from trust law which are more generous to plaintiffs might be applicable to the equitable calculation of compensation. Certainly, in *Guerin*, such principles were applied in a manner helpful to the plaintiff Indian band. It is unclear, however, whether, more generally, in claims for equitable compensation for breach of fiduciary duty, it will prove to be true that, as in trust law, "considerations of causation, foreseeability and remoteness do not readily enter into the matter".[113] The role of causation as a concept in the context of equitable compensation was raised in both *Canson* and *Hodgkinson*.

The role of causation in the law of civil obligation is a vast and

---

[109] *Supra*, note 107, at 82.

[110] See, for example, *Fern Brand Waxes Ltd. v. Pearl* (1972), 29 D.L.R. (3d) 662 (Ont. C.A.); *Worobel Estate v. Worobel* (1988), 67 O.R. (2d) 151 (H.C.J.).

[111] See, for example, *Huff v. Price* (1990), 51 B.C.L.R. (2d) 282, 46 C.P.C. (2d) 209, 76 D.L.R. (4th) 138 (C.A.); *Schauenberg Industries Ltd. v. Borowski* (1979), 25 O.R. (2d) 737, 8 B.L.R. 164, 50 C.P.R. (2d) 69, 101 D.L.R. (3d) 701 (H.C.).

[112] Ontario Law Reform Commission, *Report on Exemplary Damages* (Toronto: 1991), at 71-74, over the dissent of Commissioner Earl A. Cherniak Q.C.

[113] *Re Dawson* (1966), 84 W.N. (N.S.W.) 399 at 404. See, generally, Gummow, "Compensation for Breach of Fiduciary Duty" in Youdan (ed.), *Equity, Fiduciaries and Trusts* (Toronto: Carswell, 1989); Davies, "Equitable Compensation: Causation, Foreseeability and Remoteness" in Waters (ed.), *Equity, Fiduciaries and Trusts, 1993* (Toronto: Carswell, 1994).

intricate subject[114] which does not yield easily to generalization or the brief sketch. It is sufficient for present purposes to suggest that the doctrine of causation appears to function somewhat differently in the context of tort law where the principal focus is physical injury and property damage, in contract law where the preoccupation is with economic loss[115] and in trust law where a special view of the trustee's liability has developed.

In *Canson*,[116] the Supreme Court rejected the plaintiff's suggestion that a trust-like indifference to causation should provide a basis for imposing liability on the defendant solicitor for the losses caused by the work of the soils engineers and the pile driving contractor. Although both La Forest and McLachlin JJ. shared the view that a causal link between the fiduciary breach and the loss must be established, they each formulated this proposition in slightly different terms. For La Forest J., the reason for rejecting the plaintiff's argument was that he did not think "that the claim for the harm resulting from the actions of third parties can fairly be looked upon as falling within what is encompassed in restoration for the harm suffered from the breach".[117] McLachlin J., in coming to the same conclusion, emphasized that "[t]he solicitor's duty had come to an end and the plaintiffs had assumed control of the property".[118] The loss was therefore the result, not of the solicitor's breach of duty, but rather of "decisions made by the plaintiffs and those they chose to hire".[119] That is to say, McLachlin J. placed emphasis on the proposition that the plaintiffs were, in some sense, the authors of their own misfortune.

A slightly different causation issue arises in *Hodgkinson*.[120] The plaintiff's injury might be considered to have been caused by the collapse of the real estate market. If one applied a "but for" causal test, however, the defendant could be held liable for losses which would not have occurred but for the fact that the defendant persuaded the plaintiff to make the investments in question. As we have seen,[121] La Forest J., for the majority, adopted the view that a "but for" approach would be appropriate whether the claim was treated as a claim for damages for breach of contract or for equitable compensation. The minority view of McLachlin and Sopinka JJ. suggests that in a contractual damages claim, at least, the claim would be cut off by considerations of causation and remoteness.

---

[114] See, generally, Hart and Honoré, *Causation in the Law*, 2nd ed. (Oxford, Clarendon Press, 1985).

[115] *Ibid.*, cc. VI and XI.

[116] [1991] 3 S.C.R. 534, 61 B.C.L.R. (2d) 1, 9 C.C.L.T. (2d) 1, 39 C.P.R. (3d) 449, 43 E.T.R. 201, 85 D.L.R. (4th) 129, 131 N.R. 321.

[117] *Ibid.*, at 580.

[118] *Ibid.*, at 557.

[119] *Ibid.*

[120] [1994] 3 S.C.R. 377, 97 B.C.L.R. (2d) 1, 16 B.L.R. (2d) 1, 22 C.C.L.T. (2d) 1, 57 C.P.R. (3d) 1, 95 DTC 5135, 117 D.L.R. (4th) 161, 171 N.R. 245.

[121] See the text, *ante*, at notes 82-89.

On the evidence available thus far, then, there does not appear to be a basis for predicting that causation will be treated in a significantly different manner in contract rather than equity, even if it is true that on the difficult causation question raised in *Hodgkinson* the court was not of one view. To be sure, however, the potential for differential treatment of causation issues in this context, in reliance on the trust analogy, is very real.[122]

(6) Foreseeability

The related concept of foreseeability could conceivably play a slightly different role in equitable compensation cases than it does in either tort or contract. Again, it is important to emphasize that the role of foreseeability in contract and tort is not uni-dimensional. More particularly, the defendant in a deceit claim will enjoy less success in relying on the concept than a defendant in a negligence claim.[123]

In *Canson*, McLachlin J., by way of emphasizing the risk of proceeding by analogy with tort law, indicated that "La Forest J. has avoided one such pitfall in indicating that compensation for a breach of fiduciary duty will not be limited by foreseeability".[124] It is not entirely clear, however, that La Forest J. reaches the conclusion in *Canson* that foreseeability would never have a role in the calculation of equitable compensation. Indeed, the discounting of the factor of foreseeability in the analysis in *Canson* itself appears to rest on an assumption by the trial judge, accepted by the majority at the Supreme Court level, that damages for deceit offered the correct model to follow in this case.

It may well be that in other cases the deceit analogy will not be thought to be dispositive, perhaps because the fiduciary breach in question may be less offensive than that which occurred in *Canson*.[125] In any event, if La Forest J. and a majority of the court continue to espouse the view that characterization of a claim as equitable rather than common law should not lead to a different result if the underlying policy concerns are the same, it may well be that foreseeability will have some role to play in the context of equitable compensation.

---

[122] See Davies, *supra,* note 113, at 305.

[123] See, for example, *Doyle v. Olby (Ironmongers) Ltd.*, [1969] 2 Q.B. 158 at 167 (C.A.). See, generally, Brazier, *Street on Torts*, 19th ed. (London: Buttterworths, 1993), at 122.

[124] *Supra,* note 116, at 545, *per* McLachlin J.

[125] *Cf.,* Davies, *supra*, note 113, at 309. A common use of the word "fraud" should not mislead.

(7) Mitigation, Contributory Negligence, Time of Assessment and the Equitable Presumptions

In this series of Supreme Court decisions, though principally in *Canson*, there are also to be found intriguing discussions of possible differential treatment of questions such as the role to be played in equitable compensation by such concepts as mitigation,[126] contributory negligence,[127] time of assessment[128] and the equitable presumptions in cases of non-trustee fiduciary breach.[129] There are also helpful discussions of these issues in the secondary literature.[130] In the case-law, thus far, there is as yet no basis for confident prediction as to the role these concepts might play in non-trustee fiduciary cases, apart from cases like *Guerin* where the non-trustee fiduciary has control over the beneficiary's property. In *Guerin*, it is plainly the case that the court felt it was appropriate to apply trust-like presumptions in the plaintiff's favour with respect to the calculation of the value of the lost opportunity to make a profit. The reasoning of the court in *Canson*, however, strongly suggests that the presumptions are not going to play as large a role in non-trustee fiduciary breach cases, but the point has not been squarely confronted in the subsequent cases.

6. *Equitable Compensation for Other Equitable Wrongs*

The apparent expansion of the role of equitable compensation in the context of breach of fiduciary duty, raises the possibility that equitable compensation may have a more vigorous role to play in the context of other kinds of equitable wrongdoing.

---

[126] See, for example, *Canson, supra*, note 116, at 553 *per* McLachlin J., and at 581 *per* La Forest J.

[127] See *Canson, ibid.*, at 584-85 *per* La Forest J. quoting from *Day v. Mead*, [1987] 2 N.Z.L.R. 443, and at 591 *per* Stevenson J.

[128] See, for example, *Canson, ibid.*, at 554-55 *per* McLachlin J.; and *Guerin*, [1984] 2 S.C.R. 335, [1984] 6 W.W.R. 481, 59 B.C.L.R. 301, 20 E.T.R. 6, 36 R.P.R. 1, 13 D.L.R. (4th) 321 at 366, *per* Wilson J.

[129] See, *e.g.* ,*Canson, ibid.*, at 545 *per* McLachlin J.; and *Guerin, ibid.*, *per* Wilson J; and *Hodgkinson, supra*, note 120, at 441 *per* La Forest J.

[130] See Gummow, *supra*, note 113; and Davies, *supra*, note 113.

(1) Breach of Confidence[131]

Breach of the duty of confidence may arise in a contractual setting. In such cases, damages will be available for breach of contract and, unless different principles will apply, resort to equity may not be necessary. In a non-contractual setting, however, resort must be made to compensation in equity. In the English law of breach of confidence, it has long been understood that the ability to grant equitable compensation for breach of confidence rests on the jurisdiction to award compensation conferred on the courts by *Lord Cairns' Act*.[132] That jurisdiction is limited to cases where damages may be awarded in addition to or in lieu of an injunction or specific relief. Accordingly, the question arises as to whether equitable compensation is available in a case where an injunction or specific relief is neither sought nor available. In *Malone v. Com'r of Police of Metropolitan (No. 2)*,[133] Megarry V.-C., confirmed that where "there is no case for the grant of an injunction, as when the disclosure has already been made, the unsatisfactory result seems to be that no damages can be awarded under his head".[134]

In light of the recent Supreme Court jurisprudence on equitable compensation, it seems rather likely that this anomaly will be authoritatively removed on an early occasion. Indeed, the reasoning in *Lac Minerals Ltd. v. Int'l Corona Resources Ltd.*[135] offers some support for this view. In the first place, it will be recalled that in *Lac* a majority of the court took the view that the equitable remedy of constructive trust which would be available for a breach of fiduciary duty ought similarly to be available with respect to the defendant's breach of confidence. It seems unlikely that the Supreme Court would take the position that equitable compensation, though available for breach of fiduciary duty, will not be available for a breach of confidence. If this is so, the awarding of equitable compensation for breach of confidence will plainly not be dependent on *Lord Cairns' Act* and could be allowed, therefore, even in a case where no grounds exist for the seeking of an injunction. Further, though the majority in *Lac* on the remedies issue opted for constructive trust relief, the minority adopted the position that damages ought to be available, with

---

[131] See, generally, Capper, "Damages for Breach of the Equitable Duty of Confidence" (1994), 14 Leg. Stud. 313. With respect to the restitutionary remedies for breach of confidence, see further the text, *post*, at notes 145-167.

[132] *Chancery Amendment Act, 1858 (U.K.)*, 21 & 22 Vict., c. 27, and see Capper, *ibid*.

[133] [1979] 2 All E.R. 620 (Ch.D.).

[134] *Ibid.*, at 633.

[135] [1989] 2 S.C.R. 574, 36 O.A.C. 57, 69 O.R. (2d) 287*n*, 44 B.L.R. 1, 26 C..P.R. (3d) 97, 35 E.T.R. 1, 61 D.L.R. (4th) 14, 101 N.R. 239.

no apparent concern to discern whether the jurisdiction conferred by *Lord Cairns' Act* was applicable to the facts of that case.

A second anomaly might be resolved through the expansion of equitable compensation relates to non-pecuniary loss. Although damages for non-pecuniary injuries, such as mental distress and anxiety, could potentially be available in a contractual damages claim for breach of confidence, the traditional view would be that such injuries would not be compensable in equity.[136] As we have seen, in the recent equitable compensation cases, the Supreme Court has clearly indicated that equitable compensation for non-pecuniary injuries will be available in breach of fiduciary duty cases. For the reasons outlined above, it therefore seems rather likely that such claims would be possible, on equitable grounds, in breach of confidence as well.[137]

(2) Innocent Misrepresentation, Undue Influence and Unconscionability

The equitable remedy of rescission is available to set aside agreements that are induced by innocent misrepresentation or which are the product of undue influence or unconscionable dealings.[138] The remedy of rescission will not be available where the bars to rescission are applicable. Thus, for example, where *restitutio in integrum* is not possible, or where a third party's rights have intervened, rescission will not be granted. For example, where property has been acquired under a purchase agreement tainted with undue influence and the property has been resold to a third party, no relief is available and the person who has exercised such influence will essentially enjoy an ill-gotten gain. No relief is available, unless, of course, the defendant has also committed a tort such as a negligent misstatement. The traditional explanation for the fact that no relief of any kind will be available in such circumstances is that equity cannot award damages. In the light of the recent Supreme Court jurisprudence, this explanation has a rather hollow ring.

Again, it appears quite possible that on some early occasion it will be plainly recognized that equitable compensation might be available in such cases, even though the right to rescission has been barred. Indeed, a number of Canadian decisions, some of which do not appear to appreciate the controversial nature of the point, have granted relief of this kind,

---

[136] Capper, *supra*, note 131, at 327.
[137] Capper offers the appealing example of sensitive personal information disclosed by welfare authorities in an Irish case, *O'Neill v. Department of Health and Social Services (No. 2)* (1986), 5 N.I. 290; *ibid.*, at 327.
[138] See, generally, Perell, "Rescission", in this volume.

in cases of misrepresentation,[139] undue influence[140] and unconscionability.[141] Although, in some cases, courts have been inclined to achieve these results by finding the existence of a fiduciary relationship,[142] this has not invariably been the case.[143] It seems possible, then, that the more expansive view of equitable compensation emerging from the recent jurisprudence may provide a doctrinal foundation for relief of this kind.[144]

7. *Restitutionary Remedies*

We turn now to what was referred to in the introduction to this paper as the "law of restitution" with a view to briefly portraying recent developments of a remedial nature in this field. As was signalled in the introduction, there are really two different kinds of restitutionary remedies, those of a "subtraction" and those of a "disgorgement" measure. I will first describe recent developments of interest concerning the two equitable remedies in the disgorgement measure, constructive trust and accounting of profits, and then point briefly to a recent line of English cases which appear to expand the basis for allowing relief in the subtraction measure.

---

[139] See, for example, *Dusik v. Newton* (1985), 62 B.C.L.R. 1 (C.A.); and *Bank of Montreal v. Murphy*, [1986] 6 W.W.R. 610, 6 B.C.L.R. (2d) 169, 36 B.L.R. 36 (C.A.).

[140] See, for example, *Treadwell v. Martin* (1976), 67 D.L.R. (3d) 493, (N.B.C.A.).

[141] See, for example, *Paris v. Machnick* (1972), 32 D.L.R. (3d) 723, (N.S.S.C.), and *Junkin v. Junkin* (1978), 86 D.L.R. (3d) 751 (Ont. H.C.). See also *McCarthy v. Kenny*, [1939] 3 D.L.R. 556 (Ont. S.C.).

[142] See, for example, *Treadwell v. Martin, supra*, note 140.

[143] See *Dusik v. Newton, supra*, note 139.

[144] Should this occur, it will be necessary to consider whether such compensation should mirror rescissionary relief by limiting recovery to the loss of value transferred (for example, the difference between the market value and the unduly influenced contract price) or should embrace the possibility of recovering consequential losses as well. The former choice would, I would suggest, simply remove an anomaly in the existing remedial structure. The latter would convert undue influence, unconscionability and non-negligent misstatement into equitable torts, a much more dramatic move, which would not appear defensible, as a general proposition at least, on policy grounds.

(1) Constructive Trust

In Canadian law, the constructive trust is viewed as a remedial device which can be utilized by the courts to remedy cases of unjust enrichment.[145] This view, which draws from American jurisprudence to the same effect, is rather unlike the position in English law in which the constructive trust is viewed essentially as a remedy reserved for cases of breach of fiduciary duty. Once one adopts the remedial constructive trust approach, a number of interesting questions arise. In what sorts of cases, be they fiduciary duty cases or other kinds of cases, should the remedy of constructive trust be available with all the benefits that flow from granting a form of relief that normally confers equitable proprietary interests on the plaintiff?

The most important recent development in Canadian restitutionary law in this area has been the attempt, by the Supreme Court of Canada, in *Lac Minerals* to provide some guidance with respect to this important issue. In *Lac*, La Forest J. attempted to articulate criteria which might be employed in determining whether or not the special advantages of the constructive trust remedy should be made available to a plaintiff.[146] The significance of *Lac* in this regard has been canvassed in a recent volume of this lecture series[147] and need not be pursued in depth here. A brief summary of the main points made by La Forest J., however, may be of assistance.

It will be recalled that in *Lac* the plaintiff argued the claim as being founded either on breach of fiduciary duty or upon a breach of confidence. The defendant had exploited confidential information acquired by the plaintiff by acquiring neighbouring properties and developing therein an extremely valuable mining property. The plaintiff sought to impress the mine with a constructive trust. La Forest J. stated, and indeed the court held, that it was not necessary to find that the parties had a fiduciary relationship in order to engage the remedy of constructive trust.[148] Further, in La Forest J.'s view, it was not necessary to find that some pre-existing property right of the plaintiff would be vindicated by the constructive trust. Thus it was not necessary, for example, to hold that confidential information constituted "property" in order to impose constructive trust relief.[149] La Forest J. then listed a number of consider-

---

[145] *Pettkus v. Becker*, [1980] 2 S.C.R. 834, 8 E.T.R. 143, 19 R.F.L. (2d) 165, 117 D.L.R. (3d) 257, 34 N.R. 384; and see, generally, Maddaugh and McCamus, *The Law of Restitution* (Aurora: Canada Law Book, 1990), c. 5.
[146] *Supra*, note 135.
[147] McCamus, "Remedies for Breach of Fiduciary Duty" in *Special Lectures of the Law Society of Upper Canada, 1990: Fiduciary Duties* (Toronto: De Boo, 1991), at 57.
[148] *Supra*, note 135, at 675.
[149] *Ibid.*, at 677.

ations that might weigh in favour of the granting of the constructive trust remedy. First, the relief should be made available if "it is appropriate that the plaintiff receive the priority accorded to the holder of a right of property in a bankruptcy".[150] Second, La Forest J. noted that it "is the right of the property holder to have changes in value accrue to his account rather than to the account of the wrongdoer".[151] Accordingly, where this outcome is appropriate, the balance is tilted in the direction of constructive trust. A third factor, which La Forest J. thought weighed in favour of constructive trust and was particularly relevant on the facts of the *Lac* case, is that the defendant in this case "intercepted the plaintiff and thereby frustrated its efforts to obtain a specific and unique property that the courts below held would otherwise have been acquired [by the plaintiff]".[152] Fourth, "[t]he moral quality of the defendants' act may also be another consideration in determining whether a proprietary remedy is appropriate." Fifth, and this was also thought to be particularly important in *Lac* itself, the virtual impossibility of an evaluation may render this form of relief appropriate.[153] Sixth, and this factor was again particularly relevant in *Lac*, the uniqueness of the property in question may suggest that proprietary relief is desirable. Weighing these factors in the context of the facts of *Lac*, La Forest J. concluded that the constructive trust was the most appropriate remedy and therefore should be awarded, whether the defendant's liability arose in breach of confidence or in breach of fiduciary obligation.

Though it is unlikely, of course, that this shopping list of criteria will constitute the last word on the appropriateness or utility of any or all of these criteria, it is undoubtedly the case that Canadian courts will return to this richly suggestive discussion when attempting to determine whether constructive trust relief ought to be awarded. In the recent decision of the Court of Appeal for Ontario, *Ontex Resources Ltd. v. Metalore Resources Ltd.*,[154] for example, on facts somewhat similar to those of *Lac*, the court denied constructive trust relief to the plaintiff on the basis that it had failed to establish that "but for" the breach the opportunity exploited by the defendant would have been exploited by the plaintiff.

A recent decision of the Privy Council is also worthy of notice. *Attorney General for Hong Kong v. Reid*[155] undermines the authority of *Lister*

---

[150] *Ibid.*, at 678.
[151] *Ibid.*
[152] *Ibid.*
[153] *Ibid.*, at 679.
[154] (1993), 13 O.R. (3d) 229, 12 B.L.R. (2d) 226, 103 D.L.R. (4th) 158 (C.A.); leave to appeal to S.C.C. refused 12 B.L.R. (2d) 226*n*.
[155] [1994] 1 All E.R. 1 (P.C.). See Beatson, "Proprietary Claims in the Law of Restitution" (1995), 5 C.B.L.J. 66 and Waters," Proprietary Relief: Two Privy Council Decisions — A Canadian Perspective" (1995), 25 C.B.L.J. 90.

& Co. v. Stubbs,[156] which held that secret commissions or bribes obtained by a disloyal fiduciary could not be impressed with a constructive trust. A bribe could not be considered to be held, it was suggested, on the principal's behalf. In *Reid*, the Privy Council declined to follow *Lister*. The defendant Reid was a New Zealander who served as Crown Counsel in Hong Kong. Mr. Reid was rewarded handsomely and apparently regularly for suppressing prosecutions of certain criminals. He had amassed something in the order of 12.4 million Hong Kong dollars from this unseemly activity. The Attorney General for Hong Kong sought a constructive trust remedy with respect to three properties which the defendant had acquired in New Zealand with his ill-gotten gains. In granting such relief, the Privy Council swept aside the rule in *Lister v. Stubbs* and held that secret commissions and bribes were indeed held by agents on their principals' behalf and were thus amenable to the constructive trust remedy. Though the point is far from uncontroversial, it may well be that in the light of this decision and of the criticism levelled at *Lister v. Stubbs* over the years[157] Canadian courts will follow suit.

(2) Accounting of Profits

The equitable remedy of an accounting of profits[158] is the non-proprietary disgorgement remedy which is available in cases of breach of fiduciary duty or breach of confidence. As has already been indicated, disgorgement remedies are available in these contexts whether or not the plaintiff can establish that "but for" the breach of fiduciary duty or breach of the duty of confidence it would have earned the profits secured through breach by the defendant. The purpose served by the remedy is to provide a disincentive for the wrongful conduct by lifting the profits from the wrongdoing. Although these propositions appear to be well-established features of English law on this point,[159] a recent decision[160] of the Court of Appeal for Ontario appears to suggest that in the context of a claim for breach of confidence, an accounting of profits will be available only

---

[156] (1890), 45 Ch. D. 1 (C.A.).
[157] See, for example, Goff and Jones, *The Law of Restitution*, 2nd ed. (Toronto: Carswell, 1992),at 668-69; Maddaugh and McCamus, *supra*, note 145, at 619-20.
[158] See, generally, Maddaugh and McCamus, *ibid.*, at 103-05.
[159] See, generally, the discussions of fiduciary duty and breach of confidence in the texts referred to, *supra*, notes 3, 4 and 6.
[160] *Ontex Resources Ltd. v. Metalore Resources Ltd.*, *supra*, note 154, for discussion of which, see Smith, "Breach of Confidence — Constructive Trusts — Punitive Damages — Disgorgement of The Profits of Wrongdoing: *Ontex Resources Ltd. v. Metalore Resources Ltd.*" (1994), 73 Can. Bar Rev. 259.

if it can be shown that the plaintiff has suffered a loss in a sense that the opportunity exploited by the defendant is one that otherwise would have been taken up by the plaintiff. This point requires further exploration.

In brief, the facts of *Ontex Resources Ltd. v. Metalore Resources Ltd.* were the following. The plaintiff Ontex (or rather, a predecessor company) entered into an agreement in 1981 with the defendant Metalore under which the latter was to undertake certain exploration work in return for a share of the plaintiff's mining claims. The agreement imposed an obligation on Metalore to provide the plaintiff with information concerning the results of this drilling programme. The defendant deliberately and knowingly withheld such information and, having so misled the plaintiff, entered into a 1983 agreement which had the effect of reducing the plaintiff's interest in the claims. The defendant then acquired an additional 478 claims on neighbouring properties.

At trial, it was held that the conduct of the defendant provided a basis for setting aside the two agreements and, further, that the 478 claims staked by the defendant were held on the plaintiff's behalf on constructive trust. An appeal to the Court of Appeal for Ontario enjoyed success in reversing the award of constructive trust relief. As indicated above, the court concluded that the inability of the plaintiff to establish that "but for" the defendant's breach of confidence the plaintiff would have participated in staking some of the 478 claims rendered constructive trust relief inappropriate. It should be emphasized that the court's discussion is focussed on the question of the appropriateness of constructive trust relief. However, it is also mentioned in passing that "the plaintiff must prove detriment or loss to it flowing from the breach of confidence before it may obtain *any* remedy".[161] Although it may be that the court's attention was not directed, at this point, to the accounting of profits, there is at least a risk that the opinion of the court will be read as if it were a pronouncement on this issue. Such a view would certainly be inconsistent with orthodox principle, and arguably, sound public policy.

A compelling illustration of the proposition that detriment in the intended sense is not a requisite element for the granting of an accounting of profits remedy in breach of confidence cases is found in the decision

---

[161] *Ontex, ibid.*, at 187 D.L.R. (emphasis added). The court drew support from passages from the opinions in *Lac* that might be thought to be consistent with this view. However, as Smith, *ibid.*, points out, this reading appears to arise, in the main, from a confusion of the requirements for constructive trust with the elements of the cause of action in breach of confidence. In any event, the question of the availability of relief in the absence of detriment was not squarely before the Supreme Court in *Lac*, [1989] 2 S.C.R. 574, 36 O.A.C. 57, 69 O.R. (2d) 287n, 44 B.L.R. 1, 26 C.P.R. (3d) 97, 35 E.T.R. 1, 61 D.L.R. (4th) 14, 101 N.R. 239.

of the House of Lords in *Attorney General v. Observer Ltd.*,[162] the "Spycatcher" case. The publisher of the as yet unpublished memoirs of a former member of MI5 had sold serialization rights to a newspaper which then published excerpts from the volume. The breach of confidence involved was not subtle. The defendant newspaper was liable to account for all of the profits it reaped from doing so. Obviously, these are not profits that would have been enjoyed by the plaintiff's employer "but for" the defendant's breach of confidence. Lord Keith of Kinkel observed that the accounting of profits remedy rested on the principle "that no one should be permitted to gain from his own wrongdoing".[163] Further, having found that the publication by the newspaper constituted a misuse of confidential information, his Lordship went on to observe that "it would be naive to suppose that the prospect of financial gain was not one of the reasons why it did so".[164]

It may well be that the accounting will be withheld if the defendant has acted in good faith[165] or that the recovery may be reduced if the profits are attributable not only to the breach of confidence but the efforts and ideas of the defendant as well.[166] In principle, however, the remedy appears to be available whether or not the plaintiff could have exploited, in the same fashion as the defendant, the opportunity to profit from the confidential information.[167]

(3) Money Had and Received

The contemporary lawyer is likely to refer to the *quasi*-contractual claim for money had and received,[168] more simply, as a restitutionary claim for moneys paid by the plaintiff to the defendant in circumstances of unjust enrichment. Typical examples would be the recovery of moneys paid under

---

[162] [1988] 3 W.L.R. 776 (H.L.)

[163] *Ibid.*, at 788.

[164] *Ibid.*

[165] *Seager v. Copydex Ltd. (No. 2)*, [1969] 1 W.L.R. 809. Other remedies, however, may still be available.

[166] *Siddell v. Vickers* (1892), 9 R.P.C. 152 (H.C.J. Ch.D.). And see G.B. Klippert, *Unjust Enrichment* (Toronto: Butterworths, 1983), at 221-23. For discussion of this point in the context of breach of fiduciary duty, see *Warman Int'l Ltd. v. Dwyer* (1995), Aust. L.J.R. 362 at 367-70 (H.Ct.).

[167] Assuming that "harm" in some sense must exist in order to establish the claim, it is not clear why, in *Ontex*, depriving the plaintiff of the opportunity to explore various options for exploiting the valuable information withheld in that case would not meet any such requirement.

[168] See, generally, Maddaugh and McCamus, *The Law of Restitution* (Aurora: Canada Law Book, 1990), at 68-70.

a mistake, under duress or under a transaction which is unenforceable for some reason. These are cases of "unjust enrichment by subtraction". The most interesting remedial developments in the past few years on the substraction side are to be found in some recent English cases which support a broader view of the availability of this type of relief.

In *Lipkin Gorman v. Karpnale Ltd.,*[169] a firm of solicitors brought a claim against a casino owner to recover moneys stolen from the firm by one of its partners. The partner had stolen the money to indulge his habit of gambling at the London Playboy Club. The theory of the claim was that if it could be established that the moneys in the hands of the partner were properly considered to be the property of the firm, the innocent receipt of that money by the casino, provided it had not given good consideration in exchange for the money, would amount to an unjust enrichment. The plaintiff firm was not seeking to trace title to certain monies into the hands of the casino. It was bringing an *in personam* action in money had and received on the theory of unjust enrichment. A claim in conversion was not advanced, presumably on the basis that money received in good faith as currency will not be subject to such a claim.[170]

The claim enjoyed success. In order to succeed it was necessary to show that the rogue partner had gambled with firm moneys. He had acquired the funds by having cheques drawn payable to cash on client accounts at the firm's bank, which he then signed. Although the House of Lords held that the firm had no proprietary interest in any cash at the bank, the bank's indebtedness concerning these accounts constituted choses in action owned by the firm which could be traced into their product, the monies acquired by the rogue partner.[171] With respect to the requirement that it be demonstrated that the casino had not given good consideration for the moneys, the House of Lords held that neither the exchange of the cash for chips to be employed in gambling nor the service provided by the gambling itself constituted good consideration for this purpose. Accordingly, the claim in money had and received was allowed for the net receipt of moneys paid to the defendant's casino by the partner. On these somewhat unusual facts, then, it has been demonstrated once again that the "categories of unjust enrichment are never closed".[172]

The *Lipkin Gorman* decision appears to have provided support for a broader view of the availability of *in personam* restitutionary relief in

---

[169] [1992] 4 All E.R. 512 (H.L.). See, Birks, "The English Recognition of Unjust Enrichment", [1991] L.M.C.L.Q. 473; Burrows, *The Law of Restitution* (London: Butterworths, 1993), c. 4.

[170] *Ibid.*, at 517, *per* Lord Templeman.

[171] For discussion of tracing at common law, see Maddaugh and McCamus, *supra*, note 168, c. 6.

[172] Paraphrasing Morden J., as he then was, in *James More & Sons Ltd. v. University of Ottawa* (1974), 49 D.L.R. (3d) 666 (Ont. H.C.J.) at 676.

English restitutionary law. Evidence of this may be drawn from recent decisions concerning the recovery of moneys paid by banks under interest rate swap agreements with local authorities. Many banks and local authorities who had entered into such agreements were disappointed ultimately to learn that it was the view of the House of Lords that such agreements were *ultra vires* the local authorities.[173] In the wake of that decision, a series of restitutionary claims to recover moneys paid under these void agreements have been litigated. Claims in money had and received against the local authorities have enjoyed success[174] as have claims against banks in cases where the local authorities had paid more than they had received.[175] Indeed, in the case of a claim brought by a bank against a local authority,[176] the Court of Appeal held that the money was not merely recoverable in money had and received on the basis of unjust enrichment. As the purpose for which the moneys had been paid had wholly failed, it was said, the money was held by the local authority in a fiduciary capacity. For this reason it was appropriate that the award should be coupled with an award of interest. Further, the evidence demonstrated that if the defendant authority had not been paid under the swap agreement, it would not have reduced its expenditures. Rather, it would have borrowed the necessary moneys. Accordingly, it was the Court of Appeal's view that an award of compound interest from the date on which the money was first received was appropriate. The local authority was liable for the expense saved in this fashion, even though it might well have been the case that the bank had protected itself by laying off its risk in collateral agreements with other third parties. We may assume that the bank's initial disappointment upon learning of the *ultra vires* problem has been somewhat assuaged.

---

[173] *Hazell v. Hammersmith & Fulham London Borough Council,* [1992] 2 A.C. 1 (H.L.).

[174] See, for example, *Kleinwort Benson Ltd. v. South Tyneside Metropolitan Borough Council,* [1994] 4 All E.R. 972 (Q.B.); *Barclays Bank plc v. Glasgow City Council,* [1994] 4 All E.R. 865 (Q.B.). See also, *Morgan Grenfell & Co. Ltd. v. Welwyn Hatfield District Council (Islington),* [1995] 1 All E.R. 1 (Q.B.). For an analysis supporting this result on the basis of Canadian materials, see Maddaugh and McCamus, *supra,* note 168, at 322-33.

[175] See, for example, *South Tyneside Metropolitan Borough Council v. Svenska Int'l plc.,* [1995] 1 All E.R. 545 (Q.B.). And see, Maddaugh and McCamus, *ibid.,* at 333-37.

[176] *Kleinwort Benson Ltd.,* *supra,* note 174.

8. *Conclusion*

Although the two fields under review both appear to yield recent developments of some interest and importance, there are some interesting differences between them. More particularly, it is of interest to compare the two contexts as sites for doctrinal modification or reform. Reading these two bodies of recent cases, one gains the impression that reform of the law of restitution appears to have reached a greater level of maturity and stability than is manifest in the dynamics of reform at work in the field of equitable compensation. Restitutionary reform has been underway in North America for many decades. It is of particular interest that in recent years, the level of interest in and the pace of reform of restitutionary doctrine appear to have increased in both England and Australia.[177] The Canadian lawyer who wishes to keep abreast of recent developments in the law of restitution must now pay ever more careful attention to the developments in these jurisdictions. The basic principles and the new framework of analysis appear to enjoy a widely held consensus. The work of modification and reform of doctrine appears to be essentially of the anomaly-fixing variety.

Equitable compensation, on the other hand, appears to be a much less well defined body of remedial law. No doubt, this results from the fact that the recent Canadian cases have opened up an interesting range of possibilities. In this paper, I have attempted to outline some of the difficulties inherent in an expansive approach to equitable compensation, as well as some useful contributions that could be made by the doctrine. While the Supreme Court's recent discussions of equitable compensation appear to have introduced a degree of instability into the analysis of remedial issues, it must be remembered that, *Guerin* apart, a majority of the court in each of the leading cases has adopted the view that the result achieved was not dependent on resort to equitable compensation doctrine. At this stage, then, it remains unclear whether equitable compensation for breach of fiduciary duty and other equitable wrongs will evolve into a powerful new remedial weapon, or, indeed, runs the risk of becoming a doctrinal loose cannon.

---

[177] See, generally, Dickson, "Unjust Enrichment Claims: a Comparative Overview" (1995), 54 Cambridge L.J. 100.

ADMINISTRATIVE REMEDIES: TRIBUNAL CREATIVITY AND JUDICIAL CONTROL

Jeffrey G. Cowan
Terry D. Hancock*

1. Introduction

Almost 15 years ago, when the topic of "Remedies in Administrative Law "was discussed in the Law Society's Special Lecture Series, a distinguished professor of administrative law focused his paper upon a perceptive analysis of important recent developments in the law of judicial review of administrative action, particularly because his audience was composed of lawyers.[1] He eschewed a technical discussion of "the procedural and adjectival aspects" of judicial remedies, and devoted his considerable analytical talents to the substantive considerations that underlay what, given the previous state of administrative law in Canada, were the "landmark" decisions of the Supreme Court of Canada in *Nicholson v. Haldimand-Norfolk Regional Board of Com'rs of Police*[2] and *C.U.P.E., Local 963 v. New Brunswick Liquor Corp.*,[3] and their subsequent application by lower courts.

Professor Evans' chosen topic of necessity limited the scope of his paper, and he acknowledged "the practical importance of other remedies, such as appeal and review by administrative agencies and by the Cabinet, and resort to the political process, the Ombudsman, and the media".[4] He recognized that "administrative law" is not restricted to judge-made law, but encompasses the more comprehensive "law about the administration"

---

* Weir & Foulds, Toronto.
[1] Evans, "Remedies in Administrative Law", Special Lectures of the Law Society of Upper Canada *New Developments in Administrative Law* (Don Mills: Richard De Boo, 1981), at 429.
[2] [1979] 1 S.C.R. 311, 78 CLLC 14,181, 88 D.L.R. (3d) 671, 23 N.R. 410 (hereinafter *Nicholson*).
[3] [1979] 2 S.C.R. 227, 25 N.B.R. (2d) 237, 97 D.L.R. (3d) 417, 26 N.R. 341 (hereinafter *C.U.P.E.*).
[4] Evans, *supra*, note 1, at 430.

which included also the issues of "institutional design and composition, the relationship between one organ of government and another, the procedures followed by administrative agencies, and the width and variety of the powers and duties with which they are entrusted".[5]

Slightly more than ten years later, the 1992 Special Lectures on Administrative Law covered many of these latter topics, reflecting the growth of government and academic investigation and scrutiny of the structure and accountability of administrative tribunals, the methods, process and content of administrative decision-making, and the impact of the *Canadian Charter of Rights and Freedoms* (*Charter of Rights*) on these entities.[6] From the practitioner's perspective, this reflected the growing recognition that the vast bulk of administrative law is practised in conjunction with or before government officials, administrative tribunals, and politicians. Relatively few cases proceed to the courts by judicial review, and in the latter, in theory at least, on matters of jurisdiction that warrant intervention. Tribunal members now have their own general professional organizations such as the the Council of Canadian Administrative Tribunals ("CCAT") and the Society of Ontario Adjudicators and Regulators ("SOAR"), as well as specialized organizations,[7] with the objective, among others, of improving the quality of administrative process and decision-making.[8] From a pragmatic viewpoint this is necessary to earn from the courts what, to us, is their due arising from their nature, purpose and function: namely, respect for the integrity, autonomy and relative independence of their decision-making. Finally, appointments to the courts of experienced tribunal members, administrative law academics and practitioners, two of whom, the Honourable Justices Adams and Laskin, are co-panelists, assist the judiciary as an institution in understanding and respecting the composition and workings of the administrative justice system.

---

[5] *Ibid.*, at 429.

[6] Special Lectures of the Law Society of Upper Canada, *Administrative Law: Principles, Practice and Pluralism* (Scarborough; Carswell, 1992). The paper by Margot Priest, "Structure and Accountability of Administrative Agencies", *ibid.*, at 11, comprises a useful review of the many and varied studies and reports on administrative law and tribunals. Scholarship in administrative law as a general topic has been assisted in the last 15 years by new report series (*e.g.*, Administrative Law Reports, with comments and articles), specialized periodicals (*e.g.*, Canadian Journal of Administrative Law & Practice, Reid's Administrative Law and the Supreme Court Law Review with its annual Developments in Administrative Law) and by the (thankfully) continuing prolificy of leading administrative law scholars, such as Professors Evans, Janisch, MacLauchlan and Mullan, to name but four (alphabetically).

[7] Priest, *ibid.*, at 46.

[8] See the views of the Honourable Madame Justice Abella in "Canadian Administrative Tribunals: Towards Judicialization or Dejudicialization?", [1988] 2 C.J.A.L.P. 1, and "The Independence of Administrative Tribunals", [1992] 26 L. Soc. Gaz.113.

Optimists will suggest that these developments reflect progress away from the restricted, unitary "rule of law" model of administrative law so favoured by Dicey 100 years ago,[9] adopted by Chief Justice McRuer in his Report of the Royal Commission Inquiry into Civil Rights in 1968, and embedded both before and since in our jurisprudence, towards an "authentic, indigenous", functional and pluralistic model of administrative law articulated by Professors Willis and Arthurs, among others.[10] Madame Justice Wilson of the Supreme Court of Canada expressed this general feeling in *Nat'l Corn Growers Ass'n v. Canadian Import Tribunal* when she wrote:

> Canadian courts have struggled over time to move away from the picture that Dicey painted toward a more sophisticated understanding of the role of administrative tribunals in the modern Canadian state.[11]

Pessimists will argue that the Dicean rule of law ideology still prevails, creating ongoing contradictions in the law of judicial review despite protestations of a new era of curial deference. They posit that such deference is, upon analysis, one of "submissive" deference to a positivist view of prior legislative intent, of which only the courts are the true interpreters, and not deference as respect for the functional legitimacy of administrative tribunals' decisions.[12]

---

[9] Dicey, *The Law of the Constitution* (London: MacMillan, 1885).

[10] See Willis, "Three Approaches to Administrative Law: The Judicial, The Conceptual and the Functional" (1935), 1 U.T.L.J. 53; "Administrative Law in Canada" (1961), 39 C.B.R. 251, "The McRuer Report: Lawyers Values and Civil Servants' Values" (1969), 18 U.T.L.J. 351, "Canadian Administrative Law in Retrospect" (1974), 24 U.T.L.J. 225, and Arthurs, "Rethinking Administrative Law: A Slightly Dicey Business" (1979), 17 O.H.L.J. 1, and *Without the Law Administrative Justice and Legal Pluralism in Nineteenth Century England* (Toronto: University of Toronto Press, 1985). See also Craig, *Administrative Law*, 2nd ed. (London: Sweet & Maxwell, 1989) at 4-17. For a concise and simple description of these two competing concepts, see Macaulay, *Directions: Review of Ontario's Regulatory Agencies* (Toronto: Ontario Queen's Printer, 1988), at 4-3 to 4-12.

[11] [1990] 2 S.C.R. 1324 at 1366, 74 D.L.R. (4th) 449, 114 N.R. 81 (hereinafter *Nat'l Corn Grower's Ass'n*). See generally her comments in this regard at 1332-35.

[12] See particularly the two articles by Dyzenhaus, "Developments in Administrative Law: The 1991-92 Term" (1993), 4 Supreme Court L.R. (2d), and "Developments in Administrative Law: The 1992-93 Term" (1994), 5 Supreme Court L.R. 189. Such pessimism on this subject is not new. See Willis, "Canadian Administrative Law in Retrospect", *supra*, note 10, at 244 . For a similar but slightly more optimistic view see also Evans, "Judicial Review in the Supreme Court: Realism, Romance and Recidivism" (1991), 48 Admin. L.R. 255 at 272-73.

Within this context of the ongoing debate over curial deference, and consistent with the general theme of "Remedies" in this year's Special Lectures, we propose to review the approach the courts have taken towards the remedies that administrative tribunals themselves provide, as contrasted with the judicial remedies dispensed by the courts. Stated succinctly, we believe that the theory of jurisdiction, upon which the concept of judicial deference to the substance or merits of administrative decision-making is based, results in a lack of appropriate deference to the remedial powers of tribunals.

We suggest that for the tribunal member and for many practitioners, the comments of the Honourable Mr. Justice D.G. Blair of the Court of Appeal for Ontario in 1992 still hold true in 1995. They carry the authority of a distinguished judge with an appreciation of and experience in administrative law, and who had in 1985 written the judgment of that court[13] which wholeheartedly embraced the notion of curial deference in the face of a privative clause:

> I remain convinced now, as I was [in 1967], that the courts tend to look at administrative decisions from the wrong end of the telescope in search of technical flaws which might justify overturning administrative decisions rather than from the standpoint of the legislature's purpose in creating the tribunal.[14]

The recent entrenchment of the standard of review of "correctness" as it relates to the extent of administrative remedies, the inconsistency in application of a purposive approach to the interpretation of legislation granting remedial powers, the lack of a jurisdictional basis for tribunal policies and guidelines as a means of structuring administrative remedies, and the essentially static nature of legislation and the legislative process

---

[13] *Re Ontario Public Service Employees Union and Forer* (1985), 12 O.A.C. 1, 52 O.R. (2d) 705, 23 D.L.R. (4th) 97 (C.A.). A privative clause no longer automatically mandates the standard of "patent unreasonableness", just as the absence of one does not necessarily mean that the standard is one of correctness: *United Brotherhood of Carpenters & Joiners of America, Local 579 v. Bradco Construction Ltd.,* [1993] 2 S.C.R. 316 at 334, 106 Nfld. & P.E.I.R. 140, 93 CLLC 14,033, 102 D.L.R. (4th) 402, 153 N.R. 81 (hereinafter *Bradco*); *Dayco (Canada) Ltd. v. C.A.W. — Canada,* [1993] 2 S.C.R. 230 at 268 (hereinafter *Dayco*); *Pezim v. British Columbia (Superintendent of Brokers),* [1994] 2 S.C.R. 557 at 598-99, 92 B.C.L.R. (2d) 145, 14 B.L.R. (2d) 217, 114 D.L.R. (4th) 385, 168 N.R. 321 (hereinafter *Pezim*).

[14] The Honourable Justice Blair, "Comments on Judicial Review of Administrative Action by Federal and Ontario Courts" Special Lectures of the Law Society of Upper Canada, *supra,* note 6, at 439.

have resulted in a hiatus, at least in Ontario.[15] Recent legislative developments, interestingly enough, provide new remedial powers for tribunals
and some insight into how new models for decision-making may avoid,
if not substantially reduce, judicial review, and leave remedies in the hands
of those functionally suited to provide them.

2. *Administrative Remedies: Nature and Rationale*

Given the still general pre-occupation of the legal profession with judicial remedies in administrative law, we were not surprised, in our review
of the literature, that comparatively little analysis of administrative remedies, as a generic topic, was to be found. That which does exist consists
of a limited review of some of the general types of remedies given by
administrative authorities, or a discussion of the extent of specific powers
and court review of the manner of their exercise.[16]

This is not unexpected, given the vast expanse and growing specialization of administrative law, and the resultant focus on its individual component parts by those whose primary engagement is in a particular area
of the field. It is obvious that there are many different types of tribunals,
with varying purposes, functions and powers, so that any attempt to create a taxonomy of administrative remedies would require an exercise of
cataloguing and analysis that is beyond the scope of this paper. There is
no dearth of literature dealing with the particular remedies available to
particular tribunals or in particular fields of administrative law, such as
labour relations, human rights, and securities regulation, to name but a
few.

Any attempt to define, generally, administrative remedies is difficult.
As the administrative tribunals with which this subject is traditionally

---

[15] Again, the scope of this paper (and our resources) limit us to Ontario. Legislative developments within federal jurisdiction or in other provinces we must leave
to others for now.

[16] See Reid, "Remedies Available from Administrative Tribunals"; Sims, "The
Enforcement of Administrative Tribunal Orders", and McCallum, "Reconsideration, Re-hearing and Varying of Decisions in Administrative Law"
(address to the Canadian Bar Association "Protecting and Promoting Your
Clients' Interests in Administrative Proceedings", Ottawa, November 25 and
26, 1994) (unpublished); Laskin, "Enforcement Powers of Administrative Agencies" and Fuerst, "Testimonial Compulsion and the Privilege Against Self
Incrimination" in Special Lectures of the Law Society of Upper Canada, *supra*,
note 6, at 191 and 235. The *McRuer Report* (Toronto: Queen's Printer, 1968)
examined a number of the more "intrusive" powers available to government,
see Vol. I, cc. 27-37, Vol. III. See also Bryden, "Developments in Administrative Law: The 1993-94 Term" (1995), 6 S.C.L.R. (2d) 1 at 37.

associated are creatures of statute, remedies by definition must be equated
with the legislative grant of statutory powers. Like Professor Evans, our
selected topic precludes anything but an observation that remedies in this
field also comprise political process, the media, and other indirect means.[17]
The statutory power to make decisions, the discretion inherent in that exercise, and the processes and procedures leading to that decision are not
what we mean by the term "administrative remedies", although many decisions by administrative tribunals may, in a general sense, be characterized as a form of remedy. For example, the decision by the Ontario
Municipal Board not to grant approval to a zoning by-law to permit
development may provide a remedy to adjacent property owners who
oppose development, just as the grant of an exemption from requirements
under the *Securities Act* provides a remedy to the corporation that wishes
to avoid the expense and other consequences of compliance.

A general remedy in administrative law that follows the judicial model
is the right of an appeal to another administrative body that has the power
to rescind or vary the first decision. As with the courts, rights of appeal
are the creation of statute. What distinguishes administrative authorities
from the superior courts, however, is that the former do not possess the
latter's inherent jurisdiction to review the actions of "inferior" tribunals.
This common law jurisdiction of the superior courts is reinforced by the
constitutional protection afforded to them from legislative attempts to
exclude judicial review.[18]

In an effort to narrow an otherwise immense range of possibilities,
our focus is on the more traditional concept of remedy utilized by the
courts, namely the specific consequential relief granted by the tribunal
as a result of the decision it has reached, in order, to paraphrase the Oxford
English Dictionary, "to put the matter right". This concept of redress
lies at the heart of the remedies sought from and enforced by the courts.[19]
This more limited definition also removes from our review the broad and
varying powers of investigation and compulsion that administrative
authorities are given, and which form part of the resources available to
these entities to fashion the appropriate remedy.[20] The more general and

---

[17] As to the use of indirect or "soft remedies" see Dussault and Borgeat, *Administrative Law: A Treatise*, 2nd ed. (Toronto: Carswell, 1990), at 278-88.

[18] *Que. (A.G.) v. Farrah*, [1978] 2 S.C.R. 638, 86 D.L.R. (3d) 161, 21 N.R. 595;
Crevier v. Que. (A.G.), [1981] 2 S.C.R. 220, 127 D.L.R. (3d) 1, 38 N.R. 541.

[19] See, *e.g.*, Spry, *The Principles of Equitable Remedies*, 4th ed. (Toronto: Carswell, 1990) c. 1; Baker and Langan, *Snell's Equity* (London: Sweet & Maxwell, 1990), at 581 *et seq.*

[20] See, *supra,* note 16. The most recent decision of the Supreme Court of Canada
in this area is *British Columbia (Securities Com'n) v. Branch*,[1995] 2 S.C.R.
3, [1995] 5 W.W.R. 129, 97 C.C.C. (3d) 505, 38 C.R. (4th) 133, 27 C.R.R.
(2d) 189, 123 D.L.R. (4th) 462, 180 N.R. 241 (hereinafter "*Branch*").

broad remedial powers of investigation of the Ombudsman are also excluded.[21]

In general terms the remedies of which we speak might be thought as falling into one of two general categories — substantive or procedural. Substantive remedies is the larger of the two categories. These include grants of monetary awards, whether they be statutory benefits for those in need, compensation for workers injured in the course of their employment or as victims of crime, compensation for breach of legal standards in the collective bargaining system, or for expropriation of proprietary interests, or compensation for breaches of employment standards or human rights legislation. Such a sample is not meant to be exhaustive.

At the risk of over simplification, these remedies are akin to damages at common law, and depending upon the statutory context, may be composed of special, general and punitive damages.[22] Their focus generally is the redistribution of money or money's worth between parties to the decision-making process, with the party responsible for payment being sometimes the government. By contrast, another form of economic "remedy" effected by tribunals is the role they play in setting or approving tariffs or tolls and other similar pricing mechanisms. Here, by reference to the "public interest" money is distributed in a more indirect and sometimes less adversarial process.

Following our analogy with common law remedies, administrative authorities also wield considerable equitable remedial powers equivalent to mandatory orders, specific performance and injunctions granted by the courts. The myriad of possible orders under labour relations, environmental, pay equity, human rights, consumer protection, competition, and economic regulation legislation, again to name but a few, are familiar to anyone involved in administrative law. Included in this general category are the powers of tribunals to initiate and make new orders or to amend or to attach conditions to decisions as a form of relief, particularly in the field of planning and environmental law. In many ways, apart from the process, fact-finding and decision-making of administrative tribunals, these, and the monetary awards discussed above, are the essence of administrative law, certainly from the client's perspective. Knowing they exist, and persuading the tribunal to grant them, are the essential tasks of the lawyer who practises administrative law.

Procedural remedies, on the other hand, are less related to the sub-

---

[21] For the equation of investigation as a remedial power in this context see: *British Columbia Development Corp. v. Friedman*, [1984] 2 S.C.R. 447, [1985] 1 W.W.R. 193, 14 D.L.R. (4th) 129 at 145-46, 55 N.R. 298. For a discussion see Evans, "Developments in Administrative Law: The 1984-85 Term" (1986), 8 Supreme Court L.R. 1 at 7-11.

[22] See Reid, *supra*, note 16, at 1-13.

stantive content as those discussed above, but also give relief to those affected by reason of their relationship to the decision. Obvious examples are costs and interest. Others include enforcement of orders (generally by filing with a court and then utilizing court processes) and review, rehearing and reconsideration powers. Interim orders are another form of procedural remedial power, although they often will be in effect substantive orders in all but their time duration. We exclude from this category, again for time and space reasons, powers relating to the process of investigation, discovery and disclosure of information prior to a decision being made.

Finally, a general *Charter of Rights* remedy is available to those tribunals who meet the tests of jurisdiction over the subject-matter, the parties, and the remedy sought, as set out in the Supreme Court of Canada's trilogy of cases involving the application of s. 24 of the *Charter of Rights*.[23] They have the ability to make a non-binding decision that a provision of their governing legislation is invalid on Charter grounds for the purposes of the matter before them. However, the tribunal is still limited to the remedies that it may provide under its governing legislation. Following the decision of the Supreme Court of Canada in *Schachter v. Canada*,[24] some have suggested it is possible to argue that tribunals with jurisdiction to decide constitutional issues also have the power to provide remedies under s. 52 of the Charter for matters before them, at least to the extent of "reading in" an amendment to the legislation.[25] Others have lamented that the tribunal's remedial jurisdiction is limited by its statutory content and the particular proceeding involved, particularly when the legislative limit "has not been carefully crafted in light of its impact on constitutional interests".[26]

---

[23] *Douglas/Kwantlen Faculty Ass'n v. Douglas College*, [1990] 3 S.C.R. 570, [1991] 1 W.W.R. 643, 52 B.C.L.R. (2d) 68, 91 CLLC 17,002, 2 C.R.R. (2d) 157, 77 D.L.R. (4th) 94, 118 N.R. 340; *Cuddy Chicks Ltd. v. Ontario (Labour Relations Board)*, [1991] 2 S.C.R. 5 at 14, 47 O.A.C. 271, 3 O.R. (3d) 128*n*, 91 CLLC 14,024, 4 C.R.R. (2d) 1, 81 D.L.R. (4th) 121, 122 N.R. 360; *Tétreault-Godoury v. Canada (Employment & Immigration Com'n)*, [1991] 2 S.C.R. 22, 36 C.C.E.L. 117, 91 CLLC 14,023, 4 C.R.R. (2d) 12, 81 D.L.R. (4th) 358, 123 N.R. 1. Many tribunals also have the jurisdiction to determine constitutional questions relating to division of powers issues: *Northern Telecom Canada Ltd. v. Communication Workers of Canada*, [1983] 1 S.C.R. 733 at 741-42, 83 CLLC 14,048, 147 D.L.R. (3d) 1, 48 N.R. 161. See also the articles referred to in Anisman, "Jurisdiction of Administrative Tribunals to Apply the *Canadian Charter of Rights and Freedoms*" in Law Society of Upper Canada Special Lectures 1992, *supra*, note 6, at 100 (note 2).

[24] [1992] 2 S.C.R. 679, 92 CLLC 14,036, 10 C.R.R. (2d) 1, 93 D.L.R. (4th) 1, 139 N.R. 1.

[25] Anisman, *supra*, note 23, at 116-18.

[26] Pilkington, "Legislative Responsibility for the Jurisdiction of Tribunals to Adjudicate Constitutional Rights and Remedies", Law Society of Upper Canada Special Lectures 1992, *supra*, note 6, at 186.

The rationale for the grant of these remedial powers to administrative tribunals mirrors the rationale for the creation of the tribunals themselves. The complexities, statutory context and the polycentric nature of many fields of regulated activity require different processes, expertise, and decision-making skills than those utilized by the courts. Madame Justice Wilson acknowledged in 1990 that the courts as an institution had come to recognize what legislators and the public knew for far longer, and what mandated the creation of tribunals in the first place:

> . . . that [courts] may simply not be as well equipped as administrative tribunals or agencies to deal with issues which Parliament has chosen to regulate through bodies exercising delegated power, e.g. labour relations, telecommunications, financial markets and international economic relations. Careful management of these sectors often requires the use of experts who have accumulated years of experience and a specialized understanding of the activities they supervise.
>
> Courts have also come to accept that they may not be as well qualified as a given agency to provide interpretations of that agency's constitutive statute that make sense given the broad policy context within which that agency must work.[27]

Competence and expertise, and the "principle of specialization of duties"[28] are not the only reasons.[29] The traditional focus of the courts on the rights of parties and their random determination in an individual and retrospective fashion can be contrasted with the "public interest" mandate of many tribunals, and their concomitant need to take initiative on their own motion and deal with matters prospectively or as a matter of ongoing regulation of the same parties or industry. The public interest mandate often will be reinforced by broad remedial powers granted to the tribunal in the relevant legislation.[30]

The constitutional independence of the judiciary and the oft-professed lack of policy-making or legislative powers, at least in non-constitutional matters, is another explanation for the delegation of remedies to administrative tribunals. While tribunal independence and impartiality are

---

[27] *Nat'l Corn Growers Ass'n, supra*, note 11 at 1336, cited by the court in *Domtar Inc. v. Que. (C.A.L.P.)*, [1993] 2 S.C.R. 756 at 800, 49 C.C.E.L. 1, 105 D.L.R. (4th) 385, 154 N.R. 104.

[28] *Bell Canada v. Canada (C.R.T.C.)*, [1989] 1 S.C.R. 1722 at 1745-46, 60 D.L.R. (4th) 682, 97 N.R. 15, cited in *Pezim, supra*, note 13.

[29] For a concise explanation of the difference between tribunals and courts, see Macauley, *supra*, note 10, at c. 3. See also Hogg, *Constitutional Law of Canada*, 3rd ed. (Toronto: Carswell, 1992), at 7-30, and "Judicial Review: How much to We Need?" (1974), 20 McGill L.J. 175.

[30] The public interest mandate of the securities commission played an important role in the Supreme Court of Canada's decision in *Pezim, supra*, note 13 at 592-95 and *Brosseau v. Alta (Securities Com'n)*, [1989] 1 S.C.R. 301 at 314.

protected by the common law rules relating to bias and independence,[31] the statutory "bias" of tribunal structures (investigator, prosecutor and decision-maker all part of the same agency)[32] and the appointment process, the opportunities for review of tribunal decisions and decision-makers by Ministers, Cabinets, Ombudsmen, and Legislative Committees, and their recognized policy making functions[33] or requirement to consider (or to apply) policy directives of government[34] render them more amenable to innovation or the implementation of legislative will than the courts, who not only require legislative amendment to affect their decisions, but also are the final interpreters of the content of that legislation.

In some instances, and subject to the constitutional constraint of s. 96 of the *Constitution Act*,[35] administrative tribunals remove a potentially overwhelming caseload from the courts. For reasons of cost and expeditious processing, the "mass adjudication" of the administrative justice system provides more effective remedies to members of the public than the courts. In other cases the lack of judicial remedial power, an unwillingness of courts to grant a remedy, or the harshness of the common law (social assistance benefits, reinstatement or return to work powers of labour

---

[31] See *Committee for Justice & Liberty v. The NEB*, [1978] 1 S.C.R. 369, 68 D.L.R. (3d) 716, 9 N.R. 115; *Old St. Boniface Residents Ass'n Inc. v. City of Winnipeg*, [1990] 3 S.C.R. 1213, [1991] 2 W.W.R. 145, 69 Man. R. (2d) 134, 2 M.P.L.R. (2d) 217, 75 D.L.R. (4th) 385, 116 N.R. 46; *Save Richmond Farmland Society v. Richmond (Twp.)*, [1990] 3 S.C.R. 1213, [1991] 2 W.W.R. 178, 52 B.C.L.R. (2d) 145, 2 M.P.L.R. (2d) 288, 75 D.L.R. (4th) 425, 116 N.R. 68; *Consolidated Bathurst Packaging Ltd. v. Int'l Woodworkers*, [1990] 1 S.C.R. 282, 38 O.A.C. 321, 73 O.R. (2d) 676n, 90 CLLC 14,007, 68 D.L.R. (4th) 524, 105 N.R. 161; *Nfld. Telephone Co. Ltd. v. Nfld. (Board of Com'rs of Public Utilities)*, [1992] 1 S.C.R. 623, 95 Nfld. & P.E.I.R. 271, 89 D.L.R. (4th) 289, 134 N.R. 241 (hereinafter *Nfld. Telephone Co. Ltd.*); *Tremblay v. Quebec (Com'n des affaires sociales)*, [1992] 1 S.C.R. 952, 90 D.L.R. (4th) 609. For recent cases on institutional bias and independence see *Manning v. Ont. Securities Com'n* (1994), 18 O.R. (3d) 97 (Div. Ct.); affd 23 O.R. (3d) 257 (C.A.); leave to appeal to the Supreme Court of Canada refused August 17,1995 (Lamer C.J.C., LaForest and Major JJ.); and *Canadian Pacific Ltd. v. Matsqui Indian Band*, [1995] 1 S.C.C. 3, 85 F.T.R 79n, 122 D.LR. (4th) 29, 177 N.R. 325 (hereinafter "*Matsqui Indian Band*").

[32] *Brosseau v. Alberta Securities Com'n*, *supra*, note 30; *Re W.D. Latimer Co. and Bray* (1974), 6 O.R. (2d) 129, 52 D.L.R. (3d) 161 (C.A.).

[33] See, *e.g.*, *Capital Cities Com'ns Inc. v. C.R.T.C.*, [1978] 2 S.C.R. 141, 36 C.P.R. (2d) 1, 81 D.L.R. (3d) 609, 18 N.R. 181; *Consolidated Bathurst Packaging Ltd.*, *supra*, note 31; *Pezim*, *supra*, note 13.

[34] See *Planning Act*, R.S.O. 1990, c. P. 13, s. 3 (amended S.O. 1994, c. 23).

[35] *Re Residential Tenancies Act*, [1981] 1 S.C.R. 714, 123 D.L.R. (3d) 554, 37 N.R. 158 not only sets out the three step test determining the limits of s. 96 on the creation of provincial administrative tribunals, it is an example of one such legislative scheme that did not meet the tests. For a summary of the test, see *Massey-Ferguson Industries v. Gov't of Sask.*, [1981] 2 S.C.R. 413 at 429, [1981] 6 W.W.R. 596, 127 D.L.R. (3d) 513, 39 N.R. 308.

arbitrators and tribunals, and workers' compensation benefits, respectively) militate in favour of administrative remedies.

More flexible and informal procedures, more scope for public participation as opposed to observation, more flexible and specialized fact-finding,[36] often aided by less stringent standards of evidence, are additional reasons for providing remedies to administrative tribunals.

These are not all the differences between courts and administrative tribunals, but we believe they are the major ones. They assist in understanding the need to regard the existence and exercise of remedial powers by tribunal from a different perspective than that associated with judicial remedies, even though many of the remedies owe their origin to common law roots fed by the judiciary. It is important to recognize, as the courts have in the past, that the growth of our modern state and the new social, political, economic, cultural and technological issues it has generated

> . . . has necessitated the introduction of new methods for control and vindication of the policies of . . . legislation. It has involved the adaptation to the legislative and administrative regime of remedies that in another more individualistic context had been evolved and are still being exercised by the ordinary Courts.[37]

The courts have understood the need for "flexible and versatile"[38] powers, so that while tribunals strive for uniformity, coherence and stability in their decision-making, they have the necessary means of achieving "maximum regulatory effectiveness".[39] In short, the nature, functions and purposes of the administrative justice system require creativity in the exercise of remedial powers as much or more so than the courts, who themselves have maintained their integrity and acceptance by society by using both legislation and the "open ended" nature of the common law to fashion appropriate remedies. Respect for the integrity and autonomy of administrative remedies is necessary as part of the ongoing judicial and legislative definition of the constitutional relationship between generalist

---

[36] This is emphasized in *Canada (A.G.) v. Mossop*, [1993] 1 S.C.R. 554, 46 C.C.E.L. 1, 93 CLLC 17,006, 13 C.R.R. (2d) D-5, 100 D.L.R. (4th) 658, 149 N.R. 1; *University of British Columbia v. Berg*, [1993] 2 S.C.R. 353, 79 B.C.L.R. (2d) 273, 102 D.L.R. (4th) 665, 152 N.R. 99; *Large v. Stratford (City)* (1994), 16 O.R. (3d) 385, 1 C.C.E.L. (2d) 195, 94 CLLC 17,005, 110 D.L.R. (4th) 435 (C.A.), as it relates to human rights adjudication.

[37] *Tomko v. Nova Scotia (Labour Relations Board)*, [1977] 1 S.C.R. 112 at 123, 14 N.S.R. (2d) 191, 76 CLLC 14,005, 69 D.L.R. (3d) 250, 7 N.R. 317 (hereinafter *Tomko*).

[38] *Bell Canada v. C.R.T.C.*, *supra*, note 28, at 1741.

[39] *Consolidated Bathurst Packaging Ltd. v. Int'l Woodworkers*, *supra*, note 31, at 316 citing Adams, Chairman of the Ontario Labour Relations Board (as he was then).

courts, government and specialized administrative tribunals. The courts, in recent years, have accepted that some aspects of administrative process and decision-making independence do not fully accord with traditional absolute "rule of law" concepts such as "natural justice"[40] or "consistency, equality, and predictability".[41] The extent to which this recognition extends to the existence and scope of remedial powers exercised by administrative tribunals is the subject to which we next turn.

3. *Judicial Review of Administrative Remedies*

(1) Curial Deference: Generally

In Canadian administrative law, the concept of curial or judicial deference is well-known, and much discussed since the decision of the Supreme Court of Canada in *C.U.P.E.*[42] The central question of the application of the "pragmatic and functional" analysis of tribunals' statutory jurisdiction, articulated by Beetz J. in *Union des Employés de Service, Local 298 v. Bibeault*[43] and applied thereafter, has been narrowed down by L'Heureux-Dubé J. to asking "'who should answer this question, the administrative

---

[40] *Ibid.*, at 340.

[41] *Domtar Inc. v. Quebec (C.A.L.P.), supra*, note 27, at 784-801.

[42] In addition to the articles referred to at notes 1, 12, 14 and 21, *supra*, see also Langille, "Developments in Labour Law: The 1981-82 Term" (1983), 5 Sup.Ct.L.R. 225; Mullan, "Developments in Administrative Law: The 1980-81 Term" (1982), 3 Supreme Court L.R. 1; "Developments in Administrative Law: The 1982-83 Term" (1984), 6 Supreme Court L.R. 1 at 17-24; Arthurs, "Protection Against Judicial Review" (1983), R-du B 43-227; Etherington, "Arbitration, Labour Boards and the Courts in the 1980's: Romance Meets Realism" (1989), 68 C.B.R. 405; Evans, "Judicial Review in the Supreme Court: Realism, Romance and Recidivism" (1991), 48 Admin. L.R. 255; Mullan, "Judicial Deference to Executive Decision-Making: Evolving Concepts of Responsibility" (1993), 19 Queen L.J. 137; The Honourable Mr. Justice LaForest, "The Courts and Administrative Tribunals: Standards of Judicial Review of Administrative Action", Law Society of Upper Canada 1992 Special Lectures, *supra*, note 6 at 1; The Honourable Mr. Justice Vancise, "Is Double Breasting Still in Style? Judicial Review Beyond Lester", "Protecting and Promoting Your Clients' Interests in Administrative Proceedings", *supra*, note 16; MacLauchlan, "Reconciling Judicial Review" (1993), 7 C.J.A.L.P.1 (see notes 8 and 12 for additional articles), Busby, "Mapping the Maze: Supreme Court of Canada Jurisprudence on Standards of Judicial Review" (1994), 4 R.A.L. 1. and Jones, "Standards of Judicial Review", Law Society of Upper Canada, *Recent Developments in Administrative Law*, January 17, 1995.

[43] [1988] 2 S.C.R. 1048 at 1088-89, 24 Q.A.C. 244, 35 Admin. L.R. 153, 89 CLLC 14,045, 95 N.R. 161 (hereinafter *Bibeault*).

tribunal or a court of law?' It thus involves determining *who is in the best position to rule on the impugned decisions*".[44]

The courts have felt it necessary to look at the legislators' intent to answer this question. This requires an examination not only of the legislation creating and governing the administrative tribunal, together with any privative or finality clause that exists, but also the purpose of the legislation, the rationale and expertise of the tribunal and its members, and the nature of the issues before the tribunal. As others have pointed out, this reflects a continued adherence to a Dicean rule of law model of jurisdictional control by its insistence on the courts' primary and superior role in ascertaining, in the context of a particular dispute, a prior intention of the government in enacting legislation that was general and flexible enough to cover the wide area of concern and still anticipate changing circumstances.[45]

However, as a result of the most recent decision of the Supreme Court of Canada[46] concerning a CBC radio talk show host, Dale Goldhawk, it is now clear that the first step in the judicial review of an administrative tribunal's decision for error of law is to determine the appropriate standard of review by the application of this pragmatic and functional approach. Of fundamental importance is whether the question of law in issue goes to the jurisdiction of the tribunal involved. While courts must be careful not to brand as jurisdictional that which is doubtfully so, if the question decided by the tribunal is so characterized after the functional analysis has been undertaken, then the standard of review is correctness.[47] Whether a question of law determined by the tribunal is a jurisdictional

---

[44] *Domtar Inc. v. Quebec (C.A.L.P.)*, *supra*, note 27, at 772 (hereinafter *Domtar*) (emphasis in original). For an insightful analysis of this decision see Dyzenhaus, "CUPE's Spirit? Case comment: *Domtar Inc. v. Quebec (Commission d'appel en matiere de lesions professionnelles)*" (1994), 15 Admin. L.R. (2d) 73. For a recent case extending the *Domtar* analysis to the situation where an apparent operational conflict exists between two tribunals, the Canadian Radio-Television and Telecommunications Commission and a federal arbitration board, see *British Columbia Telephone Co. v. Shaw Cable Systems (B.C.) Ltd.*, [1995] S.C.J. 54, 125 D.L.R. (4th) 443.

[45] See Dyzenhaus, "Developments in Administrative Law: The 1991-92 Term" (1993), 4 Supreme Court L.R. (2d).

[46] *Canadian Broadcasting Corp. v. Canada (Labour Relations Board)*, [1995] 1 S.C.R. 157 at 178 -179, 95 CLLC 210-009, 121 D.L.R. (4th) 385, 177 N.R. 1 (hereinafter *Goldhawk*).

[47] See also *Pezim v. British Columbia (Superintendent of Brokers)*, [1994] 2 S.C.R. 557 at 589-90, 92 B.C.L.R. (2d) 145, 14 B.L.R. (2d) 217, 114 D.L.R. (4th) 385, 168 N.R. 321. Although there are five different judgments in *Goldhawk* it appears most if not all proceeded from an acceptance of this basic analysis. Differences arose because of the way the issue (the extent to which political statements of employees made outside the collective bargaining process were governed by the *Canada Labour Code*) was framed and viewed as either "within jurisdiction"

question will depend on whether the legislator intended it to be answered by the tribunal (non-jurisdictional or within jurisdiction) or the courts (jurisdictional).[48] Generally, if the question is a matter within jurisdiction, and provided there is a broad and strongly worded privative clause, its decision is subject to review only against a standard of patent unreasonableness.[49] The court reiterated in *Goldhawk* that the purpose of the patently unreasonable error test it earlier identified in *Domtar* was

> . . . ensuring that review of the correctness of an administrative interpretation does not serve, as it has in the past, as a screen for intervention based on the merits of a given decision. The process by which this standard of review has progressively been accepted by courts of law cannot be separated from the contemporary principle of curial deference, which is, in turn, closely linked with the development of administrative justice.[50]

On the subject of what is meant by "patently unreasonable" the court repeated the judgment of Cory J. in *P.S.A.C. (No. 2)*,[51] namely, "clearly irrational, that is to say evidently not in accordance with reason". Although the majority decision then spoke of not disturbing the tribunal's interpretation if the approach taken is a "reasonable" one and the meaning given is one which the statute "can reasonably bear" (*i.e.*, simple reasonable-

---

(Iacobucci J., (Lamer C.J.C., Cory and Major JJ.) L'Heureux-Dubé J. (Gonthier J.) and McLachlin J.), or not (Sopinka J.). Of those who found the question within jurisdiction, six found the interpretation not patently unreasonable, while McLachlin J. found it was. All of the court, except for McLachlin J., agreed with an alternative basis for upholding the decision which did not engage the debate over the standard of review. This was the sole ground on which LaForest J. supported the result. Other reasons for disagreement are discussed *infra*.

[48] *Supra*, note 46 at 184-85, *per* Iacobucci J., Sopinka J., in a separate opinion, frames the question of intent differently, as one whether "the determination of the matters included within the provision be left to the Board or whether it was a provision intended to limit the jurisdiction of the Board, in respect of which the Board had to be right". This concept of an intent "to limit jurisdiction" requiring the application of the correctness standard comes from his majority opinion in *Canada (A.G.) v. Public Service Alliance of Canada*, [1991] 1 S.C.R. 614, 91 CLLC 14,017, 80 D.L.R. (4th) 520, 123 N.R. 161, which itself is derived from *Syndicat des Employés de Production du Québec et L'Acadie v. Canada Labour Relations Board*, [1984] 2 S.C.R. 412 at 419, 84 CLLC 14,069, 14 D.L.R. (4th) 457, 55 N.R. 321, where, speaking for the court, Beetz J. equated the application of the "correctness" standard to the interpretation of a provision "which confers jurisdiction, that is, one which describes, lists and limits the powers of an administrative tribunal" or which is "intended to circumscribe the authority" of the tribunal.

[49] *Goldhawk, ibid.*, at 178-79.

[50] *Supra*, note 44.

[51] *Canada (A.G.) v. P.S.A.C.*, [1993] 1 S.C.R. 941 at 963-64, 93 CLLC 14,022, 101 D.L.R. (4th) 673, 150 N.R. 161 (hereinafter *P.S.A.C. (No. 2)*).

ness) it concluded later that the decision was arrived at "in a principled manner and was not irrational".[52]

While the *Goldhawk* decision attempts to consolidate and summarize existing jurisprudence of the court, differences in the judgments no doubt will permit more informed analysis and debate to continue. For example, even the "very strict test" of "clearly irrational" is one that still permits differences of opinion, as witnessed by the different conclusion reached by McLachlin J. in dissent, and Iacobucci J. for the majority, over the rationality of the decision. The courts still have not, and perhaps realistically cannot or should not attempt to articulate the more subjective factors that warrant intervention by courts for irrationality.[53] Cynics will suggest the test still permits court intervention when the decision is "wrong", and that, in the future, the Supreme Court will have to admonish others "not to brand as clearly irrational that which is doubtfully so".

Another point on which some members of the court in *Goldhawk* disagreed was the extent to which deference is to be accorded to the tribunal's interpretation of "external" legislation other than its constituting statute, in this case the obligation of the C.B.C. under the *Broadcasting Act*,[54] and its Journalistic Policy on political neutrality, as a means of justification for the actions of the C.B.C. The majority opinion written by Iacobucci J. reviewed the earlier decision of the court in *McLeod v. Egan*,[55] from which the proposition that in such a case the standard is that of correctness is thought to flow.[56] After a review of Ontario case-law on the subject,[57] Iacobucci J. stated:

---

[52] *Goldhawk, supra*, note 46, at 193-96. For a review of the uncertainty of the "definition" of patent unreasonableness in prior decisions of the court, see Evans, *supra*, note 42, 255 at 260-61.

[53] See Evans, *ibid.* The comment of former Mr. Justice Reid in *Re Hughes Boat Works Inc. and U.A.W., Local 1620* (1979), 26 O.R. (2d) 420 at 422, 102 D.L.R. (3d) 661 (Div. Ct.) bears repeating: "I would thus prefer that the subjective nature of the process be acknowledged and what we attempt to state the considerations that should be borne in mind . . . I think we should try to illustrate what will lead a court to interfere or to refrain from interfering with what a tribunal has done or decided notwithstanding a privative clause."

[54] R.S.C. 1985, c. B-9.

[55] [1975] 1 S.C.R. 517, 46 D.L.R. (3d) 150, 2 N.R. 443.

[56] See *Sask. Joint Board, Retail, Wholesale and Department Store Union v. MacDonalds Consolidated Ltd.* (1985), 43 Sask. R. 260 (C.A.); *United Brotherhood of Carpenters & Joiners of America, Local 579 v. Bradco Construction Ltd.*, [1993] 2 S.C.R. 316 at 336, 106 Nfld. & P.E.I.R. 140, 93 CLLC 14,033, 102 D.L.R. (4th) 402, 153 N.R. 81.

[57] *Haldimand-Norfolk Regional Board of Com'rs of Police v. Ont. Nurses' Ass'n* (1990), 41 O.A.C. 148 (C.A.); *Wentworth City Board of Education v. Wentworth Women Teachers' Ass'n* (1991), 35 C.C.E.L. 225, 80 D.L.R. (4th) 558 (Ont. Div. Ct.); and *Ont. Nurses' Ass'n v. Etobicoke General Hospital* (1993), 14 O.R. (3d) 40, 94 CLLC 17,017, 104 D.L.R. (4th) 379 (Div. Ct.).

As a general rule, I accept the proposition that curial deference need not be shown to an administrative tribunal in its interpretation of a general public statute other than its constituting legislation, although I would leave open the possibility that, in cases where the external statute is linked to the tribunal's mandate and is frequently encountered by it, a measure of deference may be appropriate. However, this does not mean that every time an administrative tribunal encounters an external statute in the course of its determination, the decision as a whole becomes open to review on a standard of correctness. If that were the case, it would substantially expand the scope of reviewability of administrative decisions and unjustifiably so. Moreover, it should be noted that the privative clause did not incorporate the error of law grounds. . . . This tends to indicate some level of deference should be provided.

While the Board may have to be correct in an isolated interpretation of external legislation, the standard of review of the decision as a whole, if that decision is otherwise within its jurisdiction, will be one of patent unreasonableness. Of course, the correctness of the interpretation of the external statute may affect the overall reasonableness of the decision. Whether this is the case will depend on the impact of the statutory provision on the outcome of the decision as a whole.

L'Heureux-Dubé J. (Gonthier J. concurring)[58] disagreed with Iacobucci J., only on this point, on the basis that *McLeod v. Egan* was not a case of a decision protected by a broad privative clause. In her view, but without giving reasons, the interpretation of an external statute cannot be characterized as a jurisdictional question, and the fact that the tribunal interpreted such legislation "has absolutely no effect on the appropriate standard of judicial review".[59]

McLachlin J., in dissent, also disagreed with the majority but on another basis. She was critical of the majority's reasoning that applied the functional test to the question of interpretation of external legislation, and concluded the standard was correctness. She stated that Iacobucci J. then effectively ignored this by applying a standard of patent unreasonableness to the conclusion or decision as a whole. This, she felt, downgraded the standard on an important component part and on questions of law outside a tribunal's jurisdiction to the more "global" test of patent unreasonableness. Ironically, she appears to be echoing a concern similar to that raised by Wilson J. in her dissent in *Nat'l Corn Growers Ass'n*[60] (in which McLachlin J. was part of the majority) to the effect that the process of judicial review should end when it was decided that a tribunal's interpretation of its constitutive legislation was not patently unreasonable, and ought not to extend to the general conclusion of the tribunal, including a detailed review of the evidence. A similar tension existed between

---

[58] *Goldhawk, supra,* note 46, at 187-88.
[59] *Ibid.,* at 205.
[60] [1990] 2 S.C.R. 1324 at 1348-49, 74 D.L.R. (4th) 449, 114 N.R. 81.

the majority (for which McLachlin, J. wrote) and minority in *W.W. Lester (1978) Ltd. v. United Ass'n of Journeymen & Apprentices of the Plumbing and Pipefitting Industry, Local 740*[61] over the extent to which the patently unreasonable test permitted intervention where the evidence was not "sufficient" to support the tribunal's conclusion on the application of the statute in question.[62]

In addition, as a matter of logic, she could not contemplate how an incorrect interpretation of external legislation would not make the decision within jurisdiction patently unreasonable. In the circumstances of the case, she could not see how it would be reasonable to determine an employer was guilty of an unfair labour practice under the *Canada Labour Code* if its conduct was justified under the *Broadcasting Act*. If the conclusion was based on a false premise (incorrect interpretation of external statute) it would be "unprincipled and irrational".[63]

Finally, Iacobucci J. reiterated what was the main point to be derived from his decision for the court in *Pezim*, namely, that as a result of the *Bibeault* functional analysis, the court had developed "a spectrum that ranges from the standard of patent unreasonableness at one extreme to that of correctness at the other"[64] when it comes to tribunal decisions made within their jurisdiction. As others have pointed out, the case-law of the Supreme Court that flowed after *Bibeault* introduced "a sliding scale of administrative expertise, and a graduated approach to the effect of the privative clause".[65] The degree of deference is a function of the breadth and strength of the privative clause, the comparative expertise of the tribunal and its members and the courts in general on the issue in question, whether the issue goes to the heart of the tribunal's specialized function and its expertise, including a developed tribunal jurisprudence, the extent of its policy development function and remedial powers to act in the public interest, the larger regulatory context in which the tribunal operates and the nature of the regulated industry, past deference shown to the tribunal by the courts, as well as the legislative intent evidenced by a review of the language, nature, purpose and objectives of the statute conferring authority on the tribunal. On the other hand, a full right of appeal does not necessarily warrant a standard of correctness. In *Pezim*, a review of these factors

---

[61] [1990] 3 S.C.R. 644, 88 Nfld. & P.E.I.R. 15, 91 CLLC 14,002, 76 D.L.R. (4th) 389, 123 N.R. 241 (hereinafter *Lester*).

[62] See Vancise, *supra*, note 42, at 6, who views these two decisions as in effect changing the standard of judicial review to one of appellate review. LaForest J., *supra*, note 42, at 44, however, perceives the majority decision in *Nat'l Corn Growers Ass'n* "a lot like vintage C.U.P.E." and notes that the court in both cases ended up exercising restraint in the result.

[63] *Goldhawk, supra,* note 46, at 221-22.

[64] *Ibid.*, at 178.

[65] MacLauchlan, *supra*, note 42, at 7.

led Iacobucci J. to conclude that the British Columbia Securities Commission was entitled to "considerable deference" in its determination of what constituted a "material change" for purposes of general disclosure under its Act, notwithstanding that there was a statutory right of appeal and no privative clause.[66]

The result of these developments is that despite curial deference, judicial review of administrative tribunal decision-makers will continue to flourish, at least to the extent that the myriad of tribunals that exist must be analyzed utilizing these varying factors and in relation to each different type of power or jurisdiction that they exercise in individual cases. In more general terms, however, we can begin to see the general types of tribunals to whom the most deference will be given (those involving labour relations, telecommunications, ombudsmen, privacy commissioners,[67] international economic relations) as well as those afforded little or none (human rights and labour adjudicators not protected by full privative clauses, and social assistance tribunals).[68]

In this context, then, how have the courts treated the extent and exercise of remedial powers of administrative tribunals?

(2) Curial Deference and Administrative Remedies

(a) *Generally*

Before we proceed to examine how the theory of jurisdiction has been applied by the court to the remedial powers of administrative tribunals, it is useful to provide a more general context by way of background. In this regard, curial deference is not restricted simply to interpretation by tribunals of questions of law within their jurisdiction. It may also be said to apply to the institutional setting of the tribunals as a matter of federal-provincial constitutional law, in the case-law dealing with the prematurity

---

[66] *Pezim, supra*, note 47, at 598-99. The court's analysis has been characterized as "judicial deference with a vengeance". See Corley and Disney, "Developments in Corporate and Commercial Law: The 1993-94 Term" (1995), 6 S.C.L.R. (2d) 127 at 174.

[67] See *John Doe v. Ont. (Information & Privacy Com'r)* (1993), 13 O.R. (3d) 767 at 776-83, 106 D.L.R. (4th) 140 (Div. Ct.). (Standard is patent unreasonableness where no privative clause or right of appeal.).

[68] See *Wedekind v. Ont. (Ministry of Community & Social Services)* (1994), 21 O.R. (3d) 289 at 293-8, 303, 7 C.C.E.L. (2d) 161, 121 D.L.R. (4th) 1 (C.A.); application for leave to appeal to the Supreme Court of Canada dismissed June 1, 1995 (Lamer C.J.C., Gonthier and Iacobucci JJ.) (standard of correctness on appeal from Social Assistance Review Board).

of judicial review and the availability of alternative remedies, and in the courts' approach to some common law remedies. In general terms, deference is provided to the remedial nature of the tribunal system. However, as we explain later, deference is not accorded as a standard of review to the specific determination of the existence of a remedial power by an individual tribunal.

This general deference is found, in a constitutional sense, in the jurisprudence surrounding s. 96 of the *Constitution Act, 1867*, and the creation of provincial administrative tribunals that provide remedies of a "judicial" nature that broadly conformed to the powers of the superior courts in 1867. Assuming that the first two tests of the tripartite analysis in *Re Residential Tenancies Act of Ontario*[69] have been met (area within exclusive jurisdiction of s. 96 courts at Confederation, judicial power being exercised), the final step is to determine if the modern "institutional setting" in which the power is exercised is such that its character cannot be said to be one that only the courts may exercise.[70] Stated simply, the courts have recognized and accepted that administrative remedies which are a "necessarily incidental aspect of the broader social policy goal"[71] of valid provincial legislation are not within the exclusive jurisdiction of the s. 96 courts. This constitutional analysis also takes into account that tribunals do not necessarily approach the grant of a remedy in the same fashion as a court, given, for example, and depending on the tribunal, their powers of investigation, their public interest mandate, and their ability to supervise the parties conduct prospectively, all of which differentiate them from the judiciary.[72]

Deference is also accorded, in the general sense, when courts are faced with applications for judicial review prior to the final conclusion of the

---

[69] [1981] 1 S.C.R. 174, 123 D.L.R. (3d) 554, 37 N.R. 158 (powers to evict tenants and to order compliance with rent control legislation ruled unconstitutional).

[70] *Tomko v. Nova Scotia (Labour Relations Board)*, [1977] 1 S.C.R. 112 at 120, 14 N.S.R. (2d) 191, 76 CLLC 14,005, 69 D.L.R. (3d) 250, 7 N.R. 317. See also Hogg, *Constitutional Law of Canada*, 3rd ed. (Toronto: Carswell, 1992), at 7-30 to 7-36.

[71] *Sobey's Stores Ltd. v. Yeoman*, [1989] 1 S.C.R. 238 at 282, 90 N.S.R. (2d) 271, 25 C.C.E.L. 169, 89 CLLC 14,017, 57 D.L.R. (4th) 1, 92 N.R. 179 (reinstatement power).

[72] These factors were part of the analysis in *Tomko, supra*, note 70, (cease and desist orders). See also *Labour Relations Board of Sask. v. John East Iron Works Ltd.*, [1949] A.C. 134 (reinstatement and compensation); *Int'l Brotherhood of Electrical Workers v. Winnipeg Builders Exchange*, [1967] S.C.R. 628 (injunctions relating to illegal strikes); *Massey-Ferguson Industries v. Sask.*, [1981] 2 S.C.R. 413, [1981] 6 W.W.R. 596, 127 D.L.R. (3d) 513, 39 N.R. 308 (compensation awards in public insurance scheme); *Chrysler Canada Ltd. v. Canada (Competition Tribunal)*, [1992] 2 S.C.R. 394, 7 B.L.R. (2d) 1, 42 C.P.R. (3d) 353, 92 D.L.R. (4th) 609, 138 N.R. 321 (hereinafter *Chrysler*) (enforcement of orders by punishment for contempt).

administrative process, including appeals to "higher" administrative tribunals. This is provided by the related doctrines of prematurity and adequate alternative remedy. Taken together, they combine to produce the following proposition: where the factual record is not complete, and a remedy is potentially available within the ongoing process or by further appeal within the administrative tribunal system, the court generally will decline to intervene, absent special circumstances.[73]

In many cases, this doctrine is applied for reasons that relate to the court's institutional convenience (caseload, possible mootness), the need to avoid fragmented proceedings, and to ensure a court has a complete factual record.[74] In the constitutional context, this is consistent with the court's desire not to rule on constitutional issues where it is not necessary or without the proper factual basis.[75] In other cases, however, the courts recognize that deference is mandated by the comparative expertise and competency of the tribunal, the public interest they represent, and the desire to facilitate autonomy and integrity of decision-making by letting mistakes be corrected within the "internal" appeal system of a particular institution.[76] In the slightly different context of interlocutory injunctions, the

---

[73] Doane, "Judicial Review and the Doctrine of Prematurity" (1995), 1 Reg. Boards and Admin. Law Litigation 65 at 65-66. See also Giles, "Should there be Judicial Review Where There is an Adequate Right of Appeal" (1983), 43 C.B.R. 497. For its application in the context of Charter issues, see Anisman, "Jurisdiction of Administrative Tribunals to Apply the *Canadian Charter of Rights and Freedoms*", Law Society of Upper Canada Special Lectures, 1992, at 122-24; Lepofsky, "Litigating Charter Claims Before Administrative Tribunals — Practice and Procedural Considerations", Special Lectures of the Law Society of Upper Canada *Administrative Law: Principles, Practice and Pluralism* (Scarborough: Carswell, 1992), at 161.

[74] See *University of Toronto v. Canadian Union of Education Workers, Local 2* (1988), 65 O.R. (2d) 268 at 269, 272, 52 D.L.R. (4th) 128 (Div. Ct.); *Great Atlantic & Pacific Co. of Canada Ltd. v. Ont. (Ministry of Citizenship)* (1993), 62 O.A.C. 1 at 8; *Prousky v. Law Society of Upper Canada* (1987), 61 O.R. (2d) 37, 41 D.L.R. (4th) 565 (Div. Ct.); *Haber v. Wellesley Hospital* (1988), 24 O.A.C. 239, 62 O.R. (2d) 756, 46 D.L.R. (4th) 575 (C.A.); *Canada (D.N.D.) v. Ontario (W.C.B.)* (1992), 8 Admin. L.R. (2d) 122 (Div. Ct.); *Ressel v. Board of Directors of Chiropractic (Ont.)* (1990), 41 O.A.C. 321, 4 C.R.R. (2d) D-4 (Div. Ct.); *Latif v. Ont. (Hospital Resources Com'n)* (1993), 11 O.R. (3d) 798 (Div. Ct.), as well as other cases cited by Doane, *supra*, note 73.

[75] See *Northern Telecom Ltd. v. Communication Workers of Canada*, [1980] 1 S.C.R. 115, 79 CLLC 14,211, 98 D.L.R. (3d) 1, 28 N.R. 107; *Law Society of Upper Canada v. Skapinker*, [1984] 1 S.C.R. 357, 3 O.A.C. 321, 11 C.C.C. (3d) 481, 8 C.R.R. 193, 9 D.L.R. (4th) 161, 53 N.R. 169; *Tremblay v. Daigle*, [1989] 2 S.C.R. 550, 27 Q.A.C. 81, 62 D.L.R. (4th) 634, 102 N.R. 81; *Danson v. Ont. (A.G.)*, [1990] 2 S.C.R. 1086, 41 O.A.C. 250, 74 O.R. (2d) 763n, 43 C.P.C. (2d) 165, 73 D.L.R. (4th) 686, 112 N.R. 362.

[76] See *Harelkin v. University of Regina*, [1979] 2 S.C.R. 561, [1979] 3 W.W.R. 676, 96 D.L.R. (3d) 14, 26 N.R. 364 (hereinafter *Harelkin*); *Federation of Women*

courts have deferred to the expertise and remedial flexibility of the Ontario Securities Commission as a better forum for the determination of corporate affairs.[77] In the Charter cases, the courts have also expressed a desire to obtain the tribunal's expert views on the issues, particularly as they relate to "reasonable limits" under s. 1 of the Charter. However, the doctrine is not absolute. There will be cases when the convenience or prejudice of the parties outweigh the advantages of judicial restraint, or the lack of resources and time available to the tribunal, the attempt by a tribunal to cloak itself with authority that is not conferred by statute, or the possibility that the integrity of the process could be "irrevocably compromised" will result in the court intervening before the end of the administrative decision-making process.[78]

As Martin Doane points out, this doctrine focuses attention on the competing demands of the autonomy and independence of administrative decision-making and the conceptual basis of contemporary judicial review, with the primacy it affords to procedural fairness and jurisdictional questions of law.[79] This tension arises out of the decision of the Supreme Court of Canada in *Harelkin*, and is reflected in the recent decisions of the Ontario Court of Appeal in *Howe v. Institute of Chartered Accountants of Ontario*[80] and the Supreme Court of Canada in *Canadian Pacific Ltd. v. Matsqui Indian Band*.[81]

In *Harelkin*, the majority of the court declined to exercise its discretion to quash the revocation of a student's enrollment made in violation of the rules of natural justice (committee hearing held in student's absence, without notice), because a further internal appeal to the university senate was available. Beetz J. felt the error was not of a jurisdictional nature that rendered the decision void, and that absent "exceptional circumstances", the availability of an adequate alternative remedy required the

---

Teachers' Ass'n of Ontario v. Ont. (H.R.C.) (1968), 67 O.R. (2d) 493 (Div. Ct.).

[77] See *First City Financial Corp. v. Genstar* (1981), 33 O.R. (2d) 631, 15 B.L.R. 60, 125 D.L.R. (3d) 303 (H.C.J.); *Corona Minerals Corp. v. C.S.A. Management Ltd.* (1989), 68 O.R. (2d) 425 (H.C.J.). Contrast *Bell Telephone of Canada Ltd. v. Harding Communications Ltd.*, [1979] 1 S.C.R. 395 (court injunction where regulatory agency appeared to have primary jurisdiction).

[78] See *Great Atlantic & Pacific Co. v. Ontario (Human Rights Com'n)* (1993), 13 O.R. (3d) 824 at 828, 93 CLLC 17,017, 109 D.L.R. (4th) 214 (Div. Ct.); *People First of Ontario v. Ontario (Niagara Regional Coroner)* (1992), 6 O.R. (3d) 289, 87 D.L.R. (4th) 765 (C.A.); *Algonquin Mercantile Corp. v. Enfield Corp.* (1990), 74 O.R. (2d) 457 (H.C.J.); *Chalmers v. Toronto Stock Exchange* (1989), 70 O.R. (2d) 532 (C.A.); Doane, *supra*, note 73, at 66-67 and cases cited therein at note 10.

[79] Doane, *ibid.*, at 66.

[80] (1994), 19 O.R. (3d) 483, 118 D.L.R. (4th) 129 (C.A.); leave to appeal refused 21 O.R. (3d) xvi (S.C.C.) (hereinafter *Howe*).

[81] [1995] 1 S.C.R. 3, 85 F.T.R. 79n, 122 D.L.R. (4th) 129, 177 N.R. 325.

court to exercise its discretion to refuse intervention. Dickson J., for the minority, felt there was no discretion available in the face of a jurisdictional error, which included a denial of natural justice "in all but the rarest of cases".[82]

In *Howe*, at issue was the refusal by the Discipline Committee of a professional self-governing body to order disclosure of an investigator's report to a member prior to a hearing into allegations of professional misconduct by the member based on the report. There was a right to appeal by way of new hearing to an Appeal Committee from the final decision of the Discipline Committee. The majority of the court upheld the Divisional Court's dismissal of an application of judicial review on the basis of prematurity in the face of an adequate alternative remedy. Three factors formed the basis of the decision. First, the matter arose from an interlocutory order made within jurisdiction and the full Discipline Committee could later require disclosure at the hearing.[83] Second, there was a right to a new full hearing on appeal. Third, given the point in the disciplinary process, the court could not measure the adequacy of disclosure to date against the report, so as to determine if there had been a denial of natural justice.

In his dissent, Laskin J. reiterated the validity of the dissent in *Harelkin*, namely, that a jurisdictional error did not permit application of the prematurity principle, except in exceptional cases. He felt that the majority decision in *Harelkin*, resting as it did on equivocal language that suggested a denial of natural justice did not go to jurisdiction, had, in effect, been seriously weakened by subsequent Supreme Court decisions that clearly treat denial of natural justice as jurisdictional error.[84] As it related to the timing issue, and the availability of a later appeal, he was of the opinion that "disclosure issues should be determined sooner rather

---

[82] *Supra*, note 76, at 593, 604, 610-11. For a recent case where such exceptional circumstances were found to exist (tribunal result guaranteed in law despite breach of fairness) see *Mobil Oil Canada Ltd. v. Canada-Newfoundland Offshore Petroleum Board)*, [1994] 1 S.C.R. 202, 115 Nfld. & P.E.I.R. 334, 21 Admin. L.R. 248, 111 D.L.R. (4th) 1, 163 N.R. 27.

[83] The non-binding nature of pre-hearing determinations was recently emphasized by the Divisional Court in *Oro (Twp.) v. BAFMA Inc.* (1995), 21 O.R. (3d) 483, 25 M.P.L.R. (2d) 258, 121 D.L.R. (4th) 538.

[84] *Howe, supra*, note 80, at 505-06, citing *Cardinal v. Director of Kent Institution*, [1985] 2 S.C.R. 643, [1986] 1 W.W.R. 577, 69 B.C.L.R. 255, 23 C.C.C. (3d) 118, 49 C.R. (3d) 35, 24 D.L.R. (4th) 44, 63 N.R. 353 and *Universite du Québec à Trois-Rivieres v. Larocque*, [1993] 1 S.C.R. 471, 93 CLLC 14,020, 101 D.L.R. (4th) 494, 148 N.R. 209. See also *Re Alta. Union of Provincial Employees and Olds College Board of Governors*, [1982] 1 S.C.R. 923, 21 Alta. L.R. (2d) 104, 136 D.L.R. (3d) 1, 42 N.R. 559 and *Nfld. Telephone Co. Ltd. v. Nfld. (Board of Com'rs of Public Utilities)*, [1992] 1 S.C.R. 623 at 645, 95 Nfld. & P.E.I.R. 271, 89 D.L.R. (4th) 289, 134 N.R. 241.

than later" thereby avoiding "a lengthy and costly public hearing that is flawed at the outset when this court can correct the flaw now".[85]

Laskin J.'s reasoning that court intervention was warranted for jurisdictional error is based on his determination that the extent of the disclosure provided ("will say" statements of witnesses, documents to be relied up, and experts' reports) was a denial of procedural justice, placing emphasis on the need of a professional to have a proper defence to a disciplinary prosecution, and because of the importance placed on full and complete disclosure by the Supreme Court of Canada in *R. v. Stinchcombe*.[86]

Mr. Justice Laskin's position that the prematurity doctrine does not apply in the case of jurisdictional error is addressed, but not conclusively answered, in *Matsqui Indian Band*. The Supreme Court of Canada was faced with an appeal originating from a Federal Court judge's decision on a motion to strike Canadian Pacific's application for judicial review of a notice of assessment issued to it by the Band. The assessment was of its roadway that ran through the Band reserve and which it apparently owned in fee simple for some time. The Band had passed by-laws under the *Indian Act* setting up assessment tribunals, with a right of appeal to the Federal Court. The motions judge struck the application for judicial review, which sought a determination that the roadway was not "within the reserve", on the basis that the assessment tribunal system provided an adequate alternative remedy. The Federal Court of Appeal allowed an appeal and dismissed the application to strike. The Supreme Court of Canada, viewing the case as a review of the discretion of the motion judge, dismissed the appeal from the Federal Court of Appeal.

Canadian Pacific took the position that the question of whether its lands were "within the reserve", and therefore properly assessed, was a jurisdictional question. In addition, it questioned the institutional independence and impartiality of the assessment tribunals, as Band members, with an indirect financial interest in Band revenues, sat on the tribunals. Chief Justice Lamer (Cory J. concurring), applying the functional approach to jurisdiction of *Bibeault*, decided that the question of whether railway lands were "within the reserve" was a jurisdictional question which the assessment tribunals could determine, but was subject to a standard of review of correctness. Although he felt the doctrine of adequate alter-

---

[85] *Howe, ibid.*, at 506.

[86] [1991] 3 S.C.R. 326, 83 Alta. L.R. (2d) 193, 68 C.C.C. (3d) 1, 8 C.R. (4th) 277, 18 C.R.R. (2d) 210, 130 N.R. 277. The extent to which the principles in this case (a criminal matter) are applicable to administrative tribunals is a topic in itself. Contrast *Ont. (Human Rights Com'n) v. Ont. (Board of Inquiry)* (1993), 115 D.L.R. (4th) 279 (Div. Ct.) (*Stinchcombe* applied) with *CIBA — Geigy Canada Ltd. v. Canada (Patented Medicine Prices Review Board)*, [1994] 3 F.C. 425, 55 C.P.R. (3d) 482 (T.D.); 83 F.T.R. 2n, 56 C.P.R. (3d) 377, 170 N.R. 360 (C.A.) (*Stinchcombe* distd.).

native remedy had been fully discussed in *Harelkin* (including his characterization of the majority decision as applying the doctrine in cases involving lack of jurisdiction), he used the occasion to set out the factors to be considered in applying the doctrine, although this category was not a closed one. These include the convenience of the alternative remedy, the nature of the error, and the nature of the appeal tribunal (its investigatory decision-making and remedial capacities) and its procedures.

In applying these factors to the case, he found that in determining the adequacy of the administrative appeal system it was proper for the motion judge to consider the larger policy context which underlay the grant of assessment powers to the Band, namely, the encouragement of self reliance and self government. Equally, if not more, important, he defined the comparative analysis between tribunal and court as one which should determine the *adequacy* of the tribunal decision-making process, and not whether the court was a better one. Although he acknowledged the jurisdictional question was complex, he felt any suggestion that the Band tribunals were ill-equipped to consider the issue was contrary to legislative intent. The tribunal was an adequate forum for considering the issue at first instance, enabling a "far reaching and extensive inquiry" in which both sides could fully present their case.[87] In this respect he showed appropriate deference to the integrity and autonomy of the administrative tribunal.

However, Lamer C.J.C. felt the motion judge erred in not considering a relevant factor, namely that there was a reasonable apprehension of institutional bias regarding the independence of the tribunals. Such reasonable apprehension of bias meant that the tribunal did not provide an adequate alternative remedy. Thus although his decision supports the theory that the doctrine of adequate alternative remedy applies even where there is jurisdictional error, in the result he finds there is no such remedy on the facts, because of what is a jurisdictional error, namely a reasonable apprehension of bias.[88]

LaForest and Major JJ. (McLachlin J. concurring), in separate judgments, both were of the opinion that the issue of "within the reserve" was a jurisdictional question and, since this was ultimately a question for the courts to decide, the matter should proceed directly to the courts without the lengthy and "possibly needless" tribunal appeals. They did not address the possibility that the tribunal itself might answer the question in a manner that did not necessitate a resort to the courts. Although they did not address the issue of the tribunals' independence, implicit in their judgments and that of Lamer C.J.C., is the conclusion that the anticipated result was one that would bring the parties to the court. Major J.

---

[87] *Supra*, note 81, at 40-41.
[88] *Nfld. Telephone Co. Ltd.*, *supra*, note 84, at 645.

obviously felt that Lamer C.J.C. determined that the doctrine of adequate alternative remedy applies even where there is jurisdictional error, for he expressly disagrees with him on this point, preferring the dissent in *Harelkin.*

Sopinka J. (L'Heureux-Dubé, Gonthier and Iacobucci JJ. concurring) agreed with Lamer C.J.C., except on the issue of institutional independence, which he felt could only be assessed in the context of an actual hearing. The essential elements of institutional independence in *Valente v. R.*[89] need not be applied with the same rigour in the case of administrative tribunals, the context of which in this case included the policy of promoting aboriginal self government. As a result, he concluded the motion judge did not err in determining the assessment tribunals constituted an adequate alternative remedy.

It seems, therefore, that the doctrine of adequate alternative remedy applies even in the face of jurisdictional error. While the particular policy context of the *Indian Act* obviously played a role in the court's reasoning, as a matter of principle, this deference to the policy function and adequacy of the tribunal's process and decision-making capacities is to be welcomed as yet another instance of acceptance of the essential integrity of tribunal decision-making.[90]

Deference is also accorded to administrative remedies to the extent that the courts have declined jurisdiction to hear lawsuits involving issues for which administrative redress already exists. One example of this is the consistent refusal of the courts to hear wrongful dismissal claims in the face of collective agreements which contain provision for grievance arbitration or other dispute resolution, partly because of the need to ensure the binding nature of the agreement, but also because of the wider range of remedies than exist in the courts, *e.g.*, reinstatement.[91]

An analogous line of cases is that in which the courts have refused to provide remedies or indeed to find a cause of action arising out of a breach of statute where there is a comprehensive administrative and adjudicative structure for the enforcement of rights created therein neces-

---

[89] [1985] 2 S.C.R. 673, 14 O.A.C. 79, 23 C.C.C. (3d) 193, 49 C.R. (3d) 97, 19 C.R.R. 354, 24 D.L.R. (4th) 161, 37 M.V.R. 9, 64 N.R. 1.

[90] See *supra*, notes 40 and 41.

[91] See *McGavin Toastmaster Ltd. v. Ainscough*, [1976] 1 S.C.R. 718 at 724-25, [1975] 5 W.W.R. 444, 75 CLLC 14,277, 54 D.L.R. (3d) 1, 4 N.R. 618. See also *St. Anne-Nackawic Pulp & Paper Co. Ltd. v. Canadian Paperworkers Union, Local 219*, [1986] 1 S.C.R. 704, 184 A.P.R. 236, 86 CLLC 14,037, 28 D.L.R. (4th) 1 at 8-9, 68 N.R. 112 and cases cited therein, at 13; *Bergeron v. Kinsway Transport Ltd.* (1979), 23 O.R. (2d) 332, 95 D.L.R. (3d) 749 (Div. Ct.); *Bourne v. Otis Elevators Ltd.* (1984), 45 O.R. (2d) 321, 4 C.C.E.L. 1, 42 C.P.C. 12 (H.C.J.). In *Bartello v. Canada Post Corp.* (1987), 62 O.R. (2d) 652, 78 C.C.E.L. 26, 35 C.R.R. 132, 46 D.L.R. (4th) 129 (H.C.J.), this rule was held not to violate s. 15 of the Charter.

sary to achieve the objectives of the legislation.[92] Ironically, in the field of human rights, an example of one such comprehensive administrative scheme, no deference is accorded to the decisions of the tribunals which determine the rights thereunder, except as it relates to their fact-finding.[93] In the field of labour relations there is more consistency between the approach of the courts in judicial review of tribunal decision-making examined above and excluding common law causes of action arising from breach of the legislative scheme. In *St. Anne-Nackawic Pulp & Paper Co. Ltd. v. C.P.W.U.*, the Supreme Court held that the relevant labour relations legislation was so comprehensive that there was no scope for an action for damages for an illegal strike in violation of the legislation and applicable collective agreement, even where one may have existed in the past:

> What is left is an attitude of judicial deference to the arbitration process. This deference is present whether the board in question is a "statutory" or a private tribunal . . . It is based on the idea that if the courts are available to the parties as an alternative forum, violence is done to a comprehensive statutory scheme designed to govern all aspects of the relationship of the parties in a labour relations setting.[94]

Finally, the combination of a standard of patent unreasonableness and the common law doctrine of estoppel may also reinforce the autonomy of administrative remedies in appropriate circumstances. In *U.S.W., Local 14097 v. Franks*,[95] the Ontario Court of Appeal determined that the standard of judicial review of an award of compensation for termination pay made under what is now s. 68(1) of the *Employment Standards Act*[96] was that of patent unreasonableness. In *Rasanen v. Rosemount*

---

[92] See *Seneca College of Applied Arts & Technology (Bd. of Governors) v. Bhadauria*, [1981] 2 S.C.R. 111, 14 B.L.R. 157, 17 C.C.L.T. 106, 81 CLLC 14,117, 22 C.P.C. 130, 124 D.L.R. (3d) 193, 37 N.R. 468; *Ryan v. Workmens Compensation Board* (1984), 6 O.A.C. 33 (Div. Ct.); *Re Peiroo v. Minister of Employment & Immigration* (1989), 34 O.A.C. 43, 69 O.R. (2d) 253, 60 D.L.R. (4th) 574 (C.A.); leave to appeal to the Supreme Court of Canada refused (1989), 104 N.R. 319n.

[93] *Supra*, note 36. See also *Zurich Ins. Co. v. Ont. (Human Rights Com'n)*, [1992] 2 S.C.R. 321, 9 O.R. (3d) 224n, [1992] I.L.R. 1-2848, 39 M.V.R. (2d) 1, 93 D.L.R. (4th) 346, 138 N.R. 1.

[94] *Supra*, note 91, at 13-14 D.L.R. However, the concurrent jurisdiction to issue injunctions remains, *ibid.*, at 15-16.

[95] (1994), 16 O.R. (3d) 620, 94 CLLC 14,011, 2 C.C.E.L. (2d) 23, 110 D.L.R. (4th) 762 (C.A.); leave to appeal to S.C.C. refused 19 O.R. (3d) xvi, 7 C.C.E.L (2d) 41n, 178 N.R. 76n.

[96] R.S.O. 1990, c. E.14, formerly R.S.O. 1980, c. 137, s. 50(1).

Instruments Ltd.,[97] where a referee had refused to order compensation under the same section, a majority of the Ontario Court of Appeal dismissed a claim for wrongful dismissal on the basis of issue estoppel. While the court recognized the civil action and a claim under the legislation were alternative remedies, the argument that the procedure before the referee was not sufficiently "judicial" to make the decision "binding" for purposes of issue estoppel was flatly rejected by Abella J.A., a judge with experience as a tribunal chair. She found that such an argument

> . . . seriously misperceives the role and function of administrative tribunals. They were expressly created as independent bodies for the purpose of being an alternative to the judicial process, including its procedural principles. Designed to be less cumbersome, less expensive, less formal and less delayed, these impartial decision-making bodies were to resolve disputes in their area of specialization more expeditiously and more accessibly, but no less effectively or credibly.[98]

From a practical point of view, the combined effect of the two cases is one that may determine the choice between administrative and judicial remedies. The administrative remedy is likely to be more expeditious and less expensive than a trial, but the result will be tested against the standard of patent unreasonableness. By contrast, the more lengthy and expensive court remedy involving a trial will permit an appeal and the more generous standard of appellate review on questions of law.

(b) *Existence of Remedial Power: Delphic Dicta and Dicey*

Against this background of general curial deference, the question arises as to the extent of deference the courts will accord to the administrative tribunal's interpretation of its remedial powers. As noted above, the courts have determined that the need for deference arises only where the issue is not one of "jurisdiction" in the strict sense as explained in *Bibeault*. Whether a question is a "jurisdictional" one still results in disagreement among members of the Supreme Court of Canada, as witnessed

---

[97] (1994), 17 O.R. (3d) 267, 1 C.C.E.L. (2d) 161, 94 CLLC 14,024, 112 D.L.R. (4th) 683 (C.A.); leave to appeal to S.C.C. refused 19 O.R. (3d) xvi, 7 C.C.E.L. (2d) 40*n*, 178 N.R. 80*n*. For a critical review that suggests the substantial differences between a wrongful dismissal action and a claim for termination pay makes issue estoppel inappropriate. See Barnott, Case Comment (1994), 3 R.A.L. 193 at 196.

[98] *Ibid.*, at 279.

by two of the most recent cases, *Goldhawk* and *Matsqui Indian Band.*[99]

Given the room for disagreement on this issue, a true functional approach that focuses on the question asked by L'Heureux-Dubé J. in *Domtar* of "who is in the best position to decide" suggests that judicial deference be given to the tribunal's interpretation of the extent and choice of remedies available to it, the amount of deference being determined by the "spectrum" analysis articulated in *Pezim*. However, a review of the caselaw on this subject makes it clear that the "Dicean view of the rule of law and the role that the courts should play in the administration of government" so criticized by Wilson J. in *Lester*[100] still prevails.

That this might not be the case in the years following *C.U.P.E.* was suggested in two decisions of the court by Laskin C.J.C. in the early 1980s. In *Teamsters Union, Local 938 v. Massicotte,*[101] at issue was the ability of the Canada Labour Relations Board, upon a finding that a union had breached its duty of fair representation to a member, to order arbitration of the grievance that the union had failed to bring. The board was fortified by a privative clause, and Laskin C.J.C. addressed himself to whether an issue of board jurisdiction was involved. The most applicable provisions of the *Canada Labour Code* were as follows:

> 118. The Board has, in relation to any proceeding before it, power
>
> . . . . .
>
> (*p*) to decide for all purposes of this Part any question that may arise in the proceeding, including, without restricting the generality of the foregoing.
>
> . . . . .
>
> 121. The Board shall exercise such powers and perform such duties as are conferred or imposed upon it by, or as may be incidental to the attainment of the objects of, this Part including, without restricting the generality of the foregoing, the making of orders requiring compliance with the provi-

---

[99] *Supra*, notes 46 and 31. See, as well, the Ontario Court of Appeal's discussion of this issue in the context of the Pay Equity Tribunal where the court examined the general purpose and mandate of the Tribunal, the language of the constituent statute and "the specific problem the Tribunal was resolving" to hold that "The Tribunal's decisions over whether and how pay equity was achieved seem . . . to have been 'logically at the heart of the specialized jurisdiction conferred on the Board'". The standard of review was, therefore, of "patent unreasonableness" and the court upheld the Tribunal's decision. See *Ont. Nurses' Ass'n v. Ont. (Pay Equity Hearings Tribunal)* (1995), 23 O.R. (3d) 43 (C.A.) at 55, 57; revg 110 D.L.R. (4th) 260 (Ont. Div. Ct.); application for leave to appeal to the Supreme Court of Canada submitted August 21, 1995.

[100] [1990] 3 S.C.R. 644 at 651, 88 Nfld. & P.E.I.R. 15, 91 CLLC 14,002, 76 D.L.R. (4th) 389, 123 N.R. 241 (Dickson C.J., Cory, L'Heureux-Dubé JJ. concurring).

[101] [1982] 1 S.C.R. 710, 134 D.L.R. (3d) 385, 44 N.R. 340 (hereinafter *Massicotte*).

sions of this Part, with any regulation made under this Part or with any decision made in respect of a matter before the Board.

. . . . .

136.1. Where a trade union is the bargaining agent for a bargaining unit, the trade union and every representative of the trade union shall represent, fairly and without discrimination, all employees in the bargaining unit.

. . . . .

189. Where . . . the Board determines that a party to a complaint has failed to comply with subsection 136.1 . . . the Board may, by order, require the party to comply with that subsection or section and may
(a) in respect of a failure to comply with section 136.1, require a trade union to take and carry on on behalf of any employee affected by the failure or to assist any such employee to take and carry on such action or proceeding as the Board considers that the union ought to have taken and carried on on the employee's behalf or ought to have assisted the employee to take and carry on;

. . . . .

and, for the purpose of ensuring the fulfilment of the objectives of this Part, the Board may, in respect of any failure to comply with any provision to which this section applies and in addition to or in lieu of any other order that the Board is authorized to make under this section, by order, require an employer or a trade union to do or refrain from doing any thing that it is equitable to require the employer or trade union to do or refrain from doing in order to remedy or counteract any consequence of such failure to comply that is adverse to the fulfilment of those objectives.

The union alleged that the legislation contemplated arbitration between the union and employees and not by an employee on his own. Laskin C.J.C. held that the "wide remedial powers" under s. 189 entitled the board to make the impugned order. After reviewing the existing caselaw, and putting particular emphasis on the reasoning in *C.U.P.E.*, he held that if the tribunal had addressed itself to an issue arising under the legislation it administers: ". . . there can be no jurisdictional infirmity when [its] is protected in its determinations by a privative clause. It may be wrong in law in interpreting the range of powers confided to it but its decisions are nonetheless immunized from judicial review".[102] He later went on to hold:

. . . mere doubt as to correctness of a labour board interpretation of its statutory power is no ground for finding jurisdictional error, especially when the labour board is exercising powers confided to it in wide terms to resolve competing contentions. . . . It is impossible to say that the Canada Labour Relations Board asked itself the wrong question in any sense of departing from

---

[102] *Ibid.*, at 719.

the inquiry in which it was engaged. It addressed itself to the issue raised by the complaint and exercised powers in relation thereto which it clearly had. At bottom, the objection is to the consequential results of that exercise, but this is a long way from any jurisdictional issue.

In the result, I am of the opinion that there is no question of jurisdiction involved in the objection to what the Canada Labour Relations Board did. Its decision and remedial order are hence not reviewable.[103]

In *Canada (Labour Relations Board) v. Halifax Longshoremen's Ass'n*,[104] at issue was an order of the Canada Labour Relations Board directing trade unions to admit members for purposes of job-referrals at hiring halls. Although the court held that nothing in the *Canada Labour Code* gave the Board any supervisory authority over the admission of persons to union membership, the wide remedial authority under s. 189 of the Code provided the basis for the impugned remedy. The Federal Court of Appeal had held that the board was limited to the establishment of a proper non-discriminatory job referral system which it was expressly permitted to do, relying in part on the view that because s. 189(*d*) gave specific authority to the Board to make admission orders in respect of other breaches, the general remedial power was thereby limited.

Laskin C.J.C. recognized that this was one possible interpretation of the Code, but felt that:

> . . . the remedial authority given to the Board is given under such broad terms under the concluding paragraph of s. 189 as not to exclude it in a special case . . . *Even more in fashioning a remedy conferred in such broad terms is the Board's discretion to be respected than when it is challenged as exceeding its jurisdiction to determine whether there has been a breach of a substantive provision of the Code. At the same time, equitable and consequential considerations are not to be so remote from reparation of an established breach as to exceed any rational parameters. What we have here is undoubtedly a unique situation to which the board addressed a remedial authority which is not unquestionable.* What we confront then is whether in the particular situation with which the Board was seized, we should be as strict in assessing the Board's powers as we would have been in dealing with the matter at first instance . . . It is rarely a simple matter to draw a line between a lawful and unlawful exercise of power by a statutory tribunal, however ample its authority, when there are conflicting considerations addressed to the exercise of power. This Court has, over quite a number of years, thought it more consonant with the legislative objectives involved in a case such as this to be more rather than less deferential to the discharge of difficult tasks by statutory tribunals like the Board. [Emphasis added.][105]

---

[103] *Ibid.*, at 724.
[104] [1983] 1 S.C.R. 245, 144 D.L.R. (3d) 1, 46 N.R. 324 (hereinafter *Halifax Longshoremen's Ass'n)*.
[105] *Ibid.*, at 255-56.

This passage, with its emphasis on the need for deference to a tribunal's interpretation of the extent of its remedial powers, even where its authority is open to question, properly reflects an appropriate approach to the issue. It adopts the test of irrationality which is the current meaning ascribed to "patent unreasonableness" in the *Goldhawk* case. It enables the decision-maker who is the expert and most closely connected to the factual and legislative policy context to "put the matter right".

However, Laskin C.J.C. apparently understood he might be entering into "Dicey" territory, for although he upheld the Board's exercise of its remedial power, he noted:

> There is no doubt that, as already noted, we tread a narrow line and nothing said in this case can be taken to establish any general principle. There may be an area in the law relating to superior court review of other tribunals, judicial as well as administrative, where more fundamental issues arise than arise in the circumstances of these proceedings. No doubt there will be required on occasion some refinement of the proper limits of jurisdictional review where an administrative tribunal, when responding to questions of fact, must construe and apply its constitutive authority, be it contractual or statutory. Nothing herein determined should be read as bearing on such considerations, faced as we are here with a unique and narrow question arising out of the extraordinary framework of these labour relations. The remedial result here is bottomed squarely on the involvement of the complaints in an allegation of breach which was firmly established and which required redress and protection to them as individuals in addition to the redress provided by the Board to other non-union employees.

Approximately one year later, the Supreme Court again had need to interpret the extent of the same board's authority under s. 189 of the *Canada Labour Code*. In *Nat'l Bank of Canada v. Retail Clerk's Int'l Union*,[106] the board had found that the integration by the Bank of two branches was the sale of a business within the meaning of the Code, and had been motivated by anti-union reasons, thereby breaching the Code. A number of remedial actions were ordered by the board, including the creation and funding by the Bank of a trust fund to promote the objectives of the Code among all employees, and the sending of a letter by the Bank president to all employees, the content of which was to be determined, in effect, by the board. The court found that the determinations by the board of a sale and its *animus* were matters within its jurisdiction and did not disturb its findings, being guided by *C.U.P.E.* and the need for deference in this regard.

However, the court found the board exceeded its jurisdiction in ordering the two remedies noted above, without addressing the *C.U.P.E.*

---

[106] [1984] 1 S.C.R. 269, 84 CLLC 14,037, 9 D.L.R. (4th) 10, 53 N.R. 203.

standard explicitly. The court recognized that the board had authority under s. 189 to require an employer to do "anything" in order to remedy or counteract any consequence of a failure to comply with the Code that it is adverse to the fulfilment of its objectives. It stated that:

> The fact remains that a remedy ordered pursuant to s.189 must be authorized by that section. In my view, it is essential for there to be a relation between the unfair practice, its consequences, and the remedy.[107]

The court referred to both *Massicotte* and *Halifax Longshoremen's Ass'n* as examples where the remedies met this test. However, in this case, Laskin C.J.C. felt this relationship did not exist. Additional reasons of Beetz J. (Estey, McIntyre, Lamer and Wilson JJ. concurring) were to the effect that the remedies were punitive. He went on to say:

> This type of penalty is totalitarian and as such alien to the tradition of free nations like Canada, even for the repression of the most serious crimes. I cannot be persuaded that the Parliament of Canada intended to confer on the Canadian Labour Relations Board the power to impose such extreme measures, even assuming that it could confer such a power bearing in mind the *Canadian Charter of Rights and Freedoms*.[108]

In our view, this decision is consistent with the approach advocated above, because the court based its reasoning, we would argue, on a view that the remedies ordered were irrational or gave rise to a Charter issue. Both grounds are appropriate as the standard against which the determination of remedial powers ought to be measured,[109] giving deference to the autonomy of tribunal decision-making, but retaining the legitimate residual role of the judiciary to be an avenue of last resort when core principles or values have been violated, and retaining the primacy of the courts' role in Charter matters.[110]

This view of the court's residual role was expressed by Cory J., in

---

[107] *Ibid.*, at 288.

[108] *Ibid.*, at 288.

[109] That the standard of review for a tribunal's interpretation and application of the Charter is that of correctness is clear and appropriate. See *Cuddy Chicks Ltd. v. Ont. (Labour Relations Board)*, [1991] 2 S.C.R. 5, 47 O.A.C. 271, 3 O.R. (3d) 128*n*, 91 CLLC 14,024, 4 C.R.R. (2d) 1, 81 D.L.R. (4th) 121, 122 N.R. 360, and other cases cited, *supra*, note 23. This accords with the constitutional position of the Charter as the "supreme law" binding both administrative tribunals and the legislatures from which they receive their remedial powers.

[110] See the comments of The Honourable Mr. Justice LaForest, "The Courts and Administrative Tribunals: Standards of Judicial Review of Administrative Action", Law Society of Upper Canada 1992 Special Lectures, at 2.

dissent, in *Canada (A.G.) v. Public Service Alliance of Canada*[111] where he referred to *Massicotte* as the "zenith" of *C.U.P.E.*:

> The principle adopted in *C.U.P.E.* reached its zenith when it was applied in *Teamsters Union Local 938 v. Massicotte* . . . In that case, Laskin C.J. . . . stated that: "mere doubt as to correctness of a labour board interpretation of its statutory power is no ground for finding jurisdictional error, especially when the labour board is exercising powers confided to it in wide terms to resolve competing contentions.
>
> *C.U.P.E.*, and the decisions referred to above, make it clear that an administrative tribunal will, in ordinary circumstances, lose jurisdiction only if it acts in a patently unreasonable manner.

However, any possibility that the basic constraints of Dicey had been loosened by *C.U.P.E.* was negated by the subsequent decision of the court in *Syndicat des Employés de Production du Québec de L'Acadie v. C.L.R.B.*[112] There, in the context of a long ongoing dispute between the union and C.B.C. over mandatory or voluntary overtime, and after the Canada Labour Relations Board had ruled that a general refusal to work overtime constituted an illegal strike under the *Canada Labour Code*, the board ordered the parties to refer this issue of overtime to arbitration pending negotiation of a new collective agreement. At issue was the authority of the board to make this order.

By reason of s. 182 of the Code, upon determining that an illegal strike took place, the board could make an order enjoining the union and its members from continuing a strike and requiring them to go back to work. An order made under such section, by reason of s. 183.1(*a*) may be "in such terms as the board considers necessary and sufficient to meet the circumstances of the case". The court found that the determination of the legality of the strike was a matter within jurisdiction subject to deference, but the board's interpretation of its remedial powers a question of jurisdiction that warranted no deference.

Beetz J., writing for the court, held that privative clauses shielded "mere" errors of law, limiting judicial intervention to patently unreasonable errors of law. A "mere" error of law was an error made in good faith "in interpreting or applying a provision of its enabling Act, of another Act, or of an agreement or other document which it has to interpret and

---

[111] [1991] 1 S.C.R. 614, 91 CLLC 14,017, 80 D.L.R. (4th) 520 at 546, 123 N.R. 161 (hereinafter *P.S.A.C. No. 1*). However, by 1993, Cory J. had accepted the majority's view: see his decision in *P.S.A.C. (No. 2)*, [1993] 1 S.C.R. 941, 93 CLLC 14,022, 101 D.L.R. (4th) 673, 150 N.R. 161.

[112] [1984] 2 S.C.R. 412, 84 CLLC 14,069, 14 D.L.R. (4th) 457, 55 N.R. 321 (hereinafter *L'Acadie*).

apply within the limits of its jurisdiction".[113] At first blush, this would appear to include the board's interpretation of its remedial power.

However, Beetz J. went on to distinguish a "mere" error of law from a "jurisdictional error" which he defined as one which

> . . . relates generally to a provision which confers jurisdiction, that is, one which describes, lists and limits the power of an administrative tribunal, or which is [translation] *"intended to circumscribe the authority of"* that tribunal . . . [Emphasis added.][114]

He went on to examine the various remedial powers of the board, and rejected the board's general argument that, taken together with the privative clauses and liberally construed, these gave the board the power to define the remedies necessary to end the labour dispute. He then proceeded to interpret the powers given to the board in ss. 183.1(a) and 118[115] in a narrow fashion, and held that the "loose wording" of s. 121[116] could not be read so as to render unnecessary the other sections of the Code that gave remedies, *i.e.*, the general was limited by the specific, and was not intended to grant general remedial discretion.[117] This seems contrary to the more liberal approach to the same basic issue of interpretation taken by Laskin C.J.C. in *Massicotte*[118] and to us appears to be an example of the "wrong end of the telescope" approach referred to above by the Honourable Mr. Justice Blair.[119]

Beetz J. justified his interpretation by the legislative intent he felt was expressed by the specific remedial powers, and although he agreed that the same legislators intended the board's powers should be "extensive", they were not intended to be "practically unlimited".[120] Characterizing the remedy ordered as one "of a quite exceptional nature" he rejected the board's argument that it was not claiming a general power to refer to arbitration, but only to proceed with a grievance already filed and which could be justified in the special circumstances of the case. Such an approach, we suggest, misses the point as it relates to the standard of review. It suggests that the potential for unfettered discretion justifies characterization of the issue as jurisdictional to which no deference is

---

[113] *Ibid.*, at 420.

[114] *Ibid.*

[115] See *supra*, text (Code, s. 118).

[116] See *supra*, text (Code, s. 121).

[117] *Supra*, note 112, at 431-32.

[118] *Supra*, note 101. See Evans, "Developments in Administrative Law: The 1984-85 Term" (1986), 8 Supreme Court L.R. 1 at 34-35. See also Gonthier in *Bell Canada v. Canada (C.R.T.C.)*, [1989] 1 S.C.R. 1722, 60 D.L.R. (4th) 682, 97 N.R. 15 (hereinafter *Bell Canada*).

[119] *Supra,* note 14.

[120] *Supra*, note 112, at 432.

accorded. As a matter of law, no discretion is unlimited,[121] and the requirement for the rationality of the remedy to be demonstrated that was articulated in *Halifax Longshoreman's Ass'n* and *National Bank* permits the
court to intervene in appropriate cases. It seems reasonable to argue that
the remedial powers granted to the Board were not meant "to circumscribe" its authority, but rather to enhance its creativity and ability to
fashion the appropriate remedy in the circumstances it was faced with,
which the legislator could not necessarily anticipate.

Beetz J. recognized that the decision of Laskin C.J.C. in *Massicotte*
could be read as determining that a similar issue of the power to authorize an employee to proceed to arbitration was not one of jurisdiction.
He distinguished that case and *Halifax Longshoreman's Ass'n* as being
decided by reference to the wider powers under s. 189 of the Code, which
"expressly authorize it to itself define the proper remedies", and that it
was a "fundamental error" to find that s. 121 or any other section in issue
were of an identical nature. This permitted him to classify the general statement of principle in *Massicotte* that an administrative tribunal protected
by a privative clause "may be wrong in law in interpreting the range of
powers confided to it but its decisions are nonetheless immunized from
judicial review[122] as "Delphic *dicta*".[123] Given his interpretation of a
"jurisdictional" provision in a statute, and his characterization of the issue
at hand, he reasoned that it could not be logical if a tribunal could make
a jurisdictional error in embarking upon an inquiry and not commit a jurisdiction error "with impunity" at its conclusion, which was the "ultimate
purpose" of the process. As we shall suggest later, this does not follow
as a matter of principle on a more general theory of curial deference
towards remedial power, and contradicts the proper distinction made by
Laskin C.J.C. in *Massicotte* between the jurisdiction to enter into an
inquiry and the consequential results of valid exercise of that jurisdiction.

In this regard, the court's characterization of the issue as "whether
the Board has the power to attach to such a declaration [of an illegal strike]
an order referring a matter to arbitration"[124] fit neatly with the concept
of statutes that "describe, list and limit" powers of tribunals, enabling
it to classify that issue as manifestly a question of jurisdiction.

Had the question been characterized, as we would suggest, as

---

[121] *Roncarelli v. Duplessis*, [1959] S.C.R. 121, [1956] Que. Q.B. 447, 16 D.L.R.
(2d) 689. See also *Apotex v. Ont. (A.G.)* (1984), 47 O.R. (2d) 176, 11 D.L.R.
(4th) 97 (H.C.J.); leave to appeal to C.A. refused; *Re Ontario Film & Video
Appreciation Society and Ontario Board of Censors* (1983), 41 O.R. (2d) 583,
34 C.R. (3d) 73, 5 C.R.R. 373, 147 D.L.R. (3d) 58 (Div. Ct.); affd 2 O.A.C.
388, 45 O.R. (2d) 80, 38 C.R. (3d) 271, 7 C.R.R. 129, 5 D.L.R. (4th) 766.
[122] See *supra*, note 102.
[123] *Supra*, note 110, at 437.
[124] *Ibid.*, at 440.

"whether the board's interpretation of its powers was a reasonable one", the result may have been different, as Beetz J. was willing to accept the proposition advanced by the board's counsel that its interpretation of its powers was not absolutely unreasonable.[125] However, this was irrelevant, because the rigidity of the theory of jurisdiction provided that once an issue was classified as going to jurisdiction, the reasonableness of the board's interpretation was no longer the question, and it did not matter if the error in interpretation was "serious or slight", as the superior court "cannot, *without itself refusing to exercise its own jurisdiction* refrain from ruling on the correctness of that decision"[126] (emphasis added). The court does not, however, explain why it has no discretion, it just states that this flows from the classification of the error as jurisdictional.

The proposition that judicial review is not discretionary in the face of jurisdictional error, was not accepted in *Harelkin* by Beetz J. and in *Matsqui Indian Band*. The concept of deference which we advocate does not exclude judicial review in the end, but tailors it according to a spectrum based on functional criteria. The appropriateness of an approach that mandates a judicial reaction simply by a classification of function was abandoned in *Nicholson*[127] in favour of a functional approach that tailored the degree of procedural formalism according to the context of the individual case. That breaches of the duty of fairness and the rules of natural justice are "jurisdictional" and are measured against a standard of correctness is not inconsistent with judicial deference to remedial powers. Procedural norms and values are of a different character and purpose than the consequential nature of remedies, and any exercise of remedial power must accord with these essential values. In addition, the decision proceeds on the basis that if the "question" is not characterized as jurisdictional, then the only standard is that of patently unreasonableness. Developments since then have demonstrated this concern is no longer warranted as the degree of deference is a consequence of a pragmatic and functional analysis of its need and ranges along the spectrum articulated in *Pezim*.

It is only at the end of its decision that the court provides its reason for its "duty" to intervene, one that reflects a basic adherence to Dicey's original concept of the rule of law. The court expressly equated its role in judicial review of administrative tribunal decision-making with judicial review of legislative authority over constitutional matters, indicating that in such latter cases the courts do not apply a standard of patent unreasonableness:

---

[125] *Ibid.*, at 440.
[126] *Ibid.*, at 441.
[127] [1979] 1 S.C.R. 311, 78 CLLC 14,181, 88 D.L.R. (3d) 671, 23 N.R. 410.

Why would they act differently in the case of judicial review of the jurisdiction of administrative tribunals? The power of review of the courts of law has the same historic basis in both cases, and in both cases it relates to the same principles, the supremacy of the Constitution or of the law, of which the courts are the guardian.[128]

While we advocate that proper respect be given to administrative decision-making, we do not seek to elevate it to the stature of legislative power. If a tribunal grants a remedy that is unconstitutional then court intervention is mandated by the *Constitution Act*. To equate questions of statutory interpretation of the extent of remedial powers, where there is a reasonable basis for the interpretation and a rational connection between the decision of the tribunal otherwise validly made and the remedy, with judicial decision-making in the constitutional arena undercuts the rationale for any curial deference based on an acknowledgement of the legitimacy of administrative tribunals deciding questions of law involving the interpretation of their "home" statute. As discussed earlier, constitutional decision-making has, by and large, been deferential to the remedial powers granted by provincial legislation. In addition, there are functional differences between the process of tribunal decision-making and the enactment of legislation.[129]

Perhaps because of the academic criticism that greeted this formalistic approach to jurisdiction, or because of the inherent difficulty in defining the concept, Beetz J. in *Bibeault* accepted that the "fluidity of the concept of jurisdiction and the many ways in which jurisdiction is conferred on administrative tribunals"[130] required the development of the "pragmatic and functional" approach described earlier. That this is the approach to be taken is now beyond doubt in light of the subsequent decisions of the court that accept and endorse it.[131] While this may be seen as reaffirming its commitment to *C.U.P.E.* and thereby addressing

---

[128] *Supra*, note 112, at 444.

[129] Evans, "Developments in Administrative Law: The 1984-85 Term", *supra*, note 118, at 35-36. This, and the detailed critique of the decision by Langille, "Judicial Review, Judicial Recidivism and Judicial Responsibility" (1986), 17 R.G.D. 164 at 197-214 were cited by Wilson J. in her dissent in *Nat'l Corn Growers*, [1990] 2 S.C.R. 1324 at 1343-45, 74 D.L.R. (4th) 449, 114 N.R. 81.

[130] [1988] 2 S.C.R. 1048 at 1087, 24 Q.A.C. 244, 35 Admin L.R. 153, 89 CLLC 14,045, 95 N.R. 161.

[131] See *Bradco*, [1993] 2 S.C.R. 316, 106 Nfld. & P.E.I.R. 140, 93 CLLC 14,033, 102 D.L.R. (4th) 402, 153 N.R. 81; *Dayco*, [1993] 2 S.C.R. 230; *Domtar*, [1993] 2 S.C.R. 756, 49 C.C.E.L. 1, 105 D.L.R. (4th) 385, 154 N.R. 104; *Pezim*, [1994] 2 S.C.R. 557, 92 B.C.L.R. (2d) 145, 14 B.L.R. (2d) 217, 114 D.L.R. (4th) 385, 168 N.R. 321; *Goldhawk*, [1995] 1 S.C.R. 157, 95 CLLC 210-009, 121 D.L.R. (4th) 385, 177 N.R. 1; *Matsqui Indian Band*, [1995] 1 S.C.R. 3, 85 F.T.R. 79n, 122 D.L.R. (4th) 129, 177 N.R. 325.

Wilson J.'s concern over "back-sliding" in *Lester*,[132] nevertheless the focus has remained on the need for the court to define the legislators' intent, and the admission of no other standard but correctness and no deference if the question at issue "concerns a legislative provision limiting the tribunal's powers".[133] For example, the case of *Bell Canada v. CRTC*[134] involved the question of whether the CRTC had the power to order Bell Canada to make a one-time credit to its customers because it earned excess revenues as a result of an interim order approving a tariff, pending final approval. The court held that it did have the power. Although an intervenor argued that curial deference should apply, and the court adopted the principle of deference to questions of interpretation by a tribunal within its area of special expertise, it held that, as the proceeding before it was an appeal and the question of the extent of the powers conferred on the CRTC was a question of law clearly subject to appeal, the issue was to be determined on an appellate standard of correctness. The question was also stated to be one of jurisdiction because "it involved an inquiry into whether the appellant had the power to make 'the order'",[135] but this determination was not equated to a standard of review, except to say that it was not a decision which fell within the tribunal's area of special expertise and was therefore subject to the appellate standard of review. In the end, this point was not critical as the court found that the tribunal did possess the impugned power.

In *Canadian Pacific Airlines v. Canadian Air Line Pilots Ass'n*[136] at issue was the power of the Canada Labour Relations Board to order production of an employers' records during an investigation of a union's application for an amended certification. The court held that the power under s. 118 of the Code to order production did not extend outside a hearing before the board. Both the majority (Lamer C.J.C., LaForest, Gonthier and Iacobucci JJ.) and the minority (L'Heureux-Dubé J.) determined that the issue was a jurisdictional one to be measured against the standard of correctness, relying, without any analysis, upon *Bibeault*, and in the case of L'Heureux-Dubé J., upon the *L'Acadie* case. The dispute between the two was the interpretation given to the scope of the power. The majority placed considerable emphasis on the coercive nature of the power and the fact that the exercise of such powers were normally reserved "uniquely" for courts of law made them "exceptional".[137] L'Heureux-Dubé stressed that to issue the order the board did not have to decide on

---

[132] [1990] 3 S.C.R. 644 at 651, 88 Nfld. & P.E.I.R. 15, 91 CLLC 14,002, 76 D.L.R. (4th) 389, 123 N.R. 241.

[133] *Bibeault, supra*, note 130, at 1086.

[134] *Supra*, note 118.

[135] *Ibid.*, at 1735, 1747.

[136] [1993] 3 S.C.R. 724, 93 CLLC 14,062, 108 D.L.R. (4th) 1, 160 N.R. 321.

[137] *Ibid.*, at 737, 739.

a question "central to its field of expertise" as the issue was not one of industrial or labour relations law.[138] Her application of the *Bibeault* test to the legislation led her to the conclusion that the legislative intent was not to give the board the exclusive power of making a final ruling on the point in issue.

One might argue that this case can be distinguished on the basis that the issue involved procedural and not true remedial powers linked to the expertise of the board as they were in *Massicotte*, but that is not necessary. Instead of trying to divine the intent of legislatures as to their notional intent as to who should decide the issue, a truly pragmatic and functional analysis would still generate a lower level of deference upon a spectrum that did not depend upon a classification of issue as jurisdictional. Put simply, the reasons expressed by both the majority and minority answer the question raised by L'Heureux-Dubé in *Domtar* of "who is in the best position" to rule on the question. Given the nature of the power, and the comparative expertise of the courts in this area of coercive procedure, it is not unreasonable for the courts to decide the extent of the power, but without first having to characterize it as jurisdictional to justify their intervention. A similar analysis would achieve the same result as occurred in *Massicotte* and *Nat'l Bank*, but may have yielded a different result in *L'Acadie*, given the courts' acceptance that the interpretation of the legislation was not absolutely unreasonable, and the superior expertise of the board in fashioning remedies tailored to the special circumstances of labour disputes.

As these cases indicate, it is likely that the extent of remedial powers will continue to be treated as a jurisdictional question as long as the *Bibeault* test causes the courts' analytical telescope to see a grant of wide remedial powers as a jurisdictional "limit" on tribunals rather than a necessary reinforcement and enhancement of their basic function and purpose.

(c) *Scope of Remedial Powers*

Given that the existing standard of judicial review for determining the existence and extent of a tribunal's remedial powers is that of correctness, one might suggest that deference still may be accorded to a tribunal's interpretation of its jurisdiction by the court adopting a broad, purposive interpretation, and determing that the tribunal's view was indeed correct. Surprisingly, very few decisions make explicit reference to the federal or provincial *Interpretation Act* and their common direction to the courts

---

[138] *Ibid.*, at 756.

to interpret leglislation in a "broad and liberal" or "remedial" fashion.[139]

In more specific terms, while it is difficult to generalize, given the different types, purposes and functions of tribunals as well as the structure and language of their governing legislation, our review leads us to the conclusion that there is no general theme of consistency or predictability to be expected on this issue, despite the focus of the functional analysis on the overall intent of the legislature rather than on an interpretation of isolated statutory provisions.[140] A very brief review of some of the case-law dealing with some generic administrative remedies is illustrative of this situation.

(i) *Compensatory Orders*

As a remedy, damages or compensation as redress for a wrong are as necessary and effective for tribunals as the courts. Generally speaking, in this area, the courts have given a broad interpretation to the remedial powers of tribunals, even if express powers were not conferred by legislation or agreement. An early example of this is *Polymer Corp. v. O.C.A.W., Local 16-14*,[141] where McRuer C.J.H.C. held that, notwithstanding the lack of any express power and the fact the legislation provided other sanctions for breach of a collective agreement, the arbitrators had the power to award damages for breach of the agreement due to the statutory direction to an arbitrator to settle labor disputes without work stoppages and the broad wording of the agreement.

Similarly, the Divisional Court in *Re Tandy Electronics and U.S.A.*[142] gave its approval to a broad range of orders made by the Ontario Labour Relations Board to remedy unfair labour practices by the employer, including compensating the union and individual employees for monetary losses arising from the loss of opportunity to negotiate a collective agreement. The court emphasized the exclusive jurisdiction and expertise of the board in the labour relations field, its general and specific powers under then

---

[139] *Interpretation Act*, R.S.C. 1985, c. I-12, s. 12; *Interpretation Act*, R.S.O. 1990, c. I.11, s. 10.

[140] *Bibeault, supra,* note 130, at 1089, cited by Lamer C.J.C. in *Matsqui Indian Band, supra,* note 131, at 27.

[141] [1961] O.R. 176, 61 CLLC 15,341, 26 D.L.R. (2d) 609 (H.C.J.); affd [1961] O.R. 438, 28 D.L.R. (2d) 81 (C.A.); affd *sub nom. Imbleau v. Laskin*, [1962] S.C.R. 338, 62 CLLC 15,406, 33 D.L.R. (2d) 124.

[142] (1980), 30 O.R. (2d) 29, 115 D.L.R. (3d) 197 (Ont. Div. Ct.); leave to appeal to C.A. refused, 115 D.L.R. (3d) 197n.

s. 79(4) of the *Labour Relations Act* (which did not expressly cover the situation),[143] and stated:

> So long as the award of the Board is compensatory and not punitive; so long as it flows from the scope, intent and provisions of the Act itself, then the award of damages is within the jurisdiction of the Board. *The mere fact that the award of damages is novel, that the remedy is innovative, should not be a reason for finding it unreasonable.* [Emphasis added.][144]

As an aside, it is interesting that in this case the standard of review was not expressly addressed as it related to the extent of the power to award damages. Instead, the court invoked the *C.U.P.E.* standard for all three issues it considered, namely, the use by the board of findings of fact and law made by other different panels involving the company and the union, an order to cease and desist from insisting on prior individual employee consent to dues check-off, and the order of compensation.

Another example of a broad approach to damages awarded by tribunals is the decision of the Ontario Court of Appeal in *Piazza v. Airport Taxicab (Malton) Ass'n.*[145] There the court held that compensation for violation of the *Human Rights Code* in the termination of an employee was not restrained by common law principles of damages in wrongful dismissal cases. The court held that the power to order a party "to make compensation" to rectify a breach of the Code was not limited to a period of reasonable notice but could extend to the full period of unemployment. This was consistent with the requirement that human rights legislation be given a broad purposive interpretation.[146]

However, as noted, broad interpretations are not always the case. In the human rights field, for example, the Federal Court of Appeal has limited damages to a person discriminated against to actual losses that

---

[143] R.S.O. 1970, c. 232. The relevant sections gave the Board, in the event it found a contravention of the Act the obligation to "determine what . . . the employer . . . shall do . . . with respect thereto and such determination, without limiting the generality of the foregoing may include . . . (c) an order to reinstate . . . or hire . . . with or without compensation, or to compensate in lieu of hiring or reinstatement for loss of earnings".

[144] *Supra*, note 142, at 215.

[145] (1989), 34 O.A.C. 349, 69 O.R. (2d) 285, 26 C.C.E.L. 191, 60 D.L.R. (4th) 759 (C.A.). See also *Re Commodore Business Machines Ltd. and Minister of Labour* (1984), 6 O.A.C. 176, 49 O.R. (2d) 17, 84 CLLC 17,028, 13 C.R.R. 338,14 D.L.R. (4th) 118 at 120 (Div. Ct.).

[146] *Ont. (Human Rights Com'n) v. Simpson Sears Ltd.*, [1987] 1 S.C.R. 114, 17 Admin. L.R. 89, 9 C.C.E.L. 185, 86 CLLC 17,002, 23 D.L.R. (4th) 321, 64 N.R. 161; *Brennan v. R.*, [1987] 2 S.C.R. 84, 87 CLLC 17,025, 40 D.L.R. (4th) 577, 75 N.R. 303, *sub nom. Robichaud v. R.*

were reasonably foreseeable.[147] In the field of labour relations, the Supreme Court of Canada interpreted Nova Scotia legislation as not permitting the tribunal to order compensation for an employer's breach of its duty to bargain in good faith where its power in such a case was "to make an order requiring any party to the collective bargaining to do the things that in the opinion of the Board are necessary to secure compliance" with the requirement to bargain collectively.[148]

(ii) *Enforcement Orders*

The interpretation of a tribunal's enforcement powers is another area of tribunal decision-making to which the courts have generally accorded considerable scope. [149] This is illustrated by the decision of the Supreme Court of Canada in *Chrysler Canada Ltd. v. Canada (Competition Tribunal).*[150]

In *Chrysler* the majority of the court upheld the power of the federal Competition Tribunal to entertain proceedings for civil contempt of its orders, in this case the alleged failure of Chrysler to comply with an order of the Tribunal requiring it to resume the supply of car parts to a former customer. Section 8 of the Tribunal's legislation[151] gave it jurisdiction to hear and determine all applications under Part VIII of the *Competition Act* "and any matters related thereto", and with respect to the enforcement of its orders, all the powers of a superior court of record. Section 8(3) specifically required that no punishment for contempt occur unless a judicial member of the Tribunal found it appropriate.

The majority decision of Gonthier J. accepted that the common law restricted the power to punish for contempt *ex facie* to the superior courts, as established in earlier decisions of the court,[152] but that this may be modified through express statutory language. Thus, the task was whether the wording of s. 8 of the *Competition Tribunal Act* accomplished this.

---

[147] *Canada (A.G.) v. McAlpine*, [1989] 3 F.C. 530, 99 N.R. 221, 12 C.H.R.R. D/253 (C.A.)

[148] *C.U.P.E. v. Labour Relations Board (N.S.)*, [1983] 2 S.C.R. 311, 60 N.S.R. (2d) 369, 83 CLLC 12,349, 1 D.L.R. (4th) 1, 49 N.R. 107.

[149] Laskin, "Enforcement Powers of Administrative Agencies", Special Lectures, Law Society of Upper Canada, 1992, at 226.

[150] [1992] 2 S.C.R. 394, 7 B.L.R. (2d) 1, 42 C.P.R. (3d) 353, 92 D.L.R. (4th) 609, 138 N.R. 321 (hereinafter *Chrysler*).

[151] *Competition Tribunal Act*, R.S.C. 1985, c. 19 (2nd Supp.).

[152] *C.B.C. v. Cordeau*, [1979] 2 S.C.R. 618, 48 C.C.C. (2d) 289, 14 C.P.C. 60, 101 D.L.R. (3d) 24, 28 N.R. 541, *sub nom. C.B.C. v. Que. Police Com'n.*

Distinguishing this task from the strict interpretation required of a stat-ute that deprived superior courts of jursidiction, the court held that:

> Barring constitutional considerations, if a statute, read in context and given its ordinary meaning, clearly confers upon an inferior tribunal a jurisdiction that is enjoyed by the superior court at common law, while not depriving the superior court of its jurisdiction, it should be given effect.[153]

Assuming, without deciding if s. 96 of the *Constitution Act, 1867* applied to federally appointed tribunals, the court held the contempt power was necessarily incidental to the proper functioning of the Tribunal in its institutional setting, as only a specialized tribunal like it could properly ensure the enforcement of the orders it makes.

In interpreting the extent of s. 8 of the *Competition Tribunal Act*, a functional and purposive approach led the court to conclude that the Tribunal's jurisdiction to hear and determine "any matter related" to applications before it meant that its jurisdiction did not terminate upon its determination of an application, but extended to the enforcement of an order made pursuant to the application. Reasoning that the common law gave the Tribunal jurisdiction over incidental and ancillary matters arising in the hearing and determination of an application, the phrase "any matters related thereto" must be given meaning by relating to matters out-side the hearing and determination of an application. Similarly, since inferior courts have common law powers over contempt *in facie*, specific reference to contempt proceedings in the section was felt to be indicative of an intent to give powers beyond those ordinarily exercised by tribunals. The court was willing to read the sections as enhancing the remedial powers of the Tribunal rather than as limiting them. The fact that there were other sanctions for breach of orders did not detract from this, as those sections sought punishment, not compliance, were retrospective and not prospec-tive, did not allow "flexibility", and were applicable before a criminal court with the consequential loss of the Tribunal's expertise.

The dissent of McLachlin J. exhibits a restrictive approach to the inter-pretative task. Finding the section ambiguous, she applied a stringent stan-dard of construction flowing from the common law presumption that inferior tribunals are strictly limited to punishment of contempt *in facie*. This presumption, together with the lack of clear language in the statute, led her to the conclusion Parliament could not have intended to grant the Tribunal the power to enforce its final orders by punishing for contempt.[154] While acknowledging that the majority's interpretation of "any matters related thereto" was a possible interpretation, it was not to be preferred

---

[153] *Supra*, note 150, at 615 D.L.R.
[154] *Ibid.*, at 630.

to the more restrictive one adopted by Iacobucci C.J. (as he then was) in the Federal Court of Appeal that limited such matters to rehearing of the application and not to its consequential order. In functional terms, she disagreed with the majority's emphasis on the expertise and need for effectiveness as a rationale for finding the Tribunal had the power to punish for contempt *ex facie*. She was of the opinion that the range of remedies available under the legislation, including a civil action for damages, did not justify the assumption that extraordinary contempt powers were necessary. The lack of an express provision for filing the Tribunal's orders with a superior court for enforcement was not to be determinative either, as this was an inherent and remedial jurisdiction of the courts in any event, and this gap could also indicate an intent that enforcement was to be restricted to the criminal and civil remedies set out elsewhere in the legislation. Finally, she disagreed that the Tribunal's expertise would be wasted or lost, as it was neither necessary for enforcement nor could it be provided to a criminal court by the prosecution utilizing this expertise or by the Tribunal seeking intervenor status.

At the heart of these two competing "visions", when one removes the legal technicalities of both (*e.g.*, the majority relying upon the differences between the English and French versions of s. 8 of the legislation), is a basic functional policy question — and not one of jurisdiction — relating to the appropriateness of the remedy in the regulatory context of the Tribunal. While the presence of a member of the judiciary on the Tribunal, and the concomitant need for his or her approval of the appropriateness and exercise of any contempt power, soften the strength of the majority decision, it still recognizes and accepts the need for and ability of administrative tribunals to exercise remedial powers traditionally, if not exclusively, the prerogative of the superior courts.

Similar acceptance of the integrity of tribunal decision-making is found in the court's decision in *U.N.A. v. Alta. (A.G.)*,[155] where McLaughlin J., this time writing the majority decision, upheld a finding of criminal contempt for violating a labour tribunal's order. The legislation did not permit the superior court to examine the validity of the order, and this was challenged as contrary to s. 96 of the *Constitution Act, 1867*. This was rejected by the majority, who reasoned that the superior court's jurisdiction was not diminished by this provision, but instead was given additional powers by which the tribunal could enforce its orders. McLaughlin J., apparently mollified by fact that, consistent with her dissent in *Chrysler*, the contempt proceedings were heard by a superior court and not the tribunal, indicated that it was not a question of jurisdiction, but one of legislative policy as to whether breach of a tribunal's order was to be

---

[155] [1992] 2 S.C.R. 901, 1 Alta. L.R. (3d) 129, 71 C.C.C. (3d) 225, 92 CLLC 14,023, 13 C.R. (4th) 1, 9 C.R.R. (2d) 29, 89 D.L.R. (4th) 609, 135 N.R. 321.

equated with breach of a court order, which was achieved by the statute permitting filing of the order with the court and its enforcement as if it was a court order. Regardless of the extraordinary and serious nature of the contempt power, the court did not find it necessary for s. 96 judges to be able to go behind the validity of the tribunal order which was the basis of the contempt or that such proceedings could flow only from breach of court orders. This constituted a recognition of the modern reality of tribunal decision-making and an acceptance of its integrity that is consistent with "real" deference based on mutual respect:

> Against the argument that the contempt power is so serious that it should be available for breaches of orders actually made by s. 96 judges, can be raised the argument that in reality important portions of our laws are administered not only by s.96 judges but by inferior tribunals, and that these decisions, like court decisions, form part of the law and deserve respect and consequently the support of the contempt power.[156]

(iii) *Mandatory Orders*

Somewhat paradoxically, it is in this area of remedial powers that the tension between tribunal creativity and judicial control is most evident and most disparate. In some areas, such as human rights legislation, the remedial power is general and broad. For example, under the *Ontario Human Rights Code*, where a finding of discrimination and breach of the Code is made, a board of inquiry may "direct the party to do anything that, in the opinion of the Board, the party ought to do to achieve compliance with the Act, both in respect of the complaint and in respect of future practices".[157] The wide range of non-monetary orders made under the provision confirm the legislative intent "to encourage broad creativity in the area of awards".[158] While no deference is paid to human rights decision-making on the merits, apart from fact finding, as noted previously,[159] generally speaking the courts have not disturbed the remedial orders made by tribunals that were correct in their interpretation of the substantive provisions of the legislation.[160]

On the other hand, in the field of labour relations, as we have seen, and perhaps because the remedial powers of tribunals are combinations

---

[156] *Ibid.*, at 939. See Laskin, *supra*, note 149, at 226.

[157] R.S.O. 1990, c. H.19, s. 41(1)(*a*).

[158] Keene, *Human Rights in Ontario*, 2nd ed. (Thompson Canada: Toronto, 1992), at 367-68.

[159] *Supra*, note 36.

[160] See Keene, *supra*, note 158.

of specific, general and consequential ones, there has been greater scope for judicial intervention. For example, prior to *C.U.P.E.*, the Ontario Divisional Court in *Re Samuel Cooper & Co. Ltd. and I.L.G.W.U.*[161] upheld the power of an arbitrator to order an employer to require employees to become union members, to check off union dues and to contribute to benefit funds. It reasoned that the general legislated policy of final and binding settlement by arbitration, and the creation of specialized tribunals to effect this objective, meant that such tribunals "ought to have the necessary powers to achieve such results".[162] The jurisdiction of the arbitrator was sufficiently wide "to encompass a full range of remedy", which was not limited by the legislation.[163]

Similarly, in the immediate "afterglow" of *C.U.P.E.*, the Divisional Court in *Re Tandy Electronics* upheld the tribunal's order that the employer cease and desist from insisting on a term in a collective agreement that employees advise the employer individually that they wished union dues to be deducted from their wages, as it had found this to be aimed at avoiding a collective agreement and undermining the union. The court viewed this exercise of an express cease and desist power as a "reasonable rather than patently unreasonable" one even if it had an indirect effect of imposing a term of a collective agreement on the parties, for which it had no direct power.[164] As we have noted, the Supreme Court of Canada at this time gave wide scope to a tribunal's interpretation of its remedial powers (*Masicotte, Halifax Longshoremen's Ass'n*) provided there was a rational connection between the primary decision and its consequential remedy (*Nat'l Bank*). However, *L'Acadie* and subsequent cases tightened the noose of jurisdictional theory on this concept both with respect to the standard of review and the restricted interpretation of the statutory provisions in question.

(iv) *Interim Orders*

A similar contrast may be found in cases dealing with interim orders. Before *C.U.P.E.*, for example, the Federal Court of Appeal held that

---

[161] [1973] 2 O.R. 841, 35 D.L.R. (3d) 501 (Div. Ct.).

[162] *Ibid.,* at 506.

[163] *Ibid.*

[164] *Supra*, note 142, at 214. In *C.U.P.E. v. Labour Relations Board (N.S.)*, *supra*, note 148, at 12,353 the Supreme Court of Canada held that the remedial powers of the tribunal did not permit it to impose terms of a collective agreement. It noted that in *Tandy* there was no similar power, and the indirect effect noted by the Divisional Court, but did not "pursue this matter", as it did not arise in the case.

despite the lack of express statutory authority, the National Energy Board was empowered by necessary implication to order a regulated company to file financial information not already in existence in the form specified by the board.[165] The court found that the nature of the economic issues within the board's jurisdiction and its public convenience and necessity mandate as a regulator made the challenged power "necessary to the effective exercise of the board's jurisdiction",[166] and the board need not wait to extract the information by *viva voce* evidence in a hearing.

In *Bell Canada v. Canada (C.R.T.C.)*,[167] the Supreme Court of Canada upheld the power of the C.R.T.C. to order Bell Canada to grant a one-time credit to customers to remedy excess revenues generated by interim rates approved by the C.R.T.C. pending a rate hearing. The C.R.T.C. had jurisdiction under the *Railway Act* to approve telephone tolls if they were "just and reasonable" and by reason of s. 340(5) "[i]n all other matters not expressly provided for in this section, the Commission may make orders with respect to all matters relating to . . . tolls".[168] In addition, it had general powers to make interim orders and to review, rescind, change, alter or vary any order made by it or re-hear any application before deciding it.[169]

The court's judgment, written by Gonthier J., introduced the concept of deference to tribunals not protected by privative clauses based on the principle of "specialization of duties",[170] which led to the "spectrum analysis" now accepted in *Pezim* and *Goldhawk*. However, the issue of the power of the C.R.T.C. to review its interim order and to make the credit order was characterized as a jurisdictional one not within its area of specialized expertise so that no deference was to be accorded to its interpretation of its powers.

Notwithstanding this strict standard of review, Gonthier J. upheld the C.R.T.C.'s interpretation of its remedial powers, after reviewing the tribunal's overall purpose, function and legislative context. He felt that the legislative scheme demonstrated an intent to give the tribunal "flexible and versatile" powers to ensure telephone rates were just and reasonable, thus giving emphasis to the public interest mandate of the C.R.T.C. More important, from our perspective, was his recognition that it was open to him to give a restricted interpretation of the legislation, as was the case in *L'Acadie* (which is not mentioned in the judgment), and his rejection such an approach:

---

[165] *Re Interprovincial Pipe Line Ltd. and National Engergy Board* (1977), 78 D.L.R. (3d) 401.
[166] *Ibid.*, at 405.
[167] [1989] 1 S.C.R. 1722, 60 D.L.R. (4th) 682, 97 N.R. 15.
[168] *Railway Act*, R.S.C. 1985, c. R.3, ss. 334-340.
[169] *National Transportation Act*, R.S.C. 1985, c. N.20, ss. 60, 66.
[170] *Supra*, note 167, at 1740.

Although the power granted by s. 340(5) [of the *Railway Act, supra*] could be construed restrictively by the application of the ejusdem generis rule, I do not think that such an interpretation is warranted. Section 340(5) is but one indication of the legislator's intention to give the appellant all the powers necessary to ensure that the principle . . . that all rates should be just and reasonable, be observed at all time.[171]

Put simply, the legislation was interpreted not so as to limit the remedial power but to support, if not enhance, it.

Equally important, Gonthier J. recognized that there was no clear or express statutory power to revisit the period when the interim rates were in force, but did not interpret the tribunal's review power, as had the Federal Court of Appeal, as restricted by the presumption against retroactivity. Nor did the fact that another tribunal, the National Energy Board, had such explicit statutory powers cause him to give a more limited interpretation. He invoked the doctrine of necessary implication to sustain the autonomy of the tribunal in achieving its legislated purpose:

The powers of any administrative tribunal must of course be stated in its enabling statute but they may also exist by necessary implication from the wording of the act, its structure and its purpose. *Although courts must refrain from unduly broadening the powers of such regulatory authorities through judicial law-making, they must also avoid sterilizing those powers through overly technical interpretations of enabling statutes.* [Emphasis added.][172]

This purposive and liberal interpretation of the remedial powers of the C.R.T.C. appears at odds with the strict and technical interpretative approach taken by Beetz J. in *L'Acadie*. As we have noted, that decision was not referred to by Gonthier J. The two can be reconciled only by distinguishing the different statutory schemes. In *Bell Canada* the policy-making function of determining "just and reasonable" rates for all consumers in the public interest provided the basis for the decision. In *L'Acadie* the dispute was between employer and union, not involving the general public, and the policy-making function of the tribunal was not so much "public interest" as it was to ensure the collecting bargaining dynamic, as much as possible, determined the outcome rather than the tribunal.

These differences in approach are reflected in the majority and minority decisions of the Supreme Court in *Canadian Pacific Airlines v. Canadian Air Line Pilots Ass'n*, discussed previously.[173] There,

---

[171] *Ibid.*, at 1738-39.
[172] *Ibid.*, at 1756.
[173] [1993] 3 S.C.R. 724, 93 CLLC 14,062, 108 D.L.R. (4th) 1, 160 N.R. 321.

Gonthier J. applied *L'Acadie* and distinguished his decisions both in *Chrysler Canada* and *Bell Canada* in holding that the labour tribunal could only compel production of documents in a formal hearing and not prior to it. He held that the general residual and incidental powers in s. 121 of the *Canada Labour Code* could not be construed so as to give the tribunal powers broader than those expressly provided in s. 118(*a*).[174] As noted previously, the effect of the exercise of the power ("coercive") and its nature ("judicial"), led Gonthier J. to the conclusion that an extension of the power from the hearing context to the administrative context would be "an exceptional enlargement of its application. The power cannot be envisaged to be so broad in the absence of clear wording to that effect."[175] It should be noted, however, that if powers to order production are expressly granted, as part of regulatory and administrative powers, the court has not found them to be so coercive as to be inconsistent with ss. 7 and 8 of the Charter.[176]

He distinguished his decision in *Bell Canada* as a case of remedial powers existing by necessary implication, where a denial of the powers would be inconsistent with the purposes of the tribunal. In *C.A.L.P.A.*, Gonthier J. found no conflict between the general purposes of the tribunal and the restriction of its powers of production, given the judicial nature of the power and his conclusion that such a restriction would not "unduly impair" the other activities of the Board.[177] He distinguished *Chrysler Canada* on the basis of the plain meaning of the words in question, the breadth of the statutory provisions, and established principles of interpre-

---

[174] The two sections provided as follows:

> 118. The Board has, in relation to any proceeding before it, power (a) to summon and enforce the attandance of witnesses and compel them to give oral or written evidence on oath and to produce such documents and things as the Board deems requisite to the full investigation and consideration of any matter within its jurisdiction that is before the Board in the proceeding.
>
> . . . . .
>
> 121. The Board shall exercise such powers and perform such duties as are conferred or imposed upon it by, or as may be incidental to the attainment of the objects of, this Part including, without restricting the generality of the foregoing, the making of orders requiring compliance with the provisions of this Part, with any regulation made under this Part or with any decision made in respect of a matter before the Board.

[175] *Supra*, note 173, at 739.

[176] *Thomson Newspapers Ltd. v. Canada (Director of Investigation & Research)*, [1990] 1 S.C.R. 425, 39 O.A.C. 161, 54 C.C.C. (3d) 417, 29 C.P.R. (3d) 97, 76 C.R. (3d) 129, 47 C.R.R. 1, 67 D.L.R. (4th) 161, 106 N.R. 161; *British Columbia (Securities Com'n) v. Branch*, [1995] 2 S.C.R. 3, [1995] 5 W.W.R. 129, 97 C.C.C. (3d) 305, 38 C.R. (4th) 133, 27 C.R.R. (2d) 189, 123 D.L.R. (4th) 462, 180 N.R. 241.

[177] *Supra*, note 173, at 746.

tation. Furthermore, the nature of the power was the same as the context in which it was to be exercised, ie. both were judicial, and the statute provided procedural safeguards specific to the exercise of the power.[178]

The dissent of L'Heureux-Dubé J. focused the debate on the majority's classification of function approach in determining that a restrictive interpretation flowed from the judicial nature of the power. Although, as noted earlier, she determined that the standard of review was that of correctness, she echoed the spirit of *C.U.P.E.* in her approach to the interpretative function of the court:

> A conclusion that the order of an administrative tribunal is subject to a strict standard of judicial review does not, however, mean that a *limiting or literal interpretation* necessarily governs the way in which powers conferred by its enabling Act should be read . . . The pragmatic and functional approach . . . is the very opposite of a textual and formalistic approach. The analysis of . . . Gonthier J. begins and is primarily concerned with a literal and gramatical interpretation. I definitely cannot agree with such an interpretation . . .[179] [Emphasis added.]

Her reading of the legislative intent was different, emphasizing the tribunal's completeness of control over its own procedure, a hallmark of tribunal autonomy, and that its statutory function in the complex field of labour relations required its ability to intervene in the collective bargaining process to be "both flexible and effective".[180] By unduly emphasizing the classification of the power as judicial, she felt the majority "runs the risk of masking this special dimension of the board's function and in so doing, of bypassing the particular nature of its role".[181] She felt that Gonthier J. himself had pointed out the risk of making classification of function determinative in an earlier case, where he had observed:

> One should beware of trying to pigeon hole the role of the Tribunal within a "judicial" or "administrative" model. This Court has since long warned of the dangers of relying on too tight a dichotomy between these models of decision (*Nicholson v. Haldimand-Norfolk Regional Board of Commissioners of Police*, [1979] 1 S.C.R. 311 at p. 325).[182]

Her review of the legislative context led her to the conclusion that the tribunal was not under a duty to hold a hearing in order to exercise

---

[178] *Ibid,.* at 744.
[179] *Ibid.*, at 757.
[180] *Ibid.*, at 758.
[181] *Ibid.*, at 759.
[182] *Chrysler Canada Ltd. v. Canada (Competition Tribunal)*, [1992] 2 S.C.R. 394 at 418, 7 B.L.R. (2d) 1, 42 C.P.R. (3d) 353, 92 D.L.R. (4th) 609.

the power, nor that procedural norms of fairness required it to do so, as concerns over objections to admissibility, relevance and privilege could be addressed in writing, and the tribunal's decision were subject to internal appeal (its power to vary or rescind its own decisions) and external control by judicial review. The interpretation by the majority, she felt, had the effect of excluding the fundamental principle that the tribunal should have complete control over its procedure, rather than "preserving the ultimate purpose of the Board, which is that the action it takes shall be flexible and effective, [which] is more consistent here with Parliament's primary intent".[183]

Finally, in answer to the majority's view that the power did not arise by necessary implication, as the restriction on it was not inconsistent with the tribunal's overall purpose, she neatly turned the argument around, stating that:

> The Board's primary purpose is not inconsistent with a power to order the filing of documents and to require intervenors to testify in writing outside *viva voce* hearings. On the contrary, the effect of such a power is to increase the Board's efficacy, by allowing it to dispose of matters without a *viva voce* hearing and facilitating the settlement of issues by non-litigous means.[184]

(v) *Review and Rehearing Orders*

The ability of a tribunal to rehear a matter is perhaps the most interesting example of the evolution of administrative law away from the Dicean model. That is, a final decision of a court cannot be reopened unless there has been a slip in drawing up the formal judgment[185] or where there has been an error in expressing the manifest intention of the court.[186] Historically, the courts had the power to rehear, but this power was replaced through the *Judicature Act*s which transferred the power to the appeal courts.[187] Thus the doctrine of *functus officio* — "a task performed" — became deeply rooted in our legal system and the primary rationale for prohibiting the reconsideration of a final decision. Stated more succinctly,

---

[183] *Supra*, note 173, at 760.
[184] *Ibid.*
[185] *Re St. Nazaire Co.* (1879), 12 Ch. D. 88.
[186] *Paper Machinery Ltd. v. J.O. Ross Engr. Corp.*, [1934] S.C.R. 186, [1934] 2 D.L.R. 239.
[187] See *Courts of Justice Act*, R.S.O. 1990, c. C.43, ss. 6 and 132. For the seminal discussion of the history of the courts and the judiciary see Lederman, "The Independence of the Judiciary" (1956), 24 Can. Bar Rev. 1.

once the trial court had performed its task — rendered a decision — only an appellate court could review or reconsider the decision.

By contrast, there are several tribunals which are given express statutory powers to amend, vary, rescind, or reconsider a final decision it has made, including the Ontario Municipal Board,[188] the Ontario Highway Transport Board,[189] the Canadian Transport Commission,[190] and the Social Assistance Review Board.[191]

To the extent that the courts have exercised control over a tribunal's rehearing, the focus has tended to be primarily on the question of whether the tribunal has the power to rehear a final decision. In that regard, the jurisprudence has, historically, been of familiar jurisdictional themes: (i) the tribunal must be "correct" in determining its jurisdiction to rehear a matter; and (ii) the power to rehear may be express or implied. More recently, however, the courts have considered the complexities of *functus officio* in the administrative law context.

The ability of a tribunal to rehear a final decision raises general issues of finality, encapsulated in the doctrine of *functus officio*, but it also raises unique administrative law issues. When should a rehearing be held? At what point does the court exercise its supervisory role? Should the same board members, if available, sit on the rehearing? Is there a reasonable apprehension of bias created by rehearing the matter? Does the tribunal start afresh or only on particular issues? How do rehearings operate within any requirement to pursue and exhaust alternative remedies and/or prematurity?

A tribunal's express statutory authority to rehear or reconsider can, due to the complexities of administrative law, achieve almost chimeric qualities. In *Re Parent Cartage Ltd. and Ont. Highway Transport Board*, [192] the Ontario Highway Transport Board's express power to rehear, at any time, any of its decisions arose under its enabling statute, the *Ontario Highway Transport Board Act*.[193] The competitors of Parent Cartage Ltd. requested, and were granted, a review of the Board's decision, pursuant to the *Public Vehicles Act*,[194] which had granted the company a certificate of "public necessity and convenience". In the bifurcated licensing

---

[188] *Ontario Municipal Board Act*, R.S.O. 1990, c. O.28, s. 43 (hereinafter *OMB Act*).

[189] *Ontario Highway Transport Board Act*, R.S.O. 1990, c. O.19, s. 16 (hereinafter *OHTB Act*).

[190] *National Transportation Act, 1987*, R.S.C. 1985, c. 28 (3rd Supp.), s. 41.

[191] *Family Benefits Act*, R.S.O. 1990, c. F.2, s. 14(7).

[192] (1970), 26 O.R. (2d) 83, 102 D.L.R. (3d) 117 (C.A.); revg 20 O.R. (2d) 219, 87 D.L.R. (3d) 144 (Div. Ct.) (hereinafter *Re Parent Cartage*).

[193] *Supra*, note 185.

[194] *Public Vehicles Act*, R.S.O. 1990, c. P.54.

regime created by the *PVA*, the board's certificate was the necessary precondition to the issuance of a public vehicle operating licence by the Minister. The basis for the competitors' request was that the principal of the company had given evidence in a board proceeding that the company was not charging rates as filed under the legislation. The remedy sought by the competitors was to amend or revoke the terms of the certificate of public necessity and convenience, and by implication, the operating licence of Parent Cartage.

The crux of the issue was the apparent conflict between the Board's authority to rehear under the *OHTB Act* and the bifurcated licensing mechanism created by the *Public Vehicles Act*. That is, while the Ontario Highway Transport Board had the power to review its decisions pursuant to its constituent statute, only the Minister, pursuant to the *Public Vehicles Act* could issue and subsequently initiate a review of a licence by requesting a report from the board. Moreover, only the Minister, after considering the board's non-binding report, could suspend, cancel, revoke, or amend that licence. The Court of Appeal held that the board was without statutory authority to conduct the review it proposed to do because the Board had "by-passed" that statutory process.[195]

Of significance in the Court of Appeal's reasoning was that the rehearing powers of the board could not be resorted to in this instance because the issue - *i.e.*, an alleged contravention of the licence — did not "bear on the original decision" of public necessity and convenience made under the *Public Vehicles Act*.[196] In effect, the board was not holding a "rehearing" as contemplated by the *Ontario Highway Transport Board Act*, but a "licence review" under the *Public Vehicles Act*. This was a distinction with a difference insofar as it determined the appropriate statutory mechanism which could be invoked, and the concomitant jurisdiction of the board. The complexity of the rehearing power arose from the bifurcation of the decision-making process which, at first blush, appeared to be a conflict of statutes but was, as the Court of Appeal correctly determined, a conflict of jurisdiction.

In the absence of an express statutory power to rehear, the courts have, nonetheless, in certain instances determined that tribunals have an implied authority to reconsider their decisions. This particularly arises in cases where a rehearing is based on new evidence not available, despite due diligence, at the original hearing.

In *Grillas v. Canada (Minister of Manpower & Immigration)*,[197] the appellant was denied entry into Canada and ordered deported by the Immigration Appeal Review Board. He subsequently was granted a rehearing

---

[195] *Supra*, note 192, at 89-90.
[196] *Ibid.*, at 91.
[197] [1972] S.C.R. 577 at 580-81, 23 D.L.R. (3d) 1 (hereinafter *Grillas*).

on the grounds that there was new evidence that he would be subject to unusual hardship if he were returned to his homeland. The rehearing, heard by two of the three members from the original panel plus one other member, confirmed the original decision. The appellant appealed the rehearing, raising as one ground of appeal that the rehearing had been before a differently constituted panel.

The preliminary issue before the Supreme Court of Canada was whether the Immigration Appeal Review Board had the jurisdiction to rehear the matter in the absence of an express statutory authority. The court answered in the affirmative, holding that the board had an "equitable" jurisdiction under its constituent statute which was a continuing jurisdiction, and not one which had to be exercised "once and for all".[198] The rationale for this was that the intent of the *Immigration Appeal Board Act* was to ameliorate the "lot" of those persons subject to a deportation order.[199] Therefore, the court reasoned, the board had the jurisdiction to hear further evidence in cases it deemed proper, particularly as there were no rights of appeal from the board's decision except on points of law.[200] Until the appellant had actually been physically deported, the court held, the board could return to its original decision. Although characterizing the issue as one of jurisdiction, the Supreme Court did not discuss the appropriate standard of review.

Significantly, the court, having found the implied authority for a rehearing, rejected the argument raised by the Minister that the board was *functus officio*. Citing the English authorities dealing with the doctrine in the judicial context, the court held that the same reasoning did not apply to the board because there was no appeal except on a question of law.[201] The court, further, found "no merit" in the appellant's argument that he was entitled to a rehearing before the same panel members, citing a lack of authority for this proposition, that the appellant had suffered no injustice, and that he was treated fairly in two processes.[202]

In *Re Lornex Mining Corp.*[203] the court applied *Grillas* to the British Columbia Human Rights Commission. The Commission had reopened its earlier decision to dismiss a complaint of sex discrimination when the complainant provided new evidence to support her contention that her employer was providing her male peers with gratuitious, on-site accommodation at the company's mine as an employee benefit not available to her. The employer challenged the reopening on the basis that the Commission had no specific statutory jurisdiction for a rehearing.

---

[198] *Ibid.*, at 582 and 590.
[199] *Ibid.*
[200] *Ibid.*, at 589.
[201] *Ibid.*
[202] *Ibid.*, at 584.
[203] [1976] 5 W.W.R. 554, 69 D.L.R. (3d) 705 (B.C.S.C.) (hereinafter *Re Lornex*).

The court acknowledged that there was no appellate tribunal and that the Commission had conceded that it was applying beneficial legislation. Consequently, where, as in *Grillas*, there was additional evidence, the Commission had, by implication, the right to reopen the hearing.[204] However, the court in *Re Lornex* interpreted *Grillas* to limit that jurisdiction to the new evidence adduced, and stated that the power to alter the original decision was contingent upon the new evidence.[205] In so holding, the court in *Re Lornex* accepted uncritically the "questionable proposition",[206] espoused in *Grillas*, that a rehearing power could be implied, but limited to fresh evidence cases in cases of "beneficial" legislation.

The analysis by the Supreme Court in *Grillas* was perhaps not as rigorous as it could have been. That is, it appeared that the Supreme Court tacitly assumed the rehearing power and appeared to be influenced by the absence of an appeal right and the presumed beneficial nature of the legislation.[207] The court in *Re Lornex* merely repeated the analysis. Consequently, the decision raised problematic questions of when a tribunal's authority to rehear would be implied - *i.e.*, only where there was no appellate tribunal, "beneficial" legislation and new evidence not previously available — and of the application of *functus officio* to administrative tribunals which did not have express rehearing powers. These were questions to be addressed by a later court.

The question of implied rehearing authority and *functus officio* were revisited by the Supreme Court of Canada in *Chandler v. Alta. Ass'n of Architects*.[208] The Practice Review Board of the Alberta Association of Architects, on its own initiative, sought to review the practice of individual members of a group of architects who had filed for bankruptcy. Although the Practice Review Board clearly stated that its hearing was restricted to a practice review — as distinct from the complaint review/disciplinary process — the board proceeded to make specific findings of unprofessional conduct and recommended to the Council of the Association that the Council impose fines in excess of $100,000 and suspensions. The architects and the corporate entities applied for *certiorari* to quash the findings on the basis that the Practice Review Board had made findings of unprofessional conduct, the purview of the Complaint Review Committee under the *Architects Act*.[209] The trial judge granted the order for

---

[204] *Ibid.*, at 557-58.

[205] *Ibid.*, at 559.

[206] Macdonald, "Reopenings, Rehearings and Reconsiderations in Administrative Law: *Re Lornex Mining Corporation and Bukwa*" (1979), 17 Osgoode Hall L. J. 207 at 209.

[207] *Ibid.*, at 216.

[208] [1989] 2 S.C.R. 848, [1989] 6 W.W.R. 521, 70 Alta. L.R. (2d) 193, 62 D.L.R. (4th) 577, 99 N.R. 277 (hereinafter *Chandler*).

[209] R.S.A. 1980, c. A-44.1, s.9(1)(*j*.1) [en. 1981, c. 5, s. 6].

certiorari which was upheld by the Court of Appeal for different reasons. After the Court of Appeal's decision, the Practice Review Board gave notice that it intended to continue the original hearing in order to give consideration to preparing a further report to the Council concerning a referral of the matter to the Complaint Review Committee. The architects obtained an order of prohibition from the Court of Queen's Bench on the basis that the Practice Review Board had exercised its jurisdiction and was *functus officio*. The Queen's Bench order was vacated and overturned by the Court of Appeal on the basis that the Practice Review Board had not exercised its jurisdiction in the original hearing to recommend a referral to the Complaint Review Committee.

Writing for the majority, Sopinka J. acknowledged that it was not uncommon for tribunals to have specific statutory authority to rehear.[210] Citing the English authorities for *functus officio*, Sopinka J. held that the decision in *Grillas* did not go so far as to preclude the application of the doctrine to administrative tribunals. Subject to three exceptions, Sopinka J. reasoned that a flexible application of *functus officio* should be made to tribunals which are subject to appeal on points of law:

> I do not understand Martland J. [in *Grillas*] to go so far as to hold that *functus officio* has no application to administrative tribunals. Apart from the English practice, which is based on a reluctance to amend or reopen formal judgments, there is sound policy reason for recognizing the finality of proceedings before administrative tribunals. As a general rule, once such a tribunal has reached a final decision in respect to the matter that is before it in accordance with its enabling statute, that decision cannot be revisited because the tribunal has changed its mind, made an error within jurisdiction or because there has been a change in circumstances. It can only do so if authorized by statute or if there is a slip or error within the exceptions enunciated in *Paper Machinery Ltd. v Ross Engr. Corp.*, *supra*.
>
> To this extent, the principle of *functus officio* applies. It is based, however, on the policy ground which favours finality of proceedings rather than the rule which was developed with respect to formal judgments of a court whose decision was subject to a full appeal. For this reason, I am of the opinion that its application must be more flexible and less formalistic in respect to decisions of administrative tribunals which are subject to appeal only on a point of law. Justice may require the reopening of administrative proceedings in order to provide relief which would otherwise be available on appeal.
>
> Accordingly, the principle should not be strictly applied where there are indications in the enabling statute that a decision can be reopened in order to enable the tribunal to discharge the function to it by enabling legislation. This was the situation in *Grillas*, *supra*.[211]

---

[210] *Supra*, note 208, at 536-37.
[211] *Ibid.*, at 541-42.

Sopinka J. further distinguished a proceeding where the tribunal, such as the Practice Review Board, had not disposed of an issue — *i.e.*, the recommendation of the referral to the Complaint Review Committee. In Sopinka J.'s view, the tribunal ought to be allowed to complete its statutory task.[212] By implication, this would not be a "rehearing" but the completion of a continuing hearing. This situation could also be distinguished from the case where the Board's decision was a nullity[213] in which, by definition, the second process could not be a rehearing since the first hearing was void, and required the board to start afresh.[214]

In effect, the majority in *Chandler* characterized the actions of the Practice Review Board as a "continuation" of its statutory function and avoided the rehearing quagmire. If the tribunal had not discharged its statutory duty, it would be permitted to return to its hearing process. By implication, the court's discussion of *functus officio* was, therefore, not germane to the determination but illuminating as to the limitations the court appeared to be placing on rehearings in the absence of express statutory provisions.

The *Chandler* and *Grillas* analyses were combined and applied in a second fresh evidence case involving the British Columbia Human Rights Council and its exercise of discretion in its investigation process.[215] The British Columbia Court of Queen's Bench held that the Council had an equitable but discretionary jurisdiction to reinvestigate a complaint in the appropriate case as the doctrine of *functus officio* had to be applied in the flexible manner contemplated by the court in *Chandler*. Moreover, the Council could not fetter its discretion, as it had, by instituting a policy of not reopening an investigation.[216] The decision was appealed by the Attorney-General of British Columbia, the British Columbia Council of

---

[212] *Ibid.*, at 542.

[213] See *Lange v. Maple Ridge School District No. 42* (1978), 9 B.C.L.R. 232 (S.C.); *Posluns v. Toronto Stock Exchange*, [1968] S.C.R. 330, 67 D.L.R. (2d) 165; *Trizec Equities Ltd. v. Area Assessor Burnaby-New Westminster* (1983), 45 B.C.L.R. 258, 147 D.L.R. (3d) 637, 22 M.P.L.R. 318 (S.C.).

[214] *Supra*, note 208, at 543.

[215] *Zutter v. B.C. (Council of Human Rights)* (1995), 3 B.C.L.R. (3d) 321, 10 C.C.E.L. (2d) 287, 122 D.L.R. (4th) 665 at 674-75 (C.A.); affg (1993), 82 B.C.L.R. (2d) 240, 49 C.C.E.L. 273 at 285-86; leave to appeal to the Supreme Court of Canada was filed July 14, 1995.

[216] Compare this to the exercise of discretion of the Minister of Revenue where the doctrine of *functus officio* did not apply to the discretionary exercise of an official: *MacMillan Bloedel v. R.* (1985), 60 B.C.L.R. 145. For cases dealing with the equitable jurisdiction of a tribunal to reconsider see as well: *Re Ombudsman of Ontario and R. in right of Ontario* (1979), 26 O.R. (2d) 434, 103 D.L.R. (3d) 117 (H.C.); affd 30 O.R. (2d) 768, 117 D.L.R. (3d) 613 (C.A.); *Canada (A.G.) v. Grover* (1994), 80 F.T.R. 256. See also, *Brown v. Troia Investments Inc.* (1995), 22 O.R. (3d) 637 (Div. Ct.).

Human Rights and the Respondent to the human rights complaint who argued that the Council did not have an equitable jurisdiction to reconsider its decision to discontinue the complaint and that the consitutuent statute rendered its decision "final" and, therefore, *functus officio*. The B.C. Court of Appeal rejected these arguments, holding that the legislation, while it did not contain any express or implied "impediment to the ability" of the Council to reconsider, had a sufficient "indication" permiting it to do so in the interests of justice and fairness.

It is apparent from the court's dicta in *Chandler* that the flexible application of *functus officio* to rehearings in the absence of express statutory provisions will require at least three conditions precedent: (1) there must be no appeal except on points of law; (2) the legislation must be "beneficial" in nature, and (3) there must be fresh evidence not previously available despite due diligence. Moreover, the requirement of finality will preclude those tribunals from reopening their proceedings if the tribunal: (1) has changed its mind; (2) made an error within its jurisdiction, and (3) decides there are changed circumstances. While the court articulated a flexible approach to the application of *functus officio*, there remain several outstanding issues. What is "beneficial" legislation particularly in light of the *Interpretations Act*[217] which deems all Acts to be "remedial" and to "receive fair, large and liberal construction and interpretation as will best ensure the attainment of the object of the Act"? What is the threshold for new evidence which will require the tribunal to reconsider its decision and how will that affect any subsequent review of the tribunal's decision particularly if the original decision is upheld? What is the application, if any, of *Chandler* to other tribunals that do not operate under "beneficial" legislation and have limited appeal rights?

The flexible application of *functus officio* shows a "new willingness to structure procedure which will enhance tribunal's ability to fulfil their statutory mandate while freeing them from strict legal doctrines emanating from practices by courts".[218] As such, *Chandler* would appear to foster deference but in rather restricted circumstances. In the broader context of "implied authority" for rehearings, *Chandler* raises problematic questions about fashioning remedies consistent with legal constraints.

It is interesting to note that the use of the rehearing remedy, particularly in cases where the express power exists, has not been considered an alternative to judicial intervention. From a review of the reported case-law, it does not appear that rehearings are part of the requirement of

---

[217] R.S.O. 1990, c. I.11, s. 10.
[218] See McCallum, "Reconsideration, Re-hearing and Varying of Decisions in Administrative Law" (address to Canadian Bar Association), Ottawa, November 25 and 26, 1994, unpublished, at 2-3.

parties to exhaust all alternative remedies before seeking the court's intervention.[219] Rather, in *Brett v. Ont. (Board of Directors of Physiotherapy)*[220] the court refused to order a rehearing in a disciplinary case where the tribunal had heard all of the evidence and made findings which the court found to be patently unreasonable. The court acknowledged that it had no discretion to deny a rehearing but that it could refuse to order one, particularly in this case where it felt a rehearing would be unfair. In so holding, the court recognized that, pragmatically, a party may not want to return to a tribunal to make similar arguments rejected by the tribunal in the original hearing, thereby incurring unnecessary costs and further delays.[221] Hence, while there may be flexibility in the application of *functus officio*, the aggrieved party is also given flexibility to choose the forum in which to obtain the relief sought, an option not otherwise available to the civil litigant.

(vi) *Cabinet Review*

Appeals to Cabinet from the decision of an administrative tribunal are a particularly *sui generis* remedy which, like rehearings, avoid or circumvent the judicial process. While the tribunal itself is not dispensing the remedy, the executive branch is permitted, in certain instances, to intervene in the administrative decision-making process. The essential theoretical construct of cabinet appeals is that of political accountability, a

---

[219] See for example, *Pronto Cabs Ltd. v. Metropolitan Licensing Com'n of Metropolitan Toronto* (1982), 39 O.R. (2d) 488 (Div. Ct.); *R. v. Burns* (1983), 41 O.R. (2d) 774, 5 C.C.C. (3d) 381, 5 C.R.R. 214, 148 D.L.R. (3d) 188 (H.C.J.); *Woodglen & Co. and City of North York* (1983), 42 O.R. (2d) 385, 23 M.P.L.R. 13, 149 D.L.R. (3d) 186 (Div. Ct.); *Ont. (A.G.) v. Rae* (1983), 44 O.R. (2d) 493, 40 C.P.C. 68, 16 C.R.R. 276, 37 R.F.L. (2d) 16, 4 D.L.R. (4th) 465 (H.C.J.); *Re Williams and Kemptville (Bd. of Directors) District Hospital* (1986), 55 O.R. (2d) 633 (H.C.J.); *Taylor v. Metropolitan Toronto (Mun.) (Metropolitan Licensing Com'n)* (1989), 36 O.A.C. 363, 70 O.R. (2d) 733, 63 D.L.R. (4th) 599 (Div. Ct.). Contrast *Martini v. Toronto (City)* (1989), 32 O.A.C. 52, 68 O.R. (2d) 73, 41 M.P.L.R. 220, 57 D.L.R. (4th) 481 (Div. Ct.); affd 36 O.A.C. 47, 70 O.R. (2d) 637, 64 D.L.R. (4th) 382 (C.A.); *550551 Ont. Ltd. v. Framingham* (1991), 4 O.R. (3d) 571, 4 B.L.R. (3d) 75, 5 C.B.R. (3d) 204, 91 CLLC 14,031, 82 D.L.R. (4th) 731 (Div. Ct.).

[220] (1993), 104 D.L.R. (4th) 421 (Ont. C.A.) at 425-26.

[221] An exception to this is the CRTC wherein the parties regularly seek the Commission's reconsideration. One of the most well-known cases involved Call-Net Telecommunications Inc. a company which used a combination of cabinet appeals and applications for reconsideration to operate for over 300 days in contravention of a C.R.T.C. ruling. See Hancock, "Regulated Competition: Resale and Sharing in Telecommunications" (1992), 2 M.C.L.R. 251.

subject beyond the scope of this paper.[222] The concept accepts that tribunals exercise no general inherent jurisdiction, and, as creatures of statutes, ought to be subject, in appropriate circumstances, to the broad public policy dictates of the cabinet.[223]

While courts have exercised jurisdictional control over rehearings, they have circumscribed the judicial role in reviewing cabinet appeals. Courts have carefully created a demarcation between statutory appeals and judicial review applications — where the scope of review is that of a spectrum between "correctness" and "patent unreasonableness" — and appeals to the Lieutenant-Governor in Council, characterizing "cabinet appeals" as somewhat oxymoronic.[224] However, in the context of appeals from administrative tribunals, the courts have clearly stated that the decisions of the Lieutenant Governor in Council are reviewable as they are not crown prerogatives but are made pursuant to a statutory provision.[225]

In *Canada (A.G.) v. Inuit Tapirisat of Canada*,[226] the Supreme Court of Canada rejected the proposition that procedural fairness applied to cabinet decisions of a broad and legislative nature. Consequently, the cabinet was not required to grant access to the information provided to it by the petitioner Bell Canada, to permit the intervenors before the CRTC to participate in the cabinet petition process, and/or to give reasons. The Supreme Court reasoned that application of the duty of fairness decisions about broad based policy questions such as telephone rates was determined by reference to the statutory context which, in this case, gave the cabinet

---

[222] It is sometimes referred to as "selective accountability". See Hartle, *Public Policy Decision-making and Regulation* (Toronto: Institute for Research on Public Policy, 1979) at 132-33.

[223] For a more comprehensive analysis of this point, see Janisch, "The Role of Independent Regulatory Agencies in Canada" (1978), 27 U.N.B. L. Rev. 83 at 88 and "Independence of Administrative Tribunals: In Praise of Structural Heretics" (1987), 1 C.J.A.L.P.; Harris, "The Courts and the Cabinet: 'Unfastening the Buckel'", [1989] Pub. L. 251 at 254; Rankin, "The Cabinets and the Courts: Political Tribunals and Judicial Tribunals", 3 C.J.A.L.P. 301 at 323.

[224] *Re C.P. Express and Snow* (1981), 32 O.R. (2d) 45 (C.A.); affg 31 O.R. (2d) 120 (Div. Ct.). "Cabinet appeals" are a misnomer which imparts, through semantics, expectations of rights to traditional legal concepts of judicial appeals: See Lawrence, "Powers of the Governor in Council over Administrative Tribunals: Appeals and Directions" (1988), C.J.A.L.P. 327 at 328.

[225] *Re Davisville Investment Co. and City of Toronto* (1977), 15 O.R. (2d) 553 at 556 and 559, 2 M.P.L.R. 81 (C.A.) (hereinafter *Re Davisville*). The Supreme Court of Canada has also held unequivocally that the decisions of the federal cabinet are subject to review under the *Charter of Rights*: *Operation Dismantle Inc. v. R.*, [1985] 1 S.C.R. 441 at 455-56, 12 Admin. L.R. 16, 13 C.R.R. 287, 18 D.L.R. (4th) 481, 59 N.R. 1 (hereinafter *Operation Dismantle*).

[226] [1980] 2 S.C.R. 735 at 739, 115 D.L.R. (3d) 1, 33 N.R. 304 (hereinafter *Innuit Tapirisat*).

wide powers to review the CRTC's decision.[227] The decision is, moreover, illustrative of the court's reliance upon statutory interpretation to avoid articulating its hesitation to interfere with the cabinet's decision. The court clearly indicated that the cabinet must act in accordance with the rule of law by exercising statutory powers (which in this case, the court interpreted broadly) but made reference to the particular nature of the cabinet's function when discussing the cabinet's "technique of review".[228] It was not until *Operation Dismantle* that the court began to express its recognition of the particular deference it would give to the cabinet in a non-Charter context.

While the Supreme Court in *Inuit Tapirisat* determined the extent of procedural fairness required in cabinet appeals, the decision was silent on the issue of substantive review, if any, of cabinet decisions. That is, the cabinet generally does not give reasons for its decisions, particularly in the area of telecommunications where appeals have been somewhat common, but the cabinet is not, by virtue of *Inuit Tapirisat*, precluded from giving reasons.[229] The degree of deference that would be given to the reasons for the cabinet's decision is an interesting question which would likely compel the courts to evaluate the relationship between the executive branch and the judiciary and, possibly, re-evaluate the requirements of procedural fairness.

A subsidiary issue raised by *Innuit Tapirisat*, but not disposed of, is the application of deference to cabinet decisions involving individual concerns.[230] In a manner reminiscent of the pre-*Nicholson* cases, where the court's preoccupation was that of "*judicial*" and "*quasi*-judicial" functions, the demarcation in *Inuit Tapirisat* between legislative and non-legislative functions of cabinet would appear to make deference contingent upon classification. As Professor Mullan has persuasively argued, this analytical approach is cloaked in a tenuous presumption of political

---

[227] See also *Nat'l Anti-Poverty Organization v. Canada (A.G.)*, [1989] 3 F.C. 684, 28 F.T.R. 160*n*, 26 C.P.R. (3d) 440, 60 D.L.R. (4th) 712 at 725, 99 N.R. 181 (hereinafter *NAPO*).

[228] *Supra*, note 226, at 753. The court defined this merely to refer to the cabinet's ability to resort to staff and department personnel.

[229] This is not entirely beyond the realm of possibility. Telesat Canada appealed the rate decision concerning the Anik "E" generation of satellites to the cabinet. A political furor erupted over the appeal because the government had a controlling interest in the company and had announced in the budget prior to the decision that the government was intending to privatize the company. As a result, in what was an unprecedented move, the cabinet, in P.C. Order 1991-1145 (June 20, 1991) the cabinet not only varied the order of the CRTC but gave reasons for the variation.

[230] See for example *Homex Realty & Development Co. Ltd. v. Village of Wyoming*, [1980] 2 S.C.R. 1011, 13 M.P.L.R. 234, 116 D.L.R. (3d) 1, 33 N.R. 475, where the issue was a municipal by-law.

accountability[231] (no government having ever fallen or cabinet minister resigned because of an error in the exercise of its statutory right to change a tribunal decision) and creates a false distinction, for purposes of judicial review, between a tribunal's and the cabinet's exercise of statutory authority premised, in reality, more on who is deciding and less on function. As such, the potential for classifying as "legislative" a cabinet decision which is "doubtfully so" is increased without a compelling analysis of how and why we distinguish executive (as used in the broadest sense) from tribunal decision making.[232]

(vii) *Costs*

Costs awards in the administrative law context best illustrate the grafting of judicial concepts on to polycentric decision-making processes involving a plurality of interests before administrative tribunals. An administrative tribunal often does not, *per se*, adjudicate a *lis inter partes*, thereby negating the historical rationale for the awarding of costs in civil litigation. As there are no winners and losers, strictly speaking, as a result of a tribunal's decision, the purpose of costs in administrative tribunal proceedings is primarily focussed on facilitating public participation rather than on awarding costs to the winner.[233] However, the purposes for costs awarded by administrative tribunals are as diverse as the tribunals themselves.[234]

Particularly as it pertains to costs, the patchwork of statutory provisions conferring any power complicates, perhaps unnecessarily, the issue. Some tribunals have wide powers to award costs, while others are more circumscribed or have none at all.

Judicial considerations of administrative tribunal cost remedies have: (i) applied jurisdictional analysis of whether the power to award costs is express or implied; (ii) interpreted the meaning of "costs" as grafted on to the administrative law context. Thus, in *Reference Re National*

---

[231] Mullan, "Judicial Deference to Executive Decision-Making: Evolving Concepts of Responsibility" (1993), 19 Queen L.J. 137 at 158.

[232] Professor Mullan compares this analysis to the United Kingdom where the courts have addressed this issue in a more cogent manner. He attributes this to the larger role played by the Minister and/or Ministry in England in administrative decisions when compared to the Canadian experience. *Ibid.*, at 147-48.

[233] See Fox, "Case Comment *Bell Canada v. CRTC*" (1986), 17 Admin. L. R. 206.

[234] MacCauley, *Directions: Review of Ontario's Regulatory Agencies* (Toronto: Ontario Queen's Printer, 1988), Vol. 2, at 27, argues persuasively that it is the tribunal which should decide the purpose in the particular circumstances of the case.

Energy Board Act,[235] the Federal Court of Appeal relied on "familiar and straightforward principles of statutory interpretation"[236] holding that the NEB could not award costs to intervenors without express statutory authority. The NEB's alleged power to award costs, the court reasoned, was not a "necessary or proper" exercise of its jurisdiction,[237] nor did that power arise by necessary implication.[238] In so holding, the court appeared to rely principally upon the absence of any previous cost awards in the NEB's history since its inception in 1959 (while disposing of innumerable applications) while other federal tribunals had been given specific legislative powers to award costs.

The jurisdictional analysis applied by the court in *Reference Re National Energy Board Act* was consistent with earlier judicial pronouncements concerning interim awards of costs and intervenor funding. Arguably as a consequence of the rise of "consumerism" in the 1980s, administrative tribunals were grappling with the requests by, in particular, participants in regulatory proceedings, for funds. The reaction by the courts was unequivocal: without specific statutory authority a tribunal could not award interim costs or provide intervenor funding, notwithstanding the tribunal's laudable objective of promoting public participation.[239] By 1988, however, the provincial government had alleviated some of the issues concerning intervenor costs by enacting the *Intervenor Funding Project Act*[240] which permitted the tribunals enumerated to require a "propo-

---

[235] (1986), 19 Admin. L.R. 302 (hereinafter *Reference Re National Energy Board Act*).

[236] See Fox, Case Comment, "Reference Re National Energy Board Act" (1986), 19 Admin. L.R. 302.

[237] *Ibid.*, at 311.

[238] *Ibid.*, at 314. For this proposition the court relied upon two earlier cases concerning the doctrine of jurisdiction by necessary implication. See *Interprovincial Pipeline Ltd. v. National Energy Board*, [1978] 1 F.C. 601 at 608 (C.A.) and *Canadian Broadcasting League v. C.R.T.C.*, [1983] 1 F.C. 182 at 192-93, 67 C.P.R. (2d) 49, 138 D.L.R. (3d) 512, 43 N.R. 77 (C.A.); affd [1985] 1 S.C.R. 174, 57 N.R. 76. See as well, *C.U.P.E. v. Labour Relations Board (N.S.)*, [1983] 2 S.C.R. 311, 60 N.S.R. (2d) 369, 83 CLLC 12,349, 1 D.L.R. (4th) 1, 49 N.R. 107, where the court held that the power to award costs did not arise by implication from the power to "secure compliance".

[239] *Re Ontario Energy Board* (1985), 11 O.A.C. 26, 51 O.R. (2d) 333, 2 C.P.C. (2d) 226, 19 D.L.R. (4th) 753 (Div. Ct.); leave to appeal refused 15 Admin. L.R. 86 at 122n; *Hamilton-Wentworth (Reg. Mun.) v. Hamilton-Wentworth Save the Valley Committee Inc.* (1985), 11 O.A.C. 8, 51 O.R. (2d) 23, 2 C.P.C. (2d) 117, 19 D.L.R. (4th) 356 (Div. Ct.); add'l reasons at 51 O.R.(2d) 43. See also *C.U.P.E. v. Labour Relations Board (N.S.)*, *supra*, note 238.

[240] S.O. 1988, c. 71. The Act contained a clause which repealed the Act on April 1, 1992 or on such date as proclamed by the Lieutenant Governor. By Proclamation of the Lieutenant Governor on March 11, 1992, the Act will not be repealed until April 1, 1996 unless the Lieutenant Governor makes further proclamation. See *Intervenor Funding Project Act*, R.S.O. 1990, c. I.13, s. 16, and *Ontario Gazette*, 1992, Vol. 125-13, 707.

nent'' to pay intervenor funding as ordered by a board before a hearing commenced.[241]

While *Reference Re National Energy Board Act* established the framework for the jurisdictional question, the Supreme Court in *Bell Canada v. Canada (C.R.T.C.)*[242] established the framework for the content of that jurisdiction. The C.R.T.C. was empowered to grant, at its discretion, ''the costs of and incidental to any proceeding''[243] pursuant to its constitutent statute the *National Transportation Act*.[244] The question before the Supreme Court was whether the principle of indemnification as used by the courts should apply equally to administrative tribunals, particularly in this case where the intervenors had other sources of funding and were not necessarily incurring the costs claimed.[245] After a comprehensive discussion of the lower court cases on this issue, and acknowledging the need for public participation by a public intervenor, the Supreme Court held that ''costs must carry the general connotation of being for the purpose of indemnification or compensation''[246] but refrained from importing completely the principle of indemnification from the courts into the administrative tribunal forum. The intuitive logic employed by the Supreme Court was that the term ''cost'' could not be construed in a manner ''quite different or foreign'' to the general sense of the word, and that the Commission had a right to take a broad view of its application, the result of which was to foster public interest intervenors. As a result, the court upheld the award of the assessment officer and paid one intervenor, the Consumers Association of Canada, its costs notwithstanding that it had other sources of funds and another intervenor, the National Anti-poverty Organization, its costs notwithstanding that a separate organization, the Public Interest Advocacy Centre (''PIAC'') had incurred the costs and there was no obligation to reimburse PIAC.

---

[241] For a more comprehensive analysis of intervenor funding see McWilliams, ''Ontario's *Intervenor Funding Project Act*: The Experience of the Ontario Energy Board'' (1991), 5 C.J.A.L.P. 203; Jeffrey, ''Ontario's *Intervenor Funding Project Act*'' (1989), 3 C.J.A.L.P. 69; J. Keeping, ''Intervenors' Costs'' (1989-1990), 3 C.J.A.L.P. 81; McGowan, ''A Review of the Intervenor Funding Project Should Be Considered'' (1995), 2 Regulatory Boards and Admin. Law Litigation 1 at 77.

[242] (1985), 17 Admin. L.R. 205 (hereinafter *Bell Canada*).

[243] Section 43 of the *Railway Act*, R.S.C. 1970, c. R-2 defined costs as follows: ''costs includes fees, counsel fees and expenses'' which was incorporated into the *National Transportation Act*.

[244] R.S.C. 1970, c. N-17, s. 73.

[245] *Supra*, note 242, at 223.

[246] *Ibid.*, at 228. This was consistent with the Divisional Court's interpretation in *Hamilton-Wentworth (Reg. Mun.) v. Hamilton-Wentworth Save the Valley Committee Inc.*, *supra*, note 239, at 41, which held that costs must be given an ''ordinary legal meaning''.

The general principle of indemnification, established in *Bell Canada v. Canada (C.R.T.C.)*, has been applied by tribunals in several instances, and has attracted the supervisory jurisidiction of the court. Consistent with the line of authority in civil litigation, the principle has not been extended to costs of salaried counsel.[247] In human rights cases, the term "costs" has been given an expansive meaning to encompass the remedial nature of the legislation and includes loss of pay, loss of promotion, and time for hearing preparation[248] but the board of inquiry has no inherent jurisidiction to award costs and cannot award costs to a "complainant" in the absence of express statutory authority.[249]

The power of a tribunal to award costs has several pragmatic consequences. It undoubtedly fosters pluralism in the administrative law process, and permits the tribunal to exercise its discretion in rewarding responsible participation. It is this consideration of responsible participation, however, which has perhaps hindered any broad based legislative reform, such as amendments to the *Statutory Powers Procedure Act*. Responsible participation can be a nebulous concept and the source of tension between the funding proponent and the participant. From our perspective, however, the tribunal is the best person to decide, having regard to all of the circumstances, but there is a need to develop guidelines, which delineate the purpose of and criteria for awarding costs. This would effectively leave the cost decision in the appropriate forum and obviate the need for familiar and protracted debates of jurisdiction.

(viii) *Summary*

This brief review of case-law indicates to us that Mr. Justice Blair's "telescope" analogy referred to earlier remains an apt description of the state of judicial attitudes to the interpretation and exercise of remedial powers by administrative tribunals. Only where the statute very clearly provides the power, or its exercise is obviously necessary to achieve the core function of the tribunal will the courts defer to the tribunal's interpretation of its powers. Traditional theories of jurisdiction and classifi-

---

[247] *Feldman v. Law Society of Upper Canada* (1989), 68 O.R. (2d) 157 at 165, 33 C.P.C. (2d) 213 (Div. Ct.).

[248] *Johnson v. East York Board of Education (No. 2)* (1991), 17 C.H.R.R. D/175 at D/194. For more general cases of broad interpretation of the Human Rights Commission's costs jurisdiction see also: *Re Ontario Human Rights Com'n and O'Malley*, [1985] 2 S.C.R. 536; *Robichaud v. R.*, [1987] 2 S.C.R. 84, 8 C.H.R.R. D/4326, 87 CLLC 17,025, 40 D.L.R. (4th) 577, 75 N.R. 303. In the federal human rights context see *Cashin v. CBC*, [1988] 3 F.C. 494, 20 C.C.E.L. 203, 88 CLLC 17,019, 86 N.R. 24 (C.A.).

[249] *Ont. (Liquor Control Board) v. Ont. (Human Rights Com'n)* (1988), 9 C.H.R.R. D/4868 at D/4875.

cation of function still guide the interpretative task of the courts. That this need not be the case is shown in the dissent of Madame Justice L'Heureux-Dubé in *Canadian Pacific Airlines v. Canadian Airline Pilots Ass'n*, where she deftly terms the telescope around, and views the tribunal landscape from a different, but more truly "pragmatic and functional" judicial perspective. That this still is the minority view in general is reflected by the recent decision of the Supreme Court of Canada in *Shell Canada Products Ltd. v. Vancouver*.[250]

In *Shell Canada Products Ltd.*, the court split five to four[251] in determining that City of Vancouver resolutions not to do business with Shell (which had been invited in the past to tender for supply services) until it divested itself of its South Africa assets, as a symbolic guesture by the City of its opposition to apartheid, were *ultra vires* and amounted to unauthorized discrimination. At issue was whether the resolutions were authorized under the municipality's constitutive legislation. In effect, the majority held that the elected representatives of the city could not refuse to do business with Shell because of its conduct beyond municipal boundaries. The majority and minority judgments illustrate two competing approaches of the court to interpreting decision-making powers of statutory entities, in this case elected politicians, the nature of which the court has recognized as a basis for modifying judicial standards of impartiality.[252]

Sopinka J., writing for the majority, recognized the statutory prohibition in the *Vancouver Charter*[253] which prevented a resolution from being invalidated on the grounds of unreasonableness, instead relying on traditional jurisdictional doctrines to find that the municipality had not acted "only for municipal purposes". He relied on the court's earlier decisions to the effect that as creatures of statute, municipalities

> . . . may exercise only those powers expressly conferred by statute, these powers necessarily or fairly implied by the expressed power in the statute, and those indispensible powers essential and not merely convenient to the effectuation of the purposes of the corporation.[254]

---

[250] [1994] 1 S.C.R. 231, 88 B.C.L.R. (2d) 145, 20 Admin. L.R. (2d) 202, 20 M.P.L.R. (2d) 1, 110 D.L.R. (4th) 1, 163 N.R. 81.

[251] Sopinka J. (LaForest, Cory, Iacobucci, Major JJ.) in the majority; McLachlin J. (Lamer C.J.C., L'Heureux-Dubé, Gonthier JJ.) dissenting.

[252] *Old St. Boniface Residents Ass'n Inc. v. Winnipeg (City)*, [1990] 3 S.C.R. 1170, [1991] 2 W.W.R. 145, 69 Man. R. (2d) 134, 2 M.P.L.R. (2d) 217, 75 D.L.R. (4th) 385, 116 N.R. 46; *Save Richmond Farmland Society v. Richmond (Twp.)*, [1990] 3 S.C.R. 1213, [1991] 2 W.W.R. 178, 52 B.C.L.R. (2d) 145, 2 M.P.L.R. (2d) 288, 75 D.L.R. (4th) 425, 116 N.R. 68.

[253] S.B.C. 1953, c. 55, s. 148.

[254] *R. v. Sharma,* [1993] 1 S.C.R. 650 at 668, 79 C.C.C. (3d) 142, 19 C.R. (4th) 329, 14 M.P.L.R. (2d) 35, 100 D.L.R. (4th) 167, 149 N.R. 169; see also *R. v. Greenbaum*, [1993] 1 S.C.R. 674 at 687, 79 C.C.C. (3d) 158, 19 C.R. (4th) 347, 14 M.P.L.R. (2d) 1, 100 D.L.R. (4th) 183, 149 N.R. 114.

The *Vancouver Charter* in s. 189 defined the general power of the elected Council as one to "provide for the good rule and government of the City". Finding that the purpose of the resolutions was to affect matters beyond territorial boundaries of the municipality without any identifiable benefit to the citizens, Sopinka J. held this was neither expressly or impliedly authorized by s.189, and was unrelated to carrying into effect the intent and purposes of the legislation.[255]

The minority of the court dissented squarely on the interpretative approach to be taken by the court in reviewing municipal decision-making, favouring a broad, liberal and non-interventionist one out of respect to the elected nature of the Council and its effective functioning without having to expend public monies on defending their decisions before judges. This led them to conclude that the "object of judicial review of municipal powers should be to accord municipalities the autonomy clearly warranted".[256] This "broader, more deferential" judicial approach was seen to be consistent with the "flexible, more deferential" approach adopted by the court in *C.U.P.E.*, *Bell Canada, Nat'l Corn Growers Ass'n* and *Domtar*.[257] This selective choice of the *C.U.P.E.* case-law is interesting, whether intentional or not, as the "Delphic dicta" of Laskin C.J.C. was recalled as justification for judicial deference:

> The Court has repeatedly stressed the need for sensitivity to context and to the special expertise of tribunals. Where such expertise is established, deference may be warranted even to a tribunal's interpretation of its statutory powers: *I.A.T., Local 938 v. Massicotte*, [1982] 1 S.C.R. 710. There can be little justification for holding decisions on the welfare of citizens by municipal councillors to a higher standard of review than the decision of non-elected statutory boards and agencies.[258]

The minority judgment then looked at the purpose of the resolutions, finding that it did not exceed a legitimate municipal concern, giving a broad meaning to what was encompassed by "good rule and government" such that it included the psychological (and not just material) welfare of the citizens in the collective exercise of a community expression of disapproval of a course of conduct. Accepting the evolution and sophistication of municipal government, the minority felt that the scope of valid municipal

---

[255] *Supra*, note 250, at 222 Admin. L.R. He also felt that the resolutions were unauthorized discrimination, particularly because the city continued to do business with Chevron, which also had South African interests and were arguably prohibited under the no grant of special rights and privileges section in the legislation.

[256] *Ibid.*, at 231.

[257] *Ibid.*, at 232.

[258] *Ibid.*, at 232-33.

purposes should be expanded to reflect the current reality in recognition that "matters which transcend municipal boundaries may properly serve as motives for municipal decisions".[259] In our view, the minority decision properly points out that the majority's decision that the purpose of the resolutions was a matter external to the interests of the municipality begs the question of who ought to decide this issue, the courts or the democratically elected representatives of the citizens. Without expressly referring to the pragmatic and functional analysis of *Bibeault*, the minority answered the central question of "who is in the best position to decide" clearly in favour of the municipality, consistent with a principle articulated by the court in 1945:

> Upon the question of public interest, courts have recognized that the municipal council, familiar with local conditions, is in the best position of all parties to determine what is or is not in the public interest.[260]

These differences in approach to the interpretation of decision-making powers, when taken with a jurisdictional analysis that denies a role for judicial deference, lead us to conclude that the existing concepts and attitudes of judicial review do not provide sufficient scope of a consistent and predictable nature that ensures tribunals generally have the necessary legal means to exercise remedial powers in a flexible and innovative manner. Possible answers to this conundrum of tribunal creativity and judicial control are next examined.

4. Deference or Dicey? Possible Answers

(1) Renewed Judicial Deference

The theory of jurisdiction as applied to tribunal remedies is premised on a certain syllogistic logic. Tribunals are creatures of statute. Remedies granted by a tribunal must be within the tribunal's statutory authority. Therefore, any remedy not grounded in the tribunal's jurisdiction, determined by reference to the purpose of the legislation, is subject to judicial control measured against a standard of correctness. The spectrum of judicial control now exercised by reference to standards ranging from correctness to patent unreasonableness articulated by the Supreme Court in *Pezim*, and now *Goldhawk*, compels a more cogent analysis of deter-

---

[259] *Ibid.*, at 240.
[260] *Kuchma v. Tache (Rural Mun.)*, [1945] S.C.R. 234 at 243, *per* Estey J.

mining the limits which ought to be placed on tribunal creativity.

At the risk of over-simplification and repetition, deference conditioned by the formalistic classification of jurisdictional errors is precisely what Dickson J. warned against in *C.U.P.E.* Moreover, jurisdictional errors are a rather facile and blunt manner in which judicial control is exercised over administrative tribunals without addressing the fundamental question: *Who is the best person to make the decision, bearing in mind a purposive approach to interpreting the constituent statute, and the functional differences of courts and tribunals?* Stated this way, the analytical focus is the nexus between the remedy and the reasonable basis for its creation or use as a matter of achieving the purpose of the applicable legislation.

We suggest no more than a return to the approach adopted by the Supreme Court of Canada in *Massicotte* and *Halifax Longshoreman's Ass'n* discussed above, particularly where remedial powers are provided in broad and general terms. The Delphic oracle was not always ambiguous; in some cases the advice was prophetic and authoritative.[261] The court's approach in *L'Acadie* was articulated when the choice of standards was rigid, demanding either correctness or patent unreasonableness. Since then, a spectrum of judicial deference has emerged which we suggest is the appropriate analysis for remedial powers, provided it is not conditioned by a prior characterization of the issue as non-jurisdictional. As others have pointed out, "there is no reason in principle why [a tribunal's] interpretation of its remedial powers should be any less a question of specialist knowledge than other issues pertaining to the exercise of its powers".[262]

The decision in *L'Acadie* also equated remedial power with the power of the tribunal to enter into the inquiry in the first place, ignoring that remedial powers have no independent operation. They flow from the exercise of the primary jurisdiction of the tribunal. In a sense, their exercise is that of a collateral jurisdiction, and the irony of *L'Acadie* is that while it eschewed and all but rejected the "preliminary" or "collateral"

---

[261] See, *e.g.*, Grimal (ed.), *Larousse World Mythology* (Chartwell, 1977), at 169, 171. Although a common dictionary definition equates the term "delphic" with ambiguity, an oracle is also defined as a person who provides wise, authoritative and influential pronouncements.

[262] Mullan, "Developments in Administrative Law: The 1982-83 Term" (1984), 6 Supreme Court L.R. 1 at 14. See also his comments at (1985), 7 Sup.Ct. L.R. at 16. In *L'Acadie*, [1984] 2 S.C.R. 412, 84 CLLC 14,069, 14 D.L.R. (4th) 457, 55 N.R. 321, the court did not quarrel with the reasonableness of the solution, but was guided, we suggest, by the fact that the particular remedy was available through a separate mechanism and different decision-maker. Had that not been the case, and had the Court adopted a purposive interpretation of the legislation, one can only speculate as to the result.

doctrine that had so bedevilled the court previously as it related the primary jurisdiction of the tribunal, it embedded a similar doctrine as it relates to the consequential and remedial jurisdiction of the tribunal. Where government has provided a statutory scheme to guide human conduct, it is dubious to assert there was no intent to provide effective remedies that can be related rationally to the purpose of the legislation and the circumstances that give rise to their exercise. The evolution of the administrative justice system is such that the words of Holt C.J. apply equally to courts and tribunals:

> If the plaintiff has a right, he must of necessity have a means to indicate and maintain it, and a remedy if he is injured in the exercise or enjoyment of it; and indeed it is a vain thing to imagine a right without a remedy; for want of right and want of remedy are reciprocal.[263]

Similarly, the concern that any other standard but correctness may confer unlimited or unwarranted jurisdiction is groundless, as judicial deference does not replace the legitimate, residual and indeed constitutional function of the courts to ensure that core concepts of rationality, fairness and constitutionally protected values and rights are not violated by the exercise of statutory powers. It instead recognizes and respects the integrity of the "judicial" decision-making of the administrative tribunal, without concern for potential as opposed to actual transgression of these norms. It applies particularly to those tribunals which exercise powers in the public interest:

> . . . if the Commission were to act *mala fide*, perversely, maliciously, arbitrarily or capriciously, it would have misused its powers, and be open to correction in this court. But when the Commission has acted *bona fide*, with an obvious and honest concern for the public interest, and with evidence to support its opinion, the prospect that the breadth of its discretion might someday tempt it to place itself above the law by misusing that discretion is not something that makes the existence of the discretion bad *per se*, and requires the decision to be struck down.[264]

Finally, this renewed concept of judicial deference to remedies fashioned by administrative decision-makers is consistent with the developing principle of "comity" in the fields of private and public international conflict of laws articulated by the Supreme Court of Canada in a number

---

[263] *Ashley v. White* (1703), 92 E.R. 126, quoted in *Orchard v. Tunney*, [1957] S.C.R. 436, *per* Rand J.

[264] *C.T.C. Dealer Holdings v. Ont. Securities Com'n* (1987), 21 O.A.C. 216, 59 O.R. (2d) 79, 35 B.L.R. 117, 37 D.L.R. (4th) 94 at 113 (Div. Ct.).

of recent decisions.[265] There, as we suggest is also the case in public law, the court has had to deal with respect for the diversity and differences of other legal decision-making systems and seek "to find a workable balance between diversity and uniformity".[266] At the heart of this concept is deference to and tolerance of the territorial integrity of another jurisdiction and its application of its law within that limit. Absent a breach of "overriding norms", comity requires respect for the decisions taken and hesitancy to interfere.[267] The parochial attidude that "the substantial ends of justice would require that this court should pursue its own better means of determining both the law and the fact of the case" is now recognized as no longer appropriate.[268]

As with the principle of comity, judicial review of administrative remedial powers must develop doctrines that prevent judicial "overreaching" and restrict the exercise of jurisdiction over tribunals with the appropriate powers and expertise. The principle of judicial deference is consistent with the requirement that courts exercise jurisdiction over extraterritorial or transnational transactions "only if it has a real and substantial connection" (a term not yet fully defined) with the subject matter of the litigation.[269] For example, in human rights decision-making and Charter questions, judicial review on a strict standard has been justified by reference to, in effect, the "real and substantial" expertise and constitutional function of the courts. The lack of such a "connection" to the regulation of securities markets is the essence of *Pezim*. The recognition of the territorial integrity of a tribunal as related to its powers of enforcement or enforcing its decision is fundamental to the decisions in *Chrysler Canada* and *U.N.A. v. Alberta*. Finally, the validity of the analogy and consistency between the two general principles is demonstrated by corollary doctrines which flow from each: the doctrine of *forum non conveniens* where a court may refuse jurisdiction where there is a more convenient or appropriate forum elsewhere[270] and the doctrine of adequate alternative remedy in administrative law.

---

[265] *Morguard Investments Ltd. v. De Savoye*, [1990] 3 S.C.R. 1077 at 1096, 1106, [1991] 2 W.W.R. 217, 52 B.C.L.R. (2d) 160, 46 C.P.C. (2d) 1, 15 R.P.R. (2d) 1, 76 D.L.R. (4th) 256, 122 N.R. 81; *Amchem Products Inc. v. B.C. (Workers' Compensation Board)*, [1993] 1 S.C.R. 897 at 912, 913, [1993] 3 W.W.R. 441, 77 B.C.L.R. (2d) 62, 14 C.P.C. (3d) 1, 102 D.L.R. (4th) 96, 150 N.R. 321; *Hunt v. T & N plc*, [1993] 4 S.C.R. 289 at 295-96, 321, 325, [1994] 1 W.W.R. 129, 85 B.C.L.R. (2d) 1, 21 C.P.C. (3d) 269, 109 D.L.R. (4th) 16; *Jensen v. Tolofson*, [1994] 3 S.C.R. 1022, [1995] 1 W.W.R. 609 at 625-27, 100 B.C.L.R. (2d) 1, 22 C.C.L.T. (2d) 173, 32 C.P.C. (3d) 141, 120 D.L.R. (4th) 289, 175 N.R. 161.

[266] *Hunt v. T & N plc, ibid.*, at 295-96.

[267] *Jensen v. Tolofson, supra*, note 265, at 625.

[268] *Amchem Products Inc. v. B.C. (Workers Compensation Board), supra*, note 265, at 912.

[269] *Jensen v. Tolofson, supra*, note 265, at 627.

[270] *Amchem Products Inc., supra*, note 265, at 921-23; *Jensen v. Tolofson, ibid.*, at 627.

(2) Legislative Responses

The intuitive logic of the jurisdictional theory is the requirement that the "creature of statute" operate pursuant to a statute. There is a certain tension created, however, between this Dicean logic and the evolution of the complexity of disputes before administrative tribunals. This tension is exacerbated by the static nature of legislation conferring the remedial power upon tribunals, the result of which is to make the issue ripe for judicial control. Stated more positively, the inertia of constituent statutes creates an imperfect regulatory instrument in the evolution of subject-matters before tribunals and shifts the forum for decision-making to the judiciary because of that imperfection. This is the essence of the jurisdictional quagmire.

(a) *Specific Powers*

Given that legislative intent is the fundamental basis for jurisdictional analysis, one solution is to enact legislative amendments to confer specific remedial powers on tribunals. The diversity of administrative tribunals makes this a daunting task, however, as the rationale for conferring or not conferring powers on, for example, the Animal Care Review Board or the Agricultural Licencing and Registration Review Board[271] may be entirely different for the Ontario Racing Commission[272] notwithstanding that these tribunals have jurisdiction over animals. Omnibus legislation conferring a laundry list of remedies upon a laundry list of tribunals likely could not accommodate the individualistic requirements of particular tribunals nor anticipate all situations.

The objective of this legislative solution, in our view, is to craft remedial powers which are neither too general so as to create omnipotent tribunal "fiefdoms"[273] with wide and undefined powers or so specific as to restrict the tribunal's creativity unduly, thereby replacing it with judicial control and necessitating further legislative initiatives. The need for specific amendment may not arise in the absence of a judicial decision that the tribunal's powers do not extend to the specific proposal. As the decision in *L'Acadie* demonstrates, enumerating specific powers may

---

[271] See *Ontario Society for the Prevention of Cruelty to Animals Act*, R.S.O 1990, c. O.36, s. 16; *Animals for Research Act*, R.S.O. 1990, c. A.22.

[272] *Racing Commission Act*, R.S.O. 1990, c. R.2.

[273] Janisch, "Administrative Tribunals and the Law" (1988), 2 C.J.A.L.P. 263 at 264-66 and "Policy Making in Regulation: Towards a New Definition of the Status of Independent Regulatory Agencies in Canada" (1979), 17 Osgoode Hall L. J. 46.

undercut the extent of general powers. Pragmatically, the political nature of the legislative process may prevent specific or even general powers from being crafted onto existing legislation in an expeditious fashion. In the absence of political will, legislative amendments perceived to be controversial are unlikely to be enacted.[274] Historically, legislative amendments in the administrative law context have been the result of "crises" particularly in the wake of judicial pronouncements, such as occurred in security regulation,[275] telecommunication competition[276] and intervenor funding[277].

(b) *General Powers: The Statutory Powers Procedure Act*

Given the need for express or necessarily implied statutory authority for remedial powers, and given the inconsistency of the interpretative approaches taken by the courts, particularly where there is a mixture of specific and general powers, one legislative response has been to provide general powers to all tribunals that exercise statutory powers of decision. In Ontario, this is accomplished by the *Statutory Powers Procedure Act*.[278] Up until recently, however, it did not grant remedial powers to tribunals to which it applies except for contempt proceedings by stated case to the Divisional Court, and the enforcement of tribunal orders as if they were court orders upon filing of certified copies of final orders with the Ontario Court (General Division).[279]

Effective April 1, 1995, numerous amendments to the *SPPA* were made as part of an omnibus bill amending or repealing over 140 statutes,

---

[274] For example, despite the 1992 ruling of Krever J.A. that the *Canadian Human Rights Act* must be read so as to include "sexual orientation", the Act has not been amended, apparently due to its controversial nature, notwithstanding that the government chose not appeal the decision to the Supreme Court of Canada: *Haig and Birch v. Canada (A.G.)* (1992), 9 O.R. (3d) 449. See also text *infra* with respect to S.P.P.A. amendments.

[275] *Ainsley Financial Corp. v. Ont. Securities Com'n* (1993), 14 O.R. (3d) 280, 10 B.L.R. (2d) 173, 106 D.L.R. (4th) 507 (Gen. Div.); affd 21 O.R.(3d) 104, 121 D.L.R. (4th) 79 (C.A.) (hereinafter *Ainsley*).

[276] See *Competition in the Provision of Public Long Distance Voice Telephone Services and Related Resale and Sharing Issues*, CRTC Telecom. Decision 91-12 (May 16, 1992); leave to appeal denied (*sub nom. British Columbia Telephone Co. v. C.R.T.C.* (July 22, 1992) (Dec. No. 86-A-359) (F.C.A.) which preceded the enactment of the *Telecommunications Act*, S.C. 1993, c. 38.

[277] *Supra*, note 239.

[278] R.S.O. 1990, c. S.22 (hereinafter *SPPA*).

[279] Sections 13 [am. 1994, c. 27, s. 56(27)] and 19 [rep. & sub., *ibid.*, s. 56(35)] respectively.

the object of which was to improve general government efficiency.[280] The background to these amendments and the primary role played by S.O.A.R. is well-documented and described elsewhere.[281] Suffice it to say that S.O.A.R., influenced by the Macauley Report and its call for a new "enabling" philosophy of administrative law, sought from the provincial government fairly extensive and substantive statutory powers of general application[282] including, for example, the powers to award costs (including costs to the tribunal), to dismiss vexatious proceedings, to continue proceedings even where the applicant had withdrawn or discontinued, and to state a case in writing to the courts, as well as the abolition of petitions to Cabinet.

The nature of the consultation process and a political dynamic that included a crowded legislative agenda and a government that was unwilling to delay omnibus legislation if specific provisions were controversial resulted in only some of the proposals by S.O.A.R. being adopted, and none of those listed above. As participants in the process, personal experience validates our suggestion that a process of legislative amendments of a general nature for all tribunals will not assist to any significant degree the need for timely amendment of tribunal powers to face changing circumstances.

From a remedial perspective, two express powers were provided by the amendments. However, they are subordinate to the specific provisions of a tribunal's governing legislation. First, tribunals may make interim orders and decisions with or without conditions, and without giving reasons.[283] Unlike many of the other new procedural powers given (orders for discovery and production between parties, prehearing conferences, electronic hearings) this power is not conditioned by the need to have enacted rules governing the exercise of the powers. In our view, the exercise of this power will inevitably generate judicial review as conflict arises over the scope and effect of conditions added to decisions, as well as the open-ended nature of the power to make interim orders. While the exercise of the discretion must be consistent with and promote the policy and objects

---

[280] *Statute Law Amendment Act (Government Management and Services)*, S.O. 1994, c. 27. For an overview of the amendments see Cowan, "New Procedural Powers Given to Ontario Tribunals" (1995), 2 Regulatory Boards and Admin. Law Litigation 1 at 82.

[281] See Priest and Burton, "Amendments to the *Statutory Powers Procedure Act*", and Sprague, "Provincial and Federal Administrative Procedure — Legislation: Current Developments", in Law Society of Canada, *Recent Developments in Administrative Law*, January 17, 1995.

[282] "A Proposal to Amend the Statutory Powers Procedure Act", Society of Ontario Adjudicators and Regulators, December, 1993.

[283] Section 16.1 [en. 1994, c. 27, s. 56(32)].

of the legislation governing the tribunal,[284] the courts have tended to restrict the scope of review given to conditions attached to statutory decisions provided they are otherwise authorized and relevant to the exercise of the power.[285]

The other general remedial power expressly provided by the amendments is that which permits a tribunal on its own initiative or or at the insistence of a party to review a final order or decision and vary, suspend or cancel it, provided it has enacted rules of procedure dealing with the exercise of this power.[286] How and when this general power of review will be exercised remains to be seen, and will depend upon a number of factors, such as whether there is significant or material new evidence which was not available at the time of the original proceeding, material changes in circumstances such as a change in legislation or government policy as it relates to the decision in issue, the tribunal made a material error of law or fact such that a different result would be likely had the error not been made, the extent to which any party or person has relied on the decision and will be affected by the review process, and generally whether the public interest in the finality of the tribunal's decision is outweighed by the prejudice to the person seeking the review or who would benefit from it.[287]

---

[284] See, *e.g.*, *Padfield v. Minister of Agriculture*, [1968] A.C. 997, *Multi Malls Inc. v. Minister of Transportation* (1976), 14 O.R. (2d) 49, 73 D.L.R. (3d) 18 (C.A.); *Re Doctors Hospital and Minister of Health* (1976), 12 O.R. (2d) 164, 1 C.P.C. 232, 68 D.L.R. (3d) 220 (Div. Ct.).

[285] See, *e.g.*, *Associated Provincial Picture Houses v. Wednesbury Corp.*, [1948] 1 K.B. 223 at 230, upholding a condition to municipal licence that could not be said to be "so unreasonable that no reasonable authority could ever have come to it". See more generally caselaw here in Ontario dealing with conditions to planning approvals. *Mills v. York (Reg. Mun.) Land Division Committee* (1975), 9 O.R. (2d) 349, 60 D.L.R. (3d) 405 (Div. Ct.); *Pinetree Dev. Co. and Ministry of Housing* (1976), 14 O.R. (2d) 687 (Div. Ct.); Re Sorokolit and Peel *(Reg. Mun.)* (1977), 16 O.R. (2d) 607, 2 M.P.L.R. 249, 78 D.L.R. (3d) 715 (Div. Ct.); *Re Hay and Burlington (City)* (1980), 31 O.R. (2d) 467, 119 D.L.R. (3d) 160 (Div. Ct.); revd 38 O.R. (2d) 476, 22 R.P.R. 108, 16 M.P.L.R. 292, 131 D.L.R. (3d) 600 (C.A.); *Jay-Del Developments Ltd. v. Durham (Reg. Mun.)* (1977), 4 M.P.L.R. 132 (H.C.J.); *First City Shopping Centre Group v. Gloucester (City)* (1990), 25 O.M.B.R. 9 (O.M.B.); affd 27 O.M.B.R. 457 (Div. Ct.); *Kally's Restaurant Inc. v. Scarborough (City)* (1991), 12 O.R. (3d) 312, 14 M.P.L.R. (2d) 117, 99 D.L.R. (4th) 381 (Div. Ct.).

[286] Section 21.2 [en. 1994, c. 27, s. 56(36)]. Section 19, dealing with enforcement of tribunal orders, has been amended in a minor way so as to provide a statutory direction to the sheriff to enforce a tribunal's order for the payment of money as if it were a writ of execution.

[287] These factors originate from discussions and proposals of SOAR's Model Rules Committee which has developed proposals for rules that precondition the exercise of the review power.

(c) *Rule Making Powers: The Ontario Securities Commission*

As posited earlier, legislative amendments in the context of administrative tribunals have been largely reactive to problems created by, as Phillip Anisman has accurately described it, regulation without authority.[288] That is, some tribunals have attempted to overcome legislative inertia by issuing subordinate "legislation" in the form of guidelines, policy statements and/or directives and using them in fashioning remedies which promote, in particular, the tribunal's policy-making objectives. These attempts by tribunals have not received deference by the courts except in cases of express statutory authority and illustrate how the complex spectrum of decision making models from adjudication to policy making, upon which tribunals rely to discharge their statutory mandates, are sometimes hindered by "anesthetized legislation".[289]

The problem of static legislation in the evolution of complex regulation crystallized for the Ontario Securities Commission in *Ainsley Financial Corp.* [290] As early as 1949, the Ontario Securities Commission had begun issuing a myriad of policy statements and guidelines.[291] It was not until 1992, however, when the Commission issued a draft policy statement purporting to regulate the marketing and sale of penny stocks that the legitimacy of this form of Commission regulation was challenged in the courts. The basis for the challenge was that the draft policy had the potential for the imposition of sanctions pursuant to the *Securities Act*.[292] The parties to the application had diametrically opposed interpretations on whether the draft policy could or would lead to those sanctions.

Acknowledging that it was "sound administrative practice" for an administrative tribunal to issue non-binding guidelines[293] or other instruments, the courts confirmed the earlier jurisprudence that these instruments could not have effect in a manner contrary to a statutory provision or regulation.[294] As the impugned policy in this case was characterized

---

[288] Anisman, "Regulation without Authority: The Ontario Securities Commission" (1994), 7 C.J.A.L.P. 195.

[289] See Janisch, "The Choice of Decision-making Method: Adjudication, Policies and Rulemaking", Law Society of Upper Canada, Special Lectures, 1992, at 259.

[290] *Supra*, note 275.

[291] Anisman, *supra*, note 288, at 197-98.

[292] R.S.O. 1990, c. S.5.

[293] Which Professor Janisch points out are "part of what the Law Reform Commission of Canada felicitously called 'law elaboration' ": *supra*, note 289, at 265.

[294] *Ainsley*, *supra*, note 276, at 108-09. The court relied upon the following cases for this proposition: *Hopedale Developments Ltd. v. Oakville (Town)*, [1965] 1 O.R. 259, 47 D.L.R. (2d) 482 (C.A.); *Maple Lodge Farms Ltd. v. Canada*, [1982] 2 S.C.R. 2, 137 D.L.R. (3d) 658, 44 N.R. 354; *Capital Cities Communications Inc. v. Canadian Radio-television & Telecommunications Com'n*, [1978]

as being mandatory on the basis that it prescribed forms and made specific reference to the Commission "public interest" jurisdiction[295], it could not be imposed without appropriate statutory authority.

The reasoning in *Ainsley* was consistent with the Supreme Court in *Pezim* where Iacobucci J., in dicta, addressed the legal status of policy guidelines:

> . . . the Commission's primary role is to administer and apply the *Securities Act*. It also plays a policy development role. Thus, this is an additional basis for deference. *However, it is important to note that the Commission's policy-making role is limited. By that, I mean that their policies cannot be elevated to the status of law; they are not to be treated as legal pronouncements absent legal authority mandating such treatment.*
>
> Thus, on precedent, principal and policy, I concluded as a general proposition that the decisions of the Commission, falling within its expertise, warrant judicial deference. [Emphasis added.][296]

The *Ainsley* case is illustrative of judicial control being exerted over what has been described as "regulatory hubris".[297] The Securities Commission, with a long history of securities regulation, had believed that its experience/expertise conferred upon it jurisdiction to regulate, through its policy statement process, participants in the securities markets. In this regard, judicial review was, of necessity created by legislative imperfections, a blunt instrument of jurisdictional control which did not substitute for the Commission's experience but made legislative amendments imperative.

As a result of the decision, however, an Ontario government report led to the enactment of amendments to the *Securities Act*[298] which conferred rule making power upon the Commission.[299] The new s. 143 of the

---

2 S.C.R. 141, 36 C.P.R. (2d) 1, 81 D.L.R. (3d) 609, 18 N.R. 181; *Friends of Oldman River Society v. Canada (Minister of Transport)*, [1992] 1 S.C.R. 3, [1992] 2 W.W.R. 193, 84 Alta. L.R. (2d) 129, 88 D.L.R. (4th) 1, 132 N.R. 321. See as well *Law Society of Upper Canada v. Ont. (A.G.)* (1995), 21 O.R. (3d) 666, 121 D.L.R. (4th) 369 (Gen. Div.).

[295] By implication, the "public interest jurisidiction" conferred upon the Commision included its penal powers. The court recognized that there was no "bright line" which separated guidelines from a mandatory provision, and stated that analytical focus must be the "thrust of the language in its entirety and not on isolated words or passages". *Supra*, note 275, at 110.

[296] *Ibid.*, at 111.

[297] *Supra*, note 288, at 239.

[298] *Securities Amendment Act*, S.O. 1994, c. 33. See Ontario Task Force on Securities Regulation, *Responsibility and Responsiveness* (Toronto: Queen's Printer, 1994).

[299] For a comprehensive discussion of this issue, see Anisman, *supra*, note 288.

Securities Act permits the the Commission to institute "notice and comment" type proceedings for a prescribed range of rules which are specifically exempted from the *Regulations Act*. The Commission publishes in its *Bulletin* notice of the proposed rule and must allow "interested persons and companies" to make written representations within a period of at least 90 days. The Commission is exempted from the notice requirement in certain instances such as urgency or where the rule does not result in a material change to existing rules. After the notice and comment period, the Commission is required to deliver to the Minister copies of the notices, a summary of any representations made and documents submitted, and any other material documents. The accountability mechanism is the Minister's power to approve or reject the rule within 60 days of delivery. If it is approved by the Minister, the rule takes effect in 15 days after approval, unless the Minister otherwise specifies.

Rule making is a remedy which illustrates a fusion, and arguably a synergy, of policy making and adjudication. As described by Professor Janisch, "a rule is of general application [*i.e.*, policy making] and an order of particular application [*i.e.*, adjudication]".[300] In the administrative law context, rule making is, therefore, a delicate blend of decision making models which must, on principles of fairness, balance "'pre-knowledge' of a particular issue and 'pre-judging' a future case".[301] It is a new instrument of administrative regulation in Canada, but one which has been used in the United States for almost 20 years. Consequently, the American system is of some assistance in providing an anlysis of its potential effectiveness and for addressing the issue of deference.

Since 1976, rule making in American tribunals has increasingly become a integral part of administrative law.[302] Codified, at the Federal level, in the *Administrative Procedure Act*, 5 USCS, s. 553, there are two types of rule making procedures: (1) "on the record" rule making which

---

[300] *Ibid.*, at 264.

[301] See Smart "Comments on Institutional Decision-Making: Did the Supreme Court Get It Right", in Law Society of Upper Canada, *Recent Developments in Administrative Law*, January 17, 1995, at 9. It also raises the issue of reasonable apprehension of bias when panel members who determined the rule then dispose of a case concerning the policy such as in *E.A. Manning Ltd. v. Ont. Securities Com'n* (1994), 18 O.R. (3d) 97 (Div. Ct.); affd 23 O.R. (3d) 257, 125 D.L.R. (4th) 305 (C.A.); leave to appeal to the Supreme Court of Canada dismissed August 17, 1995, 125 D.L.R. (4th) 305*n* (Lamer C.J.C., La Forest and Major JJ.). It is interesting to note that the Court of Appeal in *E.A. Manning*, held that in the absence of any evidence to the contrary, it must be presumed that the members will "act fairly and impartially in discharging their adjudicative responsibilities".

[302] See Janisch, "Administrative Tribunals and the Law", *supra*, note 273, at 277-80; and "The Choice of Decision-making Method", *supra*, note 289, at 275.

is rarely used because of its trial type proceeding; and (2) notice and comment rulemaking where tribunal publishes notices of proposed rules and permits participants to comment, make written or oral submissions, and/or file data.[303] By contrast, rule making has not been adopted by and large in Canada. Instead, we have opted for a more incremental approach to participation through regulations passed after notice and comment type procedures, or with little consusltation at all.[304]

There are several benefits of rule making to the administrative decision making process. Primarily, rule making procedures permit public participation in the regulatory process and the concomitant legitimacy created by that public participation.[305] Additionally, it promotes consistency of policy-making objectives and streamlines tribunal decision making, a corollary of which is to reallocate a tribunal's scarce resources to more complex cases.[306] Shifting the "minutiae" of detail from the legislators to the regulatory participants[307] is an appropriate choice of decision-making model. The key to the success of rule making is an effective consultative process combined with appropriate review processes.

Rule making is not, however, a panacea to the tension between tribunal creativity and judicial control. It challenges the tribunal's adjudicative creativity and can create rigidity in the tribunal's policy making function. From a practitioner's perspective, there is a need to prevent the creation of tribunal "fiefdoms" and to permit some form of supervision either through the courts or the legislators.[308] It may not, for instance, be an appropriate mechanism for tribunals which do not have established jurisprudence or which are disposing of cases in a rapidly changing area of the law.[309] Parliament may, in certain cases, have deliberately and legitimately chosen to retain its control over policy decisions. Moreover, there may be other effective means of addressing the tribunal's particular circumstances such as grouping cases of similar issues and deciding leading cases with expanded panels. Finally, there is a need to clarify and streamline policy directives, guidelines, in order to provide a cogent instrument by which the goals of rule making can be achieved.[310] These concerns,

---

[303] Janisch, "The Choice of Decision-making Model", *ibid.*, at 275.

[304] *Ibid.*

[305] For other benefits see *ibid.*, at 266-70.

[306] See Symes "The Choice of Decision-making Method: A Chair Responds", Law Society of Upper Canada, Special Lectures, 1992, at 317, and Fraser "Rule-making: A Cautionary Comment", *ibid.*, at 327.

[307] See Athurs, "Regulation-making: The Creative Opportunities of the Inevitable" (1970), 8 Alta. L. Rev. 315.

[308] Anisman has the comprehensive analysis of the checks and balances. See *supra*, note 288.

[309] Symes uses Employment and Pay Equity as her examples. *Supra*, note 306.

[310] *Supra*, note 288.

however, merely illustrate the need for flexibility in the application of the process to the unique circumstances of administrative tribunals. In this sense, the real advantage of rule making is that the process can craft the appropriate application in combination with other solutions.

As an issue of judicial control over remedies, rule making does not eliminate the question of deference. It merely shifts the subject of deference from the cabinet to the tribunal, and arguably compels the courts to engage in an *Innuit Tapirisat* analysis. It was implicit in *Innuit Tapirisat* that the court was making a distinction between broad based "legislative" actions taken by the cabinet pursuant to legislation and matters of individual concern in which the cabinet was deciding. On procedural matters, the court refused to extend the scope of judicial review because, in our view, the accountability of elected officials implementing policy took precedence. In rule making, the accountability of the policy-making entity is more circumspect. While tribunals do not face the electorate at regular intervals, they are "accutely accountable" to their respective Ministers in more pragmatic ways through budgets, appointments and reappointments to the tribunal, and reports. This accountability is not the form courts usually consider when determining deference on policy issues and contributes to the reluctance by courts to permit tribunals to make decisions of far-reaching implication without clear jurisdiction.

From the perspective of the regulated, the success of rule making is contingent upon the consultative process resulting in advantageous rules. From the perspective of the regulator, the success of rule making is contingent upon containing the process. Some economists would consider this scenario ripe for the application of the regulatory "capture theory". This theory postulates that the powerful participant will advance its own self-interest and "capture" the regulator whose alleged complicity is motivated by the continuation of the regulation.[311] Stated more succinctly, the participant wants to maintain and contain the regulator rather than eliminating regulation. In the context of rulemaking and deference, a court may scrupulously review the rules made by an "industry club" to ensure that the purpose of the legislation and not the "club members" is achieved. When those rules are promulgated by elected officials, the issue of deference is arguably more compelling.

Consequently, we can expect challenges to rules will proliferate, and that the courts may apply their deference analysis more vigorously because the forum has shifted away from the cabinet on an issue which can be

---

[311] For a more comprehensive analysis of this theory see Posner, "Theories of Economic Regulation" (1974), 5 Bell J. Economics No. 2 334; Stigler, "The Theory of Economic Regulation" (1971), 2 Bell J. Economics No. 1 3; Wenders, *The Economics of Telecommunications Regulation Theory and Policy* (Cambridge: Ballinger, 1987).

easily characterized as legislative. In this regard, in the United States, for example, the number of applications for judicial review of rules has increased substantially over the years, accounting for almost one half of the applications.[312] In the recent decision in *Law Society of Upper Canada v. Ont. (A.G.)*[313] wherein the court held that the Law Society's power to "make rules relating to the affairs of the Society" including for "providing for the time and manner of and methods and procedures for the election of benchers" did not encompass the proposed change for a "regional bencher" election. In the court's view, this issue did not constitute the business of the Society, but was a power retained by the legislators.[314] In so holding, the court was clearly circumscribing the "over-extension" of the rule making powers of the Law Society because it determined that the proposal was an important issue of self-governance requiring legislative approval. As such, the case is the harbinger of the deference analysis the courts will undoubtedly be compelled to consider as rulemaking emerges in the administrative law context.

(d) *Legislated Policy*

Legislated policy is an alternative model of policy making which has emerged in the planning and development area of administrative law. In contrast to rule making, where the proposed rule is decided through the tribunal process and approved by the executive branch of government, legislated policy is structurally opposite. That is, in legislated policy, the Minister (and/or the executive) issues policy instruments which are given legal status before the tribunal. Although achieved by a different route, the result is similar to rule making in that there is the fusion of the tribunal's adjudicative and policy making functions created by the policy. There are, however, fundamentally different deference issues created by the nature of the decision-maker.

The proclamation of substantial changes to the *Planning Act*[315] on March 28, 1995, is a timely illustration of the legislated policy model. Prior to this enactment, the Ontario Municipal Board, among other entities, in disposing of planning matters pursuant to the *Planning Act*, was

---

[312] See Townsend, "The Growing Irrelevance of Judicial Review: Administrative Law and the Entrepreneurial Culture" (1993), 6 C.J.A.L.P. 79 at 88.

[313] *Supra*, note 294, at 676.

[314] *Ibid.*, at 679-80.

[315] "An Act to revise the Ontario Planning and Development Act and the Municipal Conflict of Interest Act, to amend the Planning Act and the Municipal Act and to amend other statutes related to planning and municipal matters", 3rd Session, 35th Legislature, Ontario 43 Elizabeth II, 1994.

required to "have regard to policy statements issued" under the *Planning Act*, but left the implementation of policy statements to the Board's discretion in the adjudicative process. Section 3 of the former *Planning Act*[316] delineated the consultative process by which policy statements were to be issued and approved by the Lieutenant-Governor in Council and mandated their use as follows:

> 3(1) The Minister, or the Minister together with any other minister of the Crown, may from time to time issue policy statements that have been approved by the Lieutenant Governor in Council on matters relating to municipal planning that in the opinion of the Minister are of provincial interest.
>
> (2) Before issuing a policy statement, the Minister shall confer with such municipal, provincial, federal or other officials and bodies or persons as the Minister considers have an interest in the proposed statement.
>
> (3) In exercising any authority that affects any planning matter, the council of every municipality, every local board, every minister of the Crown and every ministry, board, commission or agency of the government, including the Municipal Board and Ontario Hydro, shall have regard to policy statements issued under subsection (1).

Matters of provincial interest were described in s. 2 to include:

(*a*) the protection of the natural environment, including the agricultural resource base of the Province, and the management of natural resources;

(*b*) the protection of features of significant natural, architectural, historical or archaeological interest;

(*c*) the supply, efficient use and conservation of energy;

(*d*) the provision of major communication, servicing and transportation facilities;

(*e*) the equitable distribution of educational, health and other social facilities;

(*f*) the co-ordination of planning activities of municipalities and other public bodies;

(*g*) the resolution of planning conflicts involving municipalities and other public bodies;

(*h*) the health and safety of the population;

(*i*) the protection of the financial and economic well-being of the province and its municipalities; and

(*j*) the provision of a range of housing types.

The new *Planning Act* has elevated the status of policy in the decision-making process in several respects, expanded the scope of "matters of

[316] R.S.O. 1990, c. P.13.

provincial interest", and has made the policy issues more complex. Stated succinctly, the amendments to the *Planning Act* create a two-tiered regime of policy instruments: (i) the Comprehensive Set of Policy Statements ["CSPS"] which are approved by Cabinet and are broadly worded statements of general provincial policy; and (ii) the Implementation Guidelines which, pursuant to Policy G-3 under the CSPS, are "advisory and will provide information on the meaning of the policies and illustrate ways for policies to be implemented".[317] There is a further level of policy instrument, not specifically referred to in the legislation, in the form of Technical Manuals which will be issued by the appropriate Ministry. In contrast to the previous *Planning Act* the decisions of the Ontario Municipal Board and the advice of government agencies must be "consistent" with the CSPS. Subsection 3(5) and (6) of the *Planning Act* now provide as follows:

> 3(5) A decision of the council of a municipality, local board, planning board, the Minister and the Municipal Board under this Act and such decisions under any other Act may be prescribed shall be consistent with policy statements issued under subsection (1).
>
> (6) With respect to any planning matter under this Act, the comments, submissions or advice provided by a minister or a ministry, board, commission or agency of the government or Ontario Hydro shall be consistent with policy statements issued under subsection (1).

In addition, matters of provincial interest have been expanded to include:

    (a) the protection of ecological sytems, including natural reas, features and functions;

    (b) the protection of the agricultural resources of the Province;

    (c) the conservation and management of natural resources and the mineral resource base;

    (d) the conservation of features of significant architectural, cultural, historical, archaeological or scientific interest;

    (e) the supply, efficient use and conservation of energy and water;

    (f) the adequate provision and efficient use of communication, transportation, sewage and water services and waste management systems;

    (g) the minimization of waste;

    (h) the orderly development of safe and healthy communities;

    (i) the adequate provision and distribution of educational, health, social, cultural and recreational facilities;

---

[317] Some are technical advice while others are "best practices". For a more complete analysis of the amendments see Brown, "Implementing Provincial Policy Statements" and McQuaid, "Policy Statements Under the Act" in *Bill 163 — The New Planning Act: It's the Law!* (Canadian Bar Association — Ontario, 1995 Institute of Continueing Legal Education, February 10, 1995).

(j) the adequate provision of a full range of housing;

(k) the adequate provision of employment opportunities;

(l) the protection of the financial and economic well-being of the Province and its municipalities;

(m) the co-ordination of planning activities of public bodies;

(n) the resolution of planning conflicts involving public and private interests;

(o) the protection of public health and safety;

(p) the appropriate location of growth and development;

(q) any other matters prescribed, 1994.

Under the *Planning Act*,[318] which first introduced policy statements to the planning process, four policy statements were issued by the Lieutenant-Governor in Council along with several "statement like" policies issued by various Ministries, and policies issued by other Ministers. In what has become something of a planning "tome", there are now in excess of 70 CSPSs with equal number of Implementation Guidelines and Technical Manuals. Irrespective of their content and elevated legal status, the sheer volume of these policy instruments creates a daunting decision making process. A critical analysis of this model is, however, beyond the scope of this paper, but several issues have been raised by others including problems of conflicting policies and protracted hearings caused by the quantity and quality of the CSPSs.[319]

As it pertains to issues of deference, legislated policies, because they are issued by Cabinet, albeit after consultation, raise interesting questions of accountability and reviewability. This analysis, however, must be considered in light of the jurisprudence regarding policy matters before the Ontario Municipal Board. In the planning context, the courts have recognized and given deference to the polycentric judicial and administrative policy making functions of the Ontario Municipal Board, requiring the board to "'act judicially' but not beyond the sense that the parties are to be accorded a full and fair hearing and their submissions considered".[320] Moreover, the Divisional Court has recently held that, consistent with *Pezim*, the Ontario Municipal Board, is an expert tribunal in land compensation hearings[321] and in deciding policy matters arising out of

---

[318] S.O. 1983, c. 1.

[319] McQuaid, *supra*, note 317, at 4-6.

[320] *Re Cloverdale Shopping Centre Ltd. and Township of Etobicoke*, [1966] 2 O.R. 439 at 450, 57 D.L.R. (2d) 206 (C.A.).

[321] *Tanenbaum Estate v. Ont. (Minister of Transportation & Communication)* (1994), 54 L.C.R. 161 (Ont. Div. Ct.) at 162.

official plans.[322] This deference, in the wake of *Pezim*, would appear to signal that the scope of review of the OMB will be much less stringent because of a functional analysis of the OMB's role and its expertise. Such deference is bolstered, in our view, by the "top down" approach to its policy-making function created by the new amendments to the *Planning Act*. That policy structure creates at least the appearance of accountability, an important element of deference. However, it can be expected that the catalyst of review of the legislated policy will be intra-jurisdictional, to the extent that conflicts in policies and their implementation will place the OMB in a difficult dilemma, rather than conflicts with the purpose for which the tribunal was created.

5. *Conclusion*

In his seminal book on theories of regulation,[323] Professor Marver Bernstein examined American tribunals and formulated the "life cycle" theory. The theory postulates that all tribunals have four stages of life which directly impact upon the effectiveness of their regulation: (i) gestation (ii) growth (iii) maturity; and (iv) death. The fervor which precedes and culminates in the creation of the tribunal (gestation) is followed by youthful optimism (growth). Slowly, however, a process of devitalization begins as the conflicts amongst the regulated increase and the tribunal realizes that its objects were ill-defined in its youth and that it is faced with heavily judicialized procedures, the major result of which "is a myopic view of the public interest which rationalizes the regulatory *status quo*".[324]

---

[322] *Oro (Twp.) v. BAFMA Inc.* (1995), 21 O.R. (3d) 483 at 499-500, 25 M.P.L.R. (2d) 258, 121 D.L.R. (4th) 538. Previous decisions of the courts, decided prior to the *Planning Act* of 1983, have held that the Ontario Municipal Board was at liberty to accept a Minister's policy statement contained in a letter to the Board (but not be bound by it), *Innisfil (Twp.) v. City of Barrie* (1977), 17 O.R. (2d) 277 (Div. Ct.); leave to appeal to the C. A. reserved), but held that the Board erred when it did not permit cross-examination or the opportunity to call evidence to refute the policy contained therein: *Innisfil (Twp.) v. Vespra (Twp.)* (1981), 123 D.L.R. (3d) 530. However, in *Brennan v. Ont. (Minister of Municipal Affairs)* (1988), 27 O.A.C. 223, 63 O.R. (2d) 236, 48 R.P.R. 210, 47 D.L.R. (4th) 11, the court held that the Board had erred in accepting a Minister's letter because the Minister had not complied with the procedural requirements of the *Planning Act* of 1983 and therefore, the Board could not rely upon the letter as a statement of policy.

[323] *Regulating Business by Independent Commission* (Princeton: New Jersey Press, 1955). See also Khan, *The Economics of Regulation: Principles and Institutions*, Vols. 1 and 2 (New York: John Wiley & Sons, 1970).

[324] *Ibid.*, at 89.

The participants play a major role in this devitalization by constantly challenging the tribunal's authority. At each stage of its life cycle, the tribunal is faced with competing values of regulation, and seeks to find ways in which to perform its tasks and avoid the "debility and decline of old age" and death.[325]

We are entering an era where "new" instruments are being sought to make adminstrative tribunals more effective in the decisions they make and the remedies they provide, partly in response to judicial developments. We are discovering that anachronistic legislation is inhibiting the objective of *C.U.P.E.*, with formalistic theories of jurisdiction becoming, in some instances, a "sheer veneer" for controlling tribunal creativity. The potential for debilitating the "mature" tribunal and rendering it ineffective is not remote.

Our response to this tension is to suggest a renewed theory of judicial deference, premised on a determination of the best person to decide the issue, having regard to the purpose of the relevant legislation and the functional attributes that distinguish courts and tribunals. This is particularly important for tribunals which perform adjudicative and policy-making functions and which must fashion remedies to meet the particular imperatives and complexity of the issues before them when the pace of change and the nature of the issues render the legislative process inefficient or ineffective.

---

[325] *Ibid.*, at 91.

REMEDIES AGAINST GOVERNMENT: THE INTERSECTION OF PUBLIC LAW AND PRIVATE LAW

David Sgayias, Q.C.[1]

1. *Introduction*

When asked about remedies against government, one lawyer may immediately think of judicial review. Another may think of damages. Neither will necessarily think first of non-judicial strategies to remedy the problem. The thesis of this paper is that public law and private law remedies should be considered together, and along with non-judicial solutions, when challenging government action or inaction and its consequences.

There is a tendency to treat remedies in public law and private law as quite independent subjects. Indeed, the organization of this set of lectures might reflect that tendency: remedies in public and administrative law is treated as a topic as distinct from damages, restitution and the like. This compartmentalization is quite natural. Administrative law remedies developed independently, at a time when private law remedies against government did not exist or were severely circumscribed. The prerogative writs have been used to control government for several hundred years, the law of tort for only 50.[2] This compartmentalization is also reflected in, and encouraged by, the jurisdictional and procedural separation of public law and private law remedies. Judicial review and damages usually must be pursued in different courts or by different procedures.[3]

---

[1] Senior General Counsel, Department of Justice, Ottawa. The views expressed herein are those of the author and do not purport to represent the views of the Department of Justice.

[2] General liability in tort was not imposed on the Crown until the 1950's: *Crown Liability Act*, S.C. 1952-53, c. 30; *The Proceedings Against the Crown Act*, 1952, S.O. 1952, c. 78.

[3] Federally, judicial review is obtained by application in either the Federal Court, Trial Division or the Federal Court of Appeal: *Federal Court Act*, R.S.C. 1985, c. F-7, ss. 18, 18.1, 28. Damages against the Crown can be pursued in the Federal Court, Trial Division or in the superior court of a province: *Federal Court*

Despite this compartmentalization, public law and private law remedies do intersect. They can be directed at the same wrong. For example, a cancellation of a commercial fishing licence may attract an application for judicial review. It may also attract an action in damages in respect of the financial loss suffered by reason of the cancellation.[4] It may attract one but not the other. The remedies intersect because public law and private law intersect. The activities of government are regulated by both systems. In the example, both the public law and the private law may impose obligations upon government when it comes to cancelling the fishing licence.

This paper attempts to explore, in a preliminary way, some of the points of intersection of public law and private law. The approach is to review the remedies available against government in respect of excesses of power and government promises. The focus is Ministers and their officials, as opposed to more formally established administrative tribunals. This division is somewhat artificial: it must be acknowledged that Ministers and officials may exercise decision-making powers not far removed in kind from those reposed in administrative tribunals. Nevertheless, the division is practical: activities of Ministers and officials are more likely to attract private law consequences and may serve as points for the analysis of the intersection of public law and private law. It is in this context that one is more likely to be able to identify, and possibly analyze, how public law and private law remedies interact, fit together or conflict.

2. *Alternatives to Judicial Remedies*

This may seem an unlikely place to begin. One might expect to see any discussion of extra-judicial remedies tacked on at the end of this paper. Here, however, alternatives to judicial remedies are given pride of place. This is because it is too easy to focus on the remedies the law provides and neglect the other solutions that may be available to avoid or to right a government wrong. It is useful to pause and identify some of the alternatives that may be available to the remedies, if any, provided by either public law or private law.

Extra-judicial remedies are very much a mixed bag. The range from

---

Act, s. 17; *Crown Liability and Proceedings Act*, R.S.C. 1985, c. C-50, s. 21. In Ontario, judicial review is obtained in the Divisional Court: *Judicial Review Procedure Act*, R.S.O. 1990, c. J.1, s. 6. An action for damages against the provincial Crown would proceed in the General Division.

[4] See *LaPointe v. Canada (Minister of Fisheries and Oceans)* (1992), 51 F.T.R. 161.

attempting to persuade a government official to reconsider the matter, to urging the legislature to enact a scheme of compensation. What they have in common is that they can, on occasion, provide the aggrieved person with a solution not available, or not easily or surely available, from the court.

(1) Further Consideration

Many decisions taken by Ministers and their officials are not final. When faced with an adverse result, the first recourse may well be to attempt to persuade the official, the official's superior, the official's superior's superior, or the Minister to consider the matter further. Government is not a monolith; it is a collection of individuals organized into a hierarchy. Hierarchies are made to be climbed.

The availability of further consideration depends upon the nature and terms of power being exercised. The question is whether that power attracts the principle of *functus officio*. That principle can apply to decisions of administrative tribunals. In *Chandler v. Alta. Ass'n of Architects*, [5] Mr. Justice Sopinka stated, for the majority:

> . . . there is a sound policy reason for recognizing the finality of proceedings before administrative tribunals. As a general rule, once such a tribunal has reached a final decision in respect of the matter that is before it in accordance with its enabling statute, that decision cannot be revisited because the tribunal has changed its mind, made an error within jurisdiction or because there has been a change of circumstances. It can only do so if authorized by statute or if there has been a slip or error within the exceptions enunciated in *Paper Machinery Ltd. v. J.O. Ross Engineering Corp., supra.*
>
> To this extent, the principle of *functus officio* applies. It is based, however, on the policy ground which favours finality of proceedings rather than the rule which was developed with respect to formal judgments of the court whose decision was subject to a full appeal. For this reason I am of the opinion that its application must be more flexible and less formalistic in respect to the decisions of administrative tribunals which are subject to appeal only on a point of law. Justice may require the reopening of administrative proceedings in order to provide relief which would otherwise be available on appeal.[6]

The principle of *functus officio* will only come into play if the decision at issue is final. Most of the day to day decisions of government are

---

[5] [1989] 2 S.C.R. 848, [1989]6 W.W.R. 521, 70 Alta. L.R. (2d) 193, 62 D.L.R. (4th) 577, 99 N.R. 277.
[6] *Ibid.*, at 861-62.

not final. The general rule is that powers may be exercised from time to time.[7] A licence or a subsidy refused today may be granted tomorrow. It is probably only where the power is adjudicative that the principle of *functus officio* applies. This has been put another way: the principle does not apply where the power is purely administrative.[8] The principle of *functus officio* will also not apply where the statute has expressly or impliedly conferred a continuing jurisdiction, for example, to appoint a board to hear a grievance [9] or to exercise equitable jurisdiction in immigration appeals.[10]

The practical side of the matter is that except where more than the rights of one person are involved, it is unlikely that anyone will object if the aggrieved person persuades the government official to take another look at the matter. This may involve persuading the official not only that the merits of the matter deserve reconsideration, but also that there is no statutory impediment to do so. If that can be accomplished, there will be no one to raise the *functus officio* banner.

(2) Ex Gratia Payments

It is not always necessary to establish legal liability to obtain compensation for a loss suffered by reason of government action or inaction. It is open to the government to make payments on an *ex gratia* basis. In the federal sphere, the deputy heads of government departments possess the authority to make *ex gratia* payments.[11] Deputy heads may make payments in the public interest for loss or expenditure incurred for which there is no legal liability on the part of the Crown. This is usually a remedy of last resort: *ex gratia* payments are to be made where no other source of compensation is available. Nevertheless, seeking an *ex gratia* payment may prove more successful than pursuing a claim that would face serious legal obstacles. A modest *ex gratia* payment in hand may be preferable to the risks of pursuing a weak legal claim.

---

[7] See *Interpretation Act*, R.S.C. 1985, c. I-21, s. 31(3); and consider *Parkes Rural Distribution Pty Ltd. v. Glasson* (1986), 7 N.S.W.L.R. 332 (C.A.).

[8] *McDonald's Corp. v. Canada (Registrar of Trade Marks)* (1987), 15 C.P.R. (3d) 462, 10 F.T.R. 195; revd. [1989] 3 F.C. 267, 23 C.I.P.R. 161, 24 C.P.R. (3d) 463, 100 N.R. 396.

[9] *Metropolitan Separate School Board v. Ontario (Minister of Education)* (1988), 64 O.R. (2d) 730, 50 D.L.R. (4th) 570 (Div. Ct.).

[10] *Clancy v. Minister of Employment & Immigration* (1988), 86 N.R. 301 (Fed. C.A.).

[11] Policy on Claims and *Ex Gratia* Payments, in the Treasury Board Manual on Material, Risk and Common Services (Government of Canada).

There are occasions where the government may provide a broader based programme of *ex gratia* payments. Two recent examples are the federal schemes to provide payments to persons who contracted the HIV virus from blood transfusions and to persons who underwent experimental treatment at the Allan Memorial Institute during the 1950's. These programmes provide modest amounts of compensation in situations where the legal liability could well prove very difficult to establish.

(3) Compensation Schemes

A step beyond *ex gratia* payments are compensation schemes established by legislation. An interesting example of such a scheme is the Quebec programme of indemnities for victims of immunization.[12] It is interesting because the scheme was established to fill a gap identified in the Supreme Court of Canada in *Lapierre v. Que. (A.G.)*.[13] In that case, the plaintiff's daughter had died as a result of having been vaccinated against measles as part of a government programme. No fault could be established. At trial, the plaintiff succeeded. The trial judge found liability on the basis that loss suffered by an individual for the benefit of the community should be borne by the community. This approach was rejected by the Supreme Court of Canada, which held that the civil law did not admit any such no-fault liability.[14] The court added that an obligation to compensate in circumstances such as those of the case before it would be an excellent thing. The legislative response was to establish a comprehensive programme to compensate persons injured by reason of such programmes, retroactively to cover the plaintiff.

Admittedly, such legislative solutions will be few and far between. However, where the moral claim is persuasive and the cases sympathetic, pursuing such a solution should not be dismissed out of hand.

(4) R. v. R. Prosecutions

An aggrieved person may complain that the government is failing to comply with its own legislation. Environmental complaints often have such an element. An adjoining landowner or a member of the public may take

---

[12] *Public Health Protection Act*, R.S.Q. c. P-35, ss. 16.1-16.11, as added by S.Q. 1985, c. 23.

[13] [1985] 1 S.C.R. 241, 32 C.C.L.T. 233, 16 D.L.R. (4th) 554, 58 N.R. 161.

[14] *Ibid.*, at 259. The court also rejected liability based on a theory of risk.

exception to the government's failure to meet its own regulatory standards. Where compliance with those standards is objective, a prosecution of the Crown may well be an effective technique to encourage compliance and deter future failures to comply.

This remedy is being used in the federal sphere. Charges have been laid under the *Canadian Environmental Protection Act*[15] (ocean-dumping), the *Fisheries Act*[16] (protection of fish habitats), and the *Canada Labour Code*[17] (occupational health and safety). The accused in these prosecutions has been Her Majesty the Queen as represented by the Minister of the offending department.

What the aggrieved person must do is rouse the interest of the department responsible for enforcement of the legislation. The aggrieved person may find a sympathetic ear in the department whose standards are being flaunted. That does not mean to say a prosecution will result. The enforcing department will most likely first seek to obtain compliance through other enforcement measures. Nevertheless, the threat of prosecution provides the enforcing department with clout. That may place the enforcing department in a stronger situation to ensure regulatory standards are met than the aggrieved person could ever hope to achieve.

(5) A Regulatory Efficiency Act

In some situations, the desired remedy may be exemption from the allegedly burdensome regulatory scheme. Bill C-62,[18] currently before the House of Commons, proposes a legislative solution. The Regulatory Efficiency Act would permit the Governor in Council to designate regulations that may be the subject of compliance plans.[19] The person who is subject to the regulations could propose a compliance plan that would establish alternative means to achieve the regulatory goals.[20] If accepted, the compliance plan would apply in place of the regulations.[21] Such plans would

---

[15] R.S.C. 1985, c. 16 (4th Supp.); see, for example, *Canada (Ministère de l'Environnement) v. Canada (Ministère des Travaux publics)* (1992), 10 C.E.L.R. (N.S.) 135 (C.Q.).

[16] R.S.C. 1985, c. F-14; see, for example, *R. v. British Columbia*, [1992] 4 W.W.R. 490, 66 B.C.L.R. (2d) 84 (S.C.).

[17] R.S.C. 1985, c. L-2.

[18] Bill C-62, An Act to provide for the achievement of regulatory goals through alternatives to designated regulations and through administrative agreements, First reading, December 6, 1994.

[19] *Ibid.*, s. 4.

[20] *Ibid.*, s. 5.

[21] *Ibid.*, s. 10.

allow the regulatory scheme to be tailored to meet the circumstances and peculiarities of particular cases.

(6) Summary

The non-judicial solutions discussed above are more closely associated with public law than with private law. In the case of injuries from immunization programmes, a legislative solution was required because the private law did not provide a remedy. *Ex gratia* payments, whether on the basis of legislation or on the basis of policy, are essentially public law solutions provided in cases to which the private law does not extend.

To some degree, these non-judicial remedies may represent an effort to find a public law solution to a public law problem. In this way, their role is somewhat similar to that of the private law remedies that will be discussed below: to supplement, but not supplant, the solutions provided by the public law.

3. *Remedies respecting Excesses of Power*

Excesses of power by government can attract public law or private law remedies, or a combination of the two. The question for consideration is the relationship between the two classes of remedy. This question has attracted little judicial comment. One explanation may be that there is not seen to be a relationship. Another may be that the principal public law and private law remedies, judicial review and damages respectively, are rarely available in the same proceeding[22] and rarely need be discussed together.

(1) Judicial Review

Excesses of power by Ministers and officials are generally subject to challenge by way of an application for judicial review. There are two principal avenues of attack: the Minister or official has exceeded his or her authority under statute or the statute itself is invalid and does not afford the authority purportedly exercised. The judicial review remedy is directed at the Minister or official, rather than the government as an entity. This

---

[22] *Supra*, note 3.

is understandable. The prerogative writs are not generally available against the Crown.[23] Neither is the modern application for judicial review.[24] The focus must necessarily be not the powers of the Crown, but the powers purportedly granted by statute to a particular Minister or official. If the Minister or official is merely carrying out the responsibilities of the Crown, judicial review is not available.[25] An exception may be developing. The Crown itself may be susceptible to judicial review remedies where the excess of power infringes the Constitution. In *Lévesque v. Can.(A.G.)*[26] it was held that restrictions on voting by inmates of penitentiaries offended the *Canadian Charter of Rights and Freedoms*. *Mandamus* was issued against the Crown, as well as certain officials, to take steps to permit the inmates to vote. It was held that ss. 24 and 32 of the *Charter of Rights* abrogate the common law rule and enable the court to issue *mandamus* against the Crown.[27]

Further evidence of emerging exception is the decision of the Supreme Court of Canada in *Air Canada v. B.C. (A.G.)*[28] In an earlier action, the plaintiff had obtained a declaration that certain provincial tax legislation was invalid. The plaintiff then sought to bring an action by petition of right against the provincial Crown for return of the taxes paid. The Attorney General of British Columbia recommended that the Lieutenant Governor deny the fiat, which, under the Crown proceedings legislation of the time, blocked the action. The plaintiff successfully applied for *mandamus* to compel the Attorney General to recommend that the fiat be granted. The court reasoned that it was not open to the Crown to foreclose an action for redress for benefits obtained pursuant to an unconstitutional statute.

The *Lévesque* and *Air Canada* decisions suggest that the remedial immunity of the Crown will give way to constitutional imperatives. A remedy may be available against the Crown directly where the exercise of power is challenged as unconstitutional. In these cases, relief against the Crown was essential. The aggrieved persons could not point to any unfilled statutory obligation or excess of statutory power on the part of a Minister or official.

Judicial review has its limits as a means to redress excesses of power. It will be available where the excess of power is by Ministers or officials

---

[23] Hogg, *Liability of the Crown*, 2nd ed. (1989), at 33-34, 36-37.

[24] See, for example, *M.N.R. v. Creative Shoes Ltd.*, [1972] F.C. 993 (C.A.), leave to appeal refused [1972] F.C. 1425 (C.A.).

[25] *R. v. Lords Com'rs of the Treasury* (1872), L.R. 7 Q.B. 387. See the discussion *infra* under "Injunction".

[26] [1986] 2 F.C. 287, 20 C.R.R. 15, 25 D.L.R. (4th) 184 (T.D.).

[27] *Ibid.*, at 296-97.

[28] [1986] 2 S.C.R. 539, [1987] 1 W.W.R. 304, 8 B.C.L.R. (2d) 273, 32 D.L.R. (4th) 1, 72 N.R. 135.

exercising statutory powers. It will not be available where the excess of power is by the Crown, or by Ministers or officials who merely act on the Crown's behalf, unless the excess of power offends the Constitution. Furthermore, judicial review does not purport to be an all-purpose remedy. An aggrieved person will often not be satisfied with an order quashing or prohibiting the exercise of a statutory power. In the *Air Canada* case, obtaining a declaration that the tax was invalid was not enough: the plaintiff wanted the money back. While judicial review aided the plaintiff in pursuing that claim, recovery of the tax was the matter for a separate proceeding which looked, at least on its face, to be one founded upon the ordinary private law.[29]

(2) Declaration and Injunction

Declaration and injunction are remedies which straddle public law and private law. They find their origins in the equitable principles of the private law. They have been adopted and made full-fledged members of the family of judicial review remedies.

(a) *Declaration*

Declaration is a means of challenging excesses of power by government without having to confront the immunity of the Crown from coercive remedies such as prohibition and *mandamus*. That absence of coercion is of no practical disadvantage. Declarations will be invariably honoured by governments.[30] The issue determined by declaration becomes *res judicata* between the parties and the judgment a binding precedent. Indeed, the declaration binds the Crown in similar cases involving persons not parties to the judgment.[31]

Declaratory relief may also be attractive because of its reach. A declaration may be granted in aid of extra-judicial claims. This issue arose in

---

[29] In the event, that separate proceeding came to be determined on public law grounds: *Air Canada v. British Columbia*, [1989] 1 S.C.R. 1161 at 1195-1210, [1989] 4 W.W.R. 97, 36 B.C.L.R. (2d) 145, 41 C.R.R. 308, 59 D.L.R. (4th) 161, 95 N.R. 1.

[30] *Finlay v. Canada (Minister of Finance)*, [1990] 2 F.C. 790 at 816, 37 F.T.R. 160n, 71 D.L.R. (4th) 422, 115 N.R. 321 (C.A.); revd [1993] 1 S.C.R. 1080, 101 D.L.R. (4th) 567, 150 N.R. 81.

[31] *LeBar v. Canada*, [1989] 1 F.C. 603, 46 C.C.C. (3d) 103, 90 N.R. 5 (C.A.).

Landreville v. R.[32] The plaintiff, a former judge, sought to attack a report of a commissioner into his conduct. A declaration as to the validity of the report would have no legal effect: it was merely a recommendation and no action had been or would be taken on the basis of the report. The plaintiff contended that the declaration would help to restore his reputation and to incite the government to compensate him for damage suffered as a consequence of the commission of inquiry. The court concluded that it had the jurisdiction to make a declaration which, though devoid of legal effect, would serve some useful purpose.[33] (In fact, the plaintiff was eventually compensated by the government.)

In the same vein, declaratory relief can be used to challenge past excesses of power that are now for all intents and purposes academic. In *Dumont v. Can. (A.G.)*[34] the plaintiffs sought declarations as to the validity of legislation from the 1870's and 1880's, long since spent. The Manitoba Court of Appeal struck the action as academic. The Supreme Court of Canada reversed. Mme. Justice Wilson stated:

> The Court is of the view also that the subject matter of the dispute, inasmuch as it involves the constitutionality of legislation ancillary to the *Manitoba Act, 1870* is justiciable in the courts and that declaratory relief may be granted in the discretion of the court in aid of extra-judicial claims in an appropriate case.[35]

Declaration is not always the solution. Such relief is discretionary and will not ordinarily be granted where an adequate alternative remedy exists.[36] The cases in this respect arise primarily in the public law context. It must be remembered that declaration is an equitable remedy and, therefore, declaration is discretionary in the private law context as well.[37]

---

[32] [1973] F.C. 1223 (T.D.).

[33] *Ibid.*, at 1230.

[34] [1990] 1 S.C.R. 279, [1990] 4 W.W.R. 127, 65 Man. R. (2d) 182, 67 D.L.R. (4th) 159*n*, 105 N.R. 228.

[35] *Ibid.*, at 280. See also *Montana Band v. Canada*, [1991] 2 F.C. 30, 40 F.T.R. 86, 120 N.R. 200 (C.A.); *Johns v. Australian Securities Com'n* (1993), 116 A.L.R. 277 (H.C.).

[36] *Terrasses Zarolega Inc. v. Olympic Installations Board*, [1981] 1 S.C.R. 94 at 106-107, 23 L.C.R. 97, 124 D.L.R. (3d) 204, 38 N.R. 411; *Canada (Auditor General) v. Canada (Minister of Energy, Mines & Resources)*, [1989] 2 S.C.R. 49 at 88 *et seq.*, 61 D.L.R. (4th) 604, 97 N.R. 241; *Kourtessis v. M.N.R.*, [1993] 2 S.C.R. 53 at 84-87, 115-16, 78 B.C.L.R. (2d) 257, 81 C.C.C. (3d) 286, 20 C.R. (4th) 104, 14 C.R.R. (2d) 193, 102 D.L.R. (4th) 456, 93 DTC 5137, 153 N.R. 1.

[37] *Lewis v. Green*, [1905] 2 Ch. 340 (Ch. D.).

(b) *Injunction*

The availability of injunction as either a public law or private law remedy for excesses of power by government is severely curtailed by the immunity of the Crown. At common law, the Crown is immune from injunctive relief.[38] That immunity has been codified in Crown proceedings legislation. For example, s. 22 of the federal *Crown Liability and Proceedings Act* provides:

> 22(1) Where in proceedings against the Crown any relief is sought that might, in proceedings between persons, be granted by way of injunction or specific performance, a court shall not, as against the Crown' grant an injunction or make an order for specific performance, but in lieu thereof may make an order declaratory of the rights of the parties.
>
> (2) A court shall not in any proceedings grant relief or make an order against a servant of the Crown that it is not competent to grant or make against the Crown.[39]

Neither the common law[40] nor provisions such as section 22[41] protect Ministers and officials when they act beyond their statutory authority. However, where the Ministers and officials are merely carrying out the responsibilities of the Crown, they cannot be enjoined.[42] This distinction was summarized by Strayer J. (as he then was) in *Pacific Salmon Industries Inc. v. R.*:

> The real distinction, it appears to me, is based on the nature of the functions which the government official happens to be performing at any given time. If those functions are lawfully authorized, then injunctions are not available to prohibit their performance . . . If on the other hand, they are not lawfully authorized, they are susceptible to being enjoined . . .[43]

As with *mandamus*, discussed above, the immunity from injunctive relief

---

[38] *Grand Council of Crees of Que. v. R.*, [1982] 1 F.C. 599, 124 D.L.R. (3d) 574, 41 N.R. 257 (C.A.).

[39] Section 22. To similar effect: *Proceedings Against the Crown Act*, R.S.O. 1990, c. P.27, s. 14.

[40] *Lodge v. Minister of Employment & Immigration*, [1979] 1 F.C. 775, 94 D.L.R. (3d) 326, 25 N.R. 437 (C.A.).

[41] *MacLean v. Liquor Licence Board of Ontario* (1975), 9 O.R. (2d) 597 (Div. Ct.); *Canada (A. G.) v. Sask. Water Corp.*, [1992] 4 W.W.R. 712, 109 Sask. R. 241 (C.A.).

[42] *Grand Council of Crees of Que. v. R.*, *supra*, note 38; *Peralta v. Ont. (Minister of Natural Resources)* (1984), 46 C.P.C. 218 (Ont. H.C.); leave to appeal refused 46 C.P.C. 229 (Ont. H.C.).

[43] [1985] 1 F.C. 504 at 512, 3 C.P.R. (3d) 289 (T.D.).

may admit of an exception where the relief is sought to prevent a violation of the Constitution.[44]

While the cases mentioned above arose in the public law context, the distinction between authorized and unauthorized actions of government officials finds its origins in private law jurisprudence. The Canadian source case is *Conseil des ports nationaux v. Langelier*.[45] There the plaintiff landowners sought an injunction to restrain the National Harbours Board from carrying out certain works which it was alleged would injuriously affect their properties. The board, which was a statutory Crown agent, raised the immunity of the Crown. The plea was rejected. The Supreme Court of Canada held that a Crown agent who commits a wrong is personally liable to the person injured.[46] Status as an agent of the Crown does not provide protection where the agent acts without legal justification. Therefore, it appears that whether a claim for injunctive relief against a Minister or government official arises under the public law or the private law, the inquiry is the same: is there statutory authority for the allegedly wrongful act? If so, that public law displaces the ordinary public law regime.

(c) *Interlocutory Relief*

Immunity from injunction is a significant limitation on the availability of interlocutory relief where it is alleged that there is an excess of power by government. Apart from the particular case of constitutional claims discussed above,[47] interlocutory relief will not be available when the alleged wrong is being, or about to be, committed not by or on behalf of the Crown.

There has been some suggestion that the solution is an "interim declaration."[48] This would mesh with provisions such as s. 22 of the *Crown Liability and Proceedings Act* which contemplate declaratory relief in lieu of injunctive relief. However, the courts have generally rejected the interim

---

[44] *Can. (A.G.) v. Law Society of British Columbia*, [1982] 2 S.C.R. 307 at 329-31, [1982] 5 W.W.R. 289, 37 B.C.L.R. 145, 19 B.L.R. 234, 66 C.P.R. (2d) 1, 137 D.L.R. (3d) 1, 43 N.R. 451; *Société Abestos v. Société nationale de L'amiante*, [1979] C.A. 342 (Que. C.A.); *Van Mulligan v. Saskatchewan Housing Corp.* (1982), 23 Sask. R. 66 (Q.B.).

[45] [1969] S.C.R. 60.

[46] *Ibid.*, at 71-75. See also: *Bolton v. Forest Pest Management Institute*, [1985] 6 W.W.R. 562, 6 B.C.L.R. 126, 21 D.L.R. (4th) 242 (C.A.); *M. v. Home Office*, [1993] 3 All E.R. 537 (H. L.).

[47] See the cases at notes 26, 28, 46.

[48] Zamir and Woolf, *The Declaratory Judgment*, 2nd ed. (1993), at 299.

declaration as unknown at law and inconsistent with the finality attaching to any declaration of rights.[49] Despite the preponderance of the authorities, the interim declaration has been employed[50] and has been suggested to be a remedy available where the government is deliberately flouting the law.[51]

(3) Damages

Judicial review may not fully answer the aggrieved person's concerns. At the beginning of this paper, an example was offered as to the unlawful cancellation of a commercial fishing licence.[52] The licence holder brought a successful application for judicial review to set aside the cancellation. The licence holder then brought an action for damages, both general damages to compensate him for losses suffered by reason of not being able to fish and punitive damages because of the allegedly high-handed conduct of the Minister. Damages were awarded on both counts.

Consider another example, drawn from the same general regulatory scheme. In this case, a fishing company sought a commercial fishing licence. The Minister authorized its issuance and so advised the company. Other members of the fishing community complained, loudly and publicly. The Minister changed his mind and stopped the licence being issued. The aggrieved fishing company did not seek to compel the issuance of the licence, but sued for damages. At trial the company succeeded, but not on appeal.[53]

In both these examples, the Minister was held to have exceeded his statutory authority and acted *ultra vires*. However, that excess of jurisdiction did not lead *ipso facto* to an award of damages suffered by the

---

[49] *Arctic Offshore Marine Services Ltd. v. R.*, [1986] 2 C.T.C. 179, 4 F.T.R. 183, 11 C.E.R. 363 (F.C.T.D.); *Canada (A.G.) v. Gould*, [1984] 1 F.C. 1133 (C.A.); affd [1984] 2 S.C.R. 124; *Shaw v. British Columbia*, [1982] 6 W.W.R. 718, 40 B.C.L.R. 290, 31 C.P.C. 132, 140 D.L.R. (3d) 178 (B.C.S.C.); *Ominayak v. Norcen Energy Resources Ltd.* (1982), 23 Alta. L.R. (3d) 284 (Q.B.); *Sankey v. Minister of Transport*, [1979] 1 F.C. 134 (T.D.); *MacLean v. Liquor Licence Board of Ontario* (1975), 9 O.R. (2d) 597 (Div. Ct.); *Canadian Industrial Gas & Oil Ltd. v. Saskatchewan*, [1974] 4 W.W.R. 557 (Sask. Q.B.). See also: *Ex parte Smith, Kline, French*, [1989] 2 W.L.R. 378 (H.L.).

[50] *Peralta v. Ont. (Minister of Natural Resources)*, *supra*, note 42.

[51] *Loomis v. Ont. (Minister of Agriculture & Food)* (1993), 16 O.R. (3d) 188 at 191-92, 22 C.P.C. (3d) 396, 108 D.L.R. (4th) 330 (Div. Ct.).

[52] (1992), 51 F.T.R. 161.

[53] *Comeau's Sea Foods Ltd. v. Canada (Minister of Fisheries & Oceans)*, [1992] 3 F.C. 54, 54 F.T.R. 20 (T.D.); reversed [1995] 2 F.C. 467, 24 C.C.L.T. (2d) 1, 123 D.L.R. (4th) 180, 179 N.R. 241 (C.A.).

aggrieved party as a result of the Minister's excess of power. Some element beyond the excess of power was required. The possible nature of this element may be discovered by considering the torts of misfeasance in public office and negligence.

(a) *Misfeasance in Public Office*

In the first example, the *Lapointe* case, damages were awarded not merely because the Minister had acted *ultra vires*, but because he had acted with the knowledge that he lacked lawful authority to cancel the licence. That conscious disregard for the law led to liability for the loss sustained by the licence holder.[54]

Knowingly or maliciously acting in excess of authority is the essence of the tort of misfeasance in public office. The classic Canadian case is *Roncarelli v. Duplessis*.[55] There, the Premier of Quebec was held liable for damages flowing from the unlawful termination of a liquor licence. Liability attached because the Premier acted in bad faith, seeking to punish the licence holder for his support of Jehovah's Witnesses.

Liability will not attach merely because a Minister or official acts *ultra vires*.[56] This is consistent with the position taken by the Supreme Court of Canada in *Canada v. Sask. Wheat Pool*[57] that there is no nominate tort of breach of statutory duty. Mr. Justice Dickson (as he then was) remarked:

> . . . there seems little in the way of defensible policy for holding a defendant who breached a statutory duty unwittingly to be negligent and obligated to pay even though not at fault.[58]

More than mere breach of statute is required in order to attract liability in damages.

Something more than mere breach of statute is present where the Minister or official actually knows that he or she is acting *ultra vires* and goes ahead anyway, knowing injury may be caused to the person who is the object of the *ultra vires* action. That constitutes misfeasance in public

---

[54] *Supra*, note 52, at 166-67.

[55] [1959] S.C.R. 121.

[56] Hogg, *Liability of the Crown*, 2nd ed. (1989), at 111, 113-15. See also discussion of *Welbridge Holdings Ltd. v. Metropolitan Corp. of Greater Winnipeg, infra*, note 67.

[57] [1983] 1 S.C.R. 205, [1983] 3 W.W.R. 97, 23 C.C.L.T. 121, 143 D.L.R. (3d) 9, 45 N.R. 425.

[58] *Ibid.*, at 224.

office.[59] However, the knowledge element of this tort will usually be very difficult to prove. Ministers and officials rarely give reasons for their actions. Actual malice is rarely displayed publicly. At the upper levels of decision-making, public interest privilege may limit access to information. Indeed, in the federal sphere, Cabinet documents are absolutely privileged.[60] The circumstances of the decision-making may be unknowable.[61]

(b) Negligence

In the second example, the *Comeau's Sea Foods* case, there was no evidence of knowledge on the part of the Minister that he lacked the statutory authority to stop the issuance of the licence. The Minister never addressed his mind to the question. Obviously, there could be no liability for misfeasance in public office. The question was instead whether there could be liability in negligence.

The liability of public authorities in negligence has received much judicial attention in the last few years. It is beyond the scope of this paper to attempt to review and analyze the jurisprudence in this area. That is available elsewhere.[62]

The focus of the jurisprudence and academic commentary has been the two-part test proposed by Lord Wilberforce in *Anns v. Merton London Borough Council* and adopted by the Supreme Court of Canada in *Kamloops v. Nielsen*:

---

[59] *Dunlop v. Woollahra Municipal Council*, [1981] 1 All E.R. 1202 (J.C.P.C.); *Burgoin SA v. Ministry of Agriculture, Fisheries & Food*, [1985] 3 All E.R. 585 (C.A.).

[60] *Canada Evidence Act*, R.S.C. 1985, c. C-5, s. 39; *Can. (A.G.) v. Central Cartage Co.*, [1990] 2 F.C. 641 (C.A.), leave to appeal refused 128 N.R. 319 (S.C.C.). There is no similar legislation in Ontario and the court may weigh competing public interests and order the production of Cabinet documents: *Carey v. Ontario*, [1986] 2 S.C.R. 637, 20 O.A.C. 81, 58 O.R. (2d) 352, 30 C.C.C. (3d) 498, 14 C.P.C. (2d) 10, 35 D.L.R. (4th) 161, 72 N.R. 81.

[61] Consider: *Thorne's Hardware Ltd. v. R.*, [1983] 1 S.C.R. 106 at 111-13, 143 D.L.R. (3d) 577, 46 N.R. 91.

[62] Klar, "Falling Boulders, Falling Trees, and Icy Highways: The Policy/Operational Test Revisited" (1994), 33 Alta. L. Rev. 167; Perell, "Negligence Claims against Public Authorities" (1994), 16 Advocates' Q. 222; Reynolds and Hicks, "New Directions for the Civil Liability of Public Authorities in Canada" (1992), 71 Can. Bar Rev. 1; Cohen, "Government Liability for Economic Losses: The Case of Regulatory Failure" (1992), 20 Can. Bus. L.J. 215; Woodall, "Private Law Liability of Public Authorities for Negligent Inspection and Regulation" (1992), 37 McGill L.J. 83; Garant, "La Responsabilité civile de la puissance publique: du clair obscure au nébleux" (1991), 32 C. de D. 745.

. . . in order to decide whether or not a private law duty of care existed, two questions must be asked:

(1) is there a sufficiently close relationship between the parties (the local authority and the person who has suffered the damage) so that, in the reasonable contemplation of the authority, carelessness on its part might cause damage to that person? If so,

(2) are there any considerations which ought to negative or limit (a) the scope of the duty and (b) the class of persons to whom it is owed or (c) the damages to which a breach of it may give rise?[63]

The issue which has animated the jurisdictional and academic debate is the nature and extent of policy decisions which do not attract a duty of care. The rationale for the policy exemption is explained by Mr. Justice Cory in *Just v. British Columbia*:

> The Crown . . . must be free to govern and make true policy decisions without becoming subject to tort liability as a result of those decisions.
>
> . . . . .
>
> True policy decisions should be exempt from tortious claims so that governments are not restricted in making decisions based upon social, political or economic factors.[64]

The task is to characterize the particular government activity as policy or operations.[65] This analysis provides no obvious answer where the complaint is that the government exceeded its powers. In such cases, the decisions taken by Ministers and officials may well have been based upon the social, political or economic factors that earmark policy decisions. If taken within authority, such decisions will not be subjected to a duty of care. The situation is less clear where such policy decisions are taken without authority.

If liability in negligence is to attach for an excess of power, it would

---

[63] *Kamloops v. Nielsen*, [1984] 2 S.C.R. 2 at 10-11, 66 B.C.L.R. 273, 29 C.C.L.T. 97, 26 M.P.L.R. 81, 10 D.L.R. (4th) 641, 54 N.R. 1. The test has been confirmed in *Just v. British Columbia*, [1989] 2 S.C.R. 1228 at 1235-36, [1990] 1 W.W.R. 385, 41 B.C.L.R. (2d) 350, 1 C.C.L.T. (2d) 1, 18 M.V.R. (2d) 1, 64 D.L.R. (4th) 689, 103 N.R. 1. See also *Winnipeg Condominium Corp. No. 36 v. Bird Construction Co.*, [1995] 1 S.C.R. 85 at 108-09, [1995] 3 W.W.R. 85, 100 Man. R. (2d) 241, 23 C.C.L.T. (2d) 1, 43 R.P.R. (2d) 1, 121 D.L.R. (4th) 193, 176 N.R. 321.

[64] *Ibid.*, at 1239.

[65] See *Brown v. British Columbia (Minister of Transportation & Highways)*, [1994] 1 S.C.R. 420, 89 B.C.L.R. (2d) 1, 19 C.C.L.T. (2d) 268, 2 M.V.R. (3d) 43, 112 D.L.R. (4th) 1, 164 N.R. 161; *Swinamer v. N.S. (A.G.)* , [1994] 1 S.C.R. 445, 129 N.S.R. (2d) 321, 19 C.C.L.T. (2d) 233, 112 D.L.R. (4th) 18, 163 N.R. 291.

seem that the duty involved is a duty on the part of the Minister or official to take reasonable care that he or she has the authority to be exercised. Under this theory, liability is imposed not for erring in law, but erring negligently. That raises the question of how to define the standard of care to be expected of the decision-maker. Will the decision-maker be at fault for failing to seek legal advice? A second opinion? Prior judicial approval? The difficulty of the application of this theory led the Judicial Committee in *Rowling v. Takaro Properties Ltd.*[66] to doubt wisdom of imposing such a duty.

Excluding liability for mistakes as to the extent of powers would be consistent with the approach taken where the error occurs in exercise of legislative or *quasi*-judicial powers. The application of private law remedies to such powers was considered by the Supreme Court of Canada in *Welbridge Holdings Ltd. v. Metropolitan Corp. of Greater Winnipeg.*[67] The plaintiffs sought to recover damages in negligence in respect of loss suffered by reason of the municipality enacting an invalid bylaw. The court rejected liability in damages. Mr. Justice Laskin (as he then was) explained:

> Its public character, involving its political and social responsibility to all those who live and work within its territorial limits, distinguishes it, even as respects its exercise of any quasi-judicial function, from the position of a voluntary or statutory body such as a trade union or trade association which may have quasi-judicial and contractual obligations in dealing with its members: cf. *Abbott v. Sullivan*; *Orchard v. Tunney*. A municipality at what may be called the operating level is different in kind from the same municipality at the legislative or quasi-judicial level where it is exercising discretionary statutory authority. In exercising such authority, a municipality (no less than a provincial Legislature or the Parliament of Canada) may act beyond its powers in the ultimate view of a Court, albeit it acted on the advice of counsel. It would be incredible to say in such circumstances that it owed a duty of care giving rise to liability in damages for its breach. "Invalidity is not the test of fault and it should not be the test of liability": see Davis, 3 *Administrative Law Treatise*, 1958, at p. 487.[68]

The municipality is not liable in negligence when it acts beyond its legislative or quasi-judicial powers. That excess of jurisdiction does not transform a policy decision into an operational one. This analysis could also apply where a Minister or government official acts beyond his or her discretionary powers. That excess of jurisdiction does not transform what would appear to be a policy decision into an operational one attracting

---

[66] [1988] 1 A.C. 473 at 500-02 (J.C.P.C.).
[67] [1971] S.C.R. 957.
[68] *Ibid.*, at 968-69.

a duty of care. There is no basis for limiting the proposition that invalidity is not the test of fault to legislative and quasi-judicial functions.

The Supreme Court of Canada decisions which have come after *Kamloops v. Nielsen* have dealt with situations of alleged negligence in providing government services and have not had to confront the issue of liability for an excess of power. The extent of statutory authority has only been raised from the opposite direction: when does statutory authority provide a defence.[69] However, it would appear that that issue arises only after a finding that the decision or action is operational in nature. The Supreme Court of Canada has not addressed the issue of an excess of power in making what would be a policy decision since its decision in *Welbridge Holdings*.

(c) *Charter Damages*

Liability for damages for excess of power also arises in the context of the *Charter of Rights*. The availability of damages in Charter cases has received scholarly analysis,[70] but only limited judicial consideration. One of the issues yet to be settled is whether a damages remedy fashioned under subs. 24(1) of the Charter should only be available where there has been bad faith or malice.

The small body of jurisprudence developed so far exhibits little enthusiasm for the development of a non-fault remedy, whereby infringement of the Charter, without more, would provide the basis for an award of damages. However, there is support for the non-fault approach that can be found in the decision of the Judicial Committee in *Maharaj v. Attorney General of Trinidad and Tobago (No. 1)*,[71] where a barrister who had been imprisoned for contempt of court in contravention of his constitutional rights claimed damages against the Crown. The plaintiff invoked a constitutional provision providing that a person whose consti-

---

[69] *Tock v. St. John's Metropolitan Area Board*, [1989] 2 S.C.R. 1181, 82 Nfld. & P.E.I.R. 181, 1 C.C.L.T. (2d) 113, 47 M.P.L.R. 113, 64 D.L.R. (4th) 620, 104 N.R. 241.

[70] Pilkington, "Damages as a Remedy for Infringement of the Canadian Charter of Rights and Freedoms" (1984), 62 Can. Bar Rev. 517; Pilkington, "Monetary Redress for Charter Infringement" in Sharpe, ed., *Charter Litigation* (1987); Cooper-Stephenson, *Charter Damage Claims* (1990).

[71] [1979] A.C. 385 (J.C.P.C.). This decision has been referred to but not yet adopted by Canadian courts: *Germain v. The Queen* (1984), 10 C.R.R. 232 at 243-44 (Alta. Q.B.); *Rogne v. Canada* (1986), 1 F.T.R. 234; *Oag v. Canada*, [1986] 1 F.C. 472 at 482-83, 22 C.R.R. 171, 23 C.C.C. (3d) 20 (T.D.); reversed without consideration of this point [1987] 2 F.C. 511, 33 C.C.C. (3d) 430, 73 N.R. 149 (C.A.); *Tucker v. Steetley Industries Ltd.* (1987), 9 F.T.R. 307 at 311.

tutional rights had been infringed could apply to the court for redress. The Attorney General argued that the judge who had infringed the plaintiff's rights was immune from suit and, in any event, the Crown was not vicariously liable for the judge's actions. The Judicial Committee accepted the judge was immune, but held that the Crown could nevertheless be held liable in damages. The redress provision of the constitution created a new, direct liability on the part of the Crown; Lord Diplock stated:

> . . . no change is involved in the rule that a judge cannot be made personally liable for what he has done when acting or purporting to act in a judicial capacity. The claim for redress under section 6(1) for what has been done by a judge is a claim against the state for what has been done in the exercise of the judicial power of the state. This is not vicarious liability; it is a liability of the state itself. It is not a liability in tort at all; it is a liability in the public law of the state, not of the judge himself, which has been newly created by section 6(1) and (2) of the Constitution.[72]

In *Maharaj*, the constitutional remedy in damages is seen as a matter of public law, having nothing to do with the ordinary principles of private law.[73] On the other hand, the Canadian approach, as discussed above, has been to look to the private law to provide a remedy in damages for excesses of power. That is reflected by some of the early cases dealing with the availability of damages in Charter cases. For example, in *Crown Trust Co. v. R.*[74] it was held that an action in damages for the seizure of the plaintiffs' assets under the authority of a statutory provision alleged to be inconsistent with the Charter would not lie in the absence of any allegation of wrongful conduct, bad faith, negligence or collateral purpose. Similarly, in *Lagiorgia v. R.*,[75] the court declined to award damages in respect of a seizure made in violation of the Charter because it was done in good faith and in accordance with the law as it was understood to be.

Another indication of the approach that may be taken to a Charter

---

[72] *Ibid.*, at 399.

[73] *Ibid.*, at 396-97.

[74] (1986), 54 O.R. (2d) 79 at 86-87 (Div. Ct.).

[75] [1985] 1 F.C. 438, 16 C.P.R. (3d) 74, 18 C.R.R. 348, [1985] 2 CTC 25, 85 DTC 5419 (T.D.); varied, without consideration of this point, [1987] 3 F.C. 28, 35 C.C.C. (3d) 445, 16 C.P.R. (3d) 74, 57 C.R. (3d) 284, 33 C.R.R. 372, [1987] 1 CTC 424, 87 DTC 5245, 42 D.L.R. (4th) 764 (C.A.). See also *Mills v. R.*, [1986] 1 S.C.R. 863 at 948, 16 O.A.C. 81, 58 O.R. (2d) 543, 26 C.C.C. (3d) 481, 52 C.R. (3d) 1, 21 C.R.R. 76, 29 D.L.R. (4th) 161; *Vespoli v. M.N.R.* (1984), 55 N.R. 269 at 272 (Fed. C.A.); *Kohn v. Globerman*, [1986] 4 W.W.R. 1, 39 Man. R. (2d) 263, 36 C.C.L.T. 60, 20 C.R.R. 49, 27 D.L.R. (4th) 583 at 599 (C.A.); *Scorpio Rising Software Inc. v. Sask. (A.G.)* (1986), 46 Sask. R. 230 (Q.B.).

remedy in damages comes from the cases where the aggrieved person has advanced a damage claim both under the ordinary law and under subs. 24(1) of the Charter. The two causes of action have been seen to be coincident. In *Prète v. Ontario*,[76] the plaintiff sought damages for having been wrongfully subjected to a preferred indictment for murder. It was held that there was no difference between a cause of action for breach of the Charter and one for malicious prosecution.[77] Damages were awarded on the ordinary common law basis.

Subsection 24(1) of the Charter provides the courts with the opportunity to develop a public law approach to damages for excesses of power. That opportunity has not yet been exploited. The private law continues to be the reference point for the development of a remedy in damages for excesses of power.

(4) Relationship of Judicial Review and Damages

What distinguishes judicial review and damages as remedies for excesses of power is the mental element. Judicial review is not necessarily concerned with the knowledge or motives of the Minister or official exercising the power. Sometimes knowledge or motives may come into the determination of whether the statutory power has been exceeded. However, it is the excess of power *per se*, and not the reasons for the excess of power, that triggers a judicial review remedy.

An excess of power, without more, does not entitle an aggrieved person to damages. Fault must be proven. The mental element is critical. It may be necessary to prove that the Minister or official acted in bad faith or with actual knowledge of the lack of power. Even if a remedy is available in negligence, the mental element remains essential, although an objective reasonableness test as to knowledge is substituted.

Commonly, resort will be had to judicial review, and any action in damages will follow. Judicial review will usually give quicker and more direct relief. Furthermore, a successful application for judicial review may prevent or limit the financial loss that could be suffered by reason of the excess of power.

On occasion, the aggrieved person may choose to proceed directly with an action in damages. That raises the question whether the choice not to seek judicial review will have an effect on the recovery of damages.

---

[76] (1990), 47 C.R.R. 307 (Ont. H.C.J.); revd 16 O.R. (3d) 161, 18 C.C.L.T. (2d) 54, 18 C.R.R. (2d) 291, 110 D.L.R. (4th) 94; leave to appeal to S.C.C. refused 17 O.R. (3d) xvi, 20 C.C.L.T. (2d) 319*n*, 175 N.R. 322*n*.

[77] *Ibid.*, at 311.

In *Comeau's Sea Foods*, the aggrieved plaintiff fishing company did not seek *mandamus* to compel the issuance of the fishing licence. The plaintiff chose instead to sue for damages. Arguably, a timely order of *mandamus* would have allowed the company to fish and thereby avoid the financial loss. Two of the judges[78] in the Federal Court of Appeal suggested that the choice not to seek judicial review might be shown to be a failure on the part of the plaintiff to mitigate its loss.

The third appellate judge[79] in *Comeau's Sea Foods* adopted a different approach. Mr. Justice Stone reasoned that the availability of adequate administrative law remedies by way of judicial review is a consideration to be taken into account in deciding whether the existence of a *prima facie* duty of care should be negative. His Lordship concluded that the *mandamus* had been available to the plaintiff and that negated any duty of care that may have arisen because the foreseeability of loss if the plaintiff were not issued the licence. The availability of judicial review did not reduce the plaintiff's claim but eliminated it.

The reasoning adopted by Mr. Justice Sone suggests that the policy decision exception is not the only consideration that may negative the existence of a duty of care. The second branch of the *Anns* test is open-ended and speaks of "any considerations which ought to negative" private law duty. Its purpose is to determine whether the law should impose, over and above public law powers and duties, a private law duty enabling suits for damages. Mr. Justice Stone's conclusion that the availability of the public law remedy negated a private law solution does not appear to be inconsistent in the *Anns* approach.

4. *Remedies respecting Government Promises*

Government makes promises on a daily basis. Not surprisingly, government does not keep all its promises. The aggrieved person who seeks to hold government to its promises faces an array of public law and private law options. The intent here is to identify some of the remedial solutions that government promises may attract.

---

[78] *Comeau's Sea Foods Ltd.*, [1995] 2 F.C. 467, 24 C.C.L.T. (2d) 1, 123 D.L.R. (4th) 180, 179 N.R. 241, *per* Linden J.A., at 523 [F.C.], and *per* Robertson J.A., at 537-538 [F.C.].

[79] *Ibid.*, per Stone J.A., at 485-488 [F.C.]. See also *Wirth v. Vancouver (City)*, [1988] 4 W.W.R. 72 , 24 B.C.L.R. (2d) 117, 43 C.C.L.T. 209, 49 D.L.R. (4th) 153(S.C.); affd [1990] 6 W.W.R. 225, 47 B.C.L.R. (2d) 340, 3 C.C.L.T. (2d) 282, 50 M.P.L.R. 105, 71 D.L.R. (4th) 745 (C.A.).

(1) Contracts

Government can be held liable on its contracts.[80] A government promise which leads to the formation of a contract can be enforced by way of an action in damages. However, government contracts cannot be enforced by way of orders of specific performance. Specific performance is unavailable on essentially the same basis that injunctive relief cannot be obtained.[81]

The dispute often focuses on whether a contract has come into existence. This may involve a consideration of the authority of the Minister or official to enter into a contract on behalf of the government. Legislation may appear to limit the authority to contract and bind the government. Such legislation has been interpreted narrowly, so as not to exclude the normal rules of agency but merely to establish directory rules of indoor management.[82] The presumption has been in favour of the private law.

A government promise will lead to the formation of a contract only where there is a requisite intention to contract. Absent such intention, no contract can arise.[83] This issue has arisen in cases of programmes for subsidies and grants. Offers made in such programmes do not necessarily give rise to a contractual relationship between the government and the potential recipient.[84]

An intention to create contractual relations may be difficult to find where the subject-matter is the subject of a regulatory scheme. There may be no intention to graft onto the statutory relationship some additional contractual obligations. Thus, in *Comeau's Sea Foods* the trial judge refused to characterize the Minister's authorization of a fishing licence as giving rise to a contractual obligation to issue the licence as promised.[85]

There is also a line of cases to the effect that a Minister or official with discretionary power may not by contract limit the future exercise of

---

[80] The Crown is liable in contract at common law: *Bank of Montreal v. (A.G.) (Que.)*, [1979] 1 S.C.R. 565 at 574; Hogg, *Liability of the Crown*, 2nd ed. (1989), at 159-60; Lordon, *Crown Law* (1990), at 293 *et seq.*

[81] *Gauthier v. R.* (1915), 15 Ex.C.R. 444; *Crown Liability and Proceedings Act*, s. 22; *Proceedings Against the Crown Act*, s. 14.

[82] *R. v. Transworld Shipping Ltd.*, [1976] 1 F.C. 159 (C.A.); *Verrault (J.E.) & Fils Ltée v. Que. (A.G.)*, [1977] 1 S.C.R. 41; *R. v. CAE Industries Ltd.*, [1986] 1 F.C. 129, [1985] 5 W.W.R. 481, 30 B.L.R. 236, 20 D.L.R. (4th) 347, 61 N.R. 19 (C.A.), leave to appeal refused 20 D.L.R. (4th) 347*n* (S.C.C.); *Sommerville Belkin Industries Ltd. v. Manitoba*, [1988] 3 W.W.R. 523 (Man. C.A.).

[83] Fridman, *The Law of Contract in Canada*, 3rd ed. (1994), at 26-31.

[84] *B.C. (A.G.) v. Esquimalt & Nanaimo Railway Co.*, [1950] 1 D.L.R. 305 (J.C.P.C.); but compare *Grant v. N.B.* (1973), 35 D.L.R. (3d) 141 (N.B.C.A).

[85] *Supra*, note 53, at 69-70 (T.D.). The Federal Court of Appeal affirmed the trial judge on this issue.

that discretion.[86] That approach has been effectively criticized by Professor Hogg.[87] A better view may be that the existence of a discretionary power to be exercised in the future may militate against, but not preclude, the existence of the requisite intention to create contractual relations.

The requirement of an intention to create contractual relations is by no means insurmountable. Quite the opposite. Even "political promises" may exhibit a sufficient intention to be contractually bound. In *R. v. CAE Industries Ltd.*,[88] the federal government had encountered public objection to the transfer of an aircraft maintenance work from Winnipeg to Montreal. The plaintiff company was considering taking over and operating the Winnipeg facilities. Ministers provided a letter to the company indicating, *inter alia*, that the government would employ its best efforts to supply the company with additional work. The court held there was a contract. In doing so, the court rejected the argument that there had been no intention to contract. That intention could be ascertained from the surrounding circumstances, including the government's subsequent efforts to carry out what had been promised. The government was unable to discharge its heavy onus of establishing no intention to contract.

There may be some modest similarity between the analysis of finding intent to create contractual relations and the *Anns* test as to a duty of care in negligence. Both start from a relationship between government and the individual that is founded upon a public law foundation, usually statutory. The question then becomes whether private law obligations, be they in contract or negligence, are to be added to the statutory relationship. The ultimate policy decision for the courts is the same: to what degree will the exercise of public law responsibilities be circumscribed by the imposition of private law obligations?

Damages may not always be the desired remedy. This is illustrated by the attempts to subject the government contracting process to supervision by way of judicial review remedies. *Thomas C. Assaly Corp. v. Canada*[89] is an example of an attempt that was successful. Mr. Justice Strayer quashed the Minister's decision to reject the applicant's tender to provide premises for a government department. His Lordship found

---

[86] *R. v. Dominion of Canada Postage Stamp Vending Co.*, [1930] S.C.R. 500 at 506; *Vancouver v. Registrar, Vancouver Land Registration District (No. 2) Pty Ltd. v. Chalk*, [1975] A.C. 520 at 533-36 (J.C.P.C.); *Petrocorp Exploration Ltd. v. Butcher* (1991), 122 N.R. 379 at 391-92 (J.C.P.C.). See also: Dussault and Borgeat, *Administrative Law: A Treatise*, 2nd ed. (1985), vol. 1, at 545-47.

[87] Hogg, *supra*, note 80, at 170-72.

[88] *Supra*, note 82.

[89] (1990), 34 F.T.R. 156.

a breach of procedural fairness and considered that the private law remedies would not be adequate alternatives to judicial review:

> What is involved here is the fairness of the administrative process by
> which decisions are made among tenderers who have been invited to bid on
> the basis of certain conditions and understandings. While a denial of fair-
> ness may also amount to breach of contract that is a much more difficult
> issue which, as I have pointed out in the *Glenview* case, would require a trial
> involving difficult issues of fact and law. Essentially the same would be true
> of an action in tort for misrepresentation. I cannot therefore view such actions
> for damages as adequate alternatives to the administrative law remedy of
> certiorari to which the applicant has demonstrated its entitlement now. The
> public law remedy of certiorari cannot only be realized without delay to either
> party but can also give the applicant a chance at the contract itself, some-
> thing the private law contractual remedies cannot now feasibly accomplish
> for the reasons I stated in *Glenview*.[90]

The ordinary law of contract recognizes a remedy in damages available to an unsuccessful bidder where the owner has failed to observe the
terms of the tendering process.[91] Such actions have succeeded where the
government has changed the rules of the game in midstream.[92] This remedy
appears to be directed, at least in part, at promoting the integrity of the
contracting process. Mr. Justice Strayer appeared to see a benefit in sup-
plementing this private law remedy with a judicial review on a public law
basis.

The beachhead in *Assaly* has not led to a full force invasion of public law remedies into the tendering process. Other judges have rejected
the existence of a duty of fairness.[93] The regulations as to government
contracting have been seen as merely indoor management rules.[94] Tendering has been characterized as the general conduct of government business and not the exercise of statutory powers subject to judicial review.[95]
In short, despite its public law aspects tendering has been treated as an
activity of government governed by the contract law of general application.

---

[90] *Ibid.*, at 159.
[91] *R. in right of Ontario v. Ron Engineering & Construction (Eastern) Ltd.*, [1981]
    1 S.C.R. 111, 13 B.L.R. 72, 119 D.L.R. (3d) 267, 35 N.R. 40.
[92] See, for example, *Canamerican Auto Lease & Rental Ltd. v. Canada*, [1987]
    3 F.C. 144 (C.A.).
[93] *St. Lawrence Cement Inc. v. Ont. (Minister of Transportation)* (1991), 3 O.R.
    (3d) 130 (Gen. Div.).
[94] *Socanav Inc. v. N.W.T. (Com'r)*, [1993] N.W.T.R. 364 (S.C.).
[95] *J.G. Morgan Development Corp. v. Canada (Minister of Public Works)*, [1992]
    3 F.C. 783 (T.D.); *Volker Stevin NWT (92) Ltd. v. N.W.T. (Com'r)* (1993),
    15 Admin. L.R. (2d) 211 (N.W.T.S.C.).

(2) Promissory Estoppel

Where government promises fall short of forming contracts, resort is often had to the doctrine of estoppel to prevent a minister or official from going back on a promise. The class of estoppel at issue is promissory estoppel. It is described as follows:

> 1071. Promissory estoppel. When one party has, by his words or conduct, made to the other a clear and unequivocal promise or assurance which was intended to affect the legal relations between them and to be acted on accordingly, then, once the other party has taken him at his word and acted on it, the one who gave the promise or assurance cannot afterwards be allowed to revert to their previous legal relations as if no such promise or assurance had been made by him, but he must accept their legal relations subject to the qualification which he himself has so introduced . . . It differs from estoppel [by representation] in that the representation relied upon need not be one of present fact.[96]

There is a point of view that estoppel does not bind the Crown.[97] It is difficult to accept that proposition without qualification.[98] There clearly are cases where the Crown has been estopped from going back on assurances intended to be relied on.[99] The proper question would appear to be not whether estoppel binds the Crown, but when does it not bind the Crown.

Estoppel will be of little or no assistance in obtaining a remedy where the Minister or official has made a representation in contravention of a statutory provision. Attempts to use estoppel to hold the government to advice given by officials as to the interpretation and application of taxing and similar statutes have proven singularly unsuccessful.[100] Shortly put, liability is to be determined under the statute, not under an official's opinion.

It is difficult to be unequivocal as to the operation of estoppel where there is no direct conflict with the statute. There is authority for the proposition that estoppel cannot operate to prevent the exercise by Ministers

---

[96] *Halsbury's Laws of England*, 4th ed. (revised), vol. 16, para. 1071.
[97] Lyman, "Estoppel and the Crown" (1978), 9 Man. L. J. 15.
[98] Professor Hogg does not accept it at all: *supra*, note 80, at 189.
[99] The classic case is *Robertson v. Minister of Pensions*, [1949] 1 K.B. 227 (C.A.). See also: *Re Bella Vista Restaurant* (1982), 41 B.C.L.R. 283 (C.A.); *Laker Airways Ltd. v. Department of Trade*, [1977] 2 All E.R. 182 (C.A.).
[100] *M.N.R. v. Inland Industries Ltd.*, [1974] S.C.R. 514; *Granger v. Canada (Employment & Immigration Com'n)*, [1986] 3 F.C. 70, 29 D.L.R. (4th) 501, 69 N.R. 212 (C.A.); affd [1989] 1 S.C.R. 141, 91 N.R. 141.

and officials of their statutory powers.[101] There is also authority for the competing proposition that a Minister or official can be estopped from denying that the representation in question was the exercise of the statutory power.[102] It has been suggested that the real issue is not so much one of estoppel as a question of whether or not the statutory power has been exercised. Patrick McDonald has proposed:

> A public authority cannot be estopped from exercising its powers. But once the authority has decided that a particular exercise of power is appropriate, it must accordingly, at least where there has been reliance on that decision. A promise of future executive action is binding precisely because it necessarily involves a decision that the promised action is an appropriate exercise of the power. To this point, nothing more is involved than the proposition that decisions made cannot be reconsidered, even though they may not have been implemented by executive action.[103]

There have been attempts to take estoppel beyond its use as a tool to establish entitlement to public law remedies and to raise it to the status of a remedy on its own. This is the effort to found a cause of action on promissory estoppel. At issue is whether there is a cause of action in damages where the representor fails to fulfil that promise. For example, in *Comeau's Sea Foods*, the plaintiff sought to claim damages founded on a promissory estoppel alleged to arise form the Minister's representation that a licence had been authorized. The trial judge held that promissory estoppel could not give a cause of action.[104]

There may be a place for damages for promissory estoppel in public law. There is something to be said for holding Ministers and officials liable for promises they make with knowledge they will be relied upon. There is some possible analogy to the knowledge component required for liability in tort. Such a remedy in damages would also bear some resemblance

---

[101] *Maritime Electric Co. v. General Dairies Ltd.*, [1937] A.C. 610 (J.C.P.C.); *Rootkin v. Kent County Council*, [1981] 2 All E.R. 227 (C.A.); *Kenora (Town) Hydro Electric Com'n v. Vacationland Dairy Co-operative Ltd.* (1992), 7 O.R. (3d) 385, 88 D.L.R. (4th) 725 (C.A.); affd. [1994] 1 S.C.R. 80, 110 D.L.R. (4th) 449, 162 N.R. 241.

[102] *Laker Airways Ltd. v. Department of Trade, supra,* note 99; *Re: Bella Vista Restaurant, supra,* note 92; *Husky Oil Ltd. v. M.N.R.* (1991), 44 F.T.R. 18. The case of *Violi v. Superintendent of Immigration*, [1965] S.C.R. 232, is sometimes cited in support of this proposition. It appears to be a case of *functus officio* or exhaustion of a statutory discretion, rather than one of estoppel.

[103] McDonald, "Contradictory Government Action: Estoppel of Statutory Authorities" (1979), 17 Osgoode Hall L.J. 160.

[104] [1992] 3 F.C. 54 at 68-69, 54 F.T.R. 20. The Federal Court of Appeal affirmed the trial judge on this point, [1995] 2 F.C. 467, 24 C.C.L.T. (2d) 1, 123 D.L.R. (4th) 180, 179 N.R. 241. See also: *Coombe v. Coombe*, [1951] 1 All E.R. 767 at 770 (C.A.); *Fridman, supra,* note 82, at 124.

to a claim in negligent misrepresentation, but with respect to promises of future action rather than representations of existing fact. If such a remedy were to develop, it should do so in conjunction with liability in negligence and should be subject to similar public policy considerations to limit its application where decisions are taken on social, political and economic bases.

Before leaving estoppel, it is appropriate to note the doctrine of legitimate expectations. That doctrine has been invoked to hold Ministers and officials to promises. Representations may give rise to legitimate expectations that a particular procedure will be followed.[105] It may then be a breach of the duty of procedural fairness to depart from that procedure. The doctrine is of limited utility. It is essentially a component of the duty to afford procedural fairness. The doctrine provides only a procedural remedy. It does not guarantee a particular substantive result.[106]

5. Conclusion

It is obvious that remedies against government mix public law and private law. It is less obvious that there has been any systematic approach to the admixture. There are examples of conscious efforts to adjust the private law to accommodate private law concerns. The policy exception to liability in negligence is one example. Another is the adjustment of the law of restitution to incorporate public law concerns restricting the recovery of *ultra vires* taxes.[107]

There would appear to be other points of intersection of the public and private law that merit a similar conscious analysis. For example, there is room for a comprehensive approach to liability in damages for excesses of power that would reconcile the nature of the mental element required. Similarly, the interrelationship of judicial review and damages needs to be critically examined, to determine how best those two remedies can be employed to respond to not only excesses of power, but also control of the government contracting process.

---

[105] *Bendahmane v. Canada (Minister of Employment & Immigration*, [1989] 3 F.C. 16, 61 D.L.R. (4th) 313, 95 N.R. 385 (C.A.); *R. v. Liverpool Corp., ex p. Liverpool Taxi Fleet Operators' Ass'n*, [1972] 2 Q.B. 299 (C.A.).

[106] *Reference re Canada Assistance Plan*, [1991] 2 S.C.R. 525 at 557-58, [1991] 6 W.W.R. 1, 58 B.C.L.R. (2d) 1, 83 D.L.R. (4th) 297, 127 N.R. 161; *Ontario Nursing Home Ass'n v. Ont.* (1990), 74 O.R. (2d) 364 at 380 (H.C.).

[107] *Air Canada v. British Columbia*, [1989] 1 S.C.R. 1161 at 1195-1210, [1989] 4 W.W.R. 97, 36 B.C.L.R. (2d) 145, 41 C.R.R. 308, 59 D.L.R. (4th) 161, 95 N.R. 1. It was held that the restitution of taxes paid under a mistake as to the constitutional validity of a statute was governed by public law.

PRINCIPLES AND PROOFS IN THE LAW OF REMEDIES: EMERGING TACTICAL ISSUES RELATED TO ADMINISTRATIVE LAW REMEDIES

Eleanore A. Cronk

1. *Introduction*

The purpose of this paper is to raise for consideration by practitioners certain emerging tactical issues arising from recent administrative law jurisprudence relating to remedies. A more extensive discussion of many of the recent cases has been undertaken by other speakers during the course of these Special Lectures. I propose, however, to comment on some of the tactical issues arising in relation to:

(1) intervention applications;
(2) the timing of applications for judicial review;
(3) bias issues;
(4) recent amendments to the *Statutory Powers Procedure Act* (Ontario);[1]
(5) certain advocacy issues concerning the conduct of proceedings;
(6) standards of review and the changing features of curial deference, and
(7) the relevance to administrative tribunals of the *"functus officio"* doctrine.

---

[1] R.S.O. 1990, c. S.22.

2. *Issues at the Hearing Stage*

(1) Intervention Applications

Intervention at an administrative tribunal hearing by various public interest or advocacy group representatives is not new. In recent years, particularly since introduction of the *Canadian Charter of Rights and Freedoms* and consideration of its role in the process of social change, the courts have interpreted intervention rules so as to broaden the circumstances in which public interest intervention might be sought successfully. It has been said in this regard:

> This expanded approach to public interest intervention, like reformed public interest standing law, provides an important mechanism for access to the justice system to address non-traditional interests in particular. The developments have been especially important for disadvantaged groups and environmental concerns. However, intervention law remains in transition with the result that principles are unevenly applied and substantive changes are still needed and likely to occur.[2]

Generally, permission to participate as an intervenor in administrative tribunal hearings has been granted more frequently and in wider circumstances than has been the case in the courts. Robert W. Macaulay, in *Practice and Procedure Before Administrative Tribunals*, has observed:

> The permission or right to participate in agency hearings in Canada has always been much more democratically practised by agencies than by the Canadian courts. There are unfortunately some exceptions to this general rule, lamentably, usually at the hands of agencies which are chaired by lawyers with insufficient practical administrative experience.

> Most agencies in Canada are very open about who and what they will recognize, largely because most agencies have a duty to represent and consider the public interest in addition to any particular interest of a party appearing before the agency in a given matter. It is patently difficult for an agency to consider the public interest if a member of the public is excluded from giving evidence or otherwise taking part in the proceedings. Agencies, on the whole, have adopted a low hearth of interest as an entrance requirement. The basic test that is most often applied is that of relevance. If what the person seeking to participate has to say or to bring to the hearing is relevant, the person ought to be able to participate.

> Further, it is far better to err on the open side of admission in the early stages

---

[2] Orton, *Public Interest Intervention,* Canadian Bar Association — Ontario, 1992 Annual Institute of Continuing Legal Education January 31, 1992, at 1.

of a hearing before ruling at a later date that the evidence or participation of the person is not helpful to the procedures and considerations of the agency.

Patently, there is an exception to this general view, that is, where the mandating legislation makes it very clear — and I repeat "very clear" that such a person is not to be heard by the agency. However, even then, I would be of the view that there is very little legislation to that effect in Canada, and whatever there is, is likely contrary to the *Charter of Rights* in which case the agency ought to so find and declare, where appropriate, that the constraint is unconstitutional.[3]

Under the *Rules of Civil Procedure*[4] in Ontario, the courts are permitted under Rule 13 to grant leave to non-parties to intervene in a pending proceeding in two different circumstances. Under rule 13.01 a non-party may seek leave of the courts to intervene *as an added party* on any one of three grounds, namely, that the person seeking to intervene has an interest in the subject-matter of the proceeding or that they may be adversely affected by the outcome or that there exists between the persons seeking to intervene and one or more of the parties to the proceeding, a question of law or fact in common with one or more of the questions in issue in the proceeding. As noted in the commentary to the Rules, this procedure contemplates that such intervention may lead to the intervenor becoming involved in the fact-finding process. On a motion of this kind the courts are obliged to consider whether the intervention will unduly delay or prejudice the determination of the rights of the parties to the proceeding.

Leave to intervene may also be sought under rule 13.02 *as a "friend of the court"*. Intervention on this basis is for the purpose of rendering assistance to the court *by way of argument*. The intervenor does not become a party to the proceeding but retains the status of a "friend of the court". Such intervention may be sought either by a non-party on their own motion or by the court.

As will be apparent, Rule 13 in both dimensions provides a broad basis for the granting of intervenor status in civil proceedings. Since the advent of the *Charter of Rights* it has been more widely relied upon.

There is a developed body of case-law relating to public interest intervention applications in matters pending before the courts. Apart from the Ontario *Rules of Civil Procedure*, the recently amended *Federal Court of Canada Rules*[5] and the *Supreme Court of Canada Rules*[6] specifically

---

[3] Macaulay and Sprague, *Practice and Procedure Before Administrative Tribunals* (Carswell, 1994), Vol. 1, at 9-24 — 9-25.

[4] R.R.O. 1990, Reg. 194.

[5] C.R.C. 1978, c. 663.

[6] C.R.C. 1978, c. 1512.

provide for intervention in delineated circumstances. Generally, on an application for intervenor status to address public interest issues, the applicant must be able to demonstrate that they have an "interest" in the proceeding or its outcome and that they will make a useful contribution to the deliberations of the court or provide a different perspective that will inform the court's deliberations.

The authority of administrative tribunals to grant intervenor status, where the enabling legislation of the relevant tribunal does not expressly provide for intervention, has been considered in a number of cases. In *Society of Composers, Authors & Music Publishers of Canada v. Canada (Copyright Board)*,[7] the Copyright Board directed that an applicant under the *Copyright Act*[8] (Canada) for a statement of proposed royalties, give specific notice to a category of licencee potentially to be affected by an increase in the tariffs filed as part of the proposed statement of royalties. The Board also granted intervenor status to a radio station which had filed objections out of time and, further, recognized certain participation rights for the radio station in relation to certain of the tariffs at issue in the case, including the right to attend any hearings concerning specified tariffs. The applicant applied to the Federal Court (Trial Division) under s. 18 of the *Federal Court Act*[9] (Canada) for judicial review of the Board's rulings. This resulted in various further applications being made to the court for intervenor status, including applications by three cable television services who had filed timely objections as users of the various tariffs, for intervenor status before the Board on the basis that they had an interest in the determination of whether the Board had jurisdiction to accord intervenor status to persons or groups who were not "users" of the relevant tariffs. Mr. Justice Mackay of the Federal Court (Trial Division) held:

> It is my conclusion that the Board does have the authority to grant intervenor status to those parties that, in its discretion, the Board judges to be in a position to contribute to resolution of the issues before the Board. They may be users who have not filed timely objection or they may be others whose particular interest would, in the opinion of the Board, warrant their involvement in its proceedings as intervenors.
>
> . . . . .
>
> In my view, the authority to grant intervenor status, and the authority to determine procedural rights of individual intervenors is within the implicit authority of the Board as a necessary incident in the discharge of its role in the public interest. It is implicit within the terms of subs. 66.7(1), as a power in relation to "matters necessary or proper for the due exercise of its jurisdiction", a power akin to that "vested in a superior court of record".

---

[7] (1993), 16 Admin. L. R. (2d) 187 (F.C.T.D.).
[8] R.S.C. 1985, c. C-42.
[9] R.S.C. 1985, c. F-7.

I note again there are numerous references in modern case law to the principle that administrative tribunals are now recognized generally as masters of their own procedures subject only to limitations arising from express or implied limitations by statute or by the general law. A number of decisions referring to that perspective are concerned with the authority to permit intervention by interested parties who are not otherwise before a tribunal . . .[10]

Thus, even in the absence of express authority to grant intervenor status to applicants, the Federal Court (Trial Division) held that for tribunals required to discharge specific duties in the public interest, the authority to determine the rights of intervenor applicants was necessarily incidental to the fulfillment of a public interest statutory mandate. In addition, the authority of administrative tribunals to regulate their own procedures, either by formal regulation or hearings-specific rulings, by implication authorized such tribunals to order the conduct of hearings and arrangements for those hearings. In this latter regard, Mr. Justice MacKay commented:

Clearly the role of the Board, to consider in the public interest, proposed royalties, objections and any replies to those, and to certify approved royalties, by implication authorizes the conduct of hearings by the Board, and authority in relation to arrangements for those hearings is vested in the Board primarily under subs. 66.7(1) and, in relation to the development of regulations for such proceedings, under subs. 66.6(1). The fact that no such regulations had been made is also not of significance in my view . . .[11]

Similarly, in the earlier case of *Canada (Director of Investigation & Research under the Combines Investigation Act) v. Nfld. Telephone Co.*,[12] in which the Supreme Court of Canada was concerned with whether provincial public utilities boards in Newfoundland and New Brunswick had authority to permit intervention in utilities regulations hearings, it was held that the boards had discretionary authority by implication to permit interventions as necessary to the effective exercise of an express general power to "make all necessary examinations and inquiries" in the general supervision of all public utilities. Thus, an implicit discretionary authority to permit interventions was recognized, flowing from an express supervisory responsibility.

Interventions in one form or another have become commonplace in contemporary administrative law proceedings. There have been many instances, for example, of successful intervention applications in proceedings involving:

---

[10] *Supra*, note 7, at 212.

[11] *Ibid.*, at 212-13.

[12] [1987] 2 S.C.R. 466 at 480, 68 Nfld. & P.E.I.R. 1, 20 C.P.R. (3d) 19, 45 D.L.R. (4th) 570, 80 N.R. 321.

(1) Charter-based issues or challenges, brought by equality seeking or disadvantaged groups who wish to ensure that proceedings involving the determination of Charter issues will be informed by the potential impact of rulings on people and groups who are not immediate parties to the proceedings;

(2) major public works or policy regulation matters as, for example, in the environmental and utilities regulation fields; and

(3) in the professional discipline area, particularly in cases involving allegations of sexual impropriety or sexual assault. In these cases, complainants or persons who allegedly suffered abuse are now routinely seeking standing before discipline committee panels.

The *Intervenor Funding Project Act*[13] (Ontario) provided for a system of intervenor funding in cases before a Joint Board (that is, a Board comprised of representatives of the Ontario Municipal Board and the Environmental Assessment Board of Ontario) under the *Consolidated Hearings Act*[14] (Ontario). This legislation provided statutory authority for the involvement of intervenors in a variety of environmental and planning-related hearings. Under the *Intervenor Funding Project Act,* identified tribunals were permitted to award funding to intervenors in advance of a hearing, on a stipulated scale, with the potential that this would be supplemented by a full costs award at the end of the proceeding.

Certain other developments in Ontario have also expanded the range of administrative law cases in which the involvement of intervenors is now mandated. In January 1994 the *Regulated Health Professions Act, 1991*[15] (Ontario) was introduced, governing some 21 health professions in the Province. Under that Act, and the *Health Professions Procedural Code*[16] (the "Code") which accompanied it, specific authority was granted to discipline committee panels to allow non-party participation at discipline committee hearings. Section 41.1 of the Code reads as follows:

> 41.1(1) A panel may allow a person who is not a party to participate in a hearing if,
>> (a) the good character, propriety of conduct or competence of the person is an issue at the hearing; or
>> (b) the participation of the person, would, in the opinion of the panel, be of assistance to the panel.
>
> (2) The panel shall determine the extent to which a person who is allowed to participate may do so and, without limiting the generality of this, the panel may allow the person to make oral or written submissions, to lead evidence and to cross-examine witnesses.

---

[13] R.S.O. 1990, c. I.13.
[14] R.S.O. 1990, c. C.29.
[15] S.O. 1991, c. 18.
[16] *Ibid.*

As appears from s. 41.1, discipline committee panels now have broad *statutory* authority to grant intervenor status in the form of non-party participation rights. The panels have a broad discretion to determine the manner and extent of such participation which, specifically, may include the right to make submissions, to lead evidence and to cross-examine witnesses.

The practice of discipline committee panels in granting intervenor status since introduction of the Code has been predictable. Such status is usually granted, on terms, particularly to complainants in sexual impropriety cases. The orders of discipline committee panels in this regard, however, have varied greatly on the question of the extent of the permitted or useful participation.

Of particular concern to respondents in discipline committee proceedings is the prospect that intervenors will be permitted to lead evidence, separate and apart from evidence led by prosecutors on behalf of the relevant regulatory body. It was not unusual in the past, prior to introduction of the *Regulated Health Professions Act, 1991* and the Code, for intervenors to participate in argument, either by making oral or written submissions or both. Where the intervenor was an alleged "victim" of the suggested conduct, usually such submissions were confined to those relating to *impact of the alleged events* on the person who allegedly suffered the harm inflicted by the practitioner. Under the authority of s. 41.1 of the Code, however, there now exists in statutory terms an expanded basis upon which intervenors may seek to make submissions.

In some recent instances, for example, intervenors have been permitted to make submissions on the issue of penalty, the admissibility of evidence, disclosure and production issues and, generally, on the procedures to apply relating to the receipt of evidence from particular types of witnesses. In two instances of which this writer is aware, persons granted intervenor status before discipline committee panels sought to make submissions on the issue of whether an agreed statement of facts and joint penalty submissions, agreed upon by the prosecutor on behalf of the regulatory body and the affected practitioner, should be received at all by the discipline committee panel and, if received, on the issue of the weight to be attributed to such joint submissions.

The rulings of discipline committees vary considerably on the extent to which intervenors will be permitted to participate. To date it may fairly be said that there is no consistency in approach between the discipline committee panels of various health professions in the province, or among various panels of the same College or Colleges. Thus, for example, in a number of rulings made since January 1994 by health profession discipline committees, the extent of permitted participation by complainants and their counsel in discipline committee hearings has been very broad and, in some instances, has extended to issues of relevancy, privacy, privilege and admissibility or other evidentiary issues. In other instances the extent of permitted participation has been limited to submissions only on stipulated issues and has specifically excluded the right to lead evidence or cross-examine witnesses.

In addition to this development in the professional discipline field, introduction in Ontario of the *Class Proceedings Act*[17] (Ontario) has now significantly increased the possibilities for expanded public interest litigation. This development, coupled with major reform in the law of standing, has signalled a liberalized approach generally to standing in the areas of constitutional and administrative law.

These observations do not address the evolving basis on which leave to intervene is being granted on applications for judicial review or on statutory appeals, to which the *Rules of Civil Procedure* specifically apply. In these situations, generally, the matters to be considered in determining whether intervenor status will be granted include the nature of the case, the issues which arise, the likelihood of the applicant being able to make a useful contribution to the resolution of the matter without causing prejudice or injustice to the parties to the proceeding, and whether a ''value-added'' contribution is likely, having regard to the special expertise or insight which the proposed intervenor would bring to the issues facing the court.[18]

In administrative proceedings, it is clear now that intervenor status may be granted by the presiding tribunal either pursuant to express statutory authority in that regard (as, for example, under the *Regulated Health Professions Act, 1991* (Ontario)) or, alternatively, as a necessary incident to the powers and authority of those tribunals vested in whole or in part with a public interest protection mandate.

For practitioners in the administrative law field, therefore, a series of threshold questions arise:

---

[17] S.O. 1992, c. 6.
[18] See, for example, *Hill v. Church of Scientology of Toronto* (1993), 69 O.A.C. 67, 18 O.R. (3d) 385, 20 C.C.L.T. (2d) 129, 114 D.L.R. (4th) 1 (C.A.); leave to appeal granted 20 O.R. (3d) xv, 180 N.R. 240*n*; *Christian Horizons v. Ontario Human Rights Com'n* (1993), 14 O.R. (3d) 374, 17 C.R.R. (2d) D-6 (Div. Ct.); *Doe v. Information & Privacy Com'r (Ont.)* (1992), 53 O.A.C. 236 (Div. Ct.); *Rudolph v. Canada (Minister of Employment & Immigration)* (1992), 16 Imm. L. R. (2d) 110 (Fed. C.A.); *Goudreau v. Falher Consolidated School Dist. No. 69*, [1993] 4 W.W.R. 434, 8 Alta. L. R. (3d) 205, 16 C.P.C. (3d) 295 (C.A.); *Peel (Reg. Mun.) v. Great Atlantic & Pacific Co. of Canada Ltd.* (1990), 74 O.R. (2d) 164, 45 C.P.C. (2d) 1, 2 C.R.R. (2d) 327 (C.A.); and *MacMillan Bloedel Ltd. v. Mullin*, [1985] 3 W.W.R. 380, 66 B.C.L.R. 207, 50 C.P.C. 298, 13 C.R.R. 283 (C.A.).

- who are the parties to the hearing and is there any obligation on one or more of the parties to the hearing to provide notice of the proceedings to other potentially interested persons or groups;
- who are the prospective intervenors to the hearing, and on what basis might such intervenor status be sought;
- on what basis might intervenor status be challenged or opposed given the circumstances of the case and the nature of the matters at issue;
- if intervenor status or participation rights are to be granted by the presiding tribunal, on what basis should such rights be granted and, specifically, what submissions should be made regarding the extent of participation of identified prospective intervenors;
- if the participation rights to be granted include the right to lead evidence or to cross-examine witnesses, what disclosure and/or production rights or obligations, if any, apply; and
- if intervenor status is to be granted, what impact should and will this have on the order of proceedings as, for example, the order of cross-examination and the order of argument and submissions both during the progress of the hearing and at its conclusion?

All of these issues require careful consideration prior to and at the outset of the hearing, both by those seeking or supporting intervention and by those opposing it.

(2) Timing of Applications for Judicial Review: The "Barrier of Prematurity"

In many administrative law hearings an underlying and continuing issue confronted by practitioners is whether recourse to the courts is available in the face of adverse rulings made by the tribunal during the course of the proceedings. The courts in Ontario do not encourage applications for judicial review of preliminary rulings or interlocutory orders of an administrative tribunal where the proceedings in which such rulings or orders were made is still in progress. This is particularly so where the party affected adversely by the ruling or order has a right of appeal available at the conclusion of the proceedings. A fulsome review of the existing authorities on this issue is set out in the dissenting opinion of Mr. Justice Laskin in *Howe v. Institute of Chartered Accountants of Ontario (Professional Conduct Committee)*,[19] a decision of the Ontario Court of Appeal

---

[19] (1994), 19 O.R. (3d) 483, 118 D.L.R. (4th) 129 (C.A.), application for leave to appeal to the Supreme Court of Canada dismissed February 2, 1995, 21 O.R. (3d) xvi.

in which the issue of prematurity in the context of a judicial review application was before the court.

The decision in *Howe* has generated much controversy and has received considerable attention by the administrative law bar since its release in August 1994. The factual context for the decision concerned a ruling by the chair of a provincial discipline committee in which disclosure of an investigator's report concerning the suggested misconduct of an accountant who subsequently was charged with disciplinary offences was considered and reviewed. The author of the report was to be called as a witness by the prosecutors before the discipline committee. Before the hearing commenced and before a panel had been selected to conduct the hearing, a pre-hearing disclosure motion was brought before the chair of the discipline committee in which production of the investigator's report was unsuccessfully sought. The applicant then applied to the Divisional Court for an order setting aside the decision of the discipline committee under which disclosure had been denied and sought a mandatory order compelling disclosure of the report. The Divisional Court dismissed the application on the basis of prematurity, that is, on the basis that the court should not intervene with an interlocutory order of a domestic tribunal made within its jurisdiction in circumstances where an alternative remedy by way of appeal existed. The applicant then appealed to the Ontario Court of Appeal which, by majority decision, upheld the decision of the Divisional Court.

In its dismissal of the judicial review application the Divisional Court had stated:

> The Discipline Committee of the Institute has the control of its own procedures within the limits of the relevant statutes and the requirements of natural justice. The requirements of natural justice depend on the circumstances of each particular case and vary with the nature of the tribunal and the subject matter under consideration. Mr. Howe must receive procedural fairness but in the circumstances no *Charter* right is involved. What we have before us is an interlocutory order of a domestic tribunal made within its jurisdiction. In addition, we would again restate the policy of the court to discourage premature applications for judicial review when there is an adequate alternative remedy by way of appeal. In these circumstances, it is only in the most exceptional case that this court will intervene and exercise its inherent supervisory power.[20]

The majority of the Court of Appeal, in considering the decision of the Divisional Court, noted that the by-laws of the Institute of Chartered Accountants of Ontario provided that a member found guilty of any charge

---

[20] *Ibid.*, at 488-89.

by the Discipline Committee of that Institute had a right to appeal the Discipline Committee's findings or order to an Appeal Committee. In addition, in the event that there was an allegation of a denial of natural justice, the by-laws provided that the affected member of the Institute could apply to the Appeal Committee to proceed by way of a hearing *de novo*. Moreover, the decision of the Chair of the Discipline Committee, in relation to the pre-hearing motion for disclosure of the investigator's report, was not binding on the Discipline Committee and the disclosure motion could be renewed once the hearing panel had convened and the hearing was commenced. Mr. Justice Finlayson, for the majority of the Court of Appeal, ruled:

> In short, I agree with the Divisional Court that this application is premature. I think it is trite law that the court will only interfere with a preliminary ruling made by an administrative tribunal where the tribunal never had jurisdiction or has irretrievably lost it: see *Gage v. Ontario (Attorney General)* . . .
>
> . . . . .
>
> It is not at all clear that a refusal to order production of documents goes to jurisdiction . . . much less that it is a denial of natural justice or a fatal flaw to the exercise by the tribunal of that jurisdiction . . .
>
> . . . . .
>
> I do not think that we should encourage applications such as these which have the effect of fragmenting and protracting the proceedings except in the clearest of cases . . .[21]

Fundamental to the Court of Appeal's decision was the view that the refusal to order disclosure of the report in question did not clearly go to jurisdiction and that it did not clearly amount to a denial of natural justice. Were it otherwise the case law, exemplified by the decision of the Ontario Divisional Court in *Gage v. Ont. (A.G.)*,[22] would afford grounds for judicial review notwithstanding that the administrative proceedings in question were still in progress. As noted by Mr. Justice Laskin in his dissent in *Howe,* Professor de Smith commented in his seminal text, *Judicial Review of Administrative Action*:

> The existence of a right of appeal to the courts from a tribunal's decision does not deprive the courts of power to award prohibition to restrain the tribunal from acting outside its jurisdiction. Nor is the applicant obliged to have exhausted prescribed administrative means of redress before having recourse to the courts.[23]

---

[21] *Ibid.*, at 490-91.
[22] (1992), 90 D.L.R. (4th) 537 (Ont. Div. Ct.).
[23] 4th ed. (ed. by J. M. Evans), at 425.

In *Gage v. Ont. (A.G.)* the Divisional Court was concerned with the failure of a Board of Inquiry constituted under the *Metropolitan Toronto Police Force Complaints Act, 1984* (Ontario) to provide a policeman with timely written notice of its decision to order a hearing into a complaint regarding his behaviour notwithstanding a statutory obligation to provide such notice. The court concluded that this failure was a denial of natural justice which resulted in a loss of jurisdiction. In reaching this conclusion, the court commented as follows with respect to the suggested prematurity of a judicial review application:

> The Act provides the applicant, if the board finds against him on the merits, with a full right of appeal. It is the practice of this court to discourage premature applications for judicial review where there is an adequate alternative remedy by way of appeal.
>
> If there is a prospect of real unfairness through denial of natural justice or otherwise, a superior court may always exercise its inherent supervisory jurisdiction to put an end to the injustice before all the alternative remedies are exhausted . . .
>
> The board heard full evidence on the jurisdictional facts going to natural justice. That part of the record is complete and there is nothing to add. We are in as good a position to deal with that issue as we would be on an appeal from the board.
>
> The unfairness in this case is so obvious that it would be inappropriate to put the officer through a trial before a tribunal that lost jurisdiction through a denial of natural justice. Having regard to the prejudice noted above and the fundamental unfairness in the process of the commission, an appeal is not an adequate alternative remedy. This is one of those exceptional cases where the court should exercise its extraordinary jurisdiction at this stage to prevent a further denial of natural justice.[24]

Thus, where the ruling or order in issue reflects what properly may be characterized as a denial of natural justice or a fundamental unfairness, it will be regarded by the courts as a loss of jurisdiction by the tribunal or as the tribunal acting outside its jurisdiction. Under either characterization, immediate recourse to the courts by way of judicial review will be available.

In practical terms, however, it remains very difficult to identify those situations in which the ruling of the tribunal reflects a denial of natural justice. Clearly, all those who seek judicial review during the progress of an administrative tribunal's hearing will seek to characterize the alleged error as one reflecting a lack or loss of jurisdiction. Proof of denial of natural justice constitutes the loss of jurisdiction. What is more difficult to identify, is an actual denial of natural justice or the circumstances in

---

[24] *Supra*, note 22, at 553.

which this characterization will be accorded by the courts to the action taken by the tribunal.

To illustrate the lack of predictability in this area of the law, one need only contrast the majority and dissenting opinions in the *Howe* case. As earlier noted, the majority of the court in the decision of Mr. Justice Finlayson, expressed doubt as to whether a refusal to order production or disclosure of documents goes to jurisdiction at all. Even greater doubt was cast on the proposition that the refusal to order production or disclosure of documents may amount to a denial of natural justice or a fatal flaw to the exercise by a tribunal of its jurisdiction to order production or disclosure. In contrast, Mr. Justice Laskin, in the context of professional discipline proceedings, was clearly of the view that adequate disclosure was one of the requirements of natural justice and an essential element of a fair hearing. In his view, adequate disclosure was the foundation of an adequate opportunity of knowing the case which a respondent must meet, of the ability to answer it and of the opportunity for putting in his or her own case. He therefore concluded that the Institute's prosecution arm had a duty to act fairly which required disclosure of the expert report on which the charges were based in circumstances in which the author of the report was going to testify for the prosecution. The requirement for disclosure of such a report would only be obviated if the report was otherwise privileged at law.[25]

With respect to the issue of prematurity, Mr. Justice Laskin acknowledged and endorsed the principle that courts should not lightly review evidentiary or disclosure rulings made by an administrative tribunal in the midst of a hearing or before the hearing starts. Nonetheless, in his view:

> . . . where the ruling amounts to a breach of the tribunal's duty of fairness, or a breach of natural justice, then different considerations apply. A breach of natural justice amounts to or is akin to jurisdictional error; and in administrative law language, a tribunal which begins with jurisdiction to decide will lose jurisdiction or act in excess of its jurisdiction if, in the course of deciding, it breaches natural justice. . . .
>
> . . . . .
>
> Where there is jurisdictional error arising from a breach of natural justice during the course of the proceedings, a court is entitled to intervene to correct the error though the party affected has a right of appeal.[26]

Thus, while the relevant principles may be stated with some ease, application of those principles to the particular facts of a given case is

---

[25] *Supra*, note 19, at 495.
[26] *Ibid.*, at 503.

a more difficult task. What for Mr. Justice Laskin in the *Howe* case was a clear denial of natural justice, for the majority, was not clearly a denial of natural justice and, in addition, was arguably not related to jurisdiction at all.

The challenge for practitioners, therefore, in seeking judicial review during the progress of a hearing, or before the formal commencement of a hearing based on pre-hearing rulings, is to examine whether the order or ruling at issue may properly be characterized as a denial of natural justice or as being a matter of such fundamental unfairness as to constitute a fatal flaw to the exercise by the tribunal of its jurisdiction. It may fairly be said, as illustrated by the *Howe* decision, that what for some is a denial of natural justice is for others not even a threshold jurisdictional question. So long as the category of matters which constitute a denial of natural justice continues to evolve, it may be expected that judicial review applications will continue to be initiated with considerable frequency during the progress of administrative tribunal hearings. Perhaps the only practical advice which, on the state of the current law, may be offered to those who seek relief by way of judicial review in such circumstances, is that only those cases which on their facts so clearly suggest a fundamental unfairness or diminishment of the rights of one or more parties to the hearing will afford the possibility of early successful court intervention.

(3) Bias Issues in Contemporary Administrative Law Hearings

Another area of increasingly greater importance to practitioners concerns reasonable apprehension of bias and those circumstances in which members of a tribunal, or other administrative decision-makers, may be disqualified from participating in the decision-making at issue by virtue of past conduct.

In the last five years, in a series of three important decisions, the Supreme Court of Canada specifically addressed issues related to bias challenges in the administrative law field. These cases are of great importance in the context of an increasing tendency by government to appoint to specialized tribunals, individuals whose background and life experiences suggest particular expertise or familiarity with issues falling within the mandate of those tribunals. Fundamental to these cases are issues of adjudicative independence and whether the rule against reasonable apprehension of bias should be applied equally to all statutory decision-makers.

In *Old St. Boniface Residents' Ass'n v. Winnipeg (City)*[27] and *Save*

---

[27] [1990] 3 S.C.R. 1170, [1991] 2 W.W.R. 145, 69 Man. R. (2d) 134, 2 M.P.L.R. (2d) 217, 75 D.L.R. (4th) 385, 116 N.R. 46.

Richmond Farmland Society v. Richmond (Twp.),[28] the Supreme Court of Canada was concerned with whether elected municipal councillors were disqualified by bias from participation in assigned decision-making. In one case, the challenged individual had had initial discussions with a developer concerned with the decision at issue; in the other case, the particular individual had expressed strong opinions favouring development as part of an election platform. In the first case, the decision of the court suggested that so long as the challenged individual was still "capable of persuasion" on the matters at issue, no disqualifying bias existed or was to be recognized. Absent personal interest in the outcome of the matter or a level of commitment to the outcome that amounted to the "expression of a final opinion on the matter, which cannot be dislodged", a reasonable apprehension of bias sufficient to disqualify the decision-maker could be not made out.[29]

The decision of the court in the *Old St. Boniface Residents' Ass'n* case specifically recognized that certain types of decision-makers as, for example, elected city councillors who participate in planning decisions, have been elected by constituencies to represent particular points of view. The court observed that there is a spectrum of administrative bodies whose functions vary from those almost purely adjudicative to those which are political or policy-making in nature, that is, to those which more closely resemble a legislative decision-making function. Mr. Justice Sopinka set forth an "open mind" test which should apply to decision-makers falling within the latter category:

> The party alleging disqualifying bias must establish that there is a prejudgment of the matter, in fact, to the extent that any representations at variance with the view, which has been adopted, would be futile. Statements by individual members of Council while they may very well give rise to an appearance of bias will not satisfy the test unless the court concludes that they are the expression of a final opinion on the matter, which cannot be dislodged.[30]

In the companion case of *Save Richmond Farmland Society*, as noted, the conduct of a municipal councillor who had campaigned for an election favouring a residential development was at issue. The councillor in question had made statements publicly that suggested he would not change his mind despite public hearings on the issue of the suggested residential development. Mr. Justice Sopinka, adopting the approach articulated in

---

[28] [1990] 3 S.C.R. 1213, [1991] 2 W.W.R. 78, 52 B.C.L.R. (2d) 145, 2 M.P.L.R. (2d) 288, 75 D.L.R. (4th) 425, 116 N.R. 68.

[29] See Mullan, *Common and Divergent Elements of Practices of the Various Tribunals: An Overview of Present and Possible Future Developments,* Special Lectures of the Law Society of Upper Canada, 1992, at 475.

[30] *Supra*, note 27, at 1197.

Old St. Boniface Residents' Ass'n, held that the councillor should not be disqualified for bias because he did not have a completely closed mind.

In *Nfld. Telephone Co. v. Nfld. Board of Com'rs of Public Utilities*[31] at issue was the conduct of one of the Commissioners of the Newfoundland Public Utilities Board. Prior to his appointment as a Commissioner, the individual in question had been a consumer rights advocate. Upon taking office he had made a variety of public statements in which he indicated that he viewed his mandate as being to act in an adversarial role on behalf of Newfoundland consumers. After his appointment and after the Board had decided to hold a public hearing into certain accounts of Newfoundland Telephone, the Commissioner gave a newspaper interview in which he made a number of disparaging comments about senior management of Newfoundland Telephone on a variety of issues. Newfoundland Telephone then sought to have him removed from the hearing panel on the basis of the interview and other statements made by him, arguing that his conduct gave rise to a reasonable apprehension of bias. Mr. Justice Cory, speaking for the court, observed:

> It can be seen that there is a great diversity of administrative boards. Those that are primarily adjudicative in their functions will be expected to comply with the standard applicable to courts. That is to say that the conduct of the members of the Board should be such that there could be no reasonable apprehension of bias with regard to their decision. At the other end of the scale are boards with popularly elected members such as those dealing with planning and development whose members are municipal councillors. With those boards, the standard will be much more lenient. In order to disqualify the members a challenging party must establish that there has been a pre-judgment of the matter to such an extent that any representations to the contrary would be futile. Administrative boards that deal with matters of policy will be closely comparable to the boards composed of municipal councillors. For those boards, a strict application of reasonable apprehension of bias as a test might undermine the very role which has been entrusted to them by the legislature.[32]

In this context, Mr. Justice Cory recognized and affirmed that all administrative bodies owe a duty of fairness to the regulated parties whose interests they must determine. He indicated, however, that the extent of that duty of fairness will depend upon the nature and the function of the particular tribunal. He observed:

> The duty to act fairly includes the duty to provide procedural fairness to the parties. That simply cannot exist if an adjudicator is biased. It is, of course,

---

[31] [1992] 1 S.C.R. 623, 95 Nfld. & P.E.I.R. 271, 89 D.L.R. (4th) 289, 134 N.R. 241.
[32] *Ibid.*

impossible to determine the precise state of mind of an adjudicator who has made an administrative board decision. As a result, the courts have taken the position that an unbiased appearance is, in itself, an essential component of procedural fairness. To ensure fairness the conduct of members of administrative tribunals has been measured against a standard of reasonable apprehension of bias. The test is whether a reasonably informed bystander could reasonably perceive bias on the part of an adjudicator.[33]

The court in the *Nfld. Telephone* case specifically recognized that the fact alone of appointment to tribunals of representatives from known interest or advocacy groups will not support, without more, a bias challenge. The societal value in appointing to boards representatives of interested sectors of society, including those who are dedicated to forwarding the interests of consumers or other advocacy groups, is to be recognized. Moreover, members of tribunals that perform a policy formation function are not to be challengeable on the basis of suggested bias simply because of the expression of strong opinions prior to a hearing. The courts generally are to take a flexible approach, according to Mr. Justice Cory, to the problem of potential bias so that the applicable standard varies with the role and function of the tribunal or board which is being considered.

The court in *Nfld. Telephone* also suggested that there is a difference between the latitude to be afforded to adjudicators in the arena of public comment or expression of opinion depending on whether the comments are made during the investigative stage of a matter, or after a hearing has been initiated. In the former situation, the court suggested that wide licence must be given to board members to make public comments and that such comments, so long as they do not indicate "a mind so closed that any submissions would be futile", will not support a successful bias challenge. Once the matter reaches the hearing stage, however, a greater degree of discretion is required and the parties to the proceedings are entitled to expect that the conduct of the board members will be such that it will not give rise to a reasonable apprehension of bias.

On the facts of the case before the court, the relevant Commissioner of the Public Utilities Board offended the latter rule by his conduct and comments. The Commissioner's participation thereafter in the conduct of the hearing resulted in an invalid and unfair hearing. As a consequence there had been a denial of a right to a fair hearing which, in the view of the court, could not be cured by any subsequent decision of the tribunal. Thus a decision of a tribunal which denied the parties a fair hearing was not to be regarded as simply voidable but rather, as void.[34]

Ian Holloway has suggested that the court's approach in *Nfld.*

---

[33] *Ibid.*
[34] *Ibid.*

Telephone to the question of bias inappropriately distinguishes between the investigative and hearing stages of an administrative proceeding. He has questioned whether the leeway suggested at the investigative stage is appropriate, by inquiring whether there is anything "magic" about the hearing stage so as to make reasonable apprehension of bias only then objectionable.[35] Professor Mullan has expressed similar reservations:

> Similarly, there is an air of unreality in Cory J.'s judgment in the *Newfoundland Telephone Co.* case which, in effect, is no more than an instruction to a member to act with decorum at the actual hearing irrespective of how strongly he or she has expressed views on the issue prior to the hearing. No one is going to be deluded by such shams of politeness and circumspection.[36]

Where, then, does this leave the practitioner when confronted by the prospective participation in a hearing of a board member known to hold and to have expressed strong views on the matters either directly or indirectly at issue in the hearing or who, by virtue of his/her prior political or advocacy group interests, is suspected to be predisposed to a particular outcome? With the increasing frequency of expertise or background-specific appointments of tribunal members, at least in Ontario, the issue has assumed real significance in various administrative hearings. For example, in the context of environmental hearings or professional discipline proceedings, it is not unusual for the public representatives appointed to the tribunals to have been appointed specifically because of their prior involvement with identified environmental or advocacy interest groups. It is assumed that such involvement gives rise to special expertise in or familiarity with many of the societal issues underlying environmental decisions or disciplinary offences. This, in turn, has given rise to a number of bias challenges concerning such tribunal members. It is argued in this connection, in the aftermath of the *Nfld. Telephone* case, that boards and tribunals must not only be impartial, in the sense of being disinterested, they must be seen to be impartial and disinterested. Further, as a direct result of the Supreme Court's decision in *Nfld. Telephone*, the more adjudicative the function of the board or tribunal, the more impartial, disinterested and neutral it is argued that the tribunal members must be. In this context, it becomes essential to consider the nature of the tribunal and its mandate when measuring the impugned conduct of the tribunal member.[37]

---

[35] Holloway, *The Transformation of Canadian Administrative Law* (1993), 6 C.J.A.L.P. 295 at 321-22.

[36] *Supra*, note 29, at 475.

[37] See, for example, *Sparvier v. Cowessess Indian Band*, [1993] 3 F.C. 142 at 163, 63 F.T.R. 242 and *The Great Atlantic & Pacific Co. of Canada, Ltd. v. Ont. Human Rights Com'n* (1993), 93 C.L.L.C. 17,017.

Advancing or opposing a disqualification motion relating to a tribunal member on the grounds of alleged reasonable apprehension of bias is fraught with tactical difficulties for the practitioner. Obviously, those initiating such a challenge take the risk both of failure before the tribunal and subsequently in the courts and further, of so offending the challenged tribunal member that the future conduct of the hearing and the attitude of the tribunal member to the client's cause may become tainted or impaired. On the basis of *Nfld. Telephone* it is clear that the fact of prior expertise or public comment alone prior to initiation of the hearing, without more, may not be sufficient to make out a bias challenge. What must be analyzed, therefore, is the following:

- the nature of the tribunal and its statutory mandate;
- the nature of the prior involvement, expertise or public commentary by the relevant tribunal member;
- the timing of the prior involvement or commentary, that is, whether the offending statements or conduct took place before or after initiation of a hearing or during the investigative phase of the proceedings leading up to initiation of the hearing. If the latter, the exact nature of the conduct at issue is highly relevant because it must be determined whether the conduct demonstrates a "closed mind". If the former, a lower threshold applies such that engaging in the conduct itself, without more, may be sufficient to support a disqualification motion.

The recent decision of the Ontario Divisional Court in *Dulmage v. Police Complaints Com'r*[38] illustrates some of the issues. In that case the vice-president of a Toronto Chapter of an organization publicly criticized the behaviour of certain police officers who allegedly caused a public strip search of an individual to be conducted. The president of the Mississauga Chapter of the same organization was assigned to sit as a member of the board of inquiry appointed to inquire into the allegations of misconduct brought against the relevant police officers. An application was brought before the board of inquiry for an order disqualifying the board member on the basis of reasonable apprehension of bias. The board, on the disqualification motion, ultimately declined to disqualify the challenged board member. A majority of the Divisional Court concluded on the facts that inflammatory statements dealing with the very incident involved in the Board inquiry had been made by an officer of the Congress of Black Women of Canada in Toronto. The statements were made in a city closely adjacent to the City of Mississauga in which the challenged board member was the president of the local chapter of the same organization. The statements dealt with an incident which had received significant public

---

[38] (1994), 21 O.R. (3d) 356, 120 D.L.R. (4th) 590 (Div. Ct.).

attention and referred to the incident as an "outrage". The author of the statements called for the suspension of the very officers involved in the hearing. In these circumstances the court concluded that there was a reasonable apprehension of bias on the part of a reasonable person (that being the applicable test in the view of the court), such that the motion to disqualify the board member should have been allowed.

The decision of Mr. Justice Moldaver, dissenting in part, is particularly instructive. He indicated as follows:

> In my view, the board, in its reasons, quite correctly recognized that a member need not automatically withdraw solely because of statements made by a representative of an affiliated community organization about issues before the board.
>
> That acknowledged, it seems to me that once the board's attention had been drawn to such statements in the context of a motion to disqualify, the board had a duty to carefully consider a variety of factors in order to properly determine whether the allegation of reasonable apprehension of bias had been made out. These factors included:
> (a) What position did the author of the statements hold within the affiliated organization;
> (b) When the statements were made, did the author purport to make them on behalf of the entire organization or were they limited to the author's personal views or perhaps the view of a separate and distinct chapter within the organization;
> (c) What was the nature of the issue being discussed in the statements? Did the comments relate to the critical issue or issues which the board was required to decide or were they directed to peripheral, less consequential or general matters;
> (d) If the remarks were directed to the critical issue or issues, did they reflect a position of neutrality or were they pointed, direct and judgmental;
> (e) Were the remarks directed towards a private, discrete audience or were they directed to the public at large and intended for public consumption;
> (f) When, in relation to the scheduled board hearing, were the remarks made;
> (g) What position within the organization did the challenged board member hold (i) when the statements were made by the affiliated member and (ii) at the time of the scheduled hearing.[39]

The listing of these factors by Mr. Justice Moldaver, which he described as non-exhaustive, provides a blue-print for the analysis by practitioners of allegations of reasonable apprehension of bias. While the facts of the case before the court in *Dulmage* concerned statements made by a person other than the sitting tribunal member, the factors identified by Mr. Justice Moldaver for analysis can be applied readily to an analysis of potentially offending conduct by sitting board members. It should also

---

[39] *Ibid.*, at 364.

be noted, in addition to the approach to analysis outlined by Mr. Justice Moldaver, that he specifically confirmed that mere association, either past or present, on the part of a board member with an organization would not of itself satisfy the test for reasonable apprehension of bias. This was so, in his view, even when the organization, by its very nature, might be said to favour one side or the other on the matter at issue.[40]

(4) Recent Amendments to the *Statutory Powers Procedure Act* (the "*SPPA*")

Substantial reform of the *SPPA* has long been urged by both practitioners and academics alike. When first enacted in 1971, the *SPPA* served as a very useful code of minimum rules governing procedures at administrative hearings. As was to be expected, however, as developments in administrative law progressed and the number and degree of specialization of tribunals increased, the provisions of the *SPPA* became outdated and, in some instances, virtually irrelevant. In addition to developments over time, however, some have argued that the *SPPA* from the outset failed to address significant and recurring procedural aspects of administrative tribunal proceedings. Professor Mullan, for example, has argued that the *SPPA*, from introduction, attempted to fit all tribunals exercising a statutory power of decision into a single mould by imposing on administrative decision-making, generally, a formalistic and court-like process.[41] There is no doubt that the *SPPA*, by importing into the administrative law process many judicial process concepts encouraged (and, according to some, lead to) the "judicialization" of administrative tribunals. To the extent that this approach found its beginnings in the *SPPA* it was reinforced by the reaction of courts on judicial review applications over the last 20 years in which the duties and powers of tribunals and tribunal members were interpreted by analogizing to and importing concepts from traditional notions of judicial duties.

Apart from the philosophical underpinnings of the *SPPA*, it became clear over time that certain recurring practice issues were not addressed by its provisions. Perhaps most prominent of these was the absence in the *SPPA* of provision for pre-hearing procedures of any kind as, for example, relating to discovery and production; pre-hearing conferences; agreed statements of fact; written evidence submissions from experts etc. This, for the practitioner, was exacerbated by the total absence in the statute of any provision for interim relief from administrative tribunals.

---

[40] *Ibid.*, at 366.
[41] *Supra*, note 29, at 463.

In 1989 a report was commissioned by the Ontario Ministry of the Attorney-General from Robert Macaulay[42] seeking recommendations for changes to the *SPPA*. This led to the circulation in 1992 of suggested reforms for comment by various boards, tribunals and agencies. Shortly thereafter, the Society of Ontario Adjudicators and Regulators ("SOAR") undertook a review of the *SPPA* with a view to formulating specific reform recommendations. The "SOAR Proposals", as they came to be known, were circulated in 1994 to a variety of interested parties for comment. More recently, specific proposed amendments to the *SPPA* were introduced and became effective on April 1, 1995.[43]

In summary, the substantive changes contemplated by the amendments include:

(1) parties will be permitted to waive the procedural requirements of the *SPPA* and of the statute(s) under which hearings are to be held;

(2) formation of small panels of an administrative tribunal is authorized to deal with procedural or interlocutory matters;

(3) in some cases written hearings or electronic hearings in place of oral hearings will be permitted if rules are first introduced setting out the procedures to apply to such hearings;

(4) tribunals are authorized to make rules and, in the form of such rules, to require participation in pre-hearing conferences; to permit tribunal members who preside at pre-hearing conferences to make orders with respect to the conduct of the proceedings; to provide for orders relating to discovery (including, for example, the exchange of documents, the oral or written examination of a party, the exchange of witness statements, the exchange of expert witness reports, provision of particulars etc.); and for written or electronic hearings;

(5) on consent, the admission of evidence which has been received previously in another *SPPA*-governed hearing, or in an Ontario court, or court or tribunal outside of Ontario, will be permitted;

(6) the receipt of evidence in the form of witness panels is authorized;

(7) tribunals are authorized to make interim decisions and orders and to impose conditions on such decisions or orders;

(8) on consent, the consolidation of proceedings involving similar questions of fact, law or policy will be permitted or, in the absence of consent, the hearing of such proceedings sequentially or the staying of one of the proceedings until after the determination of the other, is authorized;

---

[42] Macaulay, *Directions: Review of Ontario Regulatory Agencies: Report* (Toronto, Queen's Printer, 1989).

[43] S.O. 1994, c. 27.

(9) revisions to the applicable procedures for the provision of notice of a decision to affected parties are made; and

(10) tribunals are authorized to reconsider their decisions or orders, provided they have made rules in that regard and provided further that the review takes place within a reasonable time after the decision or order is made.

The recent amendments to the *SPPA* include a number of substantive changes recommended by SOAR. Not all of SOAR's proposed amendments were adopted, however. The SOAR Proposals have been described as follows:

> SOAR proposed comprehensive changes to the SPPA to address the new realities of the administrative justice system. The changes reflect the need to give tribunals the tools and the flexibility to help them meet their mandate with fewer resources. They reflect a shift from a narrow focus on individual rights to a recognition of community rights in the effective, responsive and expeditious resolution of proceedings. And in offering alternatives to the court-like models of adjudication they recognize the maturing of an administrative justice system. The proposed name, the *Statutory Powers Act,* reflects provisions which are enabling rather than restrictive in nature. Some of the proposals mirror the specific legislation of some tribunals and the innovative practices of others. Not all measures are appropriate for all tribunals. Although the powers granted are relatively broad, the legislation would require published rules to regulate their use.[44]

This approach is to be contrasted with the following view of the current provisions of the *SPPA*:

> The existing SPPA is a primarily restrictive, rather than an enabling, statute. It prescribes minimum procedural safe-guards for individual rights. It has hampered the evolution of accessible, responsive and effective resolution of proceedings. Lawyers usually represent individual rights and are sometimes uncomfortable with the concept that the public interest also has a role in most agency proceedings. Yet it is time for the SPPA to recognize the community's rights in the fair and efficient proceedings of tribunals.[45]

Whatever the view of the limitations of the former statute and the scope of the amendments, it is clear that all administrative law practitioners in Ontario must be alert to the reforms embodied in the amendments. Practice and procedure before all tribunals governed by the amended

---

[44] Karakatsanis, *The Statutory Powers Act: Empowering Tribunals — A SOAR Proposal*, Recent Developments in Administrative Law, The Law Society of Upper Canada, January, 1995 at G-3.

[45] *Ibid.*, at G-7.

legislation will change dramatically upon its enactment. In particular, from the perspective of available remedies, emphasis should be placed on the proposed authority of tribunals to make interim orders and, following the introduction of rules, to formalize mandatory pre-hearing conferences and discovery and production procedures. In addition, the concept of continuing jurisdiction (discussed under heading 3(2) below) is encompassed in the amendments. Many of these reforms will go a long way in addressing the procedural difficulties which, for the last decade, have imbued administrative hearings in Ontario.

Of particular importance to practitioners are the provisions under the amendments which will permit tribunals to introduce rules of procedure. Many tribunals currently publish guidelines or policy directions for participants in their hearings. In many cases, however, such guidelines or policy directions lack the force of statutory authority. This has meant that these tribunals have lacked an effective enforcement mechanism by which to ensure that participants in their proceedings adhere to the established rules of procedure. In practice, many of the rules worked by force of "moral persuasion" rather than legal requirement. It is significant that under the rule-making authority, procedures may be established relating to pre-hearing disclosure and production of evidence. Once rules are introduced, they may be enforced through costs sanctions and, ultimately, by the possibility of contempt proceedings.

Also of significance are the provisions of the amendments which contemplate pre-hearing conferences and the possibility of mandatory alternative dispute resolution measures. Under current practice, to the extent that alternative dispute resolution techniques are employed by tribunals, they are often available only on a consensual basis. The amendments to the *SPPA* provide explicit authority for administrative tribunals to initiate and require such pre-hearing settlement efforts.

Finally, the new authority of tribunals to make interim orders is of profound practical significance. This, for example, could apply so as to permit interim orders setting time lines for mandatory disclosure and production orders; imposing costs sanctions for failure to abide by set time lines or as a consequence of requested adjournments; and, mandating the delivery of summaries of evidence, expert reports and written submissions on a host of issues. For the first time, under the amendments, the prospect of interim relief will be available to practitioners.

(5) Conduct of Proceedings: The Approach of Counsel and Witnesses

In developing strategies to achieve the desired outcome for a client in proceedings before an administrative tribunal, it is important not to overlook or under-emphasize the impact on ultimate success or failure of the conduct of counsel and witnesses before the tribunal. In many cases, while the duties of tribunals have become highly specialized and the training and qualifications of many tribunal members is often sophisticated within the area of their own experiences and disciplines, tribunal members are not legally trained. So long as the administrative hearing process in Ontario continues to be characterized by judicial or court-like norms (as, for example, are reflected in the *SPPA* and in the principles enunciated by the courts on judicial review) it will remain important to consider, in preparing for and planning the conduct of a case, the lack of familiarity of many tribunal members with underlying legal principles and, significantly, the rules of evidence.

Generally, I favour an approach to administrative law advocacy which might be characterized as an attitude by counsel and witnesses of "continuing, complete co-operation". Obviously, there are instances in which this type of approach is not in the client's interest. In these circumstances the advocate's duty to his or her client takes precedence and all reasonable arguments or positions should be advanced even if they run counter to and do not further the apparent objectives or expectations of the tribunal. In most situations, however, it is prudent as a practical matter to adopt an "attitude of helpfulness" to the tribunal.

This proposition can be illustrated by reference to ways in which to advance objections and deal with rulings made by the tribunal during the course of the proceedings. Usually, objections by counsel for one or more parties concern either procedural matters or evidentiary issues. On occasion, constitutional issues or arguments under the *Charter of Rights* arise. Procedural matters often involve motions for adjournments, to stay the tribunal's proceedings for alleged abuse of process or to await the outcome of pending court proceedings or rulings; to re-open one's case; to quash a summons or part of a notice of hearing; to determine the order of examination and cross-examination; and a host of other related matters. Similarly, a variety of evidentiary issues can arise relating to such matters as pre-hearing or at hearing disclosure and production issues; the admissibility of evidence; the scope of permissible cross-examination; applications for severance, etc.

The applicable case-law and precedent, in the courts and in prior decisions of the same tribunal, differ according to the nature of the issue raised and the relief sought. Thus, the legal considerations which apply on motions and objections differ, according to subject-matter. Many of the fundamental advocacy principles, however, are common to all motions and objections. I offer the following comments:

- Most tribunals, particularly those comprised of non-legally trained adjudicators, do not welcome legal objections or protracted legal motions.

Indeed, the contemporary dynamic in many administrative tribunal hearings suggests that resort to sophisticated legal or technical arguments is not only not well received in many instances but can quickly result in discomfort or frustration on the part of the hearing panel. Rightly or wrongly, many non-legally trained adjudicators perceive objections and protracted motions as "time-wasting" devices utilized by lawyers bent on complicating or delaying the proceedings. In most situations this is not in fact the case. Nonetheless, the possibility of this perception and the speed with which it can be introduced in a hearing room are matters which should not be ignored by the advocate.

- If followed, I suggest, that the client's cause is best advanced and the possibility of attaining the desired relief or remedy is furthered, if counsel takes the time and prepares his or her submissions to minimize the use of "legalese"; to explain the jurisdiction of the tribunal to make the order or ruling sought; to outline, in detail, the exact nature of the relief sought and the grounds therefor; and, generally, to shorten where possible the task of the tribunal in determining the merits of the objection or motion. Obviously, the importance of doing so will vary depending upon the sophistication of the tribunal and its familiarity with its own enabling legislation, relevant jurisprudence and legal principles. Counsel who regularly appear before the same tribunal or tribunals are quick to recognize, however, the importance of attempting to assist the tribunal in its work throughout the entirety of the proceedings.

- Where the tribunal is comprised of non-legally trained adjudicators, and has available to it the benefit of independent legal counsel, such counsel may be approached at any time in an effort to help resolve procedural or evidentiary matters at issue. It assists the work of the tribunal and advances the process to involve independent legal counsel in an effort to resolve disputed matters among counsel and to streamline the issues which must actually be dealt with by the tribunal itself.

- No tribunal appreciates or welcomes repeated objections during the course of its proceedings, or lengthy motions. As has been urged on other occasions, a careful balance must be drawn by an advocate between the need and the duty to properly and fairly represent the interests of one's client and the tactical reality of the need to avoid unnecessarily annoying the tribunal or protracting its proceedings. In respect of each proposed objection or motion, therefore, it is prudent to consider whether the objection or motion is necessary and desirable to advance the interests of the client or, alternatively, whether it carries with it too great a risk of the perception of unnecessary and avoidable "legal-wrangling". Objections or motions, when brought, should be well thought-out and clearly explained to the tribunal members, both as to necessity and merit.

- Many of the same rules, in my view, are equally applicable to witnesses. Generally, witnesses should also adopt an attitude of "helpfulness" and communicate a willingness to be of assistance to the tribunal in its search for the facts necessary to determine the matter at issue.

At the risk of belabouring the point, I suggest that it is the prudent and wise counsel who remembers that the pursuit of the desired remedy begins long before the hearing commences. From the outset of contact with the tribunal and initiation of its proceedings, throughout the entire pre-hearing stage and the hearing itself, the attitude of the tribunal to one's client and the merits of the client's cause is being shaped. Pursuit of the remedy, thus, should be borne in mind from the outset. The influence on achievement of the desired remedy of the conduct of counsel and witnesses called on behalf of a party cannot be overestimated.

3. *Post-Hearing Issues*

(1) Standards of Review and The Changing Features of Curial Deference

A full discussion of the evolving jurisprudence relating to the standards of review applicable to decisions of administrative tribunals and developments regarding curial deference is beyond the scope of this paper. Certain recent developments, however, must be highlighted because they represent issues of fundamental importance in any consideration of the remedies available from the decisions or rulings of administrative tribunals.

Early cases concerning the concept of curial deference suggested, generally, that the courts would be reluctant to interfere with an administrative decision unless the tribunal, in formulating its decision, had committed egregious error. This was epitomized in the seminal case of *C.U.P.E., Local 963 v. N.B. Liquor Corp.*[46] by the formulation by Dickson J. of the following oft-quoted standard of review:

> Was the Board's interpretation so patently unreasonable that its construction cannot be rationally supported by the relevant legislation?[47]

This standard of "patent unreasonability" was applied in a succession of cases involving a variety of administrative decision-makers in circumstances where the adjudicator's decision was not protected by a privative clause.[48] At the same time, however, there evolved the concept

---

[46] [1979] 2 S.C.R. 227, 25 N.B.R. (2d) 237, 97 D.L.R. (3d) 417, 26 N.R. 341.

[47] *Ibid.*, at 237.

[48] See, for example, *Douglas Aircraft Co. of Canada Ltd. v. McConnell*, [1980] 1 S.C.R. 245, 79 CLLC 14,221, 99 D.L.R. (3d) 385, 29 N.R. 109, and *Re A.U.P.E. and Board of Governors of Olds College*, [1982] 1 S.C.R. 923, 21 Alta. L.R. (2d) 104, 136 D.L.R. (3d) 1, 42 N.R. 559.

that within the context of review of decisions of administrative tribunals, consideration was to be given to the principle of specialization of duties. Expressed differently, this meant that curial deference was to be given by the courts to the opinion or decisions of lower tribunals on issues which fell squarely within their area of expertise and jurisdiction.[49] The concept of curial deference, in the face of specialized tribunal expertise on matters within the jurisdiction of the tribunal, when married with consideration of appropriate standards of review, led to establishment of a low threshold of deference in those situations involving jurisdictional error or where a statutory right of appeal existed in contrast to those situations in which tribunals were protected by an effective privative clause and were deciding matters within their own jurisdiction. In the latter cases, curial deference received prominence, while in the former cases it received less, if any, emphasis.

Recently, the Supreme Court of Canada comprehensively considered the appropriate standards of review which apply to decisions of administrative tribunals. In *Pezim v. British Columbia (Superintendent of Brokers)*[50] a series of decisions made by the British Columbia Securities Commission relating to disclosure requirements under the *British Columbia Securities Act* and the insider trading provisions of that legislation were at issue. The Commission, on the facts of the case, had found breaches of the disclosure requirements of the Act by several senior managers of a reporting company but also concluded that no breach of the insider trading provisions of the legislation had occurred. The Commission, in light of its findings, had suspended the relevant managers for a period of one year by removing their trading exemptions and had ordered them, amongst other matters, to pay one-third of the Commission's incurred costs. The British Columbia Court of Appeal allowed the managers' appeal. The Supreme Court of Canada restored the Commission's decision, mainly on grounds of curial deference. The analysis of the court is of considerable interest concerning the applicable standards of review for administrative tribunal decisions and, more generally, on the issue of the evolving features of curial deference.

The judgment of the Supreme Court of Canada in *Pezim* was delivered by Mr. Justice Iacobucci. He characterized the matter before the court as relating to "the appropriate standard of review for an appellate court reviewing a decision of a securities commission which is not protected by a privative clause when there exists a statutory right of appeal and where

---

[49] See *Bell Canada v. Canadian Radio-Television & Telecommunications Com'n*, [1989] 1 S.C.R. 1722 at 1745-46, 60 D.L.R. (4th) 682, 97 N.R. 15.

[50] [1994] 2 S.C.R. 557, 92 B.C.L.R. (2d) 145, 14 B.L.R. (2d) 217, 114 D.L.R. (4th) 385, 168 N.R. 321.

the case turns on a question of statutory interpretation."[51] As apparent from this characterization, it is arguable that the judgment of the court is confined to cases falling within this construct; however, as earlier suggested, there are many who regard the case as being generally instructive on applicable standards for court review in both the appellate and judicial review settings.

It is important to note in studying the decision that the British Columbia Securities Commission, under the provisions of its enabling legislation, enjoys an express public interest mandate and is vested with powers to make a number of orders where it considers that to do so is "in the public interest". The majority of the British Columbia Court of Appeal, in allowing the managers' appeal, did not expressly consider the appropriate standard of review. Mr. Justice Locke of the Court of Appeal, however, in dissent indicated that in the case of appeals from specialized tribunals "an appellate court should be slow to interfere unless the tribunal is shown to be clearly wrong either on fact or law".[52]

Mr. Justice Iacobucci, for the Supreme Court, indicated that in determining the appropriate standard of review certain general principles are to be considered:

(1) the nature of the statute; in this regard, the *British Columbia Securities Act* was to be regarded as regulatory in nature, having as its primary goal the protection of investors but, in addition, the objectives of achieving capital market efficiency and ensuring public confidence in the system. In this connection, securities regulation is to be seen as a "highly specialized activity which requires specific knowledge and expertise in what have become complex and essential capital and financial markets";[53]

(2) standards of review are to be seen as variable depending on the type of administrative agency at issue. In this regard:

The central question in ascertaining the standard of review is to determine the legislative intent in conferring jurisdiction on the administrative tribunal. In answering this question, the courts have looked at various factors. Included in the analysis is an examination of the tribunal's role or function. Also crucial is whether or not the agency's decisions are protected by a privative clause. Finally, of fundamental importance, is whether or not the question goes to the jurisdiction of the tribunal involved.

Having regard to the large number of factors relevant in determining the applicable standard of review, the courts have developed a spectrum that ranges from the standard of reasonableness to that of correctness. Courts have also enunciated a principle of deference that applies not just to the

---

[51] *Ibid.*, at 149 B.C.L.R.
[52] (1992), 66 B.C.L.R. (2d) 257 at 300, 96 D.L.R. (4th) 137 (C.A.).
[53] *Supra*, note 50, at 166 B.C.L.R.

facts as found by the tribunal, but also to the legal questions before the tribunal in the light of its role and expertise. At the reasonableness end of the spectrum, where deference is at its highest, are those cases where a tribunal protected by a true privative clause, is deciding a matter within its jurisdiction and where there is no statutory right of appeal . . .

At the correctness end of the spectrum, where deference in terms of legal questions is at its lowest, are those cases where the issues concern the interpretation of a provision limiting the tribunal's jurisdiction (jurisdictional error) or where there is a statutory right of appeal which allows the reviewing court to substitute its opinion for that of the tribunal and where the tribunal has no greater expertise than the court on the issue in question, as for example in the area of human rights . . .[54]

In Mr. Justice Iacobucci's view, the *Pezim* case fell between the two extremes. On the one hand, a statutory right of appeal existed while on the other, the appeal concerned a decision of what the court regarded as a highly specialized tribunal on an issue which "arguably goes to the core of its regulatory mandate and expertise".[55]

Mr. Justice Iacobucci outlined a series of factors which in his view warranted considerable curial deference to the decision of the Commission. These may be summarized as follows:

(1) the concept of specialization of duties as referred to in the earlier case of *Bell Canada v. Canadian Radio-Television and Telecommunications Commission*,[56] which required that deference be shown to decisions of specialized tribunals on matters falling squarely within the relevant tribunal's expertise;

(2) legislative circumstances and provisions which make clear that the tribunal at issue has been given a very broad discretion to determine what is in the public interest;

(3) a factual framework which indicates that statutory interpretation question before the tribunal have arisen in a larger factual or regulatory context which requires expertise;

(4) precedent, that is, whether the courts have shown deference in the past towards the decisions of the type of tribunal at issue; and

(5) whether the tribunal plays a significant role in policy development. In these circumstances, notwithstanding the absence of a privative clause, a higher degree of judicial deference is warranted with respect to the tribunal's interpretation of the law.[57]

Taking these factors into account, Mr. Justice Iacobucci indicated:

---

[54] *Ibid.*, at 166-67.
[55] *Ibid.*, at 167.
[56] *Supra*, note 49.
[57] *Supra*, note 50, at 167 and 170-71 B.C.L.R.

Thus on precedent, principle and policy, I conclude as a general proposition that the decisions of the Commission, falling within its expertise, warrant judicial deference.

. . . . .

In summary, having regard to the nature of the securities industry, the Commission's specialization of duties and policy development role as well as the nature of the problem before the court, considerable deference is warranted in the present case notwithstanding the fact that there is a statutory right of appeal and there is no privative clause.[58]

The decision of the Supreme Court in *Pezim* has been referred to in a number of subsequent cases. The Ontario Court of Appeal in *Ontario (Director of Income Maintenance, Ministry of Community & Social Services) v. Wedekind*[59] recently reviewed the decision in *Pezim* and concluded that, where the decision at issue is one of a specialized tribunal having broad policy-making powers, the standard of review is one of "reasonableness". This, the court suggested, is a standard of review falling somewhere between the extremes of "correctness" and "patent unreasonableness". Where, on the other hand, a statutory right of appeal is provided which allows the appellate court to substitute its opinion for that of the tribunal on questions of law or mixed questions of law and fact, and where the tribunal has no greater expertise than the court on the issue, the standard of review remains one of "correctness".[60]

In attempting to determine the applicable standard of review for a decision of an administrative tribunal, in light of the *Pezim* decision, it is necessary to consider:

- the nature of the tribunal at issue, the reason for its existence and the purpose of its enabling legislation;
- the area of expertise of its members or, more generally, the specialization of duties contemplated by the legislation;
- whether the tribunal's enabling legislation vests the tribunal with policy-making authority or regulatory powers of a general nature;
- whether the tribunal has been given an express or implied mandate to protect the public interest;
- the nature of the matter at issue and, particularly, whether it concerns statutory interpretation. If it does, it is also necessary to consider whether the interpretive issue is one which assumes or requires expertise of other than a judicial variety; and

---

[58] *Ibid.*, at 171, 172-73.
[59] (1994), 21 O.R. (3d) 289, 7 C.C.E.L. (2d) 161, 121 D.L.R. (4th) 1 (C.A.).
[60] *Ibid.*, at 296.

- whether the tribunal's enabling legislation contains a privative clause or provides for a statutory right of appeal.

These issues are more than theoretical for the practitioner. The extent to which the courts will defer to the decision of an administrative tribunal affects strategies for the conduct of the hearing as well as the prospect for relief in the courts from an adverse decision. Where the threshold for curial deference is low, the prospects for judicial intervention are correspondingly low. Stated differently, where curial deference is not easily attracted the courts are more likely to intervene. Cases in the former category, illustrated by the *Pezim* decision, involve those where the issues concern the interpretation of a provision limiting the tribunal's jurisdiction, where a statutory right of appeal is afforded in broad terms and where the tribunal at issue has no greater expertise than that of the courts on the issue in question.

To this general overview of the evolving approach to standards of review and curial deference must be added one important qualification. A series of recent cases in the Supreme Court of Canada have established that when a constitutional question is in issue, as for example an issue under the *Charter of Rights*, curial deference will not be attracted. In these circumstances the established policy of judicial non-intervention, on grounds of curial deference, will not apply.

This proposition has been established clearly in three leading cases in the Supreme Court of Canada which involved the issue of whether administrative tribunals had Charter applying authority. In *Douglas/Kwantlen Faculty Ass'n v. Douglas College,*[61] *Cuddy Chicks Ltd. v. Ontario (Labour Relations Board)*[62] and *Tétreault-Gadoury v. Canada (Employment & Immigration Com'n)*[63] it was established that certain kinds of administrative tribunals have the power to consider and apply the *Charter of Rights* and to make decisions on constitutional issues arising thereunder with the exception that no curial deference will be given to a tribunal's decisions on such issues. Only certain kinds of administrative tribunals, however, have the power to apply the Charter:

> . . . [a] tribunal at a higher level of the administrative scheme whose functions can be described as being more adjudicative in nature — that is, which frequently resolves questions of law or fact in accordance with legislative rules

---

[61] [1990] 3 S.C.R. 570, [1991] 1 W.W.R. 643, 52 B.C.L.R. (2d) 68, 91 CLLC 17,002, 2 C.R.R. (2d) 157, 77 D.L.R. (4th) 94, 118 N.R. 340.

[62] [1991] 2 S.C.R. 5, 47 O.A.C. 271, 3 O.R. (3d) 128*n*, 91 CLLC 14,024, 4 C.R.R. (2d) 1, 81 D.L.R. (4th) 121, 122 N.R. 360.

[63] [1991] 2 S.C.R. 22, 36 C.C.E.L. 117, 91 CLLC 14,023, 4 C.R.R. (2d) 12, 81 D.L.R. (4th) 358, 123 N.R. 1.

or regulations — is likely to be in a better position both to receive argument on, and to resolve constitutional questions than a tribunal which is engaged primarily in fact finding.[64]

This approach by the courts to the treatment of constitutional issues by tribunals is significant for practitioners in a number of respects. First, it is clear from the decisions of the Supreme Court of Canada that only certain kinds of tribunals may engage in Charter-based considerations or constitutional determinations. Thus, where Charter issues are raised, it is important to determine whether the tribunal at issue is of a type which the courts have recognized may apply the Charter and engage in constitutional review.

Assuming that the tribunal is one which has Charter-applying power, a lower threshold of judicial review will apply. This may lead practitioners to cast their cases in constitutional terms to minimize the prospects for curial deference and to attract the lower standard for judicial intervention. On Charter-based issues, the courts will take a broad view of the instances in which their judgments may be substituted for those of the tribunal at issue.

(2) Revisiting the "*Functus Officio*" Rule

Traditionally, the *functus officio* rule has meant that a court, once having reached its determination and made a judgment, had no power to amend or revisit the judgment. In the early case of *Paper Machinery Ltd. v. J.O. Ross Engineering Corp.*[65] it was established that the court is "*functus officio*" once having heard and disposed of a matter. There is no power to amend a judgment that has been drawn and entered except where there has been error in expressing the clear intention of the court or where a mistake was made in drawing up the judgment.

In *Chandler v. Alberta Ass'n of Architects*[66] the issue arose as to whether the *functus officio* rule applied to tribunals as well as to the courts. The majority of the court recognized that the doctrine does have application to administrative tribunals. Mr. Justice Sopinka indicated, as a general rule, that once an administrative tribunal has reached a final decision in respect of the matter at issue before it and in accordance with its jurisdiction under its enabling statute, the tribunal's decision cannot be revisited

---

[64] *Ibid.*, at 36-37.
[65] [1934] S.C.R. 186.
[66] [1989] 2 S.C.R. 848, [1989] 6 W.W.R. 521, 70 Alta. L.R. (2d) 193, 62 D.L.R. (4th) 577, 99 N.R. 277.

unless specific authority to do so exists under the tribunal's enabling statute or if there has been a mistake in drawing up the decision or an error
in expressing the manifest intention of the tribunal has occurred. Under
this approach, the well-established parameters of the *functus officio* rule
as it applies to courts have been recognized to apply to the decision-making
process of administrative tribunals.

The *Chandler* decision gives rise to a number of issues of interest to
practitioners in the administrative law field. On the clear language of the
majority decision in *Chandler*, it is evident that a tribunal, once having
made a final decision, can revisit that decision if authorized to do so by
its enabling statute or if an error has occurred in expressing the "manifest intention of the tribunal". Relief on the second ground will usually
be possible only if the tribunal itself views the record of its decision as
not fully or adequately expressing the tribunal's intent. In other words,
relief on this ground may have to originate with or be confirmed by the
tribunal itself. There may be situations where the oral reasons for decision given by a tribunal in the presence of counsel, when compared to
the final decision released by the tribunal or the final reasons for decision
will reflect inconsistencies or errors which counsel may bring to the attention of the tribunal with a view to causing the tribunal to revisit or amend
its final decision. Of broader interest, however, is the suggestion that a
tribunal's enabling legislation may confer continuing jurisdiction on the
tribunal. It is to this possibility, particularly, that practitioners should be
alert.

It has also been suggested that the majority judgment in *Chandler*
is important in two other respects. Professor McCallum, in a paper
presented in 1991 at the Seventh Annual Conference of the Canadian
Council on Administrative Tribunals, has written:

> The judgment of the majority in *Chandler* is instructive but it leaves open
> at least two important questions. One is whether the doctrine of *functus officio*
> has any application where there is a decision made under a regulatory stat-
> ute by a public officer or someone empowered under that statute to make
> decisions (in other words, not an administrative tribunal as such); the other
> is whether the reason for greater flexibility and leniency in application of
> the rule to tribunals should be restricted to those where an appeal is limited
> to questions of law or whether it should be excluded where there is a priva-
> tive or finality clause.[67]

The suggestion that application of the doctrine of *functus officio* to
administrative tribunals is subject to some flexibility emanates in part from

---

[67] McCallum, *Recent Developments in Canadian Administrative Law* (1992), 5
C.J.A.L.P. 51 at 68.

the indications in Mr. Justice Sopinka's judgment in *Chandler* that the principle may not fully apply to administrative tribunals and, further, that where it does so apply the rationale for its application flows not from the policy considerations underlining the rules developed with respect to formal judgments of the courts but rather from the policy objectives of achieving finality of proceedings. This reasoning supports the application of the doctrine to administrative tribunals. It may not support, however, extension of the doctrine to decisions made by public officers or other purely administrative decision-makers.

In *Grillas v. Canada (Minister of Manpower & Immigration)*[68] at issue was whether the Immigration Appeal Board, once having reached a decision as to whether an individual qualified as a refugee claimant, could revisit that decision on the basis of new evidence which might establish that the applicant would be subject to unusual hardship if returned to his native country. The concept of continuing jurisdiction was expressly recognized in this case. The majority of the Supreme Court of Canada held, on the particular wording of the relevant section of the Immigration Appeal Board's enabling legislation, that the Board had an equitable jurisdiction to be exercised on a continuing basis in accordance with the review circumstances set out under the Act ". . . in order to ameliorate the lot of an appellant against whom a deportation order had been made". In the result, the board had jurisdiction to reopen the applicant's appeal and to permit additional evidence.

The approach taken in *Grillas*, and confirmed in *Chandler*, suggests:

> . . . the doctrine of *functus*, insofar as it is applicable to administrative tribunals, may be excluded where the statute can be interpreted as giving an equitable jurisdiction requiring the Board or individual to continually assess a certain situation in order to fulfil the statutory mandate.[69]

The rationale for recognizing continuing jurisdiction was formulated somewhat differently in *Trizec Equities Ltd. v. Burnaby — New Westminster Area Assessor.*[70] In that case, Madam Justice McLachlin, then of the Supreme Court of British Columbia, suggested that when a tribunal makes a decision which is a nullity, it may thereafter "enter upon a proper hearing and render a valid decision".[71]

---

[68] [1972] S.C.R. 577.
[69] *Supra*, note 67, at 69.
[70] (1983), 45 B.C.L.R. 258, 22 M.P.L.R. 318, 147 D.L.R. (3d) 637 (S.C.); affd 147 D.L.R. (3d) 645*n* (C.A.).
[71] *Ibid.*, at 643 D.L.R.

Professor McCallum concluded that these authorities suggested that a tribunal might reconsider its own previous decision in at least four situations:

(1) where an order has been made which is in law a nullity;
(2) where the order it has made does not represent the intent of the tribunal;
(3) where a reconsideration is necessary to correct technical slips and errors; and
(4) where the tribunal has a continuing equitable jurisdiction.[72]

For practitioners, the prospects of relief under situations (1) and (4) are of particular interest. In the first situation, the party affected by an order which arguably is, in law, a nullity, might first be inclined to seek review of the tribunal's decision in the courts. Of interest on examination of the cases, however, is the suggestion that the tribunal itself might be approached following release of its decision or order to reconsider its order or decision and to "enter upon a proper hearing" with a view to rendering, as suggested by Madam Justice McLachlin, a "valid decision". This may imply that the tribunal is obliged to embark upon a fresh hearing.

The fourth situation identified by Professor McCallum, as established by the Supreme Court of Canada in *Chandler*, clearly invites practitioners to scrutinize closely the enabling legislation of the tribunal before whom they are appearing to determine whether a case can be made that the legislature intended the tribunal to be vested with a continuing equitable jurisdiction. This, of course, will turn on the particular wording of the legislation and on the breadth of the regulatory scheme established pursuant to the relevant statute. The strongest arguments supporting reconsideration may be made in situations where new evidence or new arguments are available and where the language of the governing statute may be said to infuse the decision-maker with continuing jurisdiction. Because this approach leaves open the possibility of a further remedy or remedies from the tribunal itself, it should be included in the practitioner's arsenal of strategies for relief.

The application of the doctrine of *functus officio* to administrative tribunals is relevant in at least one other respect. This can be illustrated by an example emanating from decisions over the last several years in the professional discipline field. In a number of instances, in imposing penalties upon individuals found to have committed an act or acts of professional misconduct, discipline committee panels have attempted to fashion terms or conditions attaching to the licences or certificates of the affected practitioners in such a way as to trigger reappearance before the same or a

---

[72] *Supra*, note 67, at 70.

differently constituted discipline committee panel in the event of non-compliance or inadequate compliance with a particular term or condition. Thus, for example, where a course of continuing education or mandatory re-training is imposed as a term of the continuance of the licence to practise, there have been instances in which a discipline committee panel has provided by its penalty order that non-compliance or lack of success with the re-education or training programme by the practitioner will cause the matter to be brought on again before the same discipline committee panel. Such an order can be seen as an effort by a tribunal to signal or assert continuing jurisdiction. Unless this approach can be traced to statutory language which suggests the basis for continuing jurisdiction, there is a strong argument that such an order exceeds the jurisdiction of the tribunal and that the tribunal cannot re-entertain at some future date an appropriate or re-cast penalty.

As earlier noted, the amendments to the *SPPA* authorize tribunals to reconsider their decisions or orders once rules in that regard have been introduced and subject to the proviso that the review is timely in relation to the date of the original decision or order. This, in essence, expressly authorizes continuing jurisdiction for administrative tribunals, within a reasonable time period. This will provide much greater flexibility for tribunals to enforce effectively their decisions and to ensure that material new evidence can be considered so long as it arises within a reasonable period after the original determination is made. It may also promote practical difficulties, however, as continuing jurisdiction underminds the finality of the decision-making process and introduces uncertainty for the parties affected by administrative tribunal decisions. Presumably, the rules to be introduced by each tribunal will stipulate specifically the time within which reconsideration or review of an original decision or order may take place. If this is not the case, considerable uncertainty will be introduced to the administrative hearing process.

INDEX